D0758351

Black Soldiers
in Blue

The
University
of
North
Carolina
Press
Chapel Hill
and London

Black Soldiers in Blue

African American Troops
in the Civil War Era

Edited by
John David Smith

2002

© 2002 The University of North Carolina Press
All rights reserved
Manufactured in the United States of America

Designed by Jacquline Johnson
Set in Bembo
by Tseng Information Systems, Inc.

The paper in this book meets the guidelines for
permanence and durability of the Committee on
Production Guidelines for Book Longevity
of the Council on Library Resources.

Frontispiece: "The Battle at Milliken's Bend—Sketched by
Mr. Theodore R. Davis" (*Harper's Weekly*, July 4, 1863,
N.C. Division of Historical Resources, Raleigh).

Library of Congress Cataloging-in-Publication Data
Black soldiers in blue : African American troops in the
Civil War era / edited by John David Smith.
p. cm.
Includes bibliographical references and index.
ISBN 0-8078-2741-x (cloth : alk. paper)
1. United States—History—Civil War, 1861–1865—
Participation, African American.   2. United States. Army—
African American troops—History—19th century.   3. African
American soldiers—History—19th century.   4. United
States—History—Civil War, 1861–1865—Campaigns.
I. Smith, John David, 1949–
E540.N3 B63   2002
973.7'415—dc21
2002005060

06 05 04 03 02   5 4 3 2 1

Wieder für Sylvie

CONTENTS

ILLUSTRATIONS
AND MAPS
꧁✿꧂

Illustrations

Maps

ACKNOWLEDGMENTS

I began planning this book in 1996. David Perry, my editor at the University of North Carolina Press, expressed early interest in the project, provided ongoing advice and encouragement, and guided the book through the publication process. I am most grateful for his support and patience during the long editorial process, especially in 1998–99 when I served on the faculty of the Ludwig-Maximilians-Universität, Munich, Germany. Gary W. Gallagher also advised me throughout the project, helping me to conceptualize the volume, to identify contributions and contributors, and to hammer out details. Ira Berlin suggested contributors. Joseph T. Glatthaar and an anonymous reader for the University of North Carolina Press critiqued the book manuscript thoroughly and offered many useful suggestions that strengthened the volume considerably. As usual, Jeffrey J. Crow, William C. Harris, and Randall M. Miller advised me and rescued me from committing errors of fact and from infelicities of style. Reginald F. Hildebrand and Shana R. Hutchins shared with me their expertise, respectively, on the religious lives and the historiography of the U.S. Colored Troops. William W. Freehling cheered me on from the Commonwealth. Richard W. Slatta complied cheerfully and successfully with my seemingly endless requests. Sebastian Hierl, Cindy Levine, Mimi Riggs, Ann Rothe, and Marihelen Stringham of the D. H. Hill Library at North Carolina State University obtained research materials for my use with their characteristic dispatch and good humor. Sharon Baggett, Jason Burton, and Stephen A. Ross served as my graduate research assistants. Charles R. Bowery, Jr., David E. Brown, Ruth Bryan, Tiffany Charles, Jerry Cotten, Elizabeth Dunn, Kate Flaherty, James Grossman, Peter Harrington, Walter B. Hill, Jr., Jesse R. Lankford, Jr., Betsy Lowenstein, Linda McCormick, Bernard McTigue, Stephen E. Massengill,

Anne Miller, Valerie Miller, Nelson Morgan, Janie C. Morris, Gerald J. Pro-
kopowicz, David M. Reel, Claudia Rivers, Philip Lapsansky, Cindy Van
Horn, Michael Vorenberg, and Alan Westmoreland facilitated my obtaining
illustrations and gaining permissions. Noah Andre Trudeau generously provided the book's maps. Kay Banning prepared the index. Paula Wald served
as my project editor, and Paul Betz was the copyeditor. Finally, I wish to
thank the thirteen authors whose essays, in addition to my own, make up
Black Soldiers in Blue.

INTRODUCTION

African Americans of the Civil War era understood what historians understand now—that emancipation and the use of blacks as armed soldiers were defining moments in the history of the race. Writing in September 1863, G. E. Hystuns, who became a noncommissioned officer in the famous 54th Massachusetts Volunteers, wrote that arming his fellow blacks would erase "that semblance of inferiority of our race, which cruel Slavery has created." He predicted that "if there is one spark of manhood running in the blood of the Race that has resisted the . . . waves of oppression, the school of the soldier will fan it to a glowing flame." Thirteen years later, during the American Centennial, the Civil War veteran and pioneer black historian George Washington Williams celebrated the moment "when the life of our nation hung upon the thread of uncertainty, the slave threw down his hoe, took up his musket, and saved the country." Williams was certain that "when the history of this country is written in truth—when Freedom counts her jewels and reviews her glorious army of martyrs—the negro will be there." This, according to historian David W. Blight, was the "emancipationist vision" of the war.[1]

Over the last four decades, historians have made great strides in integrating the "emancipationist vision" of the war into mainstream Civil War scholarship. Important books by Dudley Taylor Cornish, James M. McPherson, Ira Berlin, Joseph T. Glatthaar, Noah Andre Trudeau, and others have documented, narrated, and analyzed the military service of the almost 179,000 African Americans who fought against the Confederates, suppressing their rebellion and destroying slavery. This corpus of scholarship, together with Edward Zwick's powerful 1989 film *Glory*, has raised scholarly and public consciousness of the vital role and varied experiences of

African American soldiers in the Union war effort. "Blacks alone did not win the war," Glatthaar emphasizes, "but timely and extensive support from them contributed significantly and may have made the difference between a Union victory and stalemate or defeat." Scholars today generally agree with Glatthaar that African Americans "tipped the delicate balance of power squarely in favor of the North."[2]

This collection of fourteen essays on African American troops in the Union Army has been inspired by and builds on the rich arsenal of recent works concerning blacks in the Civil War. The articles draw on the latest research in African American, military, and social history. They narrate widely, probe deeply, and examine analytically how blacks fought for their freedom and their citizenship and the broad military, political, and social significance of their armed service. Half of the essays focus specifically on the role of the U.S. Colored Troops (USCT) in combat; they provide the fullest, most up-to-date treatment of battles in which black troops were engaged. Because the courageous but ill-fated charge of the 54th Massachusetts Volunteers on Battery Wagner (July 18, 1863) has received extensive analysis from historians, it is not the subject of an essay here.[3] Readers will, however, find an examination of the regiment's commander, Colonel Robert Gould Shaw, in Chapter 11. The remaining essays treat relatively little-known aspects of the USCT. Collectively, the articles in *Black Soldiers in Blue* add meaning and context to the Civil War military experience and suggest implications for understanding African American life in the postwar world.

The book begins with John David Smith's essay, an overview of President Abraham Lincoln's seemingly circuitous wartime path to emancipation and the enlistment and military service of black soldiers. During the war, Lincoln's critics, most notably Frederick Douglass, denounced him loudly for his lethargy in freeing and arming the slaves, and many twentieth-century scholars followed suit. Smith, however, argues that Lincoln "charted a far more linear course toward freedom than his nineteenth-century critics and modern historians have recognized." Though others—including abolitionists, generals, and politicians—prodded and pushed him to emancipate the slaves and to mobilize black soldiers, for the first year and a half of the war Lincoln, always determined to keep the Union intact, acted cautiously on the question of slavery. He advocated gradual, compensated emancipation and voluntary colonization, declaring in August 1862, "What I do about slavery, and the colored race, I do because it helps to save the Union." Convinced, finally, in late 1862 that emancipation and military recruitment of blacks were vital to suppress the rebellion, Lincoln set in motion the processes of liberating slaves in Rebel territory and mustering into service blacks in the North, the occupied South, and eventually the loyal slave or border states. By war's end, blacks constituted between 9 and 10 percent of all Union troops who served in the war. In his article Smith assesses the recruitment, organization, mobilization, and battlefield performance of the USCT. "In exchange for the hardships and indignities they endured . . . ," he concludes, "the U.S. Colored Troops carried out various military duties and in the process surprised a doubting Northern public and their severest and most racist critics."

In the first of the combat studies, Lawrence Lee Hewitt narrates and analyzes the role of the two regiments of Louisiana's Native Guards who fought at Port Hudson, Louisiana (May 27, 1863), the first significant assault by black troops in the war. Hewitt sketches the history of the black units, composed of free blacks who had earlier cast their lot with the Confederacy, and subsequently their role in attacking key Confederate fortifications north of Baton Rouge. Sifting through the layers of meaning regarding the battle's significance, he defends the inexperienced Native Guards' battlefield performance. "Their baptism of fire came from an order to accomplish the impossible. No one could blame them for withdrawing after scores of their comrades · lay dead and dying, many floating in water too deep to wade." He interprets the service of the Louisiana Native Guards at Port Hudson as a pivotal moment in the war, one that provided Lincoln considerable "propaganda" in his joint program of emancipation and military enlistment. The blacks' participation in the battle proved to many skeptical white Northerners that African Americans could indeed fight. Their efforts smoothed the way for the systematic recruitment and utilization of USCT regiments for the remainder of the war.

So too did the performance of black troops two weeks later at Milliken's Bend, Louisiana (June 7, 1863), the subject of Richard Lowe's essay; this was another action that resulted from the struggle for control of the Mississippi River. Former Louisiana and Mississippi slaves, the men who fought at Milliken's Bend were part of General Lorenzo Thomas's Mississippi Valley recruiting initiative in the winter and spring of 1863. Though the black troops garrisoned at Milliken's Bend were inadequately trained (the 1st Mississippi Volunteers of African Descent received their weapons only one day before the battle), the raw Texas recruits in Confederate general Henry E. McCulloch's brigade were little better prepared for combat. As Lowe explains, the vicious attack by the Rebels on the levee at Milliken's Bend quickly developed into "close-in, skull-smashing fighting" that ranked as "one of the bloodiest small engagements of the war." So fierce was the Confederate assault that the Union troops retreated to the riverbank, only to be saved by the protection of the heavy guns of the ironclad USS *Choctaw*. As additional Federal ships appeared, the Confederates withdrew. Analyzing the heavy loss sustained by the black troops (the 9th Louisiana Volunteers of African Descent lost 67.4 percent of those engaged in the action), Lowe questions allegations that the Confederates gave the blacks "no quarter." "Stories of black flags and skulls and crossbones were circulated later," he writes, "almost entirely by men who had not been on the gory levee at Milliken's Bend." Although it was of negligible strategic importance to either side, Lowe argues that the engagement nevertheless proved "that black Americans could fight and die for Union and freedom as well as anyone, white or black, famous or obscure."

Arthur W. Bergeron, Jr.'s narrative and analysis of the role of black soldiers at the Battle of Olustee (February 20, 1864) underscores how the African American units often were poorly prepared for combat and mismanaged by their white commanders. Of the three regiments of blacks engaged in the action designed to bring Florida back into the Union, the 8th USCT had yet to complete its training. After occupying Jacksonville on February 7, Union general Truman Seymour's troops marched westward largely unopposed until they fell into a trap set by Confederate general Joseph Finegan at Olustee. Outnumbered and outflanked, the Union troops sustained heavy losses and retreated in disarray, especially after some of their field commanders fell. The 8th USCT alone had 310 men killed, wounded, or missing from among the 565 soldiers in the regiment who entered the battle. Even though following the engagement some white soldiers accused the black troops of cowardice, Bergeron maintains that at Olustee "most of the men of the three USCT regiments demonstrated their willingness to fight and indeed fought bravely under adverse odds."

Ever since the capture of the Federal garrison at Fort Pillow, Tennessee, on April 12, 1864, participants, polemicists, and historians have debated whether or not Confederate general Nathan Bedford Forrest's men slaughtered the black troops stationed there—the 6th U.S. Colored Heavy Artillery and the 2nd U.S. Colored Light Artillery. Carefully analyzing the primary sources, John Cimprich identifies two conflicting interpretations of what caused the deaths of approximately two-thirds of the blacks in the battle. On the one hand, Federal sources point to what one contemporary described as an "indiscriminant slaughter." According to this interpretation, Confederate soldiers, furious at facing African Americans in combat, murdered the blacks as they tried to surrender. "Given the number of survivors and interviewers," Cimprich explains, "it seems highly unlikely that the story originated in peer pressure or collaborative lying." Confederate evidence, on the other hand, charged that, rather than surrendering, the Federal troops continued to fight or attempted to escape and thus were killed in the line of battle. After taking stock of all available evidence, Cimprich concludes that a massacre did indeed occur at Fort Pillow. "The decision of some Federals to flee or resist may have unnecessarily increased their side's casualties after the fort fell," he notes, "but early accounts from both sides speak of numerous individual efforts to surrender."

William Glenn Robertson examines closely the service of two all-black divisions (General George G. Meade's Fourth Division, Ninth Corps, Army of the Potomac, and General Benjamin F. Butler's Third Division, Eighteenth Corps, Army of the James) in the 1864 campaign in Virginia. Assessing the June 15 attack on Petersburg's outer defenses by Butler's Third Division, Robertson identifies a connection between the general's confidence in his men and the black troops' determination, pluck, and resiliency. Their fighting and heavy losses at New Market Heights on September 29 "served to make the point that African American soldiers could take heavy punishment and still continue to function as dependable combat units." Black soldiers in Meade's Fourth Division, however, fared less well, according to Robertson, a reflection of their general's belief that the USCT served best as fatigue laborers, not fighters. Challenging contemporary observers and modern historians alike, Robertson argues that before the Battle of the Crater the Fourth Division spent so much time performing manual labor "that it had only rudimentary training at best." "If the division had led the assault at the crater," he explains, "it would have been the fighting spirit of the men that altered the outcome, not its pre-battle preparations." Robertson concludes that the combination of inexperienced blacks troops and incompetent white officers cost the USCT heavy casualties not just at the debacle at the crater but throughout the bloody Virginia campaign. Mismanagement circumscribed the African Americans' potential and effectiveness as combat soldiers.

The USCT who fought at the Battle of Saltville, Virginia, on October 2, 1864, the subject of Thomas D. Mays's article, also experienced poor leadership and incomplete organization. But, as Mays explains, the blacks suffered mainly from the racist rage of Confederate troops who murdered mostly wounded black prisoners in the battle's aftermath. The engagement resulted when Union general Stephen Gano Burbridge launched an expedition from eastern Kentucky into Southwest Virginia to destroy the region's saltworks that were vital to the deteriorating Confederate war effort. Among Burbridge's force were 600 men from the hastily assembled and poorly equipped 5th U.S. Colored Cavalry. Despite Burbridge's numerical superiority over the Confederates at Saltville, a ragtag assemblage of Rebels held a strong defensive position and repulsed his troops, forcing the Union soldiers to retreat and, inexplicably, to abandon their wounded. Basing his narrative on accounts by Union and Confederate observers, Mays documents how Confederates, led by guerrilla leader Champ Ferguson, executed an undeterminable number of injured black captives. Though historians disagree as to the extent of the "massacre" at Saltville, Mays interprets the killings as symptomatic of what many Confederates "felt [about] the presence of blacks on the battlefield"; for them it "raised the stakes from that of a war for Southern independence to that of an armed slave uprising."

By 1864, as Anne J. Bailey explains in her essay, the men of the USCT had proven their battle effectiveness in eastern campaigns and in engagements in the Mississippi Valley, yet influential officers, most notably General William T. Sherman, resisted their use in combat, preferring to employ blacks as manual laborers. Sherman was adamant in his disapproval of black troops, considering them untrustworthy for front-line service and believing that their employment as soldiers would lower the morale of his white troops. As a result he refused to cooperate with the government's recruitment efforts, threatening to arrest recruiters in the Western Theater of Operations. Ironically, however, as Bailey notes, Sherman's commander at Nashville, General George H. Thomas, was forced to rely on some inexperienced regiments of USCT in the bloody battle on December 15–16, 1864. Though the black brigades endured frightful casualties in the battle (the 13th USCT, for example, lost almost 40 percent of its effectives), the African Americans generally performed well in defeating General John B. Hood's Confederate Army of Tennessee. "For the black soldier," Bailey writes, "the battle at Nashville was a chance to strike another blow against slavery. More significantly, many black soldiers as well as their white officers knew that how well the men performed would have implications far beyond the battlefield."

Credit for much of the success in recruiting and mobilizing black troops, as Michael T. Meier argues, belongs to Adjutant General of the Army Lorenzo Thomas (1804–75). Known as an arrogant, vain, and verbose papershuffler, a desk officer despised and distrusted by Secretary of War Edwin M. Stanton, Thomas nevertheless assumed the immense task of raising and administering black troops in the Mississippi Valley in March 1863, two months before the establishment of the Bureau for Colored Troops. Dispatched on a seemingly unimportant inspection tour of the region by Stanton, Thomas surprisingly used the trip to champion the cause of black enlistments and exhibited uncharacteristic commitment, flexibility, and zeal. He brought order and direction to the recruitment process along the Mississippi, convincing thousands of black refugees to enlist and white soldiers to cast their lot as officers with the new USCT. In overcoming prejudice and layers of military bureaucracy, Meier explains, Thomas had by 1865 "brought uniformity to the size of the new black regiments, involved many commands in their recruitment, and eased the path of their acceptance into a skeptical U.S. Army." His efforts eventually resulted in the recruitment of more than 70,000 black soldiers.

Noah Andre Trudeau examines the contributions of one branch of the black soldiers in blue generally ignored by historians—the seven regiments of U.S. Colored Cavalry (USCC). Encountering shortages of horses, inadequate equipage and supplies, and the "racist cultural blindness" of white troops and military administrators alike, the USCC nonetheless generally fought credibly. According to Trudeau, mounted black troops performed proportionally less fatigue duty than black infantrymen but still rarely served in major campaigns with white cavalry troops. "The likely posting for a black mounted regiment," he maintains, "was outpost duty where its strength was dispersed across a wide area. Scouting, raiding, and reconnaissances made up most of its wartime activities." An exception was the participation of the 3rd USCC in General Benjamin H. Grierson's 450-mile cavalry raid through eastern and central Mississippi in December 1864 and January 1865. In addition to destroying railroad track, bridges, telegraph lines, locomotives, and war matériel, the troopers liberated 1,000 slaves. The all-black 5th Massachusetts Cavalry, commanded by Colonel Charles Francis Adams, Jr., was among the first regiments of U.S. troops to enter Richmond upon its capture on April 3, 1865.

Both contemporary observers and later historians have underscored the close relationship between the USCT's battlefield performance and the quality of its officers' leadership. Keith Wilson's article examines how the backgrounds and experiences of three officers in the Department of the South—Thomas Wentworth Higginson, James Montgomery, and Robert Gould Shaw—influenced the treatment of their men and their definition of acceptable modes of warfare. Higginson (1823–1911) was a militant Massachusetts abolitionist and an intellectual who commanded black troops as a means of uplifting the former slaves, winning the war, and punishing their ex-masters. Shaw (1837–63) was descended from elite New Englanders and, while committed to abolitionism, served with the USCT more from a sense of military honor and noblesse oblige than from a commitment to abolitionist doctrine. Montgomery (1814–71), a frontier clergyman and schoolteacher, fought alongside John Brown in Kansas and interpreted the Civil War as a holy crusade against the sins of slavery. His religious zeal and experiences with guerrilla warfare in Kansas led Montgomery to use his black troops to wage "hard war" on the South's civilian population. In June 1863, for example, companies of Montgomery's 2nd South Carolina Volunteers and Shaw's 54th Massachusetts Volunteers raided Darien, Georgia, burning and plundering the town. Though Montgomery judged his "western" warfare an appropriate means for ex-slaves to gain revenge on their former masters, Higginson and Shaw considered such tactics "uncivilized" and in conflict with the rules of legitimate war. "Essentially paternalist in outlook," Wilson explains, "Shaw and Higginson believed that black troops were emotionally unstable and lacking in self-reliance. They therefore feared how blacks would perform in guerrilla warfare." Wilson interprets the Department of the South as a crucible both for the evolving role of African Americans as soldiers and for the changing manner in which the Northern armies fought the war.

Black soldiers of course had their own visions of the war's meaning, but, as Edwin S. Redkey suggests in his essay, the vast majority remain too anonymous for any composite picture. The Reverend Henry McNeal Turner (1834–1915), who served as one of fourteen black chaplains in the USCT, is a notable exception. According to Redkey, the war provided Turner "an intense, invigorating crucible for his energetic talents." A free black from South Carolina, Turner ministered an African Methodist Episcopal Church (AME) congregation in Washington before the war. Following the Emancipation Proclamation, he recruited black troops for the 1st USCT, cared for the spiritual needs of that regiment in the Petersburg and Fort Fisher campaigns, and later received a commission as a chaplain in the Freedmen's Bureau. A pioneer African American journalist, Turner used the pages of the AME's *Christian Recorder* and the *Weekly Anglo-African* of New York to attack slavery, to celebrate the military attainments of the USCT, to criticize the injustices endured by black troops, to proselytize for the AME Church, and to promote himself. As the war drew to a close, Turner employed the "Gospel of Freedom" to win converts for the AME Church from among the freedpeople, competing with other sects, most notably the Methodist Episcopal Church, South, and the African Methodist Episcopal Zion Church, for the souls of the former slaves. In later years he became an influential Georgia politician, an AME bishop, and an emigrationist, but, as Redkey concludes, Turner had "found his life's work in his two years as an army chaplain."

Following the defeat of the Confederacy in April 1865, the War Department employed USCT regiments as occupation troops throughout the South. In his article, Robert J. Zalimas, Jr., examines minutely the experiences of African American troops garrisoned in Charleston, South Carolina, as provost guards. Not surprisingly, the black soldiers encountered a hostile reception from native white Charlestonians. But they also clashed repeatedly with Northern white regiments posted in the city who openly challenged the authority of blacks as military policemen. This culminated in the bloody race riot with white troops of July 8–10, 1865, which, according to Zalimas, "brought to light the frustrations of many African American soldiers in their struggle to gain respect within the Union ranks." Zalimas interprets the tensions between the black and white occupation troops as the result of assertiveness on the part of the African American soldiers and civilians, as indicative of the refusal of white Northerners and Southerners to grant blacks full citizenship, and as reflective of the move by white Southerners during Reconstruction to resort to racial violence to keep African Americans in check. Charleston's race riot influenced the War Department to continue the wartime policy of giving black soldiers undesirable, rural assignments, thereby segregating the occupation forces and leaving the freedpeople in urban centers to the mercy of white troops and native white Southerners.

In the final essay, Richard Reid analyzes the postwar experiences and readjustment of African American veterans from one state, North Carolina, who fought in the USCT. During the last two years of the war, North Carolina's northeastern counties, occupied by Federal forces since 1862, contributed four regiments to the USCT. Examining the postwar settlement patterns of the black North Carolinians, Reid explains that "[t]he more extensive their service outside the state, the less likely it is that one can locate the veterans within North Carolina in their later years." Those who resided in North Carolina tended to live in the eastern part of the state, near where they had been born and had entered the service. These USCT veterans lived in close proximity to one another, offering mutual aid and protection against violent white supremacists. Though most of the veterans clustered in the coastal region and eastern cities—areas with the largest black political activity during Reconstruction and after—Reid maintains that the former soldiers had little direct political involvement. Poor, rural, uneducated, and black (as distinct from mulatto), North Carolina's USCT veterans fit poorly into the profile of the state's upwardly mobile Reconstruction-era black politicians and merchants. Instead, the veterans generally suffered from the same range of financial, physical, and emotional difficulties that the majority of former soldiers of both races encountered upon their discharge. While they left the military with few tangible rewards, Reid concludes, the men nonetheless "could draw great comfort from knowing that they had played a major role in freeing the slaves and launching the freedom generation."

That, of course, was no small achievement. Few Americans in 1861, not even Frederick Douglass and other champions of black enlistment, could have envisioned the broad contributions that Lincoln's black soldiers in blue made to the Union war effort. The president's halting but ultimately inexorable emancipation plan paved the way for African Americans to take an active role in demolishing slavery. As the essays in this book suggest, the men of the U.S. Colored Troops became agents of liberation for their fellow blacks, exhibiting extraordinary bravery, sacrifice, and toughness. Subject to across-the-board discrimination from friend and foe alike, the USCT nevertheless persevered, overcoming innumerable indignities with patience, persistence, and pride. Almost 38,000 died in the cause of freedom. "As a soldier in the Union Army," Dudley T. Cornish concludes, "the American Negro proved his manhood and established a strong claim to equality of treatment and opportunity." The vital nexus of Lincoln's program of emancipation and black military service broke the chains of slavery, freed four million slaves, and spirited African Americans forward to fight new battles for true freedom and the fruits of American life.[4]

Notes

1. G. E. Hystuns quoted in Nick Salvatore, *We All Got History: The Memory Books of Amos Webber* (New York: Times Books/Random House, 1996), 115; George Washington Williams, *The American Negro from 1776 to 1876, Oration Delivered at Avondale, Ohio* (Cincinnati: Robert Clarke and Company, 1876), 24, 25; David W. Blight, *Race and Reunion: The Civil War in American Memory* (Cambridge: Harvard University Press, 2001), 2.
2. Dudley Taylor Cornish, *The Sable Arm: Negro Troops in the Union Army, 1861–1865* (1956; New York: W. W. Norton, 1966); James M. McPherson, *The Struggle for Equality: Abolitionists and the Negro in the Civil War and Reconstruction* (Princeton:

Princeton University Press, 1964); James M. McPherson, ed., *The Negro's Civil War: How American Negroes Felt and Acted during the War for the Union* (1965; New York: Vintage Books, 1967); Ira Berlin, Joseph P. Reidy, and Leslie S. Rowland, eds., *The Black Military Experience* (Cambridge: Cambridge University Press, 1982); Joseph T. Glatthaar, *Forged in Battle: The Civil War Alliance of Black Soldiers and White Officers* (New York: Free Press, 1990); Noah Andre Trudeau, *Like Men of War: Black Troops in the Civil War, 1862–1865* (Boston: Little, Brown, 1998); Joseph T. Glatthaar, "Black Glory: The African-American Role in Union History," in Gabor S. Borritt, ed., *Why the Confederacy Lost* (New York: Oxford University Press, 1992), 138.

3. See Peter Burchard, *One Gallant Rush: Robert Gould Shaw and His Brave Black Regiment* (New York: St. Martin's Press, 1965); Russell Duncan, ed., *Blue-Eyed Child of Fortune: The Civil War Letters of Robert Gould Shaw* (Athens: University of Georgia Press, 1992); Russell Duncan, *Where Death and Glory Meet: Colonel Robert Gould Shaw and the 54th Massachusetts Infantry* (Athens: University of Georgia Press, 1999); and Martin H. Blatt, Thomas J. Brown, and Donald Yacovone, eds., *Hope and Glory: Essays on the Legacy of the 54th Massachusetts Regiment* (Amherst: University of Massachusetts Press, 2001).

4. Cornish, *The Sable Arm*, 291.

Black Soldiers in Blue

LET US ALL BE GRATEFUL THAT WE HAVE COLORED TROOPS THAT WILL FIGHT

John David Smith

When President Abraham Lincoln's September 22, 1862, preliminary Emancipation Proclamation went quietly into effect on Thursday, January 1, 1863, Secretary of the Navy Gideon Welles pronounced it "a broad step . . . a landmark in history"—an "extraordinary and radical measure—almost revolutionary in its character." But few persons in the North or the South envisioned what historian James M. McPherson has termed the "revolution of freedom"—"the greatest social revolution in American history"—that ensued as the Civil War, with the preservation of the Union at stake, became a war of black liberation. On New Year's Day, "all persons held as slaves within any state . . . then . . . in rebellion against the United States" became "thenceforward, and forever free."[1]

In his final Emancipation Proclamation Lincoln issued on January 1, the president added a new paragraph authorizing that suitable emancipated slaves "will be received into the armed service of the United States to garrison forts, positions, stations, and other places, and to man vessels of all sorts in said service." This passage signaled a major reversal in policy because since the start of the war the U.S. Army had turned away free black volunteers. Lincoln's revised text, however, signified more than his changes in attitude and in policy during the last months of 1862. Soon after the war had commenced, he in fact had begun to move cautiously, carefully, but consistently toward emancipation and the enlistment of African American soldiers. The politics of emancipation and the politics of black enlistment always were closely entwined, and Lincoln's final Emancipation Proclamation underscored the vital nexus in the president's thinking between the two policies. So too, historian Joseph P. Reidy explains, were "military expediency" and "the North's commitment to emancipation." It is essential to remember, Reidy insists, "that . . . without a Union victory there would be no emancipation." Lincoln's decision to free and then employ blacks in the U.S. Army would rank among his boldest, most controversial, and most important measures.[2]

In August 1863, after black troops had first proven their mettle under fire, Lincoln explained to his critics that some of his commanders, including opponents of abolition and the Republican Party, "believe the emancipation policy, and the use of colored troops, constitute the heaviest blow yet dealt to the rebellion; and that, at least one of those important successes, could not have been achieved when it was, but for the aid of black soldiers." "You say you will not fight to free negroes," the president declared, adding wryly, "[s]ome of them are willing to fight for you." Lincoln predicted that when the war finally ended, "there will be some black men who can remember that with silent tongue, and clenched teeth, and steady eye, and well-poised bayonet, they have helped mankind on to this great consummation; while, I fear, there will be some white ones, unable to forget that, with malignant heart, and deceitful speech, they have strove to hinder it." In April 1864 the president recalled that he experimented with arming Northern free blacks and Southern ex-slaves with "a clear conviction of duty . . . to turn that element of strength to account; and I am responsible for it to the American people, to the Christian world, to history, and on my final account, to God."[3]

A harbinger of radical racial change, the freeing and arming of the slaves elicited a mountain of comments from both supporters and opponents of emancipation. For example, General John White Geary, a brigade commander in the Union army, remarked that "[t]he President's proclimation [*sic*] is the most important public document ever issued by an officer of our Government, and although I believe it, in itself, to be correct, I tremble for the consequences." Responding to newspaper reports of Lincoln's proclamation, another officer of antislavery convictions, Lieutenant John Quincy Adams Campbell of the 5th Iowa Infantry, proclaimed January 1, 1863, "the day of our nation's second birth. God bless and help Abraham Lincoln— help him to 'break every yoke and let the oppressed go free.' The President has placed the Union pry under the corner stone of the Confederacy and the structure *will* fall." In a pamphlet circulated widely in the North in 1863, George H. Boker proclaimed: "We are raising a black army. We are thus incurring a solemn obligation to abolish slavery wherever our flag flies. . . . When we do this, we shall have taken the last step in our difficult path, and shall have reached the goal, the natural, inevitable, fitting and triumphant end of the war, *emancipation*—the one essential condition to peace and Union."[4]

Not surprisingly, abolitionists, African Americans, and others sympathetic to the slaves welcomed Lincoln's final proclamation. But many expressed disappointment, disillusionment, and frustration because the president's edict only "freed" slaves in territory still under Confederate control. According to historian Russell F. Weigley, "Lincoln freed only the slaves it was not in his power to free." To be fair to the president, however, his proclamation in fact did free many slaves along the Mississippi River, in eastern North Carolina, on the Sea Islands along the Atlantic coast, and in pockets throughout the Confederacy. Nonetheless, Lincoln's critics interpreted the restrained, legalistic wording of the Emancipation Proclamation as indicative of his overall lethargy in freeing and arming the slaves, and they complained that he followed the lead of others and rarely defined policy himself. "Indeed," historian Michael Vorenberg notes correctly, "in all matters concerning slavery, Lincoln was more restrained than most of his Republican colleagues." The president's critics struggled making the transformation from what historian George M. Fredrickson has correctly termed "the celestial politics of moral reform to the earthly politics of President Lincoln."[5]

On September 25, 1862, for example, the fiery abolitionist William Lloyd Garrison remarked that

> [t]he President's Proclamation is certainly matter for great rejoicing, as far as it goes for the liberation of those in bondage; but it leaves slavery, as a system or practice, still to exist in all the so-called loyal Slave States, under the old constitutional guaranties, even to slave-hunting in the Free States, in accordance with the wicked Fugitive Slave Law. It postpones emancipation in the Rebel States until the 1st of January next, except as the slaves of rebel masters may escape to the Federal lines. What was wanted, what is still needed, is a proclamation, distinctly announcing the total abolition of slavery.

The abolitionist Moncure Conway agreed, faulting Lincoln for not going far enough in his final proclamation, for failing to make the war a moral crusade against slavery. After meeting with the president on January 25,

1863, Conway came away "with a conviction that the practical success of the Emancipation Proclamation was by no means certain in the hands of the author."[6]

Sergeant George E. Stephens of the all-black 54th Massachusetts Volunteers, the first black regiment recruited in the North, shared Conway's skepticism of Lincoln's commitment to black freedom. Though on New Year's Eve, 1862, Stephens predicted that the Emancipation Proclamation would wash away "the sorrows, tears, and anguish of millions" and "necessitate a general arming of the freedmen," Lincoln's actions quickly soured him on the president. Like other critics, black and white, Stephens chided Lincoln for moving too slowly to emancipate the slaves, for doing so on military— not humanitarian—grounds, and for leaving the "peculiar institution" untouched in the loyal slave states. In letters to the *Weekly Anglo-African*, published in New York, Stephens denounced "the false and indefinite policy of the Administration" for allowing slavery to continue in the border states.

"The Emancipation proclamation," he said, "should have been based as much on the righteousness of emancipation as on the great need of the measure, and then let the people see that the war for slavery and secession could be vigorously met only by war for the Union against slavery." As late as September 1864, Stephens condemned the North's emancipation policy as "the fulmination of one man, by virtue of his military authority, who proposes to free the slaves of that portion of territory over which he has no control, while those portions of slave territory under control of the Union armies is exempted, and slavery receives as much protection as it ever did. United States officers and soldiers are yet employed hunting fugitive slaves." He damned Lincoln's proclamation as "an abortion wrung from the Executive womb by necessity."[7]

Whereas Stephens complained that Lincoln's emancipation policies fell too short, others judged them as going too far. Though opposed to slavery because it contradicted "the spirit of modern progress and civilization," Charles Francis Adams, Jr., of Massachusetts nonetheless believed that setting free the slaves would have disastrous results for the freedpeople. Emancipation, he predicted, would open the South's cotton fields to free labor and modern technology and thereby destroy the slaves' "value as agricultural machines." "As to being made soldiers," Adams insisted, "they are more harm than good." At best they could perform fatigue duty. "It will be years before they can be made to stand before their old masters, unless . . . some leader of their own, some Toussaint rises, who is one of them and inspires them with confidence. Under our system and with such white officers as we give them, we might make a soldierly equal to the native Hindoo regiments in about five years." Adams also was convinced that black recruitment would prove too costly and thus "the idea of arming the blacks *as soldiers* must be abandoned."[8]

Ironically, by 1864 Adams was in command of the all-black 5th Massachusetts Cavalry. While he considered the African American competent enough to serve as an infantryman, Adams judged him unacceptable as a cavalryman. "He has not the mental vigor and energy," Adams informed his father, the U.S. diplomat Charles Francis Adams; "he cannot stand up against adversity. A sick nigger . . . at once gives up and lies down to die, the personification of humanity reduced to a wet rag. He cannot fight for life like a white man. . . . In infantry, which acts in large masses, these things are of less consequence than in cavalry . . . where individual intelligence is everything, and single men . . . have only themselves and their own nerve, intelligence and quickness to rely on." He continued: "Of the courage in action of these men, at any rate when acting in mass, there can no doubt exist; of their physical and mental and moral energy and stamina I entertain grave doubts. Retreat, defeat and exposure would tell on them more than on the whites." Generally Adams found the black troops deficient, lacking "the pride, spirit and intellectual energy of the whites." He had "little hope for them in their eternal contact with a race like ours."[9]

Like Adams, many white Northern soldiers doubted the blacks' abilities to fight and protested against freeing and arming the slaves. Some were ambivalent about Lincoln's policies. Others expressed feelings of anger and betrayal. While willing to sacrifice their lives to suppress the rebellion, they had not joined the army to liberate blacks or to serve alongside them. The pioneer African American historian George Washington Williams, an army veteran, wrote in 1888 that the black soldier entered the war surrounded by prejudice and bad faith, "persistently denied public confidence." At best, white troops "damned him with faint praise—with elevated eyebrows and elaborate pantomime. The good words of the conscientious few who felt . . . that he would fight were drowned by a babel of wrathful depreciation of him as a man and as a soldier."[10]

On September 30, 1862, for example, Lieutenant George Washington Whitman of the 51st New York Volunteers, the poet's brother, took note of the preliminary Emancipation Proclamation and remarked: "I dont know what effect it is going to have on the war, but one thing is certain, he [Lincoln] has got to lick the south before he can free the niggers . . . and unless he drives ahead and convinces the south . . . that we are bound to lick them, and it would be better for them to behave themselvs and keep their slaves, than to get licked and lose them, I dont think the proclamation will do much good." Another soldier, Corporal George W. Squier of the 44th Indiana Volunteers, predicted that the Emancipation Proclamation would have a deleterious effect on Union troops. Although Squier considered the proclamation "in itself right and intende[d] for good," he was confident that it would "add one hundred thousand men to the rebbels' army and take nearly as many *from* our army." Squier found Kentucky troops particularly unwilling "to peril their lives to, as they say, free the 'Nigger,' and many, very many from the free states are little better."[11]

Major Henry Livermore Abbott of the 20th Massachusetts Volunteers strongly opposed emancipation and expressed sentiments common among officers in the Army of the Potomac. Soon after the Emancipation Proclamation went into effect, Livermore informed his aunt: "The president's proclamation is of course received with universal disgust, particularly the part which enjoins officers to see that it is carried out. You may be sure that we shan't see to any thing of the kind." Another soldier, Corporal Thomas H. Mann of the 18th Massachusetts Volunteers, noted succinctly, "The President's Proc[lamation] will have *no* effect except in conquered territory. . . . [and] will prolong the war." Faced with the prospect of serving with black soldiers, Corporal Felix Brannigan of the 74th New York Volunteers, wrote his sister: "We don't want to fight side and side with the nigger." He asserted: "We think we are a too superior race for that."[12]

Sergeant Symmes Stillwell of the 9th New Jersey Volunteers concurred. He considered arming the slaves to be "a confession of weakness, a folly, an insult to the brave Solder [*sic*]." William C. H. Reeder, a private in the 20th Indiana Volunteers, refused to reenlist because, he said, "this war has turned out very Different from what I thought it would. . . . It is a War . . . to free the Nigars . . . and I do not propose to fight any more in such A cause." In September 1864 General William T. Sherman complained against emancipation and black recruitment. "I dont see why we cant have some sense about negros," Sherman wrote, "as well as about horses mules, iron, copper &c.— but Say nigger in the U.S. and . . . the whole country goes Crazy. . . . I like niggers *well enough* as niggers, but when fools & idiots try & make niggers better than ourselves I have an opinion." Three months before Appomattox, Sherman again groused that Northern radicals had become obsessed with "Sambo." "The South deserves all she has got for her injustice to the negro," Sherman acknowledged, "but that is no reason why we should go to the other extreme."[13]

Lincoln's proclamation had indeed transformed the war from a constitutional struggle over the maintenance of the Union to one of black liberation. Though many Northerners, the president included, wondered whether forced manumissions by the government would be tested in the courts following the war, most persons agreed that wartime emancipation signaled the death knell of slavery in America once and for all. Lincoln more than hinted at this when in July 1862 he addressed a group of border state politicians, urging them to accept gradual, compensated emancipation as military necessity and adroit economics. The president explained:

> The incidents of the war can not be avoided. If the war continue [*sic*] long, as it must, . . . the institution in your states will be extinguished by mere friction and abrasion—by the mere incidents of the war. It will be gone, and you will have nothing valuable in lieu of it. Much of it's [*sic*] value is gone already. How much better for you, and for your people, to take the step which, at once, shortens the war, and secures substantial compensation for that which is sure to be wholly lost in any other event. How much better to thus save the money which else we sink forever in the war. How much better to do it while we can, lest the war ere long render us pecuniarily unable to do it. How much better for you, as seller, and the nation as buyer, to sell out, and buy out, that without which the war could never have been, than to sink both the thing to be sold, and the price of it, in cutting one another's throats.[14]

In addition to emptying slaveholders' pocketbooks, Lincoln's emancipation policy smoothed the way for the first large-scale use of blacks as combat soldiers in American history. According to veteran white abolitionist Thomas Wentworth Higginson, one of the first to command a black regiment, the president's decision to arm African Americans was "a momentous experiment, whose ultimate results were the reorganization of the whole American army & the remoulding of the relations of two races on this continent." After 1863 blacks rushed to join the U.S. Army and don the Union blue, determined to bury slavery, to defeat the Confederates, to prove their manhood, and to earn full citizenship. "We came out in 1[8]63," a black soldier recalled, "as Valent hearted men for the Sacke of our Surffring Courntury." Many, like Georgian Hubbard Pryor of the 44th USCT, escaped from slavery, entered Federal lines, and enlisted in the Federal service. Captured in Dalton, Georgia, in October 1864, Private Pryor spent the remainder of the conflict working on Confederate labor gangs in Alabama, Mississippi, and Southwest Georgia.[15]

Battery A, 2nd U.S. Colored Artillery (Light), Department of the Cumberland, ca. 1864. (Chicago Historical Society, no. ICHi-07774)

By war's end, under Lincoln's authority, the army had raised 178,975 African American soldiers, organized in 133 infantry regiments, four independent companies, seven cavalry regiments, twelve regiments of heavy artillery, and ten companies of light artillery. Approximately 19 percent of the men were recruited in the eighteen Northern states, 24 percent in the four loyal slave or border states, and 57 percent in the eleven Confederate states. Though most of the black soldiers in blue were ex-slaves, more than 15 percent of the 1860 Northern free black population joined the Union army. All in all, African Americans accounted for between 9 and 10 percent of all Union troops who served in the war. Sixteen black enlisted men received the Medal of Honor, awarded to U.S. soldiers for the first time in 1863.[16]

Though emancipation and military enlistment revolutionized American society, since the war's outbreak in April 1861, however, Lincoln had insisted that the conflict was a constitutional struggle to keep the Union intact, not a war to destroy slavery or to arm blacks. The freeing and the mobilizing of black troops were consequences, not objectives, of the war. Opposed to slavery on moral grounds, Lincoln was convinced that as president he lacked the authority to act against the "peculiar institution" in the states where it existed. "Lincoln believed sincerely that the Emancipation Proclamation was a practical war measure," explains historian Mark E. Neely, Jr., "and not merely an excuse for proclaiming his humanitarian agenda. He was astonishingly literal-minded in his belief that it was a war measure." Neely is correct when he cautions, on the one hand, against "any easy characterization of . . . Lincoln as a consistent and crusading emancipationist." On the other hand, Neely adds, "Lincoln . . . did not have as consistently conservative an early policy on slavery as it seemed." A close reading of Lincoln's statements on emancipation and black enlistments suggests that he gave the American public more than "mixed signals" on the race question. While the president was haphazard and slow to articulate the twin polices of black emancipation and enlistment, he nevertheless charted a far more linear course toward freedom than his nineteenth-century critics and modern historians have recognized.[17]

To be sure, when summoning the militia to suppress the rebellion in April 1861, Lincoln assured white Southerners that "the utmost care will be observed . . . to avoid any devastation, any destruction of, or interference with, property, or any disturbance of peaceful citizens in any part of the country." And when in May 1861, black abolitionist Frederick Douglass clamored for "*'carrying the war into Africa.' Let the slaves and free colored people be called into service, and formed into a liberating army,*" Lincoln demurred. Early in the war, like the vast majority of Northerners, he defined the conflict, according to the Reverend John G. Fee, a Kentucky abolitionist, as a "white man's war," committed to "let the nigger stay where he is."[18]

Although some African Americans had fought in the American Revolution and the War of 1812, a point that proponents of utilizing black soldiers emphasized repeatedly, federal law since 1792 had prohibited blacks from serving in the state militias and the U.S. Army. Outraged by discussions of arming the South's slaves, the *New York Express* predicted late in 1861 that should "this be attempted to any extent, the whole world will cry out against our inhumanity, our savagery, and the sympathies of all mankind will be turned against us." This attitude was common among both Northern civilians and soldiers in the Union army until 1863 when regiments of black troops filled depleted Union armies and proved their worth in combat.[19]

Lincoln certainly realized the implications for social change that emancipation and the use of blacks as armed soldiers implied. These steps, including the possibility of placing blacks on a social and political par with whites, would challenge the nation's racial status quo—white supremacy. They would fuel the racial phobias of conservative Democrats and Republicans and would discourage white enlistments. Lincoln also worried that emancipation would alienate nonslaveholders as well as slaveholders in the loyal border states and might further work to unify opposition to the Union in the Confederate states. These were legitimate fears. "In mid-century," historian La Wanda Cox explains, "both friend and foe of racial equality recognized a close historic linkage between bearing arms and citizenship."[20]

Eventually, many Northerners, including white racists and those who opposed the military draft, supported the recruitment of blacks as a means of filling regiments and preventing the sacrifice of yet more whites. This line of reasoning, according to Joseph T. Wilson, an African American author who served with two black regiments, represented "[t]he not unnatural willingness of the white soldiers to allow the negro troops to stop the bullets that they would otherwise have to receive." "I only wish we had two hundred thousand [blacks] in our army to save the valuable lives of our white men," wrote diarist George W. Fahnestock. "When this war is over & we have summed up the entire loss of life it has imposed," Iowa governor Samuel J. Kirkwood wrote, "I shall not have any regrets if it is found that a part of the dead are *niggers* and that *all* are not white men." The heated debates over arming slaves in South Carolina that were conducted in the U.S. House of Representatives in July 1862 illustrate how the lines were drawn early in the war on the questions of emancipating slaves and mustering them into military service.[21]

Outraged by reports that in May 1862 General David Hunter was freeing and arming slaves at Port Royal, Representative Charles A. Wickliffe of Kentucky denounced Lincoln's administration for allowing black recruiting without congressional authority and implored the president "to pause in this mad and impolitic scheme of emancipation." Unimpressed by arguments that Andrew Jackson had employed black soldiers at New Orleans during the War of 1812 (Wickliffe insisted that they were "quadroons . . . not Africans"), he proclaimed blacks unfit by nature for military service. In Wickliffe's opinion, "a negro is afraid, by instinct or by nature, of a gun. Give him a bowie-knife or a John Brown pike if you want to get up a servile war, of murder, conflagration, and rapine." Another Kentuckian, Congressman Robert Mallory, backed Wickliffe's attack on Hunter's action and declared that arming blacks was "contrary to the rules that should govern a civilized nation in conducting war." Mallory fulminated: "I shrink from arming the slave, using him to shoot down white men, knowing his depraved nature as I do. I would as soon think of enlisting the Indian, and of arming him with the tomahawk and scalping knife, to be let loose upon our rebellious countrymen, as to arm the negro in this contest." While he favored using captured Southern slaves as military laborers, Mallory adamantly opposed arming them, confident that they would train their guns on their former masters and slaughter them. Like Wickliffe, Mallory was convinced that blacks were incapable of making efficient soldiers. "One shot of a cannon would disperse thirty thousand of them," he said.[22]

Pennsylvania's Thaddeus Stevens, a Republican, disagreed strongly with the criticisms of General Hunter's order freeing slaves in coastal South Carolina and Georgia. Ridiculing Mallory, Stevens asked how Southerners could consider blacks "a savage and barbarous race, if one gun will disperse an army of them?" Throughout history, so Stevens noted in lecturing his congressional colleagues, nations at war had liberated slaves and employed them against their former masters, and the U.S. government should do so as well. Freeing and arming South Carolina slaves was essential, he argued, first, to deprive the Confederacy of its labor and, second, to replace white troops from serving in the pestilent, miasmatic low country. "I am for sending the Army through the whole slave population," Stevens explained, "and asking them to come from their masters, to take the weapons which we furnish, and to join us in this war of freedom against traitors and rebels." From his point of view, once they were trained as soldiers, the black troops should be assigned "to shooting their masters if they will not submit to this Government." "I do not view it as an abolition or as an emancipation question," Stevens concluded. "I view it as the means, and the only means, of putting down this rebellion."[23]

Influenced neither by Wickliffe and Mallory's conservatism nor by Stevens's radicalism, Lincoln charted his own course on emancipation and military employment of blacks. Since 1861—long before the president issued his two emancipation proclamations—Lincoln's government had taken small, hesitant, and occasionally backward steps toward these policies. This, according to Neely, suggests that Lincoln's ideas on emancipation, while essentially "conservative," were nonetheless "in flux." In May 1861, for example, General Benjamin F. Butler, in command of U.S. troops at Fortress Monroe, Virginia, declared escaped slaves who had labored on Confederate fortifications "contraband of war." He refused to return them to their masters and instead put the slaves to work in his quartermaster department. Butler reasoned that surrendering the slaves to their owners would aid the enemy and employing them as laborers would help the Union. With no established policy of his own on the slavery question, but leaning in the direction of emancipation, Lincoln let Butler's ad hoc policy stand.[24]

Soon thereafter, in August 1861, Congress passed the First Confiscation Act authorizing the government to seize all property, including slaves, used by the Confederacy "to work or to be employed in or upon any fort, navy yard, dock, armory, ship, entrenchment, or in any military or naval service whatsoever, against the Government and lawful authority of the United States." Military commanders quickly took advantage of this legislation. Over the course of the war, according to one estimate, as many as 200,000 contrabands worked for the U.S. Army as cattle drivers, stevedores, pioneer laborers, and in other support roles. This figure probably is too conservative. McPherson maintains that while both Butler's "contraband of war" policy and the First Confiscation Act sidestepped the question of manumission, they nevertheless introduced "the thin edge of the wedge of emancipation" into Federal military policy.[25]

In August 1861 General John C. Frémont, in charge of the Department of the West in St. Louis, took emancipation into his own hands by issuing a proclamation freeing the slaves of Missouri Rebels, an unauthorized edict quickly rescinded by Lincoln. Annoyed that the general had usurped "legislative functions of the government," Lincoln also feared that emancipation would drive Kentucky and perhaps the other border slave states into the arms of the Confederates. "I think to lose Kentucky is nearly the same as to lose the whole game," Lincoln informed Senator Orville H. Browning of Illinois. "Kentucky gone, we can not hold Missouri, nor, as I think, Maryland. These all against us, and the job on our hands is too large for us." Frémont had used a sledgehammer to drive "the wedge of emancipation" too deep, and Lincoln wisely relieved him of command. Outraged by Lincoln's revocation of Frémont's order, radical abolitionist Parker Pillsbury condemned the president's "cowardly submission to Southern and border slave state dictation." "The step taken by Fremont," Fee recalled, "was in the right direction; and one from which the heart and judgment of the discerning part of the nation did not go back."[26]

Indicative of the slowly changing Northern attitude toward slavery and of his own conservatism, in his December 1861 message to Congress, Lincoln recommended that blacks freed under the First Confiscation Act be colonized voluntarily "at some place, or places, in a climate congenial to them." He also urged consideration "whether the free colored people already in the United States could not, so far as individuals may desire, be included in such colonization." Committed since the 1850s to colonization as the solution to America's "race problem," the president believed that the "physical difference" between the races was so great that each suffered from the other's presence and thus should be "separated." He considered those freedmen who rejected colonization to be "extremely selfish" because they considered only their own comfort and ignored the betterment of the entire race. By the end of 1861, Lincoln thus clearly envisioned some active Federal role in emancipating the slaves. While, as Neely suggests, the president was uncertain about just how to proceed, he was willing "at least to experiment with proposals that would alter the status quo." It is significant to note, however, that in shaping Federal policy on slavery both Congress and Lincoln were motivated more by military expediency than moral or humanitarian concern for the slaves. Lincoln's colonization proposals harked backward to an outmoded solution to what white racial conservatives considered, quite literally, to be the "Negro problem."[27]

Nonetheless, Lincoln's experimentation picked up momentum and direction in 1862. In March, Congress enacted an additional article of war that seriously undermined the Fugitive Slave Laws of 1793 and 1850. It prohibited military and naval personnel from "returning fugitives from service or labor, who may have escaped from any persons to whom such service or labor is claimed to be due." In a special message to Congress, Lincoln also asked legislators to fund gradual emancipation in the loyal slave states. Such a policy, the president argued, would discourage Delaware, Kentucky, Maryland, and Missouri from joining the Confederacy and thereby undermine the insurrection in the Rebel states. A month later, Congress not only agreed to Lincoln's request but also legislated a compensated emancipation bill for the District of Columbia that allocated $100,000 to assist blacks who wished to settle in either Haiti or Liberia. In May the president urged border state slaveholders to accept compensated emancipation and not "be blind to the signs of the times." Gradual, compensated emancipation, he assured them, "would come gently as the dews of heaven, not rending or wrecking anything. Will you not embrace it?" In June 1862 Congress went further, emancipating slaves (but without compensating their masters) in the federal territories. And in July, after the border state representatives rejected Lincoln's compensated emancipation offer, Congress passed two little-known and little-understood bills—the Second Confiscation Act and the Militia Act—that directly linked emancipation to military enlistment.[28]

The Second Confiscation Act authorized federal courts to free the slaves of persons "engaged in rebellion" and permitted the president "to employ as many persons of African descent as he may deem necessary and proper for the suppression of this rebellion, and for this purpose he may organize and use them in such manner as he may judge best for the public welfare." It offered blacks no guarantee of civil rights but provided the president with the authority to transport, colonize, and settle, "in some tropical country . . . such persons of the African race, made free by the provisions of this act, as may be willing to emigrate, having first obtained the consent of the government of said country." Reflecting on the meaning of this bill, historians James G. Randall and James M. McPherson have emphasized its serious limitations as an instrument of emancipation. In practice it liberated only those slaves who belonged to "traitors" as determined on a case-by-case basis by the federal courts. As a result, Randall concluded that "it is hard to see by what process any particular slaves could have legally established that freedom which the second Confiscation Act 'declared.'" The act was, however, as historians Benjamin P. Thomas and Harold M. Hyman put it, "a cautious way for [Secretary of War Edwin M.] Stanton and radical congressmen to empower Lincoln to enroll Negroes as soldiers and push him toward a willingness to use the power." Though the act "gave Lincoln legal authorization to use Negroes in any capacity he saw fit," the president believed that the time was not yet right to arm the blacks. As a result they continued to wield shovels and picks, not muskets and swords. Lincoln believed that placing "arms in the hands of former slaves—to use black men to kill white men—had more explosive potentialities than emancipation itself." "The significant point," Thomas and Hyman insist, "is that Lincoln thought the moment, not the idea, unpropitious."[29]

The Militia Act, which according to historian Mary Frances Berry "marked an extraordinary change in traditional military policy," emancipated Confederate bondsmen (as well as their mothers, wives, and children) who performed military service for the U.S. Army, and authorized the president "to receive into the service of the United States, for the purpose of constructing intrenchments, or performing camp service, or any other labor, or any military or naval service for which they may be found competent, persons of African descent." The bill also specified that African Americans employed by the military were to be paid "ten dollars per month and one ration, three dollars of which monthly pay may be in clothing." Five days following their passage, Lincoln issued an executive order instructing his field commanders to execute the Second Confiscation and Militia Acts. They were to "seize and use any property, real or personal, which may be necessary or convenient for . . . military purposes" and "em-

ploy as laborers . . . so many persons of African descent as can be advanta-
geously used for military and naval purposes, giving them reasonable wages
for their labor." [30]

On July 22, the same day as Lincoln's executive order, his cabinet discussed arming the slaves, a policy Secretary of the Treasury Salmon P. Chase
"warmly" endorsed. "The President was unwilling to adopt this measure,"
Chase recorded in his diary, "but proposed to issue a Proclamation, on the
basis of the Confiscation Bill, calling upon the States to return to their allegiance . . . and proclaiming the emancipation of all slaves within States
remaining in insurrection on the first of January, 1863." [31]

In 1862 Lincoln thus had moved consistently though circuitously toward
emancipation and black enlistment. He had progressed so far that Neely insists that by mid-July—contemporaneous with passage of the Second Confiscation Act—the president had already decided to free the slaves if the
Confederates did not surrender. Writing to a Louisiana Unionist soon after
enactment of the Second Confiscation Act, Lincoln explained "that what is
done, and omitted, about slaves, is done and omitted on . . . military necessity." Black leader Frederick Douglass, however, was not impressed with
what he considered to be Lincoln's inaction. In a July 4, 1862, speech he
charged that Lincoln's policies had "been calculated . . . to shield and protect slavery" and that the president had "scornfully rejected the policy of
arming the slaves, a policy naturally suggested and enforced by the nature
and necessities of the war." Two months later, in a blistering editorial in
Douglass' Monthly, the black leader branded Lincoln as little more than "an
itinerant Colonization lecturer, showing all his inconsistencies, his pride of
race and blood, his contempt for Negroes and his canting hypocrisy." Despite Lincoln's professed antislavery views, Douglass blasted him as "quite
a genuine representative of American prejudice and Negro hatred and far
more concerned for the preservation of slavery, and the favor of the Border
Slave States, than for any sentiment of magnanimity or principle of justice and humanity." Specifically, Douglass complained that Lincoln, lacking
"courage and honesty," had failed to enforce the Second Confiscation Act.
He had "evaded his obvious duty, and instead of calling the blacks to arms
and to liberty he merely authorized the military commanders to use them
as laborers, without even promising them their freedom at the end of their
term of service . . . and thus destroyed virtually the very object of the measure." [32]

Like Douglass, many historians have concluded that the president was
far less committed to emancipation and employing blacks as soldiers than

the historical record in fact suggests. They have based this interpretation on Lincoln's public statements prior to his announcement of the preliminary Emancipation Proclamation. For example, in an August 1862 public letter to Horace Greeley, editor of the *New York Tribune*, Lincoln emphasized that his only goal was to restore the Union. Greeley had criticized Lincoln for falling under the influence of border state slaveholders and for failing to implement the emancipation provisions of the Second Confiscation Act. Responding to Greeley, Lincoln explained:

> If there be those who would not save the Union, unless they could at the same time *save* slavery, I do not agree with them. If there be those who would not save the Union unless they could at the same time *destroy* slavery, I do not agree with them. My paramount object . . . *is* to save the Union, and is *not* either to save or destroy slavery. If I could save the Union without freeing *any* slave I would do it, and if I could save it by freeing *all* the slaves I would do it; and if I could save it by freeing some and leaving others alone I would also do that. What I do about slavery, and the colored race, I do because it helps to save the Union.

Having said this, Lincoln left the door open for a change in policy, adding that he remained willing "to correct errors when shown to be errors; and I shall adopt new views so fast as they shall appear to be true views." Here was Lincoln at his pragmatic best, what Neely has termed his ability "to balance short-term practicality and long-term ideals." Lincoln also differentiated between his "*official* duty" — which was to restore the Union — and his "*personal* wish that all men everywhere could be free." Ever the astute politician, Lincoln wanted to have it both ways. As late as December 1862, in his annual message to Congress, the president proposed three constitutional amendments for voluntary and compensated emancipation by 1900 with voluntary colonization. In doing so, Neely explains, Lincoln gave the border states and the Rebel states "one last chance."[33]

Lincoln sought the right moment — a military victory — to unveil his true sentiments regarding emancipation. "While he waited," Neely maintains, "Lincoln chose, without actually lying, to give the American public the impression that he was not likely to free the slaves." Though Lincoln's reasons for adapting this disingenuous strategy are unknown, he no doubt purposely gave "mixed signals" in order to keep his options open — not to commit to emancipation prematurely — should the Confederacy surrender or seek a negotiated peace settlement. He also kept a close eye on public opinion in the border states and in the Confederacy. Determined to save the Union by any means, Lincoln gradually concluded that freeing and arming the slaves were necessary steps in suppressing the rebellion. "The way these measures were to help the cause," he later wrote, "was not to be by magic, or miracles, but by inducing the colored people to come bodily over from the rebel side to ours." The promise of freedom became a prerequisite before full-scale black recruitment could become reality.[34]

The Union army actually had little "inducing" to do because just as soon as the war began, slaves flooded Federal lines in the border South and continued to inundate army camps as U.S. troops penetrated the Confederacy. Underestimating the slaves' desire to be free and to contribute to their own emancipation, and ever mindful of losing border state and Northern conservative support, from the fall of 1861 to the spring of 1862 Lincoln instructed his commanders to exclude runaway slaves from Federal lines. But the bondsmen kept coming, gradually convincing soldiers, their officers, politicians, Northern public opinion, and finally Lincoln, of their importance as a strategic weapon against the Rebels. The army generally put them to work as military laborers. "It is a military necessity," Lincoln explained in July 1862, "to have men and money; and we can get neither, in sufficient numbers, or amounts, if we keep from, or drive from, our lines, slaves coming to them." As historian Ira Berlin and his colleagues at the Freedmen and Southern Society Project have so effectively documented, "the strongest advocates of emancipation were the slaves themselves." "In time," Berlin notes, "it became evident even to the most obtuse Federal commanders that every slave who crossed into Union lines was a double gain: one subtracted from the Confederacy and one added to the Union." As "contrabands," hundreds of thousands of fugitive slaves performed all manner of skilled and semiskilled labor for the Union forces. They worked as teamsters, blacksmiths, coopers, carpenters, bakers, butchers, cooks, laundresses, servants, and performed many other duties. "With their loyalty, their labor, and their lives," Berlin adds, "slaves provided crucial muscle and blood in support of the Federal war effort." While the slaves may have "forced the issue" of emancipation on the president, as McPherson reminds us, they ultimately depended on Lincoln to free and arm them.[35]

Lincoln also was less than forthcoming on his plans to arm the blacks. In early August 1862, for example, he informed a delegation of Indianans that he could not accept their offer to recruit two regiments of African American troops. Though he would continue to employ blacks as laborers, Lincoln was unprepared at that time to enlist them as soldiers. As his justification the president asserted that "the nation could not afford to lose Kentucky at this crisis, and . . . that to arm the negroes would turn 50,000 bayonets from the loyal Border States against us that were for us." He used almost the identical language in responding to a delegation of Chicago Christians on September 13, nine days before issuing his preliminary proclamation, but added: "I am not so sure we could do much with the blacks. If we were to arm them, I fear that in a few weeks the arms would be in the hands of the rebels; and indeed thus far we have not had arms enough to equip our white troops." Responding to Lincoln's obsession with keeping Kentucky in the Union, James Russell Lowell reportedly asked, "How many times are we to save Kentucky and lose our self-respect?" Thus when Lincoln's preliminary emancipation edict finally appeared on September 22, most considered it to be a dramatic about-face, one that not only altered the direction of the war but also redefined the meaning of "freedom" in American life. The shift in the president's policy, however, was more apparent than real. Addressing Congress a month before the Emancipation Proclamation was scheduled to take effect, Lincoln explained: "In *giving* freedom to the *slave*, we *assure* freedom to the *free*—honorable alike in what we give, and what we preserve."[36]

Though white Northerners and border state Unionists defined blacks as their social, cultural, and intellectual inferiors, by late 1862 the exigencies of war forced Lincoln to reverse his emancipation policy. Union general George B. McClellan's tactical draw against Confederate general Robert E. Lee at the Battle of Antietam on September 17 provided the breakthrough Lincoln desperately needed. Not only had the timing become right, but circumstances rendered such action crucial. The war had turned into a military stalemate, and morale was low in the North. England threatened to recognize President Jefferson Davis's new government. Lincoln needed more men to fill depleted Union regiments. To a significant degree the Confederacy's military successes had depended on slavery. Bondsmen provided the agricultural and industrial labor that equipped, fed, and supplied the Confederacy's armies. Slaves constructed fortifications, repaired railroads, and freed up white men to serve in the ranks. "Slavery has been, and is yet the shield and helmet of this accursed rebellion," Douglass remarked in January 1862. A year later he congratulated Lincoln on the "amazing change" in his emancipation policy—"this amazing approximation toward the sacred truth of human liberty." "We are all liberated," by the Emancipation Proclamation, Douglass said. "The white man is liberated, the black man is liberated, the brave men now fighting the battles of their country against rebels and traitors are now liberated, and may strike . . . the Rebels, at their most sensitive point." The destruction of slavery had become a military necessity and a major Union war aim. So too was the enlistment of black troops.[37]

From the start of the war, many Northerners who favored emancipation commonly included the enlistment of blacks, free and slave, as armed soldiers as part of the nation's antislavery crusade. They led and Lincoln followed.

Weeks after the Confederates attacked Fort Sumter, for example, abolitionist Gerrit Smith predicted that further Southern aggression would transform all Northerners "into radical, uncompromising, slave-arming, slave-freeing Abolitionists." "Unless the war shall be ended very soon," Smith wrote in May 1861, "black regiments will be seen marching Southward." Soon thereafter, an anonymous New Yorker admonished the president: "Strike, in the name of God . . . free the slaves and let them swell the army of freedom, and thus save the lives of our brave men, and prevent the utter bankruptcy of the people, by bringing the war to a speedy and triumphal close." Lieutenant Robert G. Shaw of the 2nd Massachusetts Volunteers, destined to command the 54th Massachusetts Volunteers to glory in its famous assault on Battery Wagner, outside Charleston, South Carolina, agreed. Writing in August, Shaw asked: "Isn't it extraordinary that the Government won't make use of the instrument that would finish the war sooner than anything else, — viz. the slaves? . . . What a lick it would be at them [the Confederates], to call on all the blacks in the country to come and enlist in our army! They would probably make a fine army after a little drill, and could certainly be kept under better discipline than our independent Yankees." In October, Secretary of War Simon Cameron put theory into practice, instructing the commander of Federal troops at Port Royal, South Carolina, to utilize fugitive slaves in any capacity he saw fit, including organizing them in "squads" and "companies." In the following months, Cameron publicly supported the arming of the slaves as a military necessity and recommended in his annual report to Congress an army of freed slaves.[38]

As in Frémont's case, Cameron's independent move to emancipate the slaves met with Lincoln's displeasure and was overturned. In a letter to a Kentucky editor, the president, still concerned that he could lose border state and Northern conservative support, later explained his side of the story: "When, early in the war, Gen. Fremont attempted military emancipation, I forbade it, because I did not think it an indispensable necessity. When a little later, Gen. Cameron, then Secretary of War, suggested the arming of the blacks, I objected, because I did not yet think it an indispensable necessity." Influential Republican abolitionists, however, including Congressman Thaddeus Stevens and Senator Charles Sumner, sided with Cameron. In December 1861, Illinois congressman Owen Lovejoy proclaimed that it would be impossible to defeat the Southern states "without liberating their slaves and putting muskets into the hands of all who will fight for us." The Reverend John G. Fee recalled that when he learned that the government had begun recruiting blacks, "I then began to have hope of a speedy and successful termination of the war. I had from the beginning of the war continuously said, 'I do not believe we will succeed until we begin enlisting men as men—not merely white men.'"[39]

As 1862 dawned, other radical abolitionists, including Governor John A. Andrew of Massachusetts and Senator James H. Lane of Kansas, and Generals John W. Phelps and David Hunter, pressed Lincoln to enlist black troops. Their efforts were important because they underscored the eagerness of blacks to fight and alerted the nation to their potential as soldiers. Significantly, events in 1862 smoothed the way for the integration of military service of blacks into the nation's emerging emancipation policy. By the time Lincoln issued his final Emancipation Proclamation, five regiments of blacks, between 3,000 and 4,000 men, already were in service in South Carolina, Louisiana, and Kansas. As historian Dudley T. Cornish has remarked, they were "raised on a catch-as-catch-can basis with little or no control from Washington."[40]

For his part, Andrew petitioned Washington for permission to recruit free blacks in his state, which did not come to pass until January 1863. The governor was cognizant of the importance of his efforts because, as he explained to influential abolitionist Francis G. Shaw, father of Robert G. Shaw, "it will be the first colored regiment to be raised in the free States, and . . . its success or its failure will go far to elevate or to depress the estimation in which the character of the colored American will be held throughout this world." Lacking Federal authority, the irrepressible Lane nevertheless recruited, largely from among fugitive slaves from Arkansas and Missouri, what became the 1st Kansas Colored Volunteers. Mustered into service in January 1863, it became the first regiment of black troops recruited in a Northern state.[41]

Hunter and Phelps, in South Carolina and Louisiana, respectively, encountered more difficulties in their crusades to enlist black troops. According to Ira Berlin, though they were working independently, these Union generals "envisioned a slave army of liberation assaulting the Confederacy from their respective points of command." Late in 1861, for example, Hunter, then posted in Kansas, proposed invading Kentucky and then moving south, "proclaiming the negro free and arming him as I go. The Great God of the Universe has determined that this is the only way in which this war is to be ended, and the sooner it is done the better. If I am the instrument, I shall not stop short of the Gulf of Mexico, unless laid low by His Almighty hand." Hunter's superiors ignored the proposal.[42]

Writing the following year with similar apostolic conviction, Phelps requested permission from his superior, General Benjamin F. Butler, then commander of the Department of the Gulf, to arm and equip fugitive slaves at Camp Parapet near New Orleans, which had fallen to Federal forces in April 1862. "Society in the South seems to be on the point of dissolution," Phelps informed Butler, "and the best way of preventing the African from becoming instrumental in a general state of anarchy, is to enlist him in the cause of the Republic. . . . It is for the interests of the South, as well as for the North that the African should be permitted to offer his block for the temple of Freedom. Sentiments unworthy of the MAN of the present day, worthy only of another Cain could prevent such an offer from being accepted." As radical abolitionists, both Hunter and Phelps obviously were convinced that, with regard to emancipation and the enlistment of black troops, they were answerable to a "higher law" than Lincoln.[43]

In April 1862 Hunter, then commander of the Department of the South, liberated bondsmen around Fort Pulaski, Georgia, determined to put them to work as laborers. He did so without War Department authorization. In May, once more lacking government approval, he proclaimed slaves in small sections of coastal South Carolina, Georgia, and Florida free and ordered the forced enlistment as soldiers of all physically fit black men between ages eighteen and forty-five. Lincoln overruled Hunter's actions, again convinced that enlisting African American soldiers was not yet an "indispensable necessity," but the general continued recruiting blacks, seizing them while they were at work on plantations and coercing them into his Federal unit. According to an officer who later commanded black troops, Hunter's strong-armed recruiting tactic "was valuable as an example of how not to do it."[44]

In August 1862, when Stanton refused to recognize and pay his black troops, Hunter disbanded all but one company of his recruits. Stanton soon reversed himself and quietly authorized General Rufus Saxton to pick up recruiting African Americans where Hunter had left off. Disgusted by what he considered Lincoln's conservative and circuitous approach to emancipation, Garrison wrote his daughter: "The President can do nothing for *free-dom* in a direct manner, but only by circumlocution and delay. How prompt was his action against Fremont and Hunter!" By permitting Saxton to arm 5,000 "volunteers of African descent," Stanton hoped to guard coastal plantations from Confederate marauders and to deny the Rebels laborers. "A small step toward emancipation," writes historian David J. Eicher, "it was nonetheless somewhat remarkable for the time." By October 1862, Saxton began organizing the 1st South Carolina Volunteers, the first regiment of former slaves formally authorized by the War Department, under the command of Higginson. In November it participated in a coastal raid that freed more than 150 slaves. Other regiments of black South Carolinians soon followed.[45]

Phelps fared little better in southern Louisiana than Hunter had done in South Carolina. Beginning in May 1862, he made Camp Parapet a refuge for runaway slaves and instructed his men to retaliate against slaveholders who had mistreated their bondsmen. Deeply committed to emancipation and black enlistment as means to weaken the Confederacy and to turn the slaves against their former masters, Phelps implored Butler to allow him to arm the slaves in his camp. Butler refused, arguing that he lacked authority to enlist black soldiers and also doubting the necessity and quality of African American troops. Undaunted, in July 1862 Phelps raised five companies of black troops with hopes of arming them. Instead of supplying Phelps's men with guns, however, Butler ordered him to have them cut trees around the camp, not drill.

Outraged, Phelps refused to obey Butler's order and resigned his commission. "I am not willing to become the mere slave-driver which you propose," Phelps explained. He judged it "impossible to serve in this Department without doing violence to my convictions of right and public necessity." Ironically, in August 1862 Butler, then in need of reinforcements, decided "to call on Africa" and accepted the volunteers of the Louisiana Native Guards, a regiment of free blacks that previously had offered its services to the Confederates. By November Butler had mustered three regiments of Louisiana Native Guards (Union) into Federal service, making him the first Union commander to bring free blacks formally into the ranks. For the remainder of the war Butler continued to champion the use of African American troops, one of the few high-ranking generals who, according to historian Richard J. Sommers, refused to consider black soldiers as "uniformed ditchdiggers." Near the end of the war, Butler commanded the Army of the James and its Twenty-fifth Corps, "the first and only American army corps composed entirely of black units."[46]

Whereas Lincoln's government had grudgingly authorized recruitment of black soldiers in South Carolina and Louisiana on a piecemeal basis to relieve temporary manpower shortages, during 1862 the president recognized the vital connection between redirecting the war, emancipation, and military recruitment. Explaining the evolution of his policy, Lincoln recalled:

> When in March, and May, and July 1862 I made earnest, and successive appeals to the border states to favor compensated emancipation, I believed the indispensable necessity for military emancipation, and arming the blacks would come, unless averted by that measure. They declined the proposition; and I was, in my best judgment, driven to the alternative of either surrendering the Union, and with it, the Constitution, or of laying strong hand upon the colored element. I chose the latter. In choosing it, I hoped for greater gain than loss; but of this, I was not entirely confident.

Military necessity, the need to fill depleted units, the need to employ the 500,000 to 700,000 fugitive slaves who had entered Federal lines, and the need to deprive the Confederates of vital manpower convinced Lincoln in late 1862 that the time was "right" to free the Confederacy's slaves and to arm blacks, North and South.[47]

In 1863 black enlistment became the focal point of Lincoln's emancipation program and his subordinates worked to systematize and integrate black recruitment into national policy. In a widely circulated pamphlet, Henry Carey Baird urged politicians to enlist blacks with all dispatch. "By utilizing this element the Government can secure the services of 700,000 able-bodied men, acclimated to and familiar with the seat of war, and at the same time strike the Rebels a vital blow," he averred. Douglass concurred, arguing in February 1863, "Whoever sees fifty thousand well drilled colored soldiers in the United States, will see slavery abolished and the union of these States secured from rebel violence." A month later Lincoln confided to General Nathaniel P. Banks that he considered the raising of black troops "very important, if not indispensable." "The colored population is the great *available* and yet *unavailed* of, force for restoring the Union," the president informed Military Governor Andrew Johnson of Tennessee. "The bare sight of fifty thousand armed, and drilled black soldiers on the banks of the Mississippi, would end the rebellion at once."[48]

Secretary of the Treasury Salmon P. Chase agreed. "The American blacks must be called into this conflict," he told a friend in April 1863, "not as cattle, not now even as contrabands, but as men. . . . We need their good will and must make them our friends, by showing ourselves their friends. We must have them for guides, for scouts, for all military service in camps or field. . . . Thus employed, from a burden they will become a support; and the hazards, privations, and labors of the white soldiers will be proportionally diminished." In August Lincoln informed General Ulysses S. Grant that black regiments would become an invaluable "resource which, if vigorously applied now, will soon close the contest. It works doubly, weakening the enemy and strengthening us. We were not fully ripe for it until the [Mississippi] river was opened. Now, I think at least a hundred thousand can, and ought to be rapidly organized along it's [*sic*] shores, relieving all the white troops to serve elsewhere."[49]

Lincoln restated these arguments in his widely printed August letter to James C. Conkling, also reiterating a point he had made and would make many times—that no matter what happened during and after the war, emancipation would stand. Military and political events would not undo the Union's commitment to emancipation. Blacks, he explained, "like other people, act upon motives. Why should they do anything for us, if we will do nothing for them? If they stake their lives for us, they must be prompted by the strongest motive—even the promise of freedom. And the promise being made, must be kept." "Thus," Ira Berlin explains, in "1863 the Lincoln administration had tied the question of slavery to the larger issues of the nature of the war, the impact of emancipation on American society, and the role of blacks in the war effort. These issues could not be easily separated, and the insatiable demand for soldiers forced the question of black enlistment to the fore. The previously inconceivable idea of large-scale black enlistment appeared increasingly to be common cause." The character of the war had indeed changed.[50]

Despite its newfound commitment to black recruitment, Lincoln's administration continued to move casually and inefficiently—according to historian Fred A. Shannon, it was "slow, uncertain, halting, and timid"— in organizing African American units. Historian W. E. Burghardt Du Bois described the Northern government as taking "perplexed and laggard steps" toward emancipation and black enlistment. The loose, decentralized administrative structure that characterized black recruiting in early 1863 suggests perhaps a certain degree of ambivalence within the War Department over the enlistment of blacks. Or it may simply have reflected the first stages of a new and ambitious experiment.[51]

For example, early in 1863 Secretary of War Stanton authorized Massachusetts, Rhode Island, and Connecticut, but not Ohio, to recruit black regiments. Leading abolitionists, including Douglass, George L. Stearns, Richard P. Hallowell, Martin R. Delany, William Birney, Henry McNeal

Turner, and John Mercer Langston were commissioned to traverse the Northern and Midwestern states to gather recruits, but the men were to be sent back to New England to be credited to the various states' draft quotas. The door was opened to conscript Northern free blacks when, in March 1863, Congress passed the Enrollment Act, rendering "all able-bodied male citizens . . . liable to perform military duty." As the Northern regiments filled up with free blacks, Stanton authorized free state governors to send more than one thousand agents to Louisiana, North Carolina, and the Mississippi Valley to recruit slaves and fugitive slaves. Frederick Douglass admonished recruits "to fly to arms, and smite with death the power that would bury the government and your liberty in the same hopeless grave." The dream of this black leader of "carrying the war into Africa" was becoming a reality.[52]

In March 1863 Stanton dispatched Adjutant General Lorenzo Thomas to the Mississippi Valley not only to recruit blacks but also to identify white officers to command them. Overcoming all manner of racism within the ranks, Thomas succeeded brilliantly in recruiting freedmen, encouraging white noncommissioned officers to apply for commissions in black units, and in popularizing the employment of black soldiers. Though Thomas's men sometimes seized slaves and forced them into military service, he insisted that blacks be treated equally with whites and that African American regiments not be singled out for a disproportionate share of fatigue duty. By May 1, Thomas had mustered his first regiment into service—the 1st Arkansas Volunteers of African Descent. According to Dudley T. Cornish, Thomas's inspection tour "initiated the new Negro soldier policy of proceeding not by the parceling out of authority to selected individuals and states but by decree and direction of the War Department acting through the army. This step was the great turning point in the development of the movement to arm the Negro as a soldier." By year's end, Thomas had organized twenty black regiments. By war's end, he had participated in raising seventy such units, more than 40 percent of the entire number of African Americans who fought for the Union.[53]

Thomas's success in the Mississippi Valley contributed to the growing Northern support for Lincoln's emancipation program. Writing in May 1863, Attorney General Edward Bates noted that "abolition seems be the strongest rallying point" in Washington, "and men who dont care a fig about it have become all of a sudden, very zealous in that cause." He included among them Secretary of State William H. Seward and Secretary of War Stanton. A month later Whitelaw Reid, columnist for the *Cincinnati Gazette*,

Recruitment poster, U.S. Colored Troops, ca. 1863–65. (P[ierre] S. Duval, "Come and Join Us Brothers," n.d., Rare Book, Manuscript, and Special Collections Library, Duke University)

commented on the dramatic change in public opinion concerning the recruitment of African American soldiers: "The day for raising a panic over Negro enlistment has passed; and it, like confiscation, emancipation and a dozen other bitterly denounced 'Abolition measures,' has passed as an accepted fact into the history of the war."[54]

Thomas's recruiting efforts also underscored the need for a centralized system of recruitment. In May 1863 the War Department standardized the recruitment process by establishing a separate office in the Adjutant General's Office to coordinate the organization of black troops. Cornish considers the creation of the Bureau for Colored Troops "the coming of age of the American Negro soldier," "a milestone in the history of the Negro in the Civil War."[55]

Led by Assistant Adjutant General Charles W. Foster, the bureau supervised the recruitment of blacks in both the North and the South and examined officer candidates for regiments that, by the summer of 1863, were

Recruitment broadside, U.S. Colored Troops, Philadelphia, 1863.
(The Library Company of Philadelphia)

assigned numbered units in the U.S. Colored Troops (USCT). With the exception of a few black regiments formed in Connecticut, Louisiana, and Massachusetts (including the 54th and 55th Massachusetts Volunteers and the 5th Massachusetts Cavalry), all other African American units, including those previously mustered on the state level, entered Federal service and eventually were assigned numbered U.S. regimental designations. For example, under Federal auspices Higginson's 1st South Carolina Volunteers became the 33rd USCT; Lane's 1st Kansas Colored Volunteers became the 79th USCT; Butler's 1st, 2nd, and 3rd Louisiana Native Guards became, respectively, the 73rd, 74th, and 75th USCT; and the 1st Arkansas Volunteers of African Descent became the 46th USCT. No longer were African American troops enlisting to fight for particular states, but rather "for the United States—the government . . . [that] had promised them freedom." According to Cornish, the establishment of the Bureau for Colored Troops transformed black recruitment from "its original amateurish, haphazard, and volunteer basis to a new footing of professional, organized, regularized activity under central control from Washington."[56]

No matter what happened in the nation's capital, the mobilization of black troops would have failed had not African Americans enthusiastically encouraged their sons, brothers, and husbands to enlist. Meeting, for example, at a black state convention in Poughkeepsie, New York, in July 1863, "The Colored Citizens of the State of New York" declared "that men of negro lineage hold the balance of power in this contest, and . . . we should . . . throw our weight for the Government, not alone in words, but by sturdy blows. We should strike, and strike hard, to win a place in history, not as vassals, but as men and heroes." That same month Douglass, who according to historian David W. Blight interpreted the war as "an apocalyptic power that forever changed the relationship of blacks to America," once more urged his black brethren to enlist. As Douglass explained,

> Never since the world began was a better chance offered to a long enslaved and oppressed people. The opportunity is given us to be men. With one courageous resolution we may blot out the hand-writing of the ages against us. Once let the black man get upon his person the brass letters U.S.; let him get an eagle on his button, and a musket on his shoulder, and bullets in his pocket, and there is no power on the earth or under the earth which can deny that he has earned the right of citizenship in the United States. I say again, this is our chance, and woe betide us if we fail to embrace it.

Though Douglass never joined the USCT (Stanton promised him a commission that never came to pass), two of his sons, Charles and Lewis, served in the 54th Massachusetts Volunteers. A third son, Frederick, Jr., recruited black troops in Mississippi.[57]

Who were the men who volunteered to fight in the USCT? According to Norwood P. Hallowell, colonel of the 55th Massachusetts Volunteers, the regiments recruited from the free states "contained every known variety of citizen of African descent, and were recruited from every class and condition of colored society." Hallowell compiled statistics on his regiment, which he considered typical of units recruited in the North—and his soldiers were indeed a diverse lot.[58]

Of the 961 enlisted men in the 55th, the largest number (222) were born in Ohio, followed by Pennsylvania (139), Virginia (106), Indiana (97), Kentucky (68), Missouri (66), and Illinois (56). The remaining 207 men were born in eighteen states (including eleven slave states), the District of Columbia, Nova Scotia, Canada, Africa, and places "unknown." Collectively, the men had plied forty-six trades and occupations. The most common profession was farmer (596), followed by laborer (74), waiter (50), cook (27), teamster (27), sailor (20), mason and plasterer (16), and hostler and shoemaker (9 each). The recruits served in thirty-five other occupations, ranging from broom-maker to glass-grinder to confectioner. The men included 247 former slaves, 550 "pure blacks," 430 men of "mixed blood," 477 men who were literate, 319 men who could read and write, 52 church-members, and 219 married men. The average age of the recruits was twenty-three and one-fifth years, and their average height was five feet, seven-twelfths inches. The men had one thing decidedly in common. They entered camp uniformly "poor and ragged."[59]

Once mustered into service, Colonel Hallowell explained, officers employed two different methods of training the black recruits. In regiments such as the 54th and 55th Massachusetts Volunteers, composed largely of free blacks, commanders resorted to the strict discipline commonly used in drilling whites. "The unruly members of the Fifty-fourth and Fifty-fifth were stood on barrels, bucked, gagged and, if need be, shot; in fact, treated as white soldiers were in all well-disciplined regiments." In contrast, Colonel Higginson's 1st South Carolina Volunteers were ex-slaves, and he used a more "enlightened" method to train his men. "In a slave regiment," Hallowell explained, "the harsher forms of punishment were, or ought to have been, unknown, so that every suggestion of slavery might be avoided." Hallowell was convinced that whether free black or slave, once the recruit re-

*Private Charles R.
Douglass, 54th
Massachusetts Volunteers.
(Moorland-Spingarn
Research Center, Howard
University)*

Sergeant Lewis H.
Douglass, 54th
Massachusetts Volunteers.
(Moorland-Spingarn
Research Center, Howard
University)

Unidentified soldier, 55th Massachusetts Volunteers. (Alfred S. Hartwell Collection, State Library of Massachusetts)

Sergeant Jackson, 55th Massachusetts Volunteers. (Alfred S. Hartwell Collection, State Library of Massachusetts)

Unidentified soldier, 55th
Massachusetts Volunteers.
(Alfred S. Hartwell
Collection, State Library
of Massachusetts)

Unidentified soldier, 55th Massachusetts Volunteers. (Alfred S. Hartwell Collection, State Library of Massachusetts)

ceived his new uniform he was transformed into a new man. "He straightened up, grew inches taller, lifted, not shuffled, his feet, began at once to try, and to try hard, to take the position of the soldier." The colonel insisted: "For the first time in his life he found himself respected, and entrusted with duties, for the proper performance of which he would be held to a strict accountability." Under the command of competent white commanders like himself, Hallowell concluded, each black volunteer became "a possible Lord Chesterfield."[60]

Though many abolitionists, Northern free blacks, and USCT recruits assumed that African Americans would serve as officers in USCT regiments, white soldiers, U.S. government officials, and the white public in general frowned on elevating blacks to the status of commissioned officers. "The real question," Assistant Adjutant General Charles W. Foster asserted in 1864, was whether "white officers and men [were] prepared to acknowledge and obey the colored man, or officer, as a military superior?" Mirroring contemporary white supremacist views, the War Department answered in the negative, arguing that the appointment of black officers would prove unworkable if circumstances placed them in command of white enlisted men or officers. "In the black regiments," Berlin notes, "the divide of color reinforced that of rank." Blacks and their white allies objected to this policy, bombarding Washington with demands for the commissioning of capable black soldiers.[61]

These pleas fell largely on deaf ears, and only around one hundred blacks received commissions in the USCT. Roughly two-thirds of these men served early in the war in the Louisiana Native Guards until they were forced out of service by General Nathaniel P. Banks, General Benjamin F. Butler's successor as commander of the Department of the Gulf. The remaining handful of African American officers served as company-level officers, chaplains, surgeons, and, late in the war, as recruiters. None held field command. Thousands of blacks, however, "appointed from the best men of their number," did serve ably as noncommissioned officers at the regimental level (sergeant-major, quartermaster sergeant, commissary sergeant, and hospital steward) and at the company level (first sergeant, sergeant, and corporal). In doing so, black noncommissioned officers provided all manner of leadership and became vital intermediaries between white officers and black enlisted men. "While federal officials found it useful to place blacks in command over other blacks," Berlin notes, "they had no desire to revolutionize American race relations by placing blacks in command of whites." Writing back home, Private Wilbur Fisk of the 2nd Vermont Volunteers considered this arrangement a "miserable compromise to an unreasonable prejudice."[62]

Whites were not necessarily interested in commanding black units, however. Even before the War Department established the Bureau for Colored Troops, which in May 1863 instituted boards for rigorous examinations of prospective USCT officers, whites debated the merits of leading black soldiers. In July 1862, for example, Charles Francis Adams, Jr., equated command of blacks to the work of a "'nigger driver' . . . seeing that they don't run away, or shirk work or fatigue duty," and he wanted no part of it. At first Captain John William De Forest of the 12th Connecticut Volunteers found the prospect of securing a colonelcy in a black regiment attractive. "It would be a comfortable position," he wrote in October 1862. But De Forest's enthusiasm quickly faded when he learned that African American units would most likely garrison unhealthy posts, perform fatigue and pioneer labor, and "will be seldom put into battle, and will afford small chance of distinction." Whites like De Forest preferred to avoid the ridicule and abuse that awaited officers who cast their lot with black troops.[63]

Service as an officer with the USCT, however, appealed to a broad range of other whites—abolitionists and "careerists," paternalists and racists. Abolitionists included such men as Colonels Higginson, Shaw, and Nathan W. Daniels, the commander of the 2nd Louisiana Native Guard (Union). Reflecting on the qualities of his men and his service in March 1863, Daniels identified "many rough diamonds among this race" and remarked "what they need is only cultivation and opportunity. The Bonds of a half dozen centuries could not smother their inherent capacity." Grateful for the opportunity to lead blacks in combat, Daniels added: "Thank God it hath been my fortune to be a participator in the grand idea of proclaiming freedom to this much abused & tortured race. Thank God my Regiment an African one."[64]

"Careerists" were those soldiers eager to take advantage of the War Department's policy of offering promotions to men who were willing to leave their white regiments to serve in black units. They sought the higher pay, perquisites, and prestige accorded commissioned officers. The examining boards were strict, however, and about 40 percent of the almost 4,000 men who stood for the examination failed. Only 25 percent of the applicants received a USCT commission. Many of the approximately 7,000 white officers assigned to USCT regiments took advantage of these incentives and, for example, received promotions from private or sergeant to lieutenant or from captain to colonel. The promotion of battle-tested noncommissioned

Unidentified sergeant, U.S. Colored Troops. (Rare Book, Manuscript, and Special Collections Library, Duke University)

and junior officers from white to black units (almost 80 percent of the white officers had prior combat experience) provided the USCT with a generally strong leadership base. For instance, Sergeant Charles Trowbridge of the 1st New York Engineers was promoted to a captain in the 1st South Carolina Volunteers. By war's end he commanded the regiment.[65]

Few potential white officers of the USCT, however, failed to be stained by the white racism of their age. As historians Michael A. Cavanaugh and William Marvel have observed, "it took a certain liberal attitude to admit that Negroes could equal white men in combat, but it would never have done to forget these black soldiers were only a few cultural steps removed from draft animals, and required a stronger rein than their white counterparts." In March 1863, for example, Private Henry Martyn Cross of the 48th Massachusetts Volunteers informed his parents that he was studying "to fit myself for a commission." "I should be glad of a 2nd lieutenancy in a 'nigger regiment,'" Cross wrote, "if I could not do any better." Three months later, however, following what he described as the "magnificent success" of the black troops in their May 27 assault at Port Hudson, Louisiana, Cross changed his tune. "God forgive the nation for not giving in to it sooner. In *every respect* they are fully equal to any troops, and in many respects . . . *superior* to all. . . . If I ever get a commission, I hope that it will be in a 'nig. regt.'"[66]

Corporal Robert K. Beecham of the 2nd Wisconsin Volunteers also joined the USCT in order to obtain what he termed "a commission into the fraternity of military swell heads." After an exhaustive, nit-picking examination before a board of haughty officers in Washington, D.C., and six months of red tape, in December 1863 Beecham finally received his much-coveted commission and the shoulder straps of a first lieutenant in the 23rd USCT. Like Colonel Daniels, Beecham developed a close bond with his black troops, describing them as cleaner, more sober, and more respectful of white women than the white men in his former Wisconsin unit. Writing tongue-in-cheek, he described "how delightfully easy it is for a private soldier who possesses the physical manhood, the intellectual ability, and the sand in his craw to get a commission in the American army."[67]

Beecham's problems, however, paled in contrast to those of the black soldier who, according to George Washington Williams, "had enemies in his rear and enemies in his front." Aghast at the mistreatment, degradation, and discrimination under which the USCT served, *Cincinnati Gazette* columnist Whitelaw Reid complained that "every Negro we enlist goes into the field with a halter around his neck." The black troops, he said, encountered "ten-fold the dangers our white soldiers incur and none of the protections." As he prepared to enter combat in the summer of 1863, Corporal James Henry Gooding of the 54th Massachusetts Volunteers summarized the realities of black military service. "There is not a man in the regiment who does not appreciate the difficulties, the dangers, and maybe ignoble death that awaits him, if captured by the foe, and they will die upon the field rather than be hanged like a dog." Seeking relief from Secretary of War Stanton from the "Veary Hard & a Dreadfull condishion," under which his regiment suffered in New Bern, North Carolina, a soldier of the 4th USCT wrote "that i hope that the Time Shall Soon come when Shall all be Eacklize as men hear." He added: "i have read the Regulations Enough to Know that it is Rong but i Suppose that because we are colored that they think that we dont no any Better."[68]

Army recruiters had indeed promised black enlistees fair and equal treatment. But in practice the color line circumscribed virtually every aspect of black military life, mirroring racial proscriptions for free blacks in the antebellum North. The twin forces of white racism and military necessity converged on the men of the USCT, and throughout their service black soldiers received discriminatory duties, inferior assignments, inadequate care, insufficient training, and insults from white soldiers. Conditions for the USCT were generally separate and unequal to those of white troops—a condition that underscored their second-class status in the War Department's bureaucracy and in American society at large.

From the start of their military service, many white commanders believed that black troops were better suited to labor than to soldier—to dig and perform menial duties, not to fight. This is not surprising because, when welcoming blacks into "the armed service of the United States" in his final Emancipation Proclamation, Lincoln specifically directed them "to garrison forts, positions, stations, and other places." Convinced that blacks would prove inferior to whites in combat but superior to work under the hot tropical sun and in unhealthy lowlands, whites assigned black troops an excessive amount of fatigue labor, oftentimes replacing white units for these tasks. In September 1863 Private John H. Westervelt of the 1st New York Engineer Corps criticized the treatment of the black troops, saying that they were "ill used by those whose duty it is to look after their interest and see them get what Uncle Sam intends to provide for all alike both white and black." Though he denied being "a nigger worshiper," Westervelt nevertheless noted the disproportionate amount of labor that the USCT performed during the siege of Charleston. "They certainly do more fatigue duty, and I believe there is no longer any question about their [*sic*] being good fighters. They are put at the hardest as well as the meanest kinds of work. I have seen them policing (cleaning up filth and rubbish) white regiment camps. If a spirited white soldier were to do this except as punishment for some offense I think he would die first."[69]

"In many places," Berlin explains, "black soldiers found themselves doing little but constructing fortifications, digging trenches, and loading and unloading wagons and ships. White soldiers commonly assigned them the most loathsome duties such as cleaning latrines and ship bunkers, and then cursed them for doing the odious work." The posting of the USCT largely to garrison work, historian William W. Freehling argues, was most prevalent in the Union's Western army of occupation. It freed white troops, Freehling maintains, to fight in the East. "Instead of the musket," a soldier from the 20th USCT informed President Lincoln, "It is the spad and the Whelbarrow and the Axe cuting in one of the most horable swamps in Louisiana stinking and misery Men are Call to go on thes fatiuges wen sum of them are scarc Able to get Along." Another infantryman, Thomas D. Freeman of the 54th Massachusetts Volunteers, complained that "we are not Soldiers but Laborers working for Uncle Sam for nothing but our board and clothes . . . it is nothing but work from morning till night Building Batteries Hauling Guns Cleaning Bricks clearing up land for other Regiments to settle on . . . now do you call this Equality if so God help such Equality." Probably because of such protests, in General Orders No. 21, issued in June 1864, Adjutant General Lorenzo Thomas instructed his commanders to distribute labor and fatigue detail equally among soldiers of both races. General William T. Sherman nevertheless remained skeptical of the fighting qualities of blacks, preferring to employ them as "pioneers, teamsters, cooks, and servants" and only gradually experimenting with them "in the art of the Soldier, beginning with the duties of local garrison." In the last year of the war, blacks continued to perform a disproportionate amount of menial labor. Two months after Appomattox, officers of the 15th USCT still complained of the excessive fatigue duty assigned their men.[70]

Such onerous work details, along with generally insufficient and inferior regimental medical care, contributed to black soldiers' suffering from significantly higher morbidity and mortality rates than whites. Approximately one in five black soldiers died from disease as compared to roughly one of every twelve white soldiers. Though more than one-third (68,178) of the black soldiers who served in the army died, only 2,751 were killed in action. The rest were reported missing or having died from wounds or disease. According to historian Joseph T. Glatthaar, the black troops' "woeful and discriminatory medical care," resulted in more than 29,000 men dying from pneumonia, dysentery, typhoid fever, and malaria. "Very few surgeons will do precisely the same for blacks as they would for whites," remarked a surgeon assigned to a USCT regiment in 1863. "The mortality in our Regt. beats anything I ever saw," reported another officer assigned to a USCT unit in Louisiana. "They frequently drop dead in the streets, and in two or three instances have been found laying dead in the weeds some distance from camp." The 56th USCT, for example, assigned principally to garrison duty at Helena, Arkansas, lost only twenty-five officers and men in its limited military engagements, but it suffered the loss of 653 men from disease. In October 1864 a military medical board reported that an undiagnosed disease had ravaged three Missouri black regiments—the 62nd, 65th, and 67th USCT—units subjected to continuous labor at Morganzia, Louisiana. Sickness wiped out one-third of the enlistees. Later in the war Adjutant General Lorenzo Thomas inspected a USCT hospital in Nashville and observed lice-infested wards with men still clothed in the blood-soaked uniforms that they had worn in battle. "Words," Thomas said, "cannot describe the utter filthiness of what I saw." "Had these men been white soldiers," he added, "think you this would have been their condition? No!"[71]

Because many military administrators considered black troops inferior to whites, and because the War Department initially defined blacks primarily as military laborers, not soldiers, from the start of their service African American units commonly received inadequate war matériel, rations, and weapons. According to historian Susan-Mary Grant, "the nature of the duties required of them meant that their uniforms became worn out very quickly, giving them the appearance of laborers rather than of soldiers." Typical of the black military experience, the 5th USCT, a regiment of black Ohioans, endured insufficient clothing and equipage and deficient housing, forcing its commander, Lieutenant Colonel Giles W. Shurtleff, to improvise. As Berlin explains, though the USCT reportedly received the regular army ration provided white troops, the daily allotment of beef and starches catered more to the dietary preferences of white and black Northerners than to black Southerners. "For Southern black soldiers . . . the standard ration represented a sharp departure from their customary regimen of pork, cornbread, and green vegetables. As disease spread, black soldiers, who understood in their own way the connection between diet and health, indicted the army ration as one source of deteriorating health." In addition to complaining about their military diet, black troops also faulted the quantity and quality of their chow. Private Westervelt remarked that the blacks routinely congregated "around our cookhouse to get what bean or pea soup we leave. It is allowed in plentifull quantities by government and goes begging with us, but they receive it with eagerness and swallow it with voracity. Bread is served them only once a week they tell me." And in the case of at least one regiment—the 6th USCT—a supervisory committee investigated charges that the men received adulterated hardtack.[72]

As for their arms, USCT regiments, according to historian William A. Gladstone, "were issued the best weapons available to fulfill their perceived mission." All too often this translated into such "second-class" arms as the .54 caliber M1855 Austrian "Lorenz" rifled musket or third-class guns including the .69 caliber Austrian rifled musket or the .69 caliber Prussian musket. Commenting on a failed mission by a black regiment, Colonel Hallowell reported that it fought "with nearly worthless old Austrian rifles, [that were] soon after condemned." To compound problems with their outdated and malfunctioning weapons, some regiments received not only different types of muskets but ones that also fired different calibers of ammunition. As late as April 1864, General Edward W. Hincks requested that troops in his all-black division should be issued "as effective a weapon as any that are placed in the hands of white Soldiers, who go into battle with none of the peculiar disadvantages to which my men will be Subject." Specifically, Hincks wanted the blacks' "unreliable" Springfield and Enfield rifles and "Old Harpers Ferry smoothbore" muskets replaced with the latest weapons—Spencer repeating carbines or breech-loading rifles. It was imperative, Hincks implored General Benjamin F. Butler, that following the slaughter of black soldiers who tried to surrender at Fort Pillow, Tennessee (April 12, 1864), men of the Army of the James be able "to defend themselves and lessen their liability to capture." Because African American troops "cannot afford to be beaten, and will not be taken," Hincks added, they deserve "the best arm . . . that the country can afford."[73]

Long before Fort Pillow, where 66 percent of the blacks assigned to that Federal garrison were massacred by troops commanded by General Nathan Bedford Forrest, black soldiers and their white officers worried about how they would be treated—as prisoners of war or as insurrectionists—if captured by the Confederates. In 1887 Joseph T. Wilson recalled that when he and his black comrades "heard the long roll beat to arms, and the bugle sound the charge, . . . they were not to go forth to meet those who regarded them as opponents in arms, but who met them as a man in his last desperate effort for life would meet demons." Ever vigilant against slave revolt and concerned that fugitive slaves could provide intelligence to the Union forces, early in the war Confederate officers announced that slaves convicted of insurrection or of aiding the enemy would be executed. This was in line with the punishment meted out to Southern slaves convicted of insurrection since the colonial period. "For many Southerners," Cornish explains, "it was psychologically impossible to see a black man bearing arms as anything but an incipient slave uprising complete with arson, murder, pillage, and rapine."[74]

Worried, for example, that North Carolina's statutes were insufficient to punish "armed slaves & Yankees who may be found with them," in January 1863 state legislator William T. Dortch offered his legal opinion to Governor Zebulon B. Vance: "The mere fact of finding a colored person armed ought to be made a capital offence, & the presence of a Yankee with an armed negro ought also to be made capital." Robert Garlick Hill Kean, an official in the Confederate War Department, judged the recruitment of Southern slaves "a barbarity which no people, who regarded anything save the gratification of a devilish lust of revenge and hatred, could tolerate on the principle, the use of savages," he added, ". . . [was] infamous." In August 1864 Methodist preacher George Richard Browder, a slaveholder and Southern sympathizer, recorded his impressions of first observing U.S. Colored Troops in South-central Kentucky. "The sight was very revolting to me & other Kentuckians," he wrote.[75]

Jefferson Davis and his government shared these opinions and reacted to the early efforts to recruit slaves by General Hunter in South Carolina and Generals Phelps and Butler in Louisiana with outrage. In August 1862 Adjutant and Inspector General Samuel Cooper declared Hunter and Phelps "outlaws" and announced that if captured, they and their officers "employed in drilling, organizing, or instructing slaves, with a view to their armed service in this war" should be "held in close confinement for execution" as felons. When, in November 1862, Confederate troops captured six black soldiers on Georgia's Saint Catherines Island, the local commander recommended "that these negroes be made an example of. They are slaves taken with arms in hand against their masters and wearing the abolition uniform. Some swift and terrible punishment should be inflicted that their fellows may be deterred from following their example." Secretary of War James A. Seddon concurred, recommending that one of the blacks "be executed as an example."[76]

Davis reserved a special animus for Butler and his officers, declaring them "robbers and criminals deserving death." The Confederate president condemned Butler for exciting "the African slaves . . . to insurrection" and for arming them "for a servile war—a war in its nature far exceeding in horrors the most merciless atrocities of the savages." Davis damned Lincoln's preliminary Emancipation Proclamation as an "effort to excite servile war within the Confederacy" and blasted the final Emancipation Proclamation as "the most execrable measure recorded in the history of guilty man," one that would lead to insurrection by the slaves and to their ultimate "extermination." Davis announced that "all negro slaves captured in arms" and their white commissioned officers would be tried under the laws of the various Confederate states. Within weeks the Reverend Browder recorded in his diary that "confederates hang or shoot all the negroes they find in uniform & say they will give all the officers captured since the issuing of Lincolns proclamation into the hands of the State authorities to be punished for exciting insurrection. The penalty is death & this may lead to cruel & bloody retaliation. Oh the horrors of these evil times."[77]

By the spring of 1863, as Lincoln's program of freeing and arming the slaves unfolded, circumstances increasingly required that both the Confederacy and the Union clarify their official positions regarding the treatment of black U.S. troops. In April, Confederate secretary of war Seddon authorized General John C. Pemberton, commander of the Department of Mississippi and East Louisiana, to put to labor as he saw fit an African American, presumably a soldier, captured on a Federal ship. "The Department," Seddon wrote, "has determined that negroes captured will not be regarded as prisoners of war." A month later, in a joint resolution, the Confederate Congress declared that those engaged in freeing and arming the South's slaves would be "lawfully repressed by retaliation." Any white officer recruiting, training, or commanding blacks would "be deemed as inciting servile insurrection, and shall if captured be put to death or be otherwise punished at the discretion of the court." Black soldiers who fell into Confederate hands were to "be delivered to the authorities of the State or States in which they shall be captured to be dealt with according to the present or future law of such State or States."[78]

In June, General Edmund Kirby Smith, commander of the Trans-Mississippi Department, discouraged his subordinates from even capturing black soldiers or their officers and directed instead that they be given "no quarter." The Confederate War Department, however, overruled Kirby Smith's order, describing the men of the USCT as "deluded victims" who "should be received and treated with mercy and returned to their owners. A few examples might perhaps be made," an official explained, "but to refuse

them quarter would only make them, against their tendencies, fight desperately." Captured black troops thus faced several possible scenarios. Northern
free blacks might be sold into slavery; former slaves might be reenslaved and
returned to their masters; or the black soldiers might be executed for "inciting servile insurrection." Their officers might be executed or imprisoned.
Or all might be forced to perform hard labor.[79]

Mindful of Confederate threats to enslave or execute black soldiers and
to execute their officers, War Department officials in Washington outlined
in April 1863 the historical and legal bases for what they considered to be
the fair and equal treatment of the U.S. Colored Troops. General Orders
No. 100 stated clearly that black troops and their officers were to be respected
as soldiers and, if captured, treated as prisoners of war. First, a slave who
entered Union lines as a fugitive or who was captured by Northern troops
was "immediately entitled to the rights and privileges of a freeman." Second,
once men, regardless of "class, color, or condition," were "properly organized as soldiers," they must be treated by their captors as "public enemies,"
not as individuals. Third, because international law drew no color distinc-
tions between soldiers, the enslavement or sale of captured men based on
race warranted "the severest retaliation, if not redressed upon complaint."
Given that the United States could not "retaliate by enslavement," the order
declared that "therefore death must be the retaliation for this crime against
the law of nations." Legalistic and theoretical, General Orders No. 100 was
conspicuously vague and unspecific regarding how and when such "retaliation" would be implemented.[80]

Lincoln did not comment publicly on the treatment of the USCT by
the Confederates until late July 1863. He did so following allegations that
black soldiers were murdered or enslaved after the battles of Port Hudson
(May 27), Milliken's Bend (June 7), Mound Plantation (June 29) in Louisiana, and Battery Wagner (July 18) in South Carolina. Port Hudson, Milliken's Bend, and Battery Wagner marked the first use of black troops by the
U.S. Army in combat and convinced many skeptics, in both the North and
the South, that African American soldiers would fight—and would fight
bravely and with distinction. Confederate threats to give black troops and
their officers "no quarter" inspired the men of the USCT to become stubborn fighters who were loath to give up, fearful that Southern troops would
not take them alive. "Negro soldiers and their officers," Cornish explains,
thus "were bound together in a heightened esprit de corps and in a determination to die before surrendering that is rare in military annals." In 1863
Colonel Daniels wrote proudly that the men of his 2nd Louisiana Native

Guard would "fight like bloodhounds, and never surrender. Defeat in our case is worse than Death. Victory the only alternative—my men are well aware of this and will vent themselves accordingly." Recent research suggests that though eleven white USCT officers probably were executed by Southern troops, the Confederate government never carried out its threat systematically to try captured white officers for inciting insurrection.[81]

In the summer of 1863, however, Frederick Douglass, was livid over the Confederates' threats and was furious over what he considered the across-the-board second-class status accorded black soldiers. They were denied commissions as officers; they received unequal pay; and their families generally were denied humanitarian relief provided white soldiers' families. Douglass exploded with anger when he learned of the Confederates' treatment of the 54th Massachusetts Volunteers at Battery Wagner. Though in the battle the black soldiers proved that they could fight "and vindicated their sponsors, the abolitionists," the regiment paid a heavy price for its valor. Almost one-half (272) of the 600 men who attacked Battery Wagner were killed, wounded, or captured. "Think," Douglass admonished white abolitionist George L. Stearns, "of its noble and brave officers literally hacked to pieces while many of its rank and file have been sold into a slavery worse than death, and pardon me if I hesitate about . . . raising a fourth Regiment until the President shall give the same protection to them as to white soldiers." "The slaughter of blacks taken as captives," Douglass complained, "seems to affect him as little as the slaughter of beeves for the use of his army."[82]

Finally, on July 31, Lincoln issued General Orders No. 252, declaring that the government would protect all of its soldiers—irrespective of color—who became prisoners of war. "To sell or enslave any captured person on account of his color and for no offense against the laws of war is a relapse into barbarism and a crime against the civilization of the age," he declared. Specifically, Lincoln ordered that "for every soldier of the United States killed in violation of the laws of war a rebel soldier shall be executed, and for every one enslaved by the enemy or sold into slavery a rebel soldier shall be placed at hard labor . . . until the other shall be released and receive the treatment due to a prisoner of war." Despite Lincoln's threats of reprisals, throughout the war the Confederates employed captured black soldiers in forced labor battalions and in at least three other engagements in 1864 after Fort Pillow—Poison Spring in Arkansas (April 18) and Petersburg and Saltville in Virginia (July 30, October 2)—Confederate troops murdered surrendering or wounded black troops. Following the Fort Pillow massacre, Lincoln

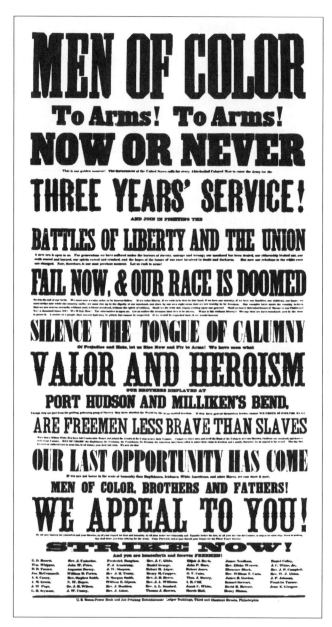

Recruitment broadside, U.S. Colored Troops, Philadelphia, 1863.
(The Library Company of Philadelphia)

admitted that while he was "determined to use the negro as a soldier, there is no way but to give him all the protection given to any other soldier. The difficulty is not in stating the principle," he said, "but in practically applying it."[83]

Probably the experiences of the men of the 8th USCT captured by the Confederates following the Battle of Olustee (February 20, 1864) were typical of the treatment accorded black prisoners of war and their white officers. In his diary Private Robert Knox Sneden of the 40th New York Volunteers observed "a dozen or more Negroes, all prisoners of war," at Andersonville, the Confederacy's notorious Georgia prison. "Nearly all are minus an arm or leg, and their wounds are yet unhealed. Many of them are gangrened and they will all surely die. They keep by themselves and are very quiet. The Rebels have removed every vestige of any uniform they once wore, and then have nothing on but old cast off jean trousers and cotton shirts. All are bareheaded, barefooted, and as thin as skeletons. Those captured who were able to work are kept at work outside by the Rebels, felling trees, making roads, etc., etc." Their officers had been sent to prisons in Richmond, Sneden added, "and are made to eat and sleep with Negroes."[84]

Though Lincoln had little control over how the Confederates treated black prisoners of war, he ultimately was successful in addressing another discrimination black soldiers experienced—unequal pay. As early as August 1862, Stanton had promised black recruits the same pay as whites ($13 per month, $3 of which constituted a clothing allowance), but in 1863 War Department solicitor William Whiting ruled that under the Militia Act of July 1862 blacks of all ranks were to be paid $10 per month with $3 withheld by the government for clothing. Framers of the act had assumed—erroneously—that African Americans who joined the army would serve not as soldiers but as laborers and, accordingly, should be paid at a lower rate than whites. Stanton confirmed the lower rate of pay for blacks in General Orders No. 163 on June 4, 1863. In response, the men of the 54th and 55th Massachusetts Volunteers protested, refusing to accept any pay that was unequal pay. "A more pitiful story of broken faith," recalled Captain Luis F. Emilio of the 54th Massachusetts Volunteers, "with attendant want and misery upon dependent ones, than this . . . cannot be told." "Notwithstanding the negroes fight so well and show so much bravery," Private Wilbur Fisk of the 2nd Vermont complained, "they have hitherto been allowed but the bare pittance of seven dollars a month."[85]

Abolitionists and the black soldiers themselves protested loudly against the inequality of pay, arguing correctly that not only had blacks performed courageously in combat, but because of their race they were also exposed to greater risks than white troops. "Colored men have a right not only to ask for equal pay for equal work," Douglass wrote in August 1863, "but that merit, not color, should be the criterion observed by Government in the distribution of places." Writing in the *New Bedford Mercury*, James Henry Gooding of the 54th Massachusetts Volunteers explained why his regiment refused to accept any pay until it was offered equal pay. "Too many of our comrades' bones lie bleaching near the walls of Fort Wagner," he said, "to subtract even one *cent* from our hard earned pay." To accept less, Gooding added, "would rob a whole race of their title to manhood, and, even make them feel, no matter how faithful, how brave they had been, that their mite towards founding liberty on a firm basis was spurned, and made mock of." "Now your Excellency," Gooding explained in a letter to Lincoln, "we have done a Soldier's Duty. Why Can't we have a Soldier's pay? . . . Now if the United States exacts uniformity of treatment of her Soldiers from the In-surgents, would it not be well and consistent to set the example herself by paying all her *Soldiers* alike?"[86]

While sympathetic to the black soldiers' feelings with regard to their un-equal pay, Lincoln urged them to be patient. According to Douglass, in Au-gust 1863 the president reminded him that many whites still doubted the wisdom of enlisting black troops, that many whites still considered the idea of black soldiers offensive, and "the fact that they were not to receive the same pay as white soldiers seemed a necessary concession to smooth the way to their employment at all as soldiers." Reportedly in a patronizing tone, Lincoln informed Douglass that because black men "had larger motives for being soldiers than white men . . . they ought to be willing to enter the service upon any condition." Eventually, Lincoln assured Douglass, the gov-ernment would equalize the pay of black and white soldiers. But the men would have to wait.[87]

However, both Douglass and African American troops in the ranks were losing "patience and faith" with Lincoln. As late as September 1864, the black leader remained dismayed at the government's "treatment of our poor black soldiers—the refusal to pay them anything like equal compensation, though it was promised them when they enlisted; the refusal to insist upon the exchange of colored prisoners, and to retaliate upon rebel prisoners when colored prisoners have been slaughtered in cold blood, although the Presi-dent has repeatedly promised thus to protect the lives of his colored sol-diers." The black soldiers held on, but they remained impatient and seethed with indignation, especially over their unequal wages. Back home, their families suffered from lack of support.[88]

The men of the 54th and 55th Massachusetts Volunteers, insulted by Federal policy, continued to refuse any pay, even a supplement offered by their state legislature to make up the difference between their promised and actual compensation. In June 1864, Colonel Edward N. Hallowell, who replaced Shaw as commander of the 54th, reported that his men, having received no pay in almost a year, were nearly mutinous. "I believe them to be entirely right, morally," Hallowell explained, "and yet military necessity has compelled me to shoot two of them." Conditions were worse in the 3rd South Carolina Volunteers where, in protest of the government's unequal pay policy, Sergeant William Walker marched his company to his captain's tent and ordered them to stack their guns. Walker asserted that because the army had failed to uphold its contract with the men, he and his men were released from duty. His superiors disagreed, and Walker was court-martialed and executed. According to Colonel Higginson, "fear of such tragedies spread a cloud of solicitude over every camp of colored soldiers for more than a year."[89]

In his December 1863 annual report, Secretary of War Stanton heaped praise on the USCT for its military performance and urged Congress to equalize their pay. "There seems to be inequality and injustice" in their wages, Stanton remarked in a gross understatement. "Soldiers of the Union, fighting under its banner, and exposing their lives in battle to uphold the government, colored troops are entitled to enjoy its justice and beneficence." Nevertheless, Lincoln and Republicans in Congress dragged their feet, indicative of considerable opposition by Democrats and conservative Republicans in recognizing the equality of black and white troops. In January 1864 Higginson informed the *New York Tribune* that the government's failure to honor its pledge to the black regiments "inflicted untold suffering . . . impaired discipline . . . relaxed loyalty, and has begun to implant a feeling of sullen distrust in the very regiments whose early career solved the problem of the nation, created a new army, and made peaceful emancipation possible." Even though in April 1864 Attorney General Bates reversed Whiting's interpretation of the Militia Act (laborers, *not* soldiers, were to receive $10 per month), thereby paving the way for equal pay, Lincoln refused to act.[90]

Two months later, on June 15, 1864, Congress finally equalized pay for black and white troops, but with a major qualification. Soldiers who had been enslaved at the start of the war would receive retroactive pay only to January 1, 1864. Men who were free at the beginning of hostilities would receive back pay to the date of their enlistment as well as bounty payments.

Determined to rectify the discrimination against soldiers who had been slaves, Higginson waged a vigorous campaign in the national press accusing the government of defrauding former slaves who served in the army and for breaking its contract with them. "Any employer," Higginson wrote to the *Tribune*, "following the example of the United States Government, may make with him [the former slave] a written agreement, receive his services, and then withhold the wages. He has no motive to honest industry, or to honesty of any kind. He is virtually a slave, and nothing else, to the end of time." Not until March 3, 1865, did Congress finally grant full retroactive pay to all black soldiers who had been promised equal pay upon mustering into the service. Two months later the War Department authorized bounties for all black recruits—slave and free—who enlisted after July 18, 1864. Slaves who enlisted before that date, however, were denied such a claim. "In the eyes of the War Department," Berlin notes, "the slaves' freedom itself was adequate bounty."[91]

In exchange for the hardships and indignities they endured—half wages, inferior medical care, inadequate weapons, inappropriate rations, insufficient training, the prospect of being enslaved or executed if captured, repeated insults from white troops, brutal punishments that smacked of slave discipline, and much more—the U.S. Colored Troops carried out various military duties and in the process surprised a doubting Northern public and their severest and most racist critics. Because of the white officers' racist, limited expectations of blacks' abilities as soldiers ("I would use Negros [*sic*] as Surplus," Sherman wrote in 1864), these troops largely garrisoned forts, escorted wagon trains, performed fatigue labor, and guarded confiscated plantations and prisoners of war. But they also participated in 449 separate military actions, thirty-nine of which were "major engagements." By the close of 1863, Secretary of War Stanton reported to Lincoln that though many persons doubted that the freed slaves had sufficient courage and could adjust to military discipline, combat experience had proven "how groundless were these apprehensions." He indicated that "[t]he slave has proved his manhood, and his capacity as an infantry soldier, at Milliken's Bend, at the assault upon Port Hudson, and the storming of Fort Wagner." Attitudes, especially in the War Department, were changing.[92]

Indeed, black soldiers fought in every military theater: in the East, the West, the Mississippi Valley, and the Trans-Mississippi. They entered combat as early as October 29, 1862 (a skirmish at Island Mound, Missouri, by the 1st Kansas Volunteers), and continued fighting until May 11–12, 1865 (skirmishes at Palmito Ranch, Texas, involving the 62nd USCT), a month

"The Negro in the War— Various Employments of the Colored Men in the Federal Army. From Sketches by C. E. F. Hillen." (Editor's collection)

after General Lee surrendered at Appomattox. To be sure, most of the black troops' fighting was limited to minor engagements or outpost scraps, removed from the major campaigns, and under the command of relatively obscure general officers. And when the black soldiers finally saw combat, historian Noah Andre Trudeau explains, "they too often entered the fight saddled with the burden of having to prove themselves worthy to their Caucasian comrades. Any misstep during an engagement, or a slip of discipline that would be forgiven a raw white unit, would be held as proof of a black unit's unreliability, a stain that no amount of blood could wash away." Repeatedly, the USCT had "to prove anew that they would fight."[93]

But fight they did, and certainly on a par with white troops. Though historian Bell Irvin Wiley complained that contemporary testimony was too biased to allow an objective evaluation of their fighting, he nevertheless concluded "that some Negro soldiers conducted themselves heroically in battle while others skulked and ran; that leadership was a crucial factor in their combat performance . . . that in offensive spurts the showing of Negroes compared favorably with that of whites of comparable background and training." In short, they discharged their duties more or less like all soldiers, irrespective of time, place, or race. Wiley was on less solid footing, however, when he argued "that units recruited in the North were more effective than those composed of recently freed slaves." Neither Wiley nor more recent scholars have unearthed evidence to support a correlation between free or slave status and military performance. Rather, as in all wars, numerous intangible factors determined how soldiers fought.[94]

For example, in such actions as the attack on the Confederate bastion at Port Hudson, Louisiana (May 27, 1863), and the engagement at New Market Heights, Virginia (September 29, 1864), Trudeau argues, the USCT "were deliberately committed to a hopeless task—not for any strategic reason, but solely to test their mettle." Despite terrible odds, however, the black troops distinguished themselves in both battles, and whites grudgingly took note. Having observed the valiant performance of the black soldiers (the 1st and 3rd Louisiana Native Guards) at the defeat at Port Hudson, a white New Yorker commented: "They charged and re-charged and didn't know what retreat meant. They lost in their two regiments some four hundred men as near as I can learn. This settles the question about niggers not fighting well. They, on the contrary, make splendid soldiers and are as good fighting men as any we have." A Massachusetts soldier agreed with this assessment of the performance of the black troops at Port Hudson. "A race of serfs stepped up to the respect of the world," he wrote with considerable prescience, "and commenced a national existence." Writing to his wife, Union colonel Benjamin H. Grierson remarked, "the negro regiments fought bravely yesterday . . . there can be no question about the good fighting qualities of negroes hereafter." Following New Market Heights, where fourteen men of the USCT received the Medal of Honor, Lieutenant Joseph J. Scroggs of the 5th USCT proclaimed that "no man dare hereafter say aught in my presence against the bravery and soldierly qualities of the colored soldiers."[95]

Raw, virtually untrained black troops, mostly ex-slaves, exhibited similar dash and grit while defending the Union garrison at Milliken's Bend, Louisiana, twenty-five miles above Vicksburg on the Mississippi River, on June 7, 1863. In this engagement three regiments (the 9th and 11th Louisiana Volunteers of African Descent and the 1st Mississippi Volunteers of African Descent) held off a larger force of Confederates in heated hand-to-hand combat. This is especially significant because the black soldiers entered battle poorly prepared and equipped with outmoded Belgian rifles. They nevertheless fought fiercely but suffered devastating losses—35 percent of the black troops were killed or wounded. The 9th Louisiana lost almost 45 percent of its men, which, according to Glatthaar, represents the highest proportional loss by a unit in a single engagement during the war. But such sacrifices and courage did not go unnoticed. "The bravery of the blacks in the battle at Milliken's Bend," Assistant Secretary of War Charles A. Dana recalled, "completely revolutionized the sentiment of the army with regard to the employment of negro troops." Accompanying General U. S. Grant's army during the Vicksburg campaign, Dana "heard prominent officers who formerly in private had sneered at the idea of the negroes fighting express themselves after that as heartily in favor of it."[96]

Having served their military "apprenticeship" in 1863, black troops gained in 1864 more opportunities to fight, distinguishing themselves in several major campaigns and in many small engagements. On February 20 three black regiments (the 54th Massachusetts Volunteers, the 1st North Carolina Colored Volunteers, and the 8th USCT) suffered heavy casualties during the Union Army's defeat at the Battle of Olustee, Florida, along the Florida, Atlantic, and Gulf Central Railroad about sixty miles west of Jacksonville. A correspondent who observed the battle reported to the *Liberator* that "[t]he rebels allowed us to penetrate, and then, with ten to our one, cut us off, meaning to 'bag' us." The 8th USCT served as one of the lead Union regiments and bore the brunt of the Confederates' intense enfilading fire. According to historian William H. Nulty, the 8th USCT was "a completely new and combat-inexperienced unit which had never even practiced firing their weapons. . . . Sent into action with weapons empty, to deploy and load their weapons while under fire, it was remarkable that they stayed where they were for an hour and a half." When the smoke of battle cleared, more than 300 of the regiment's 554 effectives were killed or wounded. The 1st North Carolina Colored lost 230 of its approximately 600 men, and the 54th Massachusetts, which covered the Union troops' withdrawal, had 86 casualties from among its roughly 495 men. To make matters worse, following the battle Confederate troops brazenly murdered wounded black prisoners. A Rebel soldier instructed his wife to "[t]ell the negroes if they could have seen how the [Northern] negroes are treated I think it would cure them of all desire to go." Another Confederate remarked that at Olustee "our men slayed the Negrows & if it had not been for the officers their would not one of them been spaired."[97]

The USCT met with more success on June 15, 1864, when the Third Division, Eighteenth Corps, led by General Edward W. Hincks, assaulted the outer defenses of the Confederate stronghold at Petersburg, Virginia. Hincks's two brigades, consisting of the 5th Massachusetts Cavalry, and the 1st, 4th, 5th, 6th, 10th, and 22nd USCT, stormed the fortified Dimmock Line that circled Petersburg south of the Appomattox River. Despite heavy casualties (almost half of the men of the 4th USCT were hit), the black troops successfully stormed the twenty-foot-thick breastworks and trenches protected by fifteen-foot ditches. They captured six Confederate batteries, including nine artillery pieces, and took 200 prisoners. Private Charles Torrey Beman of the 5th Massachusetts Cavalry remembered how "the shell, grape and canister came around us cruelly"; but "we rallied, and after a terrible charge, amidst pieces of barbarous iron, solid shot and shell, we drove the desperate greybacks from their fortifications, and gave three cheers for our victory." "It was rather interesting to see the old veterans of the A[rmy of the] P[otomac] stare when they saw the works we had captured," wrote Lieutenant Harvey Covell of the 6th USCT. Convinced that Rebel reinforcements were en route, and still skeptical of the "experiment" of employing black soldiers, Hincks's superior, Union general William F. Smith, failed to use the USCT to pursue the enemy and missed a perfect opportunity to capture Petersburg. "There was nothing—not even a military force," an exasperated General Grant later complained, "to prevent our walking in and taking possession." Smith's inaction necessitated the ten-month-long siege of Petersburg.[98]

Despite Smith's indecision and doubts about blacks as soldiers, the men

Company E, 4th U.S. Colored Troops, Fort Lincoln, D.C., ca. 1864.
(Library of Congress, no. B817-7890)

of the USCT nonetheless proved their worth at the Petersburg assault. According to McPherson, Hincks's division experienced its first real combat there "and performed well" during its baptism of fire. Summarizing their contribution to the early Petersburg campaign, Private Fisk wrote that

> The negroes were remarkably well pleased with their prowess on this occasion. It was a glorious day for them. They won great favor in the eyes of the white soldiers by their courage and bravery. I am sure I never looked upon negroes with more respect than I did upon those soldiers, and I did not hear a word of disrespect towards them from any of the boys. Yesterday they made another charge here, and it was done in excellent style. The best military critic could hardly find fault with it. In a steady straight line they advanced right over the crest of the hill and right up to the enemy's works, under a terrible fire, but without wavering or faltering, compelling the enemy to leave his works in the hands of the blacks. The stream of wounded that came pouring back, some leaning on

a comrade and some carried on stretchers, told of the bloody work they had done.

The Reverend William H. Hunter, the black chaplain of the 4th USCT, interpreted the success of the African American troops at Petersburg in millennial terms. "The 15th of June, 1864," he wrote, "is a day long to be remembered by the entire colored race on this continent. It is the day when prejudice died in the entire Army of the U.S. of America. It is the day when it was admitted that colored men were equal to the severest ordeal. It is the day in which was secured to us the rights of equality in the Army and service of the Government of the United States."[99]

Not only did Hunter speak too optimistically about the acceptance and success of blacks in the Federal forces, but six weeks later the USCT participated in one of the Union army's most famous debacles—the bloody and brutal assault on the crater created at Petersburg on July 30, 1864. Determined to find a means of penetrating the center of the Dimmock Line and end the Petersburg siege, General Ambrose Burnside, commander of the Ninth Corps, authorized coal miners from the 48th Pennsylvania Volunteers to tunnel 551 feet to the Confederate line, to pack 320 kegs of gunpowder—eight thousand pounds—under the Confederate redoubt known as Elliott's Salient, and to detonate the massive charge. Burnside selected nine rested but inexperienced USCT regiments from the Fourth Division, commanded by General Edward Ferrero, to lead the attack after the explosion and to capture Cemetery Hill behind the Confederate lines. These regiments had heretofore been employed for guard detail and fatigue labor, not combat. To prepare them for the attack, the USCT received two weeks of special tactical training (right and left wheels in double column) in order to circumvent quickly the hole that would result following the explosion that was set for 3:30 A.M. on Saturday, July 30. "In conception," McPherson explains, the plan "bid fair to become the most brilliant stroke of the war; in execution it became a tragic fiasco."[100]

In fact, the carefully planned explosion and accompanying attack seemed destined to fail. Less than twenty-four hours before the scheduled blast, Burnside's superiors, General George G. Meade and General Grant, overruled the decision to have Ferrero's black division spearhead the attack. Meade and Grant, like most high-ranking Union officers, doubted the fighting ability of black troops. They also feared that they would be accused of recklessly sacrificing black lives if the attack failed. As a result, instead of Ferrero's black troops, three divisions of white soldiers (commanded by

Guard House and Guard, 107th U.S. Colored Troops, Fort Corcoran, Arlington, Va.,
ca. 1864. (Library of Congress, no. B8184-841)

Generals James H. Ledlie, Robert B. Potter, and Orlando B. Willcox) were
staged to deploy around the periphery of the hole that would result from the
detonation of the mine and then capture Cemetery Hill. Ferrero's USCT
would follow them into battle and push on to Petersburg. Not surprisingly,
the white troops were poorly prepared for this hastily assembled plan. Ledlie
in fact never instructed his brigade commanders that they were to capture
the ridge at Cemetery Hill.[101]

After a delay (the fuses leading to the gunpowder fizzled out and had to
be relit), the tremendous explosion finally occurred at 4:44 A.M. The four
tons of powder erupted, tearing a hole 150 to 200 feet long, sixty feet wide,
and thirty feet deep in the Confederate lines. The explosion launched earth,
debris, men, and matériel hundreds of feet in the air, killing or wounding
almost 300 Rebels. Sergeant William H. Thomas of the 5th USCT remembered the explosion as "a never to be forgotten sight of death and devastation." Ledlie's white division, slow to move out of its trenches, was followed
by those of Willcox and Potter. But instead of dashing around the crater and

fanning out en route to high ground as Ferrero's division had been trained to do, the white troops moved slowly, stopping in the great crater or becoming trapped in rifle pits to its right, and quickly came under the intense fire of Confederates who, because of the lethargy of Ledlie's men, had time to regroup. Amid this chaos, Ferrero's First Brigade, consisting of the 27th, 30th, 39th, and 43rd USCT and led by Colonel Joshua K. Sigfried, entered the fray. After unsuccessfully trying to skirt to the right, the black soldiers, led by the 43rd USCT, advanced beyond the crater and engaged the Confederates in fierce hand-to-hand combat, capturing 200 prisoners. Next came Colonel Henry Goddard Thomas's Second Brigade, composed of the 19th, 23rd, 28th, 29th, and 31st USCT. These regiments, however, also soon became trapped in the crater. "Our generals had pushed us into this slaughter pen," Lieutenant Robert Beecham of the 23rd USCT remembered, "and then deserted us." Beecham recalled that as the black troops formed to try a second attack, they were "as ready to face the enemy and meet death . . . as the bravest and best soldiers that ever lived." This assault too was repulsed by torrents of enemy bullets fired by Confederates under General William Mahone. Those soldiers who were not dead or dying were driven into the crowded, deadly hole.[102]

With their commanders preoccupied irresponsibly (Burnside and Meade exchanged hostile communications during the fight; Ledlie and Ferrero drank liquor in a bombproof; Potter and Willcox stayed clear of the combat zone), the black troops, huddled and pinned down in the crater, received withering enemy artillery and rifle fire. By the time Burnside ordered a retreat, historian Benjamin Quarles explains, "the crater had become a hell. Thirsty and sun-baked, the blue-clad boys tried to break out of the death-trap and make a dash for the Union lines." When Confederate infantrymen stormed the crater, the blacks panicked and retreated, acting more like a stampeding mob than an army. According to one of their leaders, the USCT "became wild, confused, terror stricken, and . . . ran." Many who fled were picked off by Confederate riflemen as they desperately climbed up the steep sides of the hole. Some blacks were slaughtered as they tried to surrender, and others were captured, never to reach the rear. In the words of historian Noah Andre Trudeau, "Horror was piled upon horror." Lieutenant Colonel Delevan Bates of the 30th USCT recalled that "[m]any a dusky warrior had his brains knocked out with the butt of a musket, or was run thru with a bayonet while vainly imploring for mercy." "Some of the Negro prisoners," Confederate general Edward Porter Alexander recollected, "who were originally allowed to surrender . . . were afterward shot by others, & there was, without doubt, a great deal of unnecessary killing of them."[103]

The Battle of the Crater was unquestionably the USCT's darkest hour. Of the 4,500 African Americans from Ferrero's Fourth Division who entered the battle, 1,327 were hit, and 436 died. Whites suffered 2,471 casualties, including 227 deaths. The 29th USCT began the battle with 450 effectives and finished it with only 128. Writing two days after the disaster, General Grant described the battle as "the saddest affair I have witnessed in this war. Such opportunity for carrying fortifications I have never seen and do not expect again to have." In the aftermath of battle, soldiers and politicians alike made allegations, looking for scapegoats for the humiliating Union defeat. Not surprisingly, some blamed the blacks for the catastrophe. General Willcox, for example, praised the performance of his division and Potter's in the battle, but he reported that "Ledlie's division & the colored troops acted badly." A member of Willcox's staff agreed, remarking that the USCT "formed very well and advanced with much spirit till they came under hot fire, when they ignominiously broke and ran in every direction." Sergeant George F. Cram of the 105th Illinois Volunteer Infantry used their performance at the infamous crater as a justification to damn blacks as soldiers. "What a pity! When so near the most brilliant victory ever known." Cram informed his mother that "the abolitionists may talk as they please, but I tell you that colored troops cannot be depended on and that evidently caused this great defeat."[104]

Burnside disagreed. Responding to questions posed by a court of inquiry, the general refused to hold the USCT responsible for the loss. Though admitting "that the black troops broke and ran to the rear in considerable of a panic, which indicates misbehavior," Burnside insisted that

> they went in late, found in the enemy's works quite a mass of our own troops unable to advance, and during their formation, and in fact during their advance between the two lines, they were subjected to probably the hottest fire that any troops had been subjected to during the day; and I do not know that it is reasonable to suppose that after the loss of so great a portion of their officers they could have been expected to maintain their position. They certainly moved forward as gallantly under the first fire and until their ranks were broken as any troops I ever saw in action.

After sifting the conflicting evidence, the congressional Joint Committee on the Conduct of the War blamed Meade for overruling Burnside's decision to use Ferrero's black troops to lead the attack. Historian William Marvel agrees, concluding that the battle was lost "the instant . . . Meade told Burnside he could not use his fresh black troops or his plan employing divergent flank guards." "However," historian Bruce Tap argues, "it is

by no means self-evident . . . that employing black troops would have significantly altered the battle's outcome. No matter how they were trained,
they were green troops who had never experienced enemy fire; hence, it is
not certain that they would have executed the attack successfully." "Call it a
wrong decision based on right premises," Cornish concludes, in what represents perhaps the most balanced assessment of the issue. Ineptitude and
mismanagement by Burnside, Grant, and Meade, not the USCT, caused the
Union defeat at the Battle of the Crater.[105]

Though rumors of their poor showing at the crater persisted, during the
last nine months of the war no one accused the USCT of cowardice. Frederick S. Eaton, an officer of the 32nd USCT, informed readers of the *American Missionary*: "They can fight, have fought, are willing to fight, and in
no instance have they proved unworthy the important position instrusted
so judiciously to them." As the war drew to a close, the USCT repeatedly
demonstrated their valor and value as soldiers and suffered severe losses.
For example, on September 29, 1864, two brigades of General Charles J.
Paine's Third Division, Eighteenth Corps, composed of the 4th and 6th
USCT and the 5th, 36th, and 38th USCT, successfully assailed the Confederate entrenched line of defense at New Market Heights, Virginia, north
of the James River. This formidable position was a key element in the
southeastern defenses of Richmond. Overcoming rough terrain, encountering many obstructions, and confronting galling fire, the black troops
captured the enemy's works in two attacks and forced the Confederates
to retreat. Following the engagement, one of the brigade commanders,
Colonel Samuel A. Duncan, extolled the virtues of his men. "Ah! give me
the Thunder-heads & Black hearts after all," Duncan wrote. "They fought
splendidly . . . facing the red tempest of death with unflinching heroism."
Another observer, African American newspaper reporter Thomas Morris
Chester of the *Philadelphia Press*, complained that the USCT had received insufficient praise for its fighting at New Market Heights. "Every man looked
like a soldier," Chester noted, "while inflexible determination was depicted
upon every countenance. . . . Let us all be grateful that we have colored
troops that will fight."[106]

No one came to appreciate the contributions of black troops more than
President Lincoln, though he continued to justify their employment as a
matter of military expediency and paid scant attention to its meaning to
the freedpeople. "So far as tested," the president announced in December
1863, "it is difficult to say they are not as good soldiers as any. No servile insurrection, or tendency to violence or cruelty, has marked the measures of

emancipation and arming the blacks." Five months later, Lincoln remarked that the experiment of arming blacks "shows no loss by it in our foreign relations, none in our home popular sentiment, none in our white military force, — no loss by it any how or any where. On the contrary, it shows a gain of quite a hundred and thirty thousand soldiers, seamen, and laborers." As the November 1864 presidential election approached, Lincoln reiterated his appreciation of and his commitment to the USCT.

> There have been men who have proposed . . . to return to slavery the black warriors of Port Hudson & Olustee to their masters to conciliate the South. I should be damned in time & in eternity for so doing. The world shall know that I will keep my faith to friends & enemies, come what will. My enemies say I am now carrying on this war for the sole purpose of abolition. It is & will be carried on as long as I am President for the sole purpose of restoring the Union. But no human power can subdue this rebellion without using the Emancipation lever. . . . My enemies condemn my emancipation policy. Let them prove by the history of this war, that we can restore the Union without it.

Following his reelection, two brigades of USCT proved themselves worthy of Lincoln's confidence by their heroic but deadly assaults on Confederate general John B. Hood's right flank at the Battle of Nashville, Tennessee (December 15–16, 1864). In his report of the battle, Union general James B. Steedman, after acknowledging that black troops suffered the highest casualties among his command, added: "I was unable to discover that color made any difference in the fighting of my troops. All, white and black, nobly did their duty as soldiers, and evinced cheerfulness and resolution such as I have never seen excelled in any campaign of the war in which I have borne a part."[107]

As the war dragged on, Lincoln and most white Northerners slowly had reached the same conclusion. They came to recognize that Americans of African descent had become an invaluable resource to the Union military effort and had earned the rights and privileges of other Americans. Early in 1864 Lincoln explained to General James S. Wadsworth, himself a convert to the use of black soldiers, that as a race blacks had "heroically vindicated their manhood on the battle-field, where, in assisting to save the life of the Republic, they have demonstrated in blood their right to the ballot." The president admitted that though he had not set out to free and arm the slaves, circumstances warranted his actions. "I claim not to have controlled events," he explained, "but confess that events have controlled me." Uncertain of the future, Lincoln looked for divine guidance. "If God now wills the removal of a great wrong, and wills also that we . . . shall pay fairly for our complicity in that wrong, impartial history will find therein new cause to attest and revere the justice and goodness of God." The military service of the former slaves and free blacks proved the president's faith in God to be well served.[108]

Notes

1. Lincoln, "Preliminary Emancipation Proclamation," September 22, 1862, in Roy P. Basler, ed., *The Collected Works of Abraham Lincoln*, 9 vols. (New Brunswick: Rutgers University Press, 1953–55), 5:434 (hereafter cited as *Collected Works of Lincoln*); Welles diary entry, January 1, 1863, in *Diary of Gideon Welles: Secretary of the Navy under Lincoln and Johnson*, 3 vols. (Boston: Houghton Mifflin, 1911), 1:212; Gideon Welles, "The History of Emancipation," *Galaxy* 14 (December 1872): 848; James M. McPherson, *Ordeal by Fire: The Civil War and Reconstruction* (New York: Alfred A. Knopf, 1982), 349; James M. McPherson, "Lincoln the Devil," *New York Times Book Review*, August 27, 2000, 13.

2. Lincoln, "Emancipation Proclamation," January 1, 1863, in Basler, *Collected Works of Lincoln*, 6:30; Joseph P. Reidy, "Broadening Both the Letter and the Spirit of the Law: Blacks' Assertion of the Rights of Citizenship during the Civil War and Reconstruction," *Journal of the Afro-American Historical and Genealogical Society* 8 (Winter 1987): 148. On the contemporary debate over military "expediency" and "experimentation" with black troops, see "Use of Negroes as Soldiers," *New York Times*, February 16, 1863, 4:4–5.

3. Lincoln to James C. Conkling, August 26, 1863, in Basler, *Collected Works of Lincoln*, 6:408–9, 410; Lincoln, "Address at a Sanitary Fair in Baltimore," April 18, 1864, in Roy P. Basler, ed., *Abraham Lincoln: His Speeches and Writings* (Cleveland: World Publishing Company, 1946), 749.

4. Geary to Mary, September 25, 1862, in William Alan Blair, ed., *A Politician Goes to War: The Civil War Letters of John White Geary* (University Park: Pennsylvania State University Press, 1995), 56; Campbell diary entry, September 25 [1862], in Mark Grimsley and Todd D. Miller, eds., *The Union Must Stand: The Civil War Diary of John Quincy Adams Campbell, Fifth Iowa Volunteer Infantry* (Knoxville: University of Tennessee Press, 2000), 61; George H. Boker, *Washington and Jackson on Negro Soldiers; Gen. Banks on the Bravery of Negro Troops; Poem—the Second Louisiana* (Philadelphia: Printed for Gratuitous Distribution [n.p., 1863]), 15.

5. Russell F. Weigley, *A Great Civil War: A Military and Political History, 1861–1865* (Bloomington: Indiana University Press, 2000), 191; Howard C. Westwood, "Lincoln's Position on Black Enlistments," in *Black Troops, White Commanders, and Freedmen during the Civil War* (Carbondale: Southern Illinois University Press, 1992), 15; Michael Vorenberg, *Final Freedom: The Civil War, the Abolition of Slavery, and the Thirteenth Amendment* (Cambridge: Cambridge University Press, 2001),

25; George M. Fredrickson, *The Inner Civil War: Northern Intellectuals and the Crisis of the Union* (New York: Harper and Row, 1965), 120.

6. Garrison to Fanny Garrison, September 25, 1862, in Walter M. Merrill and Louis Ruchames, eds., *The Letters of William Lloyd Garrison*, 6 vols. (Cambridge, Mass.: Harvard University Press, 1971–81), 5:114; Conway quoted in John d'Entremont, *Southern Emancipator: Moncure Conway: The American Years, 1832–1865* (New York: Oxford University Press, 1987), 180.

7. Stephens to the editor, *Weekly Anglo-African* (New York), January 17, 1863, June 18, September 3, 1864, in Donald Yacovone, ed., *A Voice of Thunder: The Civil War Letters of George E. Stephens* (Urbana: University of Illinois Press, 1997), 18–19, 219, 306, 324.

8. Charles Francis Adams, Jr., to father, November 2, 1864, to Henry Adams, April 6, 1862, and to father, July 28, 1862, in Worthington Chauncey Ford, ed., *A Cycle of Adams Letters, 1861–1865*, 2 vols. (Boston: Houghton Mifflin, 1920), 2:215, 1:131, 1:171.

9. Adams to Charles Francis Adams, November 2, 1864, and to Henry Adams, September 18, 1864, in Ford, *A Cycle of Adams Letters*, 2:216–17, 219, 195.

10. George Washington Williams, *A History of the Negro Troops in the War of the Rebellion, 1861–1865* (1888; New York: Negro Universities Press, 1969), 170, 180. On Williams's military service, see John Hope Franklin, *George Washington Williams: A Biography* (Chicago: University of Chicago Press, 1985), 3–4. On the hostile response of white troops to the employment of African American soldiers, see Randall M. Miller and Jon W. Zophy, "Unwelcome Allies: Billy Yank and the Black Soldier," *Phylon: The Atlanta University Journal of Race and Culture* 39 (September 1978): 234–40. On the emerging racial perceptions of white Union soldiers during the war, see David A. Cecere, "Carrying the Home Front to War: Soldiers, Race, and New England Culture during the Civil War," in Paul A. Cimbala and Randall M. Miller, eds., *Union Soldiers and the Northern Home Front: Wartime Experiences, Postwar Adjustments* (New York: Fordham University Press, 2002), 293–323.

11. Whitman to mother, September 30, 1862, in Jerome M. Loving, ed., *Civil War Letters of George Washington Whitman* (Durham: Duke University Press, 1975), 71; Squier to Ellen, December 24, 1862 in Julie A. Doyle, John David Smith, and Richard M. McMurry, eds., *This Wilderness of War: The Civil War Letters of George W. Squier, Hoosier Volunteer* (Knoxville: University of Tennessee Press, 1998), 30.

12. Abbott to Aunt Lizzie, January 10, 1863, in Robert Garth Scott, ed., *Fallen Leaves: The Civil War Letters of Major Henry Livermore Abbott* (Kent, Ohio: Kent State University Press, 1991), 18; John J. Hennessy, ed., *Fighting with the Eighteenth Massachusetts: The Civil War Memoir of Thomas H. Mann* (Baton Rouge: Louisiana State University Press, 2000), 142; Felix Brannigan quoted in Benjamin Quarles, *The Negro in the Civil War* (1953; Boston: Little, Brown, 1969), 31.

13. Stillwell and Reeder quoted in James M. McPherson, *For Cause and Comrades:*

Why Men Fought in the Civil War (New York: Oxford University Press, 1997), 126, 128–29; Sherman to William M. McPherson, [ca. September 15–30, 1864], in Brooks D. Simpson and Jean V. Berlin, eds., *Sherman's Civil War: Selected Correspondence of William T. Sherman, 1860–1865* (Chapel Hill: University of North Carolina Press, 1999), 727; Sherman to Henry W. Halleck, January 12, 1865, in U.S. War Department, *The War of the Rebellion: A Compilation of the Official Records of the Union and Confederate Armies*, 128 vols. (Washington, D.C.: Government Printing Office, 1880–1901), 1st ser., 47 (2):37 (hereafter cited as *OR*).

14. Lincoln to James C. Conkling, August 26, 1863, in Basler, *Collected Works of Lincoln*, 6:408n; Charles Francis Adams, Jr., to Henry Adams, October 15, 1864, in Ford, *A Cycle of Adams Letters, 1861–1865*, 2:206; Lincoln, "Appeal to Border State Representatives to Favor Compensated Emancipation," July 13, 1862, in Basler, *Collected Works of Lincoln*, 5:318.

15. Higginson, "Scattered Notes about T. W. H.'s Colored Troops, 1864," quoted in Christopher Looby, ed., *The Complete Civil War Journal and Selected Letters of Thomas Wentworth Higginson* (Chicago: University of Chicago Press, 2000), 1; anonymous soldier to Edwin M. Stanton, October 2, 1865, in Ira Berlin, Joseph P. Reidy, and Leslie S. Rowland, eds., *The Black Military Experience* (Cambridge: Cambridge University Press, 1982), 654; Robert Scott Davis, Jr., "A Soldier's Story: The Records of Hubbard Pryor, Forty-fourth United States Colored Troops," *Prologue* 31 (Winter 1999): 267–68, 270. On the incentives and disincentives for blacks joining the Union army, see Gary Knoch, "Terrible Dilemmas: Black Enlistment in the Union Army during the American Civil War," *Slavery and Abolition* 18 (August 1997): 104–27.

16. C. W. Foster to E. D. Townsend, October 20, 1865, and E. D. Townsend to Edwin M. Stanton, October 20, 1866, *OR*, 3rd ser., 5:138, 1028; Dudley Taylor Cornish, *The Sable Arm: Negro Troops in the Union Army, 1861–1865* (1956; New York: W. W. Norton, 1966), 288; Joseph T. Glatthaar, *Forged in Battle: The Civil War Alliance of Black Soldiers and White Officers* (New York: Free Press, 1990), 71, appendix 2; Stephen W. Sylvia, "Medal of Honor," in Patricia L. Faust, ed., *Historical Times Illustrated Encyclopedia of the Civil War* (New York: Harper and Row, 1986), 484. For higher across-the-board enlistment figures and percentages, see Jacob Metzer, "The Records of the U.S. Colored Troops as a Historical Source: An Exploratory Examination," *Historical Methods* 14 (Summer 1981): 124 (table 1).

17. Fred A. Shannon, *The Organization and Administration of the Union Army, 1861–1865*, 2 vols. (1928; Gloucester, Mass.: Peter Smith, 1965), 2:145; Mark E. Neely, Jr., "Lincoln and the Theory of Self-Emancipation," in *The Continuing Civil War: Essays in Honor of the Civil War Round Table of Chicago*, ed. John Y. Simon and Barbara Hughett (Dayton, Ohio: Morningside, 1992), 62; Mark E. Neely, Jr., *The Fate of Liberty: Abraham Lincoln and Civil Liberties* (New York: Oxford University Press, 1991), 216; Mark E. Neely, Jr., *The Last Best Hope of*

Earth: Abraham Lincoln and the Promise of America (Cambridge, Mass.: Harvard University Press, 1993), 100, 104; Vorenberg, *Final Freedom*, 27.

18. Lincoln, "Proclamation Calling Militia and Convening Congress," April 15, 1861, in Basler, *Collected Works of Lincoln*, 4:332; Douglass, "How to End the War," *Douglass' Monthly*, May 1861, in Philip S. Foner, ed., *The Life and Writings of Frederick Douglass*, 5 vols. (New York: International Publishers, 1952–75), 3:94; Fee, *Autobiography of John G. Fee, Berea, Kentucky* (Chicago: National Christian Association, 1891), 156–57.

19. *New York Express* quoted in James M. McPherson, *The Struggle for Equality: Abolitionists and the Negro in the Civil War and Reconstruction* (1964; Princeton: Princeton University Press, 1995), 192, 194.

20. La Wanda Cox, *Lincoln and Black Freedom: A Study in Presidential Leadership* (Columbia: University of South Carolina Press, 1981), 23.

21. Joseph T. Wilson, *The Black Phalanx: African American Soldiers in the War of Independence, the War of 1812, and the Civil War* (1887; New York: Da Capo Press, 1994), 200; George W. Fahnestock quoted in J. Matthew Gallman, *The North Fights the Civil War: The Home Front* (Chicago: Ivan R. Dee, 1994), 133; Kirkwood to Henry W. Halleck, August 5, 1862, in Berlin et al., *The Black Military Experience*, 85.

22. Charles A. Wickliffe and Robert Mallory (July 5, 1862) in *Congressional Globe*, July 8, 1862, 37th Cong., 2nd sess., 1862, 3123, 3124, 3127.

23. Thaddeus Stevens (July 5, 1862) in *Congressional Globe*, July 8, 1862, 37th Cong., 2nd sess., 1862, 3127, 3125, 3126, 3127.

24. Neely, *The Last Best Hope of Earth*, 100–101, 103; Berlin et al., *The Black Military Experience*, 3–4.

25. "An Act to Confiscate Property Used for Insurrectionary Purposes," August 6, 1861, in *The Statutes at Large, Treaties, and Proclamations of the United States of America*, vol. 12, *December 5, 1859, to March 3, 1863* (Boston: Little, Brown, 1863), 319; John Syrett, "The Confiscation Acts: Efforts at Reconstruction during the Civil War" (Ph.D. diss., University of Wisconsin, 1971), chap. 1; Gallman, *The North Fights the Civil War*, 132; McPherson, *Ordeal by Fire*, 267.

26. James G. Randall, *Constitutional Problems under Lincoln*, rev. ed. (1951; Urbana: University of Illinois Press, 1964), 276, 357; Allan Nevins, *Frémont: Pathmaker of the West* (1939; Lincoln: University of Nebraska Press, 1983), 500–506; Lincoln to Orville H. Browning, September 22, 1861, in Basler, *Collected Works of Lincoln*, 4:532; Pillsbury (February 15, 1862) quoted in Stacey M. Robertson, *Parker Pillsbury: Radical Abolitionist, Male Feminist* (Ithaca: Cornell University Press, 2000), 123; Fee, *Autobiography of John G. Fee*, 157.

27. Lincoln, "Annual Message to Congress," December 3, 1861, and "Address on Colonization to a Deputation of Negroes," August 14, 1862, in Basler, *Collected Works of Lincoln*, 5:48, 371, 372; Neely, *The Last Best Hope of Earth*, 105. On the relationship between military expediency and black civil rights, see Mary Frances

Berry, *Military Necessity and Civil Rights Policy: Black Citizenship and the Constitution, 1861–1868* (Port Washington, N.Y.: Kennikat Press, 1977).

28. "An Act to Make an Additional Article of War," March 13, 1862, in *The Statutes at Large*, 354; Lincoln, "Message to Congress," March 6, 1862, in Basler, *Collected Works of Lincoln*, 5:145, 146n; Mary Tremain, *Slavery in the District of Columbia: The Policy of Congress and the Struggle for Abolition* (1892; New York: Negro Universities Press, 1969), 94; Lincoln, "Proclamation Revoking General Hunter's Order of Military Emancipation of May 9, 1862," May 19, 1862, in Basler, *Collected Works of Lincoln*, 5:223; Randall, *Constitutional Problems under Lincoln*, 365; Neely, *The Last Best Hope of Earth*, 107.

29. Mark E. Neely, Jr., "Confiscation Act of July 17, 1862," in *The Abraham Lincoln Encyclopedia* (New York: McGraw-Hill, 1982), 67–68; "An Act to Suppress Insurrection, to Punish Treason and Rebellion, to Seize and Confiscate the Property of Rebels, and for Other Purposes," July 17, 1862, in *The Statutes at Large*, 591, 592; Patricia L. Faust, "Confiscation Act of 1862," in Faust, *Historical Times Illustrated Encyclopedia of the Civil War*, 157; Randall, *Constitutional Problems under Lincoln*, 363; McPherson, "Lincoln the Devil," 12; Benjamin P. Thomas and Harold M. Hyman, *Stanton: The Life and Times of Lincoln's Secretary of War* (New York: Alfred A. Knopf, 1962), 233, 237, 238. For Lincoln's concerns about the severity and potential negative implications of the Second Confiscation Act (he threatened to veto it), see Syrett, "The Confiscation Acts," 86–87. Also see Wyatt Cunningham Hornsby, "Abraham Lincoln, Congress, the Confiscation of Property during the Civil War, and the Decision for Emancipation" (M.A. thesis, North Carolina State University, 1998).

30. Berry, *Military Necessity and Civil Rights Policy*, 42; Randall, *Constitutional Problems under Lincoln*, 363–65; "An Act to Amend the Act Calling Forth the Militia to Execute the Laws of the Union, Suppress Insurrections, and Repel Invasions . . . ," July 17, 1862, in *The Statutes at Large*, 599; General Orders No. 109, August 16, 1862 [executive order, July 22, 1862], *OR*, 3rd ser., 2:397.

31. Chase diary, July 22, 1862, in David Donald, ed., *Inside Lincoln's Cabinet: The Civil War Diaries of Salmon P. Chase* (New York: Longmans, Green, 1954), 99.

32. Neely, *The Last Best Hope of Earth*, 107–8; Lincoln to Cuthbert Bullitt, July 28, 1862, in Basler, *Collected Works of Lincoln*, 5:345; Douglass, "The Slaveholders' Rebellion" (July 4, 1862), *Douglass' Monthly*, August 1862, and "The President and His Speeches," *Douglass' Monthly*, September 1862, in Foner, *The Life and Writings of Frederick Douglass*, 3:256, 267, 268, 269.

33. Lincoln to Horace Greeley, August 22, 1862, and "Annual Message to Congress," December 1, 1862, in Basler, *Collected Works of Lincoln*, 5:388–89, 529–32; Neely, *The Fate of Liberty*, 222, 116–17.

34. Neely, *The Last Best Hope of Earth*, 110; Lincoln to Charles D. Robinson, August 17, 1864 [draft of letter never sent], in Basler, *Collected Works of Lincoln*, 7:500. On the broad, often undervalued, significance of the slaves' fleeing the

Confederacy for Union lines, see William W. Freehling, *The South vs. The South: How Anti-Confederate Southerners Shaped the Course of the Civil War* (New York: Oxford University Press, 2001), chap. 8.

35. Lincoln to Bullitt, July 28, 1862, in Basler, *Collected Works of Lincoln*, 5:345; Ira Berlin, "Emancipation and Its Meaning," in David W. Blight and Brooks D. Simpson, eds., *Union and Emancipation: Essays on Politics and Race in the Civil War Era* (Kent, Ohio: Kent State University Press, 1997), 110–11, 114; McPherson, "Who Freed the Slaves?" *Reconstruction* 2 (1994): 40.

36. Lincoln, "Remarks to a Deputation of Western Gentlemen" (August 4, 1862), *New York Tribune*, August 5, 1862, and "Reply to Emancipation Memorial Presented by Chicago Christians of All Denominations," September 13, 1862, in Basler, *Collected Works of Lincoln*, 5:356–57, 423; James Russell Lowell quoted in Nevins, *Frémont*, 507; Lincoln "Annual Message to Congress," December 1, 1862, in Basler, *Collected Works of Lincoln*, 5:537; Eric Foner, *The Story of American Freedom* (New York: W. W. Norton, 1998), 95–97.

37. Douglass, "The Reasons for Our Troubles," *Douglass' Monthly*, February 1862, and "The Proclamation and a Negro Army," *Douglass' Monthly*, March 1863, in Foner, *The Life and Writings of Frederick Douglass*, 3:204, 322.

38. McPherson, *The Struggle for Equality*, 192–93; Smith, "War Meeting in Peterboro: Speech of Gerrit Smith," April 27, 1861, and "Letter to Rev. Dr. G. C. Beckwith," May 18, 1861, in *Sermons and Speeches of Gerrit Smith* (New York: Ross & Tousey, 1861), 186, 189, 192, 196; *The War and Slavery; or, Victory Only through Emancipation* (Boston: R. F. Wallcut, 1861), 8; Shaw to Sydney Howard Gay, August 6, 1861, in Russell Duncan, ed., *Blue-Eyed Child of Fortune: The Civil War Letters of Colonel Robert Gould Shaw* (Athens: University of Georgia Press, 1992), 123; Edward Bates diary entry, November 20, 1861, in Howard K. Beale, ed., *The Diary of Edward Bates, 1859–1866* (Washington, D.C.: Government Printing Office, 1933), 203; T. Harry Williams, *Lincoln and the Radicals* (1941; Madison: University of Wisconsin Press, 1965), 59, 116.

39. Lincoln to Albert G. Hodges, April 4, 1864, in Basler, *Collected Works of Lincoln*, 7:281–82; Hans L. Trefousse, *Thaddeus Stevens: Nineteenth-Century Egalitarian* (Chapel Hill: University of North Carolina Press, 1997), 116; David Donald, *Charles Sumner and the Rights of Man* (New York: Alfred A. Knopf, 1970), 48; Edward Magdol, *Owen Lovejoy: Abolitionist in Congress* (New Brunswick: Rutgers University Press, 1967), 300; Fee, *Autobiography of John G. Fee*, 172–73.

40. Dudley T. Cornish, "African American Troops in the Union Army," in Richard N. Current, ed., *Encyclopedia of the Confederacy*, 4 vols. (New York: Simon and Schuster, 1993), 1:11.

41. John A. Andrew to Francis G. Shaw, January 30, 1863, in Berlin et al., *The Black Military Experience*, 86; Noah Andre Trudeau, *Like Men of War: Black Troops in the Civil War, 1862–1865* (Boston: Little, Brown, 1998), 71–88; Cornish, *The Sable Arm*, 72–78.

42. Berlin et al., *The Black Military Experience*, 37; Hunter to Lyman Trumbull, December 9, 1861, quoted in Edward A. Miller, Jr., *Lincoln's Abolitionist General: The Biography of David Hunter* (Columbia: University of South Carolina Press, 1997), 79.

43. Phelps to R. S. Davis, July 30, 1862, in Berlin et al., *The Black Military Experience*, 62.

44. Berlin et al., *The Black Military Experience*, 37–39; McPherson, *The Struggle for Equality*, 195–96; Lincoln to Hodges, April 4, 1864, in Basler, *Collected Works of Lincoln*, 7:282; Norwood P. Hallowell, *The Negro as a Soldier in the War of the Rebellion* (Boston: Little, Brown, 1897), 4.

45. Garrison to Fanny Garrison, September 25, 1862, in Merrill and Ruchames, *The Letters of William Lloyd Garrison*, 5:114–15; Edwin M. Stanton to Rufus Saxton, August 25, 1862, *OR*, 1st ser., 14:377–78; David J. Eicher, *The Longest Night: A Military History of the Civil War* (New York: Simon and Schuster, 2001), 336; Berlin et al., *The Black Military Experience*, 39–41. For an analysis of why Stanton authorized Saxton to arm the blacks, see Westwood, "Generals David Hunter and Rufus Saxton and Black Soldiers," in *Black Troops, White Commanders, and Freedmen During the Civil War*, 65–68.

46. Berlin et al., *The Black Military Experience*, 43, 44, 63n; Phelps to Butler, August 2, 1862, in Berlin et al., *The Black Military Experience*, 63–65, 65n; Excerpt of Testimony of General B. F. Butler [May 1, 1863], in Berlin et al., *The Black Military Experience*, 312, 315n; Richard J. Sommers, *Richmond Redeemed: The Siege of Petersburg* (Garden City, N.J.: Doubleday, 1981), 31; Mark M. Boatner III, *The Civil War Dictionary* (1959; New York: Vintage Books, 1987), 434, 585; Edward G. Longacre, "Black Troops in the Army of the James, 1863–65," *Military Affairs* 45 (February 1981): 1. On the Louisiana Native Guards, see James G. Hollandsworth, Jr., *The Louisiana Native Guards: The Black Military Experience during the Civil War* (Baton Rouge: Louisiana State University Press, 1995), and Stephen J. Ochs, *A Black Patriot and a White Priest: André Cailloux and Claude Paschal Maistre in Civil War New Orleans* (Baton Rouge: Louisiana State University Press, 2000).

47. Lincoln to Hodges, April 4, 1864, in Basler, *Collected Works of Lincoln*, 7:282; Joseph T. Glatthaar, "Black Glory: The African-American Role in Union Victory," in Gabor S. Boritt, ed., *Why the Confederacy Lost* (New York: Oxford University Press, 1992), 142.

48. Henry Carey Baird, *General Washington and General Jackson on Negro Soldiers* (Philadelphia: Henry Carey Baird, 1863), 8; Douglass, "Condition of the Country," *Douglass' Monthly*, February 1863, in Foner, *The Life and Writings of Frederick Douglass*, 3:317; Lincoln to Nathaniel P. Banks, March 29, 1863, and Lincoln to Andrew Johnson, March 26, 1863, in Basler, *Collected Works of Lincoln*, 6:154, 149.

49. Chase to George Opdyke and others, April 8, 1863, in John Niven, ed., *The Salmon P. Chase Papers*, 5 vols. to date (Kent, Ohio: Kent State University Press, 1993–), 4:8–9; Lincoln to Grant, August 9, 1863, in Basler, *Collected Works of Lincoln*, 6:374.

50. Lincoln to James C. Conkling, August 26, 1863, in Basler, *Collected Works of Lincoln*, 6:409; Berlin et al., *The Black Military Experience*, 8. For other statements by Lincoln confirming his commitment to emancipation, see Lincoln to Nathaniel P. Banks, August 5, 1863, and "Annual Message to Congress," December 8, 1863, in Basler, *Collected Works of Lincoln*, 6:365, 7:51; and Lincoln to Henry C. Wright, December 20, 1863, in Roy P. Basler and Christian O. Basler, eds., *The Collected Works of Abraham Lincoln: Second Supplement, 1848–1865* (New Brunswick: Rutgers University Press, 1990), 84.

51. Shannon, *The Organization and Administration of the Union Army, 1861–1865*, 2:145; W. E. Burghardt Du Bois, *Black Reconstruction in America: An Essay toward a History of the Part Which Black Folk Played in the Attempt to Reconstruct Democracy in America, 1860–1880* (1935; New York: Atheneum, 1973), 81.

52. Berlin et al., *The Black Military Experience*, 9–10; "An Act for Enrolling and Calling Out the National Forces, and for Other Purposes," March 3, 1863, *OR*, 3rd ser., 3:88; James B. Fry to Edwin M. Stanton, March 17, 1866, *OR*, 3rd ser., 5:662; Douglass, "Men of Color, To Arms!" (broadside), Rochester, March 21, 1863, in Foner, *The Life and Writings of Frederick Douglass*, 3:318.

53. Cornish, *The Sable Arm*, 111, 114, 117–25; Fry to Stanton, March 17, 1866, in *OR*, 3rd ser., 5:660. In June 1864, Lincoln wrote Lorenzo Thomas that recruiters in northwestern Kentucky were "seizing negroes and carrying them off without their own consent, and according to no rules whatever, except those of absolute violence." See Lincoln to Thomas, June 13, 1864, in Basler, *Collected Works of Lincoln*, 7:390.

54. Bates diary entry, May 16, 1863, in Beale, *The Diary of Edward Bates, 1859–1866*, 292; Reid, "How Philadelphia Raises Negro Soldiers," June 22, 1863, in James G. Smart, ed., *A Radical View: The "Agate" Dispatches of Whitelaw Reid, 1861–1865*, 2 vols. (Memphis: Memphis State University Press, 1976), 2:97.

55. Cornish, *The Sable Arm*, 130, 131.

56. Joseph B. Ross, comp., *Tabular Analysis of the Records of the U.S. Colored Troops and Their Predecessor Units in the National Archives of the United States* (Washington, D.C.: National Archives and Records Service, 1973), 1, 8, 11, 27; Cornish, *The Sable Arm*, 130, 131.

57. "Manifesto of the Colored Citizens of the State of New York, July 16, 1863," in C. Peter Ripley, ed., *The Black Abolitionist Papers*, 5 vols. (Chapel Hill: University of North Carolina Press, 1985–92), 5:228; David W. Blight, *Frederick Douglass' Civil War: Keeping Faith in Jubilee* (Baton Rouge: Louisiana State University Press, 1989), 240; Douglass, "Address for the Promotion of Colored Enlistments" (July 6, 1863), *Douglass' Monthly*, August 1863, in Foner, *The Life and Writings of Frederick Douglass*, 3:365; William S. McFeely, *Frederick Douglass* (New York: W. W. Norton, 1991), 224; Blight, *Frederick Douglass' Civil War*, 170.

58. On the 55th Massachusetts Volunteers, see Noah Andre Trudeau, ed., *Voices of the 55th: Letters from the 55th Massachusetts Volunteers, 1861–1865* (Dayton, Ohio: Morningside, 1996).

59. Hallowell, *The Negro as a Soldier in the War of the Rebellion*, 7, 8, 9. In at least one instance, Hallowell obviously miscalculated. The total number of men (980) he listed by race ("pure blacks" and "mixed blood") exceeded his regimental total (961) by nineteen.

60. Ibid., 9, 10, 11. Hallowell was probably referring to one of two descendants of the first earl of Chesterfield, James Stanhope (1673–1721) or Edward Stanhope (1840–93). The former had extensive combat experience in Europe; the latter was an innovative military administrator.

61. Berlin et al., *The Black Military Experience*, 304n, 434.

62. Ibid., 303, 304, 304n, 305–7, 29, 310; General Orders No. 143, May 22, 1863, *OR*, 3rd ser., 3:215; Fisk to *Montpelier Green Mountain Freeman*, June 19, 1864, in Emil Rosenblatt and Ruth Rosenblatt, eds., *Hard Marching Every Day: The Civil War Letters of Private Wilbur Fisk, 1861–1865* (1983; Lawrence: University Press of Kansas, 1992), 231. War Department orders never specifically addressed the race of those permitted to stand for examinations for commissions in USCT regiments. See General Orders No. 144, May 22, 1863, *OR*, 3rd ser., 3:216. For a compilation of the black officers, see Glatthaar, *Forged in Battle*, 279–80. Glatthaar's book is the definitive study of USCT officers.

63. Adams to Henry Adams, July 28, 1862, in Ford, *A Cycle of Adams Letters*, 1:171; John William De Forest, *A Volunteer's Adventures: A Union Captain's Record of the Civil War* (1946; Baton Rouge: Louisiana State University Press, 1996), 50–51. On the examining boards for USCT officers, see Cornish, *The Sable Arm*, 204–14.

64. Berlin et al., *The Black Military Experience*, 24; Daniels diary entries for March 26, 29, 1863, in C. P. Weaver, ed., *Thank God My Regiment an African One: The Civil War Diary of Colonel Nathan W. Daniels* (Baton Rouge: Louisiana State University Press, 1998), 64, 68.

65. Cornish, *The Sable Arm*, 213, 288; Glatthaar, *Forged in Battle*, 53, 21; Cornish, "African American Troops in the Union Army," 10, 12. For a thorough study of German-speaking immigrants who passed the examination and served as officers with the USCT, see Martin Öfele, " 'I Do Not Wish to Take the Field with Any Better Men': Deutschsprachige Einwanderer als Offiziere afroamerikanischer Truppen im amerikanischen Bürgerkrieg" (Dr. phil. diss., University of Leipzig, 1999).

66. Michael A. Cavanaugh and William Marvel, *The Petersburg Campaign: The Battle of the Crater, "The Horrid Pit," June 25–August 6, 1864* (Lynchburg, Va.: H. E. Howard, 1989), 52; Cross to parents, March 29, June 22, 1863, in William Cullen Bryant II, ed., "A Yankee Soldier Looks at the Negro," *Civil War History* 7 (June 1961): 141, 147.

67. Michael E. Stevens, ed., *As If It Were Glory: Robert Beecham's Civil War from the Iron Brigade to the Black Regiments* (Madison, Wis.: Madison House, 1998), 152, 167, 168, 159.

68. Williams, *A History of the Negro Troops in the War of the Rebellion*, 180; Reid, "How Not to Get Negro Soldiers," April 2, 1863, in Smart, *A Radical View*, 2:94, 95; Gooding in *New Bedford Mercury*, May 26, 1863, in Virginia M. Adams, ed., *On the Altar of Freedom: A Black Soldier's Civil War Letters from the Front* (Amherst: University of Massachusetts Press, 1991), 24; anonymous soldier to Stanton, October 2, 1865, in Berlin et al., *The Black Military Experience*, 654.

69. Lincoln, "Emancipation Proclamation," January 1, 1863, in Basler, *Collected Works of Lincoln*, 6:30; Westervelt diary entry, September 29, [1863], in Anita Palladino, ed., *Diary of a Yankee Engineer: The Civil War Story of John H. Westervelt, Engineer, 1st New York Volunteer Engineer Corps* (New York: Fordham University Press, 1997), 43, 44.

70. Berlin et al., *The Black Military Experience*, 484–85; Freehling, *The South vs. The South*, 150–51, 153–54; [Nimrod Rowley] to the president, [August] 1864, in Berlin et al., *The Black Military Experience*, 501; Thomas D. Freeman quoted in Susan-Mary Grant, "Fighting for Freedom: African-American Soldiers in the Civil War," in Susan-Mary Grant and Brian Holden Reid, eds., *The American Civil War: Explorations and Reconsiderations* (Harlow, England: Pearson Education Limited, 2000), 205; General Orders No. 21, June 14, 1864, in Grant and Reid, *The American Civil War*, 500–501, 487n; Sherman to John A. Spooner, July 30, 1864, in Simpson and Berlin, *Sherman's Civil War*, 678.

71. Berlin et al., *The Black Military Experience*, 633, 634, 486; Cornish, *The Sable Arm*, 288; Glatthaar, *Forged in Battle*, 190–91, 194, 195; Cornish, "African American Troops in the Union Army," 12; Thomas to Assistant Surgeon General, January 16, 1865, in Berlin et al., *The Black Military Experience*, 645.

72. Grant, "Fighting for Freedom," 203; Versalle F. Washington, *Eagles on Their Buttons: A Black Infantry Regiment in the Civil War* (Columbia: University of Missouri Press, 1999), 32–33; Berlin et al., *The Black Military Experience*, 634–35; Palladino, *Diary of a Yankee Engineer*, 44; James M. Paradis, *Strike the Blow for Freedom: The 6th United States Colored Infantry in the Civil War* (Shippensburg, Pa.: White Mane Books, 1998), 15–16.

73. William A. Gladstone, *United States Colored Troops, 1863–1867* (Gettysburg, Pa.: Thomas Publications, 1990), 72, 73; Hallowell, *The Negro as a Soldier in the War of the Rebellion*, 23; Glatthaar, *Forged in Battle*, 185–86; [Hincks] to Butler, April 29, 1864, in Berlin et al., *The Black Military Experience*, 548, 549.

74. John Cimprich and Robert C. Mainfort, Jr., eds., "Fort Pillow Revisited: New Evidence about an Old Controversy," *Civil War History* 28 (December 1982): 295; Wilson, *The Black Phalanx*, 200; Thomas D. Morris, *Southern Slavery and the Law, 1619–1860* (Chapel Hill: University of North Carolina Press, 1996), 266–71; Cornish, *The Sable Arm*, 158, 159.

75. Dortch to Vance, January 3, 1863, in Joe A. Mobley, ed., *The Papers of Zebulon Baird Vance*, vol. 2, *1863* (Raleigh: North Carolina Division of Archives and History, 1995), 7; Kean diary, August 13, 1863, in Edward Younger, ed., *Inside the*

Confederate Government: The Diary of Robert Garlick Hill Kean (1957; Baton Rouge: Louisiana State University Press, 1993), 92; Browder diary entry, August 9, 1864, in Richard L. Troutman, ed., *The Heavens Are Weeping: The Diaries of George R. Browder, 1852–1886* (Grand Rapids, Mich.: Zondervan Publishing, 1987), 182.

76. General Orders No. 60, August 21, 1862, *OR*, 1st ser., 14:599; H. W. Mercer to Brigadier-General [Thomas] Jordan, November 14, 1862, and endorsement by Seddon, n.d., *OR*, 2nd ser., 4:945, 946.

77. General Orders No. 111, A Proclamation by the President of the Confederate States, December 24, 1862, *OR*, 2nd ser., 5:796, 797; Davis to the Senate and House of Representatives of the Confederate States, January 12, 1863, *OR*, 807–8; Browder diary entry, February 7, 1863, in Troutman, *The Heavens Are Weeping*, 146.

78. Seddon to Pemberton, April 8, 1863, *OR*, 2nd ser., 5:867; "Joint Resolutions Adopted by the Confederate Congress on the Subject of Retaliation April 30–May 1, 1863," May 1, 1863, *OR*, 940, 941.

79. Kirby Smith to Samuel Cooper and enclosures, June 16, 1863, and H. L. Clay to Kirby Smith, July 13, 1863, *OR*, 2nd ser., 6:21, 22, 115.

80. General Orders No. 100, April 24, 1863, "Instructions for the Government of Armies of the United States in the Field," *OR*, 3rd ser., 3:153, 155.

81. Cornish, *The Sable Arm*, 163–68; Trudeau, *Like Men of War*, 97–102; Cornish, *The Sable Arm*, 172, 180; Daniels diary entry, March 14, 1863, in Weaver, *Thank God My Regiment an African One*, 54; James G. Hollandsworth, Jr., "The Execution of White Officers from Black Units by Confederate Forces during the Civil War," *Louisiana History* 35 (Fall 1994): 477, 483, 485, 489 (table 3).

82. Douglass to Stearns, August 1, 1863, and Douglass, "The Commander-in-Chief and His Black Soldiers," *Douglass' Monthly*, August 1863, in Foner, *The Life and Writings of Frederick Douglass*, 3:369, 370. On Battery Wagner, see Duncan, *Blue-Eyed Child of Fortune*, 52–53.

83. General Orders No. 252, July 31, 1863, *OR*, 2nd ser., 6:163; Cornish, *The Sable Arm*, 171, 172–79; Trudeau, *Like Men of War*, 179, 310–12, 167–68, 193–94, 245–47, 274; Lincoln, "Address at a Sanitary Fair in Baltimore," 749.

84. Robert Knox Sneden, *Eye of the Storm: A Civil War Odyssey*, ed. Charles E. Bryan, Jr., and Nelson D. Lankford (New York: Free Press, 2000), 225.

85. Cornish, *The Sable Arm*, 183–87; McPherson, *The Struggle for Equality*, 212–13; General Orders No. 163, June 4, 1863, *OR*, 3rd ser., 3:252; Luis F. Emilio, *A Brave Black Regiment: The History of the 54th Massachusetts, 1863–1865* (1894; New York: Da Capo Press, 1995), 221; Fisk to *Montpelier Green Mountain Freeman*, June 19, 1864, in Rosenblatt and Rosenblatt, *Hard Marching Every Day*, 231. On the question of unequal pay, see Herman Belz, "Law, Politics, and Race in the Struggle for Equal Pay during the Civil War," *Civil War History* 22 (September 1976): 197–213.

86. Douglass, "Duty of Colored Men," *Douglass' Monthly*, August 1863, in Foner, *The*

Life and Writings of Frederick Douglass, 3:373; Gooding in *New Bedford Mercury*, August 21, December 4, 1863, and Gooding to Lincoln, September 28, 1863, in Adams, *On the Altar of Freedom*, 49, 83, 119–20.

87. Douglass, *Life and Times of Frederick Douglass Written by Himself: His Early Life as a Slave, His Escape from Bondage, and His Complete History* (1892; New York: Macmillan Publishing Company, 1962), 348.

88. "Frederick Douglass on President Lincoln," *Liberator*, September 16, 1864, 1.

89. McPherson, *Struggle for Equality*, 214, 215, 217; Thomas Wentworth Higginson, "Appendix D: The Struggle for Pay," in *Army Life in a Black Regiment* (1869; Boston: Beacon Press, 1962), 280–81.

90. Stanton, "Report of the Secretary of War," December 5, 1863, in *Message of the President of the United States, and Accompanying Documents, to the Two Houses of Congress, at the Commencement of the First Session of the Thirty-Eighth Congress* (Washington, D.C.: Government Printing Office, 1863), 8; Higginson to the editor, *New York Tribune*, January 22, 1864, in *Army Life in a Black Regiment*, 284; Bates to Lincoln, April 23, 1864, *OR*, 3rd ser., 4:273–74.

91. McPherson, *Struggle for Equality*, 217; General Orders No. 215, June 22, 1864, *OR*, 3rd ser., 4:448; Higginson to the editor, *New York Tribune*, August 12, 1864, in *Army Life in a Black Regiment*, 289; General Orders No. 31, March 8, 1865, *OR*, 3rd ser., 4:1223; Cornish, *The Sable Arm*, 194–95; Fry to Stanton, March 17, 1866, *OR*, 3rd ser., 5:659–60; Berlin et al., *The Black Military Experience*, 766n.

92. Cornish, "African American Troops in the Union Army," 12; Sherman to Edwin M. Stanton, October 25, 1864, in Simpson and Berlin, *Sherman's Civil War*, 741; Trudeau, *Like Men of War*, xix; Cornish, *The Sable Arm*, 265; Stanton, "Report of the Secretary of War," 8. On "slave modes of correction" used to punish black troops, see Berlin et al., *The Black Military Experience*, 433–42.

93. Trudeau, *Like Men of War*, xix, 466.

94. Bell Irvin Wiley, *Southern Negroes, 1861–1865* (1938; New Haven: Yale University Press, 1965), 334, 336, 340; Bell Irvin Wiley, *The Life of Billy Yank: The Common Soldier of the Union* (1952; Indianapolis: Bobbs-Merrill, 1962), 314.

95. Trudeau, *Like Men of War*, 467, 44–45, 288; William H. Leckie and Shirley A. Leckie, *Unlikely Warriors: General Benjamin Grierson and His Family* (Norman: University of Oklahoma Press, 1984), 101; Joseph J. Scroggs Diary, September 29, 1864, 20, U.S. Military History Institute, Carlisle Barracks, Pa. For analyses of the role of the USCT at Port Hudson and New Market Heights, respectively, see Lawrence Lee Hewitt, *Port Hudson: Confederate Bastion on the Mississippi* (Baton Rouge: Louisiana State University Press, 1987), 175–79, and Sommers, *Richmond Redeemed*, 31–38.

96. Trudeau, *Like Men of War*, 46–58; Glatthaar, *Forged in Battle*, 134; Charles A. Dana, *Recollections of the Civil War* (1898; New York: Collier Books, 1963), 93. A detachment from the 13th Louisiana Volunteers of African Descent, a regiment that never completed its organization, also fought at Milliken's Bend. The men later

were assigned to the 1st Mississippi Regiment of African Descent. See Trudeau, *Like Men of War*, 53n.

97. Cornish, *The Sable Arm*, 265; *Liberator*, March 18, 1864, 47, quoted in Adams, *On the Altar of Freedom*, 115; Yacovone, *A Voice of Thunder*, 67; Trudeau, *Like Men of War*, 138, 152; William H. Nulty, *Confederate Florida: The Road to Olustee* (Tuscaloosa: University of Alabama Press, 1990), 203, 209, 211.

98. Trudeau, *Like Men of War*, 220–26, 228; Quarles, *The Negro in the Civil War*, 299; Beman to unidentified newspaper, June 20, 1864, in Edwin S. Redkey, ed., *A Grand Army of Black Men: Letters from African-American Soldiers in the Union Army, 1861–1865* (Cambridge: Cambridge University Press, 1992), 99; Grant to Daniel Ammen, August 14, 1864, in John Y. Simon, ed., *The Papers of Ulysses S. Grant*, 24 vols. to date (Carbondale: Southern Illinois University Press, 1967–), 12:35.

99. James M. McPherson, *Battle Cry of Freedom: The Civil War Era* (New York: Oxford University Press, 1988), 740; Fisk to the *Montpelier Green Mountain Freeman*, June 19, 1864, in Rosenblatt and Rosenblatt, *Hard Marching Every Day*, 230; Hunter to *Christian Recorder*, July 9, 1864, in Redkey, *A Grand Army of Black Men*, 102.

100. Trudeau, *Like Men of War*, 229–34; William Marvel, *Burnside* (Chapel Hill: University of North Carolina Press, 1991), 393; Cavanaugh and Marvel, *The Petersburg Campaign*, 18; McPherson, *Battle Cry of Freedom*, 758.

101. Trudeau, *Like Men of War*, 234–35; Marvel, *Burnside*, 399.

102. Thomas to Theodore D. Jervey, July 30, 1911, Theodore D. Jervey Papers, South Carolina Historical Society, Charleston, S.C.; Stevens, *As If It Were Glory*, 183, 184; Trudeau, *Like Men of War*, 236–43.

103. Marvel, *Burnside*, 404; Edward A. Miller, Jr., *The Black Civil War Soldiers of Illinois* (Columbia: University of South Carolina Press, 1998), 74; Quarles, *The Negro in the Civil War*, 304; Trudeau, *Like Men of War*, 244, 246; Edward Porter Alexander, *Fighting for the Confederacy: The Personal Recollections of General Edward Porter Alexander* (Chapel Hill: University of North Carolina Press, 1989), ed. Gary W. Gallagher, 462.

104. Trudeau, *Like Men of War*, 247; Cavanaugh and Marvel, *The Petersburg Campaign*, 128; Cornish, *The Sable Arm*, 276; Glatthaar, *Forged in Battle*, 150; Grant to Henry W. Halleck, August 1, 1864, in Simon, *The Papers of Ulysses S. Grant*, 11:361; Willcox to Eb[en] N. Willcox, August 3, 1864, and William V. Richards to Marie Willcox, August 6, 1864, in Robert Garth Scott, ed., *Forgotten Valor: The Memoirs, Journals, and Civil War Letters of Orlando B. Willcox* (Kent, Ohio: Kent State University Press, 1999), 557, 560; Cram to Mother, August 9, 1864, in Jennifer Cain Bohrnstedt, ed., *Soldiering with Sherman: The Civil War Letters of George F. Cram* (DeKalb: Northern Illinois University Press, 2000), 133.

105. Burnside testimony, August 12, 1864, *OR*, 1st ser., 40 (1):73; Marvel, *Burnside*, 411–12; Bruce Tap, *Over Lincoln's Shoulder: The Committee on the Conduct of the War* (Lawrence: University Press of Kansas, 1998), 191; Cornish, *The Sable Arm*, 274.

106. Frederick S. Eaton, "Colored Troops," *American Missionary* 8 (November 1864): 274; Trudeau, *Like Men of War*, 284–94; Glatthaar, *Forged in Battle*, 151; Chester, *Philadelphia Press*, October 17, 1864, in R. J. M. Blackett, ed., *Thomas Morris Chester, Black Civil War Correspondent: His Dispatches from the Virginia Front* (Baton Rouge: Louisiana State University Press, 1989), 150, 153.

107. Lincoln, "Annual Message to Congress," December 8, 1863, Lincoln to Hodges, April 4, 1864, and Interview with Alexander W. Randall and Joseph T. Mills, August 19, 1864, in Basler, *Collected Works of Lincoln*, 7:50, 282, 506; Trudeau, *Like Men of War*, 338–49; James B. Steedman, January 27, 1865, *OR*, 1st ser., 45 (1):508.

108. Bell Irvin Wiley, *Kingdom Coming: The Emancipation Proclamation of September 22, 1862: An Address Delivered at the Chicago Historical Society, September 21, 1962* (Chicago: Chicago Historical Society, 1963), 17; Lincoln to Wadsworth [January 1864?], Lincoln to Isaac M. Schermerhorn, September 12, 1864 [unfinished draft], and Lincoln to Albert G. Hodges, April 4, 1864, in Basler, *Collected Works of Lincoln*, 7:101, 8:2, 7:282.

AN IRONIC ROUTE
TO GLORY

Louisiana's Native Guards
at Port Hudson

Lawrence Lee Hewitt

Shortly after the firing on Fort Sumter in April 1861, free blacks in New Orleans organized the Native Guards. On May 2, Governor Thomas O. Moore authorized the addition of a regiment of Native Guards to the state militia. Though he appointed a white colonel, Henry D. Ogden, to command the regiment, all the rest of the officers he commissioned were black. White New Orleanians approved Moore's action. The *New Orleans Daily Crescent* claimed that the Native Guards "will fight the Black Republican with as much determination and gallantry as any body of white men in the service of the Confederate States."[1] Such sentiment was limited to Louisiana, however, where blacks, both slave and free, had fought with the French against the Choctaw Indians, with the Spanish against the English, and with Andrew Jackson at the Battle of New Orleans.

Existing Afro-Creole mutual aid societies formed the basis of these companies, and officers of a particular society were often elected to military office within that organization's company. President Charles Sentmanat and Secretary André Cailloux of the Friends of Order became captain and first lieutenant, respectively, of Order Company, which was designated Company C. Though some of these free blacks undoubtedly volunteered for other reasons, economics appears to have been the dominant motivation.

These individuals were the elite of black society in New Orleans: doctors, dentists, architects, and skilled craftsmen. They were well educated and, by 1860s standards, wealthy. Collectively, they owned more than $2 million worth of property. Each of the officers reportedly had a net worth of over $25,000, and several of them owned slaves. Coupled with the fact that more than eighty percent of them were of European descent, it is readily apparent why these African Americans felt a stronger bond with white, rather than slave, society.

The Native Guards quickly set about learning the lessons of soldiering. Twice they participated with white Confederate troops in massive reviews, one on November 23, 1861, and a second on January 7, 1862. By that time, the Native Guardsmen numbered approximately one thousand and were organized into thirteen companies. Three days later, however, the morning report indicated an increase in the number of absentees. Marching with the white soldiers made it clear to the Native Guardsmen that if they wanted uniforms and weapons they would have to purchase those articles themselves. Though some had already done so, others opted not to continue to participate under such conditions.

The Native Guards were not the only people distressed by what they witnessed at the January 7 review. Seeing some of the African Americans carrying weapons upset many white citizens. Their complaints undoubtedly brought about the disbandment of the regiment in February. Nonetheless, Governor Moore recalled the Native Guards on March 24, after Commodore David G. Farragut's Union fleet entered the Mississippi River downstream. Widely divergent accounts fail to explain what happened to this unit when Confederate forces evacuated the Crescent City in April 1862. A majority of the unit apparently fled north with other soldiers and rendezvoused at Camp Moore, just south of the Mississippi border. Confederate authorities there made it clear to the Native Guards that their regiment would not be mustered into the Confederate army. The unit disbanded, its members returning to New Orleans.

Major General Benjamin F. Butler commanded Union occupation forces in Louisiana. A severe shortage of soldiers, coupled with the threat of a Confederate attack on the Crescent City following the Battle of Baton Rouge on August 5, 1862, prompted Butler to appeal to blacks to join the Union army. On September 27, Butler mustered the 1st Regiment of the Native Guards into service, making it the first officially sanctioned regiment of black soldiers in the U.S. Army.

Though the unit's designation remained the same, its Union composition differed dramatically from the earlier Confederate organization. According to one source, of the 906 members of the pro-Confederate Native Guards, only 108 men (11 percent) enlisted in the Union's version. Butler's claim

"Our Colored Troops at Work—The First Louisiana Native Guards Disembarking at Fort Macombe, Louisiana.—Sketched by Our Special Artist." (Harper's Weekly, *February 28, 1863, Hargrett Rare Book and Manuscript Library, University of Georgia Libraries)*

that "the darkest of [them] is about the complexion of the late Mr. [Daniel] Webster" was certainly erroneous, as was his alleged claim that none of its members were fresh from slavery at the time of their enlistment. Only five of its black officers, including the thirty-six-year-old Cailloux, had served in the Confederate unit.[2]

Combining deceit with legal maneuvers, Butler managed to secure enough black volunteers, primarily slaves, to organize the 2nd Native Guards in October and the 3rd in November. With one exception, Butler appointed white field officers for these regiments, but all of the line officers (captains and lieutenants) in the 1st and 2nd Regiments, and some in the 3rd, were black; every one of the noncommissioned officers in the three units was black. Eleven of the line officers had held commissions in the Louisiana militia, while another ten had served in the ranks.

The colonel of the 1st Native Guards claimed that his regiment contained some of the "best blood of Louisiana," being either the offspring

"Pickets of the First Louisiana 'Native Guard' Guarding the New Orleans, Opelousas and Great Western Railroad—From a Sketch by Our Special Artist." (Frank Leslie's Illustrated Newspaper, *March 7, 1863, The Lincoln Museum, Fort Wayne, Ind., no. 4331)*

of white politicians or prominent, wealthy free blacks from New Orleans. Cigar maker Captain Cailloux proudly claimed to be the blackest man in New Orleans. Sixteen-year-old Second Lieutenant John H. Crowder may have been the youngest officer in the Union army. Both men had held similar ranks in the unit when it formed part of the pro-Confederate Louisiana State Guard.

When Nathanial P. Banks relieved Butler in December 1862, he quickly became convinced that, whatever their status had been in civilian life, blacks were not capable of serving as officers. He also thought that black officers reduced the effectiveness of white units by creating unnecessary racial tension. So Banks relegated the Native Guards to garrison duty and assigned them to locations where there were few, if any, white soldiers. He also began systematically removing black officers by any means possible, thereby stirring resentment throughout the ranks of the Native Guards.

On the other hand, reports that Banks had stated "that the colored soldiers went where the white ones dared not go" undermined the white troops' support for both him and the Native Guards. Officers of white regiments who pointed out that the Native Guards were better at drilling only increased the prejudice of their troops against the blacks.[3]

In May 1863, Banks determined to move against the Confederate stronghold at Port Hudson. Though hardly remembered today, Port Hudson, Louisiana, holds a distinct place in U.S. history. Located seventeen miles north of Baton Rouge, the town was the site of the longest true siege in American military history and the last Confederate stronghold on the Mississippi River. It was here, too, on May 27, 1863, that black soldiers in the regular U.S. Army first participated in a major assault.

While Banks moved from Alexandria via Bayou Sara toward the Confederate bastion, other units of his army struck out from New Orleans and Baton Rouge in a pincer movement designed to isolate the enemy garrison. Most of the Union soldiers who initially encircled Port Hudson came from New England or New York. Augmenting this force were five batteries of U.S. regulars; two regiments from Illinois; one each from Indiana, Michigan, and Wisconsin; and five from Louisiana. African Americans comprised two of the last.

The 1st and 3rd Native Guards advanced northward from Baton Rouge toward Plains Store, a crossroads five miles east of Port Hudson on the Bayou Sara road. On May 21, the Native Guards stood on the Union left during the Battle of Plains Store to prevent the Confederates from turning that flank. That same day Banks ordered the arrest of Colonel Spencer H. Stafford of the 1st Native Guards for "conduct to the prejudice of good order and military discipline." He had cussed out Captain J. P. Garland of the 21st Maine after Garland called one of his officers a "black son of a bitch." Following Stafford's arrest, Colonel John A. Nelson of the 3rd was placed in command of both regiments.[4]

On May 25, the Native Guards marched from the extreme left to the extreme right of Banks's investing army. Oppressive heat and thick dust made it a hard march, and every man had to carry all his personal baggage because the regiment had never been issued wagons. That night they camped by a sugarhouse near Foster's Creek.

The following morning, the 75th New York marched past the Native Guards a few miles north of Port Hudson, where the latter were guarding baggage trains and ambulances. The New Yorkers found the black troops to be impressive-looking soldiers who longed for a fight. When the African Americans advanced later that day, they appeared in good spirits, declaring along the march that "they would make no guard by taking prisoners."[5] Passing through the 38th Massachusetts, they skirmished with the Confederates on the opposite bank of Sandy Creek while some pioneers built a footbridge across the waterway. A Massachusetts soldier commented that the black soldiers performed this duty "in a cool, collected manner." Upon its completion in the early afternoon, the Native Guards crossed over and continued skirmishing with the Confederates, driving them back to enable the men of Company K, 42nd Massachusetts, to construct a 280-foot rubber pontoon bridge across the swollen stream. Even though this engagement was their first encounter with the enemy, the African Americans remained cool and stood their ground like veterans. Under artillery and musket fire for several hours, they never faltered. When the 38th Massachusetts Infantry and the 18th New York Battery took a position along the north bank of the creek to support the black troops, the Confederate infantry withdrew.

That night the Native Guards withdrew to the north bank, where they relieved the 38th Massachusetts. Those not on picket or guard duty were so exhausted that they slept despite the noise of the naval bombardment of Port Hudson. During the night the guards apparently mistook stampeding mules for a Confederate cavalry attack and fired a volley that passed over the heads of the men in the 38th Massachusetts. Fortunately, no one was hurt and things quieted quickly.[6]

Colonel William L. Rodman (38th Massachusetts) noted in his diary that he had heard Nelson bragging that "his niggers" would be the first Union troops to enter Port Hudson. Conceding that the Native Guards even impressed the Irishmen in his regiment, Rodman concluded, "if they will fight, and Port Hudson falls, the great problem of 'Will the blacks fight?' will be solved forever. It is a question of vast interest." He would have his answer the following morning.

Though the mortar vessels shelled the garrison throughout the night, the battle proper opened at about 5:30 A.M. Federal batteries began a heavy, hour-long bombardment of the Confederate center and right, as an ominous silence prevailed on their left. The upper and lower fleets approached the fortress and began firing at around 7:00 A.M., but they ceased an hour later for fear of injuring their comrades on shore. Their brief participation proved ineffective.[7]

Early on May 27, while the Confederates completed what preparations they could to meet the impending Union onslaught, Union brigadier general Godfrey Weitzel formed his men in a column of brigades. Brigadier General William Dwight's division headed the advance, Colonel Jacob Van Zandt's brigade leading off, supported by that of Colonel Stephen Thomas. Brigadier General Halbert E. Paine's division followed, Colonel Hawkes Fearing, Jr.'s brigade in front and Colonel Oliver P. Gooding's in the rear. Twelve hundred Confederate infantrymen awaited the onslaught of this overwhelming force.

The four brigades under Weitzel contained fourteen regiments that encompassed at least 6,000 soldiers, ranging from the 8th Vermont, about 900 strong, to the 298 members of the 8th New Hampshire. Weitzel began his advance at about 6:00 A.M. During the next hour, Van Zandt pushed the Confederates back through the forest and ravines in savage fighting. Though heavily outnumbered, the Southerners held their ground until threats to both their flanks forced them to withdraw within the fortifications. Both sides got severely bloodied in what amounted to a skirmish, with the Confederates losing nearly 200 men killed, wounded, or missing—including one colonel captured—40 percent of the delaying force.

But the Union column had fallen into disarray. The farther south the Federals advanced, the more they drifted to the west, trying to keep their right flank anchored on Sandy Creek, which meandered southwesterly. Steep ravines, many over thirty feet deep, and dense woods broke battle lines. To press the attack, Thomas's troops passed through the gaps of Van Zandt's exhausted and widely dispersed men. By the time the Federals gained the crest north of Little Sandy Creek any sense of organization above the regimental level had vanished.[8]

Scores of blue-clad infantrymen, confused and separated from their officers, advanced no further than the edge of the woods lining the crest. Before them lay the valley of Little Sandy Creek, broken by small hillocks and ravines, dense with pines and magnolias and the interlaced branches of felled trees. Sharpshooters sniped away from this natural cover. Beyond the basin stood the opposite crest, crowned with the yellow dirt of unfinished earthworks. Beyond the Federals could see the garrison's tents, shanties, and warehouses, as well as the church and dwellings of the village. The only

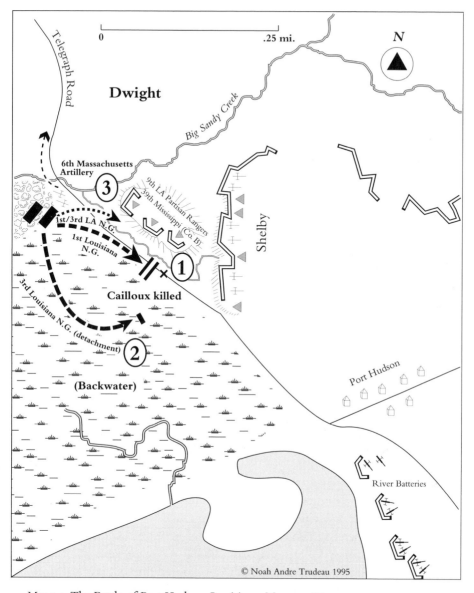

Map 2.1. The Battle of Port Hudson, Louisiana, May 27, 1863.
(Courtesy of Noah Andre Trudeau)

unobstructed route through the bottom was a wagon path leading straight into the blazing guns of the battery atop Commissary Hill.

First to respond to the challenge, Lieutenant Colonel Willoughby Babcock drew his sword and dashed ahead of the 75th New York shouting, "Come on!" A corporal leapt forward, replying, "Here goes the Colonel, boys, we won't leave the Colonel! Charge!" The rugged, obstructed valley soon dispersed the advancing 75th into squads. The same happened to the regiments that followed, and something resembling an unorganized mob struggled toward the breastworks.[9] The attacking force steadily diminished as fear, heat, humidity, and the unforgiving terrain took their toll.

While Confederate infantrymen waited for the enemy to close within musket-range, gray-clad artillerymen opened fire. Soon their shells were exploding among the advancing enemy, causing much confusion. The Confederate commander opposing Weitzel, Colonel I. G. W. Steedman, reported that the Yankees were "mowed down in whole ranks, their lines . . . soon broken, yet undismayed they rushed down the hill." Using felled trees and ravines for cover, some of the Federals approached within easy range of the rifle pits.

Pioneers followed the advancing blue-clad infantry to open roads through the woods for the artillery. Soon enough, the five batteries had un-limbered their pieces along the crest and immediately drew Confederate artillery fire. Zeroing in on a section of the 1st Maine Battery as it wheeled into position, they quickly killed one soldier and thirteen horses and wounded twelve more men. The premature discharge of another Confederate cannon hurled a rammer toward Battery F, 1st U.S. Artillery. Just before it reached the battery, it struck a tree. Ricocheting off, the whirling staff killed five or six Federals. But it was Company A of that regiment that suffered the most. The Confederates dismounted two of its guns, killed two men and fifteen horses, and wounded a lieutenant and eleven men.[10]

Yet the Confederate gunners' deadly precision succeeded only in diverting Federal artillery fire from the retreating gray-clad infantry. Captain Edmund C. Bainbridge's U.S. regulars unlimbered the six guns of Battery A next to the 6th Massachusetts's four cannon at the edge of the woods, 400 yards from the advanced lunette, which contained two twelve-pound howitzers and the 15th Arkansas. Together, the two Union batteries quickly silenced the two Confederate cannon, while other Yankee gunners pounded the Confederate artillery on Commissary Hill and riddled the large granary just to the right of the battery.

Meanwhile, three companies of the 12th Connecticut worked their way forward toward Commissary Hill. Dispersed among the fallen trees and firing as sharpshooters, they soon forced the Confederate gunners to lie behind their parapets. When they ceased firing, some of the Federals seized a ditch from which they poured an enfilading fire into the battery. Confederate efforts to oust the Yankees proved costly and futile, but the latter could advance no farther.

Just to the west, the advancing Federals saw the parapet forty yards before them blaze with a volley of musketry. The suddenness of the destruction staggered the Federals. The more courageous of them rallied quickly, however, and came on with a yell. A few of the Federals almost reached the parapet before fleeing from the withering fire. The Confederates shot them down from behind until they passed beyond range. The Federals who had actually inflicted the most damage were three companies of the 1st Louisiana (U.S.) who lined the ridge in front of the Confederates before their comrades began their assault. These men are credited with killing far more Confederates with their fire on the breastworks than the Federals in the advancing column—a clear indication of the limited number of New Yorkers participating in the final charge. Out of 700 men, the 75th New York lost only eighty-six the entire day.[11]

Farther to the west and almost in concert with Thomas's attack, the 91st and 131st New York of Van Zandt's brigade struck the lunette near Major W. K. Bennett's residence. Bullets and canister from the breastworks wreaked havoc: the 131st lost about sixty killed and wounded during the assault. While waving his sword, Union sergeant major William H. Aldis, Jr., took a minié ball in his right forearm. With his left hand and teeth, he managed to tie a dirty handkerchief about the flesh wound while keeping pace with the advance.

The obliquing of Dwight's brigades westward and the ensuing extension of the line, coupled with the fragmentation of regiments struggling through the valley, uncovered Paine's front. To fill the gap, Paine ordered Fearing's brigade forward. Fearing's men struck the breastworks at the "Bull Pen," where the Confederates slaughtered their cattle. Steedman had foreseen this possibility and requested reinforcements. Three Arkansas regiments arrived in time to check the enemy's advance. One Union officer aptly labeled the resulting engagement a "huge bushwhack."[12]

Under fire from the battery at Bennett's lunette, the 4th Wisconsin halted about 300 yards from the breastworks to dress its line. The shot and shell tore through the trees with devastating effect. One solid shot cleared an entire file from the line. When the men moved forward, they reserved their fire while struggling over and under tree trunks and through branches, all the while under a deadly hail of missiles. By twos and threes, they passed through what one officer termed "the valley of the shadow of death,"[13] and a few especially determined Federals reached the final summit.

One hundred yards away, they saw the Arkansans forming behind an irregular line of entrenchments. Confederate fire soon forced them to withdraw below the crest. But there they encountered yet another danger. Premature ignition of shells from the 1st Maine Battery caused the projectiles to explode around them, killing one man and wounding several others.

Captain John M. Stanyan thought the terrain "very peculiar, looking like the skeleton of a huge fish, the backbone representing the long ridge running from the woods towards the fortifications, and the ribs the short ridges which partially protected us in the gullies." Like many of his comrades, Stanyan had managed to find a safe refuge. But his regiment, the 8th New Hampshire, lost 124 men killed and wounded. Considering that the men were assaulting fortified defenders, a 42 percent loss was not exceptional — but it was double the percentage of casualties of any other regiment in that sector.[14]

The Confederates' determination and the timely arrival of reinforcements alone cannot explain their successful defense. The piecemeal Federal attacks contributed to their repulse, and the terrain and officer casualties helped disorganize the Federal ranks. Sheer weight of numbers, however, should have enabled the Federals to breach the fortifications. But not enough Federals reached the Rebel breastworks. Seven regiments—37 percent of the available infantry—did not assault the breastworks. And too many men had dropped out to seek safety. Admittedly, some of these soldiers acted as sharpshooters. But the paucity of casualties reflected the failure of many troops to participate in the final charge against the enemy's parapet. The Federals simply lacked the resolve needed to achieve victory.

Having failed to capture the fortifications along Little Sandy Creek, the Federals looked for any available assistance on either flank. The 1st and 3rd Louisiana Native Guards anchored the right end of the Union line. Brigadier General William Dwight had stationed both black regiments on the flank because he thought little of the ability of African Americans on a battlefield, even if they were led by the best white officers. Like many of his colleagues, he believed garrison duty in some rear area the proper place for black soldiers. "A man not distinguished for courage or sobriety," Dwight was drunk before breakfast. As did other brigade commanders that morning, Dwight issued whiskey to his troops; one Native Guardsman recalled being intoxicated when the order was given to advance.[15]

Dwight desperately wanted to breach the Confederate defenses, and he was anxious "to test the negro question," as he phrased it. He had written his mother the previous evening, "I have had the negro Regts longest in the service assigned to me, and I am going to storm a detached work with them. You may look for hard fighting, or for a complete run away . . . the garrison will of course be incensed and fight defiantly. The negro will have the fate of his race on his conduct. I shall compromise nothing in making this attack, for I regard it as an experiment."[16]

After the assault along Little Sandy Creek ground to a halt, Dwight availed himself of the opportunity to order the black regiments forward. Six companies of the 1st with nine of the 3rd Native Guards crossed the pontoon bridge. Two cannon of the 6th Massachusetts Battery and some dismounted troopers of the 1st Louisiana (U.S.) Cavalry accompanied them. The artillerymen unlimbered the cannon in the road, but after getting off only one round they were forced by enemy fire to withdraw. The infantry, however, filed to the right, where they formed a line of battle among the willow trees covering the old riverbed. Confederate gunners in two of the river batteries responded to Colonel Winchester B. Shelby's call for help by bombarding the area with shell and solid shot.

The terrain made the fortifications the Native Guards would assault the strongest at Port Hudson. With the Mississippi near its crest, backwater covered much of the floodplain along the Telegraph Road and Sandy Creek. The Federals had constructed the pontoon bridge where the road crossed the creek, one-half mile northwest of the Confederate defenses. South of the creek, the road paralleled the almost inaccessible west slope of an abrupt ridge for a quarter of a mile, at which point both road and ridge intersected the bluff.

Along the crest of this ridge, which formed an island when the Mississippi River was at flood stage, Confederate lieutenant S. D. Rhodes had deployed forty-five infantrymen of Company B, 39th Mississippi, and fifteen dismounted cavalrymen of the 9th Louisiana Battalion Partisan Rangers. Ordered to hold his position at any hazard, Rhodes must have been confident that his sixty riflemen would fight to the death. Their only alternative was to yield the crest to the enemy and be shot in the back while struggling through the water to reach about three hundred men of Colonel Shelby's 39th Mississippi who manned the rifle pits constructed along the edge of the steep bluff. Two two-pounder breechloaders augmented Rhodes's position, while two additional field pieces were positioned on Shelby's line where they could enfilade the Telegraph Road.[17]

At 10:00 A.M., the Native Guards moved forward. More than a thousand black soldiers emerged from the woods in fine order, advancing first at quick time and then double-quick toward the bluff, about six hundred yards away. Lieutenant Colonel Chauncy J. Bassett led the 1st Native Guards forward, followed closely by the 3rd under Lieutenant Colonel Henry Finnegass. Both regiments formed in a long line, two ranks deep. Shortly after the advance began, Finnegass detached his four leftmost companies under Captain John E. Quinn to support the 1st Regiment. To secure the left flank of the assaulting force, Quinn deployed one company perpendicular to the line of advance and parallel to the Confederate rifle pits on the outlying ridge.[18]

As the black soldiers rushed forward, bullets from the ridge ripped into their flank. Yet despite confusion and disorder they pressed on toward the bluff, to a point two hundred yards from the Confederate main line. At that moment Rebel artillery opened with canister, and Shelby's troops, eager to join in the fight, began firing from the bluff without orders. Canister and minié balls mowed down men in the lead ranks by the dozen. So many projectiles pierced the flag of the 1st Native Guards that it was nearly severed from its staff before an artillery shell cut the banner in two and struck Color Sergeant Anselmas Planciancois. The son of free parents, the forty-year-old illiterate mulatto fell embracing the flag, his blood and brains staining the riddled banner. Louis Leveiller and Athanase Ulgere, two corporals of the color guard, fought each other for the honor to carry the flag until a minié ball fatally wounded Leveiller, who fell atop Planciancois. Ulgere managed to retrieve the colors, taking a bullet in his left hand in the process. Captain Cailloux commanded the company nearest the color guard's position in the line. Though his left arm was shattered above the elbow early in the engagement, he refused to leave the field. With one arm dangling and the other waving his sword, Cailloux moved along the line shouting orders in both English and French to steady his men. His voice growing faint, he reached the front of his company and called to his men, "Follow me!" and "En avant, mes enfants!" (Once more, my children!). He led his men forward, reaching a point about fifty yards from the Confederate main line before an artillery shell struck him dead. Ordinary soldiers performed similar acts of valor. After an artillery shell tore off his leg below the knee, a member of the 3rd Native Guards refused to be taken to the hospital. Telling his captain to take care of himself, the enlisted man pulled himself up on a log and "Sat With his leg a swing, and bleeding and fierd [*sic*] thirty rounds of Ammunition" before being carried to the rear; he died a few days later.

Over eight feet deep and approximately forty feet across, the backwater prevented the Native Guards from reaching the main line of Confederate fortifications atop the bluff. After firing one volley, the black soldiers in front fell back in utter confusion. When they encountered Finnegass's remaining five companies in their rear, men in the second line faltered, and both regiments withdrew to the woods.[19]

While other officers attempted to rally the troops among the trees, Quinn called for volunteers to follow him into the water. But the thirty-five or forty officers and men brave enough to do so found it impossible to reach the Confederates, even by holding their rifles and cartridge boxes above their heads. Only six of these soldiers reportedly survived. Another heroic group managed to scale the projecting ridge, but all of the men were either killed by enfilading fire or captured. Barely fifteen minutes had passed from the time the black troops exited the woods until they returned to them. Although the Rebels had killed and wounded scores of the enemy, they themselves had not suffered a single casualty. Among the mortally wounded black officers was the teenage Lieutenant Crowder, who was carried from the field only to die the following day.[20]

The black soldiers found little safety in their refuge. Confederate artillery continued to rain shell and solid shot into the woods, and splinters from fragmenting trees proved almost as dangerous as the projectiles themselves. One Native Guardsman remembered, "Quite a number of men were hurt in that fight by the limbs of trees falling on them." Another recalled, "A shell from a rebel battery cut the limb of a tree and it fell on me injuring my back. It struck me across the small of the back, knocked me down and I was carried off the field."

Following Dwight's example, quasi–brigade commander Nelson remained in the rear, possibly even north of Sandy Creek. When he learned that his men had been unable to reach the enemy's breastworks, he sent an aide with a request to Dwight for permission to withdraw. "Tell Colonel Nelson I shall consider he has done nothing unless he carries the enemy's works," Dwight responded. Protesting, the aide argued that the black regiments had already suffered 50 percent casualties. Pompously, Dwight ended the argument, "Charge again, and let the impetuosity of the charge counterbalance the paucity of the numbers."[21]

Troops did not exist who could accomplish the objective Dwight had set for the African Americans. Nelson sent word to his lieutenant colonels to prepare to make another attack. Finnegass went to protest to Nelson. After being ordered back to his regiment, Finnegass departed only to return five minutes later. After senseless bantering, he finally mustered the courage to tell Nelson he would be damned if he would lead his men forward again.

Because Nelson had no inclination to lead the attack himself, he called it off. But he could not withdraw. To fool Dwight, who remained far to the rear in a drunken state, Nelson had his men continue firing. But his deception forced his men to remain among the trees and endure the shelling for hours. On June 1, Nelson diverted the blame for not pressing the attack by filing charges against Finnegass for refusing to obey orders. Other officers of the 1st Native Guards, including Captain Alcide Lewis of Company G and Second Lieutenants Louis H. Thibaut of Company H and Hippolyte St. Louis of Company E, were later dismissed for cowardice.[22]

To support Weitzel's stymied advance, Brigadier General Cuvier Grover sent the 159th New York and 25th Connecticut on a wide detour to the west to unite with Weitzel's left flank. Lieutenant Colonel Charles A. Burt moved forward under the mistaken impression that a trifling number of Confederates would oppose him and that his New Yorkers alone could breach the enemy's line. The men double-quicked down the dusty road under a murderous fire from the battery on Commissary Hill and started through the valley choked with felled trees and heavy underbrush—a combination that undoubtedly influenced several of the troops to drop out of the column. Turning west and advancing in single file, they sloshed across Little Sandy, and some of the men finally reached the side of the hill they were to assault. They waited a few tense moments for the order to charge. At 10:00 A.M., as the Native Guards moved forward a half-mile to their west, the New Yorkers rose with a terrifying yell and rushed forward, crashing through brush and bounding over the last tree only to emerge thirty yards from the breastwork, where it seemed to one Federal that "a thousand rifles were cracking our doom." Within seconds, the Federals suffered some fifty casualties. The survivors dove for cover. The colors of the 159th lay before the parapet, the standard bearer dead at their side. Sergeant Robert Buckley of the 25th Connecticut worked his way back and brought in the colors, only to be killed when he turned to pick up his gun.

When these two regiments failed to breach the defenses, Grover decided to increase the pressure even more. He extended the fighting eastward to encompass the lunette defended by the 15th Arkansas. Two hundred Arkansans lined the quarter-mile-long lunette, while the major and thirty men prepared to hold the rear "at all hazards."[23]

Grover dispatched three additional regiments of his division to engage the 15th Arkansas. Marching west, they passed through the woods littered with the dead and wounded of Weitzel's command. As the Native Guards fell back into the woods at about 10:30 A.M., these three regiments and

Gooding's brigade moved toward the lunette. The 12th Maine led the assault, followed by the 38th Massachusetts; the third wave, composed of the 31st Massachusetts, did not advance. The assaulting column received covering fire from one company of the 12th Connecticut on the right, and the 13th and 24th Connecticut on the left.

The Federals advanced in a long, crescent-shaped line that covered the Confederates' front and partly overlapped both flanks. Though his situation appeared hopeless, Colonel Benjamin W. Johnson ordered his men not to look over the parapet until the Federals were within sixty yards, at which point the Yankees let out a lusty cheer and quickened their pace. The Arkansans rose with a yell and rapidly fired volleys of buck and ball cartridges. Within ten minutes they broke the Federal center, and the Yankees fled. The absence of devastating volleys of canister from Confederate artillery, however, enabled the more steadfast of the Federals to close both wings on the center. Onward they came, only to have their center decimated a second time by Johnson's backwoodsmen. The Federals rallied a third time and advanced to within fifty yards of the works, where they dropped behind stumps and logs or sought shelter in ravines.

A steady covering fire of artillery and musketry enabled about 300 Federals, less than 30 percent of the attacking column, to move up a ravine and into the ditch surrounding the lunette. The Federals repeatedly attempted to scale the rampart, each time being bloodily repulsed. Finally a Federal officer shouted, "Are you ready?" Everyone replied in the affirmative, and the officer screamed, "Charge!" He scaled the parapet with only four men at his side. When their lifeless bodies rolled down into the ditch, their comrades were gripped with fear. When another officer shouted "Charge!" not a single man rose above the parapet. The Federals crossed bayonets with the foe and hurled sticks, dirt clods, and verbal abuse, but they quickly discovered they could neither advance nor retreat.[24]

Those infantrymen that had remained in the rear now moved to support their comrades in the advance. The 53rd Massachusetts moved up to relieve the 91st New York, and the reserve companies of the 12th Connecticut rotated with those sharpshooting at the front. The 173rd New York marched to assist the 1st Louisiana, but that unit had the right flank securely anchored on Big Sandy, and the 173rd took position in its rear. Shortly after noon, Grover relaxed his efforts because he heard nothing from the left, and Weitzel followed suit. Both men requested fresh orders and awaited their arrival or the sound of battle from the Union left before renewing their assault. Federal victory would have to be achieved elsewhere.

Without question, desperate fighting had occurred along Little Sandy Creek, but such encounters were generally isolated and short-lived and involved few men on either side. Seven of the nineteen Federal regiments on the field did not actively participate in the assault. With few exceptions, Union losses indicate that the remaining twelve made no serious effort to breach the Confederate defenses. Out of more than 8,000 blue-clad infantrymen, fewer than 700 were killed or wounded. One-fourth of these casualties occurred in the 8th New Hampshire and 4th Wisconsin, the units caught in the "huge bushwhack."[25]

The terrain prevented any organized effort by separating most of the enlisted men from their regimental officers. Once this happened, the more faint-hearted soldiers secreted themselves at a safe depth in a ravine. With little chance of embarrassment, these men remained hidden in their sanctuaries until nightfall. Few participants pressed the attack despite allegations to the contrary. This grossly exaggerated account of the performance of the 156th New York, coupled with its number of casualties, typifies the "action" of too many Federals on May 27: "In order to reach the enemy works they had to plunge through a dense forest of magnolias, choked with a thick undergrowth, brambles and wild honeysuckle, before encountering the maze of felled trees. All the time their broken ranks were subjected to a galling fire that pinned them down in ravines, woods or any shelter they could find. The protection thus gained kept their losses down, but they would always remember Port Hudson and May 27, 1863." The regiment's position indeed protected its members. The 156th New York did not suffer a single casualty. All ten of its companies were miles in the rear; three protected Banks's headquarters and seven guarded a large train of ammunition wagons.[26]

Despite the terrain, and without the aid of covering fire from two regiments and over twenty cannon, three regiments should have overwhelmed the 200 Arkansans in the lunette north of the creek. Though Johnson reported killing ninety and wounding more than 300 of the enemy in his front, many of these Federals apparently feigned death until nightfall. The combined loss of the three Federal regiments amounted to fewer than eighty men killed or wounded; virtually none of the casualties occurred in the 31st Massachusetts. One can only speculate about the consequences of that regiment's failure to participate in the final advance. Indeed, the courage of most of Grover's men did not equal that of the Native Guards, who endured a ten-hour bombardment after they had been repulsed.

Widespread Yankee shirking should not detract from those Federals who pressed the assault. The 8th New Hampshire, 131st New York, 4th Wisconsin, and the African American regiments performed gallantly. And the sharp-shooters of the 1st (U.S.) Louisiana and 12th Connecticut kept up a withering fire on the enemy. For the outnumbered Confederates, it was a hard-fought engagement. The men of the 15th Arkansas expressed their view of the fierceness of the battle by nicknaming their lunette "Fort Desperate."[27]

Banks's battle plan for May 27 was typical for the time. Most Civil War commanders favored the tactical offensive, even though those assaults seldom proved decisive, even if successful. And such endeavors proved extremely costly against fortified defenders armed with rifled weapons. In four assaults during his defense of Atlanta, John Bell Hood lost 19 percent of his command. Braxton Bragg suffered losses of 27 percent at Murfreesboro and 26 percent at Chickamauga. Robert E. Lee lost 30 percent of his army at Gettysburg, 21 percent during the Seven Days, and 19 percent at Second Manassas and Chancellorsville. And Ulysses S. Grant lost 41 percent during his offensive from the Wilderness to Cold Harbor.

A piecemeal attack by only 63 percent of the available infantry demonstrates incompetence equal to that displayed by George B. McClellan at Antietam. No force could maintain its organization while advancing over terrain such as that which fronted Steedman's position. Any chance that the Federals had of achieving victory after they descended into the valley of Little Sandy Creek depended on the individual courage and initiative displayed by the soldiers and junior officers. Their failure to breach the Confederate defenses, coupled with a loss of only 8 percent of the attacking force, strongly indicates that the Federals who entered "the valley of the shadow of death" clearly lacked the determination needed to achieve victory. A member of the 4th Massachusetts said it best: "The first charge, May 27th, was sadly disastrous,—a vast slaughter and little or nothing to compensate, except, perhaps, the proof given by the colored troops, for the first time employed in the department, that they could not only fight, but with the most determined valor."[28]

The Native Guards' assault proved the last undertaken by the Federals on their extreme right and the last in which the 1st and 3rd Louisiana Native Guards participated at Port Hudson. Even after the Mississippi River began to recede, withering fire made their sector a death trap for any attacker. Exact casualty figures for the black soldiers will never be known. Considering the number of attackers, the terrain, the lengthy shelling they had to endure, and the number and firepower of their opponents, a loss of 50 percent would not be unusual. The official casualty return for both regiments for the entire siege lists forty-four killed, 133 wounded, and three captured or missing for a total loss of 180 men. Without question, there was a cover-up within Banks's army. Official figures indicated that the blacks constituted one-twelfth of the troops on hand and suffered one-eighth of the casualties. A more reasonable estimate would be that the Native Guards who participated in the assault constituted less than one twenty-fifth of the Union soldiers present and suffered at least 20 percent of the casualties. The lowest believable accounting found by this author is 371 killed and 150 wounded out of an attacking force of 1,080 men, and these figures are reasonable only if those listed as killed include the mortally wounded and the missing. Several Confederates claimed that 250 bodies were clearly visible the following day, and the most reliable account placed this figure at 200. One indication of their casualties lay in the arms and legs piled behind their hospital the night of the twenty-seventh. Another was the recollection of one of the Native Guards that on the morning of the twenty-eighth only a third of the nine hundred present the previous morning answered roll call. Those who never returned from the Mississippi backwater to answer roll call after May 27 were listed as deserters.[29]

The performance of the black troops impressed the Union army commander. "They fought splendidly!" Banks wrote his wife. He put Dwight in command of a division and, needing every man possible, ordered additional black soldiers at Baton Rouge to hasten to the front. The difference their participation made during the siege quickly became apparent. In a letter written on June 4, a member of the 48th Massachusetts stated: "This army would be like a one-handed man, without niggers. We have two regts. of fighting nigs. and as many more of diggers. Even with these, men from the white regts. have to be detailed for working parties; 60 went from us today. The nigs. work all night, every night, planting guns and building breastworks. We shall soon be ready to open on them with fifty big guns and mortars."[30]

Quiet reigned over the battlefield throughout much of the twenty-eighth. Banks had requested the truce to carry off the wounded and bury the dead. Inexplicably, the Federals left untouched the area where the Native Guards had charged—in stark contrast to their actions elsewhere on the battlefield. The hot sun putrefied the bodies until the stench forced Confederate colonel Shelby to ask Banks's permission to bury the dead in front of his lines. Banks refused, claiming that he had no dead in that area. The rumors circulated among the Union soldiers, however, asserted "that the rebels barbarously refused the negroes burial, until the stench of their corpses made it a matter of self-preservation."[31]

On the evening of June 1, a few Confederates took advantage of the cover of darkness to examine the bodies remaining among the willow trees. Foremost among the dead were Cailloux and Planciancois. In their search for booty, they found one Native Guardsman still alive, though in agony from his wounds and lack of water. After giving Private Jake Edmund some water, they placed him on a blanket and carried him to the garrison hospital, where he was admitted shortly before midnight with a "wound in shoulder." Though he recovered enough to thank them for their efforts, Edmund died two hours later. The dying man's comrades apparently saw him carried off. When they could not locate him after the surrender, the story circulated that the Rebels had murdered all black prisoners. Other rumors spread through the Union army that the Confederates tortured and even crucified these black soldiers, but none of these charges proved true.[32]

All major engagements during the Civil War made headlines in the newspapers, but an assault by black troops drew special attention from Northern reporters. One correspondent wrote: "One negro was observed with a rebel soldier in his grasp, tearing the flesh from his face with his teeth, other weapons having failed him. After firing one volley they did not deign to load again, but went in with bayonets, and wherever they had a chance it was all up with the rebels." An illustration in *Harper's Weekly* showed the black soldiers in hand-to-hand combat atop a parapet that bristled both with cannon and an abundance of Rebels. William Lloyd Garrison's *Liberator* promised its readers that the blood shed by the Native Guardsmen at Port Hudson would "wash out the prejudices so long existing against their oppressed race."[33]

Many Yankees who fought at Port Hudson agreed with the press's view. These men believed that the black troops had fought valiantly and looked forward to the day when thousands of former slaves would swell the ranks of the Union army. A white lieutenant in the 3rd Native Guard told a fellow officer, "My Co. was apparently brave. Yet they are most contrabands, and I must say I entertained some fears as to their pluck. But I have now none." On May 28 Colonel Benjamin H. Grierson wrote his wife: "There can be no question about the good fighting quality of negroes, hereafter; that question was settled beyond a doubt yesterday." Captain Robert F. Wilkinson wrote his father on June 3: "One thing I am glad to say, that is that the black troops at P. Hudson fought & acted superbly. The theory of negro inefficiency is, I am very thankful at last thoroughly Exploded by facts. We shall shortly have a splendid army of thousands of them."[34]

Banks praised the black soldiers in his official report. He took pleasure in writing "that they answered every expectation. In many respects their conduct was heroic. No troops could be more determined or more daring.

Whatever doubt may have existed heretofore as to the efficiency of organizations of this character, the history of this day proves conclusively that the Government will find in this class of troops effective supporters and defenders. The severe test to which they were subjected, and the determined manner in which they encountered the enemy, leaves upon my mind no doubt of their ultimate success. They require only good officers, commands of limited numbers, and careful discipline, to make them excellent soldiers."[35]

Yet white officers commanding black troops often were below average in ability. Captain John C. Palfrey (U.S. Engineers) concluded that "there was a deep instinctive prejudice against serving with them and recognizing them as soldiers in equal standing. This prejudice made it hard to officer these regiments. Some men from a high sense of duty took commissions in them, but with a secret sense of self-sacrifice; others, especially men of scientific attainments, were appointed officers in them to secure the rank and pay, while always serving on detached duty; others were deterred from taking commissions in them by apprehension of the treatment to be expected in case of capture; and in general the officers held higher grades than they would have expected in white regiments." By officially endorsing the use of black soldiers in the army, Banks not only hurt his popularity with the white troops but also increased their prejudice toward the African Americans.[36]

Not everyone accepted the newspaper accounts. Confederate lieutenant Howard C. Wright gave a different evaluation of the media coverage in a letter to his mother: "The N.Y. Herald correspondence & all the Illustrations I have seen of the fighting, in Leslie & Harper, are preposterous, particularly the story about the negro troops fighting well. The story must have been gotten up for political effect." Other readers, including numerous Yankees, agreed with Wright. Colonel Halbert S. Greenleaf of the 53rd Massachusetts described the charge by the Native Guards as "an exhibition of cowardice on the part of the entire gang instead of that courageous and valiant spirit of which so much has been written." When the Rebels read that the black units had suffered six hundred casualties, they concluded that the white soldiers supporting the African Americans must have shot them. One Alabama private even reported hearing volleys of musketry from the direction the black troops fled, but apparently the Native Guardsmen fired these discharges in order to convince Dwight they were pressing the assault.[37]

The truth lay between the extremes. Despite their failure to penetrate or even reach the principal fortifications, the black soldiers deserve no criticism for their performance on May 27, 1863. Their baptism of fire came from an order to accomplish the impossible. No one could blame them for withdrawing after scores of their comrades lay dead and dying, many floating in water too deep to wade. Many white regiments failed to advance any closer than two hundred yards to the Confederate works during the attack; some hardly moved forward at all. Only the 165th New York, fighting in the afternoon on the Union left and attired in Zouave uniforms that included red pants, suffered a higher percentage of casualties. Banks even ordered one of his division commanders relieved for not attacking promptly. The black troops deserved the praise they received—even if it was somewhat exaggerated.

Abolitionist reporters and military officers made the African Americans' assault one of the turning points of the war—a turning point long overlooked by both contemporaries and historians. On June 11, 1863, the *New York Times* published extracts from Banks's report with the comment: "this official testimony settles the question that the negro race can fight with great prowess. Those black soldiers had never before been in any severe engagement. They were comparatively raw troops, and were yet subjected to the most awful ordeal that even veterans ever have to experience—the charging upon fortifications through the crash of belching batteries. The men, white or black, who will not flinch from that, will flinch from nothing. It is no longer possible to doubt the bravery and steadiness of the colored race, when rightly led."[38]

The excitement generated by the newspaper coverage of the black soldiers' charge at Port Hudson proved pivotal in convincing whites to accept the enlistment of African Americans in the U.S. Army. It also stimulated free blacks in the North to volunteer. By sponsoring a recruiting poster heralding the "VALOR AND HEROISM" displayed by the black soldiers at Port Hudson, black abolitionists in Philadelphia alone induced more than eight thousand African Americans to enlist. The bravery exhibited by black troops in the July 18 assault on Battery Wagner, outside Charleston, South Carolina, dashed any serious doubts that remained after the Native Guards' performance at Port Hudson on May 27. The black man had earned the right to fight for his freedom.[39]

Nearly 180,000 black soldiers served in the Federal army before the war ended. Though African Americans generally found themselves stationed in rear areas doing guard duty, this service freed white troops for combat and, probably of more importance, greatly reduced the number of whites drafted into service. By the spring of 1865, black troops nearly equaled in number

Confederate infantrymen present for duty throughout the South. In addition, this fresh source of manpower appeared when the war-weary North had grown tired of the seemingly endless list of casualties. The positive impact the presence of these additional soldiers had on the Union war effort should not be underestimated. Undoubtedly, the performance of black soldiers on the battlefield had some impact on the Confederate government's decision to enlist slaves in its army, although it came too late to turn the tide of the war.

Following so closely Robert E. Lee's repulse at Gettysburg and Ulysses S. Grant's capture of Vicksburg, the surrender of Port Hudson and the events that brought it about are all but forgotten today. Yet Gettysburg did not assure Lee's final defeat, or Vicksburg Grant's eventual triumph. But the propaganda generated by the Native Guards' assault at Port Hudson almost singularly convinced Northern whites to accept the enlistment of nearly 180,000 black soldiers in the Federal army.[40] Ironically, the Confederates' dogged resistance along Little Sandy Creek on May 27, 1863, hastened the participation by African Americans in the war, thereby shortening the lifespan of the Confederacy.

Notes

1. James G. Hollandsworth, Jr., *The Louisiana Native Guards: The Black Military Experience during the Civil War* (Baton Rouge: Louisiana State University Press, 1995), 2; *New Orleans Daily Crescent*, May 29, 1861; Stephen J. Ochs, *A Black Patriot and a White Priest: André Cailloux and Claude Paschal Maistre in Civil War New Orleans* (Baton Rouge: Louisiana State University Press, 2000), 68.

2. Hollandsworth, *The Louisiana Native Guards*, 1n, 4–8, 10–11, 14–18; Ochs, *Black Patriot*, 16, 70–72, 74, 76; U.S. War Department, *The War of the Rebellion: A Compilation of the Official Records of the Union and Confederate Armies*, 128 vols. (Washington, D.C.: Government Printing Office, 1880–1901), 1st ser., 15:559 (hereafter cited as *OR*).

3. Hollandsworth, *The Louisiana Native Guards*, 20–21, 24–25, 25n, 27, 119; Noah Andre Trudeau, *Like Men of War: Black Troops in the Civil War, 1862–1865* (Boston: Little, Brown, 1998), 27; Joseph T. Glatthaar, *Forged in Battle: The Civil War Alliance of Black Soldiers and White Officers* (New York: Free Press, 1990), 124–25, 176–77; Joseph T. Glatthaar, "The Civil War through the Eyes of a Sixteen-Year-Old Black Officer: The Letters of Lieutenant John H. Crowder of the 1st Louisiana Native Guards," in "Notes and Documents," *Louisiana History* 35 (Spring 1994): 202–3; George W. Powers, *The Story of the Thirty-eighth Regiment of Massachusetts Volunteers* (Cambridge, Mass.: Dakin and Metcalf, 1866), 91; Henry T. Johns, *Life with the Forty-ninth Massachusetts Volunteers* (Pittsfield, Mass.: Published for the

Author, 1864), 150; Ochs, *A Black Patriot and a White Priest*, 57 (where the quotation in the next sentence of this note appears). Contrary to depictions of him following his death, Cailloux "did not possess significant wealth, education, or property."

4. Edward Cunningham, *The Port Hudson Campaign, 1862–1863* (Baton Rouge: Louisiana State University Press, 1963), 129–30; George W. Williams, *A History of the Negro Troops in The War of the Rebellion, 1862–1865* (1888; New York: Negro Universities Press, 1969), 216–17; Joseph T. Wilson, *The Black Phalanx* (1890 ed.; New York: Arno Press, 1968), 524–25; Hollandsworth, *The Louisiana Native Guards*, 50–51, 51n; Trudeau, *Like Men of War*, 36–37. Tried, found guilty, and dismissed, Stafford successfully appealed the case after the war. On January 3, 1871, he received an honorable discharge retroactive to August 12, 1863, his date of dismissal. References to Nelson's regiment or the 3rd during this period are applied to both regiments, as they were united under Nelson.

5. L. Carroll Root, "The Experiences of a Federal Soldier in Louisiana in 1863," *Louisiana Historical Quarterly* 19 (July 1936): 657–58; Williams, *A History of the Negro Troops*, 215; Wilson, *The Black Phalanx*, 525; Richard Irwin, *History of the Nineteenth Army Corps* (1893; Baton Rouge: Elliott's Book Shop Press, 1985), 165–66. Present-day Foster's Creek was known as Little Sandy at the time of the siege. Foster's Creek at that time was a smaller stream that entered Sandy Creek from the opposite bank.

6. Trudeau, *Like Men of War*, 37; Wilson, *The Black Phalanx*, 525; Charles P. Bosson, *History of the Forty-second Regiment Infantry, Massachusetts Volunteers, 1862, 1863, 1864* (Boston: Mills, Knight & Co., 1886), 364; *OR*, 1st ser., 26:85; Powers, *The Story of the Thirty-eighth Regiment of Massachusetts Volunteers*, 91; Root, "The Experiences of a Federal Soldier," 658.

7. U.S. Navy Department, *The War of the Rebellion: Official Records of the Union and Confederate Navies*, 27 vols. (Washington, D.C.: Government Printing Office, 1894–1927), 1st ser., 20:769, 795; "Fortification and Siege of Port Hudson—Compiled by the Association of Defenders of Port Hudson; M. J. Smith, President; James Freret, Secretary," *Southern Historical Society Papers* 14 (January-December 1886): 319; Ochs, *A Black Patriot and a White Priest*, 140.

8. Irwin, *History of the Nineteenth Army Corps*, 169–70; Cunningham, *The Port Hudson Campaign*, 122; John M. Stanyan, *A History of the Eighth Regiment of New Hampshire Volunteers* (Concord, N.H.: Ira C. Evans, 1892), 245; George W. Carter, "The Fourth Wisconsin Infantry at Port Hudson," in *War Papers Read before the Commandery of the State of Wisconsin, Military Order of the Loyal Legion of the United States* (Milwaukee: Burdick, Armitage & Allen, 1903), 3:227; E. B. Quiner, *The Military History of Wisconsin* (Chicago: Clarke & Company, 1866), 503; Henry A. Willis, *The Fifty-third Regiment Massachusetts Volunteers* (Fitchburg, Mass.: Press of Blanchard & Brown, 1889), 121; Edward H. Sentell, Diary, May 27, 1863, Sentell Family Papers, New-York Historical Society, New York; *OR*, 1st ser.,

26 (1):163, 530–31; Lieutenant Peter Eltinge to Father, May 30, 1863, Eltinge-Lord Family Papers, Perkins Library, Duke University, Durham; Lawrence Lee Hewitt, "They Fought Splendidly!: The Struggle For Port Hudson" (Ph.D. diss., Louisiana State University, 1984), 213n, 226, 228, 233A, 238–39; "Fortification and Siege of Port Hudson," 319–20; [F. Y.] Dabney to [Franklin Gardner], August 24, 1863, Louisiana Historical Association Collection, Manuscript Department, Special Collections Division, Tulane University Library, New Orleans (hereafter cited as LHAC).

9. Henry Hall and James Hall, *Cayuga in the Field* (Auburn, N.Y.: Truair, Smith & Co., 1873), [sect. 2], 113–14, 257, 265.

10. *Mobile Advertiser and Register*, August 9, 1863; Jill K. Garrett and Marise P. Lightfoot, *The Civil War in Maury County, Tennessee* (n.p.: n.p., 1966), 62; "Fortification and Siege of Port Hudson," 320; Lawrence L. Hewitt, ed., *A Place Named . . . Desperate!* (Baton Rouge: VAAPR, Inc., 1982), 1, 6; Irwin, *History of the Nineteenth Army Corps*, 171; Stanyan, *A History of the Eighth Regiment of New Hampshire Volunteers*, 225–26; William E. S. Whitman and Charles H. True, *Maine in the War for the Union* (Lewiston: N. Dingley, Jr., & Co., 1865), 387; Diary of Elon P. Spink, May 27, 1863 (typescript copy in author's possession); William L. Haskin, comp., *The History of the First Regiment of Artillery* (Portland, Me.: B. Thurston and Company, 1879), 192.

11. Garrett and Lightfoot, *The Civil War in Maury County*, 62–63; Hewitt, *A Place Named . . . Desperate!*, iv–v, 5–6; Dabney to [Gardner], August 24, 1863, LHAC; Edward Young McMorries, *History of the First Regiment Alabama Volunteer Infantry C.S.A.* (1904; Freeport, N.Y.: Books for Libraries Press, 1970), 33, 62–64; John William De Forest, *A Volunteer's Adventures: A Union Captain's Record of the Civil War*, ed. James H. Croushore (New Haven: Yale University Press, 1946), 111; *OR*, 1st ser., 26 (1):163; Frank Moore, ed., *The Rebellion Record: A Diary of American Events*, 12 vols. (New York: G. P. Putnam, 1861–63; D. Van Nostrand, 1864–68), 7:268; *Mobile Advertiser and Register*, August 9, 1863; Hall and Hall, *Cayuga in the Field*, [sect. 2], 114, 118–19.

12. Irwin, *History of the Nineteenth Army Corps*, 170; *OR*, 1st ser., 26 (1):71, 163; *OR*, 1st ser., 15:1032; Wm. H. Aldis to Wife, June 3, June 7, 1863, Wm. H. Aldis, Jr., Papers, New-York Historical Society, New York; Stanyan, *A History of the Eighth Regiment of New Hampshire Volunteers*, 234–37; Hall and Hall, *Cayuga in the Field*, [sect. 2], 114; Map of Port Hudson, Camp Moore State Commemorative Area, La.; "Fortification and Siege of Port Hudson," 320.

13. Carter, "The Fourth Wisconsin Infantry at Port Hudson," 228–29.

14. Ibid., 229–30; Stanyan, *A History of the Eighth Regiment of New Hampshire Volunteers*, 226, 245.

15. Williams, *A History of Negro Troops*, 216; Stanyan, *A History of the Eighth Regiment of New Hampshire Volunteers*, 229; Garrett and Lightfoot, *The Civil War in Maury County*, 64; *OR*, 1st ser., 26 (1):529, 529n; Otis F. R. Waite, *New Hampshire in the*

Great Rebellion (Claremont: Tracy, Chase & Co., 1870), 520; Hollandsworth, *The Louisiana Native Guards*, 52.

16. [William Dwight, Jr.], to his mother, May 26, 1863, in Dwight Family Papers, Massachusetts Historical Society, Boston, cited in Hollandsworth, *The Louisiana Native Guards*, 52.

17. Irwin, *History of the Nineteenth Army Corps*, 172; Wilson, *The Black Phalanx*, 525; Bosson, *History of the Forty-second Regiment Infantry, Massachusetts*, 364; Company A, 1st Louisiana Cavalry, Muster Roll, May and June 1863, and 1st Louisiana Cavalry, Return, May 1863, roll 67, microcopy 594, Compiled Records Showing Service of Military Units in Volunteer Union Organizations, National Archives, Washington, D.C.; Shelby to [Gardner], August 5, 1863, and Dabney to [Gardner], August 24, 1863, both in LHAC; *OR*, 1st ser., 15:1027; "Fortification and Siege of Port Hudson," 321; *New Orleans Times-Democrat*, April 26, 1906; [Howard C. Wright], *Port Hudson: Its History from an Interior Point of View* (St. Francisville, La.: *St. Francisville Democrat*, 1937), 36. One source claims that because of their limited number, Shelby's men had three rifles each when the Native Guards attacked on May 27. It is more plausible, however, that Shelby's troops found these surplus weapons on the field after the fighting ended on the twenty-seventh.

18. Williams, *A History of the Negro Troops*, 216; Wilson, *The Black Phalanx*, 525–26; George H. Hepworth, *The Whip, Hoe, and Sword*, ed. Joe Gray Taylor (1864; Baton Rouge: Louisiana State University Press, 1979), 187; Hollandsworth, *The Louisiana Native Guards*, 52n, 55n.

19. William Wells Brown, *The Negro in the American Rebellion: His Heroism and His Fidelity* (Boston: Lee & Shepard, 1867), 171; P. F. de Gournay, "The Siege of Port Hudson," in "Annals of the War" (scrapbook of miscellaneous newspaper clippings), Tulane University, New Orleans; Williams, *A History of the Negro Troops*, 217–19; Shelby to [Gardner], August 5, 1863, LHAC; [Wright], *Port Hudson*, 36; Wilson, *The Black Phalanx*, 525; Bell Irvin Wiley, *Southern Negroes, 1861–1865* (1938; Baton Rouge: Louisiana State University Press, 1974), 327; Glatthaar, *Forged in Battle*, 129; Ochs, *A Black Patriot and a White Priest*, 79–80, 144. The sergeant had kept the promise he had made when first handed the flag: "Colonel, I will bring back these colors in honor or report to God the reason why." See Ochs, *A Black Patriot and a White Priest*, 141.

20. Wilson, *The Black Phalanx*, 525; J. V. Frederick, ed., "War Diary of W. C. Porter," *Arkansas Historical Quarterly* 11 (Winter 1952): 313–14; [Wright], *Port Hudson*, 36; Shelby to [Gardner], August 5, 1863, LHAC; Glatthaar, "Through the Eyes of a Black Officer," 204–6; Glatthaar, *Forged in Battle*, 129; Ochs, *A Black Patriot and a White Priest*, 148. Crowder's specific date of birth in 1846 is unknown, so he may have been seventeen at the time of his death.

21. Johns, *Life with the Forty-ninth Massachusetts Volunteers*, 254–55; [Wright], *Port Hudson*, 36; Stanyan, *A History of the Eighth Regiment of New Hampshire Volunteers*,

229; *OR*, 1st ser., 26 (1):529; Wilson, *The Black Phalanx*, 526; Ochs, *A Black Patriot and a White Priest*, 143.

22. Trudeau, *Like Men of War*, 43; Irwin, *History of the Nineteenth Army Corps*, 174; Daniel P. Smith, *Company K, First Alabama Regiment, or Three Years in the Confederate Service* (Prattville, Ala.: Published by the Survivors, 1885), 63; Dabney to [Gardner], August 24, 1863, LHAC; Wilson, *The Black Phalanx*, 525; Hollandsworth, *The Louisiana Native Guards*, 56, 56n; Ochs, *A Black Patriot and a White Priest*, 145. Nelson reported that his men made three distinct assaults and his claim is substantiated by Gardner's report of the siege, as prepared by Dabney. Both Nelson and Dabney must have considered the attempt to wade through the backwater and the scaling of the projecting ridge as independent assaults.

23. *The Twenty-fifth Regiment Connecticut Volunteers in the War of the Rebellion* (Rockville: n.p., 1913), 46–47; Irwin, *History of the Nineteenth Army Corps*, 171; *OR*, 1st ser., 26 (1):530; Thomas McManus, *Twenty-fifth Regiment Battle Fields Revisited* (Hartford: Clark & Smith, Printers, 1896), 22; William F. Tiemann, comp., *The 159th Regiment Infantry, New-York State Volunteers* (Brooklyn: William F. Tiemann, 1891), 40–41; McMorries, *History of the First Regiment Alabama Volunteer Infantry C.S.A.*, 63; W. A. Croffut and John M. Morris, *The Military and Civil History of Connecticut during the War of 1861–65* (New York: L. Bill, 1868), 410; Hewitt, *A Place Named . . . Desperate!*, 1–2, 5, 11–12.

24. Homer B. Sprague, *History of the 13th Infantry Regiment of Connecticut Volunteers* (Hartford: Case, Lockwood & Co., 1867), 139–40; Irwin, *History of the Nineteenth Army Corps*, 172; Frank M. Flinn, *Campaigning with Banks in Louisiana, '63 and '64, and with Sheridan in the Shenandoah Valley in '64 and '65* (Lynn, Mass.: Press of Thomas P. Nichols, 1887), 75; *Hampshire Gazette and Northampton Courier*, June 30, 1863; De Forest, *A Volunteer's Adventures*, 113; Hewitt, *A Place Named . . . Desperate!*, 6, 11–12; [Wright], *Port Hudson*, 34–35.

25. Willis, *The Fifty-third Regiment Massachusetts Volunteers*, 121–22; De Forest, *A Volunteer's Adventures*, 111; Philemon H. Fowler, *Memorials of William Fowler* (New York: A. D. F. Randolph & Company, 1875), 43; John C. Palfrey, "Port Hudson," in *Papers of the Military Historical Society of Massachusetts*, vol. 8, *The Mississippi Valley, Tennessee, Georgia, Alabama, 1861–1864* (Boston: Military Historical Society of Massachusetts, 1910), 40; Irwin, *History of the Nineteenth Army Corps*, 175; 12th Connecticut, Return, May 1863, roll 7, microcopy 594, Compiled Records Showing Service of Military Units in Volunteer Organizations, National Archives, Washington, D.C.; *The Twenty-fifth Regiment Connecticut Volunteers*, 47–48; Tiemann, *The 159th Regiment Infantry, New-York State Volunteers*, 41; Lieutenant Peter Eltinge to Father, May 30, 1863, Eltinge-Lord Family Papers; Hall and Hall, *Cayuga in the Field*, [sect. 2], 118–19; Powers, *The Story of the Thirty-eighth Regiment of Massachusetts Volunteers*, 94–95; Stanyan, *A History of the Eighth Regiment of New Hampshire Volunteers*, 245; William DeLoss Love, *Wisconsin in the War of the Rebellion* (Chicago: Church and Goodman, 1866), 544.

26. Will Plank, comp., *Banners and Bugles: A Record of Ulster County, New York and the Mid-Hudson Region in the Civil War* (Marlborough, N.Y.: Centennial Press, 1972), 46; Frederick Phisterer, comp., *New York in the War of the Rebellion, 1861 to 1865*, 5 vols. (Albany: J. B. Lyon Company, 1912), 5:3819; Lieutenant Peter Eltinge to Father, May 30, 1863, Eltinge-Lord Family Papers.

27. Hewitt, *A Place Named . . . Desperate!*, 15, 19; Adjutant General, *Annual Report of the Adjutant General of the State of Maine for the Year Ending December 31, 1863* (Augusta: Stevens & Sayward, 1864), 80, 405–32; Adjutant General, *Massachusetts Soldiers, Sailors, and Marines in the Civil War*, 9 vols. (Norwood: Adjutant General, 1931–37), 3:397–447, 4:1.

28. Grady McWhiney and Perry D. Jamieson, *Attack and Die: Civil War Military Tactics and the Southern Heritage* (University, Ala.: University of Alabama Press, 1982), 10–11, 19–21, 69, 72; Henry B. Maglathlin, *Company I, Fourth Massachusetts Regiment, Nine Months Volunteers, In Service, 1862–3* (Boston: Geo. C. Rand & Avery, 1863), 30.

29. Wiley, *Southern Negroes*, 327–28, 328n; Wilson, *The Black Phalanx*, 526; Diary of Lieutenant R. W. Ford (7th Texas Infantry), May 27, 1863 (typescript copy), in possession of Russell Surles, Jr., Dallas, Tex.; [Wright], *Port Hudson*, 36; Dabney to [Gardner], August 24, 1863, LHAC; Stanyan, *A History of the Eighth Regiment of New Hampshire Volunteers*, 230; de Gournay, "The Siege of Port Hudson"; Garrett and Lightfoot, *The Civil War in Maury County*, 64; Ochs, *A Black Patriot and a White Priest*, 269–71. Because Dabney, a Confederate officer, officially reported that the Native Guards made three charges, his account appears the least prejudicial of those found to date.

30. Banks to wife, May 30, 1863, N. P. Banks Papers, Essex Institute, Salem, Massachusetts; *OR*, 1st ser., 53:559; [Banks] to Commanding Officer at Baton Rouge, May 27, 1863, 10 P.M., Letters Sent, December 1862–August 1863, Department of the Gulf, Record Group 393, National Archives, Washington, D.C.; William Cullen Bryant II, ed., "A Yankee Soldier Looks at the Negro," *Civil War History* 7 (June 1961): 147.

31. McMorries, *History of the First Regiment Alabama Volunteer Infantry C.S.A.*, 64–65; *Mobile Advertiser and Register*, August 9, 1863; Johns, *Life with the Forty-ninth Massachusetts Volunteers*, 257.

32. Dudley Taylor Cornish, *The Sable Arm: Negro Troops in the Union Army, 1863–1865* (1956; New York: W. W. Norton, 1966), 144; *OR*, 1st ser., 26 (1):68, 513–18; Dabney to [Gardner], August 24, 1863, LHAC; de Gournay, "The Siege of Port Hudson"; Luther Tracy Townsend, *History of the Sixteenth Regiment, New Hampshire Volunteers* (Washington, D.C.: Norman T. Elliott, 1897), 237; Cunningham, *The Port Hudson Campaign*, 55; [Wright], *Port Hudson*, 36, 43; Lawrence L. Hewitt and Arthur W. Bergeron, Jr., eds., *Post Hospital Ledger, Port Hudson, Louisiana, 1862–1863* (Baton Rouge: Le Comite des Archives de la Louisiane, 1981), 96. Though his men tried repeatedly, they were unable to recover Cailloux's body

until the garrison surrendered. It was then sent to New Orleans, where it was buried with full honors. A few years ago, a monument was erected at Port Hudson to commemorate the fact that apparently the Confederate garrison cemetery there is the only place where soldiers from both armies were buried side by side. Those who made this discovery and were involved in erecting the monument were apparently unaware that one of the Union soldiers buried there among the Confederates was an African American.

33. Jno. Robertson, comp., *Michigan in the War* (Lansing: W. S. George & Co., 1881), 267; *Harper's Weekly*, July 18, 1863; Ochs, *A Black Patriot and a White Priest*, 149.

34. Glatthaar, *Forged in Battle*, 129; Grierson to Alice, May 28, 1863, 6 P.M., B. H. Grierson Papers, Illinois State Historical Library, Springfield; Cornish, *The Sable Arm*, 142–43; Captain Robert F. Wilkinson to father, June 3, 1863, Wilkinson Papers, New-York Historical Society, New York.

35. *OR*, 1st ser., 26 (1):45.

36. Palfrey, "Port Hudson," 36; Adjutant General, *Massachusetts Soldiers, Sailors, and Marines*, 6:770; Powers, *The Story of the Thirty-eighth Regiment of Massachusetts Volunteers*, 91.

37. [Howard C. Wright] to mother, July 16, 1863, Lieutenant H. C. Wright Letters, New-York Historical Society, New York; *New Orleans Daily Picayune*, August 19, 1863, quoting correspondent of *Chicago Times*; *OR*, 1st. ser., 26 (1):530; Charley [Moulton] to Brother and Sister, June 19, 1863, Charles Moulton Letters, Michigan Historical Collections, Bentley Historical Library, University of Michigan, Ann Arbor; Smith, *Company K*, 63, 83.

38. Cunningham, *The Port Hudson Campaign*, 55, 60–62; *OR*, 1st ser., 26 (1):509–10; Cornish, *The Sable Arm*, ix, 143.

39. Charles L. Blockson, "Escape from Slavery: The Underground Railroad," *National Geographic* 166 (July 1984): 33; E. B. and Barbara Long, *The Civil War Day by Day: An Almanac, 1861–1865* (Garden City, N.Y.: Doubleday, 1971), 363, 387; Cornish, *The Sable Arm*, 145, 155–56; Benjamin Quarles, *The Negro in the Civil War* (1953; Boston: Little, Brown, 1969), 336–37. Some historians emphasize the African Americans' performance at Milliken's Bend, Louisiana, on June 7, 1863, as having a major impact on public opinion. But the black troops in that engagement merely fought on the defensive, were protected by earthworks, and were supported by gunboats — hardly as impressive as African Americans equaling or surpassing the performance of white soldiers in a full-scale assault.

40. "Notes on the Union and Confederate Armies," in Robert Underwood Johnson and Clarence Clough Buel, eds., *Battles and Leaders of the Civil War*, 4 vols., *The Way to Appomattox* (1888; New York: Thomas Yoseloff, 1956), 4:767–68.

BATTLE ON
THE LEVEE
The Fight at
Milliken's Bend
Richard Lowe

The Union victory in the vicious little battle at Milliken's Bend, Louisiana, in June 1863 shocked Confederate soldiers and civilians and pumped new enthusiasm into the ranks of Western Federal armies. A new weapon—African American soldiers—was unsheathed at Milliken's Bend, and the black recruits, most of them field hands only a few weeks earlier, fought like veterans in the bloody hand-to-hand engagement on the banks of the Mississippi River. The use of African American soldiers in combat at Milliken's Bend and at Port Hudson, less than two weeks earlier, was the first sign that the war west of the Appalachians had entered a new phase. From the late spring of 1863 forward, black Americans would play an increasingly important role in the subjugation of the Confederacy.

Despite its significance as a new departure, Milliken's Bend has traditionally been ignored or given only scant treatment in comprehensive surveys and general reference works on the American Civil War.[1] On the other hand, studies that focus on black soldiers or the engagements in which they fought and some more recent histories do consider the battle in more detail.[2] Both the older, brief treatments and the more recent, more detailed studies agree that one remarkable feature of the story of Milliken's Bend was the inexperience of the black soldiers in blue that day in June 1863. Organized into regiments only weeks earlier, and with little drill or experience to prepare them for combat, these former slaves fought stubbornly in a hand-to-hand struggle on the Mississippi River levee northwest of Vicksburg. A white officer of these black soldiers was to say later, "Such a hand to hand conflict, such feats of daring, . . . has never in the annals of this war been equalled."[3]

Only a short while before, these black men had been slaves on cotton plantations strung along both sides of the Mississippi River near Vicksburg. In the spring of 1863, they put down their shovels and hoes and picked up Uncle Sam's muskets as part of the federal government's drive to bring African Americans into the Union's war effort. Following President Lincoln's Emancipation Proclamation on New Year's Day in 1863, Secretary of War Edwin M. Stanton sent Brigadier General Lorenzo Thomas from Washington to recruit and organize new regiments of black soldiers, mostly former slaves, in the Mississippi River valley. By mid-April, General Thomas had authorized ten such regiments (about one thousand men each) and appointed white officers from the ranks of veteran units in the region. By the time the war ended in 1865, he had enrolled more than 76,000 black soldiers for the Union.[4] Three of the earliest regiments Thomas raised provided the bulk of the Federal force that defended Milliken's Bend in early June 1863.

Appointing officers and authorizing the new regiments were relatively easy tasks. Actually filling the ranks with black recruits took more work. Many slaves in the Vicksburg region had been sent by their masters to areas far from the attractions of Union lines. Moreover, the Northern white officers assigned to recruiting duty were often condescending in their attitudes, had little experience in dealing with Southern black folk, and, consequently, sometimes failed to make much progress in signing new soldiers to the rolls of the army. One white lieutenant later recounted his ineffectual attempts to recruit among the slaves on the Louisiana side of the river: "The first plantation house we came to there were six or eight eligibles loafing around and we dismounted and proceeded to business. We found them much interested in the subject but could get no decision from them. They would not say they would not go, neither would they say they would." When the white strangers then listed the benefits of military life—pay for service performed, ample rations, new clothing—and some of the potential recruits seemed to show interest, the black women standing nearby shook their heads and pulled their men away from the presentation. For two days this recruiting detail moved from plantation to plantation, making its appeal and receiving only lukewarm responses from the black men and generally hostile reactions from the women.[5]

The dispirited white officers then turned to a man who had already joined the unit, an African American who knew how to communicate with his fellow black Southerners. This formidable individual, known as Big Jack

Jackson, accompanied the white Northerners on their next recruiting jaunt. Dressed in a sergeant's army jacket and striped military pants, armed with a musket and cartridge box, and sitting astride a horse, Jackson was probably the first black soldier these plantation hands had ever seen, and his appearance caused a stir in the slave quarters. He simply plowed through the crowds of gathering slaves, grabbing and snatching recruits in his path and ignoring the frowns and warnings of their women. The white officers merely stood back and watched Jackson work, filtering their understanding through the racism that afflicted many white Northerners as well as Southerners. "They [the slaves] did not pay much attention to me but rivited [sic] their eyes on Jack whom they must have thought a brigadier at least," a white lieutenant recalled. "Jack soon dismounted and proceeded to set these coons up in line with about as much ceremony as he would use if he was setting up so many tenpins." After marching his prizes around the grounds for a few minutes, Jackson headed them down the road toward the army camp in the distance. "When the wenches discovered that the men were being marched away they set up a terrible howl, but it did not faze Jack. He kept them going and they were soon out of sight and hearing."[6]

Although such strong-arm methods were not unknown in the recruitment of black soldiers, most African Americans apparently joined the army willingly, determined to show that they could fight for their own freedom and make their own way in the world. By the end of 1863, Lorenzo Thomas had raised more than twenty thousand black soldiers for the Union cause. Whether signed up by white officers or by men such as Jack Jackson, former slaves tramped into the ranks in the spring of 1863, gradually filling the rolls of the regiments that would fight their first battle only a few weeks later.[7]

The first few companies of the 9th Louisiana Infantry Regiment (African Descent) gathered in army camps near Vicksburg in April. Of the three black regiments that fought at Milliken's Bend, the 9th Louisiana was the best prepared—or least poorly prepared. They wore the same uniforms, used the same equipment, and consumed the same rations as white Union soldiers. A white lieutenant in the 9th Louisiana wrote his wife that "[t]hey learn very fast and I have no doubt they will make as rapid progress as white soldiers. As fast as we get them we clothe them from head to foot in precisely the same uniform that 'our boys' wear, give them tents, rations, and blankets and they are highly pleased and hardly know themselves." These black recruits began drilling in late April, and they burned twenty thousand rounds of ammunition in target practice over the same ground that their enemies would advance across on the day of the battle.[8]

About two weeks after the 9th Louisiana organized at Vicksburg, the

1st Mississippi Infantry (African Descent) was formally created at Milliken's Bend, across the river from Vicksburg and about twenty-five miles upstream. Although the men of the 1st Mississippi had been in the ranks about three weeks before the fight at Milliken's Bend, they were not as prepared for combat as the soldiers of the 9th Louisiana. Indeed, the Mississippi soldiers received their weapons only the day before the battle. The 11th Louisiana Infantry (African Descent) was organized at Milliken's Bend one week after the 1st Mississippi. Although formally created after the 1st Mississippi, the 11th Louisiana had at least been armed as soon as the men were mustered into service, sixteen days before the battle on the levee. One of the white officers of the 11th Louisiana, Lieutenant Colonel Cyrus Sears, later shook his head and wondered at the commendable performance of his men in the face of so little preparation: "All veterans, at least, must know how inadequate were sixteen days to recruit, muster, organize, arm, equip, drill—in short to make soldiers of *any* material, under *any* circumstances."[9]

The environment in which these new regiments began their training was far from ideal. Some of the Northern-born white officers, unaccustomed to dealing with black men, found it difficult to distinguish one new soldier from another: "contrabands looked alike to the unsophisticated," in the words of one officer. In addition, some Federal staff officers and supply personnel spent more time harassing the new units than providing for their needs. "The newly made officers of these troops were kept at the verge of 'brainstorm' by the studied delays, slights, sneers, snubs, and naggings of the Smart Alecks of the [supply] departments," one lieutenant colonel later complained, still fuming after fifty years. As if interference from above were not enough to frustrate the new lieutenants and captains, they had to contend with the families and friends of the recruits, milling about the training grounds in great numbers and occasionally interfering by joining in the drills. The black recruits would doubtless have benefited from standard military order and discipline, administered by experienced officers in a controlled environment, but this ideal was far from reality in the training camps near Vicksburg.[10]

In addition to the three black regiments, parts of two other Federal units manned the levees at Milliken's Bend in early June 1863—the 13th Louisiana Infantry (African Descent), not yet completely organized, and the white 23rd Iowa Infantry. The 13th Louisiana, in fact, never did complete its formal organization, and one month after the battle the men of that unit were folded into the ranks of the 1st Mississippi Infantry (African Descent). The 23rd Iowa Infantry was the only Federal unit at Milliken's Bend with battlefield experience. Organized in September 1862, the men of the 23rd Iowa had marched with General Ulysses S. Grant's army through the Louisiana swamps, crossed the Mississippi River at Bruinsburg, and fought in the bloody engagements at Port Gibson, Champion Hill, and Big Black River Bridge in Grant's campaign against Vicksburg. A detachment of the regiment, returning from Memphis where they had escorted prisoners, was assigned to the camp at Milliken's Bend the day before the battle.[11]

The Texans who assaulted the Federal camp at Milliken's Bend—the soldiers of Major General John G. Walker's Texas Infantry Division—were nearly as green as the black soldiers who opposed them. These were not veterans, as Federal officers assumed, but rather men who had no more experience under fire than the former slaves—and considerably less than the white Iowa soldiers who lined up against them. The only Confederate general and all of the Rebel regimental officers on the scene were conducting their first real battle at Milliken's Bend. And although the men in the ranks were highly experienced at marching—having marched hundreds of miles from Texas to Arkansas to Louisiana, earning them the sobriquet "Texas greyhounds"—they had virtually no time under fire and apparently had received no target practice with their ancient smoothbore muskets. Like their officers and like their enemies, they were raw material indeed for a pitched battle. Nevertheless, the black soldiers in blue and the white soldiers in gray, ready for combat or not, found themselves caught up in the struggle for control of the Mississippi River in the early summer of 1863.[12]

In late 1862 the Union's most important objective in the West was to gain control of the entire Mississippi River, from source to mouth. With the river in Federal hands, the Confederacy would be split in two, Northern commerce would flow freely downriver again, and an important psychological blow to Confederate morale would be struck by Union forces. By early 1863 the only significant Confederate strongholds remaining on the river were the fortified positions at Vicksburg, Mississippi, and Port Hudson, Louisiana, about 250 miles apart by water. By late spring, however, Federal naval assaults from the river, attempts to get at Vicksburg via an overland route from the north, other attempts to reach Vicksburg through the impassable Yazoo swamps, and the digging of canals to bypass important Confederate defenses had all failed. It appeared to some that Vicksburg could hold out indefinitely.

The most important man involved in the campaign, Major General Ulysses S. Grant, was not deterred, however. General Grant eventually determined to land his army on the west side of the Mississippi above Vicksburg, march them south through the bayous and swamps on the Louisiana shore, and cross the river to the higher ground south of Vicksburg, where he could launch a full assault on the city's defenses. For an important few weeks, his supply line on the west bank of the river would be vulnerable. Once most of his army was on the east bank of the river—dependent on their supply line stretched along the Louisiana side—Grant's army might be stymied by a forceful Confederate assault on his distant communications. A Confederate raid on his supply line several months earlier had ruined his first attempt to approach Vicksburg. In December 1862 a column of only 3,500 Confederate horsemen had wrecked Grant's plans by destroying his supply depot at Holly Springs, Mississippi, forcing him to withdraw all the way to Memphis.[13]

Some historians have written that Grant's army in the spring of 1863 was safe anyway, since he had determined to cut himself off from his communications and live off the countryside (as Grant himself later wrote), thereby eliminating any need for a secure supply line on the Louisiana shore. Historian Edwin Bearss's three-volume work on the Vicksburg campaign makes it clear that such was not the case. Grant's army continued to rely on the tenuous supply line west of the river from the time he crossed the river south of Vicksburg in late April until May 21, when a new line of communications was opened on the east bank, from the Yazoo River to the northern outskirts of Vicksburg.[14] During those three weeks the trans-Mississippi Confederates had a golden opportunity to disrupt the entire Federal campaign in the Mississippi River valley.

As usual, the Confederates west of the river dithered while Grant drove relentlessly toward Vicksburg. Lieutenant General Edmund Kirby Smith, commander of the Confederate Trans-Mississippi Department, had about thirty thousand men under arms in his department—more than enough to break Grant's thin supply line—but they were scattered across Arkansas, Louisiana, and Texas. Some of them, under Sterling Price, would eventually attack Helena, far upriver from Vicksburg, in a failed attempt to relieve the besieged Confederates on the east bank. Another force, under Richard Taylor in South Louisiana, had its hands full in the spring of 1863 with a Federal drive up Bayou Teche into central Louisiana. Still other regiments and brigades were scattered from Little Rock to the Rio Grande and were not available for an assault on Grant's communications on the west bank of the river.

One Confederate division was nearby and available, however: Major General John G. Walker's Texas infantry, the only division in either army composed of men from a single state and the largest single body of Texans in the war. Walker, a veteran of the antebellum army and an accomplished division commander in Robert E. Lee's Army of Northern Virginia during the Antietam campaign, had been transferred to the Trans-Mississippi Department in late 1862. He had taken command of his newly formed division in early January 1863 and was just learning about his officers and men in the winter and spring of 1863. His soldiers, mustered into service the previous spring and stationed near Little Rock since October 1862, had suffered terribly from disease and exposure during the cold Arkansas winter. Their numbers had dwindled from about twelve thousand at initial muster to only five thousand or fewer by the spring of 1863.[15]

On April 14, about the time that trans-Mississippi Confederates realized that Grant's army was pushing down the west bank of the Mississippi toward its crossing point south of Vicksburg, Kirby Smith ordered Walker's raw division to move from the Little Rock area to Monroe, in Northeast Louisiana. From there, Walker could move south to assist Richard Taylor in his struggle with the Federal army in central Louisiana, or Walker could strike at Grant's communications, only sixty miles east of Monroe. As it turned out, the possibilities for Walker's division were squandered. First, the division was sent south to bolster Richard Taylor in central Louisiana, but it was sent too late to do any good in that vicinity. Meanwhile, Grant's army crossed the Mississippi and exposed its supply line on the west bank. This was the moment for the trans-Mississippi Confederates to strike, but Walker's division was far away, on its march to central Louisiana. Not until late May, a week after Grant had established a new, safer supply line east of the Mississippi, did Kirby Smith send Walker's division back toward Vicksburg—to attack a line of communications that was no longer crucial to Federal success.[16]

Walker's infantry, having marched from Little Rock to Monroe and then down to Alexandria in central Louisiana, turned back north on May 28. The lead elements of the division reached the Mississippi River downstream from Vicksburg on the evening of May 30. Learning that a small force of Federals was camped near the river just a few miles away, Taylor and one of Walker's three brigades followed a local guide before daylight on May 31 to the Union camp near Perkins' Landing. Wary Federal scouts detected the approaching Confederates, however, and the officers and men of the 60th Indiana Infantry abandoned their campfires and morning coffee and took cover behind the nearby levee of the Mississippi River.[17] Not realizing that his prey had flown away, Brigadier General Henry McCulloch, commander of Walker's only brigade on the scene, put his men into line and charged across an open field into the Union camp, where the inexperienced and hungry Texans immediately broke ranks to ransack Federal tents and eat an Indiana breakfast. After a long-range artillery duel, during which only a few soldiers on either side were wounded, the Federal regiment made good its escape on a newly arrived transport ship.[18]

In the end, nothing much was accomplished in this little scrap. A Confederate brigade chased a lone Union regiment onto a riverboat; the Confederates torched the abandoned Union tents; and both sides left for other adventures before the end of the day. And yet, in the history of Walker's Texas Division, this was an important event. It was the first time the Texans, or one brigade of them at least, had ever been under fire, limited though it was. One officer in the 17th Texas Infantry wrote his daughter back in Texas, "Well I have been in one battle at last. I stood it finely not a nerve twiched or muscle trembled . . . Co F was all right so was the regiment—every body cool. Jokes & cute remarks about the shooting etc passed freely. If this is all the fear I dont mind a battle." Some individuals in McCulloch's brigade were not quite so cool. An officer in another brigade, after speaking of the affair with some of McCulloch's men, wrote his wife that "the first firing of Battle to raw troops, all confess makes them feel very strangely." An artillerist in the division described his own sensation when first under fire: "When I first came into the army and got close to fighting, I got blue in the 'gizzard.'" If some of the men in McCulloch's brigade changed gizzard color at Perkins' Landing—where they lost only one killed, two wounded, and two missing in a mostly harmless long-range artillery duel—then they were in for multicolored gizzards a week later when they fought their first real battle at Milliken's Bend.[19]

Word of the presence of Confederates on the Louisiana side of the river near Vicksburg reached General Grant by June 2, and he immediately took measures to protect the Federal camps on the west bank. He appointed Brigadier General Elias S. Dennis, a man he trusted, to take command of the District of Northeast Louisiana. Dennis had about 4,200 men—including some of the newly formed black regiments—scattered among four Federal posts along the river, including Milliken's Bend and Young's Point just up-river from Vicksburg. On June 5 Dennis learned that Confederate cavalry had occupied Richmond, Louisiana, about twenty miles west of Vicksburg. Convinced that trouble was brewing and that an attack on his posts was imminent, Dennis ordered the commander at Milliken's Bend to send out a reconnaissance party early the next day to discover the location and force of the Rebels.[20]

The Federal reconnaissance column that left Milliken's Bend before dawn on June 6 comprised two companies of Illinois cavalry and one of the new regiments of African American soldiers created in the spring of 1863, the 9th Louisiana. The reconnaissance party split into two columns a few miles out of Milliken's Bend, with the black infantry pushing southwest toward Richmond and the Illinois cavalry turning southeast toward Young's Point. Colonel Hermann Lieb, the white commander of the 9th Louisiana, approached within three miles of Richmond before he ran into a strong Confederate cavalry force. Fearing an ambush, Lieb reversed his course and was marching back toward Milliken's Bend when he spied a cloud of dust coming up from the direction of Young's Point. Hastily throwing his black soldiers into line of battle, Lieb soon discerned the source of the dust—the Illinois cavalry were racing back toward safety with Confederate horsemen close on their heels. The Federal troopers had just lost eight men killed and twenty-five wounded in a sharp clash with these Rebels, and the Illinois men were hustling back to Milliken's Bend as fast as they could gallop. A white lieutenant in the black infantry regiment lost all respect for the Federal horsemen racing toward his waiting line of foot soldiers. "When the head of the column reached us they called out, 'Save us boys for God's sake save us.' The day was hot, their jackets had been discarded, and most of them had lost their hats. They were lying on their animals' necks, wildly driving their spurs into their flanks, hanging to the pummels of their saddles for their dear lives and imploringly and piteously bawling, 'Save us, save us, save us.'" Although this version of events may have been designed to paint the lieutenant's infantry in the brightest possible colors, at least one of the Illinois cavalry admitted that he was never so happy to see a blue infantry line: "we came in sight of a line of men in bright new blue uniforms, who soon opened fire on 'our friends the enemy.'" That stopped the chase. "When we had time to look well at our men in blue, we discovered they had black faces. I had been raised an Abolitionist, yet was opposed to the plan of arming negroes before that day, but I can tell you of one who became a sudden convert right then and there, perfectly willing that negroes should have as good a right to be shot as myself."[21]

The reconnaissance is worthy of note for three reasons. First, it confirmed what earlier reports had suggested—that a sizable force of aggressive Confederates were looking for a fight in the neighborhood of Milliken's Bend and Young's Point. Second, the reaction of the white Federal cavalryman foreshadowed those of many other Americans later in the war—that is, a reversal of opinion on the subject of using African Americans to fight the Confederacy and a new respect for black soldiers. Third, the inexperienced former slaves in the 9th Louisiana regiment fired their first shots at an enemy exactly six days after McCulloch's Texans had done the same at Perkins' Landing.

When the reconnaissance party finally returned to Milliken's Bend around midday, Colonel Lieb sent a courier to General Dennis at Young's Point to inform him that Confederate columns were converging on the Union post at the bend. Dennis immediately ordered the 23rd Iowa Infantry aboard a transport and sent them upriver to Milliken's Bend. Dennis also alerted Admiral David Porter to the looming threat, and Porter dispatched the monstrous ironclad *Choctaw* to provide a shield of heavy firepower from the river. Within the Union camp at Milliken's Bend, Colonel Lieb was also preparing for trouble. He doubled the usual picket force, sent a squad of mounted infantry farther out to act as vedettes, and instructed his regimental officers to have their troops in line by 2:00 A.M.[22]

The Confederates, meanwhile, were busy with their own preparations. General Taylor, grumbling that he and Walker's division should have been set loose on South Louisiana instead of chasing Grant's shadow near Vicksburg, was further perturbed to learn from his cavalry that Grant had shifted his main supply route from the west side of the river to the east—thereby making any attack on the west bank almost meaningless. Despite this news, Taylor had no choice but to proceed with the campaign because he had direct orders from Kirby Smith to "do something for Vicksburg." The government in Richmond demanded it. Cavalry officers then gave Taylor dangerously erroneous information about the Federal garrisons on the west bank, portraying them as severely undermanned and outnumbered. When Walker's infantry arrived at Taylor's headquarters in Richmond on June 6, Taylor laid out his plan to "do something for Vicksburg."[23]

First, a detachment of Louisiana cavalry would attack the Federal post at Lake Providence, fifty miles upriver from Milliken's Bend. Meanwhile, McCulloch's infantry brigade, about fifteen hundred strong, would bag the supposedly weak garrison at Milliken's Bend, and Brigadier General James M. Hawes's brigade would simultaneously capture the allegedly undermanned Union camp at Young's Point, thirteen river miles from Milliken's Bend and halfway to Vicksburg. Two batteries of field artillery and Walker's third brigade of Texans, commanded by Colonel Horace Randal, would take position in the triangle between Milliken's Bend, Young's Point, and Richmond. Randal's regiments and the artillery could be sent to either point of assault, as the situation demanded. Taylor would remain in Richmond, and Walker would station himself at Oak Grove Plantation with

Randal's reserve brigade. Thus the highest ranking Confederate officer on the scene at Milliken's Bend would be General McCulloch, a man without formal military education, training, or experience in leading large bodies of men. Brother of the more famous Ben McCulloch, Henry was a former sheriff and U.S. marshal whose only military seasoning had taken place on the Texas frontier against the Indians.[24]

Taylor sent his brigades out of Richmond and toward their assigned positions early in the evening of June 6. "The intense heat of the weather rendered a night march desirable," Taylor later wrote, "and an attack at early dawn lessened the risk of annoyance from gunboats." With a Louisiana cavalry escort to screen their movement and guide them to their targets, Walker's men tramped out of Richmond, through Tallulah, and on to Oak Grove Plantation, about six miles away. In the darkness of a warm June night, Hawes's brigade turned right toward Young's Point, McCulloch's brigade turned left to Milliken's Bend, and Randal's brigade halted to take its place as the reserve. McCulloch had the shorter march from that point, only six miles to the Federal camp at the bend. By 3:00 A.M. his Texans had reached a point about one and one-half miles from the river. "It was so dark that I could not see our skirmishers, about one hundred yards in advance of our line of battle," one soldier in the 17th Texas wrote. "We marched with bayonets fixed and guns loaded and capped. Such feelings I never had before or since. . . . No word was spoken louder than a whisper. Every order was in a whisper as it passed from officer to man."[25]

A mile or so further on, Colonel Lieb's Federals were waiting for the silently approaching Rebels in a strong defensive position. About 150 yards from the river, an eight-foot-high levee ran parallel to the riverbank for about a quarter of a mile. Twenty-five yards beyond the levee, toward the Confederates, a fifteen-foot-high bois d'arc hedge, bristling with evil-looking thorns, paralleled the levee. A thirty-yard gap in the hedge, cut the day before the battle, gave the defenders on the left end of the Federal line a clear field of fire, but, more important, it also gave the Confederates an open path to that part of the levee. Farther out, other bois d'arc hedges and ditches bordered nearby farm fields, cutting the open ground into a maze of obstacles to the advancing Texans. Lieb had placed his men, about thirteen hundred strong, behind and near the top of the levee. The Federals had dug a trench along the inner edge of the levee, enabling them to stand and fire with some protection. On the left of the Union line, looking through the wide gap in the hedge, were the African Americans of the 9th Louisiana; to their right were the 1st Mississippi and the unattached men who would later be added to the 1st Mississippi. To the right of them was a space left for the only battle-tested Federals in the fight, the 150 white soldiers of the 23rd Iowa, now filing off a river transport to take their place in line. Anchoring the right end of the blue line was the 11th Louisiana, the largest unit on the field, with nearly 700 men.[26]

For a while the Federals behind the levee stared out into the darkness, expecting to see hordes of Rebels come flying at them at any second. Equally nervous Confederates glided silently forward, bayonets ready, not far behind the cavalry scouts a few hundred yards ahead. Suddenly, from behind one of the first bois d'arc hedges, Colonel Lieb's outer line of skirmishers fired into the advance cavalry scouts, spinning the jumpy horsemen into a panic. "The effect of so sudden and terrible a fire, from an invisible foe, was very startling and disheartening," one Confederate remembered. "No wonder the simple-minded cavalry scouts were broken, and that many of them hurried to the rear, in utter confusion, with and without muskets, hats, or coats!" They jerked their horses around and galloped away from the hedge, only to be greeted by shots from their own skirmishers, who nervously assumed that Yankee cavalry were bearing down on them. McCulloch's inexperienced skirmishers bagged three horses, but all the Louisiana cavalrymen survived the fright.[27]

McCulloch now put his four regiments into line of battle, with skirmishers thrown forward and Louisiana horsemen sent to the rear. The 16th Texas Cavalry (dismounted), the 17th Texas, and the 19th Texas lined up, left to right, on the left side of the Richmond road. Slightly behind them was the 16th Texas Infantry, held in reserve and placed on the right of the road. "As soon as it was light enough to see the further hedge [about one thousand yards away], we got glimpses of the enemy forming his line of battle," a Federal lieutenant in the 9th Louisiana remembered. "His front covered the field from hedge to hedge, double rank, elbow to elbow. . . . they had the appearance of a brigade on drill . . . we had no line of retreat here except to swim the Mississippi, and were evidently up against something this time that was extra-hazardous." In the dim morning light McCulloch's line pushed forward now, but it soon lost symmetry when the Texans were forced to cross ditches, filter through gaps in the hedges, and stumble through vines and briars. Forty years later, one soldier in the 16th Texas Infantry still remembered losing a young German friend from a skirmisher's bullet early in the advance. "My friend and I were . . . side by side and he was killed by the first volley. He pulled a small bible out of his bosom and told me to send it to his mother in Washington County." Over the last

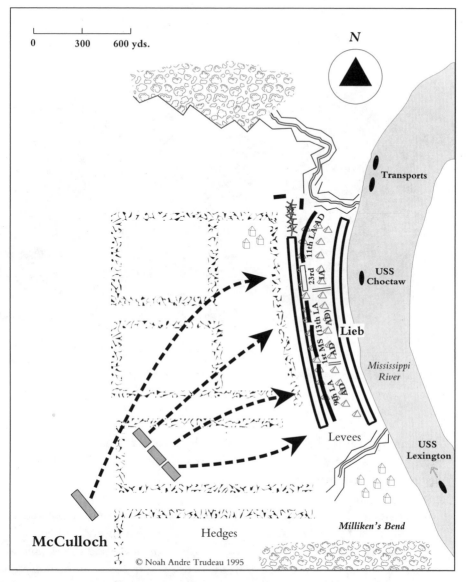

Map 3.1. The Battle of Milliken's Bend, Louisiana, June 7, 1863.
(Courtesy of Noah Andre Trudeau)

"*The Battle at Milliken's Bend—Sketched by Mr. Theodore R. Davis.*"
(Harper's Weekly, *July 4, 1863, N.C. Division of Historical Resources, Raleigh*)

two hundred yards, the Texans moved at the double-quick, all the while reforming their lines and forcing Lieb's skirmishers to fall back to the last hedge. "With yells that would make faint hearts quail, on double-quick they charged our little band," wrote one Yankee.[28]

McCulloch's line, approaching the Federal position from an oblique angle, had to halt when it reached the fifteen-foot-high hedge only twenty-five yards from the levee. The only way to get to the levee and the enemy was to file through a few openings in the hedge and re-form on the other side. A former Methodist preacher in the 17th Texas recalled the moment: "We rushed through the hedge, driving the foe before us, and they fell behind the levy, thus making their ranks four lines deep. We mounted the embankment and turned loose our war dogs, and I tell you, . . . they howled!" Lieutenant Cornwell of the 9th Louisiana painted a similar picture: "Not a shot was fired until they reached the hedge row, and then most of [our] shots went into the air. Where the hedge was down [in front of the 9th Louisiana]

they sailed up the exterior slope of the levee to meet our thin line on the top with empty guns and lowered bayonets. . . . Their guns being loaded they shot the men in their front and slowly moved down the interior slope, loading their pieces as they came." As the Confederates milled around the last hedge and ran up the levee, the men of the 23rd Iowa were racing from their river transport to their place in the center of the Union line. One of the Iowans told his wife later that "[t]he most of the white soldiers gained the spot [just in time] and commenced firing through the hedge at the Rebs about 2 rods distance, but on they came and up the steep levee and at us with the bayonet."[29]

At this point the conflict became something rare in the Civil War, a hand-to-hand fight with bayonets and clubbed muskets. While some of the Iowans were still running forward to fill the gap in the center of the Union line, others were already crossing bayonets with the onrushing Rebels. An Iowa captain recalled how "One member of the regiment and a Rebel met and at the same instant plunged their bayonets into one another, and both fell dead on the works, with their bayonets in that position. Another Rebel ran his bayonet thru one of our men, and another of our men knocked his brains out with the but [*sic*] of his musket. It was a very hot place." An Iowa private remembered that "Colonel Glasgow was bespattered with the blood and brains of his slaughtered men, beaten out with the clubbed muskets of the enemy. The contending forces were separated only by the levee and several hand-to-hand encounters took place on its top."[30]

About two hundreds yards to the left of the Iowans, Lieutenant Cornwell of the 9th Louisiana was in the thick of the death struggle. "I . . . ordered my men to keep their loads and not shoot a man if he could bayonet him, and not to pull off his gun until the muzzle was against a rebel. They were intensely excited and could not stand still. I guess I was a little excited myself, for instead of saying [the correct order to charge, 'double quick, with bayonets'] . . . , I simply said 'Now bounce them[,] Bullies.' Big Jack Jackson passed me like a rocket. With the fury of a tiger he sprang into that gang and smashed everything before him." Soon, "there was nothing left of Jack's gun but the barrel, and he was smashing in every head he could reach. . . . On the other side [of the levee] they were yelling, 'Shoot that big nigger, shoot that big nigger,' while Jack was daring the whole gang to come up there and fight him. Then a bullet reached his head and he went full length on the levee." Another officer in the 9th, a veteran of much larger battles east of the Mississippi, admitted that the carnage at Milliken's Bend was awful. "It was a horrible fight," he said, "the worst I was ever engaged in, not excluding Shiloh."[31]

After several minutes of this close-in, skull-smashing fighting, Colonel Richard Waterhouse's 19th Texas broke through on the Union left and set off a wave of Federal withdrawals from the levee, beginning with the 9th Louisiana on the left and running along the line finally to the 11th Louisiana on the far right. "They poured a murderous enfilading fire along our line, directing their fire chiefly to our officers who fell in numbers," Colonel Lieb reported. "Then, and not until they were overpowered and forced from their position, were the blacks driven back, when numbers of them sought shelter behind wagons, piles of boxes and other objects [in the camp between the levee and the river]. The others sought shelter behind the river bank." Within minutes the wave reached the recently arrived 23rd Iowa in the center of the Union line. "We had been in the ditch about three minutes, when the negroes gave way on our left and let the rebels in. They fired a terrible volley on us, right down the ditch, and were preparing to give us another, when the Colonel ordered us to fall back to the . . . [camp between the levee and the river]. We did so, when they flanked us again and we had to fall back to the river bank." In his usual bombastic style, Admiral

Porter claimed a few days later that the Iowa soldiers "stood at their post until they were slaughtered to a man," but the accounts of eyewitnesses, including Colonel Lieb, generally agreed that the Iowans were as quick to seek safety in the rear as anyone else. Indeed, after abandoning the levee, the 23rd Iowa "was seen no more," Lieb reported. Black soldiers on the far right of the Federal line, protected by a cross-levee and some cotton bales, were the last to be driven back, but only after they had poured "a heavy fire" (in General McCulloch's words) down the length of the Confederate ranks.[32]

Gradually the Federals retreated, from the levee to the camp to the river-bank, turning to fire a musket or thrust a bayonet when necessary, with the yelling Texans following close behind. Some retreating soldiers pan-icked and leaped into the river to swim out to nearby transports, but most jumped down behind the riverbank, turned, and emptied their muskets at the onrushing Rebels. The river happened to be very low, and the riverbank provided a natural earthwork. One Texan admitted to his wife that "[w]e suffered much in the assault of the inside Levy, which was strengthened by Cotton Bales, and the skill of engineers." The strong new defensive position of the Union line finally halted the Texas advance. While some Confeder-ates carried off the wounded, others rummaged through the Federal camp, searching for food and other plunder.[33]

Soon a new element was introduced into the day's proceedings—the heavy guns of the ironclad *Choctaw*. Now that the sun was up and some space divided their comrades from the Rebels, the gunners on the 1,000-ton *Choc-taw* had an opportunity to unleash their firepower. A 100-pounder rifled gun, two thirty-pounder rifles, a nine-inch smoothbore, and two twenty-four-pounder smoothbores far overmatched anything the Texans had in the vicinity. Not even the six-pounder field guns that McCulloch had thrown at the enemy at Perkins' Landing were available; the artillery had been left behind with the reserve brigade. It is not clear from surviving accounts how much actual damage the naval guns inflicted on the Confederates, but it is certain that the Rebels were awed by the 100-plus heavy shells thrown their way. Because the river was so low and because the *Choctaw* therefore had to fire over the fifteen-foot-high riverbank, the naval gunners were forced to fire blindly. Spotters on shore sent signals out to the *Choctaw* to help di-rect the fire, but many shells apparently created more dust than damage to the Rebels; and some rounds fell among Federal soldiers who had not yet reached the protection of the riverbank. Colonel Sears of the 11th Louisiana had a first-hand encounter with friendly fire: "The gun-boat men mistook a body of our men for rebels and made a target of them for several shots, before we could signal them off. From the fact that I was very unpleasantly splattered with blood, brains and flesh of one of our men, who there had his head shot off from one of our gunboats, I shall never forget that our navy did some real execution at Milliken's Bend."[34]

More Confederate blood was spilled by bayonets and musket balls than by gunboats at Milliken's Bend, but the big naval guns made the desired impression on the minds of the Texans. They scrambled back over the original levee and had to settle for firing potshots at the Federals behind the riverbank. The two lines, now separated by the 150 yards from the river to the outer levee, with the Federal camp in between, continued to exchange fire for two or three hours until further developments convinced the Confederates that the battle was over. First, they could see more riverboats steaming toward the scene, including the timberclad *Lexington*, which immediately joined the *Choctaw* in throwing shells at the Rebels. Some concluded that even more Federal ironclads were about to enter the bombardment, and others figured that heavy reinforcements were arriving by transports. Either way, the tide seemed to be turning for the Federals. In addition, the Confederates had marched all night and fought all morning, and fatigue began to slow them down, especially in the ninety-five-degree heat. The stiffened Federal resistance along the riverbank, the heat, the arrival of more riverboats, and the monstrous shells falling all around them—but especially the shells—finally convinced General McCulloch that his brigade had accomplished all that was possible. Around noon, he turned the Texans around and ordered them back to meet General Walker and the reserves at Oak Grove Plantation. From there, McCulloch's brigade and the reserve brigade returned to Richmond, and the third Confederate brigade eventually joined them after failing to capture Young's Point. The battle of Milliken's Bend was over.[35]

After the Union and Confederate surgeons had done their bloody work and the adjutants had counted out the cost of the battle, Colonel Lieb and General McCulloch made their reports. The Federals lost 101 killed, 285 wounded, and 266 men captured or missing—a total of 652 or about half the entire garrison. These numbers are somewhat misleading because many of the missing eventually came straggling back into camp. The 9th Louisiana took the brunt of the assault and suffered far more than the other units: 62 killed and 130 wounded of 285 engaged (67.4 percent). McCulloch's Texans had suffered far less heavily: 44 killed, 131 wounded, and 10 captured or missing, a total of 185 or about 12 percent of those engaged. The 17th Texas lost 92 men, about 20 percent of its total manpower. Despite their inexperience, the Yankees and Rebels of Milliken's Bend had fought one of the bloodiest small engagements of the war.[36]

The large number of killed and wounded men among the soldiers of the 9th Louisiana raises the possibility that many of the black soldiers were massacred, killed after they were wounded or captured.[37] Certainly there were reports after the battle that the Texans had shouted "no quarter" as they came over the outer levee. Some Union accounts even claimed that the Confederates fought under a "black flag" or a "skull and crossbones flag." Three reports by Federals who actually fought in the battle are damning at first glance, but their inconsistency raises some doubts. Lieutenant Colonel Cyrus Sears of the 11th Louisiana Infantry claimed forty-five years later that the Texans "fought us under the skull, coffin and cross bones (black) flag." Since Sears wrote nearly half a century after the fact and since some of his comrades claimed that he had spent the better part of the fight hiding behind the riverbank, his account seems insufficient in itself to settle the matter. Colonel Lieb's detailed official report of the battle, written the day after the engagement, seems much more reliable. According to Lieb, when the Confederates reached the levee, "they came madly on with cries of 'No quarters for white officers, kill the damned Abolitionists, but spare the niggers &c.'" Captain Miller of the 9th Louisiana wrote only that some Rebels shouted "no quarters."[38]

Although the excited nerves and adrenaline of men in their first combat—especially men who recoiled at the very idea of black soldiers—may well have led some individual Confederates to shoot wounded black soldiers or others who had thrown down their arms, the Texans apparently had no prearranged plan or order to massacre the African American soldiers in blue at Milliken's Bend. Colonel Lieb's specific recollection indicates that the Texans were shouting that black soldiers should be spared, and General McCulloch on the day after the battle discussed how black captives should be returned to slavery.[39] In fact, in their planning for the battle, the Confederates seem not even to have considered the question of black soldiers—their officers were confused after the battle about what to do with the African American captives.[40] Confederate survivors boasted of several dozen black prisoners taken during the fight, and later newspaper reports indicated that those prisoners were turned over to army authorities.[41] Lieutenant Colonel Sears of the 11th Louisiana, no friend of the Rebels, reported that the African American prisoners were taken to Texas, put to work for the Confederacy, and released by General George Custer at the end of the war.[42] It seems certain that the ragged Texans, some of them barefoot and most of them without uniforms, had no special flags for such occasions. Stories of black flags and skulls and crossbones were circulated later, almost entirely by men who had not been on the gory levee at Milliken's Bend.[43]

Although an organized and predetermined effort to massacre black soldiers probably did not occur at Milliken's Bend, it appears that Confederate authorities in Monroe may have executed two captured white officers of black regiments. When General Grant heard rumors about executions of prisoners taken at Milliken's Bend, he wrote General Taylor, asking for an explanation. Taylor huffily denied the allegations and claimed that he had given no such orders, and Grant let the matter drop. Nevertheless, a careful examination of the affair concludes that Second Lieutenant George L. Conn of the 9th Louisiana Infantry and Captain Corydon Heath of the 11th Louisiana may well have been executed days after the battle by officers not under Taylor's command.[44]

As often happened in this war, the men on both sides claimed to have whipped the other. Rank-and-file Texans remembered that they had broken the blue line at the point of the bayonet and pushed the Federals back to the water's edge. General Taylor was not so happy with the result. He considered the whole exercise a waste of time and resources that should have been focused on South Louisiana. The men in blue concentrated on the bottom line of the day—the ultimate retreat of the Confederates and the survival of the Federal camp.[45] In the larger context of the war, of course, the battle at Milliken's Bend had little strategic importance. The original purpose of the Confederate strike at Milliken's Bend—to break Grant's supply line—could not have been accomplished even if the Rebels had wiped out the entire Union garrison. Grant's main line of communication was secure on the other side of the river. In that sense, the Confederates had lost the battle before the first shots were fired from behind that outer bois d'arc hedge.

Although the battle made no significant difference in the outcome of Grant's Vicksburg campaign, it did send a shiver of excitement through the ranks of the Union army along the Mississippi River. Many Northern white soldiers and officers had expressed doubts about the fighting ability of former slaves. Could men accustomed to taking orders from white masters stand up to Southern white soldiers? Could they stand fire? Were they intelligent enough to learn drill and the use of their weapons? Such doubts were a reflection of the racism that afflicted white Americans in general in the mid-nineteenth century. The performance of their black comrades at Milliken's Bend may not have erased all vestiges of such racial thinking, but the vicious hand-to-hand struggle on the levee near Milliken's Bend created new respect for African American fighting men.

Captain M. M. Miller of Galena, Illinois, an officer in the 9th Louisiana Infantry, described the battle in a letter written three days later. Every man but one in Captain Miller's company of thirty-three was either killed or wounded, and he had no doubts at all about the black man's willingness and ability to fight for freedom and Union.

> I never felt more grieved and sick at heart than when I saw how my brave soldiers had been slaughtered, one with six wounds, all the rest with two or three, none less than two wounds. Two of my colored sergeants were killed, both brave, noble men; always prompt, vigilant, and ready for the fray. I never more wish to hear the expression. "The niggers wont fight." Come with me 100 yards from where I sit and I can show you the wounds that cover the bodies of 16 as brave, loyal, and patriotic soldiers as ever drew bead on a rebel.[46]

Even Federal soldiers not in the battle soon heard stories of how fiercely the African Americans had fought. A soldier in the military hospital at Milliken's Bend discussed the fight with other white men who had been there. "All concur in saying that the negroes fougt [sic] like tigers," he wrote to his father in Illinois. "The negroes on that day demonstrated their character as fighting men. They were all raw recruits and had just recieved [sic] their arms still they fought like veterans, affording a convincing argument to those who are disposed to cavil with the policy of employing negroes to bear arms against our enemies." An Ohio soldier in the same hospital came to the same conclusion about the black enlisted men. "Poor fellows, they had bad wounds, pretty well cut up, although only a few weeks in their new life. Their gallant conduct illicited [sic] the praise of the whites who say the nigger will fight and no mistake. Not many white regiments would stand the attack of Sunday," he wrote his brother. To drive the point home, he added that "the rebs were Texas rangers, a bloodthirsty set."[47]

The new esteem traveled from the survivors of the fight to comrades-in-arms in other units, and from there back to families and newspapers in Northern towns and cities in the Midwest. Indeed, admiration for the courage and grit of the former slaves of Mississippi and Louisiana rose to the highest reaches of the federal government. Assistant Secretary of War Charles A. Dana, traveling with Grant's army during the drive on Vicksburg, reported to Secretary of War Stanton that "the sentiment of this army with regard to the employment of negro troops has been revolutionized by the bravery of the blacks in the recent battle of Milliken's Bend. Prominent officers, who used in private to sneer at the idea, are now heartily in favor of it." Unfortunately for the veterans of Milliken's Bend, their story was barely noted in the columns of the large Eastern newspapers and magazines in New York, Washington, Philadelphia, and Boston. Many Eastern news readers then, and generations of Americans since, have assumed that the first black regiment to stand tall in a pitched battle was the 54th Massachusetts Infantry at Fort Wagner, six weeks after Milliken's Bend. Nevertheless, the obscure African American soldiers of Port Hudson and Milliken's Bend had shown the way for other more famous black units that would seize the imagination of the American people, from the 54th Massachusetts of the Civil War to the Tuskegee airmen of World War II.[48]

Even the Confederates at Milliken's Bend testified to the rugged resistance of the black soldiers at the levee. General McCulloch himself admitted that "this charge was resisted by the negro portion of the enemy's force with considerable obstinacy." McCulloch lamented that "our loss of 184 in killed, wounded and missing, shows but too painfully how firm was the resistance of the foe." A soldier in the 16th Texas Infantry wrote that the levee was taken only "after some hard fighting." Another member of the same regiment recalled later that "bayonets were crossed, and muskets clubbed, and the struggle indeed became a close and deadly one." If Confederates in the Mississippi River valley had harbored doubts about the effectiveness of African American soldiers, Port Hudson and Milliken's Bend seemed to settle the question.[49]

Southern civilians seemed even more surprised by the performance of the former slaves in blue. Kate Stone, a refugee from a nearby plantation, simply could not believe reports that the black soldiers "fought like mad demons." Stone recorded her puzzlement in her diary: "It is hard to believe that Southern soldiers—and Texans at that—have been whipped by a mongrel crew of white and black Yankees." Another Louisiana woman wrote in her own diary: "it is said that . . . the negroes fought desperately, and would not give up until our men clubbed muskets upon them . . . it is terrible to think of such a battle as this, white men and freemen fighting with their slaves, and to be killed by such a hand, the very soul revolts from it, O, may this be the last." But it was only one of the first. Black regiments would be used in increasing numbers for the rest of the war in the West: in the Union victory at Honey Springs (Indian Territory) six weeks later, in the occupation of the lower Texas coast five months later, on the Red River campaign, at the Battle of Jenkins' Ferry, at the Battle of Nashville, and in the capture of Mobile. With their performance on the levee, the field hands of Louisiana and Mississippi introduced Southern whites to a new and ominous phase of the war.[50]

Despite its limited strategic significance, the struggle on the levee and the riverbank is worth remembering. For only the second time in the history of the nation, regiments of black Americans had stood and fought under the American flag in a general engagement, for the Union and for their own freedom. The first occasion had been at Port Hudson near Baton Rouge only eleven days earlier. Milliken's Bend sent shivers of excitement and renewed enthusiasm through the Union army in the Mississippi River valley, even among those formerly skeptical about the use of black troops. Western Confederates, military and civilian, also realized that the war had taken on a new character. The former-slaves-turned soldiers of Louisiana and Mississippi have not received the same respect and attention that the men of the 54th Massachusetts received for their assault on Fort Wagner six weeks later, but the Western African Americans demonstrated for all to see that black Americans could fight and die for Union and freedom as well as anyone, white or black, famous or obscure.

Notes

1. In his four-volume treatment of the Civil War, Allan Nevins devoted a grand total of eleven words to Milliken's Bend. See Nevins, *The War for the Union*, 4 vols. (New York: Scribner, 1959–71), 3:6. J. G. Randall and David Donald did not even mention the engagement in their 1969 synthesis, *The Civil War and Reconstruction* (Lexington, Mass.: D. C. Heath, 1969), and Peter J. Parish summarized the event in half a sentence in his own synthesis, *The American Civil War* (New York: Holmes & Meier, 1975), 259. The pertinent volume in the West Point Military History Series grants one sentence to this battle; see Timothy H. Donovan, Jr., et al., *The American Civil War*, West Point Military History Series (Wayne, N.J.: Avery Publishing Group, 1987), 118. Three standard reference works on the Civil War do not include entries on Milliken's Bend. See Mark Mayo Boatner III, *The Civil War Dictionary* (New York: David McKay, 1988); Patricia L. Faust, ed., *Historical Times Illustrated Encyclopedia of the Civil War* (New York: Harper and Row, 1986); Richard N. Current, ed., *Encyclopedia of the Confederacy*, 4 vols. (New York: Simon and Schuster, 1993).

2. See Dudley Taylor Cornish, *The Sable Arm: Negro Troops in the Union Army, 1861–1865* (New York: Longmans, Green, 1956), 144–45, 163–65; Joseph T. Glatthaar, *Forged in Battle: The Civil War Alliance of Black Soldiers and White Officers* (New York: Free Press, 1990), 130–35; Noah Andre Trudeau, *Like Men of War: Black Troops in the Civil War, 1862–1865* (Boston: Little, Brown, 1998); James M. McPherson, *Battle Cry of Freedom: The Civil War Era* (New York: Oxford University Press, 1988), 633–34; Edwin Bearss, *The Campaign for Vicksburg*, 3 vols. (Dayton, Ohio: Morningside, 1985–86), 3:1153–83; Terrence J. Winschel, "To

Rescue Gibraltar: John Walker's Texas Division and Its Expedition to Relieve Fortress Vicksburg," *Civil War Regiments* 3 (1993): 33–58. Noah Andre Trudeau graciously shared copies of important documents for the writing of this essay.

3. David Cornwell, "Dan Caverno: A True Tale of American Life on the Farm, in a Country Store, and in the Volunteer Army," 136–37, David Cornwell Papers, Civil War Miscellaneous Collection, U.S. Army Military History Institute, Carlisle Barracks, Pa. For examples from more recent accounts, see the works cited in notes 1 and 2 above.

4. Cornish, *The Sable Arm*, 112–26; Ira Berlin, Joseph P. Reidy, and Leslie S. Rowland, eds., *The Black Military Experience* (New York: Cambridge University Press, 1982), 9–16, 116–22; Glatthaar, *Forged in Battle*, 37–38, 67–71; U.S. War Department, *The War of the Rebellion: A Compilation of the Official Records of the Union and Confederate Armies*, 128 vols. (Washington, D.C.: Government Printing Office, 1880–1901), 3rd ser., 5:121, 124 (hereafter cited as *OR*).

5. Cornwell, "Dan Caverno," 122–23. On the reluctance to enlist among some African Americans, see Gary Kynoch, "Terrible Dilemmas: Black Enlistment in the Union Army during the American Civil War," *Slavery and Abolition* 18 (August 1997): 104–27.

6. Cornwell, "Dan Caverno," 123–24.

7. For examples of abusive recruiting, see Berlin et al., *The Black Military Experience*, 150–60. For Thomas's recruiting figures, see *OR*, 3rd ser., 3:1190.

8. Jacob Bruner to Dear Wife, April 28, 1863, Jacob Bruner Papers, Ohio Historical Society, Columbus; Cornwell, "Dan Caverno," 128; Frederick H. Dyer, *A Compendium of the War of the Rebellion*, 2 vols. (1908; Dayton, Ohio: Broadfoot Publishing Company and Morningside, 1994), 2:1214. The 9th Louisiana Infantry would later be designated the 1st Mississippi Heavy Artillery (African Descent) and then the 63rd U.S. Colored Troops (ibid.).

9. Cyrus Sears, *Paper of Cyrus Sears, Read before the Ohio Commandery of the Loyal Legion, October 7th 1908* (Columbus, Ohio: F. J. Heer Printing Co., 1909), 7; Dyer, *A Compendium of the War of the Rebellion*, 2:1214–15, 1344; "Distances from N. Orleans to St. Louis," John C. Black and Family Papers, Illinois State Historical Library, Springfield; annual return of the 1st Mississippi Volunteers (African Descent), in "The Negro in the Military Service of the United States, 1639–1886," Records of the Adjutant General's Office, Record Group 94, microfilm M858, roll 2, 2143, National Archives, Washington, D.C. (hereafter cited as "The Negro"). The 1st Mississippi was later designated the 51st U.S. Colored Troops; the 11th Louisiana, the 49th U.S. Colored Troops (Dyer, *A Compendium of the War of the Rebellion*, 2:1215, 1344).

10. Sears, *Paper of Cyrus Sears*, 12.

11. Dyer, *A Compendium of the War of the Rebellion*, 2:1174; Trudeau, *Like Men of War*, 53n; A. A. Stuart, *Iowa Colonels and Regiments: Being a History of Iowa Regiments in the War of the Rebellion* (Des Moines, Iowa: Mills & Co., 1865), 391.

12. Inspection Report, Walker's Division, May 27, 1863, J. L. Brent Papers, Collection 55-L, Louisiana Historical Association Collection, Howard-Tilton Memorial Library, Tulane University, New Orleans; Current, *Encyclopedia of the Confederacy*, 4:1462.

13. Bearss, *The Campaign for Vicksburg*, 1:287–347; Robert G. Hartje, *Van Dorn: The Life and Times of a Confederate General* (Nashville, Tenn.: Vanderbilt University Press, 1967), 247–70.

14. Bearss, *The Campaign for Vicksburg*, 1:345, 2:447, 449, 459, 461, 470, 480–81, 3:791–92.

15. Ezra J. Warner, *Generals in Gray: Lives of the Confederate Commanders* (Baton Rouge: Louisiana State University Press, 1959), 319–20.

16. *OR*, 1st ser., 15:1041; Bearss, *The Campaign for Vicksburg*, 3:1168–69; Winschel, "To Rescue Gibraltar," 42–43.

17. McCulloch's and Walker's reports are reprinted in Joseph Palmer Blessington, *The Campaigns of Walker's Texas Division*, with an introduction by Norman D. Brown and T. Michael Parrish (1875; Austin, Tex.: State House Press, 1994), 87–92, 119–20.

18. U.S. Navy Department, *The Official Records of the Union and Confederate Navies in the War of the Rebellion*, 31 vols. (Washington, D.C.: Government Printing Office, 1894–1927), 1st ser., 25:147–48; Paul H. Silverstone, *Warships of the Civil War Navies* (Annapolis, Md.: Naval Institute Press, 1989), 151; Norman D. Brown, ed., *Journey to Pleasant Hill: The Civil War Letters of Captain Elijah P. Petty, Walker's Texas Division, C.S.A.* (San Antonio: Institute of Texan Cultures, 1982), 231–32.

19. E. P. Petty to My Dear Daughter, June 1, 1863, in Brown, *Journey to Pleasant Hill*, 231–32; Theophilus Perry to Dear Harriet, June 1, 1863, Theophilus Perry Letters, Presley Carter Person Papers, Duke University Library, Durham, N.C.; Sam Wright to My dear Mother, July 4, 1862, Samuel J. Wright Civil War Letters, box 13, Skipper Steely Collection, Texas A&M University at Commerce Library, Commerce, Tex.; McCulloch's report on casualties, in Blessington, *The Campaigns of Walker's Division*, 91.

20. *OR*, 1st ser., 24 (1):93; ibid., (2):447–48, 458; ibid., (3):375, 508.

21. Lieutenant Cornwell's account and Lieb's report, June 8, 1863, in Cornwell, "Dan Caverno," 130, 136–37; account by F. W. Sedgwick, Co. A, 10th Illinois Cavalry, in *Washington National Tribune*, December 7, 1905; *OR*, 1st ser., 24 (2):447, 458.

22. Lieb's report, in Cornwell, "Dan Caverno," 136; *OR*, 1st ser., 24 (2):453; *The Official Records of the Union and Confederate Navies*, 1st ser., 25:163.

23. *OR*, 1st ser., 24 (2):457; Bearss, *The Campaign for Vicksburg*, 3:1174, 1177; Richard Taylor, *Destruction and Reconstruction: Personal Experiences of the Late War*, with an introduction by T. Michael Parrish (1879; New York: Da Capo Press, 1995), 136.

24. *OR*, 1st ser., 24 (2):458–59, 469; Taylor, *Destruction and Reconstruction*, 136; Report of Brigadier General J. M. Hawes, June 8, 1863, John G. Walker Papers, Southern

Historical Collection, University of North Carolina, Chapel Hill; Warner, *Generals in Gray*, 201; Faust, *Historical Times Illustrated Encyclopedia of the Civil War*, 458–59.

25. *OR*, 1st ser., 24 (2):458; Peter W. Gravis, *Twenty-five Years on the Outside Row of the Northwest Conference: Autobiography of Rev. Peter W. Gravis* (1892; Brownwood, Tex.: Cross Timbers Press, 1966), 28; Blessington, *The Campaigns of Walker's Texas Division*, 94.

26. Lieutenant Cornwell's account, in Cornwell, "Dan Caverno," 131, 132; Sears, *Paper of Cyrus Sears*, 13; G. G. Edwards, "Fight at Milliken's Bend, Miss. [*sic*]," *Rebellion Record* 7 (1869): document 8, 12–13; Captain W. M. Little to his wife, June 9, 1863, *Washington National Tribune*, January 13, 1916. The estimates of Federal strength during the fight range from 1,100 to 1,400 . Lieutenant Cornwell's estimate (1,328), because it is more detailed and precise than any others, seems most reliable (Cornwell, "Dan Caverno," 132, 139).

27. Blessington, *The Campaigns of Walker's Texas Division*, 95; *OR*, 1st ser., 24 (2):467.

28. Cornwell, "Dan Caverno," 132; Mamie Yeary, comp., *Reminiscences of the Boys in Gray, 1861–1865* (1912; Dayton, Ohio: Morningside, 1986), 665–66; Edwards, "Fight at Milliken's Bend," 12; *OR*, 1st ser., 24 (2):467; Blessington, *The Campaigns of Walker's Texas Division*, 97–98.

29. Gravis, *Twenty-five Years on the Outside Row of the Northwest Conference*, 28; Cornwell, "Dan Caverno," 133; Robert Henry to Dear Wife, June 12, 1863, Robert W. Henry Letters, State Historical Society of Iowa, Des Moines; *OR*, 1st ser., 24 (2):462–63, 467.

30. Captain W. M. Little to his wife, June 9, 1863, *Washington National Tribune*, January 13, 1916; Robert Henry to Dear Wife, June 12, 1863, Robert W. Henry Letters.

31. Cornwell, "Dan Caverno," 133; account of Captain Matthew M. Miller in William Eliot Furness, "The Negro As a Soldier," *Military Essays and Recollections: Papers Read before the Commandery of the State of Illinois, Military Order of the Loyal Legion of the United States* (Chicago: A. C. McClurg and Co., 1894), 475.

32. Lieb's report, in Cornwell, "Dan Caverno," 137; Captain W. M. Little to his wife, June 9, 1863, *Washington National Tribune*, January 13, 1916; *The Official Records of the Union and Confederate Navies*, 1st ser., 25:162; *OR*, 1st ser., 24 (2):468.

33. Your Husband (Theophilus Perry) to Dear Harriet, June 11, 1863, Theophilus Perry Letters; Lieb's report, in Cornwell, "Dan Caverno," 137; Captain W. M. Little to his wife, June 9, 1863, *Washington National Tribune*, January 13, 1916; Robert Henry to Dear Wife, June 12, 1863, Robert W. Henry Letters; Gravis, *Twenty-five Years on the Outside Row of the Northwest Conference*, 28; Edwards, "Fight at Milliken's Bend," 12–13; Sears, *Paper of Cyrus Sears*, 6; *Confederate Veteran* 8 (February 1900): 67; John G. Walker, "The War of Secession West of the Mississippi River during the Years 1863–4–& 5," 29, in John G. Walker Papers; Blessington, *The Campaigns of Walker's Texas Division*, 100.

34. Sears, *Paper of Cyrus Sears*, 15–16; Silverstone, *Warships of the Civil War Navies*, 157;

James Russell Soley, "Naval Operations in the Vicksburg Campaign," in Robert Underwood Johnson and Clarence Clough Buel, eds., *Battles and Leaders of the Civil War*, 4 vols. (New York: Century, 1887–88), 3:570.

35. *OR*, 1st ser., 24 (2):447–48, 453–54, 459, 464, 469; Lieb's report, in Cornwell, "Dan Caverno," 137; Walker, "The War of Secession," 29; Blessington, *The Campaigns of Walker's Division*, 100; Yeary, *Reminiscences of the Boys in Gray*, 609–10; Furness, "The Negro As a Soldier," 477; Edwards, "Fight at Milliken's Bend," 12; Harvey Alexander Wallace Diary, 1829–65, entry of June 7, 1863, Southwest Arkansas Regional Archives, Washington, Ark.

36. *OR*, 1st ser., 24 (2):447–48, 470; Glatthaar, *Forged in Battle*, 134; Boatner, *The Civil War Dictionary*, 301; William F. Fox, *Regimental Losses in the American Civil War, 1861–1865* (Albany, N.Y.: Albany Publishing Co., 1889), 54; Cornwell, "Dan Caverno," 132. The name and the description of the wound for each Confederate casualty are available in "Confederate States Army Casualties: Lists and Narrative Reports, 1861–1865," War Department Collection of Confederate Records, Record Group 109, microfilm M836, roll 2, National Archives, Washington, D.C.

37. One recent account of the Battle of the Crater mentions Milliken's Bend as a "possible candidate" for listing as a massacre (Bryce A. Suderow, "The Battle of the Crater: The Civil War's Worst Massacre," *Civil War History* 43 [September 1997]: 224). The overall number of deaths among black soldiers at Milliken's Bend (95 of 1,223 engaged, or 7.8 percent) was far less proportionally than the 63.9 percent of African American soldiers killed at a widely acknowledged massacre, Fort Pillow, Tennessee, in April 1864, raising serious doubts about Milliken's Bend as a massacre. See Fox, *Regimental Losses in the American Civil War*, 54 (for deaths); Cornwell, "Dan Caverno," 132 (for numbers engaged); John Cimprich and Robert C. Mainfort, Jr., "The Fort Pillow Massacre: A Statistical Note," *Journal of American History* 76 (December 1989): 836.

38. Sears, *Paper of Cyrus Sears*, 15; Cornwell, "Dan Caverno," 136–37, 138–40; *OR*, 3rd ser., 3:454.

39. For McCulloch's statements about returning captured black soldiers to slavery, see *OR*, 1st ser., 24 (2):468–69. Private B. G. Goodrich of the 16th Texas Infantry scoffed at later reports of a massacre: "With their usual disregard of truth, the Yankees accused us of shouting 'No quarter,' but the Sixteenth Infantry captured an entire company of negroes." See *Confederate Veteran* 8 (February 1900): 67.

40. For confusion about how to handle black prisoners, see *OR*, 1st ser., 24 (2):459; T. Michael Parrish, *Richard Taylor: Soldier Prince of Dixie* (Chapel Hill: University of North Carolina Press, 1992), 292–93.

41. For Confederate statements about the capture of black prisoners, see Blessington, *The Campaigns of Walker's Texas Division*, 99–100; Taylor, *Destruction and Reconstruction*, 136; Ned [Cade] to Dear Wife, June 8[?], 1863, Edward W. and Allie Cade Correspondence, John Q. Anderson Collection, Texas State Library

and Archives Commission, Austin; Henry McCulloch's report, *OR*, 1st ser., 24 (2):468; Walker's special order, June 20, 1863, reprinted in *Austin (Tex.) Tri-Weekly State Gazette*, August 20, 1863. The *Shreveport (La.) News* reported on June 13 that sixty black prisoners from Milliken's Bend had been escorted to Monroe on June 11.

42. Sears, *Paper of Cyrus Sears*, 15. One of the captives, Vincent Dickerson of the 1st Mississippi Infantry, continued his fight for equal rights after the war by serving as a Republican in the Louisiana House of Representatives from 1874 to 1892 (Eric Foner, *Freedom's Lawmakers: A Directory of Black Officeholders during Reconstruction* [New York: Oxford University Press, 1993], 63).

43. For later allegations about black flags and the killing of prisoners, all repeated by men who had not been in the fight and nearly all including erroneous information, see, for example, *Washington National Tribune*, December 7, 1905; *Burlington (Iowa) Weekly Hawk-Eye*, June 27, 1863; *Keokuk (Iowa) Daily Gate City*, June 12, 1863; *New Orleans Times Picayune*, June 23, 1863; Furness, "The Negro As a Soldier," 475; *Harper's Weekly* 7 (July 4, 1863): 427, and *Harper's Weekly* 8 (May 21, 1864): 334.

44. *OR*, 1st ser., 24 (3):425–26, 443–44, 469 (Grant-Taylor correspondence); James G. Hollandsworth, Jr., "The Execution of White Officers from Black Units by Confederate Forces during the Civil War," *Louisiana History* 35 (Fall 1994): 479, 489.

45. For the opinions of rank-and-file Confederates, see Yeary, *Reminiscences of the Boys in Gray*, 609–10, 759–60; Gravis, *Twenty-five Years on the Outside Row of the Northwest Conference*, 28; *Confederate Veteran* 8 (February 1900): 67; Blessington, *The Campaigns of Walker's Texas Division*, 96–97. Taylor's assessment is in his *Destruction and Reconstruction*, 136. Federal judgments are in Lieb's report, in Cornwell, "Dan Caverno," 134, 137; Sears, *Paper of Cyrus Sears*, 15–16; Soley, "Naval Operations in the Vicksburg Campaign," 570; *OR*, 1st ser., 24 (1):95 and (2):453–54; Ulysses S. Grant, "The Vicksburg Campaign," in Johnson and Buel, *Battles and Leaders of the Civil War*, 3:524–25; Henry Burrell to Dear Bro., June 17, 1863, Henry Burrell Papers, U.S. Army Military History Institute, Carlisle Barracks, Pa.; Furness, "The Negro As a Soldier," 477; extract from 1863 annual return of 5th U.S. Colored Artillery-Heavy (formerly the 9th Louisiana Infantry, African Descent), "The Negro," roll 2, 2141–42.

46. M. M. Miller to Dear Aunt, June 10, 1863, reprinted in *OR*, 3rd ser., 3:454.

47. Charles Otto Henthorn to Dear Father, June 10, 1863, Charles Otto Henthorn Papers, Clements Library, University of Michigan, Ann Arbor; Frank [McGregor] to [his brother], June 9, 1863, Frank McGregor Papers, U.S. Army Military History Institute, Carlisle Barracks, Pa.

48. Charles A. Dana to Edwin Stanton, June 22, 1863, *OR*, 1st ser., 24 (1):106. Captain M. M. Miller's account of the battle originally appeared in the *Galena (Ill.) Advertiser*. Other Midwestern newspapers that published reports of the fight in-

cluded the *Burlington (Iowa) Weekly Hawk-Eye* (July 4, 1863), the *Keokuk (Iowa) Daily Gate City* (June 12, 1863), the *Cincinnati Gazette* (reprinted in the *New Orleans Times Picayune,* June 28, 1863), and doubtless more. The *New York Herald,* June 19, 1863, printed a letter from a post-battle visitor at Milliken's Bend; the *New York Times* printed a second-hand dispatch from Cairo, Illinois (reprinted in the *New Orleans Times Picayune,* June 23, 1863); and *Harper's Weekly* 7 (July 4, 1863): 427, reprinted a short second-hand account of the battle.

49. *OR,* 1st ser., 24 (2):467; *Austin Tri-Weekly State Gazette,* June 23, 1863; *Confederate Veteran* 8 (February 1900): 67; Blessington, *The Campaigns of Walker's Texas Division,* 97.

50. John Q. Anderson, ed., *Brokenburn: The Journal of Kate Stone, 1861–1868* (Baton Rouge: Louisiana State University Press, 1955), 218, 219; Sarah L. Wadley, Private Journal, June 9, 1863, Southern Historical Collection, University of North Carolina, Chapel Hill.

4

THE BATTLE
OF OLUSTEE

Arthur W. Bergeron, Jr.

The Battle of Olustee, also known as Ocean Pond, occurred on February 20, 1864, and was a part of the largest campaign waged in the state of Florida during the Civil War. Three black regiments constituted a part of the Union forces engaged: the 54th Massachusetts Infantry, the 1st North Carolina Colored Infantry, and the 8th U.S. Colored Infantry. Only one of these units, the now famous 54th Massachusetts, had seen combat prior to the battle. In fact, the men of the 8th USCT had not even completed their training. Like engagements before it, Olustee would turn into a proving ground for black soldiers. Had the valor shown by other regiments at Port Hudson and Milliken's Bend been anomalies, or could these men indeed fight as well as their white comrades?

Until early 1864, Florida had seen little in the way of military actions. The Union government had had no incentives to invade the state even though Confederate armies drew large amounts of foodstuffs from it, primarily salt, beef, pork, and sugar. When in January 1864 President Abraham Lincoln gave his approval for an expedition, the operation was meant to have primarily a political agenda—the restoration of Florida to the Union in time for it to send a pro-Lincoln delegation to the Republican National Convention. The previous December, the president had issued a Proclamation of Amnesty and Reconstruction. Under its provisions, a seceded state could come back into the Union when only 10 percent of its 1860 voters had taken an oath of allegiance.

Major General Quincy A. Gillmore, commander of the Department of the South, had submitted a proposal for an invasion of Florida in that same month. He hoped to use a mixture of white and black troops to take Florida back from the Confederacy. The expedition would capture vital transportation routes, cut off the flow of supplies from the peninsula, bring thousands of freed slaves into the Federal army, and allow the export of cotton and timber to the North. Union troops would land at Jacksonville and move into the interior along the Florida, Atlantic, and Gulf Central Railroad and capture the town of Baldwin. From there, the force could proceed westward toward the capital at Tallahassee or southwestward along the Florida Railroad toward Gainesville and the Gulf Coast.[1]

When he received word to proceed, Gillmore selected Brigadier General Truman Seymour to command the expedition. The new commander of the District of Florida was a thirty-nine-year-old native of Vermont and graduate of the U.S. Military Academy. Seymour received two brevets during the Mexican War, was a drawing instructor at West Point, and fought in the Seminole War. As a member of the 1st U.S. Artillery, he became a part of the garrison at Fort Sumter and received a brevet for gallantry defending the post. Promoted to brigadier general on April 28, 1862, Seymour performed well in a number of battles in Virginia before he was assigned to participate in the attack on Charleston in the summer of 1863.

Men of Seymour's command, which included the 54th Massachusetts, conducted the famous assault on Battery Wagner on July 18. Six months later, a reporter for the *New York Tribune* accused the general of sending the black regiment ahead of his white troops so that they would draw most of the Confederate fire. This accusation, as well as one concerning racial prejudice, had no basis in fact. Seymour believed strongly in giving these men an opportunity to prove their fighting abilities and had expressed publicly his desire to help local freedmen in any way he could.[2] Seymour suffered a severe wound from the explosion of an artillery shell while accompanying the second wave of attackers as they moved against Battery Wagner. He returned to duty in December and received command of the Florida expedition.[3]

The Federals occupied Jacksonville without any real opposition on February 7. The following afternoon, Seymour moved a part of his force toward Camp Finegan, about eight miles west of the town, which fell after a short fight. Union forces reached Baldwin on February 9. The Confederate commander in the area, Brigadier General Joseph Finegan did not have sufficient numbers of men to contest Seymour's advance and withdrew his men toward Lake City. Finegan requested reinforcements and had his troops begin to erect earthworks across the Florida, Atlantic, and Gulf

Central Railroad just east of Olustee Station. General Pierre G. T. Beauregard ordered men southward from Georgia, and by February 20 Finegan had a force of about 5,000 men.[4]

When Seymour's force marched westward on the morning of the twentieth, it numbered approximately 5,500 men. The black regiments were organized in two different commands. Colonel Joseph R. Hawley's brigade included the 8th U.S. Colored Troops. Commanded by Colonel Charles W. Fribley, the regiment had present twenty-one officers and 544 enlisted men. Fribley's unit, composed primarily of free blacks from Pennsylvania, had completed its organization at Camp William Penn in Philadelphia on December 4. Traveling by ship, the men left for New York on January 16 and reached Hilton Head a few days later. Fribley had served as a captain in the 84th Pennsylvania and won the confidence of his troops during his brief association with the regiment during its training.[5]

Colonel James Montgomery, commander of the 2nd South Carolina Colored Volunteers and a radical abolitionist who had worked with John Brown and James H. Lane in Kansas, led a brigade composed of the 1st North Carolina Colored Volunteers and the 54th Massachusetts Infantry. The 1st North Carolina had organized at New Bern, North Carolina, and Portsmouth, Virginia, and entered service on June 30, 1863. Almost all of the enlisted men of the regiment had been slaves. Though they had seen duty along the South Carolina coast, they had worked primarily as laborers and on garrison duty and had received inferior weapons. The regiment's colonel, James C. Beecher, had gone on leave, so Lieutenant Colonel William N. Reed led the unit during the campaign. Approximately 600 men were present at the time. Just prior to the operation, the regiment had been redesignated as the 35th United States Colored Troops but maintained its original name until after the battle.[6]

The 54th Massachusetts Volunteers was organized in May 1863 at Readville; the unit consisted of free blacks from Massachusetts and Pennsylvania. Colonel Robert Gould Shaw had led his men to immortality in the attack on Battery Wagner the following July. Edward N. Hallowell, who received a wound in that assault, had succeeded to command of the regiment after Shaw's death. He had approximately thirteen officers and 480 enlisted men under him during the battle. Clearly, Hallowell's troops were the only battle-hardened of the three black regiments in Seymour's force.[7]

Having concentrated near Barber's Ford, just west of Baldwin, the Union army broke camp before seven o'clock on the morning of February 20. Hawley's brigade followed the cavalry; Colonel William B. Barton's all white brigade marched behind Hawley's; and Montgomery's brigade brought up the rear. Sergeant George E. Stephens of the 54th Massachusetts described the day as "a most delightful one." He recalled, "The springs and rivulets along the line of march reminded us of the cool, refreshing waters of the Sea Islands!" Not everything on the route seemed so appealing, however. Stephens commented on the sterile countryside: "You can see nothing but pine woods, marsh, and every five or ten miles a cluster of dilapidated, deserted huts, with no sign of agricultural thriftiness."[8] Another participant complained that the men really did not get much rest, even though they stopped for brief periods each hour. They also had little opportunity to eat more than "a mouthful of food." This soldier described the march as passing "over a road of loose sand, or boggy turf, or covered knee-deep with mud or water" and felt that the army was "weary, exhausted, faint, hungry, and ill-conditioned" when it met the enemy.[9]

By noon, the main part of the column had reached Sanderson, and the advance cavalry elements made contact with Finegan's Confederates about fifteen minutes later. Hawley sent forward the 7th Connecticut and some artillery. About two o'clock the men from the Nutmeg State drove the Confederate pickets in on their earthworks near Olustee. Soon the Federals found themselves outnumbered, under heavy fire, and their flanks threatened. About 3:00 P.M., the 7th Connecticut received orders to fall back, and Hawley directed the 8th USCT and 7th New Hampshire to move to the support of the artillery. Fribley's men had been aware of skirmishing to the front, but, as Lieutenant Oliver W. Norton of Company K recalled, "we paid little attention to it."[10]

The New Hampshire regiment moved to the right of the road, and Fribley's men formed to the left. According to Norton, one of Seymour's aides ordered the 8th USCT to "double quick, march!" He wrote to his sister, "We turned into the woods and ran in the direction of the firing for half a mile, when the head of the column reached our batteries." At that point, Seymour, whom Norton snidely called "the presiding genius," directed Fribley to move his regiment into the developing battle.[11] Sergeant Major Rufus Jones remembered: "The Eighth, having been on the railroad for a short distance, was ordered to change direction to the right, and received orders to go into the fight."[12]

Both Norton and Jones agreed that their regiment was ill prepared to go into combat so quickly. Jones stated that the soldiers did not have an opportunity to drop their knapsacks. He estimated that about half of the men had not even loaded their weapons. Norton's letters confirmed this situation

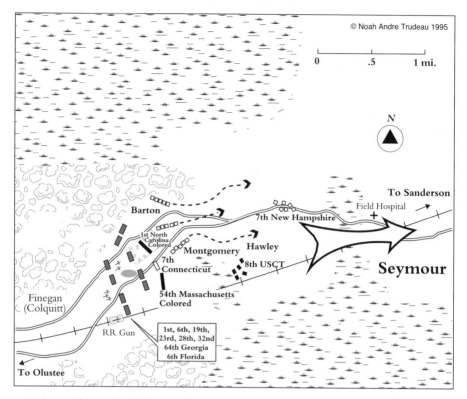

Map 4.1. The Battle of Olustee, Florida, February 20, 1864.
(Courtesy of Noah Andre Trudeau)

and concluded, "No new regiment ever went into their first fight in more unfavorable circumstances." He complained that most of their training had concentrated on parade-ground maneuvers rather than learning how to fire their rifles. "Colonel Fribley," he said "had applied time and again for permission to practice his regiment in target firing, and been always refused."[13] Fribley still expected his men to perform well. After the war, a member of the 40th Massachusetts Mounted Infantry wrote of speaking with the colonel as the 8th USCT moved forward: "As he passed me I said, 'I am glad you are here.' He replied, 'I am glad to be here. If I can get these fellows under fire in good shape, they will give a good account of themselves.'"[14]

Due to confusion in or misunderstanding of orders from Hawley, the 7th New Hampshire did not form its lines properly. As heavy fire from the Confederate lines tore into them, the men wavered and then broke for the rear. Fribley's blacks then began to take the brunt of the rain of bullets and artillery shells. The regiment's left flank had no protection from an enfilading fire from that direction. Inexperience soon began to show. According to an account given by Norton, "At first they were stunned, bewildered, and knew not what to do. They curled to the ground, and as men fell around them they seemed terribly scared." In similar words, he wrote his father, "They behaved as any one acquainted with them would have expected. They were stunned, bewildered, and, as the balls came hissing past or crashing through heads, arms and legs, they curled to the ground like frightened sheep in a hailstorm."[15]

The Massachusetts soldier who had spoken to Fribley presented an equally unflattering description of the reaction of the blacks to the storm of bullets: "Wherever there was a tree you would see them in single file, strung out like a file of men inquiring at the general delivery of the post office where mails come only at long intervals. . . . They soon commenced stepping to the rear; one wounded through the hand, and startled at the sight of his own blood, would drop his rifle, and with the help of two or three able-bodied comrades, would form a procession toward some safe retreat."[16] The scream of artillery projectiles was a new sound to these men and added to their terror. Dr. Charles P. Heichold, the regimental surgeon, wrote that they "commenced dropping like leaves in autumn."[17]

As his losses began to mount, Fribley decided to order a retreat to prevent useless casualties. The regiment started to withdraw, firing as best they could. Lieutenant Norton wrote that many of the men "gathered in groups like frightened sheep."[18] Confederate fire poured into these knots of soldiers. Three color sergeants and five men of the color guard fell. While the colonel attempted to organize his troops, a bullet through the heart felled him, and he died a few minutes later. According to one eyewitness, Fribley "did not cease for a moment to encourage and rally his men, and by his gallant behavior proved himself to be an officer of no ordinary merit."[19] Major Loren Burritt received wounds in both legs. Command devolved on Captain Romanzo C. Bailey, who directed the 8th USCT off of the battlefield. Unlike the soldiers of the 7th New Hampshire, the blacks did not scatter but took up a position behind Colonel Montgomery's men then arriving to enter the fray.[20]

Seymour had brought up Barton's three New York regiments after the collapse of the 7th New Hampshire and placed them to the right of the 8th USCT. When the latter unit retreated, Barton's men had to extend their lines. The Union position became extremely precarious, and at this point the 54th Massachusetts arrived on the field. Montgomery's brigade had been about six miles away when the battle began. The sound of the struggle caused the colonel to push forward his veteran regiment. Sergeant George Stephens recalled that the men of the 54th Massachusetts were "in heavy marching order, with knapsacks, haversacks, canteens, and every other appurtenance of the soldier."[21] They quickly threw off their gear and went in at the double-quick. As the regiment took position on the army's left flank, the blacks let out what one soldier described as "a hearty cheer."[22] Their appearance at that critical moment prevented the Confederates from turning the flank.

When the regiment reached the scene of fighting, its band took up a position at the side of the road. Their music "burst out on the sulphureous air" as the soldiers dropped their knapsacks and began forming their line. A veteran recalled being able to hear the band's "soul-stirring strains" over the clamor of the artillery and musketry fire and the yells of the troops of both sides. The sounds of "The Star Spangled Banner" seemed to give the men new energy. Even the nearby New York troops seemed to respond to the national anthem, and some of the retreating New Hampshire soldiers halted to try to assist in this phase of the battle.[23]

Colonel Hallowell's regiment opened fire and halted a Confederate charge. The men's enthusiasm continued, and Captain Luis F. Emilio remembered that they shouted, "Three cheers for Massachusetts and seven dollars a month!"[24] Some of the men attempted to run forward to engage the Confederates, while others made a rush toward some of the enemy cannon. Hallowell had to restrain their excitement and keep his line intact. According to Sergeant Stephens, "Johnny Reb could not stand" the heavy fire poured out by the Massachusetts regiment.[25] Finegan's men did not slacken their fire for long, however, and soon renewed the barrage of musketry and artillery. Some of the exploding shells tore branches and limbs from the trees, and these fell among the soldiers causing more casualties.[26]

Thinking he might drive back the Confederate left flank, Seymour brought the 1st North Carolina Colored in on the right of Barton's New Yorkers. The general reported that Lieutenant Colonel Reed put his men in line "in the most brilliant manner."[27] A reporter from the *Philadelphia Press* noted that the men came up "with a yell on the double-quick."[28] All around them, these men saw the dead and the dying, but they formed up and began returning the Confederate fire. Quickly, Reed was mortally wounded, and Major Archibald Bogle received severe wounds. Unable to advance as Seymour had wished, the North Carolinians were left to stand and take the punishment that the other Union troops had had to bear for so many hours.

"Battle of Olustee, Fla.," 1894. (Anne S. K. Brown Military Collection, John Hay Library, Brown University)

A minié ball shattered the right arm of the regiment's color sergeant. He knelt down and held the flag with his left arm until another soldier forced him to relinquish it.[29]

Clearly, the battle was going against the Federals, and Seymour recognized the necessity of retreat to avoid having his force completely overrun. As Confederate troops threatened both of his flanks, it appeared they might get into the Union rear. About dusk, Seymour ordered the 54th Massachusetts, the 1st North Carolina Colored, the 7th Connecticut, and the mounted infantry to form a rear guard as the rest of the army moved eastward. A Massachusetts soldier wrote: "the men had no idea of obeying the firm order, and it was repeated by Col. Hallowell three times before the order was obeyed."[30] Sergeant Stephens recalled, "it was a sorrowing spectacle to see our little army, so hopeful and so gallant, in such precipitate retreat."[31] According to an officer of the 1st North Carolina Colored, "Our retreat was steady and cool."[32]

Seymour's defeated army fell back all the way to Barber's Ford, which it reached about midnight. Many of the wounded remained on the battlefield, although men of all the regiments attempted to assist their fallen comrades to safety when they could. The official casualty report showed 1,861 men had been killed or wounded or were missing. Of the three black regiments engaged at Olustee, the 8th USCT suffered the heaviest losses: forty-nine men killed, 188 wounded, and seventy-three missing. The 1st North Carolina Colored lost twenty-two men killed, 131 wounded, and seventy-seven missing. Though heavily engaged, the 54th Massachusetts had only thirteen men killed, sixty-five wounded, and eight missing. By contrast, Finegan's Confederates had suffered only 961 men killed, wounded, and missing. Five artillery pieces and some 1,600 small arms fell into Confederate hands.[33]

The 8th USCT lost its national flag during the engagement. While trying to protect some of the Union cannon, Confederate fire decimated the color guard and caused high casualties in the color company. Lieutenant Elijah Lewis saw the banner on the ground, picked it up, and carried it to the battery in an attempt to rally a force to protect the guns. At the recommendation of Lieutenant Norton, Lewis handed the flag to one of the cannoneers and then tried to help form a line. The attention of both of these officers and of Lieutenant Alfred F. Ely, who also tried to bring troops up to the guns, quickly became fixed on their respective tasks. When Captain Bailey ordered a retreat from the spot, the colors remained with the artilleryman. He either dropped the flag or became a casualty, thus leaving it on the field.[34]

Wounded black soldiers who were also left on the battlefield and those who fell uninjured into Confederate hands feared what might happen to them. A private in the 2nd Florida Cavalry Regiment recalled after the war the words that his lieutenant colonel had said in a short speech before the battle: "General Seamore's [*sic*] Army is made up largely of negroes from Georgia and South Carolina, who have come to steal, pillage, run over the state and murder, kill and rape our wives, daughters and sweethearts. Let's teach them a lesson. I shall not take any negro prisoners in this fight."[35] Although some Confederates killed a few wounded prisoners, no wholesale massacre of the blacks occurred. A Massachusetts newspaperman reported several weeks later "that our wounded officers and men are well treated by the enemy without regard to color, or regiment."[36]

Although exact numbers are not known, seventy or more black prisoners of war ended up in Camp Sumter, near Andersonville, Georgia. The Confederates had taken these men, along with Major Bogle of the 1st North Carolina and other white officers, to Tallahassee after the battle and held them there for several weeks. About mid-March, they began moving the

captives by rail, steamer, and wagon to Andersonville. All of the men had arrived there by the end of that month. They eventually established an area of
their own close to the prison's south gate. Because of orders issued by Lieutenant General Ulysses S. Grant, no chance of release by exchange existed
for them until early 1865. The men were placed on work details, the tasks of
which included the burial of men who died in the prison. William Marvel,
in his study of Andersonville, acknowledged that some blacks received punishment by whipping but concluded, "Individual guards committed some
petty cruelties against them, but for the most part the prison authorities
treated their black prisoners little differently than they did the white ones;
they seemed to reserve their greatest animosity for the white officers who
served with the Colored Troops."[37]

From Barber's Ford, Seymour withdrew his army the following morning
back to Jacksonville. Most of the men worked night and day to throw up
or improve upon earthwork fortifications in case the Confederates pursued
and attacked the town. Some troops worked for several days immediately
after the battle to get the wounded not left at Olustee back to the safety
of the lines at Jacksonville. They used seven cars available on the railroad as
transportation. No engine was available, so the soldiers rounded up horses
to pull the cars. Finally that night, the engineers managed to get a locomo-
tive operating, but it was too late for the men to use it. Nearly three hundred wounded men, both black and white, were moved aboard the steamer
Cosmopolitan and taken to hospitals in Beaufort.[38]

Seymour again came under attack for his treatment of the black soldiers
of the army. A correspondent of the *New York Times* came to his defense,
saying that the general was not a man "to over-indulge any of his troops,
either white or colored." This writer cautioned the friends of the black regiments that no one had any grounds for complaining about Seymour's attitude. He went on to present an assessment of the conduct of those men in
words that reflected his own prejudices: "The value of the colored soldiers
has been thoroughly tested, and as far as my experience goes, it is equal to
that of white troops, when the latter are within supporting distance. They
must have an example to go by. In my opinion, it would be a fearful mistake
to send a body of colored troops into a fight without having nearby a force
of white soldiers. While I do not believe in crowding the colored soldiers,
I do not believe in placing him above the white one, for it is the latter after
all that we must depend upon to achieve our signal victories."[39]

Most contemporary accounts expressed at least qualified praise of the role
of the black soldiers in the battle. Sergeant Stephens of the 54th Massachu-

setts wrote in a letter that Seymour had been quoted as saying "that the Fifty-fourth 'is the only colored regiment that is worth a d——n.'" Yet the general's official report stated that they "behaved creditably," and he commended the men of the 1st North Carolina Colored and the 54th Massachusetts for behaving "like veterans."[40] A reporter for the *Boston Journal* wrote that he heard "loud praises" for the blacks and concluded that they "did nobly."[41] In even stronger words, a correspondent with the 1st North Carolina Colored informed his readers how that regiment handled itself: "Henceforth the long disputed question: will the negro fight? Can he be made available in this our nation's conflict? is irrevocably settled. Events have proven it beyond cavil. Say to the world, that the negro will fight and earn the long desired boon of liberty to his down trodden race."[42]

A correspondent who reported the actions of the 8th USCT commented that he found criticism of that unit unfair. He pointed out that the regiment had not been engaged with the Confederates before and that the soldiers "had never been sufficiently practiced in target firing—many of the men, so far as their officers knew, never having fired a gun." Captain John Hamilton of Battery E, 3rd U.S. Artillery, who had received severe wounds while fighting near the 8th USCT, told the newspaperman: "The men did not know how to use their rifles; the rebels were behind trees shooting the negroes down every moment, and though I used severe language in rallying them, I felt sorry for the poor fellows. I did not see one of their officers or men who showed cowardice." The reporter also quoted the words of a Confederate officer who, during a truce several days after the battle, was asked about the conduct of the black troops: "They stood killing d——d well, but they didn't hurt us much." In conclusion, the correspondent told his editor: "Train them thoroughly in firing at target until they have confidence in their weapons, and on the whole, are rather anxious to try their effect on human bodies (this is the natural effect of such training), and if they have brave officers they will fight as well as the average of mankind."[43] Reflecting this opinion of the performance of the black troops, Captain Romanzo Bailey of the 8th USCT concluded that "both officers and men did their duty to the extent of their ability."[44] In similar words, Lieutenant Oliver Norton of the same regiment informed his father, "I don't claim that they fought well, only as well as they could."[45]

The most negative comments about the performance of the three regiments came from a member of the 40th Massachusetts Mounted Infantry. He wrote of the 8th USCT: "As might be expected of them, as is, to some extent, true of all new troops, particularly when they have lost their commanding officer, they were a mob, a mob of negroes." Because the regiment had taken a relatively large number of men onto the field, this man speculated that "the straggling, undisciplined cowards were never missed" as they went toward the rear. He was particularly outraged that the blacks had allowed their major to fall into Confederate hands, saying that if they "had been soldiers, [they] would have rescued him at once, and easily."[46]

In spite of these criticisms, evidence suggests that most of the men of the three USCT regiments demonstrated their willingness to fight and indeed fought bravely under adverse odds at the Battle of Olustee. Seymour probably expected too much from the two untried black units and mismanaged them during the engagement. Rather than placing the African American troops in critical positions on his battle line where heavy Confederate fire might demoralize them, he might have used them to support the more veteran regiments. Nevertheless, the black soldiers acquitted themselves as well as the majority of the white soldiers on the field and could take pride in how they conducted themselves at Olustee.

Notes

1. William H. Nulty, *Confederate Florida: The Road to Olustee* (Tuscaloosa: University of Alabama Press, 1990); U.S. War Department, *War of the Rebellion: A Compilation of the Official Records of the Union and Confederate Armies*, 128 vols. (Washington, D.C.: Government Printing Office, 1880–1901), 1st ser., 35 (1):276 (hereafter cited as *OR*). Nulty's book is the most comprehensive study of the campaign. An older work is George F. Baltzell, "The Battle of Olustee (Ocean Pond), Florida," *Florida Historical Quarterly* 9 (April 1931): 199–223. The most recent study of the role of the black units at Olustee appears in Noah Andre Trudeau, *Like Men of War: Black Troops in the Civil War, 1861–1865* (New York: Little, Brown, 1998).

2. Ezra J. Warner, *Generals in Blue: Lives of the Union Commanders* (Baton Rouge: Louisiana State University Press, 1964), 432–33; John T. Hubbell and James W. Geary, eds., *Biographical Dictionary of the Union: Northern Leaders of the Civil War* (Westport, Conn.: Greenwood Press, 1995), 467; Stephen R. Wise, *Gate of Hell: Campaign for Charleston Harbor, 1863* (Columbia: University of South Carolina Press, 1994), 99–100. See also John C. Waugh, *The Class of 1846: From West Point to Appomattox: Stonewall Jackson, George McClellan and Their Brothers* (New York: Warner Books, 1994), 183–84.

3. Warner, *Generals in Blue*, 433.

4. *OR*, 1st ser., 35 (1):276, 281–82, 295–96, 321–22, 330–31; Joseph T. Wilson, *The Black Phalanx: A History of the Negro Soldiers of the United States in the Wars of 1775–1812, 1861–'65* (Hartford: American Publishing Company, 1888), 265.

5. *OR*, 1st ser., 35 (1):298, 312; Frederick H. Dyer, *A Compendium of the War of the*

Rebellion, 3 vols. (1908; New York: Thomas Yoseloff, 1959), 3:1725; Wilson, *The Black Phalanx*, 265.

6. Dudley Taylor Cornish, *The Sable Arm: Negro Troops in the Union Army, 1861–1865* (New York: W. W. Norton, 1966), 70, 72–74, 104; Richard Reid, "Raising the African Brigade: Early Black Recruitment in Civil War North Carolina," *North Carolina Historical Review* 70 (July 1993): 266–97; Dyer, *A Compendium of the War of the Rebellion*, 3:1472, 1729; *New York Times*, March 1, 1864.

7. Dyer, *A Compendium of the War of the Rebellion*, 3:1266; Cornish, *The Sable Arm*, 106; *OR*, 1st ser., 35 (1):315. See also Luis F. Emilio, *A Brave Black Regiment: History of the 54th Massachusetts Volunteer Infantry* (Boston: Boston Book Company, 1894) and Peter Burchard, *One Gallant Rush: Robert Gould Shaw and His Brave Black Regiment* (New York: St. Martin's Press, 1965).

8. Donald Yacovone, ed., *A Voice of Thunder: The Civil War Letters of George E. Stephens* (Urbana: University of Illinois Press, 1997), 295; *OR*, 1st ser., 35 (1):288, 303, 315.

9. *New York Times*, March 1, 1864.

10. Oliver W. Norton, *Army Letters, 1861–1865* (Dayton, Ohio: Morningside, 1990), 198; *OR*, 1st ser., 35 (1):288–89, 303–4; Wilson, *The Black Phalanx*, 266.

11. Norton, *Army Letters*, 198; *OR*, 1st ser., 35 (1):311–12.

12. *Christian Recorder*, April 16, 1864 (hereafter cited as *CR*).

13. Ibid.; Norton, *Army Letters*, 198, 202.

14. "Bronte" to Editor, *Army and Navy Journal*, July 24, 1875, 798.

15. Norton, *Army Letters*, 198, 202; *OR*, 1st ser., 35 (1):289, 304, 311.

16. *Army and Navy Journal*, July 24, 1875, 798.

17. *Brookville Republican*, March 23, 1864.

18. Norton, *Army Letters*, 198–99, 202; *OR*, 1st ser., 35 (1):312.

19. *New York Times*, March 1, 1864.

20. *OR*, 1st ser., 35 (1):312–14; *Army and Navy Journal*, July 24, 1875, 798; Norton, *Army Letters*, 199, 202; *CR*, April 16, 1864; *Philadelphia Press*, March 10, 1864.

21. Yacovone, *A Voice of Thunder*, 296; *OR*, 1st ser., 35 (1):289, 315; *Boston Journal*, March 2, 1864; *Worcester (Mass.) Aegis and Transcript*, April 2, 1864; Emilio, *A Brave Black Regiment*, 162; Wilson, *The Black Phalanx*, 267.

22. *Burlington (Vt.) Free Press*, March 22, 1864.

23. Wilson, *The Black Phalanx*, 267.

24. Emilio, *A Brave Black Regiment*, 163.

25. Yacovone, *A Voice of Thunder*, 296–97; Emilio, *A Brave Black Regiment*, 165–66.

26. *Xenia (Ohio) Torchlight*, March 16, 1864.

27. *OR*, 1st ser., 35 (1):289.

28. *Philadelphia Press*, March 16, 1864.

29. *OR*, 1st ser., 35 (1):289; *Worcester Aegis and Transcript*, April 2, 1864; *New York Herald*, March 1, 1864.

30. *Burlington Free Press*, March 22, 1864; *OR*, 1st ser., 35 (1):289, 315; Yacovone, *A Voice of Thunder*, 298.

31. Yacovone, *A Voice of Thunder*, 297.

32. *Weekly Anglo-African* (New York), March 26, 1864.

33. *OR*, 1st ser., 35 (1):298, 312, 315, 337, 342; Virginia Matzke Adams, ed., *On the Altar of Freedom: A Black Soldier's Civil War Letters from the Front* (Amherst: University of Massachusetts Press, 1991), 114–15; *New York Times*, March 1, 8, 1864. In his study of the campaign, William Nulty pointed out that "on the basis of the percentage of casualties, the battle of Olustee was the third bloodiest of the entire war" (*Confederate Florida*, 203).

34. *OR*, 1st ser., 35 (1):312–14; Norton, *Army Letters*, 199; *Boston Journal*, March 2, 1864.

35. Lawrence Jackson, "As I Saw and Remember the Battle of Olustee, Which Was Fought February 20, 1864," copy in Olustee Battlefield Museum.

36. *Worcester Aegis and Transcript*, April 2, 1864. See also Nulty, *Confederate Florida*, 210–13, and Trudeau, *Like Men of War*, 151.

37. William Marvel, *Andersonville: The Last Depot* (Chapel Hill: University of North Carolina Press, 1994), 41–44, 154–55.

38. *New York Times*, March 1, 1864; Wilson, *The Black Phalanx*, 267.

39. *New York Times*, March 14, 1864.

40. Yacovone, *A Voice of Thunder*, 297; *OR*, 1st ser., 35 (1):290.

41. *Boston Journal*, March 2, 1864.

42. *Worcester Aegis and Transcript*, April 2, 1864.

43. *Army and Navy Journal*, May 7, 1864, 614.

44. *OR*, 1st ser., 35 (1):312.

45. Norton, *Army Letters*, 204.

46. *Army and Navy Journal*, July 24, 1875, 798.

THE FORT PILLOW MASSACRE
Assessing the Evidence
John Cimprich

At dawn on April 12, 1864, a force of some 1,500 Confederates began a surprise attack on Fort Pillow, a post in Tennessee about fifty miles north of Memphis. The Federal garrison consisted of around 600 men. Detachments from the 6th U.S. Colored Heavy Artillery (USCHA) and the 2nd U.S. Colored Light Artillery composed about half of the garrison, while Major William F. Bradford's Tennessee Cavalry Battalion of white Unionists made up the rest. By 2:00 P.M. the outnumbered Federals had retreated to an inner fortification on a bluff above the Mississippi River, while the Confederates held ravines to the north and east as well as barracks cabins to the south. Major General Nathan Bedford Forrest, the Confederate commander, then called a truce to request the fort's surrender. Bradford, the Federal leader at that point, refused. Around 3:15 the Confederates charged and gained control of the fort. Controversy would arise about the subsequent events, which ended with almost half of the garrison dead. The survivors called it a massacre of men who tried to surrender; the Confederates claimed that the Federals refused to stop fighting or fleeing. Since 1973 most historians who have written about the incident have judged it a massacre.[1] But during the Civil War the public learned about the event piecemeal over time—like an unfolding mystery story. In that fashion but with the larger pool of evidence available today, this essay offers a critical examination of the primary sources and their treatment by recent historians.

Federal Sources

On the morning following the battle the Union gunboat *Silver Cloud* and the passenger steamer *Platte Valley* landed at the fort after Confederates offered a truce for turning over wounded Federals. Other vessels stopped later in the day. Most of the first pieces of Federal evidence came from newspaper correspondents and military personnel aboard these ships, and most of the authors obtained a highly consistent story from survivors about a massacre after the fort's fall. The fullest version, appearing in the *Missouri Democrat*, summarized separate interviews with Private Daniel W. Harrison (Bradford's battalion), Corporal Jacob Wilson (6th USCHA), and Dr. Charles Fitch (post surgeon). Each witness's later testimony was consistent with that given on April 13.[2]

From ten second-hand accounts and three first-hand ones completed very soon after the incident, a basic narrative of the event emerged. The larger force of Confederates assaulting the fort overwhelmed the garrison. Routed Federals fled down the bluff, found themselves surrounded, and tried to surrender only to discover that few Confederates would grant quarter. Many, especially among the blacks, died before the massacre ended. Given the number of survivors and interviewers, it seems highly unlikely that the story originated in peer pressure or collaborative lying. Furthermore, a statistical analysis published in 1989 has confirmed the disproportionate number of African American casualties.[3]

Some of the reporters and Federals asked Confederate officers about the incident. According to several accounts, Brigadier General James Chalmers, Forrest's second-in-command at the battle, and a few other officers admitted that a massacre occurred because they could not control enlisted men infuriated by fighting blacks. The Federal government was pursuing a controversial policy in recruiting blacks, especially runaway Southern slaves, during the war. Before the attack on Fort Pillow, none of the Confederates present had engaged in close combat with African American troops. Chalmers stressed that neither he nor Forrest had ordered the massacre. One journalist who talked to a number of enemy officers found that most claimed the numerous deaths resulted from the Federals' refusal to surrender.[4] The reporting parties obviously could have distorted their enemies' statements, but the same two versions of the event would also appear in early Confederate documents.

On April 14 some wounded arrived in Memphis, and the *Memphis Bulletin* reported that an "indiscriminant massacre" had taken place at Fort Pillow.

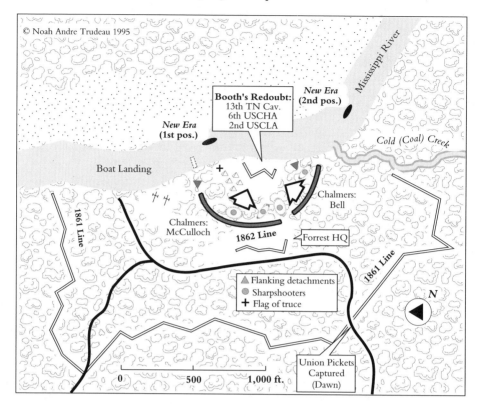

Map 5.1. The Massacre at Fort Pillow, Tennessee, April 12, 1864.
(Courtesy of Noah Andre Trudeau)

The same day, while delivering wounded men to an upriver hospital, the *Platte Valley* stopped at Cairo, Illinois, and an Associated Press (AP) telegram from that town spread the news across the North. The AP report stated that Confederates gained the upper hand by moving troops closer during the truce (a claim made as well in a report the same day by Lieutenant Daniel Van Horne, a survivor from the 6th USCHA). The AP dispatch, which incorrectly implied that a massacre occurred after the fort's surrender, also accused the enemy of killing civilians and burning to death some wounded Federals. Another AP dispatch on April 15 charged the enemy with burying some of the wounded alive. The new details about additional atrocities probably originated with the survivors who would soon give similar testimony about the incident. On April 16 Secretary of War Edwin Stanton ordered an army investigation; two days later the congressional Joint Committee on the Conduct of the War decided to study the matter as well.[5]

Army investigators collected sworn affidavits from twenty-seven survivors, mostly soldiers but also a few civilians, between April 17 and 30. Several different individuals conducted the effort. The results seem to indicate that they had directions to take short, factual statements from witnesses about what they saw happen and who the people involved were. The set of documents additionally included Lieutenant Van Horn's report, as well as statements, some sworn and some not, by eight visitors to the fort on the day after the incident.[6]

The army documents elaborate on several allegations related to the massacre. Two Federals said that they watched the enemy kill civilians. Three women witnesses reported finding on April 13 the burning body of a Federal who seemed nailed to wood planks. Six soldiers claimed Confederates violated the truce by moving closer to the fort, although a deponent who had fought at a canon port near the barracks disproved stories that Confederates took those cabins during the truce.[7] The congressional subcommittee would look more deeply into these matters.

Overlapping their work with that of the army investigators, Senator Benjamin F. Wade, a Radical Republican, and Congressman Daniel Gooch, a more moderate member of the same party, conducted interviews with fifty-one survivors and a variety of other people between April 22 and 26. Besides taking more affidavits than the army investigators did, they generally obtained longer and more specific statements. Their questions appeared in the record, which was not true of most of the army affidavits. They usually began with an open-ended query—such as "What did you see done there?"—and then moved to requests for either elaboration of a statement or more detail on a specific allegation raised in newspapers. Forrest later claimed that the narrower questioning amounted to leading the witnesses. However, Wade and Gooch conducted a legislative inquiry seeking detailed and concrete information regarding all the particular charges appearing in newspapers, rather than a trial in which most queries with "yes" or "no" answers would have been excluded as leading questions. Furthermore, witnesses do not appear to have been led, for far more stated that they did not see the burning or burying of wounded Federals than did. A few reported that they did not observe Confederates violating the truce or killing civilians. To their credit, the interrogators always drew a distinction between seeing an act and hearing talk about it. Their questions also avoided emotional phrasing.[8]

All of the eyewitnesses described the culminating events at Fort Pillow as a massacre. The congressmen often asked about soldiers' wounds and

*"The War in Tennessee—Rebel Massacre of the Union Troops after the Surrender at Fort Pillow, April 12." (*Frank Leslie's Illustrated Newspaper, *May 7, 1864, Hargrett Rare Book and Manuscript Library, University of Georgia Libraries)*

learned that most occurred after the fort fell. Soldiers also reported that the massacring Confederates stressed their hostility toward black soldiers for "fighting against your master" and toward white Unionists who "fight side by side with niggers."[9] This testimony provided much corroboration for the evidence about the occurrence of a massacre.

The two members of Congress obtained more testimony about the subsidiary allegations than the army did, although this still involved relatively few witnesses. Several speakers reported truce violations similar to those described in the army affidavits. One of these witnesses had noticed Confederate officers moving with men into the fort's trench, something much later verified by one of those officers. While early Confederate documents show that they first entered ravines and barracks close to the fort before the truce, an illegitimate reinforcement of those forces may have occurred during the truce.[10]

Three soldiers reported the killing of black women and children. Testimony from Federal sailors mentioned burying one or two women in the fort on April 13. One wounded black woman reached the army hospital at Mound City, Illinois, only to die there. Workers would find two children's graves in the fort in 1868 but without any indication of when they died.[11] So, Confederates did kill at least a few women either accidentally or deliberately.

The evidence regarding the charge that Confederates buried wounded Federals resembles that concerning the killing of civilians. On April 13 sailors dug out one barely alive soldier who died soon afterward. Another soldier, Private Daniel Tyler of the 6th USCHA, admitted that he was acting dead for fear of being killed when others picked him up and tossed him into a burial trench. A Confederate noticed that he was alive and rescued him. Crews could have buried other Federals feigning death or unconscious from severe wounds. A Confederate newspaper correspondent admitted in May 1864 that for the fun of seeing their "resurrection" he deliberately buried some Federals who were acting dead.[12] Only a few individuals participated in this activity, which may not have been intentional murder.

Several witnesses encountered burnt bodies, two of which seemed nailed to wooden planks. Two Federals claimed to have seen cabins of wounded Federals set afire on the morning of April 13. The Confederates set the blazes in haste during a bombardment by the *Silver Cloud* before the truce. Lieutenant Mack Leaming of Bradford's battalion noted that the hut where he had rested was torched just as Confederates received a warning that men remained inside. His testimony did not specifically attribute fault to the Confederates, as would a report written nine months later, possibly after angry brooding. Several Federals testified that Confederates helped them out of huts or tents before starting fires.[13] Proof of the deliberate burning of wounded Federals therefore is limited and lacks support from other types of evidence. Testimony about the subsidiary charges the congressmen made either sounded inconclusive or could only substantiate wrongdoing on a small scale.

The congressional committee held that the massacre flowed from a hostile Confederate policy toward black troops, but it did not directly comment on what several witnesses implied: that Forrest permitted the massacre. Jacob Thompson, a contraband cook, claimed to recognize Forrest during the massacre yet described the general's appearance incorrectly. Sergeant Benjamin Robinson saw an officer whom Confederates referred to as Forrest. Several soldiers heard Confederates say that Forrest ordered the massacre. On the other hand, one Federal reported hearing an officer shout that Forrest wanted prisoners protected, and several watched officers trying to stop the killing.[14]

Forrest later charged the committee with bias against the Confederates. Hostile and unqualified statements in the congressional report supported him to some degree. However, nothing backed his assertion that Federal soldiers received instructions to give prepared testimony. In fact, in an April 17 letter to relatives Charley Robinson, a civilian combatant who could not have come under military pressure, corroborated several points raised by the two investigations. He affirmed that some Confederates sneaked into the fort's trench during the truce, that Federals fled down the bluff, and that an ugly massacre ensued when Federals tried to surrender after throwing down their guns. Further support for these points came from the *Missouri Democrat*'s interview with Edward B. Benton, another civilian who fought at the fort, and from an unpublished report by Charles Fitch, a contract surgeon. Robinson, Benton, and Fitch composed their accounts at about the same time.[15]

Lonnie E. Maness, a historian who rejects the massacre thesis, has questioned the reliability of Fitch's report on account of incorrect statements about the removal of all women and children from the fort, the occupation of the barracks in violation of the truce, and the number of captured Federals. The log of the Federal gunboat (No. 7 or *New Era*) agrees with Fitch's statement that "the women, children and most of the Citizens of the Fort, had got into a coal barge, and were towed by the Gun Boat, No. 7, Up the River." Apparently, everyone around the river landing did not know of the few remaining individuals mentioned by three other witnesses. Forty black women and children captured by Forrest's men most likely were caught in the fort's contraband camp or at Edward Benton's plantation. The quarters of Benton's contracted laborers lay just beyond the fort's outer earthworks.[16] In regard to the alleged violation of the truce, Fitch, who could not have seen it from his field hospital on the riverbank, carelessly repeated an inaccurate story circulated by some other survivors. That alone should not discredit him. As for the captured Federals, Fitch referred only to the group of 101 to which he belonged, rather than to all of the prisoners, as Maness has assumed. Captives came to the river landing from several different locations on April 13 for paroling. No one present that day had a solid knowledge of all the incident's statistics. Maness has also speculated that a very reluctant Fitch caved in to peer pressure to write a falsified report. Fitch, however, had made all the same major points about a massacre in his April 13 interview with the *Missouri Democrat* reporter. He did not testify in the army or congressional investigations probably because he had received a leave to recuperate from his wound at home in Iowa.[17]

After the war only two Federal survivors wrote about the incident. Neither responded to the defensive arguments hammered out by postwar Confederate writers, and both kept their comments brief. Dr. Fitch wrote a letter to Confederate general Chalmers in which he gave a brief description of the massacre but exonerated both Chalmers and Forrest from responsibility. Lieutenant Thomas McClure, though, declared that he heard the two enemy generals speak approvingly of the massacre.[18] While the generals may have had such thoughts, that did not prove that they initiated or permitted the incident. The occurrence of a spontaneous massacre is the more common theme running through the Federal evidence.

Confederate Evidence

Confederate diary entries for April 12 and letters written shortly afterward all agreed that the Federals at Fort Pillow suffered a high death toll. Estimates ranged from 65 percent to 86 percent. Most of these documents simply celebrated the victory without elaboration. Forrest's letter to Confederate president Jefferson Davis on April 15 blamed the Federals for continuing to fight or attempting to escape rather than surrendering. He also made the claim, unique among all the early sources, that Federals retreated, rather than fled, to the riverbank.[19] This claim could have several different origins. Forrest and other Confederates, who stayed on top of the bluff, may not have heard or seen the events that took place primarily on the riverbank. Very soon after the incident, subordinates could have misinformed Forrest; or — out of a sincere belief in his comrades' innocence — he may have begun rationalizing the question of who was to blame by attributing culpability to the other side. If he knew about the massacre, then he quickly covered it up with denials and rationalizations. The current body of evidence does not resolve the matter.

In a dispatch to the *Mobile Advertiser and Register*, however, the correspondent "Vidette" stated that "an indiscriminate slaughter followed [the battle.] . . . The fort ran with blood; many jumped into the river and drowned or [were] shot." Sergeant Achilles V. Clark's letter to his sisters elaborated more vividly:

> Our men were so exasperated by the Yankees' threats of no quarter that they gave but little. The slaughter was awful. Words cannot describe the

*"Massacre at Fort Pillow, Tennessee, detail." (*Harper's Weekly, *April 30, 1864, N.C. Division of Historical Resources, Raleigh)*

scene. The poor deluded negroes would run up to our men fall on their knees and with uplifted hands scream for mercy but they were ordered to their feet and then shot down. The whitte [*sic*] men fared but little better. Their fort turned out to be a great slaughter pen. Blood, human blood stood about in pools and brains could have been gathered up in any quantity. I with several others tried to stop the butchery and at one time had partially succeeded. but [*sic*] Gen. Forrest ordered them shot down like dogs.

Clark and another Confederate writer held that bantering between the lines during the truce before the final assault had stirred up the Confederate ranks.[20]

The historian Lonnie E. Maness has judged Clark an unreliable source because of the sergeant's supposed errors regarding the number of defenders, the time of the final charge, the location of most of the killing, and Forrest's role. Clark did erroneously give the Federal garrison's size as 790. However, Forrest and most other Confederate sources also overestimated their enemy's numbers as between 700 and 800 men, apparently because of something misleading in the captured post records. Maness has Clark placing the final assault at 2:20, presumably because Clark stated that "[a]t 2 P.M. Gen. Forrest demanded a surrender and gave twenty minutes to consider," but Clark actually mentioned no specific time for the attack. Because of Bradford's delaying tactics and Forrest's final battle preparations, the charge probably came at about 3:15 (the time given in the New Era's log). The sergeant did not explicitly say where most of the killing occurred, although he focused his attention on the riverbank. Maness believes that it took place mostly in the fort, but the matter is at least debatable. Despite all of Maness's suspicions, Clark conveys the sincerity of a conscientious man troubled by what he had observed, as indicated by the line "In as much as I am a member of Forrest's Cavalry modesty would direct that I say nothing in our praise nor will I but will tell you . . . what was done and leave you to judge whether or not we acted well or ill."[21] Furthermore, it seems very hard to believe that in a family letter a Confederate would falsely accuse his comrades of committing a massacre.

Sergeant Clark did not explain why he thought Forrest had ordered a massacre. He would have been incorrect if he had placed Forrest in the melee after Confederates entered the fort, for the general observed the charge from outside and then focused first on redirecting captured artillery against the gunboat New Era. But neither Clark nor any one else ever explicitly claimed to have heard Forrest issue a massacre order. As a young man who had enlisted just a few months earlier, the sergeant may have believed Confederates who went about the battlefield shouting that Forrest had ordered that blacks be killed. It is possible that the general called for a massacre after the charge's success, but several witnesses stated that he soon ordered the shooting stopped. Surgeon Samuel H. Caldwell reported to his wife a story that "[t]hey refused to surrender—which incensed our men & if General Forrest had not run between our men & the Yanks with his pistol and sabre drawn not a man would have been spared."[22] Leaving aside the question of whether or not Caldwell, whose duties kept him in the rear, had heard an accurate account, no sensible commander would try to halt only his side's firing while the enemy persisted in fighting.

Confederates first experienced the hostile Federal reaction to the incident through pointed questions, which Union reporters and officers directed toward the small group present on April 13 during the truce for releasing wounded Federals. Those Confederates included Major Charles Anderson, three cavalrymen detached from Forrest's escort, General Chalmers, and Chalmers's staff. Forrest and the rest of his escort had already left the fort. Only Anderson and the detached escort members rejoined Forrest at Jackson, Tennessee, where someone composed the first defensive account of the incident on April 18. Probably not enough time had elapsed for the writer to have seen the allegations in Northern newspapers. The letter, signed "Memphis," appeared in the *Memphis Appeal*, which at the time was being published in Atlanta. It admitted that "[t]he sight of negro soldiers stirred the bosoms of our soldiers with courageous madness," but it emphasized that "the enemy would not surrender." They either kept firing or trying to escape, so that "[n]ot the first sign of surrender was ever given." Furthermore, "Gen. Forrest expected a surrender after entering the fort, and anxiously looked for it as he witnessed the carnage." The correspondent mentioned that the Federals failed to lower their flag as a sign of group surrender, which was true, but giving such a signal would have been difficult to do after the rout. Unlike some of the other early accounts, the one provided by "Memphis" implied that no Federal attempted an individual surrender.[23]

Shortly after the "Memphis" letter, "Marion" from the 2nd Tennessee Cavalry, which had moved from Fort Pillow to Okolona, Mississippi, wrote to the *Mobile Advertiser and Register*. He stated that the final charge routed the Federals and that "the whites received quarter, but the negroes were shown no mercy."[24] The letter from "Marion" was the last Confederate document to appear in 1864 that acknowledged that a massacre had occurred. Once Federal outrage became well known, subsequent Confederate statements took on a defensive tone.

By April 25 Forrest knew about the Union newspapers' allegations against his army and had decided to write a rebuttal. His expanded report of April 26 held that the Federals "retreated toward the river, arms in hand and firing back, and their colors flying," in a "short but desperate struggle." He reduced his estimate of the time of the final fight from thirty to twenty minutes, the same figure an undated report by Major Anderson gave. Anderson, who commanded a force engaged below the bluff, definitely knew what happened there. He endorsed Forrest's view about Federal casualties, and thus, if a massacre did occur, he either rationalized it away or tried to hide his men's guilt. Chalmers's report, completed on May 7, ignored the massacre issue and only referred to numerous Federal casualties caused by efforts at escaping rather than surrendering. In mid-May Isham G. Harris, the exiled Confederate governor of Tennessee who had accompanied Forrest's army, gave a newspaper interview in which he, like the general, contended that most of the Federals kept up a desperate defense. Yet he not only reported seeing a Federal rout below the bluff; he also admitted that "a few, black and white, threw down their arms and made signs of surrender." Harris excused their deaths because "in the heat, din, and confusion of a fire of such close quarters there was no chance of discrimination."[25]

On May 13 the *Memphis Appeal* published a letter from Forrest's headquarters by "G.W.A." (if the "G." was a typo, the author likely was Charles W. Anderson). "G.W.A." registered the first claim that many Federals were drunk. Both sides during the Civil War made repeated use of this common propagandist device for discrediting opponents who put up a particularly tough fight. After several millennia of experience with alcohol, society knew that it harmed both judgment and effectiveness. A mass distribution of liquor during a battle would have demonstrated extreme foolishness and would hardly have gone unmentioned by so many Federal witnesses. Several members of Bradford's battalion and one officer of the 6th USCHA had already accused each other's units of cowardly flight before the Confederates.[26] The new allegation was a highly questionable one.

Forrest explicitly denied the occurrence of a massacre in correspondence with a Federal general in June 1864. He stressed that "[i]n all my operations since the war began I have conducted the war on civilized principles." In an interview at the war's end he implied that blacks made inherently untruthful witnesses. He also endorsed the allegation of Federal drunkenness and asserted that open whiskey and beer barrels in the fort proved it, although he did not profess to having seen the barrels himself. In 1868 Forrest's authorized biography specified Colonel Clark Barteau of the 2nd Tennessee Cavalry as the source of this information. Barteau may have felt impelled to defend a portion of his regiment, which, like Anderson's men, played a major role in the action below the bluff.[27]

Thomas Jordan and John P. Pryor based the first Forrest biography largely on his memory and records. The work contains a highly defensive chapter on Fort Pillow so often consulted by subsequent writers that it crystallized the orthodox pro-Confederate view of the incident. Its key arguments for explaining the high Union death toll were that (1) Federal depredations provoked Confederates to fight hard; (2) drunkenness made the Federals irrational; and (3) the Federals desperately resisted surrender much too long.

Only the last allegation had appeared immediately after the incident and was consistently repeated by many witnesses, including Forrest. Thus it carries the most weight. Although numerous Federals testified that their side threw down weapons in an attempt to surrender, a Confederate refusal to grant quarter could easily have motivated some to seek escape or to continue fighting. One Northern newspaper interview with wounded men in the hospital reported exactly that. The low number of Confederate casualties could indicate that ongoing Federal resistance was light. Most significantly, the admission of a massacre by several Confederates undermined the argument that desperate resistance caused the high death toll.[28]

The contention about Federal depredations appeared rarely before 1868. Before the battle Forrest had only complained about the confinement of a local preacher without charge at Fort Pillow, but three days after the battle he blamed all West Tennessee Unionist regiments for "oppression, murder, and plunder." The specifics he mentioned involved only Colonel Fielding Hurst's poorly disciplined regiment, which may have tarred the reputations of the others. Bradford's battalion certainly appropriated food and horses from civilians, as did both the fort's preceding Federal garrison and Forrest's army. Bradford arrested only one of his men for looting, and, even if he was a poor disciplinarian, the unit merely served two months at the fort. Jordan and Pryor in 1868 added rape to the charges, probably as an embroiderment, since Forrest's men had no reason to withhold the allegation earlier (one Confederate had publicly accused black troops of rape during the Brice's Crossroads campaign in June 1864). The protection of women's honor and sexual purity figured prominently in the postwar "Lost Cause" movement, which defended and glorified the Confederates as morally upright crusaders. The only antagonistic act charged against the black troops in the 1868 Forrest biography was that of having "indulged in provoking, impudent jeers" during the truce. Both previous Confederate sources that mentioned this talk blamed it on the entire garrison, rather than singling out the blacks.[29]

Jordan and Pryor denied the subsidiary allegations made by the Federals. The truce violation issue alone received much attention. They asserted that "in large part" it arose from Federal misunderstanding of Forrest's decision to move several companies under Anderson to the riverbank during the truce to stop steamboats from landing with reinforcements. But no Federal specifically mentioned any movement in that direction, thus weakening the argument.[30]

Jordan and Pryor's most extreme contention was that the war code of Western civilization permitted unrestricted killing when an enemy refused to surrender an untenable position. No subsequent writer explicitly repeated this self-serving argument, but many hinted at agreement by emphasizing the post's rejection of Forrest's surrender request, as if that justified killing all Federals until Forrest stopped the fighting by having the Federal flag cut down. Major Anderson notably stressed that he had strict orders to "fight everything '*blue*' between wind and water until yonder flag comes down."[31] This argument may constitute the key rationalization for the killing.

Because ex-Confederates like Forrest gradually regained cultural and political dominance in the South on a platform of unified white supremacy, the biography helped to place the "Lost Cause" version of the war in the center of Southern identity and to lionize the general as a folk hero. Many subsequent accounts by Confederates present at Fort Pillow followed Jordan and Pryor's lead by stressing Federal depredations, drunkenness, and desperate fighting. Several appeared in the *Confederate Veteran*, a mouthpiece of "Lost Cause" thinking.[32] However, just six ex-Confederates (all but one responding to an 1898 questionnaire) joined Barteau in specifically stating that they saw whiskey barrels in the fort; none of them mentioned the beer Barteau thought he saw.[33] A semantic issue clouds this matter. A large amount of liquor was unquestionably found by Confederates within Fort Pillow in traders' warehouses, but those buildings sat away from the inner fort where the battle occurred. Some of the witnesses could have meant nothing more than that.[34]

A few postwar reminiscences made major admissions about the incident. Most significantly, John W. Carroll, like several witnesses in the Federal investigations, reported that "while the flag of truce was up, Captain James Stinett and I with some picked men crawled up close under the guns to be ready in case they refused to surrender, to prevent them from discharging their cannon into our ranks, which we successfully did." Several Confederates granted that some Federals tried to surrender, and William J. Shaw admitted that some of his comrades refused to accept surrendering Federals. Thomas F. Berry alone acknowledged that a massacre occurred.[35]

Berry's 1914 version of events, however, contained a slew of factual errors. Distorted memories appeared in others' narratives too. Both Berry and G. A. Hanson told the completely spurious story that the garrison officially surrendered to stop the Confederates' fire and then dishonorably resumed the shooting. James Dinkins in 1897 became the only eyewitness to make the questionable assertions that the black units participated in depredations, including the rape of white women, that Confederates fought their way into the fort's trench before the truce, and that many Federals died by falling down the bluff. Some reduced the time of the final round of fighting to fifteen minutes or less. Ex-Confederates writing long after the controversial incident often sounded excessively defensive as they grasped for numerous and sometimes imaginary straws of argument.[36]

To counter the congressional report's sworn testimony, John Wyeth, a Forrest admirer, sent in 1898 a number of Confederate witnesses copies of the report and requested sworn affidavits about the incident in return. Recurrent phrasing in the responses suggests that he asked them to comment on certain controversial points: (1) "that the testimony of certain witnesses made before the subcommittee of the United States Congress, stating that a massacre of the garrison took place after the fort was captured, is false," (2) that Confederates did nothing that justified the congressional report, (3) that the garrison never surrendered but either kept fighting or sought escape, (4) that the respondent saw whiskey in the fort, and (5) that the Federals acted drunk. Wyeth claimed that his deponents unanimously swore agreement to the first three points; nearly all affirmed Federal drunkenness and the sighting of whiskey. Unfortunately, nothing remains of the affidavits today other than what the author included in his book: one full document and some excerpts. Since Wyeth's directions and his analysis of the resulting affidavits may have been open to self-serving interpretations, historians would benefit from seeing the documents. Contrary to a claim by Wyeth, Anderson's affidavit, the one fully given, did not say he saw the whiskey.[37] These matters raise questions about Wyeth's interpretation of the now missing documents.

Conclusions

The primary sources for the Fort Pillow incident contain many conflicting statements. The historian must carefully evaluate each author's motives and role in the event, as well as each recollection's closeness in time to April 12, 1864. In 1958 the historian Albert Castel, using little more than the congressional report and published army documents, argued that while the Federal evidence very consistently supported the charge that Federals were massacred, all the subsidiary charges seemed questionable. Castel's seminal essay also pointed out inconsistencies in the defensive statements of Confederates.[38]

Other evidence found since then in newspapers, rare books, and document collections corroborates Castel's views, except for his doubts about a truce violation and civilian casualties. These documents include the early Confederate admissions of a massacre. It becomes clear that Confederate defensiveness arose in response to Federal criticism. Pieces of Federal evidence located in the last thirty years fit with the rest in exhibiting much consistency on the essential point that a massacre occurred.[39] The decision of some Federals to flee or resist may have unnecessarily increased their side's casualties after the fort fell, but early accounts from both sides speak of numerous individual efforts to surrender. Consequently, nearly all historians publishing on the subject today hold that a massacre took place, that some

Confederates tried to cover it up, and that some Northerners tried to exploit the event to aid the war effort.[40]

Notes

1. Richard L. Fuchs, *An Unerring Fire: The Massacre at Fort Pillow* (Rutherford, N.J.: Farleigh Dickinson University Press, 1994), 55–58; John Cimprich and Robert C. Mainfort, Jr., "The Fort Pillow Massacre: A Statistical Note," *Journal of American History* 76 (December 1989): 831–33; John Cimprich and Robert C. Mainfort, Jr., eds., "Fort Pillow Revisited: New Evidence about an Old Controversy," *Civil War History* 28 (December 1982): 294. Bradford's battalion at first called itself the 13th Tennessee Cavalry, but—because another unit had already received that designation—it became the 14th in August 1864.

2. *Missouri Democrat* (St. Louis), April 16, 1864; *St. Louis Union*, April 16, 1864; U.S. Navy Department, *Official Records of the Union and Confederate Navies in the War of the Rebellion*, 31 vols. (Washington, D.C.: Government Printing Office, 1894–1927), 1st ser., 26:225–26 (hereafter cited as *ORN*); *Illinois State Journal* (Springfield), April 18, 1864; *Cincinnati Commercial*, April 20, 1864; *New York Times*, May 3, 1864; U.S. War Department, *The War of the Rebellion: A Compilation of the Official Records of the Union and Confederate Armies*, 128 vols. (Washington, D.C.: Government Printing Office, 1880–1901), 1st ser., 32 (1):539, 558, 563, 568–69, 571 (hereafter cited as *OR*); "Fort Pillow Massacre," U.S. Congress, *House Report* (serial 1206), 38th Cong., 1st sess., No. 63, 35; John Cimprich and Robert C. Mainfort, Jr., eds., "Dr. Fitch's Report on the Fort Pillow Massacre," *Tennessee Historical Quarterly* 44 (Spring 1985): 28–37.

3. Accounts other than those listed in n. 2 are *OR*, 1st ser., 32 (1):566–67, 570; *ORN*, 1st ser., 26:220. On casualty figures, see Cimprich and Mainfort, "The Fort Pillow Massacre," 835–36.

4. *Missouri Democrat*, April 16, 1864; *St. Louis Union*, April 16, 1864; *ORN*, 1st ser., 26:225–26; *OR*, 1st ser., 32 (1):558; *New York Times*, May 3, 1864; Brian S. Wills, *A Battle from the Start: The Life of Nathan Bedford Forrest* (New York: HarperCollins, 1992), 176–77.

5. *OR*, 1st ser., 32 (1):570, (3):381; *House Report* (serial 1206), No. 63, 1. The AP dispatches were printed on April 15 and 16.

6. *OR*, 1st ser., 32 (1):519–71.

7. Ibid., 522–25, 527, 530, 532–33, 569.

8. *House Report* (serial 1206), No. 63, 15–95.

9. Ibid., 22, 36.

10. *House Report* (serial 1206), No. 63, 4–5, 43, 47, 51, 86, 120; Fuchs, *An Unerring Fire*, 103.

11. *House Report* (serial 1206), No. 63, 26, 46, 50, 58–59, 90; *New Era* Log, April 13, 1864, Record Group (RG) 24, National Archives (NA), Washington, D.C.; Rolls

of Remains at Ft. Pillow, 1867, Cemetery Files (Memphis), RG 92, NA; Mound City Hospital Register #125, 9, RG 94, NA.

12. *House Report* (serial 1206), No. 63, 18, 87, 95; *Memphis Appeal* (Atlanta), June 14, 1864.

13. *House Report* (serial 1206), No. 63, 27, 30–31, 40, 42, 44, 50, 82, 91; *OR*, 1st ser., 32 (1):562; Thomas Jordan and J. P. Pryor, *The Campaigns of Lieut. Gen. N. B. Forrest and of Forrest's Cavalry* (New York: Blelock & Company, 1869), 445.

14. *House Report* (serial 1206), No. 63, 18, 26, 30, 34, 40, 44–47.

15. LeRoy P. Graf et al., eds., *The Papers of Andrew Johnson*, 16 vols. (Knoxville: University of Tennessee Press, 1967–2000), 11:484–85; George Bodnia, ed., "Fort Pillow 'Massacre': Observations of a Minnesotan," *Minnesota History* 43 (Spring 1973): 188; *Missouri Democrat*, April 22, 1864; Cimprich and Mainfort, "Dr. Fitch's Report," 31–36.

16. Lonnie E. Maness, "The Fort Pillow Massacre: Fact or Fiction," *Tennessee Historical Quarterly* 45 (Winter 1986): 294; *New Era* Log, April 12, 1864; Cimprich and Mainfort, "Dr. Fitch's Report," 30–31, 38; *House Report* (serial 1206), No. 63, 26, 46, 50; *OR*, 1st ser., 32 (1):616; *Missouri Democrat*, April 16, 22, 1864; Mound City Hospital Register #125, 9, RG 94, NA.

17. *OR*, 1st ser., 32 (1):535, 562; *ORN*, 1st ser., 26:222; Maness, "The Fort Pillow Massacre," 295; *Missouri Democrat*, April 16, 1864; Charles Fitch file, Personal Papers of Physicians, RG 94, NA.

18. C. Fitch, "Capture of Fort Pillow—Vindication of General Chalmers by a Federal Officer," *Southern Historical Society Papers* 7 (October 1879): 440–41; Thomas W. McClure, "The Fort Pillow Massacre," in Ward Edwards, *Lion-Hearted Luke, or, The Plan to Capture Mosby: A Story of Perilous Adventure in the Rebellion* (New York: Novelist, 1884), 22.

19. William W. Cherster, ed., "Diary of Captain Elisha Tompkin Hollis," *West Tennessee Historical Society Papers* 39 (1985): 96; W. R. Dyer Diary, April 12, 1864, Tennessee State Library and Archives, Nashville, Tenn.; Alex M. Jones to Sally J. Jones, April 15, 1864, Jones-Black Family Papers, University of Memphis Library, Memphis, Tenn.; Cimprich and Mainfort, "Fort Pillow Revisited," 299–300; *OR*, 1st ser., 32 (1):612.

20. Cimprich and Mainfort, "Fort Pillow Revisited," 297, 299, 301.

21. Maness, "The Fort Pillow Massacre," 293, 295; Cimprich and Mainfort, "Fort Pillow Revisited," 299–300; *OR*, 1st ser., 32 (1):599; Dyer Diary, April 12, 1864; *New Era* Log, April 12, 1864.

22. A. V. Clark Compiled Service Record (Russell's 20th Tennessee Cavalry), RG 109, NA; Cimprich and Mainfort, "Fort Pillow Revisited," 297–300; *ORN*, 1st ser., 26:224; *OR*, 1st ser., 32 (1):615.

23. *OR*, 1st ser., 32 (1):598, 612; Jordan and Pryor, *The Campaigns of Lieut. Gen. N. B. Forrest*, 444, 454; Charles W. Anderson, "The True Story of Fort Pillow," *Confederate Veteran* 3 (November 1895): 324; *Memphis Appeal*, May 2, 1864.

24. *Mobile Advertiser and Register*, April 26, 1864.

25. *OR*, 1st ser., 32 (3):822, (1):597, 615–16, 621; *Mobile Advertiser and Register*, May 7, 1864.

26. *Memphis Appeal*, May 13, 1864; Bell Irvin Wiley, *The Life of Johnny Reb: The Common Soldier of the Confederacy* (Indianapolis: Bobbs-Merrill, 1943), 311; Bell Irvin Wiley, *The Life of Billy Yank: The Common Soldier of the Union* (Indianapolis: Bobbs-Merrill, 1952), 349–50; Reid Mitchell, *Civil War Soldiers* (New York: Viking, 1988), 30, 218; Cimprich and Mainfort, "Fort Pillow Revisited," 305; *OR*, 1st ser., 32 (1):523–26, 531–32, 539.

27. *OR*, 1st ser., 32 (1):586; Frank Moore, ed., *The Rebellion Record: A Diary of American Events*, 11 vols. (New York: D. Van Nostrand, 1861–68), vol. 8, poetry section, 56; Jordan and Pryor, *The Campaigns of Lieut. Gen. N. B. Forrest*, 439–40.

28. Jordan and Pryor, *The Campaigns of Lieut. Gen. N. B. Forrest*, viii, 434–39, 442–43; Cimprich and Mainfort, "Fort Pillow Revisited," 295; excerpt from *Cairo News*, April 16, 1864, in *Philadelphia Inquirer*, April 24, 1864.

29. *OR*, 1st ser., 32 (3):117, (1):612; Charles L. Lufkin, " 'Not Heard from since April 12, 1864': The Thirteenth Tennessee Cavalry, U.S.A.," *Tennessee Historical Quarterly* 45 (Summer 1986): 137–41; Testimony, 10, 16, Hattie Lanier file, Congressional Jurisdiction Cases, RG 123, NA; Robert C. Mainfort, Jr., and Patricia Coats, eds., "Soldiering at Fort Pillow, 1862–1864: An Excerpt from the Civil War Memoirs of Addison Sleeth," *West Tennessee Historical Society Papers* 36 (1982): 82; James M. Christenburg CSR (Bradford's Tennessee Cavalry Battalion), RG 94, NA; Jordan and Pryor, *The Campaigns of Lieut. Gen. N. B. Forrest*, 434; Cimprich and Mainfort, "Fort Pillow Revisited," 299, 301. For the only Confederate eyewitnesses who later repeated the allegation that the black troops acted in a particularly insulting manner, see James Dinkins, *Personal Recollections and Experiences in the Confederate Army* (Cincinnati: Robert Clarke Company, 1897), 152; John A. Wyeth, *The Life of General Nathan Bedford Forrest* (New York: Harper & Brothers, 1899), 385.

30. Jordan and Pryor, *The Campaigns of Lieut. Gen. N. B. Forrest*, 432–33, 450–53.

31. Ibid., 445, 448; *Memphis Appeal*, June 23, 1864; Anderson, "The True Story of Fort Pillow," 323, 326–27; Wyeth, *The Life of General Nathan Bedford Forrest*, 384–85.

32. Charles Reagan Wilson, *Baptized in Blood: The Religion of the Lost Cause* (Athens: University of Georgia Press, 1980), 39–43, 100, 139–43; Gaines M. Foster, *Ghosts of the Confederacy: Defeat, the Lost Cause, and the Emergence of the New South, 1865–1913* (New York: Oxford University Press, 1987), 195–96; Lois D. Bejack, ed., "The Journal of a Civil War 'Commando' — DeWitt Clinton Fort," *West Tennessee Historical Society Papers* 2 (1948): 19–20; [G. A. Hanson], *Minor Incidents of the Late War* (Bartow, Fla.: Sessions, Barker, and Kilpatrick, Publishers, 1878), 72; James R. Chalmers, *The Storming of Fort Pillow: A Personal Explanation* (Washington, D.C.: Government Printing Office, 1879); Richard R. Hancock, *Hancock's Diary* (Nashville: Brandon Printing Company, 1887), 351, 360, 367; Anderson,

"The True Story of Fort Pillow," 325; Dinkins, *Personal Recollections and Experiences*, 150–54; Thomas F. Berry, *Four Years with Morgan and Forrest* (Oklahoma City: Harlow-Ratliff Company, 1914), 220–21; Theodore Brewer, "Storming Fort Pillow," *Confederate Veteran* 33 (December 1925): 459, 478; Wyeth, *The Life of General Nathan Bedford Forrest*, 384–89.

33. Hancock, *Hancock's Diary*, 367; Wyeth, *The Life of General Nathan Bedford Forrest*, 384, 387, 389.

34. Cimprich and Mainfort, "Fort Pillow Revisited," 305.

35. John W. Carroll, *Autobiography and Reminiscences* (Henderson, Tenn.: n.p., 1898), 29; Bejack, "The Journal of a 'Civil War Commando,'" 20; Hancock, *Hancock's Diary*, 361; Wyeth, *The Life of General Nathan Bedford Forrest*, 390; Berry, *Four Years with Morgan and Forrest*, 220–21.

36. Berry, *Four Years with Morgan and Forrest*, 220–21; Hanson, *Minor Incidents of the Late War*, 72; Dinkins, *Personal Recollections and Experiences*, 150, 152, 154; Hancock, *Hancock's Diary*, 361; Wyeth, *The Life of General Nathan Bedford Forrest*, 384; James Chalmers, "Forrest and His Campaigns," *Southern Historical Society Papers* 6 (October 1879): 470; Chalmers, *The Storming of Fort Pillow*.

37. Wyeth, *The Life of General Nathan Bedford Forrest*, 382–90.

38. Albert Castel, "The Fort Pillow Massacre: A Fresh Examination of the Evidence," *Civil War History* 4 (March 1958): 45, 48–50. Nearly all relevant Federal military documents appear in *OR* or *ORN*.

39. Cimprich and Mainfort, "Fort Pillow Revisited," 294–305; Cimprich and Mainfort, "Dr. Fitch's Report," 28–39; Carroll, *Autobiography and Reminiscences*, 29.

40. Wills, *A Battle from the Start*, 190–93; Fuchs, *An Unerring Fire*, 112; Noah Andre Trudeau, *Like Men of War: Black Troops in the Civil War, 1862–1865* (Boston: Little, Brown, 1998), 166–68; Jack Hurst, *Nathan Bedford Forrest: A Biography* (New York: Alfred A. Knopf, 1993), 174. Among recent works, only two reject the massacre interpretation: Lonnie E. Maness, *An Untutored Genius: The Military Career of General Nathan Bedford Forrest* (Oxford, Miss.: Guild Bindery Press, 1990), 230–60, and Roy Morris, Jr., "Fort Pillow: Massacre or Madness?" *America's Civil War* 13 (November 2000): 32.

6

FROM THE
CRATER TO NEW
MARKET HEIGHTS
A Tale of Two Divisions
William Glenn Robertson

By the opening of the 1864 spring campaign in Virginia, African American units had already proven themselves capable soldiers in the Mississippi Valley and on the South Atlantic coast. In Virginia, however, they had yet to see any duty beyond the most mundane camp, fatigue, and engineering details. Nevertheless, when the two primary Federal armies in Virginia began offensive operations in May 1864, their ranks included seventeen African American combat units. In the Army of the Potomac, a division of the Ninth Army Corps consisted entirely of infantry regiments of the U.S. Colored Troops (USCT). Similarly, in the Army of the James, African American infantry regiments made up a full infantry division in the Eighteenth Army Corps. In addition, the Army of the James included two African American cavalry regiments and one African American artillery battery among its combat formations. Too few to be dominant, yet too many to be ignored, these African American units would clearly play a role in the coming campaign. The nature and scope of that role remained unclear as the armies left their winter quarters and marched toward an uncertain future. The positive performance of African American troops at Milliken's Bend, Port Hudson, and Battery Wagner notwithstanding, the black soldiers in the Army of the Potomac and the Army of the James knew that they were controversial adjuncts to white armies in the primary theater of operations and that their activities would be watched carefully and judged critically.[1]

Although each Federal army began the spring campaign in Virginia with the same number of African American infantry regiments (seven) and the same organizational structure (single divisions of two brigades each), the attitude toward black units differed significantly between the Army of the Potomac and the Army of the James. The Army of the Potomac was commanded by Major General George G. Meade, victor of the Battle of Gettysburg. Associated with Meade's command but not originally part of it was the Ninth Army Corps of Major General Ambrose Burnside. Because he technically outranked Meade, Burnside reported directly to Lieutenant General Ulysses S. Grant, general in chief of all the armies of the Union, who made his headquarters with the Army of the Potomac. Burnside's Ninth Army Corps thus was something of an anomaly among the four infantry corps that constituted the combined command, and Burnside's poor reputation armywide (stemming from his disastrous tenure as army commander at Fredericksburg in 1862) made a bad situation worse. Thus Brigadier General Edward Ferrero's all-black Fourth Division, Ninth Army Corps, represented a controversial experiment within an outcast corps commanded by an officer with no standing at army headquarters. Ferrero's men entered upon the campaign burdened not only with prejudice against their race but also with prejudice against their parent unit and its commander. At the beginning of the spring campaign, the black division in the Army of the Potomac could have little hope of playing a major role in the momentous events about to unfold.[2]

In Major General Benjamin Butler's Army of the James, Brigadier General Edward Hincks's Third Division, Eighteenth Army Corps, labored under somewhat more favorable conditions than Ferrero's men in the Army of the Potomac. Commander not only of the Army of the James but also of the encompassing Department of Virginia and North Carolina, Butler by May 1864 had become a firm believer in the capabilities of African American units. A nonprofessional soldier but a professional politician, he had long maintained a reputation for championing the cause of America's downtrodden classes. While commanding in New Orleans in 1862 he had come to see both the justice and the utility of arming blacks in the struggle to preserve the Union. His convictions, whether held philosophically or expediently, inclined Butler toward the recruitment, organization, and sustainment of all-black units wherever he held command. By May 1864 Butler had gathered within his department enough African American regiments to form a two-brigade division. He chose the white officers of the division with care; he established schools to educate the enlisted men; and he devised a supporting infrastructure to care for the soldier's families. Perhaps most important of all, in stark contrast to the views held by the leaders of the Army of the Potomac, Butler proposed to give Hincks's division major responsibilities as soon as the campaign opened. Racial prejudice was by no means absent from the Army of the James, as the testimony of numerous witnesses affirms, but the army's commander did not share that prejudice.[3]

When the Army of the James began offensive operations on May 5, 1864, in accord with Grant's master plan, Butler was true to his promise to employ black troops in significant roles. The plan called for the Army of the James to sail as far up the James River toward Richmond as possible, then seize and fortify a base from which to threaten the Confederate capital. The chosen site for the base was Bermuda Hundred, a triangular peninsula of land between the James and Appomattox Rivers. Protected on two sides by water, the fortified camp was vulnerable only if Confederates could interdict its line of supply, which followed the James back to Hampton Roads. At two points downstream from Bermuda Hundred the channel narrowed sufficiently to permit Confederate artillery to interdict river traffic from adjacent bluffs. Those two points, Fort Powhatan and Wilson's Wharf, would have to be occupied by Federal units to protect the vessels bringing the necessities of life to the Army of the James. Just south of Bermuda Hundred and across the mouth of the Appomattox River from it was a spit of land known as City Point, the occupation of which would protect transports anchored off Bermuda Hundred Landing and provide a beachhead south of the Appomattox if needed in the future. While not as glamorous as marching on Richmond itself, the mission of protecting the line of communications of the Army of the James was critical to the ultimate success of Butler's expedition. He therefore assigned an entire division to seize and hold City Point, Fort Powhatan, and Wilson's Wharf.[4]

The division chosen to protect Butler's line of communications was Hincks's Third Division, Eighteenth Army Corps. As a citizen-soldier from Maine, age thirty-four, Hincks had compiled by May 1864 a distinguished combat record culminating in two wounds at Antietam. Promoted to brigadier general in November 1862, he had eventually come to command the prisoner of war camp at Point Lookout, Maryland, where black units had been part of his guard force. Hincks's Third Division consisted of two brigades: Brigadier General Edward Wild's First Brigade (1st, 10th, 22nd, and 37th USCT), and Colonel Samuel Duncan's Second Brigade (4th, 5th, and 6th USCT). An ardent abolitionist, Wild, thirty-eight, had lost an arm as a colonel at South Mountain in 1862. Upon recuperating from his wound and being promoted to brigadier general, he had recruited and organized many of the troops he now led. In contrast, Duncan, almost twenty-eight, had seen no action as a major in the Washington defenses and had escaped that dreary fate by being commissioned colonel of the 4th USCT in November 1863. Now he led the brigade to which the 4th belonged. Of the seven regiments in the two brigades, five had been organized in the summer and fall of 1863, and the other two early in 1864. None had seen significant combat, but the 4th, 5th, and 6th USCT of Duncan's brigade had participated in numerous expeditions and several small skirmishes on the Peninsula in February and March. Duncan's unit clearly was the more experienced of Hincks's two brigades.[5]

Early on the morning of May 5, Butler's Army of the James ascended the James River from Hampton Roads with Hincks's division in the lead. On reaching Wilson's Wharf, the Federal armada dropped off half of Wild's brigade (1st and 22nd USCT, and two sections of Battery B, 2nd U.S. Colored Light Artillery), then continued upstream. At Fort Powhatan the process was repeated as Wild's remaining regiments scrambled ashore. Still in the lead, Hincks reached City Point by midafternoon and landed all of Duncan's brigade, plus the last section of Battery B. While the remaining five divisions of the Army of the James continued upriver to Bermuda Hundred Landing, Hincks's men began to fortify their three enclaves on the James River shore. The works at Wilson's Wharf and Fort Powhatan would remain small throughout the campaign, but the City Point defenses were much more extensive because of their proximity to the Confederate citadel of Petersburg. As the main army began its operations against Petersburg and Richmond from its own fortified base, Hincks both aggressively reconnoitered toward Petersburg and expanded the City Point enclave. On May 12 with Duncan's brigade he began construction of Fort Converse, centerpiece of a fourth enclave, on the south bank of the Appomattox River a few miles upstream from City Point and across from Butler's headquarters at Point of Rocks.[6]

Throughout the remainder of May and the first half of June, Hincks's division improved its scattered posts and faithfully protected the line of communications of the Army of the James. Although none of Hincks's infantry participated in the actions culminating in the Battle of Drewry's Bluff, the Third Division remained busy in its own sector. On May 16 a foraging party from City Point was ambushed, losing seven men from the 37th USCT. Two days later a Confederate probe tested Fort Converse, but the garrison easily held its ground. On May 21 it was Fort Powhatan's turn to repulse a Confederate reconnaissance without loss. More serious was the action at Wilson's Wharf on May 24, when a large Confederate cavalry force strongly attacked the works. In a five-hour fight, Brigadier General Wild and the 1st and 10th USCT, supported by the gunboat USS *Dawn*, drove off the attackers at a cost of twenty-two casualties. Nothing further of note occurred until June 9, when Edward Hincks himself led two regiments from Fort Converse toward Petersburg, a rail junction critical to Richmond's survival, as part of an expedition commanded by Major General Quincy Gillmore. Gillmore's timidity cost the Union an opportunity to break into Petersburg when it was lightly defended, and Hincks's men returned to their base without loss. This episode ended the Bermuda Hundred campaign. During that campaign the men of the Third Division had become seasoned soldiers, performing well in a variety of tasks. They would be heard from again.[7]

While the Army of the James had been conducting operations against Confederate forces south of Richmond, Generals Grant and Meade had been slowly fighting their way southward with the Army of the Potomac. By mid-June Grant had decided to transfer Meade's army south of the James River and attempt to gain possession of Petersburg. The enclave established at Bermuda Hundred–City Point by Butler would provide the initial bridgehead for the Army of the Potomac and become its forward supply base as well. Grant ordered Petersburg's defenses to be assaulted by Major General William Smith's Eighteenth Army Corps from the Army of the James, supported by units of the Army of the Potomac as they arrived. Smith and most of his corps had been on detached duty with Meade's army since late May and had participated heavily in the disastrous assault at Cold Harbor in early June. Returned to Bermuda Hundred by water, the corps prepared to move against Petersburg's eastern defenses early on the morning of June 15. In accord with an earlier order from Butler, Hincks gathered a two-brigade force to assist Smith. Colonel Samuel Duncan commanded one brigade, consisting of his own 4th, 5th, and 6th USCT, augmented by the 22nd USCT. Hincks also formed a provisional brigade under Colonel John H. Holman, age twenty-eight, the commander of the 1st USCT. Holman's brigade consisted of his own regiment and one wing of the all-black 5th Massachusetts Cavalry (dismounted). One of the two artillery batteries accompanying the column was Battery B, 2nd Colored Light Artillery. All told, Hincks's division numbered 3,747 officers and men.[8]

Hincks's command began its advance from Broadway Landing on the Appomattox River before dawn on June 15, closely following a screen of troopers from Brigadier General August Kautz's cavalry division. Three miles from the river Kautz's men received fire from a Confederate artillery battery posted behind works straddling the road at the Baylor farm. As the cavalrymen displaced to the left, Hincks brought up Duncan's brigade to replace them. Duncan deployed his four regiments in a single line of battle: from left to right, the 6th, 4th, 22nd, and 5th USCT. Holman's brigade, which included the ill-trained, disgruntled, and dismounted 5th Massachusetts Cavalry, formed a second line behind Duncan. To get to the enemy artillery, Duncan's men had to traverse a tangled, swampy belt of woods, then cross several hundred yards of open ground. Passing through the timber with some difficulty, the infantrymen suddenly confronted their foe, who proved to be a Confederate cavalry brigade and a battery. Before Duncan could arrange a coordinated advance, a portion of the 4th regiment rushed forward impetuously and, without support, was shattered at a cost of 120 casualties. The rout of the 4th was compounded by the actions of some soldiers in Holman's second line, who fired into Duncan's retreating men and then fled in panic themselves. The situation was fast degenerating into a debacle when Colonel Joseph B. Kiddoo of the 22nd regiment led a charge of his own unit and the adjoining 5th USCT that drove the Confederates from their works, captured one gun, and saved the division's honor.[9]

With Baylor's farm secure by 8:00 A.M., Hincks's men rested briefly, then resumed their advance toward Petersburg with Holman's brigade now in the lead. The corps commander's plan placed Hincks's division on the left of a three-division advance, so Hincks moved his column over to the Jordan's Point Road and proceeded toward the city on that axis. By 11:00 A.M. his skirmishers had driven in a few Confederate pickets and confronted the formidable earthworks of the Dimmock Line, Petersburg's main line of defense. Unknown to the Federals, the fortifications were only lightly garrisoned by a single Confederate brigade supported by citizen reserves. For several hours the Eighteenth Corps waited impatiently while Smith arranged his units and made a series of personal reconnaissances. At last, around 7:00 P.M., Smith ordered a general advance by heavy skirmish lines. In Hincks's division, Holman's brigade was on the left and Duncan's brigade on the right. Because the 5th Massachusetts Cavalry had virtually no training in infantry tactics and had performed so badly at Baylor's farm, Holman placed it in reserve and advanced only with his own 1st USCT. On Holman's right, Duncan formed his command in two lines: from left to right, the 22nd and 4th regiments in the front line and the 6th and 5th regiments in the second. Thus weighted, the division's right faced the Confederate defenses centered on Battery 7 of the Dimmock Line.[10]

On receiving the order to advance, heavy skirmish lines from the 1st,

22nd, and 4th USCT surged toward the Confederate line. Led by Major John Cook, skirmishers of the 22nd regiment raced forward to Battery 7, circled behind it, and stormed it from the rear. They were quickly joined by elements of the 1st and 4th regiments. Duncan then sent forward the remainder of the 22nd and 4th regiments to secure the ground gained. Upon reforming his regiment, Colonel Kiddoo of the 22nd turned it to the left and commenced an advance on Battery 8. Supported by elements of the 1st USCT under Lieutenant Colonel Elias Wright, Kiddoo and his men crossed a ravine and chased the defenders of Battery 8 from their position. While Kiddoo consolidated his gains, Lieutenant Colonel George Rogers brought up the 4th USCT and, under the direct orders of corps commander Smith, continued the advance southward toward Battery 9. Seeing his approach in the gathering darkness, the outnumbered defenders withdrew from Battery 9, relinquishing Batteries 10 and 11 as well in their haste to disengage. By the time the firing ceased, Hincks's command had opened a wide path through the Dimmock Line. Coupled with Federal gains made on Hincks's right by the remainder of the Eighteenth Corps, the ground seized by the black units offered a grand opportunity to capture Petersburg.[11]

Unfortunately, the Army of the Potomac, which began to arrive on the field late on June 15, bungled its attacks on June 16–18, and Petersburg was not taken. Hincks's division took little part in those attacks, being moved to the right near the Appomattox River and placed in support of another Eighteenth Corps division for several days. The battle on June 15 had been costly to the division, resulting in more than 550 killed, wounded, and missing. Duncan's brigade had borne the brunt of the fight, losing forty-four killed, 317 wounded, and seventeen missing, for a total of 378. In addition, limited action on June 18 cost Duncan another thirty-seven casualties. Grievous as they were, the losses indicated that the African American contingent in the Army of the James was as willing to suffer and die for the Union cause as any other unit. Hincks and Duncan were especially fulsome in their praise in their after-action reports, the former noting that "we have a sufficient proof that colored men, when properly officered, instructed, and drilled, will make most excellent infantry of the line, and may be used as such soldiers to great advantage." The only sour note struck during June 15 came with reports that some men of Duncan's brigade attacked Confederates in Battery 6 who had already surrendered to white troops, killing at least one before they were restrained. That isolated incident notwithstanding, the performance of Hincks's Third Division indicated that Benjamin Butler's faith in his black units had not been misplaced.[12]

While Hincks's men were building a reputation in the Army of the James, their compatriots in the Army of the Potomac were not faring so well. The all-black Fourth Division, Ninth Army Corps, began the spring campaign on May 4 under Brigadier General Edward Ferrero. Thirty-three years of age, Ferrero had been born in Spain to Italian parents but had been brought to America in infancy. A dancing master by trade, he won through his prewar militia experience in New York the colonelcy of the 51st New York Infantry Regiment in 1861. His brigade command at Second Manassas, Antietam, and Fredericksburg was undistinguished, and Ferrero's initial appointment as brigadier general failed to receive Senate confirmation. Reappointed in 1863, he commanded a Ninth Corps brigade at Vicksburg and a division of the corps at Knoxville, again without distinction. When the reorganized corps was transferred to the Eastern Theater early in 1864, Ferrero received command of the Fourth Division. Although his brigade had seized the famous Burnside's Bridge at Antietam in September 1862, his subordinates rightfully received the credit for that exploit, and rumors held that his division had charged without his orders at Knoxville. His lackluster command style hardly suited a controversial formation like the Fourth Division.[13]

Ferrero's new command at the opening of the spring campaign consisted of two infantry brigades. The First Brigade, commanded by Colonel Joshua Sigfried, age thirty-one, included four regiments, the 27th, 30th, 39th, and 43rd USCT. A volunteer officer, Sigfried had spent most of the war as major and colonel of the 48th Pennsylvania Infantry Regiment before coming to the brigade. None of his regiments had been formed earlier than mid-January 1864 and two, the 27th (seven companies) and 43rd (six companies) marched to war on May 4 with their organization incomplete. Colonel Henry Thomas, age twenty-seven, commanded Ferrero's Second Brigade. An attorney in civil life, Thomas had seen action at First Bull Run as a captain in the 5th Maine Infantry Regiment. He had then received a similar commission in the newly formed 11th U.S. Infantry Regiment but had quickly been detailed to recruiting duty. For much of 1863 that duty involved recruiting and organizing black regiments. Commissioned colonel of the 19th USCT in January 1864, Thomas gained brigade command just as the campaign opened. His brigade consisted of the 19th and 23rd regiments plus a detachment of the 30th Connecticut (Colored) Infantry. The first two units had begun their formation in December 1863, but the Connecticut detachment had been in service less than two months. Like Sigfried's command, Thomas's men were innocent of combat experience and were still learning the rudiments of soldiering when the Ninth Corps began the spring campaign.[14]

Ferrero's Fourth Division left Manassas Junction, Virginia, on May 4 en route to join the Ninth Corps, which was itself concentrating to advance with the Army of the Potomac. On May 6 it crossed the Rapidan River at Germanna Ford and established a position guarding the crossing. As the Battle of the Wilderness erupted not far to the south, Ferrero received a flurry of orders that ultimately assigned the Fourth Division to the temporary control of Major General John Sedgwick of the Sixth Army Corps. Ferrero's mission was to link the Army of the Potomac to the Germanna crossing, while at the same time shielding the army's massive trains. On May 7 the division moved to the vicinity of Chancellorsville to protect the thousands of wagons on which Meade's forces depended for sustenance. For a time, Ferrero's troops came under the command of Major General Philip Sheridan, but Sheridan would not long content himself with guarding wagons. As the Army of the Potomac left the Wilderness and headed for another encounter with the Confederates at Spotsylvania Court House, Ferrero's men remained behind as the right flank guard for the army and security for its wagon trains. Thus deployed in a screen west and south of Fredericksburg the Fourth Division had its first taste of action on May 15. On that day Confederate cavalry drove in Federal horsemen near Piney Branch Church, and Ferrero sent the 23rd USCT of the Second Brigade to restore the position. At a cost of a few wounded the regiment easily repulsed the enemy. Four days later a similar Confederate probe was deflected without loss.[15]

The train-guard mission given to Ferrero's division in the midst of the crisis in the Wilderness now assumed an unexpected permanency. For the next month, under Meade's direct orders, the division moved with the wagons as they creaked and groaned their way southward behind the advancing Federal army. By May 24, when Burnside's Ninth Corps officially became part of the Army of the Potomac, Grant and Meade had tired of the stalemate around Spotsylvania Court House and had swung southeastward in a futile attempt to outflank the Confederates. Dutifully shepherding their charges in the army's rear, Ferrero's men slogged through Bowling Green and took up a position around Milford Station while Grant and Meade confronted the enemy at the North Anna River. Finding the North Anna position untenable in late May, Grant sent Meade's forces looping southeastward in still another flanking move. Again, the Fourth Division guarded the trains as they followed the army across the Mattaponi and Pamunkey Rivers. June 1 found Ferrero south of the Pamunkey River in the vicinity of

Haw's Shop. For nearly two weeks the division remained between Haw's Shop and Old Church protecting the trains and the army's far right, while Grant and Meade struggled with the Confederates at Cold Harbor. During that period, the only items of note were the arrival of the newly organized 29th USCT to join Thomas's Second Brigade on June 8 and a small skirmish with Confederate cavalry at Old Church on June 10.[16]

Grant's decision to transfer the Army of the Potomac south of the James River meant little to Ferrero's Fourth Division, whose mission remained unchanged. Following the trains, the division passed through New Kent Court House, crossed the Chickahominy River and on June 17 marched over the great James River pontoon bridge to the river's south bank. Unknown to Ferrero, the initial assaults on the Petersburg lines were culminating unsuccessfully, and the army's forward progress was momentarily halted. Ferrero probably also was unaware of a proposal by Burnside to transfer the black division to Butler's army in exchange for white units that had previously been a part of the Ninth Corps. Although Grant and Meade did not oppose the switch, the proposal died because the white units in question were scattered in several states. On arriving near Meade's headquarters on June 18, Ferrero received orders to relinquish control of the wagons and report to his parent unit. Two days later Burnside placed the division in a reserve position in the corps sector. On the following day he proposed to assault the Confederate works with Ferrero's men, proving that his earlier request for their transfer did not reflect dissatisfaction with their abilities. Nothing came of the proposal, and Ferrero's men remained where they were, heavily engaged in fatigue duty on the fortifications, until June 27. On that day the division was sent to Prince George Court House in the army's rear, to guard against a possible Confederate cavalry raid. No Confederates materialized, but another regiment, the 28th USCT, joined Thomas's brigade on June 30.[17]

On the last day of June Ferrero received orders from Meade to move his division westward to the Jerusalem Plank Road and report to Major General Winfield Hancock of the Second Corps. Hardly had the division arrived when new orders sent Ferrero's men eastward to the intersection of the Baxter Road and Blackwater Swamp. Meade was rearranging his corps, and Ferrero's division now became the left unit of the army's left flank. On the evening of July 9 the Fourth Division returned to its old position on the Jerusalem Plank Road and to the control of Hancock's Second Corps. Hancock placed Ferrero's men on the left of his entrenched line and levied large numbers of them for fatigue duty on the fortifications. Within three days, Meade had decided to withdraw Hancock's corps from the line and place it in reserve behind the army's left. Ferrero's men thus were placed in the works they were building and now connected on their right with Major General Gouverneur Warren's Fifth Army Corps. On the evening of July 10 Meade assigned Ferrero's division to Warren. While willing to have Ferrero's men occupy and improve the works, Meade did not want them to picket their front, telling Hancock "I do not like relying on the colored troops for this duty in so important a position, and would prefer employing them on working party." Meade's sentiments were echoed by his engineers, who openly preferred using black troops for fatigue duty instead of white units.[18]

By July 14 the levies on his command for working parties had become so great that Ferrero registered a complaint with Warren. Receiving no relief, Ferrero complained again three days later, this time to his nominal parent unit, the Ninth Corps. By this time the division commander had even greater reason to be concerned. Earlier in the month Burnside had told Ferrero that his division would lead an assault on the Confederate works after the successful completion of a mining operation then taking place on the front of the Ninth Corps. Beginning in late June, coal miners from the 48th Pennsylvania Infantry of Robert Potter's division had started driving an underground shaft from Potter's advanced lines toward the Confederate works little more than one hundred yards away. With no encouragement, much derision and, indeed, considerable obstruction from Grant, Meade, and their respective staffs, Burnside and his coal miners pressed forward with their project into the month of July. Anticipating success in the mining, the corps commander thought long and hard about the composition of the storming party that would charge the Confederate position following the great explosion. Burnside's three white divisions had seen hard service since the beginning of the spring campaign and according to the corps inspector general were in no condition to make the assault. In contrast, Ferrero's men, while untried, were fresh and eager to prove their mettle. Given that analysis, Burnside selected the Fourth Division for the storming column.[19]

According to Burnside's later testimony, he chose Ferrero's command at least three weeks before the explosion of the mine. Once selected, Ferrero was invited to survey the ground and to devise an attack plan. He viewed the position as safely as Confederate sharpshooters permitted and eventually offered a plan to Burnside. In Ferrero's formulation the leading regiments would diverge to left and right as they approached the crater created by the mine and advance perpendicularly to the Confederate trenches, thereby forming strong shoulders to the penetration. Once the lodgment was obtained and secured, the remainder of the division would advance as rapidly as possible toward the high ground of Cemetery Hill five hundred yards behind the main Confederate line. Burnside approved the plan and left it to Ferrero to educate his troops in their respective roles and train them accordingly. No doubt Ferrero meant to do just that, but his division was not freed of other responsibilities to prepare for the coming ordeal. Indeed, Ferrero's men through the first half of July shuttled from army control to Second Corps control to Fifth Corps control. While its superiors changed often, the division's mission remained the same: picket its front with a quarter of the division strength while digging trenches and building forts with the remainder. The division's facility with pick and shovel, coupled with his doubts as to its fighting ability, caused Warren on July 18 to renew a suggestion to Meade that Ferrero's men do nothing but fatigue work for the remainder of the siege. Warren had work for the men to do, and that work did not include preparing for an assault on Burnside's front.[20]

As if Ferrero's problems with Warren were not enough to occupy him, the division commander also was beset by personal difficulties during the middle of July. Originally commissioned brigadier general in late 1862, he had not been confirmed by the U.S. Senate, and the commission lapsed. Nominated again by the War Department, to rank from May 6, 1863, he was now notified that the new appointment had lapsed as well because of Senate inaction. Efforts to rectify the matter proceeded on two fronts. Grant on July 15 sent a telegram to Secretary of War Stanton praising Ferrero in extravagant terms and asking that his nomination to brigadier general be resubmitted. Stanton responded affirmatively the next day, renominating Ferrero with his old date of May 6, 1863. Meanwhile, Ferrero personally sought to be relieved of his command so that he could go to Washington to argue his case. Early on July 21 Meade approved his formal request, and Ferrero departed instantly on the morning mail boat from City Point. His departure was so hasty that he left important paperwork unsigned. Aware that the mine was nearing completion and that his division was assigned to lead the subsequent attack, Ferrero nevertheless left the theater without a definite return date. To replace him as division commander, Burnside picked Brigadier General Julius White, who had arrived earlier in the month and was an unassigned officer at Ninth Corps headquarters.[21]

A nonprofessional soldier from New York, Julius White, almost forty-eight, had been a lawyer, politician, and customs collector before the war. Upon the outbreak of hostilities he had raised a regiment in the Chicago area, the 37th Illinois Infantry. A brigade commander at the Battle of Pea

Ridge, he had been promoted to brigadier general in June 1862. Transferred to the Eastern Theater, he had led his small command into the fortified position at Harpers Ferry in September 1862 but had refused to assume command from the colonel in charge of the post. When that officer was killed, White surrendered Harpers Ferry and its entire garrison to Stonewall Jackson. Arrested for this questionable behavior, White was subsequently exonerated, but his upward mobility was seriously curtailed. Transferred to the Department of Ohio in early 1863, White had gone to work for Burnside and had briefly commanded a small division in operations around Knoxville, Tennessee, that fall. He had joined the Ninth Corps on July 9, 1864, but had had no assignment until Ferrero's unexpected departure created a vacancy in the Fourth Division. If Ferrero did not return, White would have to lead the division in the coming assault. Perhaps to that end, Special Order 194, which authorized Ferrero's relief, also transferred his Fourth Division back to Burnside's direct control.[22]

On July 22 elements of the Second Corps relieved the Fourth Division from its position on the left of the army, and White's men returned to the Ninth Corps sector. For a few days the division was not in the line and may have engaged in some training for the forthcoming assault, although the documentary record is silent on this point. The respite was brief, however, because on the evening of July 25 Burnside used Sigfried's First Brigade to relieve a brigade of Orlando Willcox's Third Division in the trenches. On the next day, Hancock's Second Corps left the Petersburg lines to demonstrate north of the James River. Hancock's departure caused Meade to direct Burnside to send a division to reoccupy the trenches formerly held by Ferrero on the left of Warren's Fifth Corps. Because it was familiar with the position, Burnside picked the Fourth Division and ordered White to reunite its two brigades. The movement had hardly begun when Meade's original order was suspended. When the process resumed on July 27, White was instructed to use Thomas's Second Brigade and a brigade of Willcox's, leaving Sigfried's men in the Ninth Corps trenches. The following day, the mine was charged with powder and was pronounced ready for use. The Fourth Division, however, remained split, with the division commander and one of its two brigades on detached service guarding the far left of the army's entrenched line.[23]

While White was dividing the Fourth Division into two widely separated parts, turmoil erupted within the highest command echelons of the Army of the Potomac. On July 26 Meade demanded to see Burnside's plan for assaulting the Confederate position. In great detail Burnside explained what would happen, including the fact that the Fourth Division would comprise the initial attack wave. The corps commander seemed unaware that Meade had little confidence in the black division as a combat unit; nor was he sensitive to the political ramifications of a bloody failure by Ferrero's men. Unlike Burnside, Meade feared an abolitionist outcry if the division met disaster, an argument he would later raise privately with Grant. Two days thereafter Burnside visited Meade's headquarters to make final coordination for the attack. He was startled when Meade told him that under no circumstances could the Fourth Division lead the assault. Burnside argued for his original plan so strenuously that Meade grudgingly agreed to lay the question before Grant later that day. Hearing nothing from Meade for almost forty-eight hours, Burnside assumed Grant had left the plan unchanged. During a meeting between Burnside and several of his division commanders around midday on July 29, Meade suddenly appeared and announced that Grant had forbidden the Fourth Division to lead the assault. Crushed, Burnside and Brigadier Generals James Ledlie, Robert Potter, and Orlando Willcox struggled to select another division to spearhead the attack. At last, Burnside had the division commanders draw lots. In this way Ledlie's First Division received the mission. Julius White, acting commander of the Fourth Division, was present for none of the deliberations.[24]

Ledlie's First Division was the poorest possible choice to lead the attack, and its commander would soon be exposed as an incompetent and a disgrace. White, no doubt, was relieved that he would not have to lead the Fourth Division into the maelstrom following the explosion of the mine. His mood improved further when Ferrero suddenly appeared late in the afternoon and asked to resume command of his division. Meade's headquarters approved Ferrero's reinstatement at 7:00 P.M. on July 29, barely eight hours before the mine was to be exploded. Momentarily without a command, White was made Burnside's chief of staff, replacing John Parke, who had become ill. With both the plan and one of his division commanders changed, Burnside during the evening published a circular detailing the revised scheme of maneuver. Ledlie's First Division was to pass through the breach made by the mine and seize Cemetery Hill several hundred yards beyond it. Willcox's Third Division was to follow Ledlie, then turn to the left and form a protective shoulder for the penetration. Potter's Second Division was to follow Willcox and establish a similar blocking position to the right of the breach. Finally, Ferrero's Fourth Division would follow Ledlie's track, pass through the First Division and enter the Petersburg suburb of Blandford. All was to begin as soon as the mine exploded, which was scheduled for 3:30 A.M. on July 30, just a few hours hence.[25]

According to Colonel Henry Thomas, commander of Ferrero's Second Brigade, he did not learn that the Fourth Division had been replaced in the order of assault until 11:00 P.M. on July 29. Thomas and his men were keenly disappointed at losing an opportunity to prove themselves to the remainder of the Army of the Potomac. Nevertheless, they loyally took position behind Potter's Second Division in the darkness and waited for new orders. At 3:30 A.M. no explosion was heard; the fuse had extinguished itself. Reignited under heroic circumstances by men of the 48th Pennsylvania, the mine finally erupted just before 4:45 A.M. According to the Confederate sector commander, Major General Bushrod Johnson, the blast created a crater "135 feet in length, 97 feet in breadth, and 30 feet deep." First Ledlie's division, then Willcox's, and finally Potter's charged forward to the smoking depression where a large stretch of Confederate earthworks moments before had been located. Instead of pressing forward toward Cemetery Hill as required by the plan, Ledlie's men mostly gathered in and around the crater. There they busied themselves gawking at the devastation and digging out dazed, half-buried Confederates. The division commander neither went forward with nor supervised his men, and he indeed may never have instructed his two brigade commanders about their objective. Willcox on Ledlie's left and Potter on Ledlie's right both got brigades into the Confederate trenches emanating from the crater, but without a continued advance by the First Division they were unable to do more than cling to their limited gains. The Confederate response, which had initially been slow in coming, now began to build, making the Federal position increasingly tenuous.[26]

While Burnside's three white divisions clogged the crater and the surrounding trenches, Ferrero's Fourth Division waited apprehensively for ninety minutes in a communication trench behind the Union front line. There they were subjected to the ghastly sight of badly wounded men being carried to the rear, shrieking in agony. Near the head of the trench was a bombproof shelter, formerly a regimental command post but now an aid station manned by surgeons. Finding the way forward blocked by troops from the other divisions, Ferrero ducked inside the bombproof. There he found Brigadier General Ledlie, already under the influence of alcohol, and several surgeons. Ferrero spent some time there, responding to every order to advance that he would do so as soon as the way in front cleared. At last a peremptory order arrived for Ferrero from Burnside, and he moved to obey. He soon met Lieutenant Colonel Charles Loring, the corps inspector general, who countermanded the order on his own authority until he could confirm that such indeed was Burnside's wish. On learning that Burnside was responding to a similar order from Meade, Loring gave Ferrero permis-

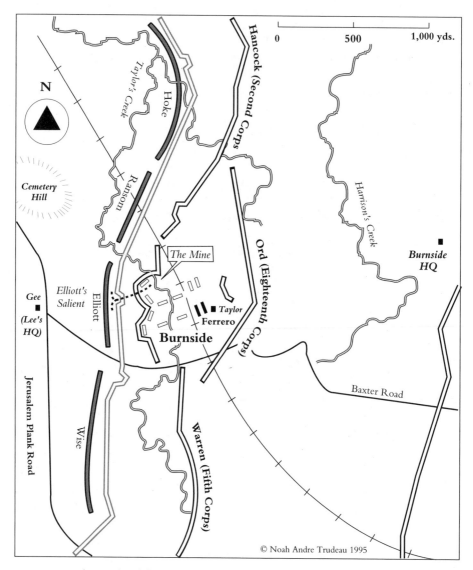

Map 6.1. The Battle of the Crater, Petersburg, Virginia, July 30, 1864.
(Courtesy of Noah Andre Trudeau)

sion to take his division forward. Sigfried's First Brigade was in the lead, followed by Thomas's Second Brigade, all closely massed. Around 7:30 A.M., or perhaps a little earlier, the men of the Fourth Division climbed out of the Federal trenches and sprinted forward toward the upturned earth that marked the lip of the crater.[27]

Reaching the enormous depression created by the mine, Sigfried's brigade found a scene of almost indescribable chaos. Before them was the crater, clogged with hundreds of men and debris of all kinds. Behind it and on both sides was a warren of trenches and bombproof shelters, also filled with soldiers. For units that were well trained in the linear tactics of the day, this maze of holes and passageways would have represented a difficult obstacle to an advance; for the inexperienced Fourth Division, it presented an almost insurmountable barrier. Nevertheless, Sigfried's men plunged forward into the roiling mass of humanity. With extreme effort, most of the First Brigade pressed through the throng in the crater and entered the web of trenches and traverses behind it. There they were halted by the crowds of men from preceding divisions. Meanwhile, one of Sigfried's regiments, the 43rd USCT, peeled off to the right and tried to expand the breach until it too was stopped by the crush of other units. Sigfried's instructions called for him to form beyond the crater on the right of the division line, but he was unable to extract his regiments from the mob to do so. Severe casualties among his officers, including two regimental commanders, so impeded Sigfried's efforts to advance that no further forward movement occurred in the First Brigade. After about an hour, the brigade fell back with everyone else, either taking refuge in the crater or continuing on to the Federal trenches.[28]

Colonel Henry Thomas's Second Brigade followed Sigfried's command to the crater. Thomas's regiments were moving "left in front," anticipating the requirement to form on the left of the division line beyond the crater. Seeing Sigfried's problems in the crater itself, Thomas took his regiments to the right, thus causing them to form with the rear rank in the front line, an undesirable formation for the best-trained units. This tactical error almost instantly proved inconsequential, however, because Thomas's regiments soon lost all formation in the trench complex to the right of the crater. Gathering the 28th and 29th regiments, Thomas attempted to charge into the open ground beyond the trench maze but was unable to get the men forward. While trying to devise another effort, he received a written order from Ferrero to make an extreme effort to seize the crest of Cemetery Hill several hundred unreachable yards in front. This time Thomas added part of the 23rd regiment to the 28th and 29th, the only units in hand. The 31st regiment was in shambles, having lost all its field officers, and the 19th had been trapped behind the mob from other commands. Led by Lieutenant Colonel John Bross of the 29th, the attack began heroically, but it ran head-on into a fierce Confederate counterattack and collapsed. Bross and many others were killed, causing the survivors to panic. White and black alike, Federal troops scrambled for safety in the trench complex and crater to the rear. Some continued back to the Federal lines, but large numbers cowered in the crater and adjacent works, fearing to cross the fire-swept ground to safety.[29]

By 8:30 A.M. all Federal offensive efforts around the crater had ceased, and the Confederates began methodical counterattacks that gradually retook the trenches surrounding the depression on three sides. Eventually they pushed up to the crater itself, which was packed so tightly with men that some could hardly raise their arms in self-defense. Enraged to find that they were fighting African Americans, many Confederates refused to permit the surrender of beaten foes, black or white. The evidence from both sides is overwhelming that racial hatred turned an already brutal struggle into heinous atrocities as the Federal perimeter inexorably contracted. Down the slope in the Federal lines, Ferrero could see nothing as he was buffeted by fleeing, panic-stricken soldiers of his own and other divisions, so he again visited the comfortable bombproof with its convivial surgeons. Farther to the rear in Fort Morton, where the view was much better, Burnside could see clearly that unless the Ninth Corps was assisted by other corps, the assault would fail. That assistance was not forthcoming, and at 9:15 A.M. Meade told Burnside to withdraw his command. It took three hours to get that order into the crater, where all unit cohesion had broken down. Burnside ordered Ferrero to dig a trench from the Federal lines to the crater for evacuation purposes, but it was too late for such pitiful efforts to have any effect. By midafternoon, with the surrender of the last dazed survivors in the crater, the battle was over.[30]

The Battle of the Crater cost the Ninth Corps 473 killed, 1,646 wounded, and 1,356 captured or missing, for a total of 3,475 officers and men. Although it was the last to enter the fight, Ferrero's Fourth Division suffered a total loss of 1,327 men, 38 percent of the corps total and more than the losses of the First and Third Divisions combined. Of the seventy-one officers of the Ninth Corps killed or mortally wounded in the battle, seventeen came from the Fourth Division. In Colonel Thomas's words: "Whether we fought well or not, the scores of our dead lying as thick as if mowed down by the hand of some mighty reaper and the terrible loss of officers can best attest." Of the twenty-four Medals of Honor subsequently awarded to participants in the battle, only four recipients came from the Fourth Division, all from Sigfried's First Brigade. Three of the four were white officers, but the final medal winner was Sergeant Decatur Dorsey of the 39th USCT. The citation for Dorsey's medal, awarded November 8, 1865, read: "Planted his colors on the Confederate works in advance of his regiment, and when the regiment was driven back to the Union works he carried the colors there and bravely rallied the men."[31]

After the debacle many participants asserted that if the Fourth Division had been allowed to lead the storming column, the results might have been more satisfactory to the Union cause. Much was made of the fact that the Fourth Division had trained vigorously to be the lead division, only to be swept aside by political considerations. In the ensuing official inquiries Meade spoke of this specialized training, as did Burnside, Potter, Willcox, and Ferrero. Nearly twenty years later, Second Brigade commander Henry Thomas made a similar claim, and Colonel Delavan Bates, commander of the 30th regiment, echoed him in 1891. This testimony notwithstanding, close analysis of the Fourth Division's activities during the month of July shows there was little time for such training. Indeed, for most of the month the division was not even under Ninth Corps control and its commander complained repeatedly about the large amounts of fatigue duty required of his troops by other officers. If it was conducted at all, the assault training could only have taken place between July 22, when the division returned to Ninth Corps control, and July 27, when the brigades went back into the line. During that period Ferrero was absent in Washington, and the passive, ineffectual Julius White commanded the division. In fact, the very idea that the Fourth Division was specially prepared for the assault was ridiculed by a junior officer in the 23rd USCT, who categorically denied in his memoirs that any such training occurred. The history of the Fourth Division prior to July 30, 1864, proves that it had only rudimentary training at best. If the division had led the assault at the crater, it would have been the fighting spirit of the men that altered the outcome, not its pre-battle preparations.[32]

While the survivors of Ferrero's Fourth Division recuperated and their compatriots captured at the crater were marched ignominiously through the streets of Petersburg, the spotlight shifted back to the black formations in the Army of the James. Immediately prior to Burnside's attack on the crater, Grant had sent Hancock's Second Corps across the James River in the vicinity of Deep Bottom to distract Confederate attention from the Petersburg front. That demonstration had come to nothing, but Grant saw that the same approach might have further utility later. In August Grant received information leading him to believe that the Confederates were detaching significant numbers of troops from the Richmond-Petersburg lines for duty in the Shenandoah Valley. Another Federal thrust north of the James from Deep Bottom might force the recall of those Confederate units and prevent further detachments. Accordingly, Grant sent Hancock again to Deep Bottom in mid-August. In addition to his own corps, Hancock received control of part of Major General David Birney's Tenth Army Corps from the Army of the James. Birney provided six infantry brigades for the operation, including a newly formed separate brigade of black regiments commanded by his older brother, William Birney.[33]

Formed only on August 12, a day before it joined the operation, Brigadier General William Birney's brigade consisted of the 29th Connecticut (Colored) Infantry Regiment and the 7th, 8th, and 9th USCT. The Connecticut regiment had been formed only in March 1864, but the others had been in service since the late fall of 1863. The 7th and 8th regiments had spent their prior service in Florida around the town of Jacksonville, while the 29th and 9th had been stationed at Hilton Head and Beaufort, South Carolina. All of the regiments had participated in minor expeditions and skirmishes, but only the 8th had significant battle experience; nor had they served together as a brigade until Birney's unit was formed. William Birney, forty-five, was the son of the famous abolitionist James Birney. A lawyer and publisher before the war, he had spent the first part of the conflict with the 4th New Jersey Infantry but had seen little action. In May 1863 he had been appointed colonel of the 22nd USCT and simultaneously nominated to brigadier general's rank. After spending the remainder of 1863 organizing new black regiments, he had held various administrative commands in the Department of the South until arriving at Bermuda Hundred and organizing his new command just before the Deep Bottom operation began.[34]

Although not all of the 29th Connecticut had yet arrived from South Carolina, Birney moved his brigade into the Deep Bottom enclave with the remainder of the Tenth Corps during the early morning hours of August 14. The Tenth Corps had the decidedly junior role on that day, with pride of place going to Hancock's Second Corps on the right, beyond Bailey's Creek. Neither Federal corps made many gains on August 14, so Hancock ordered the bulk of David Birney's Tenth Corps to reposition itself on the right of the Second Corps for a new attack on the Confederate left. Because Birney was slow to get into position, the attack was postponed a day. On August 16, the Tenth Corps assaulted the Confederate line north of Fussell's Mill. Two of William Birney's regiments were on the right of the corps and participated in the seizure of the Confederate line in their front. The remainder of the brigade, the 8th USCT and the 29th Connecticut, held the Deep Bottom fortifications on the Federal left and did not participate in the charge. Although a Confederate counterattack soon ejected the Tenth Corps from its gains, Hancock believed that its troops had done well, and he complimented them all, including William Birney's brigade, in his report. The fight had been relatively small, and Birney's part in it minor, but the brigade had now experienced combat for the first time. The cost was a total of 136 men killed, wounded, and missing, all but twelve of them in the 7th and 9th regiments. On August 20 Hancock ended the operations at Deep Bottom and the troops, including Birney's brigade, returned to the south bank of the James.[35]

A little over five weeks later, Grant again sent a large force across the James to strike from the enclave at Deep Bottom. Planned for the end of September 1864, the new operation represented the secondary portion of Grant's latest effort to crush Confederate resistance around Petersburg and end the war in central Virginia. The main effort would be a drive by Meade's army southwest of Petersburg, but Grant added a strong thrust north of the James at the urging of Benjamin Butler. Butler hoped that Confederate focus on Petersburg and corresponding weakness on the Peninsula would permit him to break through the Confederate capital's multiple defense lines and seize the city itself. To ensure success, Butler planned to use the bulk of the Army of the James, leaving only a skeleton force to guard his Bermuda Hundred base. Butler divided his mobile force into two wings: the left wing, under Major General Edward Ord, consisted of two divisions of Ord's own Eighteenth Corps; the right wing, under David Birney, contained two divisions of his own Tenth Corps, the separate African American brigade of William Birney, plus the black division of the Eighteenth Corps. According to Butler's detailed plan, Ord's wing was to cross the James near Aiken's Landing, advance up the Varina Road, break into the Confederate defensive complex at Chaffin's Bluff, then drive up the Osborne Turnpike to Richmond. Meanwhile, Birney's wing was to advance from the Deep Bottom bridgehead, carry the Confederate works at New Market Heights, and drive on Richmond via the New Market Road. Finally, Brigadier General August Kautz's cavalry division would follow Birney, cross to the Darbytown Road and enter the Confederate capital by that route.[36]

The black units in the Army of the James had undergone considerable re-organization since their last major operation. In the Tenth Corps, William Birney's command briefly had risen to division status by absorbing a brigade from the Eighteenth Corps, but by September 24 he had reverted again to command of a separate brigade. At the same time his original four regiments were augmented by a battalion from the 45th USCT. In the Eighteenth Corps, Edward Hincks, commander of the Third Division since the beginning of the campaign, departed the theater on July 1 because of ill health. Caretakers ran the division until August 3, when Brigadier General Charles Paine took command. A lawyer and protégé of Butler's, Paine, age thirty-one, had been an officer in several Massachusetts regiments until March 1862. Commissioned colonel of the 2nd Louisiana, a black regiment in the Department of the Gulf, Paine had risen rapidly to brigade command and had seen action at Port Hudson. Leaving his regiment in early 1864 to take a position on Butler's staff, he had been rewarded with an appointment as brigadier general in July and division command in August. Formerly a two-brigade division, Paine's unit now consisted of three brigades. Colonel John Holman's First Brigade had three regiments, the 1st, 22nd, and 37th USCT, all of which had participated in the campaign from the beginning. Colonel Alonzo Draper's Second Brigade was composed of the 5th, 36th, and 38th USCT. The 5th had originally been part of Duncan's brigade in May, and the others were new arrivals from elsewhere in Butler's department. Finally, Colonel Samuel Duncan commanded the Third Brigade, now comprising the 4th, 6th, and 10th USCT.[37]

Butler's drive on Richmond began badly late on September 28 when David Birney's Tenth Corps made an exceedingly disorganized march to Deep Bottom. Early on September 29, Birney placed Paine's Third Division of the Eighteenth Corps on his left, supported by a division of the Tenth Corps, while on his right a Tenth Corps division was in front, followed by William Birney's brigade. When his men came upon the Confederate works at the foot of New Market Heights, the corps commander ordered his right to fix the enemy while his left stormed the position. Thus Paine's black brigades would carry the brunt of the battle. Facing the Confederate works beyond Four Mile Creek, Paine ordered Duncan to deploy the Third Brigade for an attack. Having left the 10th USCT at City Point, Duncan had only two regiments available, so Paine gave him the dismounted troopers of the 2nd U.S. Colored Cavalry to serve as skirmishers on his right. Behind Duncan waited Holman's First Brigade and to his left rear formed Draper's Second Brigade, but Paine gave neither commander any orders to support the Third Brigade when it attacked at 5:30 A.M. Struggling through the ravine of Four Mile Creek, Duncan's men next encountered two lines of obstructions. Trying to pass the slashing, they were riddled by deadly accurate small-arms fire. Many of the brigade, including Duncan himself, went down in the entanglements, wounded or dead. A few men heroically continued forward and actually broke into the Confederate line. Unsupported, they soon were either killed or captured. The brigade's survivors, now under Colonel John Ames, hastened rearward to the cover of the ravine. Duncan's brigade had been committed alone and was wrecked the same way.[38]

Having learning nothing from the defeat of Duncan's small force, Paine next committed Draper's Second Brigade over virtually the same terrain and without significant support from Holman's First Brigade in rear. Like Duncan before him, Draper first had to negotiate the swampy ravine of Four Mile Creek, then find a way through the two lines of abatis and slashing in front of the Confederate works. When the three regiments of the brigade reached the entanglements they lost momentum and halted to engage the dimly seen enemy in a firefight. Unaware that their best hope of survival lay in continuing the charge, two of Draper's regiments, the inexperienced 36th and 38th USCT, especially remained rooted in place. Try as he might, the twenty-nine-year-old Draper was unable to get his men to cease firing and resume the advance. So the brigade stood in the slashing and traded shots with the Confederate defenders for at least thirty minutes. Losses quickly mounted, but the men could not be brought under positive control for some time. At last, as the Confederate fire slackened, Draper encouraged the troops near him to raise a shout and press forward. Their example was infectious, and the whole brigade surged ahead, up to and over the works. Draper's men did not stop until they had scaled the crest of New Market Heights itself, driving off Confederate batteries that had bolstered the defense.[39]

The fight at New Market Heights cost Paine's Third Division more than eight hundred casualties, heavily concentrated in Duncan's and Draper's brigades. Duncan's two regiments had been wrecked, with losses approaching four hundred. Draper had suffered nearly as many casualties, most incurred during that horrible half-hour in the slashing. Such losses, terrible though they were, served to make the point that African American soldiers could take heavy punishment and still continue to function as dependable combat units. When he suggested to David Birney before the battle that Paine's division be given the leading role at New Market Heights, Benjamin Butler had just such a result in mind. Riding over the field afterward, Butler was visibly touched by the sacrifice exacted from the men of the Third Division. More tangibly, he awarded nearly two hundred medals for valor of his own design to members of the division who had especially distinguished themselves. Equally charitable, by its own standards, was the War Department, which ultimately awarded fourteen Medals of Honor to black Third Division soldiers for heroic service at New Market Heights. In Duncan's brigade, three members of the 4th regiment and two soldiers of the 6th were so honored. The most famous exploit was that of Sergeant Major Christian Fleetwood of the 4th, who saved one of the regimental flags and rallied survivors after the regiment's bloody repulse. More successful in the battle, Draper's brigade garnered nine Medals of Honor, four in the 5th USCT, three in the 38th, and two in the 36th. Of these fourteen Medals of Honor, twelve were awarded on April 6, 1865, before the war ended.[40]

While subtracting nothing from the valorous deeds of Paine's Third Division, analysis of the New Market Heights action requires that it be placed within the larger context of the entire operation. The Confederate position below the heights was an advance line only and was lightly held on September 29. Furthermore, the Confederate defenders were already evacuating the position when Draper's regiments made their final charge. The Confederates were leaving because Butler's left wing under Edward Ord was threatening their main position behind Richmond's intermediate defense line. Ord's two divisions later that morning captured Fort Harrison, a key position on that line. To expand the rupture in the Confederate defenses, Butler called David Birney's wing forward from its triumph at New Market Heights. Birney initially moved west with his Tenth Corps units, momentarily leaving Paine's division behind to secure its hard-won gains. Eventually Birney confronted the Confederate intermediate line in the vicinity of Fort Gilmer, a strong work north of the captured Fort Harrison. After a personal reconnaissance the corps commander deployed his troops for a two-pronged attack on the Fort Gilmer salient. Robert Foster's Tenth Corps division, with support from Paine's now arriving troops, would assault the salient from the north. At the same time William Birney's African American brigade, with the assistance of part of Brigadier General Alfred Terry's division, would attack the fort from the east.[41]

What should have been a coordinated attack quickly degenerated into more piecemeal assaults. Foster struck first, but in a long, thin formation that dissipated his strength. When his white units faltered far short of their objective, Foster requested and received the 5th USCT from Draper's brigade of Paine's division as a reinforcement. The losses at New Market

Heights momentarily forgotten, the 5th regiment swept forward past Foster's men. They actually reached a point within one hundred yards of Fort Gilmer before being forced to withdraw with a loss of nearly one hundred more casualties. Some time after Foster's repulse, William Birney finally deployed his brigade in front of the east face of the Confederate fort. Birney had only three usable regiments, the 7th, 8th, and 9th USCT, because he dared not use the inexperienced battalion of the 45th regiment and the 29th Connecticut had not arrived. Rather than make one strong thrust, Birney unaccountably elected to attack piecemeal. The 9th regiment charged first and was quickly thrown back. Next came the 8th USCT, which Birney ordered forward four companies at a time, a formation that guaranteed failure. With those examples before him, Birney ordered his last regiment, the 9th USCT, to charge with only a battalion of four companies in skirmish order. Numbering just under two hundred officers and men, Captain Julius Weiss's battalion advanced with an élan unseen since the war was young. Taking almost 50 percent casualties, they made it into the fort's moat but could go no farther. Three attempts to scale the parapet collapsed in shambles, but there was no retreat. Eventually the survivors of the battalion were all forced into captivity, having gained nothing but everlasting glory. Birney's abysmal tactical performance cost his brigade nearly four hundred men.[42]

Following its failure before Fort Gilmer, the Tenth Corps moved southward and joined the Eighteenth Corps around Fort Harrison. During the night of September 29–30 Paine's division and Birney's brigade occupied several positions either in or to the right of the captured Confederate fort. On the next morning Paine was told to transfer his command to the left of the Federal line and extend toward the river. With Confederate counterattack imminent, Paine was unable to move, and he thus was in place just to the right of Fort Harrison when the enemy advanced. The Confederate thrust aimed for the fort itself, but Paine's sector also received considerable attention. To assist Paine, William Birney sent the 7th and 9th regiments, plus the battalion of the 45th USCT, to ensure that the Federal position would hold. Fortunately for the Federals, the two assaulting Confederate divisions coordinated their actions no better than had the Tenth Corps on the previous day. Fort Harrison would remain in Federal hands. Defense of the position, however, cost Paine an additional hundred casualties and Birney nearly fifty. That night Birney's brigade relieved Paine's division from its hard-won position, and the latter occupied a new line linking Butler's left with the James River. For the next month both Paine's and Birney's commands remained in place as the Army of the James consolidated its foothold in Richmond's outer defenses.[43]

During the remainder of 1864, the African American formations of the Army of the James and the Army of the Potomac cut timber, dug trenches, and moved supplies as the Union siege lines expanded westward. In late October Butler mounted a demonstration north of the James in support of a major thrust by Meade's army southwest of Petersburg. The skirmishing on the Darbytown Road and somewhat heavier fighting around Fair Oaks involved participation by a total of four African American brigades, two from each corps. When the troops returned to their camps on October 28, major offensive operations below Richmond ended for the black formations in the Army of the James. Similarly, the black division in the Army of the Potomac found little to do in the Petersburg trenches, and in November Grant transferred it to Butler's army at Bermuda Hundred. On December 3, 1864, a major reorganization of the Army of the James resulted in the creation of two new army corps from existing formations. The white units of the old Tenth and Eighteenth Corps became the new Twenty-fourth Corps, while the African American units of both corps became the all-black Twenty-fifth Corps. Two of the three division commanders were Charles Paine and William Birney, while among the nine brigade commanders were Samuel Duncan, Alonzo Draper, and Henry Thomas. Exactly four months later, on April 3, 1865, the First Division of the corps was among the first Federal troops to enter Richmond. A reporter who watched them march into the Confederate citadel wrote: "the survivors of those who fell in the disastrous assault of the 'crater' at Petersburg have had the post of honor in the final consummation."[44]

A comparison of the experiences of the two African American divisions in Virginia in 1864 yields few insights surprising to a military historian, but several points instructive to a wider audience are nevertheless worthy of mention. First, the general tone established within a command by its senior leader does make a difference. Benjamin Butler believed in his black formations, gave them significant missions, and brought them along slowly. Thus they grew in experience and capability over time. Ambrose Burnside also believed in his black units, but the attitude of Meade and his staff was so prejudicial against both the corps commander and Ferrero's division that efforts to use them intelligently foundered. Moreover, Burnside's lax leadership style let Ferrero neglect to provide his men the training they needed to survive. Second, inexperienced troops of any racial background display similar characteristics. Green units tend to be either overexuberant in the charge, like Duncan's regiments at Baylor's farm, or are inclined to panic at the slightest setback, as some of Ferrero's men did at the crater. Steadiness under fire came with experience, for white and black troops alike. Third, throughout the ages incompetent commanders regularly kill good soldiers through egregious blunders on the battlefield. Among the officers of black units, zeal for the cause of abolition did not necessarily equate to tactical proficiency, as the actions of William Birney so unfortunately proved. The Battle of the Crater clearly showed that incompetent leaders could inadvertently slaughter black and white men indiscriminately. Finally, the 1864 Virginia campaign illuminated two paths toward the goal of integrating black soldiers into the nation's military structure. Unfortunately, for many years the example of Benjamin Butler's Army of the James was set aside in favor of the ruinous course adopted by George Meade's Army of the Potomac.

Notes

1. Organizational charts of the Army of the Potomac and the Army of the James can be found in U.S. War Department, *The War of the Rebellion: A Compilation of the Official Records of the Union and Confederate Armies*, 128 vols. (Washington, D.C.: Government Printing Office, 1880–1901), 1st ser., 36 (1):106–19 (hereafter cited as *OR*). At the beginning of May 1864 the Ninth Army Corps was technically not a part of the Army of the Potomac but only unofficially associated with it. It formally became part of the Army of the Potomac on May 24, 1864.

2. The peculiar situation of Burnside and his corps in early May 1864 is delineated in William Marvel, *Burnside* (Chapel Hill: University of North Carolina Press, 1991), 346–47, and in Gordon C. Rhea, *The Battle of the Wilderness, May 5–6, 1864* (Baton Rouge: Louisiana State University Press, 1994), 48. Typical of the Army of the Potomac's attitude toward African American units at this time is the oft-quoted observation of Colonel Theodore Lyman of Meade's staff on May 7: "A division of black troops, under General Ferrero, and belonging to the 9th Corps, marched up and massed in a hollow near by. As I looked at them, my soul was troubled and I would gladly have seen them marched back to Washington. Can we not fight our own battles, without calling on these humble hewers of wood and drawers of water, to be bayonetted by the unsparing Southerners? We do not dare trust them in the line of battle. Ah, you may make speeches at home, but here, where it is life or death, we dare not risk it. They have been put to guard the trains and have repulsed one or two little cavalry attacks in a creditable manner; but God help them if the grey-backed infantry attack them!" George R. Agassiz, ed., *Meade's Headquarters, 1863–1865: Letters of Colonel Theodore Lyman from the Wilderness to Appomattox* (Boston: Atlantic Monthly Press, 1922), 102.

3. Butler's views and actions in regard to African American units serving in the Army of the James are best summarized in Edward G. Longacre, *Army of Amateurs: General Benjamin F. Butler and the Army of the James, 1863–1865* (Mechanicsburg, Pa.: Stackpole Books, 1997), 50–58.

4. Butler's plan and the role of black units in it are fully described in William Glenn Robertson, *Back Door to Richmond: The Bermuda Hundred Campaign, April–June 1864* (Newark, Del.: University of Delaware Press, 1987), 21–22, 59–61. The plan also called for Colonel Robert M. West's 1st and 2nd U.S. Colored Cavalry Regiments to parallel the army's waterborne advance on the Virginia Peninsula to its right.

5. Ezra J. Warner, *Generals in Blue: Lives of the Union Commanders* (Baton Rouge: Louisiana State University Press, 1964), 229–30, 557–58; Mark Mayo Boatner III, *Civil War Dictionary* (New York: David McKay Company, 1959), 251; Roger D. Hunt and Jack R. Brown, *Brevet Brigadier Generals in Blue* (Gaithersburg, Md.: Olde Soldier Books, 1990), 177; *OR*, 1st ser., 33:268–69; Frederick H. Dyer, *A Compendium of the War of the Rebellion*, 3 vols. (1908; New York: Thomas Yoseloff, 1959), 3:1723–25, 1727, 1730.

6. *OR*, 1st ser., 36 (2):165–66; Robertson, *Back Door to Richmond*, 60–61, 115; Dyer, *A Compendium of the War of the Rebellion*, 3:1724.

7. *OR*, 1st ser., 36 (2):166–70, 269–72, 306–8; Robertson, *Back Door to Richmond*, 231, 239–40. Detesting Gillmore, Butler had originally planned for Hincks to lead the expedition on June 9; but Gillmore stood on his rank, and Butler reluctantly relegated Hincks to a supporting role. For a detailed treatment of the June 9 operation, see William Glenn Robertson, *The Petersburg Campaign: The Battle of Old Men and Young Boys, June 9, 1864* (Lynchburg, Va.: H. E. Howard, Inc., 1989).

8. Thomas J. Howe, *The Petersburg Campaign: Wasted Valor, June 15–18, 1864* (Lynchburg, Va.: H. E. Howard, Inc., 1988), 10–21; *OR*, 1st ser., 40 (1):720–21; Dyer, *A Compendium of the War of the Rebellion*, 3:1240; Hunt and Brown, *Brevet Brigadier Generals*, 291. Holman commanded the provisional brigade because its nominal commander, Brigadier General Edward Wild, was under arrest for insubordination. See *OR*, 1st ser., 40 (2):202.

9. *OR*, 1st ser., 40 (1):720–21, 724; *OR*, 1st ser., 51 (1):265–66; Howe, *The Petersburg Campaign*, 22–24.

10. *OR*, 1st ser., 40 (1):721–22, 724–25; *OR*, 1st ser., 51 (1):264, 266–67.

11. *OR*, 1st ser., 40 (1):722–23, 725–26; *OR*, 1st ser., 51 (1):264, 267–68; Howe, *The Petersburg Campaign*, 33–35. Although it remains useful for context, Howe's account, both text and map, is somewhat at variance with the after-action reports in its placement of units.

12. *OR*, 1st ser., 40 (1):236–37, 722–23; *OR*, 1st ser., 51 (1):269; Howe, *The Petersburg Campaign*, 35. An eyewitness account of the atrocity can be found in a letter of Hermon Clarke of the 117th New York Infantry, quoted in Harry F. Jackson and Thomas F. O'Donnell, *Back Home in Oneida: Hermon Clarke and His Letters* (Syra-

cuse, N.Y.: Syracuse University Press, 1965), 142. For a modern account of the role of black troops in the initial Petersburg assaults, see Noah Andre Trudeau, *Like Men of War: Black Troops in the Civil War, 1862–1865* (Boston: Little, Brown, 1998), 220–27.

13. Warner, *Generals in Blue*, 150–51; Boatner, *Civil War Dictionary*, 277.

14. Hunt and Brown, *Brevet Brigadier Generals*, 558; Boatner, *Civil War Dictionary*, 761, 836; Warner, *Generals in Blue*, 502; *OR*, 1st ser., 36 (1):114; Janet B. Hewett, ed., *Supplement to the Official Records of the Union and Confederate Armies* (Wilmington, N.C.: Broadfoot Publishing Company, 1995–98), ser. 89:530–40, 582–89, 619–26, 673–99, 814–21, ser. 90:11–22; Dyer, *A Compendium of the War of the Rebellion*, 3:1016, 1726–28, 1730–31.

15. *OR*, 1st ser., 36 (1):986–89; Michael E. Stevens, ed., *As If It Were Glory: Robert Beecham's Civil War from the Iron Brigade to the Black Regiments* (Madison, Wis.: Madison House, 1998), 169.

16. *OR*, 1st ser., 36 (1):989–91; Hewett, *Supplement to the Official Records of the Union and Confederate Armies*, ser. 89:633, 638, 700. During this period the detachment of the 30th Connecticut (Colored) Infantry in Thomas's brigade was merged into and henceforth was known as the 31st USCT.

17. *OR*, 1st ser., 40 (1):594–95; *OR*, 1st ser., 40 (2):137, 139, 194, 207–8, 251, 282–84, 462–63, 467, 472; Hewett, *Supplement to the Official Records of the Union and Confederate Armies*, ser. 89:626–27.

18. *OR*, 40 (1):595; *OR*, 40 (2):525, 529, 561, 569, 587; *OR*, 40 (3):101, 131, 144, 166, 182, 187, 192, 196, 236.

19. *OR*, 1st ser., 40 (3):237, 304; *Report of the Committee on the Conduct of the War on the Attack on Petersburg, on the 30th Day of July, 1864* (Washington, D.C.: Government Printing Office, 1865), 14, 104; Michael A. Cavanaugh and William Marvel, *The Petersburg Campaign: The Battle of the Crater, "The Horrid Pit," June 25–August 6, 1864* (Lynchburg, Va.: H. E. Howard, Inc., 1989), 4–10, 16–17; Marvel, *Burnside*, 391–93.

20. *Report of the Committee on the Conduct of the War*, 14–18; *OR*, 1st ser., 40 (1): 59, 136; *OR*, 1st ser., 40 (3):101, 131, 196, 240, 320.

21. Boatner, *Civil War Dictionary*, 277; Warner, *Generals in Blue*, 151; *OR*, 1st ser., 40 (3): 99, 252, 292, 352–53, 364, 369, 373.

22. Boatner, *Civil War Dictionary*, 914; Warner, *Generals in Blue*, 556–57; *OR*, 1st ser., 40 (3):99, 364.

23. *OR*, 1st ser., 40 (3):390–91, 478–79, 481, 526–27, 531, 613; Cavanaugh and Marvel, *The Petersburg Campaign*, 20, 28.

24. *OR*, 1st ser., 40 (1):46, 60–62; *OR*, 1st ser., 40 (3):608; *Report of the Committee on the Conduct of the War*, 17–18, 42, 55–56, 125; Cavanaugh and Marvel, *The Petersburg Campaign*, 19–23; Marvel, *Burnside*, 394–96.

25. Warner, *Generals in Blue*, 277; *OR*, 1st ser., 40 (3):609–12; Cavanaugh and Marvel, *The Petersburg Campaign*, 24.

26. Henry Goddard Thomas, "The Colored Troops at Petersburg," in Robert Under-

wood Johnson and Clarence Clough Buel, eds., *Battles and Leaders of the Civil War*, 4 vols. (New York: Century Company, 1884), 4:563; Cavanaugh and Marvel, *The Petersburg Campaign*, 37–49; Marvel, *Burnside*, 398–404; OR, 1st ser., 40 (1):788.

27. Thomas, "The Colored Troops at Petersburg," 564; OR, 1st ser., 40 (1):103–4, 118–19; *Report of the Committee on the Conduct of the War*, 105.

28. OR, 1st ser., 40 (1):596–97; Cavanaugh and Marvel, *The Petersburg Campaign*, 56–58, 85, 89; Pia Seija Seagrave, ed., *A Boy Lieutenant: Memoirs of Freeman S. Bowley, 30th United States Colored Troops Officer* (1906; Fredericksburg, Va.: Sergeant Kirkland's Museum and Historical Society, 1997), 83–86.

29. OR, 1st ser., 40 (1):104–7, 598–99; Thomas, "The Colored Troops at Petersburg," 564–67; *Report of the Committee on the Conduct of the War*, 121–22; Stevens, *As If It Were Glory*, 182–85; Cavanaugh and Marvel, *The Petersburg Campaign*, 57–58, 85, 88.

30. OR, 1st ser., 40 (1):93, 103–4, 119, 128, 529, 595–99; Cavanaugh and Marvel, *The Petersburg Campaign*, 87–103; Marvel, *Burnside*, 405–8; George S. Bernard, ed., *War Talks of Confederate Veterans* (Petersburg, Va.: Fenn & Owen, 1892), 159–60. Following the battle, Ferrero was among the officers censured by the army court of inquiry for dereliction of duty.

31. OR, 1st ser., 40 (1):246–48, 250; Cavanaugh and Marvel, *The Petersburg Campaign*, 131–33; Thomas Truxtun Moebs, *Black Soldiers—Black Sailors—Black Ink: Research Guide on African-Americans in U.S. Military History, 1526–1900* (Chesapeake Bay, Va.: Moebs Publishing Company, 1994), 1307.

32. OR, 1st ser., 40 (1):59, 74; *Report of the Committee on the Conduct of the War*, 42, 91, 102, 119; Thomas, "The Colored Troops at Petersburg," 563; Bernard, *War Talks of Confederate Veterans*, 183; Stevens, *As If It Were Glory*, 178–79. Long after the event, Ferrero repeated the story of much preliminary preparation by the division in conversation with Orlando Willcox, but his absence during the period in question tends to lessen his credibility on that point. See Robert Garth Scott, ed., *Forgotten Valor: The Memoirs, Journals, and Civil War Letters of Orlando B. Willcox* (Kent, Ohio: Kent State University Press, 1999), 554–55. A graphic account of the actions of Ferrero's division in the Battle of the Crater can be found in Trudeau, *Like Men of War*, 228–51.

33. Stevens, *As If It Were Glory*, 191–93; Frank J. Welcher, *The Union Army, 1861–1865: Organization and Operations*, vol. 1, *The Eastern Theater* (Bloomington: Indiana University Press, 1989), 852, 861; Boatner, *Civil War Dictionary*, 230; OR, 42 (1):216–17.

34. OR, 1st ser., 42 (1):120; OR, 1st ser., 42 (2):101, 138–39; Dyer, *A Compendium of the War of the Rebellion*, 3:1016, 1725; Warner, *Generals in Blue*, 35; Boatner, *Civil War Dictionary*, 65; Richard J. Sommers, *Richmond Redeemed: The Siege at Petersburg* (Garden City, N.Y.: Doubleday, 1981), 88.

35. OR, 1st ser., 42 (1):120, 217–21, 779–80; OR, 1st ser., 42 (2):182, 188, 209; Welcher, *The Union Army*, 862–64; Boatner, *Civil War Dictionary*, 230–31.

36. Sommers, *Richmond Redeemed*, 4–8, 18–21; Welcher, *The Union Army*, 872–73, 875; Longacre, *Army of Amateurs*, 211–12.

37. Welcher, *The Union Army*, 452–53, 482–83; Warner, *Generals in Blue*, 354–55; Boatner, *Civil War Dictionary*, 615; Sommers, *Richmond Redeemed*, 31; OR, 1st ser., 42 (2):622, 1026, 1044.

38. Welcher, *The Union Army*, 876; Sommers, *Richmond Redeemed*, 27–28, 31, 34–36; OR, 1st ser., 42 (1):110; OR, 1st ser., 42 (2):552.

39. Sommers, *Richmond Redeemed*, 36–37; OR, 1st ser., 42 (1):819–20.

40. OR, 1st ser., 42 (1):136, 820; Sommers, *Richmond Redeemed*, 31; Benjamin F. Butler, *Autobiography and Personal Reminiscences of Major-General Benj. F. Butler: Butler's Book* (Boston: A. M. Thayer & Co., 1892), 742–43; Moebs, *Black Soldiers*, 1305–12; Walter F. Beyer and Oscar F. Keydel, eds., *Deeds of Valor: How America's Civil War Heroes Won the Medal of Honor* (1903; Stamford, Conn.: Longmeadow Press, 1994), 434–35; Senate Committee on Veterans' Affairs, *Medal of Honor Recipients 1863–1978*, 96th Cong., 1st sess., 1979, S. Committee Print No. 3:25, 27, 40, 88, 93, 109, 112, 117, 119, 129, 136–37, 189–90, 197, 246–47. Trudeau provides an excellent secondary account of the New Market Heights engagement in *Like Men of War*, 284–94.

41. Sommers, *Richmond Redeemed*, 37–38, 80–82; Welcher, *The Union Army*, 877–78.

42. Sommers, *Richmond Redeemed*, 84–92; OR, 42 (1):134, 772–75, 778, 780–81, 820. See also Trudeau, *Like Men of War*, 294–300.

43. Sommers, *Richmond Redeemed*, 119, 121, 131–32, 137, 141, 147, 151; Welcher, *The Union Army*, 887–88; OR, 1st ser., 42 (1):773, 775, 778, 781, 818.

44. Welcher, *Union Army*, 437, 504–7, 892–93; OR, 1st ser., 42 (1):771–77, 779, 814, 818–19; OR, 1st ser., 42 (3):651, 702, 791; Longacre, *Army of Amateurs*, 301.

7

THE BATTLE
OF SALTVILLE

Thomas D. Mays

On October 2, 1864, near the Southwest Virginia town of Saltville, Confederate forces commanded by General John S. Williams repulsed an invading Union army under General Stephen Gano Burbridge. The battle would have been remembered as a small affair, confined to the footnotes of history, if it were not for what took place the next morning. What started as an inconsequential but intense mountain battle degenerated into a no-quarter racial massacre. When the fighting ended, Confederate troops, disregarding their commanders' orders, began killing many of the wounded black troops that had fallen into their hands. The murders would continue for almost a week. Both Union and Confederate eyewitness accounts and regimental records demonstrate that the murders at Saltville were among the worst atrocities of the American Civil War.[1]

Saltville was not, however, the only massacre of black troops in the Civil War. By the end of 1864 battlefield atrocities had become far too common. Confederates were known to have killed black Union prisoners on several occasions, one of the most infamous having been at Fort Pillow, Tennessee, on April 12, 1864. Preeminent Civil War historian Bell I. Wiley, after editing a Southern confession to the executions at Saltville, noted, "It appears that Saltville deserves more than Fort Pillow to be called a massacre." Although historians agree that Fort Pillow remains the most notorious racial massacre of the war, the Battle of Saltville should be rated as equally brutal.[2]

Most witnesses agreed that the Federal forces at Fort Pillow had refused an offer to surrender and that Confederates rushing the works granted no quarter to black troops defending the fort. Although Confederate general

Nathan Bedford Forrest's actions at Fort Pillow are inexcusable, his men committed the murders during the heat of battle after the garrison had refused to surrender. The situation at Saltville was quite different. The men killed at Saltville were prisoners, mostly wounded, and were murdered in the days following the fight.[3]

In the fall of 1864, as General Ulysses S. Grant tightened his noose around the Confederacy, the natural resources of Southwest Virginia gained in importance as Southern supplies became scarce. Salt from the area was vital to the Confederates, who depended on the Virginia and Tennessee Railroad, which ran from Tennessee and points south to Lynchburg and on to Richmond to distribute it.

Possibly in an effort to save his failing reputation, Federal general Stephen Gano Burbridge pressed for permission to lead an expedition from Kentucky against the saltworks of Southwest Virginia. Although he remained loyal to the Union, he was a plantation owner. Early in the war Burbridge had earned a respectable reputation at the Battle of Shiloh and later was credited with rebuffing John Hunt Morgan's Ohio raid. Yet as commander of the District of Kentucky his inept and tyrannical behavior had alienated most Union supporters. Burbridge had no tolerance for dissent and jailed many who publicly opposed his policies.[4]

While General Burbridge planned his invasion the Confederates were facing many setbacks. On September 2 General William T. Sherman's forces had captured the vital transportation hub of Atlanta, Georgia. In Virginia, Confederate general Jubal A. Early's small army operating in the Shenandoah Valley had met stunning defeat at Winchester and Fisher's Hill. These setbacks opened the way for General Philip H. Sheridan's Union army to advance up the valley. At Petersburg, General Ulysses S. Grant tightened his headlock on General Robert E. Lee's Army of Northern Virginia.

In Southwest Virginia, Confederate general John Echols, recuperating from wounds, recognized that the fall of Atlanta would free Federal forces for a possible raid on the area. On his arrival in the department, Echols admitted that he "found everything in the worst possible condition." Many of the troops in the department were unarmed; others were mutinous; and many lacked regimental organization. Should the Federals advance, Echols believed he would "have serious fears of the result."[5]

During the fall of 1864, Echols, despite many problems, did all in his power to organize the defenses in Southwest Virginia. He mobilized and reorganized the local reserve forces, noting in the process that they would make good troops "if they had not had the power to select their own officers."[6] In addition to the threat of a Federal attack, pro-Union sentiment was strong in both Southwest Virginia and in East Tennessee, and the area had become a refuge for hundreds of Confederate deserters.[7]

Authorities in Richmond heeded General Echols's warnings. On September 27 Confederate secretary of war James A. Seddon ordered General John C. Breckinridge, a former vice president of the United States, to return to Southwest Virginia and take personal command.[8] Although a political general, Breckinridge had proven himself a competent military commander. In May 1864 he had saved the Shenandoah Valley from destruction at the Battle of New Market. There his ragtag army, including the Keydets of the Virginia Military Institute, had defeated a Federal invading army of superior numbers. But by the time Breckinridge was ordered back to the department, Burbridge's Union army was already on the move.

On September 20, 1864, the Federal campaign began as the main force of three brigades of Kentucky cavalry and mounted infantry headed east from Mount Sterling, Kentucky. Four days later six hundred men of the as yet unorganized 5th U.S. Colored Cavalry (USCC) joined Burbridge's army at Prestonburg, Kentucky.[9]

The blacks Burbridge planned to employ in the raid would pose a special problem. Even though Lincoln's plan for arming ex-slaves to fight their former masters had matured by 1864, Kentucky presented a dilemma to the Lincoln government. It was a loyal slave state. The Emancipation Proclamation failed to free any Kentucky slaves; even so, many abolitionists pressed for the arming of blacks in the state. By enlisting the support of white units and offering promotions to members who would officer the blacks, the army defused some of the negative reaction blacks would otherwise have received in the service. The army then established boards to test the qualifications of potential officers, thereby creating possibly the best-trained officer corps in the service.[10]

In early 1864 General Burbridge issued General Order No. 24, which authorized the raising of black units composed of freedmen and ex-slaves. The order admitted slaves at the "request" of their owners. Whites in the state reacted violently to the arming of their former slaves. Captain James Fidler, an enlisting officer in Lebanon, Kentucky, witnessed his black recruits mobbed and beaten in the streets. When the white 13th Kentucky Cavalry arrived in Lebanon early in June, Fidler found that he too was a target for violence. On June 10 Fidler narrowly missed being killed by a shot fired at him by a sniper in the town. Later one of Fidler's black recruits recorded his experience in verse:[11]

Captain Fidler's come to town,
　With his abolition papers;
He swears he is one of Lincoln's men,
　He's cutting almighty capers.

Captain Fidler's come to town,
　With his abolition triggers,
He swears he's one of Lincoln's men,
　"Enlisting all the niggers." . . .

My old massa's come to town,
　Cutting a Southern figure;
What's the matter with the man?
　Lincoln's got his niggers?

Some folks say this "almighty fuss
　Is getting worse and bigger";
Some folks say "its worse and worse,"
　Because I am a "nigger."

We'll get our colored regiments strung
　Out in a line of battle;
I'll bet my money agin the South
　The rebels will skedaddle.[12]

But pressure on recruiting officers began to ease in the state when the white population realized that black units would help offset Kentucky's draft quota. Many changed their attitudes as they realized that a black man could stop a Confederate bullet just as effectively as a white man. The Federals took advantage of the opportunity by ordering slaves in the state enrolled without regard to the wishes of their owners. On June 30 Adjutant General Lorenzo Thomas gave permission for the officers of the 5th USCC to start selecting recruits for the regiment.[13]

Colonel James Brisbin, a well-known abolitionist, eventually became commander of the 5th. His first duty was enlisting blacks at Camp Nelson, a camp of instruction south of Louisville, where he trained the new volunteers for the regiment. Camp Nelson served as a primary recruitment center, quartermaster and commissary depot, and hospital facility for the Union army in the West. Eleven regiments of black troops would serve

Private Samuel Truehart, Company E, 5th U.S. Colored Cavalry.
(Courtesy of David E. Brown)

there, making it the third largest African American recruitment camp in the nation. The camp was also home to thousands of black women and children who were refugees following their husbands and fathers into the protection of the Union army.[14]

The organization of the 5th proceeded slowly in the summer and fall of 1864. Many of the companies were recruited at Camp Nelson, while others were enlisted in nearby towns including Lebanon, Louisville, and Lexington. The majority of the men were ex-slaves who had enlisted for three years. One company became a dumping ground for draftees and conscripts. Of eighty-three men in Company L, fifty-three were substitutes and ten were draftees.[15]

Under the army's organizational plans, the officers of the 5th USCC were to be whites selected by a board; the noncommissioned officers were to be chosen from black men in the ranks. Yet, with almost an entire regiment of ex-slaves, the officers found it difficult to find men literate enough to handle the tasks assigned to sergeants. Lieutenant Colonel L. Henry Carpenter asked for permission to appoint experienced white soldiers as noncommissioned officers. "Scarcely any of the Coloredmen enlisted into this regiment can read or write," he stated. It is unclear how Carpenter solved the problem, but it would be months before he would be able to train the men needed for efficient operation.[16]

While many white Kentuckians continued to harass Federal authorities in their efforts to recruit black troops, some Union officers made matters worse. Captain Thomas Branch of the 5th contributed to the problem by confiscating slaves for the regiment and then accepting bribes from their owners for their return. Slave owners would pay Branch one hundred dollars, and in return he agreed to release the slaves and give the owners their enlistment contracts. On receiving the money he gave the slaves' enlistment papers to the owners and kept the slaves for the regiment. He also threatened to kill slave owners who would not cooperate with him. Branch was eventually punished, but not until he had disfranchised many "loyal" Kentuckians.[17]

When word of Burbridge's raid reached them, the men of the 5th USCC still had not been organized into a regiment. Some had not even enlisted; only a few of their officers had been appointed, and even fewer noncommissioned officers were at their posts. The officers hastily placed the unit in a temporary organization. Command of the group went to Colonel James F. Wade, who would eventually command the 6th USCC. With the assistance of Colonel James Brisbin, the officers hurriedly attempted to organize an untrained mob of recruits into some semblance of order. The men of the

5th were issued Enfield infantry rifles (weapons useless to mounted men as they could not be loaded from horseback) and untrained horses.[18]

On joining Burbridge's force at Prestonburg, Kentucky, Brisbin observed that his men "were made the subject of much ridicule and many insulting remarks by the white troops, and in some instances petty outrages, such as pulling off the caps of the colored soldiers, stealing their horses etc." While it was common for veteran regiments to tease green troops, the harassment of the 5th had ugly racial overtones. Brisbin concluded that "these insults, as well as the jeers and taunts that they would not fight, were borne by the colored soldiers patiently . . . in no instance did I hear colored soldiers make any reply to insulting language used toward [them] by white troops."[19]

Burbridge placed the black troops with General Nathaniel C. McLean's Kentucky Division. His plan called for three separate columns. He would march directly on the saltworks with McLean's Kentucky Division while the other two units would create a diversion before joining his force. Burbridge personally took command of McLean's division. The force consisted of mounted infantry, cavalry, and six mountain howitzers. In all Burbridge would have over 4,000 men. The two diversionary columns included General Jacob Ammen's 800 troops who were to hold Bull's Gap, Tennessee, blocking the Virginia and Tennessee Railroad, while General Alvan C. Gillem advanced on Jonesboro, Tennessee, with 1,650 men. Ammen and Gillem would then link up and join Burbridge for the raid on Saltville.[20]

On September 27 Burbridge's army left Prestonburg, advanced through Pikeville, pushed a small party of Confederate pickets from its path, and camped for the night. There Burbridge prepared his men for the rough passage through the mountains of Southwest Virginia. He ordered the baggage train to the rear; each horse then was loaded with two bushels of corn to be carried behind the saddle. Burbridge's entire force was mounted and traveled without wagons or ambulances; mules carried the six small mountain howitzers that served as artillery. The weapons could be carried by mules by strapping the wheels and barrels to the animals' backs.[21]

During the next four days, Confederates in Colonel Henry L. Giltner's small 300-man Kentucky cavalry brigade did all in its power to slow the Federal advance. They blocked roads and ravines and set ambushes at every turn in the road, forcing the Federals to deploy and drive them from each obstacle. As the majority of both Giltner's Confederate command and Burbridge's Federals were Kentuckians, the fighting became personal. Neighbor fought neighbor and former slaves faced slave owners as the Kentuckians brought their personal feuds into Virginia.

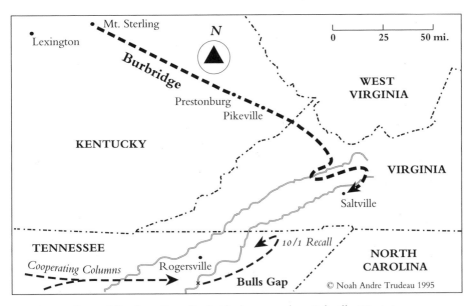

Map 7.1. General Stephen Gano Burbridge's approach to Saltville, Virginia, September 27, 1864. (Courtesy of Noah Andre Trudeau)

By the night of October 1, the Federals had pushed Giltner's men within two miles of Saltville. The small town had only Giltner's brigade and the local militia to protect it. Yet instead of immediately attacking and capturing the saltworks before reinforcements arrived, Burbridge ordered his men to camp for the night.[22]

During the day in Saltville, the militia from the counties of Southwest Virginia attempted to organize. On arriving in town, seventeen-year-old Second Lieutenant John H. Wise joined Colonel Robert Preston's militia unit. Wise had attended Virginia Military Institute and had seen combat with the Keydets at the Battle of New Market. Although quite young, Wise used his father's political connections as ex-governor and general to secure a commission in the Virginia militia. When Wise reported to Colonel Preston, he found that "Colonel Bob" was "short, thick-set, and had an immense snow-white beard, extending nearly to his sword-belt." Wise concluded that Preston's "appearance, figure[,] beard, merry twinkling eye, and ruddy face instantly suggested Santa Claus." He found Preston's Southwest Virginia reserves in "every stage of manhood, from immature boyhood to decrepit old age. One of his companies drawn up in line looked as irregular as a pile of barrel-hoops. There was no pretense of uniforms; they wore everything, from straw hats to coon-skin caps." Their Belgian rifles and cartridge boxes provided the unit's only vestige of a uniform military appearance.[23]

In Saltville that evening, Colonel Preston reported to Brigadier General Alfred E. Jackson, who was in the process of organizing the Southwest Virginia militia units. His troops referred to Jackson as "Mudwall" or "Mudfence" in a rather uncharitable comparison to the famous Thomas J. "Stonewall" Jackson, *the* Jackson of the Confederate army. When Preston arrived, the young Wise overheard the general saying: "Kernel . . . my men tell me the Yanks have a lot of nigger soldiers along. Do you think you reserves will fight niggers?" "Fight'em?" replied Preston, "by ——, Sir, they'll eat'em up! No! Not eat'em up! That's too much! By ——, Sir, we'll cut'em up!"[24]

As the night set in around Saltville, reserves and regular troops began to filter in. Like Burbridge, Federal general Gillem's diversionary force enjoyed success on October 1, but then new orders, canceling the entire Saltville raid, turned them back. Gillem had united with Ammen's command in order to push the Confederates from Jonesboro, Tennessee. After a brief skirmish at Jonesboro on September 29, the Federals pushed John Vaughn's Confederate command back to Carter's Station on the Watauga River. On October 1 Gillem forced the Confederates from their works along the river. He was preparing to join Burbridge's main force at Saltville when a courier arrived with word that Confederate general Nathan Bedford Forrest threatened Sherman's supply line to Atlanta. Sherman canceled Burbridge's entire operation and ordered him into Tennessee to block Forrest. Gillem immediately started for Tennessee, but Burbridge failed to receive news of the order for another two days.[25]

Bivouacked near Saltville, Burbridge may have been content to rest on his laurels. He had just crossed some of the most rugged terrain in the eastern part of the country. Although opposed by Colonel Giltner's undermanned veterans, Burbridge had easily brushed all resistance aside. The next morning, October 2, Burbridge expected to find only the remnants of Giltner's beaten brigade along with the local militia. He had no reason to anticipate much resistance from the "old men and boys" of Southwest Virginia.

But the Confederates did indeed find help. On the morning of October 2 the Rebels assembled about 2,800 troops to face 4,500 Federals. At Saltville the Southern forces were commanded by General John S. Williams at the front, while the overall commander of the department, Major General John C. Breckinridge, funneled reinforcements from nearby Abingdon. The Rebel defensive line at Saltville followed the rough terrain surrounding

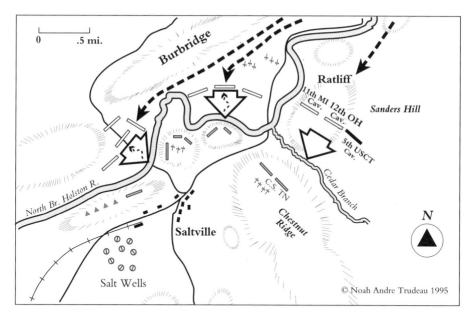

Map 7.2. The Massacre at Saltville, Virginia, October 2, 1864.
(Courtesy of Noah Andre Trudeau)

the town. Northeast of town, Sanders Hill and Chestnut Ridge dominated the area. Between the two hills ran Cedar Branch, a small stream in a deep ravine that passed close to "Governor" James Sanders's house and emptied into the North Fork of the Holston River near the river road ford. To the left of the ford the Confederates had fortified the yard of a small log church near Elizabeth Cemetery.

The main attack came on the Confederate right along Chestnut Ridge in front of John S. Williams's division, including the small brigades of George G. Dibrell and Felix H. Robertson and the guerrilla company of Champ Ferguson. While Ferguson remains an obscure figure to many historians, he was one of the most notorious guerrillas of the war. Driven out of the foothills of Kentucky by Unionists early in the war, he formed a gang of backwoodsmen in Tennessee who then occupied themselves with attacking local loyalists. By the time of the Saltville raid, Ferguson and his gang had been incorporated into the Rebel army.

About halfway up Chestnut Ridge, the defenders had dug a series of rifle pits; their main works were along the crest of the hill. The attack on the forward line came as the Federals advanced down Sanders' Hill and up Chestnut Ridge in front of Williams's men. The battle began in earnest around

10:00 A.M. as the Federals made a series of dismounted charges upon Chestnut Ridge. The Yankees decided to attack on foot after realizing the strength of the Confederate position. After two unsuccessful attempts to take the works, Robert Ratliff's brigade prepared to make a final charge up the ridge. This time the 5th USCC, 12th Ohio Cavalry, and 11th Michigan Cavalry made a dismounted assault up the hill. Accounting for horse holders and stragglers, around 400 men of the 5th USCC fell in line with the rest of the brigade.[26]

As the Federal battle line formed, Dibrell's Confederate scouts could hear a speech given to Ratliff's brigade by an officer whom they assumed to be Burbridge. The officer encouraged the men in their efforts and stated that depriving the Confederates of the saltworks would do more to bring down the Confederacy than the capture of Richmond.[27]

After the speech, Ratliff's brigade advanced down an overgrown ravine behind Sanders's farm, crossed Cedar Branch, and then moved up Chestnut Ridge. Confederate and Federal skirmishers met in the dense undergrowth in the ravine. One Federal observed: "More than once duels took place between individuals at a distance of not more than half-a-dozen paces—each firing at a noise heard beyond until a groan or cessation of the firing announced that the heard but unseen enemy was dead. At other times a rebel would pop out from behind a tree or rock only a few feet from an advancing Yankee, and then it was the quickest and surest shot of the two who lived to tell the story."[28]

Sergeant Jeremiah Davis, the guidon bearer for Company H, 12th Ohio Cavalry, found himself in a hand-to-hand fight for his colors with a Confederate. With no help in sight, and only the flag for a weapon, Davis "harpooned his enemy with the sharp spear head of the flagstaff—the brazen point passing through the rebel and appearing between his lower ribs on the opposite side." After much in-close fighting, the Federals emerged from the undergrowth in front of the Confederate works.[29]

When the Confederates saw that many of the advancing Federal troops were black, they became enraged. "The cry was raised that we were fighting negroes," recalled one Southerner, "the first we ever met." Lieutenant John Web, his brother Thomas, and several others of the 8th Tennessee Cavalry jumped from behind the Confederate breastworks and attacked the blacks with their pistols. The blacks killed John Web and wounded the others as they drove the Confederates back to the works.[30]

As the Federals advanced, they found a gap in the line between Robertson's brigade on the left and some of the reserves on the right. Robertson had withdrawn his brigade without warning and left Dibrell's brigade almost surrounded, leaving a large gap in the center of the Confederate line. The Federal attackers took full advantage of the opportunity and pressed the Confederates to the top of the ridge. Armed with Spencer repeating carbines, the men of the 11th Michigan Cavalry and 12th Ohio Cavalry had an advantage over Dibrell's and Ferguson's men. Yet as the day progressed the men in Ratliff's brigade began to run low on ammunition.[31]

Many Federals were impressed by the performance of the blacks in the charge. An officer of the 13th Kentucky (U.S.) Cavalry admitted that he "never thought they would fight until he saw them there." He added that he "never saw troops fight like they did. The rebels were firing on them with grape and canister and were mowing them down by the scores but others kept straight on." After leading the blacks as they took the Confederate works, Colonel James Brisbin, commander of the 5th USCC, noted: "I have seen white troops fight in twenty-seven battles and I never saw any fight better" than the blacks.[32]

Several of the young boys in Colonel Robert Preston's Virginia militia had been "sighting their guns and showing how they would shoot a nigger, if they had a chance." The breach in the left of the line gave the boys their opportunity. Half of Preston's reserves went up Chestnut Ridge. The militia fought with Ratliff's brigade for fifteen minutes until the line stabilized. The militia then returned to its place in reserve with the loss of one or two men.[33]

After the attack on the Confederate right, Burbridge made two more unsupported assaults on the Southern lines. One came on the center, and the last on the far left. But by the end of the day, after some desperate fighting, the Rebel lines still held. The Federals had temporarily broken the Confederate line with the charge of the black troops, but without reinforcement they would have to fall back. With the timely arrival of Southern reinforcements and the unexpected tenacity of the local reserves, Williams won the day.[34]

At about 5:00 P.M. Burbridge decided to retreat. Ratliff's cavalry, including the black troops, held the Confederate works until dark. At nightfall the Federals, out of ammunition and energy, pulled back from their advance position. They built large fires in order to deceive the Confederates into thinking that they remained, but Burbridge's force retreated, leaving most of its dead and wounded on the field.[35]

Upon Burbridge's withdrawal from the field, some Confederates advanced into the vacant Union position. Silas Sims, a member of the 4th Kentucky (CSA) Cavalry, found a dead Federal officer who had been hit in the head by an artillery shell. Sims reached into his haversack, brought forth a handful of salt, and, according to one witness, poured it into the open skull. "There," he said to the corpse, "you came for some salt, now take some."[36]

After dark Confederate captain Edward O. Guerrant and his aide, George Dallas Mosgrove of the 4th Kentucky Cavalry, met with General Felix Robertson. Mosgrove noted that Robertson "was the youngest looking General in the army, apparently not more than twenty-four years of age." During the meeting the "gallant and handsome" Robertson, who had fought on the right with Ferguson, proudly informed Guerrant that "he had killed nearly all the negroes."[37]

The black troops knew what was coming, aware that some of the men the Confederates captured during the battle had already been murdered. As Burbridge began his retreat, many seriously wounded black soldiers attempted to follow. Colonel Brisbin looked on in horror as he "saw one man riding with his arm off, another shot through the lungs, and another shot through both hips," all attempting to evade the Confederates. He reported later that at least 118 of the 400 men of the 5th USCC who took part in the fight were killed, wounded or missing.[38]

The next morning, October 3, as the battlefield lay enveloped in a blanket of fog, firing along the line prompted Mosgrove to think that a new Federal attack was under way. As Mosgrove later recalled: "Presently I heard a shot, then another and another until the firing swelled to the volume of a skirmish line." He then mounted his horse and rode forward to ascertain the source of the shooting. Arriving in front of Ferguson's, Dibrell's, and Robertson's men on Chestnut Ridge, he "found the Tennesseans were killing negroes. . . . Hearing more firing at the front, I cautiously rode forward and came upon a squad of Tennesseans, mad and excited to the highest degree. They were shooting every wounded negro they could find. Hearing firing on other parts of the field, I knew the same awful work was going on all about me."[39]

Mosgrove was appalled at the scene, yet he admitted that it would have been futile (if not dangerous) to attempt to stop it. He observed that "[s]ome were so slightly wounded that they could run, but when they ran from the muzzle of one pistol it was only to be confronted by another."[40]

Guerrant also heard the firing and noted in his diary, "Scouts were sent [and] went all over the field and the continual sing of the rifle, sung the death knell of many a poor negro who was unfortunate enough not to be killed yesterday. Our men took no negro prisoners. Great numbers of them were killed yesterday and today."[41]

Henry Shocker, a wounded prisoner from the 12th Ohio Cavalry, watched in horror as the guerrilla chief Champ Ferguson calmly walked about the battlefield killing black and white prisoners.[42]

Shocker got a good look at the outlaw at Saltville. Ferguson was dressed in a butternut uniform without insignia. He had on a black plug hat that covered his long black hair. His beard was also long and untrimmed, presenting a fierce appearance.[43] Shocker first spotted Ferguson walking along Chestnut Ridge "pointing his revolver down at the prisoners that were laying down on the field." Shocker looked on as he "heard the report of a revolver and heard the men hollering." He had just spent the night lying by a wounded friend, Crawford Henselwood. When he saw Ferguson heading their way, Shocker crawled off and hid. Henselwood was not so lucky. When the guerrilla found Henselwood, he asked him why he had come there "to fight with the damn! niggers." Ferguson then asked him: "Where will you have it, in the back or the face?" Henselwood sat up and begged; "For God's sake don't kill me soldier!" "I heard the report of a pistol," Shocker recalled, "and saw my partner fall over and he was dead." Ferguson then walked over to the Sanders house, where the wounded were being collected.[44]

Soon Shocker spotted two Confederate soldiers and asked them to take him to the hospital. He had been wounded in the calf, and the Southerners agreed to help him. Along the way the Rebels stopped in the hollow between Chestnut Ridge and Sanders's home when they saw Ferguson emerge from the house leading two black soldiers. One of the Confederates said, "Wait and lets see what he does with them." The witnesses paused as Ferguson led his prisoners up the hollow. "I saw him shoot the niggers after he took them in the hollow there," added Shocker. Then, "He came and got two more niggers out of that log cabin," Shocker continued; "I heard the report of a pistol not long afterwards." Shocker spent the rest of the morning at Sanders's before being moved a few miles away to Emory and Henry College, a school that the Confederates had converted into a general hospital.[45]

The Sanders house had been the center of Ratliff's Union line. Many of the men who had been wounded in the charge were brought to the farm and left there during the retreat. Confederate witness George D. Mosgrove found seven or eight slightly wounded blacks in a cabin. The men were lined up with their backs against the walls. As Mosgrove stepped in "a pistol-shot from the door caused me to turn and observe a boy, not more than sixteen years old, with a pistol in each hand." Mosgrove told the boy to hold his fire as he jumped out of the way. He then added, "In less time than I can write it, the boy had shot every negro in the room."[46]

Orange Sells of the 12th Ohio Cavalry also witnessed some of the murders at the cabin. "I think I saw eight or ten killed after the fight," he noted. "They were all soldiers and all wounded but one." The killing was widespread, Sells added: "I heard guns firing around there—all over—every place—it was like a skirmish."[47]

Lieutenant George W. Cutler of the 11th Michigan Cavalry looked on as eight or nine blacks were killed at Sanders's. "They were all prisoners and all wounded," he continued. As for the killers, "I could not say whether they were citizens or soldiers. They were dressed alike." The Rebels, he noted, "all appeared to be commanding themselves." Although many Confederates were local civilians called up as reserves, at that point in the war the veteran Southern regiments as well as Ferguson's guerrillas were also known for their nonmilitary appearance.[48]

Later in the morning Mosgrove watched as Generals Breckinridge and Basil Duke, along with other officers, rode to the front. The scene infuriated Breckinridge. "With blazing eyes and thunderous tones," Mosgrove recalled, the former vice president of the United States "ordered that the massacre should be stopped. He rode away and—the shooting went on. The men could not be restrained." Mosgrove asserted that he did not see any Kentuckians of his unit involved in the murders, although he admitted that they could have been. He blamed the work on the Tennessee troops, including those of Felix H. Robertson and George D. Dibrell.[49]

Mosgrove later found a young black lad "who seemed to think he was in no danger." A youthful Confederate approached him and drew his pistol, "and then the little mulatto jumped behind a sapling not larger than a man's arm, and cried out that General Duke had ordered him to remain there until he should return." It was no use. In another moment the little mulatto was a corpse.[50]

On October 3 word reached Richmond of the Confederate victory. General Echols wrote the commander of the reserve forces in Virginia, General James L. Kemper, commending him on the fine performance of this militia. He added, "There were two or three regiments of negro troops, which were badly cut up."[51]

On October 4 General Robert E. Lee issued an official report of the battle to Confederate secretary of war James A. Seddon. Lee informed Seddon that the "enemy attacked Saltville on the 2nd instant and received a bloody repulse. They retired during the night in confusion . . . leaving most of their dead and wounded on our hands. . . . All our troops behave well." Yet after several days, the truth about the battle began to emerge in Richmond as the murders continued around Saltville. The killing would go on for six days after the fight.[52]

In Southwest Virginia Federal surgeon William H. Gardner remained after the battle and continued to work with the wounded at Emory and Henry. The hospital had served both the Federal and Confederate wounded. One night a few days after the fight, Gardner watched as several men forced their way past the Confederate staff at the hospital and murdered two blacks in their beds.[53]

Confederates visited the hospital several times, and at one point Union prisoner Henry Shocker again found himself face to face with the guerrilla Champ Ferguson. As he was lying in bed at Emory and Henry, Ferguson and one of his men, Lieutenant William Hildreth, entered the room. Shocker was sharing the room with a young wounded soldier from the 11th Michigan Cavalry. The men entered, pulled up chairs, and greeted them with a pleasant inquiry: "How are you getting along boys?" Ferguson asked them what regiments they were in, and Shocker told him he was with the 12th Ohio Cavalry, stationed in Kentucky. "I suppose you have heard of me," replied the outlaw. "My name is Champ Ferguson."[54]

Hildreth recognized the 11th Michigan boy. He turned to Ferguson proclaiming, "There's that boy. I saved his life." He went on to explain how he found the prisoner on the battlefield surrounded by wounded black troops. He had saved his life by taking him to safety. "If I had seen you lying among niggers," Ferguson interrupted, "it would have been all day with you then." Hildreth changed the subject and inquired if the boy had any money. He replied in the negative, and the guerrilla handed him ten Confederate dollars to keep him in tobacco money while he was a prisoner.[55]

Ferguson then turned back to Shocker and got to the business at hand. "Do you know Lieutenant Smith?" he asked. Shocker replied that he did not. Ferguson grew angry. "Yes you do," he flew back, "you damnd yankee, you know him well enough but you don't want to know him now." "Well," he continued, "do you know where he is then?" Shocker refused to answer and the two got up to leave. As he reached the door Ferguson added, "I have a *be*grudge against Smith. We'll find him."[56]

Ferguson was searching for Lieutenant Elza C. Smith of the 13th Kentucky Cavalry. The twenty-nine-year-old Smith was a relative of Ferguson's first wife. He had joined the 13th in Clinton County, Kentucky, in 1863 and had spent much of his service chasing down guerrillas like Ferguson. Prior to the Saltville raid Smith had been placed in charge of transporting one of the region's most notorious guerrillas, Colonel Oliver P. Hamilton. Smith was leading a detail that was to transport the prisoner from Lexington to Camp Nelson, Kentucky, when, according to Smith, Hamilton attempted to flee and was killed. Hamilton had been a close friend of Ferguson, and many Southerners believed the killing had been deliberate. Ferguson intended to treat Smith in kind.[57]

Ferguson soon found Smith in an upstairs room. Smith looked up and asked, "Champ is that you?" Ferguson walked up to the bed and lifted his musket in his left hand and slapped it with his right while asking, "Smith do you see this?" Smith tried to lift his head and begged: "Champ, for God's sake dont shoot me here!"[58]

Ferguson pointed the barrel of the gun within a few inches of Smith's head and pulled the trigger. The hammer snapped but failed to ignite the priming cap. The outlaw had to pull it back and try again three times before the charge went off. A witness described how Smith was "shot through the head—the ball entered the left side of the forehead then passed through and tore off the top of the skull. His brains were oozing out on the pillow." Ferguson's partner Hildreth had been standing by with a carbine in one hand and a pistol in the other. He spoke up, "Champ, be sure your work is well done." Ferguson looked down on the body and concluded, "He is damned dead."[59]

After killing Smith, Ferguson turned his attention to another wounded prisoner, Smith's commander, Colonel Charles Hanson of the 13th Kentucky Cavalry. This time the Confederate hospital staff—at the risk of their own lives—intervened and talked Ferguson out of his plan. The next day the Confederates defused the situation in Southwest Virginia by moving the surviving wounded prisoners to Lynchburg. On October 8 the hospital sent sixty-one prisoners east. Meanwhile Ferguson quietly left the department.[60]

By the end of the week, the Richmond papers were proclaiming a great Southern victory in Southwest Virginia over Burbridge and his army. The *Richmond Enquirer* ran a column that segregated Union casualties:

Killed, (Yankee Whites)	106
Negroes,	150
Wounded, (Whites)	80
Negroes,	6

The editor of the *Enquirer* felt no need to explain the disparity in numbers between the eighty wounded whites and six wounded blacks.[61]

The *Richmond Dispatch* joined in with an editorial that praised the Confederates and mocked the black troops: "They routed Burbridge and all his 'niggers,' horse, foot and dragoon. Abundant as the article was in that region, they could not put a grain of salt on the tails of the flying black birds. The coat-tails, we mean, which stuck so straight that little boys might have played marbles on them." The editor added that: "The country had since been infested with birds of the same color, but greater respectability. They are turkey-buzzards this time, and they come in quest of Yankee carcasses."[62]

While some Confederates gloated, many Union witnesses to the massacre refused to put the incident behind them. Following his parole and return to Federal lines, surgeon Gardner of the 30th Kentucky Infantry filed a full report on Ferguson and the Saltville massacre. The document traveled up the chain of command with many endorsements and then went on to the secretary of war in Washington. General Nathaniel McLean endorsed the report with a demand that the murderers be delivered for punishment to Union authorities. "In case of refusal [he urged] that immediate retaliation be enforced upon such Confederate prisoners as we may have in our possession, man for man." On October 18 Federal couriers delivered Gardner's report to Lee's headquarters by a truce boat.[63]

Breckinridge had already informed Lee of the murders, and he added that one of the generals at Saltville had taken part in the killings. On October 21 General Lee's aide-de-camp reported to Breckinridge that the general was "much pained to hear of the treatment the negro prisoners are reported to have received, and agrees with you in entirely condemning it. That a general officer should have been guilty of the crime you mention meets with his unqualified reprobation. He directs that if the officer is still in your department you should prefer charges against him and bring him to trial."[64]

One of the leaders of the killings may indeed have been a high ranking Confederate officer. Texas general Felix H. Robertson may have directed some of the killings. Yet Robertson slipped away from Southwest Virginia and out of Breckinridge's department to join General Joseph Wheeler's cavalry in Georgia. While leaving the department, Robertson and his brigade became completely insubordinate to Confederate authority. They refused to follow orders and terrorized all communities they passed. Shortly after arriving in Georgia, Robertson was severely wounded near Augusta at Buckhead Creek at the end of November 1864. He never returned to duty and avoided any inquiry of the massacre. The Confederate Congress did, however, take notice. Robertson had been recommended for promotion from the rank of colonel to brigadier general prior to the massacre and was already acting in that capacity, but after the murders the Congress refused to confirm the promotion. This may have been directly caused by his actions at Saltville. Later, he returned to his home in Texas and began a profitable law career in Waco. Ironically, when Robertson died in 1928, it was noted that he was the last Confederate "general" to pass away.[65]

Following the battle, it took some time for the disorganized Union raiders to sort out what had happened. After the Federal forces made their disorderly retreat back to Kentucky, the 5th USCC reported having lost 118 of its 400 men. But, as time progressed, many who were lost on the campaign drifted back into camp. With the poor leadership and organization of the regiment at the time, it is difficult to make an exact judgment as to how many men were murdered at Saltville. Few officers and noncommissioned officers were at their posts at the time of the battle.[66] A few of the men originally listed as missing in action had deserted during the campaign. Samuel Harrison of Company G, for example, later returned to the unit and was court-martialed for desertion. Alex Young of Company L came back to the regiment in April 1865; a court-martial sentenced him to one year at hard labor for deserting at Saltville.[67]

The men of the 5th USCC had no doubt as to the fate of the majority of their missing comrades. Colonel James F. Wade noted on the October 1864 muster roll that his men at Saltville had "participated in a very severe engagement losing a large number of killed and wounded and missing; those who fell into the hands of the enemy were supposed to have been murdered."[68] Many of the company returns also listed troops as being left wounded on the field and later murdered by Ferguson and their Confederate captors. Lieutenant Augustus Flint of Company E reported that the twelve men missing from his company were killed by the Confederates. The commander of Company C noted that he left eight wounded men on the field at Saltville and was unsure of their fate. Men from white units also attempted to make sense of the events after the battle. The historian of the 12th Ohio Cavalry recorded that Jacob C. Pence had been listed as missing at Saltville and that he was "supposed to have been killed by Champ Ferguson."[69]

In Kentucky General Burbridge continued in his efforts to apprehend Ferguson. Under a flag of truce, Burbridge informed Confederate general Duke that he considered the murder of Lieutenant Smith as "one of the most diabolical acts of the war." He also added that if the Federals captured Ferguson and his band, "they would not be treated as prisoners." Although the Confederates had no desire to turn Ferguson over to the U.S. government, they also had no intention of letting Ferguson get away with murder.[70]

This time the guerrilla had gone too far. It was one thing for him to wage a private war with his neighbors while isolated in the back hills of Kentucky and Tennessee. It was quite another to brutally murder wounded prisoners while serving with an organized army. This act could not go unpunished.

Before Breckinridge was able to press charges against Ferguson and Hildreth, they had left the department and joined Wheeler's cavalry in Georgia. While in Georgia, General George Dibrell had camp guards arrest him for an unspecified infraction. After that incident Wheeler had little more trouble out of the guerrilla while he served with the Southern cavalry.[71]

Some time in January or February Breckinridge ordered Ferguson and Hildreth to return to Southwest Virginia to face a court-martial for the murder of Smith. They were held in Wytheville during the remainder of the winter. As the Confederates investigated the case, Breckinridge asked Wheeler if he had any idea of just who had authorized Ferguson to raise his band. Wheeler looked into it and reported back that it was his understanding that General Kirby Smith had authorized Ferguson to raise a company "for service on the Kentucky border."[72]

But the Confederates were unable to make their case against Ferguson. After Richmond fell on April 5, 1865, General Echols released Ferguson and Hildreth and ordered them back to the army. Echols let them go "in view of the long arrest to which they have been subjected and the impracticability of procuring witnesses for the trial of their cases." That was not surprising because many of the troops who had witnessed the massacre were no longer in the department; others obviously condoned the killings by their own participation. The witnesses were also aware that Ferguson led a gang of killers. With the Confederate government no longer able to enforce law and order, it was doubtful that they could have safely testified against Ferguson. Before the end of April 1865, the Confederate government finally collapsed. As happened with Robertson, the culminating events of the war overshadowed Southern efforts to prosecute Ferguson. It seemed that the Confederate guerrilla would quite literally get away with murder.[73]

During the final months of the war, the 5th USCC would return to Saltville. The area had vital resources that Union authorities could not ignore. In December 1864 General George Stoneman, the new commander of the Department of the Ohio, launched his own raid into Virginia. Stoneman's plan was to return to Southwest Virginia with Burbridge and remove Breckinridge as a threat.[74]

The Union raiders again included the 5th USCC as well as the newly created 6th USCC. The survivors of the massacre were more than ready to avenge Saltville. On December 17–18, outnumbering the Confederates four to one, the Federals took on Breckinridge along the Holston River about a mile outside Marion, Virginia. After two days of indecisive action, Breckinridge withdrew with his command.[75]

Following Breckinridge's retreat, the Federals were finally free to take the resources of Southwest Virginia. On December 20 Stoneman captured Saltville and began destroying the works. He also did considerable damage to the lead mines, the Virginia and Tennessee Railroad, and the towns of Abingdon, Wytheville, and Bristol. While the damage to the railroad and saltworks could be repaired, the government stores destroyed in the towns could not be replaced.[76]

The black troops performed admirably in Marion and continued to add to their hard-won reputation. Even former enemies praised their performance. They had won their spurs and would remain on active duty for almost a year after Appomattox. On March 16, 1866, as the 5th USCC held its final formation in Helena, Arkansas, the men were aware that over fifty of their comrades were missing: the men who never returned from Saltville. The horse-soldiers had paid the full price for their freedom.[77]

As for Burbridge, a few months after his Saltville debacle he was relieved of command. Most likely his demise was caused by his controversial handling of civilian affairs in Kentucky and his botched raid on Saltville. He was despised by Federals as well as Confederates; both sides were delighted to see his rule come to an end.[78]

As for the murderers, Champ Ferguson became the only person ever brought to justice for the massacre at Saltville. After Appomattox, Ferguson continued with his personal feuding in Tennessee and was eventually captured by the Federals. Had he laid down his arms like most other former Confederates, he likely would have been permitted to disappear into obscurity. Many former Tennessee and Kentucky guerrillas quietly slipped into Texas after the war. But Ferguson chose to continue the fight.[79]

On May 25, 1865, the Federals captured Ferguson and brought him to Nashville where they charged him with the murder of Lieutenant Elza Smith as well as of "twelve soldiers whose names are unknown, at Saltville, Virginia," and "two negro soldiers, names unknown, while lying wounded in prison, at Saltville." But the Saltville massacre was only one brief chapter in the guerrilla's savage career. Numerous pro-Union and even many former Confederate eyewitnesses testified in brutal detail about Ferguson's personal civil war in the mountains of Tennessee, Kentucky, and Virginia.

"Champ Ferguson and His Guard." (Harper's Weekly, *September 23, 1865, courtesy of* Thomas D. Mays)

The evidence was overwhelming, and the military court-martial found him guilty of murdering fifty-three men and convicted him as a "border rebel guerrilla, robber and murderer." Ironically, the prosecution failed to convince the jury that Ferguson was responsible for the killing of the blacks at Saltville. Perhaps they were sure they had an air-tight case as it was. He was acquitted on that charge.[80]

Ferguson denied having anything to do with the battlefield killings. In one interview he refused to admit taking part in the battle or in the murders the next day. In another, he conceded, "I only killed one of them [the blacks]. The others were killed, but I had no hand in it, and did not know it was done till the next day." He then bragged that "my men did it." In another interview Ferguson claimed that the twelve blacks he was charged with murdering were killed by members of another guerrilla command at Saltville, "and they were fairly killed in battle." "Besides," he added, "[t]here were thirty instead of twelve that fell on that day, and it was all in a regular fight."[81]

On October 20, 1865, Ferguson was hanged. Standing silently nearby as witnesses to the execution were the men of the 15th U.S. Colored Troops,

"Execution of Champ Ferguson, October 20, 1865." (Frank Leslie's Illustrated
Newspaper, *November 11, 1865, courtesy of Thomas D. Mays)*

whose presence added a bit of poetic justice to the end of Ferguson's brutal life.[82]

The Saltville massacre was not an isolated incident. The massacre demonstrates one of the factors that cause the "rules of war" to break down on
the battlefield. In warfare of every age, as differences in religion, race, and
culture are combined to dehumanize the enemy, the chance for a massacre
of prisoners increases. As the war aims of the Union broadened from the
preservation of the Union to include the liberation of blacks, many white
Southerners felt threatened. Brought up on stories of Nat Turner's rebellion
and the recent memory of John Brown, many whites felt that the presence
of blacks on the battlefield raised the stakes from that of a war for Southern
independence to that of an armed slave uprising. Neither side could expect
quarter to be given.

Notes

1. William Marvel, "The Battle of Saltville: Massacre or Myth?" *Blue and Gray
  Magazine* 8 (August 1991): 10–19, 46–60; William Marvel, *The Battles for Saltville:
  Southwest Virginia in the Civil War* (Lynchburg, Va.: H. E. Howard, Inc., 1992);

U.S. War Department, *The War of the Rebellion: A Compilation of the Official Records of the Union and Confederate Armies*, 128 vols. (Washington, D.C.: Government Printing Office, 1880–1901), 1st ser., 49 (1):765 (hereafter cited as *OR*).

2. George Dallas Mosgrove, *Kentucky Cavaliers in Dixie: Reminiscences of a Confederate Cavalryman*, ed. Bell I. Wiley (Jackson, Tenn.: McCowart-Mercer Press, 1957), xix.

3. For an interesting comparison of contrasting interpretations, see Albert Castel, "The Fort Pillow Massacre: A Fresh Examination of the Evidence," *Civil War History* 4 (March 1958): 37–50, and John Cimprich and Robert C. Mainfort, "Fort Pillow Revisited: New Evidence about an Old Controversy," *Civil War History* 28 (December 1982): 293–306. For an overview, see Brainerd Dyer, "The Treatment of Colored Union Troops by the Confederates, 1861–1865," *Journal of Negro History* 20 (July 1935): 273–86.

4. William C. Davis, "Massacre at Saltville," *Civil War Times Illustrated* 9 (February 1971): 4.

5. *OR*, 1st ser., 43 (2):864–66.

6. Ibid.

7. Ibid.

8. *OR*, 1st ser., 39 (2):887.

9. *OR*, 1st ser., 39 (1):556.

10. Dudley Taylor Cornish, *The Sable Arm: Blacks Troops in the Union Army, 1861–1865* (New York: Longmans, Green, 1956), 205–6.

11. Morris J. MacGregor and Bernard C. Nalty, eds., *Blacks in the United States Armed Forces: Basic Documents*, 13 vols. (Wilmington: Scholarly Resources, 1977), 1:7–9.

12. James M. McPherson, *The Negro's Civil War* (1965; New York: Ballantine Books, 1991), 211–12; the poem was originally published in the *Anglo-African* (New York), September 24, 1864.

13. McPherson, *The Negro's Civil War*, 211–12; *OR*, 3rd ser., 5:122.

14. W. Stephen McBride, "More Than a Depot: Camp Nelson," *Kentucky Civil War Journal* 1 (March 1997): 7–13.

15. *OR*, 3rd ser., 5:122; "Regimental Personal Descriptions, Orders, Letters, Guard Reports, Council of Administration, Funds Accounts, Telegrams and Clothing Accounts of Noncommissioned Staff," vol. 1, "5th United States Colored Cavalry," Record Group 94, National Archives, Washington, D.C. (hereafter cited as NARG 94).

16. Lieutenant Colonel L. Henry Carpenter, 5th USCC, to Captain O. Bates Dickson, NARG 94.

17. Joseph T. Glatthaar, *Forged in Battle: The Civil War Alliance of Black Soldiers and White Officers* (1990; New York: Meridian, 1991), 68.

18. Muster Roll of the Field and Staff of the 5th United States Colored Cavalry, NARG 94, box 5317.

19. *OR*, 1st ser., 39 (1):557.

20. Ibid., 556.

21. F. H. Mason, *The Twelfth Ohio Cavalry: A Record of Its Organization and Services in the War of the Rebellion, Together with a Complete Roster of the Regiment* (Cleveland: Nevins, 1871), 59–61.

22. Thomas D. Mays, "The Price of Freedom: The Battle of Saltville and the Massacre of the Fifth United States Colored Cavalry" (master's thesis, Virginia Polytechnic Institute and State University, 1992), 6–30.

23. John S. Wise, *The End of an Era* (Boston: Houghton, Mifflin, 1901), 374–75.

24. Ibid., 379.

25. Ibid., 558.

26. Mays, "The Price of Freedom," 40–42; *OR*, 1st ser., 39 (1):557.

27. John Barrien Lindsley, ed., *The Military Annals of Tennessee, Confederate* (Nashville: J. M. Lindsley & Company, 1886), 671.

28. Mason, *The Twelfth Ohio Cavalry*, 64.

29. *OR*, 1st ser., 39 (1):557.

30. George B. Guild, *A Brief Narrative of the Fourth Tennessee Cavalry Regiment* (Franklin, Tenn.: Cool Springs Press, 1996), 100; Lindsley, *The Military Annals of Tennessee*, 671.

31. Lindsley, *The Military Annals of Tennessee*, 671; Mason, *The Twelfth Ohio Cavalry*, 65; John Robertson, comp., *Michigan in the Civil War* (Lansing: W. S. George & Company, 1882), 573.

32. Glatthaar, *Forged in Battle*, 165; *OR*, 1st ser., 39 (1):557.

33. Wise, *The End of an Era*, 382; Mays, "The Price of Freedom," 58; R. A. Brock, *Hardesty's Historical and Geographical Encyclopedia . . . Special Virginia Edition* (Richmond: Frank B. Painter, 1884), 95.

34. Thomas D. Mays, *The Saltville Massacre* (Fort Worth: Ryan Place, 1995), 49–53.

35. Mason, *The Twelfth Ohio Cavalry*, 67; Mosgrove, *Kentucky Cavaliers in Dixie*, 203, 205.

36. Mosgrove, *Kentucky Cavaliers in Dixie*, 203, 205, 203.

37. Ibid., 200, 205; Mays, "The Price of Freedom," 59; Guerrant Diary, October 2, 1864, Southern Historical Collection, University of North Carolina at Chapel Hill.

38. Guerrant Diary, October 2, 1864.

39. Mosgrove, *Kentucky Cavaliers in Dixie*, 206–7; Guerrant Diary, October 2–3, 1864.

40. Mosgrove, *Kentucky Cavaliers*, 206–7.

41. Guerrant Diary, October 3, 1864.

42. For a complete biography of Ferguson, see Thomas D. Mays, "Cumberland Blood: Champ Ferguson's Civil War" (Ph.D. diss., Texas Christian University, 1996).

43. Henry Shocker testimony, August 1, 1865, Transcript from the Trial of Champ Ferguson, Record Group 153, mm 2997, National Archives, Washington, D.C. (hereafter referenced by name of witness and date of testimony, NARG 153).

44. Ibid.

45. Ibid.

46. Mosgrove, *Kentucky Cavaliers in Dixie*, 207.

47. Orange Sells testimony, August 12, 1865, NARG 153.

48. George W. Cutler testimony, July 31, 1865, NARG 153.

49. Mosgrove, *Kentucky Cavaliers in Dixie*, 208.

50. Ibid., 207.

51. *OR*, 1st ser., 39 (1):560.

52. *OR*, 1st ser., 39 (3):786.

53. *OR*, 1st ser., 39 (1):554.

54. Henry Shocker testimony, August 1, 1865, NARG 153.

55. Ibid.

56. Ibid.; Mason, *The Twelfth Ohio Cavalry*, 70.

57. Orange Sells testimony, August 12, 1865, NARG 153; Compiled Service Records of Union Soldiers Who Served in Organizations from the State of Kentucky, 13th Kentucky Cavalry, Record Group 109, roll 126, National Archives, Washington, D.C. Smith's record notes that he was "Wounded Saltville on Oct. 2nd/ 64 left in hospital where he was killed by guerrillas Oct. 7/64."

58. Orange Sells testimony, August 12, 1865, NARG 153.

59. Ibid.; A. J. Watkins testimony, July 31, 1865, NARG 153; *OR*, 1st ser., 39 (1):554.

60. *OR*, 1st ser., 39 (1):554, 556, 557, 561; Mason, *The Twelfth Ohio Cavalry*, 70.

61. *Richmond Enquirer*, October 8, 1864.

62. *Richmond Dispatch*, October 6, 1864.

63. *OR*, 1st ser., 39 (1):554.

64. *OR*, 2nd ser., 7:1020.

65. Marcus J. Wright and Harold B. Simpson, eds., *Texas in the War 1861–1865* (Hillsboro, Tex.: Hill Junior College Press, 1965), 90.

66. Glatthaar, *Forged in Battle*, 317.

67. NARG 94, box 10.

68. Muster Roll of the Field and Staff of the 5th USCC, NARG 94, box 5317.

69. Monthly Return for Co. E., 5th USCC for October 1864, NARG 94, box 5317; Mason, *The Twelfth Ohio Cavalry*, 29, 70; Return for Co. C., 5th USCC, NARG 94, box 5317. Eventually, five of Flint's missing men in Company E were accounted for.

70. *OR*, 1st ser., 49 (1):765.

71. "Document 'O,'" NARG 153; Joseph Wheeler testimony, August 28, 1865, NARG 153.

72. Joseph Wheeler testimony, August 28, 1865, NARG 153.

73. Ibid.

74. William C. Davis, *Breckinridge: Statesman, Soldier, Symbol* (Baton Rouge: Louisiana State University Press, 1974), 465–77.

75. Return of the Fifth Regiment of the United States Colored Cavalry, Colonel James S. Brisbin, October 1864, NARG 94, box 5316; Descriptive Roll for the

5th United States Colored Cavalry, NARG 94; Mosgrove, *Kentucky Cavaliers in Dixie*, 234–42.

76. Mosgrove, *Kentucky Cavaliers in Dixie*, 234–42.

77. I am indebted here to David and Phillis Brown for their research in the National Archives. Return of the Fifth Regiment of the United States Colored Cavalry, Colonel James S. Brisbin, October 1864, NARG 94, box 5316; Descriptive Roll for the 5th United States Colored Cavalry, NARG 94; Mosgrove, *Kentucky Cavaliers in Dixie*, 234–42.

78. Thomas Speed, R. M. Kelley, and Alfred Pirtle, *The Union Regiments of Kentucky* (Louisville: Courier-Journal Job Printing Company, 1897), 67.

79. Mays, "Cumberland Blood," 176–202.

80. Ibid.; Thurman Sensing, *Champ Ferguson: Confederate Guerrilla* (Nashville, Tenn.: Vanderbilt University Press, 1942), vii, 247, 251.

81. *Nashville Union*, October 12, 1865; *Nashville Dispatch*, October 22, 1865. Former Confederate soldier George B. Guild remembered fighting alongside Ferguson at Saltville and noted that "Champ Ferguson and his followers participated actively at Saltville." See Guild, *A Brief Narrative of the Fourth Tennessee Cavalry Regiment*, 102.

82. Davis, "Massacre at Saltville," 48.

8

THE USCT IN THE
CONFEDERATE HEARTLAND, 1864
Anne J. Bailey

Emancipation struck a deathblow to bondage, but newly freed slaves found liberation offered few tangible rewards in the occupied South. Even before the Union government made emancipation the official policy, many Northerners argued that Washington bureaucrats had to demonstrate a true commitment to change. One way to fulfill that obligation and at the same time guarantee the promise of legal freedom was to allow African Americans to join the army. But until Lincoln issued his Emancipation Proclamation, Northern legislators had not embraced the idea of blacks in Union blue with enthusiasm. Although black Northerners and white abolitionists had long argued the benefits of enlisting African Americans, the majority of Northern citizens felt uncomfortable with what an armed black man would mean to society at large. Even after the War Department sanctioned black enlistments, there were Union-occupied regions in the South that lagged behind. In the Confederate heartland of Tennessee the administration had to balance the loyalty of law-abiding slaveholders against the army's need for more manpower. Not everyone agreed with Lincoln's policy, and some generals refused to include black regiments in white combat armies, preferring instead to use African American enlistees for garrison duty, as laborers and railroad guards, or in other menial positions. They balked at using blacks in meaningful roles that would allow them to fight alongside white soldiers. Major General William Tecumseh Sherman was one of those commanders who simply refused to consider using blacks in combat.[1]

Moreover, it was impossible to ignore Sherman's defiance, for as 1864 opened he commanded the vast Western Theater. He had assumed this position after Ulysses S. Grant had left for Washington to become general in chief, and he had definite ideas about what should happen in the West. Sherman's strong friendship with Grant allowed him to operate fairly independently, and his connection to the powerful Republican senator John Sherman, who was his brother, and the prestige of having a father-in-law who had served as the nation's first secretary of the interior gave him an added edge. Ever vigilant about political threats to his armies, he carefully watched the efforts of Northern recruiters operating in the Confederate heartland.[2]

Far from Washington, the president, and meddling administrators in the War Department, commanders in the Western Theater always had enjoyed more freedom of action than their counterparts in the East. Throughout the war Sherman avoided making public comments on most political issues, but privately he was quite knowledgeable about what went on in Washington. In June 1862, Senator Sherman had told "Cump," as the general was known to the family, that Lincoln was "honest & patriotic" but lacked "dignity, order & energy" and would fail at any business except "pettifogging." John Sherman even considered supporting a War Democrat in the 1864 election, writing that he would back almost anyone except "our Monkey President." The anti-administration press agreed, calling Lincoln a "gorilla," even a "black gorilla" for his decision to arm black men. While General Sherman recognized that the demise of slavery foreshadowed change, he told his wife Ellen just months before the war ended that he still opposed blacks as soldiers. He had no objection to treating a black man "as free," but he did not think a former slave should be "hunted and badgered to make a soldier of when his family is left back on the plantations. I am right and won't Change."[3]

Sherman's personal opinion had meant little to the overall Union war effort while he served under Grant in the West. Grant had not openly defied his president on the issue of black soldiers, but had quietly used them in a variety of ancillary ways along the Mississippi River, thus avoiding the sticky issue of placing blacks in combat units. In 1863, after the president had openly encouraged black enrollment and expected his generals to comply, both Grant and Nathaniel P. Banks, who commanded the Department of the Gulf, had stationed black troops at numerous points along the Mississippi River. As an unexpected outcome, black soldiers engaged white Confederates in the fighting at Port Hudson and Milliken's Bend, Louisiana, in the summer of 1863. Public awareness of blacks in Union blue grew as the Northern press reported on their progress as soldiers. The number of African American units also continued to rise, increasing their visibility. By October 1864 there were 140 black regiments in the field with a reported strength of almost 102,000. Black troops were beginning to have more opportunities to engage in battle in almost every theater, except, of course, black men with the armies under Sherman's direct control.[4]

On this one issue Sherman would refuse his president, even to the point of insubordination. When the War Department first started recruiting blacks, Sherman had written his wife Ellen that he could not bring himself to place black soldiers "with arms in positions of danger and trust." He even told his men that "they should be used for some side purpose & not be brigaded with white men," while he wrote his brother that he did not believe blacks ready for the front lines. He conceded that he might one day change his opinion, but at the time he felt that the army was better served with blacks doing the manual labor that would then allow the white soldiers to win the war.[5]

Because of his visibility as a commander of a major department in 1864, Sherman stood out as one of the administration's strongest opponents when it came to integrating white armies. Yet his words only reflected the feelings of many of his men, for a significant number of soldiers in the Western armies came from the Midwest, where racism was widespread. In the spring of 1863 Sherman had told Ellen, "I would prefer to have this a white man's war, & provide for the negroes after the Storm. . . . With my opinion of negroes and my experience, yea prejudice I cannot trust them yet." Writing to his brother nine days later he bluntly reiterated, "I won't trust [blacks] to fight yet." Again mirroring what many of his soldiers felt, he believed blacks should be kept in jobs that were not that different from what slaves were doing for the Confederate army.[6]

As a result, Sherman announced a ban on black recruiting in 1864. During the campaign for Atlanta, Sherman believed he needed every white soldier at the front; he therefore wanted all the blacks in the army to serve as the work force. In June he issued an order stating that recruiting officers could not "enlist as soldiers any negroes who are profitably employed" by the army. Defeating the Confederate Army of Tennessee was his objective, and he would not allow outsiders to impede military operations. To make it clear, he warned that any recruiter who interfered "with the necessary gangs of hired negroes" would be arrested and, if necessary, imprisoned.[7]

Moreover, as his armies advanced toward Atlanta, Sherman knew that his military victories would protect him from censure from his superiors. He even lectured Lorenzo Thomas, who was charged with recruiting black troops along the Mississippi River. "I believe that negroes better serve the

Army as teamsters, pioneers, and servants, and have no objection to the surplus, if any, being enlisted as soldiers, but I must have labor and a large quantity of it. I confess I would prefer 300 negroes armed with spades and axes than 1,000 as soldiers." Based on service in the lower South during his service in the Old Army and his prewar days as head of a military school in Louisiana, he confidently added: "I think I understand the negro as well as anybody" and believe he "must pass through a probationary state before he is qualified for utter and complete freedom." The soldier issue was, therefore, an "open question" and one he admitted "should be fairly and honestly tested." But he also pointed out that blacks were "as scarce in North Georgia as in Ohio." He told one recruiter that it was "a waste of time" to recruit in Northwest Georgia for he had not "seen an able bodied man black or white there fit for a soldier who was not in this Army or the one opposed to it."[8]

Because of the political power of the Unionist slave owners in Tennessee, recruiting black soldiers in the Confederate heartland had not begun until late in 1863. Boston businessman George L. Stearns, who had organized the 54th and 55th Massachusetts, had been ordered to Nashville in September to raise black units in the Department of the Cumberland. Using private funds collected in Massachusetts to pay his recruiters, he raised six regiments before resigning. As a result of his efforts, the *Nashville Daily Press* reported in October: "Our citizens yesterday saw, for the first time, a regiment of colored troops marching through the streets of Nashville," but "the novelty of armed negro troops elicited many remarks about the policy of the Administration in raising them—both pro and con."[9]

Black recruitment continued into 1864 when Stearns's chief assistant, Captain Reuben D. Mussey of the 19th U.S. Infantry, became colonel of the 100th USCT and commissioner for the organization of U.S. Colored Troops in Middle and East Tennessee in February. That same month a local paper reported that "Tennessee has furnished 30,000 white troops to the Union Army" and noted that "she has given equally as good a report of herself in regard to the formation of colored troops. Already upwards of twelve thousand colored troops have been enlisted." But even Governor Andrew Johnson had opposed efforts to arm blacks at first, believing they should remain laborers. Still, as the number of contraband continued to grow, recruiting centers sprouted at Gallatin, Shelbyville, Murfreesboro, and Clarksville.[10]

Nonetheless, Union recruiters continued to have trouble with Sherman. In July, the general told one Northern recruiter that he considered himself a friend of the black man, but he would not budge on his decision to use them exclusively in traditional roles such as cooks, servants, laborers, and teamsters. He did concede that he might allow "others gradually to experiment in the art of the Soldier, beginning with the duties of the local Garrisons, such as we had at Memphis, Vicksburg, Natchez, Nashville, and Chattanooga." He lectured a recruiter, telling him that blacks were in a transition state and were therefore "not the equal of the white man." It was "unjust to the brave [white] soldiers and volunteers . . . to place them on a par" with blacks.[11]

The letter contained harsh words that would only stir up Sherman's critics. On receiving a copy of Sherman's correspondence, Reuben Mussey forwarded it up the line with a cover letter that stated that he could not endorse what Sherman said about enlisting blacks because he thought the general was "fully two years behind the time." Moreover, although Mussey was too astute to criticize Sherman publicly, he emphasized his point by adding, "and when I say two years I mean two of those century like years which we are living."[12]

Sherman's letter created quite a stir when it appeared in Northern newspapers. He wrote a friend that he "thought it would never get into the press. . . . I lay low." He added that he liked blacks if they remained in their place, "but when fools and idiots [meaning white recruiters] try to make [them] better than ourselves, I have an opinion." He pointedly told Chief of Staff Henry W. Halleck that a black man might be as good as a white man for stopping a bullet, but "a sand-bag is better." Could they skirmish and do picket duty, and improvise when necessary? he asked. "I say no," he answered. In June, when Lorenzo Thomas had been in the West organizing black units, the secretary of war had asked him to talk to Sherman about the subject. "I have seen your recent order respecting the enlistment of negroes," Thomas wrote of Sherman's threat to arrest recruiters and added that he thought it would "almost altogether stop recruiting with your army. I don't know under what circumstances it was issued," he admitted, "but the imprisonment of officers for disobedience seems to me a harsh measure." Two days later he pointed out that blacks were coming in to join "very rapidly," and he needed the general's cooperation. Even Lincoln reminded Sherman that the law regarding black recruitment was "a law" and "must be treated as such by all of us." More to the point, the commander in chief concluded, "May I ask therefore that you will give your hearty co-operation?"[13]

But Sherman had no intention of changing his attitude, even though he told the president, "I have the highest veneration for the law, and will respect it always, however it conflicts with my opinion of its propriety." He had told a recruiter that some might say he had "peculiar notions" on the subject, but he could "assure" him that those notions were "shared by a large portion of our fighting men." Clearly, one of his goals was to protect the morale of his soldiers, and he would oppose anyone, even his commander in chief, if that was endangered by integration. As events turned out, Sherman's capture of Atlanta made him a Northern hero and strengthened his position in the argument. Although not openly political, he knew exactly how important the fall of Atlanta was to the Republican Party. The Democrats, who had attacked Lincoln for the huge number of casualties in Grant's army in the early summer, could no longer claim the Northern war was a failure, and Sherman continued to ignore Washington's pleas that he include black soldiers in his white armies.[14]

Yet perhaps one of the great ironies of history is that Sherman, with all of his prejudices and objections to the use of former slaves as soldiers in white armies, would be the sole individual responsible for African American soldiers participating in a major battle in the Western Theater. Less than four months after Sherman captured Atlanta, black soldiers would fight alongside white soldiers, and together they would face the Western Theater's main Rebel army in battle in the Confederate heartland.

After the fall of Atlanta in September, Sherman planned a strategy that would bring war to the people, a march across the heart of Georgia to the coast. Yet this scheme meant that he would turn away from the Confederate Army of Tennessee, the army he had faced in battle since May. Although he was not sure what the Confederate commander would do, he hoped that the weakened Rebel army would turn north toward the Ohio River rather than follow him south. To prepare for such an event, he ordered Major General George H. Thomas to pull together a defense at Nashville, Tennessee. Sherman felt confident that with reinforcements coming to Thomas from Missouri the Union army could handle anything the Confederates might try.[15]

Thomas faced an unenviable task. He had to draw together an army out of scattered Union units. To do so, he did not have the option of refusing garrison troops composed of African American soldiers and their white officers. Moreover, Thomas did not have the political pull of Sherman, for he was a Virginian in a Northern army, and he lacked the support of influential allies in Washington that Sherman enjoyed. A competent and respected soldier, Thomas also believed, unlike Sherman, that he had to follow the instructions of his commander in chief. So in the autumn of 1864, scores of African Americans in garrisons scattered from Mississippi to Georgia headed for Nashville.[16]

While Union troops converged on the Tennessee capital, other Northern soldiers had to deal with the Confederate army as it moved west, away from Georgia. When the Rebels approached Decatur, Alabama, a possible location for crossing the Tennessee River, they found the garrison stronger than anticipated. One of the units hurried from Chattanooga to prevent the Confederates from fording the river was the 14th U.S. Colored Troops (USCT). This regiment, composed of former slaves, had been organized by Colonel Thomas J. Morgan at Gallatin, Tennessee, in late 1863. The recruits accepted by Morgan had come from men already working for the army in traditional jobs as wagon drivers and cooks. The colonel handpicked them according to their motivation to fight for freedom and then tried to instill a sense of pride that would help them become examples to other blacks. Strict discipline was a necessary component if he ever hoped to see his regiment selected for battle.[17]

Morgan had worked hard to have his black regiment recognized. One method he used to make his unit stand out was to organize the companies according to height. "When the regiment was full," he recalled, "the four center companies were all composed of tall men, the flanking companies of men of medium height, while the little men were sandwiched between." He was proud of his accomplishments and even bragged that his men "drill well, and go through the evolutions with as much grace and ease as any regiment in the service." He had finally seen his men selected for an active role in the war, for they had successfully defended Dalton, Georgia, against a Rebel cavalry raid in the late summer. Now, in October, Morgan received orders to reinforce the threatened garrison at Decatur.[18]

When the Confederate army arrived, the Union defenders were ready. The fighting was not much of a contest because after some skirmishing the Confederate commander, John Bell Hood, decided the garrison was too heavily defended and moved on west in search of an easier place to ford the river. But the black troops of the 14th USCT distinguished themselves by charging a Rebel position. "The affair did not last much more than 20 minutes," recalled a Union soldier, "and the colored boys had to fall down along the water's edge under the bank of the river, while the enemy ran along above them, and shot down on them." Still, Morgan heaped praise on the determined assault, and as the regiment returned to the Union lines, the white officers "mounted the parapet and gave it three rousing cheers." As a result, a black sergeant turned to a white superior and said, "Captain, we've got it at last." Moreover, Morgan told his men that their conduct had "elicited praises and cheers from all who witnessed it—It is no small event for a black regiment to receive three hearty cheers from a regiment of white men; and yet the 14th deserved the compliment." This would not be the last time the 14th USCT would encounter Hood's army. After the Confederates crossed the Tennessee River and headed north, Morgan's regiment was one of those ordered to join Thomas at Nashville.[19]

In the Tennessee capital, the Union commander hurried to strengthen the city's fortifications. Thomas grumbled that Sherman had taken most of the best units on his march across Georgia, leaving him with only a skeleton army to stop the Confederate advance toward the Ohio River. This was an overstatement; Thomas's troops included veterans from the Fourth Corps and a portion of the Twenty-third Corps, seasoned soldiers who fought Hood's advance into Tennessee at the little town of Franklin on November 30. Moreover, an additional 10,000 hardened veterans under A. J. Smith were on their way from Missouri. But to meet the emergency in case Smith did not arrive before Hood, Thomas needed all the garrison troops, including various units of railroad guards and reserve battalions. They would man the trenches around Nashville as the Rebel army dug in on the outskirts of the city.

One provisional division to arrive at Nashville from Chattanooga was commanded by James B. Steedman. Besides having three brigades composed of men who had not rejoined their commands serving with Sherman, Steedman brought two brigades of African Americans. The 1st Colored Brigade, under Colonel Thomas J. Morgan, included the 14th, 16th, 17th, 18th, and 44th USCT. The 2nd Colored Brigade, commanded by Colonel Charles R. Thompson, was made up of the 12th, 13th, and 100th USCT and the Kansas Light Artillery, 1st battery. Even Steedman, who had supported Stephen Douglas's Democratic Party in 1860, admitted, "I wonder what my Democratic friends . . . would think of me if they knew I was fighting" with black troops.[20]

Obviously, the black soldiers had little real combat experience. The 12th and 13th USCT, composed of contrabands, had just come from West Tennessee, where they had been guarding the railroads. An officer in the 12th commented: "From slavery to freedom was itself a grand transition; but to become Union soldiers was a still bigger promotion, exceeding their most sanguine hopes—a privilege estimated at its full value." A soldier in the 13th USCT bragged that the troops were "the bravest set of men on the Western continent. They think nothing of routing the guerrillas, that roam at large in the wilds of Tennessee."[21]

Still, the coming battle would test the courage of the African American troops, and opinions varied over how well they would meet the challenge. Men like Colonel Morgan were convinced they would succeed. When organizing the 14th USCT, he had interviewed each prospective soldier personally and remembered that after he had told one former slave that he might lose his life if he enlisted, the hopeful recruit had responded, "but my people will be free." For the black soldier, the battle at Nashville was a chance to strike another blow against slavery. More significantly, many black soldiers as well as their white officers knew that how well the men performed would have implications far beyond the battlefield.[22]

Thomas planned an attack on the Confederate line outside Nashville for the morning of December 15. The Virginian knew that his superiors back east had tired of delays, for his numerous postponements had worn Washington's patience thin. As he outlined his strategy, Thomas picked Steedman's provisional division to initiate a diversion on the left, with Morgan leading the advance. The move was a feint, Steedman pointed out to Morgan, intended to make Hood believe that it was the main attack, "and lead him to support his right by weakening his left," where Thomas intended to strike the main blow. The plan seemed simple enough; after Morgan surveyed the enemy position, he concluded that his men only needed to silence some Rebel rifle pits.[23]

This was the opportunity that many African American soldiers had eagerly anticipated and one that men like Sherman had sought to avoid—black soldiers fighting on the front line in an army of white soldiers. This development was clear to the men in the three regiments involved. The skirmish line consisted of the 14th USCT, followed by the 17th USCT under Colonel William R. Shafter and then the 44th USCT under Colonel Lewis Johnson. As the line advanced toward the Confederate position on the morning of December 15, a new era had dawned for these black soldiers.[24]

Unfortunately for the black units, the Confederates had laid a trap. Shafter had no trouble pushing back the Rebels until he reached a man-made ravine where the tracks of the Nashville and Chattanooga line ran through a cut in the hill about twenty feet long. Without realizing it, Shafter was moving toward a concealed lunette, where silent soldiers in gray patiently watched the enemy approach. The Rebel gunners, hidden behind a parapet with heavy head-logs on top and a ditch in front, waited until the Union troops reached the ravine before opening fire on the line in blue. The blacks, startled and frightened by the flash and roar of the cannon, raced for safety.[25]

The flight turned into chaos, and in a matter of minutes two of Shafter's regiments disintegrated. "It was an awful battle," he later wrote his sister. Several officers and scores of soldiers had died. Among the casualties was his sister's husband, a captain in the 17th USCT. When Shafter found his brother-in-law's body, even his clothes had been taken by Rebel soldiers.[26]

It is not unusual for men in their first battle to panic, and black soldiers,

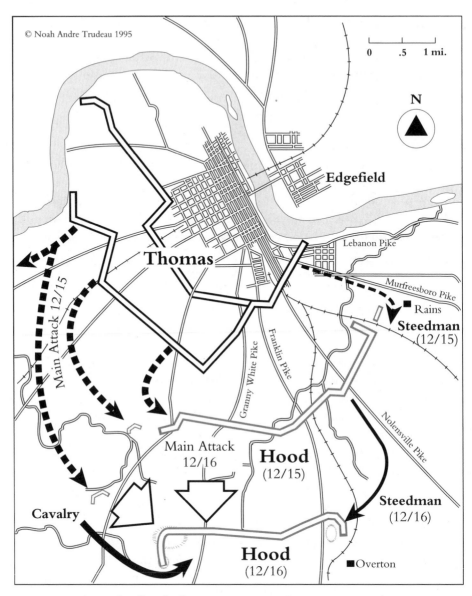

© Noah Andre Trudeau 1995

0   .5   1 mi.

N

Edgefield

Lebanon Pike

Thomas

Murfreesboro Pike

Rains

Steedman
(12/15)

Main Attack 12/15

Granny White Pike

Franklin Pike

Nolensville Pike

Main Attack
12/16

Hood
(12/15)

Steedman
(12/16)

Cavalry

Hood
(12/16)

Overton

Map 8.1. The Battle of Nashville, Tennessee, December 15–16, 1864.
(Courtesy of Noah Andre Trudeau)

afraid of what capture meant to an escaped slave, ran in every direction. Most of the casualties were from the 14th USCT, the unit that had led the advance. Troops in the 44th USCT, also anxious to avoid death or capture when they saw what was happening in their front, had fled up a nearby pike. Moreover, white Union regiments that tried to take the Rebel position also fell back, and one commander reported that some of the white troops "behaved in the most cowardly and disgraceful manner." Thus the diversion on the east of the Confederate line failed.[27]

The Confederate reaction to black soldiers was fierce. Two days before the battle, a Texas soldier had written in his diary, "The Yanks have been fighting our picket line with negroes, for nearly a week, and we have killed several so close that they can't get them. So they remain where they fell froze as hard as a log," implying that this shameful treatment would not have befallen a white soldier. Another Southerner, Arkansan Philip Stephenson, left a vivid account of the racial prejudice. "This was the first time that we of the Army of Tennessee had ever met our former slaves in battle," he announced. "It excited in our men the intensest indignation, but that indignation expressed itself in a way peculiarly ominous and yet quite natural for the 'masters.'" Stephenson later wrote: "As soon as it was found out that the men advancing upon them were Negroes, a deliberate policy was adopted. It was to let them come almost to the works before a shot was to be fired, and then the whole line was to rise up and empty their guns into them." The results had been deadly. "On the darkies came, slowly and wavering enough for that silence was terribly significant," added Stephenson. "On they came, closer and closer, until, as our men said afterward, they could see the whites of their eyes. *Then* up rose the line of grey and crash went that deadly volley of lead full into the poor fellows' faces. The carnage was awful. It is doubtful if a single bullet missed."[28]

Although the black regiments had suffered heavy casualties, the Union army succeeded in driving the Confederates back before the day ended. During a long cold night both sides prepared for the battle they knew would resume at first light. Not all African American units had fought on the first day; there were still some ready for battle, and anxious black soldiers hoped that their chance would come with the first rays of light on November 16.[29]

Indeed, the second day of fighting at Nashville gave black soldiers another chance to face the Confederate Army of Tennessee. Although Thomas had pushed the Confederate line back, he had not defeated Hood and he planned to strike again. Thomas still meant for the main attack to come in the west, but Brigadier General Thomas J. Wood thought he saw an opportunity to turn the Confederate flank by hitting an outcropping known as Overton Hill on the east end of the Rebel line. Steedman agreed, and the two commanders planned an attack for midafternoon. The units selected were from Steedman's provisional division, made up of the 100th USCT and 12th USCT. They would be followed in the advance by the 13th USCT. A small contingent of white infantry, with a few black troops, would provide support. The African American soldiers recognized the peril of the undertaking, for the assault was to be on a strongly fortified position. To reach the objective, the soldiers would have to cross a boggy plowed field, and the sticky mud would hamper every step. So, as the soldiers made preparations for the charge, some asked friends or white officers to hold their personal belongings. "This and little talk among themselves showed a settled resolution, to unflinchingly face death in the cause of freedom and nationality," observed a captain in the 100th USCT.[30]

One Confederate gunner on Overton Hill recalled that the black soldiers advanced "in splendid order." When the Confederates fired, the black soldiers were so close together that "every shot from Rebel muskets and cannon was telling with fearful effect," reported a captain with the 12th USCT. Moreover, for men in the 13th USCT this was their first time under fire. "There were very few negroes who retreated in our front," declared a Confederate, "and none were at their post when the firing ceased; for we fired as long as there was anything to shoot at."[31]

Confederate reinforcements soon arrived to bolster the line, and a Rebel general later reported that the black soldiers "came only to die. I have seen most of the battle-fields of the West, but never saw dead men thicker than in front of my two right regiments." The general had to stop his troops from pursuing the retreating line, and the Rebels finally settled for capturing some regimental flags. One carried the words, "Thirteenth Regiment U.S. Colored Infantry, Presented by the colored ladies of Murfreesboro." A Union surgeon who treated the wounded declared, "Don't tell me negroes won't fight!"; he told his family, "I know better." The 13th USCT suffered 220 casualties in its first battle, nearly 40 percent of the regiment's strength. Thomas had not expected the loss on that part of the line to be very high, for the main attack was in the west. But the fighting on Overton Hill exacted around one-third of the total casualties for the entire two-day battle.[32]

Even General Thomas admitted that the black soldiers had acquitted themselves well. In a conversation before the battle, he had told General Morgan that he did not think blacks could fight in the open field. Perhaps they could be used behind breastworks, but he was not willing to go further.

After the fighting at Overton Hill, as Thomas rode across the battlefield, he was heard to say, "Gentlemen, the question is settled; negroes will fight."[33]

For the Confederates, the greatest blow to their traditional perception of the old social order came after the battle ended. As the Rebel army retreated in disarray, an Arkansas soldier noted that his pursuers were black. "Oh woeful humiliation," he moaned. "The faces of Negroes! Pushed on by white soldiers in their rear, but *there*, nevertheless in the front rank of those our men were running from. . . . Such was the battle of Nashville."[34]

Moreover, one outcome that Sherman could not have anticipated was that the Tennessee campaign brought the issue of black soldiers in the army to the political forefront as officers praised the fighting abilities of the black troops. Hood's campaign was both the first time that many Union soldiers in the Western armies had fought with African Americans and the first time that the Rebel Army of Tennessee had faced black troops in a major battle. Overall, black soldiers had acquitted themselves well in their first major battle in the Western Theater, although they paid a high price for that distinction.

While Sherman did not know about the part that blacks played in the battle at Nashville, he faced a new challenge to his policy concerning black soldiers in his army. After he safely reached Savannah on his March to the Sea, Washington sent men from the 110th USCT to join Sherman's army. To no one's surprise, he immediately put the men to work as laborers, teamsters, and servants. Reports even surfaced that white soldiers persecuted the African Americans and that some were killed. One Union soldier stated that blacks should be "taught to know their place & behave civilly." Obviously the government had to stop such behavior, and Henry Halleck told Sherman that he would make many enemies among the Radical Republicans if he persisted with his policy. With pressure from above, Sherman changed his official stance if not his personal belief about the inclusion of black soldiers in his army. On the march through the Carolinas, the soldiers from the 110th USCT accompanied his white army.[35]

Still, the battle of Nashville had been a major event for those black men who only months before had been slaves. Perhaps it is fitting that Reuben Mussey, who had been responsible for raising some of the men who fought in the battle wrote, "I rode over the ground in front of the Fort [after the first day's battle]. Black and white dead lay side by side. Death had known no distinction of color, nor had Valor, for the blacks were as near the enemy's line, as were the whites." And the commander of the 100th USCT, Henry Stone, in congratulating his men in February 1864, had added: "For the first time in the memorable history of the Army of the Cumberland . . . the blood of white and black men had flowed freely together for the great Cause which is to give freedom, unity, manhood and peace to all men, of whatever birth or complexion." While this equality was not to be, the experience of being a soldier in a combat situation had laid the groundwork for growing self-esteem and self-confidence. Moreover, that experience had provided former slaves with the basic skills required to survive in a white world. One soldier wrote from Nashville in 1865, "We Wish to have some benefit of education To make ourselves capable of business In the Future . . . We wish to become a People capable of self support as we are Capable of being soldiers." The noted black abolitionist Frederick Douglass had predicted earlier in the war, "Once let the black man get upon his person the brass letters U.S.; let him get an eagle on his button, and a musket on his shoulder and bullets in his pocket, and there is no power on the earth or under the earth which can deny that he has earned the right of citizenship in the United States."[36]

Notes

1. Even as late as the autumn of 1864, slaveholders in occupied Tennessee who were loyal to the Union retained ownership of their slaves. When their slaves joined the army, the Union government promised compensation, and the slaves were not legally free until their term of enlistment ended. Keeping loyal slaveholders happy, but also providing for emancipation, was a complicated matter.
2. Sherman, who commanded the Military Division of the Mississippi, was in charge of operations in the Western Theater. It is the purpose of this paper to look only at his reaction to Union recruiting efforts in the Confederate heartland from late 1863 until 1865. While there were black units enlisted in the army prior to 1863 and successful recruiting efforts in many areas of the occupied South, this was not the case in Union-held Tennessee, northern Alabama, and Georgia.
3. Neither Grant nor Sherman knew Abraham Lincoln well. Indeed, Sherman met the president only twice during the war. The first was a brief encounter in 1861 when Sherman was hoping for a commission in the Union army, and the second was in March 1865 after Sherman had become a military hero. Still, Sherman knew what his brother thought of the president. Late in 1863, John Sherman concluded that Lincoln would leave office in 1864 "with the reputation of an honest clown." Ironically, Sherman's capture of Atlanta gave Lincoln the needed military boost to win reelection and made John realize he had to back the party candidate. John, however, did not like Lincoln personally. See Michael Fellman, "Lincoln and Sherman," in Gabor S. Boritt, ed., *Lincoln's Generals* (1994; New York: Oxford University Press, 1995), 127. While there are a number of fine biographies of Sherman, the best of the most recent accounts

are Lee Kennett, *Sherman: A Soldier's Life* (New York: HarperCollins, 2001); Stanley P. Hirshson, *A White Tecumseh: A Biography of General William T. Sherman* (New York: John Wiley & Sons, 1997); John F. Marszalek, *Sherman: A Soldier's Passion for Order* (New York: The Free Press, 1993); and Michael Fellman, *Citizen Sherman: A Life of William Tecumseh Sherman* (New York: Random House, 1995). Other useful books include William T. Sherman, *Memoirs of General William T. Sherman*, 2 vols. (1875; New York: Da Capo Press, 1984); Charles Royster, *The Destructive War: William Tecumseh Sherman, Stonewall Jackson, and the Americans* (New York: Alfred A. Knopf, 1994); and Lloyd Lewis, *Sherman: Fighting Prophet* (1932; Lincoln: University of Nebraska Press, 1993). For the excerpt of the letter, see William T. Sherman to Ellen Sherman, January 15, 1865, in Brooks D. Simpson and Jean V. Berlin, eds., *Sherman's Civil War: Selected Correspondence of William T. Sherman, 1860–1865* (Chapel Hill: University of North Carolina Press, 1999), 798.

4. C. W. Foster to the Adjutant-General U.S. Army, October 20, 1864, U.S. War Department, *The War of the Rebellion: A Compilation of the Official Records of the Union and Confederate Armies*, 128 vols. (Washington, D.C.: Government Printing Office, 1880–1901), 3rd ser., 4:789 (hereafter cited as *OR*). For more on the recruitment of black soldiers, see Joseph T. Glatthaar, *Forged in Battle: The Civil War Alliance of Black Soldiers and White Officers* (New York: Free Press, 1990); Benjamin Quarles, *The Negro in the Civil War* (1953; New York: Da Capo Press, 1989); Dudley Taylor Cornish: *The Sable Arm: Black Troops in the Union Army, 1861–1865* (1956; Lawrence: University Press of Kansas, 1987); James M. McPherson, *The Negro's Civil War: How American Blacks Felt and Acted during the War for the Union* (1965; New York: Ballantine Books, 1991); and Ira Berlin, Joseph P. Reidy, and Leslie S. Rowland, eds., *Freedom's Soldiers: The Black Military Experience in the Civil War* (New York: Cambridge University Press, 1998) (hereafter cited as Berlin et al., *Freedom's Soldiers*). Grant also had to deal with the prisoner-of-war issue, and angry words passed between the general and the Confederate government over the treatment of blacks captured in battle. But Grant was no longer in charge of the department when the most notorious incident, Nathan Bedford Forrest's attack on Fort Pillow, happened in the spring of 1864. For more on locating information on black soldiers, see Budge Weidman, "Preserving the Legacy of the United States Colored Troops," *Prologue: Quarterly of the National Archives and Records Administration* 29 (Summer 1997): 90–94.

5. William T. Sherman to Ellen Sherman, April 17, 1863, in Simpson and Berlin, *Sherman's Civil War*, 454; William T. Sherman to John Sherman, April 26, 1863, William T. Sherman Papers, Manuscript Division, Library of Congress. For the quotes, see also Fellman, "Lincoln and Sherman," 141–42.

6. William T. Sherman to Ellen Sherman, April 17, 1863, in Simpson and Berlin, *Sherman's Civil War*, 454; William T. Sherman to John Sherman, April 26, 1863, Sherman Papers. For the quotes, see Fellman, "Lincoln and Sherman," 141–42.

7. Special Field Order No. 16, June 3, 1864, *OR*, 3rd ser., 4:434.

8. William T. Sherman to Lorenzo Thomas, June 21, 1864, *OR*, 1st ser., 39 (2):132; W. T. Sherman to John A. Spooner, July 30, 1864, enclosed in R. D. Mussey to Major [Charles W. Foster?], August 2, 1864, M-583 1864, Letters Received, ser. 360, Colored Troops Division, Record Group (RG) 94, Records of the Adjutant General's Office, National Archives, Washington, D.C., quoted in Ira Berlin, Joseph P. Reidy, and Leslie S. Rowland, eds., *The Black Military Experience* (New York: Cambridge University Press, 1982), 110–11. Notwithstanding Sherman's evaluation of Georgia, at least 3,486 African American Georgians and more than 2,300 white Georgians joined the Federal army. See Robert S. Davis, Jr., "White and Black in Blue: The Recruitment of Federal Units in Civil War North Georgia," *Georgia Historical Quarterly* 85 (Fall 2001): 347–74. See also Clarence L. Mohr, *On the Threshold of Freedom: Masters and Slaves in Civil War Georgia* (Athens: University of Georgia Press, 1986).

9. Stearns had also been one of the "Secret Six," a group of abolitionists who had financed John Brown's plans to liberate the slaves in Virginia in 1859. Mussey later reported that Stearns "found that the raising of colored troops was, if not opposed, regarded with distrust and suspicion by influential loyal Tennesseans, and some time elapsed before harmonious relations were established between Major Stearns and these gentlemen." Reuben D. Mussey to C. W. Foster, October 10, 1864, *OR*, 3rd ser., 4:763–74; *Nashville Daily Press*, October 3, 1863; Special Field Order No. 243, September 8, 1863, *OR*, 3rd ser., 3:786–87; Special Orders No. 15, February 9, 1864, *OR*, 3rd ser., 4:90; Cornish, *The Sable Arm*, 235–38, 248–49.

10. Tennessee would furnish around 20,000 black soldiers. Under Lincoln's directive, "Slaves of loyal citizens may be enlisted into the service of the United States with their master's consent." The governor finally agreed to allow other blacks to enlist without their owner's consent if the government would give a voucher to the owner promising compensation (not to exceed a bounty) upon the granting of emancipation papers. Neither slaves of loyal citizens nor slaves of rebel or disloyal masters would be actually free until the expiration of their military service. These were instructions directly from Abraham Lincoln as stated in a letter from E. M. Stanton to George L. Stearns, September 16, 1863, *OR*, 3rd ser., 3:816; *Nashville Daily Times and True Union*, February 27, 1864. See also Cornish, *The Sable Arm*, 237; Berlin et al., *The Black Military Experience*, 122–26; Stephen V. Ash, *Middle Tennessee Society Transformed, 1860–1870: War and Peace in the Upper South* (Baton Rouge: Louisiana State University Press, 1988); and Benjamin Franklin Cooling, *Fort Donelson's Legacy: War and Society in Kentucky and Tennessee, 1862–1863* (Knoxville: University of Tennessee Press, 1997).

11. William T. Sherman to John A. Spooner, July 30, 1864, quoted in Berlin et al., *The Black Military Experience*, 110–11.

12. R. D. Mussey to [Charles W. Foster?], August 2, 1864, quoted in Berlin et al., *The Black Military Experience*, 110–11.

13. Lincoln also told Sherman, "It is not for the War Department, or myself, to restrain, or modify the law in it's [sic] execution, further than actual necessity may require. . . . We here, will do what we consistently can to save you from difficulties arising out of it." Abraham Lincoln to William T. Sherman, July 18, 1864, in Roy P. Basler, ed., *The Collected Works of Abraham Lincoln*, 9 vols. (New Brunswick: Rutgers University Press, 1953), 7:449–50. For the other quotes, see William T. Sherman to William M. McPherson, [c. September 1864], William T. Sherman Papers, Huntington Library, San Marino, Calif., quoted in Fellman, "Lincoln and Sherman," 146; William T. Sherman to Henry Halleck, September 4, 1864, *OR*, 1st ser., 38 (5):792–93; Lorenzo Thomas to William T. Sherman, June 20, 1864, *OR*, 1st ser., 38 (4):542–43; Lorenzo Thomas to William T. Sherman, June 22, 1864, *OR*, 1st ser., 571–72; Lorenzo Thomas to William T. Sherman, June 19, 1864, *OR*, 3rd ser., 4:436 (same as June 20 letter); Fellman, *Citizen Sherman*, 158–60. Thomas also told the secretary of war that he thought Sherman's threat to arrest recruiters was "especially harsh." Lorenzo Thomas to Edwin Stanton, June 15, 1864, *OR*, 3rd ser., 4:433–34. Nonetheless, Sherman referred to recruiters as "unscrupulous State agents," and added that raising Union units in the occupied South was the "height of folly."

14. William T. Sherman to Abraham Lincoln, July 21, 1864, *OR*, 1st ser., 38 (5):210; William T. Sherman to John A. Spooner, July 30, 1864, quoted in Berlin et al., *The Black Military Experience*, 111. See also two letters, both William T. Sherman to Henry Halleck, July 14, 1864, *OR*, 1st ser., 38 (5):136–37. The quote is from the second, received on the fifteenth, in which Sherman told Halleck that he would not permit recruiting, "and I will not have a set of fellows here hanging about on any such pretenses."

15. Sherman correctly predicted Hood's plan of action. He did march his army north instead of following Sherman across Georgia. For more on the Confederate strategy, see Anne J. Bailey, *The Chessboard of War: Sherman and Hood in the Autumn Campaigns of 1864* (Lincoln: University of Nebraska Press, 2000); Wiley Sword, *The Confederacy's Last Hurrah: Spring Hill, Franklin, and Nashville* (1992; Lawrence: University Press of Kansas, 1993); James Lee McDonough and Thomas L. Connelly, *Five Tragic Hours: The Battle of Franklin* (Knoxville: University of Tennessee Press, 1983); Stanley F. Horn, *The Decisive Battle of Nashville* (1956; Baton Rouge: Louisiana State University Press, 1984); Jacob Cox, *The March to the Sea: Franklin and Nashville* (1882; New York: Jack Brussel, n.d.); Jacob Cox, *The Battle of Franklin, Tennessee, November 30, 1864* (1897; Dayton, Ohio: Morningside, 1983); Albert Castel, *Decision in the West: The Atlanta Campaign of 1864* (Lawrence: University Press of Kansas, 1992); Thomas L. Connelly, *Autumn of Glory: The Army of Tennessee, 1862–1865* (Baton Rouge: Louisiana State University Press, 1971); Stanley F. Horn, *The Army of Tennessee: A Military History* (Indianapolis: Bobbs-Merrill, 1941); Richard M. McMurry, *John Bell Hood and the War for Southern Independence* (Lexington: University Press of Kentucky,

1982). A popular version of the Nashville campaign is Winston Groom, *Shrouds of Glory—From Atlanta to Nashville: The Last Great Campaign of the Civil War* (New York: Atlantic Monthly Press, 1995).

16. Sherman had anticipated that Brigadier General Andrew Jackson Smith and his 10,000 soldiers would be able to join Thomas at Nashville, thus giving Thomas ample numbers to face the Rebel army. But bad weather made Smith's transfer slow and arduous, and it quickly became clear to Thomas that he might have to face the Confederate army with the troops at hand.

17. When Morgan set about to organize the regiment, he started with men of all ages, dressed in anything from a uniform to "the clothes in which they had left the plantations." The 14th USCT was formally organized in January 1864, and all the noncommissioned officers were black; Morgan noted that "had the war continued two years longer, many of them would have been competent as commissioned officers." Thomas J. Morgan, "Reminiscences of Service with Colored Troops in the Army of the Cumberland, 1863–65," in *Personal Narratives of Events in the War of the Rebellion, being Papers read before the Rhode Island Soldiers and Sailors Historical Society*, 3rd ser. (Providence: Rhode Island Soldiers and Sailors Historical Society, 1885), no. 13, 11–48.

18. The action at Dalton had occurred on August 14–15. Noah Andre Trudeau, *Like Men of War: Black Troops in the Civil War, 1862–1865* (Boston: Little, Brown, 1998), 276–77; Morgan, "Reminiscences of Service with Colored Troops," 11–48. See also Frederick H. Dyer, *A Compendium of the War of the Rebellion*, 3 vols. (Des Moines, Iowa: Dyer Publishing Company, 1908), 3:1726.

19. Trudeau, *Like Men of War*, 282; Morgan, "Reminiscences of Service with Colored Troops," 11–48; General Orders No. 50, H'd. Q'r's. 14th U.S. Col'd. Infantry, 23 Nov. 1864, General Orders, 14th USCI, Regimental Books and Papers USCT, RG 94, quoted in Berlin et al., *The Black Military Experience*, 559.

20. Men in the 44th USCT had already faced Hood's army when they had been garrison troops at Dalton, Georgia. Hood had captured the town, a stop on the Western and Atlantic Railroad, in October when trying to draw Sherman out of Atlanta. Although the entire command had surrendered, some had escaped, and, with additional new recruits, Colonel Lewis Johnson had rebuilt the regiment. For more on Dalton, see Bailey, *The Chessboard of War*, 34–38. For an account of one of the prisoners, see Robert S. Davis, Jr., "A Soldier's Story: The Records of Hubbard Pryor, Forty-fourth United States Colored Troops," *Prologue: The Quarterly of the National Archives and Records Administration* 31 (Winter 1999): 267–72. See also Trudeau, *Like Men of War*, 340.

21. The 12th USCT was originally the 2nd Alabama. The men had been impressed in the summer of 1862 to work as laborers on the fortifications at Nashville. At Nashville they had received poor treatment, and a Union recruiter later observed that "the change from the irregular and irresponsible treatment they received as laborers to that they had as soldiers was very grateful to them."

The 13th was raised soon after, and also ordered to Nashville. Both regiments were eventually transferred to duty guarding the railroad in West Tennessee. See Reuben D. Mussey to C. W. Foster, October 10, 1864, *OR*, 3rd ser., 4:763–74; Trudeau, *Like Men of War*, 336–37.

22. Trudeau, *Like Men of War*, 276–77. For more on African American soldiers at Nashville, see Bailey, *The Chessboard of War*, 148–50, 152–54, 159–61.

23. Thomas had told Henry Halleck in Washington that he did not have enough men to attack the Confederate army and would have to operate on the defensive until Smith's reinforcements arrived from Missouri. His two corps numbered 12,000 and 10,000, respectively, and his cavalry a mere 3,000. Moreover, his cavalry had informed him that the estimated strength of the Confederate army was between 30,000 and 35,000 soldiers, with sixty pieces of artillery and some 10,000 cavalry. This was an exaggeration (one Confederate report said the army crossed the Tennessee River with 30,600 men), but it still meant that Thomas was outnumbered. The result of Thomas's concern was that garrison troops throughout the region headed for Nashville. He believed that using black soldiers in the trenches might work, but he did not anticipate using them in a combat situation because he did not think they could stand the test. See Trudeau, *Like Men of War*, 340–41; Organization of the U.S. Forces, commanded by Major General George H. Thomas, at the battle of Nashville, Tenn., December 15–16, 1864, *OR*, 1st ser., 45 (1):94; Morgan, "Reminiscences of Service with Colored Troops," 11–48.

24. The 14th USCT had been organized by Morgan from contrabands coming into Gallatin, Tennessee; the 17th USCT was organized at Murfreesboro; and the 44th USCT, also made up of contrabands, had been organized at Chattanooga and did post and garrison duty in Georgia at both Rome and Dalton. Reuben D. Mussey to C. W. Foster, October 10, 1864, *OR*, 3rd ser., 4:763–74. See also Report of Thomas J. Morgan, January 16, 1865, *OR*, 1st ser., 45 (1):536.

25. Later gaining fame as "Pecos Bill," the thirty-year-old, Michigan-born Shafter would fail to gain recognition in Civil War narratives, but he found a place in history by leading the army in Cuba during the Spanish-American War in 1898.

26. Trudeau, *Like Men of War*, 343; Sword, *The Confederacy's Last Hurrah*, 325, 357.

27. One need only read accounts of the Battle of First Bull Run (Manassas) in the summer of 1861 to see that fear was just as common among white soldiers in their first battle: inexperienced Union soldiers broke and ran back toward Washington, D.C., in disarray. Colonel Morgan wrote in his after-action report, "The troops under my command have, as a whole, behaved well, and if they failed to accomplish all I expected it was my fault, not theirs; I was deceived as to the character of the work built by the enemy on the 14th." Report of Thomas J. Morgan, January 16, 1865, *OR*, 1st ser., 45 (1):536–37. Steedman reported, "All, white and black, nobly did their duty as soldiers"; Report of James B. Steedman, January 27, 1865, *OR*, 1st ser., 45 (1):508.

28. Samuel T. Foster, *One of Cleburne's Command: The Civil War Reminiscences and Diary of Capt. Samuel T. Foster, Granbury's Texas Brigade, CSA,* ed. Norman D. Brown (Austin: University of Texas Press, 1980), 153; Philip Daingerfield Stephenson, *The Civil War Memoir of Philip Daingerfield Stephenson, D.D.* (Conway, Ark.: University of Central Arkansas Press, 1995), 320. Very few diaries and memoirs mention black soldiers. It is particularly interesting that Stephenson was so taken by the fighting ability of blacks that he mentioned it on several occasions.

29. Morgan later told an audience, "Thus the first day's fight wore away. It had been for us a severe but glorious day. Over three hundred of my command had fallen, but everywhere our army was successful. . . . General Steadman [*sic*] congratulated us, saying his only fear had been that we might fight too hard. We had done all he desired, and more. Colored soldiers had again fought side by side with white troops; they had mingled together in the charge; they had supported each other; they had assisted each other from the field when wounded, and they lay side by side in death. The survivors rejoiced together over a hard fought field, won by a common valor." Morgan, "Reminiscences of Service with Colored Troops," 11–48.

30. The 100th USCT, composed of the first black men openly recruited in Kentucky, was organized in June 1863 and sent to garrison the Nashville and Northwestern Railroad. The 12th USCT and 13th USCT had also been stationed on the Nashville and Northwestern Railroad as laborers and as guards to other laborers. Reuben D. Mussey to C. W. Foster, October 10, 1864, *OR,* 3rd ser., 4:763–74. See also Trudeau, *Like Men of War,* 345.

31. Trudeau, *Like Men of War,* 344–46.

32. Report of James T. Holtzclaw, January 12, 1865, *OR,* 1st ser., 45 (1):705; Report of James B. Steedman, January 27, 1865, *OR,* 1st ser., 45 (1):507; Sword, *The Confederacy's Last Hurrah,* 362–63. There were several instances of bravery: after the color bearer of the 13th USCT was shot down, a second man carried the colors until he was hit, and five more men went down carrying them. "The last color-bearer shook the flag over the rebel works but it was snatched from his hand, and he was shot. Every one of the color-guard was either killed or wounded," wrote Reuben D. Mussey. See [Reuben D. Mussey] to Captain C. P. Brown, December 21, 1864, vol. 221 DC, 364–68, Letters Sent by the Commissioner, ser. 1141, Organization of U.S. Colored Troops, Dept. of the Cumberland, RG 393 (1), quoted in Berlin et al., *The Black Military Experience,* 561–63. Frederick H. Dyer in *A Compendium of the War of the Rebellion,* 3:1726, indicates that the regiment lost four officers and eighty-six enlisted men killed or mortally wounded during the war and that 265 men died of disease.

33. Thomas, who died in 1870, could neither deny nor support this version of his comment, for Morgan said it long after Thomas's death. Since Morgan wanted to put the best face on his command of black troops, it was certainly convenient

to believe that he had swayed his commanding general. Bearing in mind that
he was a Virginian and former slave owner, one can only guess at Thomas's true
opinion of black soldiers. It is hard to believe that, as a graduate of West Point
and former instructor at the academy, he would have supported equality in the
armies. Morgan, "Reminiscences of Service with Colored Troops," 148. Still, at
a convention of white Unionists in Nashville in January 1865, black Tennesseans asked the delegates to consider abolishing slavery. They used the argument
that the "Government has asked the colored man to fight for its preservation
and gladly has he done it. It can afford to trust him with a vote as safely as it
trusted him with a bayonet." In pressing for the right to vote, the blacks declared
"what higher order of citizen is there than the soldier? . . . The colored man will
vote by instinct with the Union party, just as uniformly as he fights with the
Union army." See Berlin et al., *Freedom's Soldiers*, 147; Ira Berlin, Barbara J. Fields,
Steven F. Miller, Joseph P. Reidy, and Leslie S. Rowland, eds., *Free at Last: A
Documentary History of Slavery, Freedom, and the Civil War* (New York: New Press,
1992), 499.

34. Stephenson, *The Civil War Memoir of Philip Daingerfield Stephenson*, 332.

35. Fellman, *Citizen Sherman*, 163, 166; Joseph T. Glatthaar, *The March to the Sea and
    Beyond: Sherman's Troops in the Savannah and Carolinas Campaign* (New York: New
    York University Press, 1985), 57; Sherman, *Memoirs of General William T. Sher-
    man*, 2:248. The 110th USCT was organized at Pulaski in November 1863 as the
    2nd Alabama Colored Infantry. Its designation was changed to the 110th USCT
    on June 25, 1864. It is unclear exactly why the 110th was selected or exactly how
    it ended up being sent to Sherman. Perhaps the greatest irony was that the 110th
    accompanied Sherman on his march through the Carolinas, but what specific
    role the soldiers were allowed to play in the march is unknown. See also Orga-
    nization of Union Forces commanded by Major General William T. Sherman,
    January–April 1865; Return of Casualties in the Union Forces, January 1–April 6,
    1865; Roster of the Command of John A. Logan, January 7–March 31, 1865, *OR*,
    1st ser., 47 (1):48, 69, 238; and Marszalek, *Sherman*, 315.

36. Although African Americans did not obtain equality at the end of the war,
    they would gain citizenship, a citizenship that was partially helped along by
    the more than 179,000 black men who wore the Union blue. For the quotes,
    see [Reuben D. Mussey] to C. P. Brown, December 21, 1864, vol. 2221 DC, 364–
    68, Letters Sent by the Commissioner, ser. 1141, Organization of U.S. Colored
    Troops, Dept. of the Cumberland, RG 393 Pt. I; General Orders No. 5, Head
    Quarters, 100th Regt. U.S. Colored Infantry, February 2, 1865, General Orders,
    100th USCI, Regimental Books and Papers USCT, RG 94, quoted in Berlin
    et al., *The Black Military Experience*, 562–63. Unfortunately, the black soldiers did
    not win the respect of everyone. In February 1865 conditions in the hospital
    at Nashville that housed the wounded black soldiers were so bad that Adjutant
    General Lorenzo Thomas complained to the assistant surgeon general, "Had

these men been white soldiers, think you this would have been their condition? No! And yet the Black fell side by side of the White with their faces to the Foe, at the very apex of the abbatis [*sic*]." Still, some had "suffered in filth for weeks." See [Lorenzo Thomas] to Colonel R. C. Wood, January 16, 1865, L. Thomas Letters and Orders, Generals' Papers and Books, ser. 159, RG 94, quoted in Berlin et al., *The Black Military Experience*, 645–46. For the Frederick Douglass quote, see Douglass, "Address for the Promotion of Colored Enlistments" (July 6, 1863), *Douglass' Monthly*, August 1863, in Philip S. Foner, ed., *The Life and Writings of Frederick Douglass*, 5 vols. (New York: International Publishers, 1952–75), 3:365; and McPherson, *The Negro's Civil War*, 163. The letter from the black soldier is John Sweeny, October 8, 1865, quoted in Berlin et al., *The Black Military Experience*, 161–62. It should be pointed out that their military service did not always improve the conditions in which black men lived. In some cases, their families suffered because of that service, and the men were themselves treated badly. In August 1865 a black soldier wrote from Chattanooga of Colonel Lewis Johnson of the 44th USCT: "[I]f he Don't look out he will git apple cart tumbled he has been kicking some of the Boys but the[y] say the[y] will stop that or stop his life." Unsigned to E. M. Stanton, August 22, 1865, A-345 1865, Letters Received, ser. 360, Colored Troops Division, RG 94, quoted in Berlin et al., *The Black Military Experience*, 773–74.

9

LORENZO THOMAS AND THE RECRUITMENT OF BLACKS IN THE MISSISSIPPI VALLEY, 1863–1865

Michael T. Meier

On March 25, 1863, Lorenzo Thomas, a U.S. Military Academy graduate, a long-time staff officer, and now adjutant general of the army, was ordered to the Mississippi Valley to recruit and organize regiments of blacks. Secretary of War Edwin Stanton's order gave Thomas wide latitude, a most peculiar situation given that, as some scholars argue, he "detested" the adjutant general. Certainly, Stanton did not trust him.[1] Nevertheless, when Thomas arrived in the Mississippi Valley, he found that the commanders who handled the immense problems created by refugees coming behind their lines lacked direction and that their efforts differed from officer to officer. There was no system to recruit the able-bodied among the refugees for use as soldiers, nor were there plans to employ those not physically fit for military service. If Thomas had thoughts about dealing with such a chaotic situation, he had not expressed them. On the other hand, he had the power of the secretary of war to experiment with solutions. The adjutant general's views on the role of blacks in the army had not been tested, and his thoughts on slavery or emancipation seemed murky, if he had any at all. Indeed, until the army ordered him to act, he seems not to have given such weighty problems much thought.[2] The tinderbox issue of using blacks in combat eluded Thomas, and racial equality was to him an unfamiliar concept. To effect quick solutions to the troubles he found in the Mississippi Valley, he used the method he understood best—he issued orders. By doing so, he brought uniformity to the size of the new black regiments, involved many commands in their recruitment, and eased the path of their acceptance into a skeptical U.S. Army.

For blacks wanting to serve in the Union army as fighting soldiers, 1863 was a pivotal year. The Emancipation Proclamation was announced in January. In February, Massachusetts governor John A. Andrew, with the approval of the War Department, appointed George L. Stearns to recruit blacks for the famed 54th and 55th Massachusetts Infantries.[3] By March, the War Department had decided on a policy regarding the use of blacks in the army. In May, the War Department took control of all black recruitment by creating the Bureau for Colored Troops as part of the Adjutant General's Office.[4] In June, Stearns, no longer a civilian, was awarded a major's rank with the responsibility of recruiting blacks for the army. He later concentrated his formidable talents with the Army of the Cumberland in Tennessee.[5] By October, the Bureau for Colored Troops reported that fifty-eight black regiments were active.[6] The phlegmatic Old Army had rarely seen events turn so quickly.

Almost from the beginning of the war, however, the use of blacks was left to the discretion of the local commander. Distrust of blacks as soldiers was pervasive, and many officers held that if blacks were to be used at all, it was to be as laborers, cooks, teamsters, or servants. Arming and using them as fighting men were issues gingerly approached. General David Hunter in South Carolina discovered as much when in 1862, to the chagrin of his superiors, he zealously organized the 1st South Carolina Infantry, which was composed of former slaves. His efforts failed, and Hunter was transferred out of the Department of the South, leaving his successor, General Rufus Saxton, to repair the damage.[7] In Louisiana, Major General Benjamin F. Butler, after a period of reluctance and a dispute with Brigadier General John Phelps over the use of blacks, came around and recruited three black regiments of former Confederate Louisiana Native Guards in September 1862. Significantly, these units were officered by blacks,[8] an unsavory issue for white officers that would surface under Butler's successor, Major General Nathaniel Banks. By February 1863, Banks reported that the regiments of Louisiana Native Guards had a strength of 900 men in each, while a company of Louisiana Native Guards Artillery and a fourth artillery regiment also were being raised. According to Banks, these regiments conformed to regulations, each having ten complete companies. Banks's aim was to replace the black officers with whites "as vacancies occur . . ., being entirely satisfied that the appointment of Colored officers is detrimental to the service." The officers of the yet-to-materialize fourth regiment would be white.[9]

Blacks had been flocking to the Union camps in Arkansas, Missouri, and Illinois, even before Lincoln's Emancipation Proclamation. Here chaos characterized the situation. Commanders could not point to a policy for guidance, and frustration became commonplace. Writing from his headquarters at Helena, Arkansas, in mid-January 1863, Colonel Cyrus Bussey pleaded with Missouri Department commander, Major General Samuel R. Curtis, that "there are a great many Negro men, women and children coming into our lines since the proclamation; many are leaving their homes. I am at a loss to know what to do with them, and would be pleased to receive some instructions from you."[10] Curtis did not have much advice to give, for there were problems in Missouri as well. To Brigadier General Benjamin Prentiss, Curtis wrote from St. Louis on March 9, 1863, that Prentiss's letter of February 28, had arrived along "with a boat-load of negroes" and that the department had "more of these, unfortunately, than I know what to do with. The State of Missouri must not be made the depot for the paupers of Arkansas, and it is not a safe way of disposing of free negroes, because the laws of this State are such as to endanger the freedom of persons of African descent."[11] With many efforts taking place on behalf of former slaves, and events coming to a head, there was an obvious need for a national policy concerning the use of blacks in the army.

Setting a policy was impossible until Congress passed the Second Confiscation Act and the Militia Act in the summer of 1862. Among the powers granted the president was the freedom to use blacks for labor or "any military or naval service for which they may be found competent."[12] Even though the door had been opened, field commanders still remained in the dark for almost a year. On March 31, 1863, however, General in Chief Henry W. Halleck, in an unofficial letter to Major General U. S. Grant, commander of the Army of the Tennessee, shed some light on this troublesome issue. The Lincoln administration wanted to damage the productive capacity of the South, he said, and allowing slaves to escape and come behind the Federal lines would help ruin the Southern economy by withdrawing a productive piece of it. Whites would have to harvest the crops, and "every slave withdrawn from the enemy, is equivalent to a white man put *hors de combat*."[13] Blacks could be used to defend forts and camps, Halleck thought, and they would be particularly useful during the "sickly season." Halleck informed Grant that the coming summer would see much organizing of blacks, and if they could not be used in battle, they "certainly can be used with advantage as laborers, teamsters, cooks, &c." The army was to use them to its advantage.

The War Department had received reports, so said Halleck, that some commands had discouraged "the negroes from coming under our protection." They had received ill treatment and had been forced to return to their masters. This was poor policy, the general in chief advised, and it violated orders of the War Department. It was the duty of every officer, regardless of his thinking on the matter, "to cheerfully and honestly endeavor to carry out the measures so adopted." Whatever the opinion of individual commanders might be, blacks had to be tried, and Grant was to carry out the policy in his particular theater of war. From his perch in Washington, Halleck advised Grant that the "character" of the war had changed. Any hope of peace was gone now. Peace would have to be won through war: "we must conquer the rebels, or be conquered by them."[14]

The order of March 25 was wide-ranging and gave Thomas a significant amount of leverage. The inspection tour was to take him first to Cairo, Illinois, to take note of the "military condition" while paying particular attention to the black refugees flooding the city. Stanton wanted to know how they were being treated by the army. The secretary gave Thomas authority to issue orders designed to provide "humane and proper treatment in respect to food, clothing, compensation for their service, and what ever is necessary to enable them to support themselves and to furnish useful service in any capacity to the Government." Thomas was to make similar observations at Columbus, Kentucky, at Memphis, Tennessee, and at the numerous posts on his way to General Ulysses S. Grant's headquarters at Milliken's Bend, Louisiana. At each stop, he was to explain the U.S. government's policy to the troops toward the "use of the colored population emancipated by the Presidents proclamation," especially their use as soldiers. In Thomas's mind, the most important section of his orders instructed him to work out a plan for organizing blacks into military units and finding officers willing to command them. He could reassign men from other regiments and promote enlisted men to officer rank if they qualified. Thomas could appoint officers for brigades, regiments, and companies and was to see to their supplies and uniforms. Through all of this, the adjutant general was to communicate frequently with the War Department, being candid as to the state of things.[15]

Thomas had limited familiarity with slaves. He did not come from a large family, and his father, Evan Thomas, never owned slaves.[16] The elder Thomas was a long time register of wills for the probate court of New Castle, Delaware,[17] who in 1819 was anxious to have the fifteen-year-old Lorenzo go to the U.S. Military Academy.[18] Letters were sent to President James Monroe and Secretary of War John C. Calhoun extolling young Lorenzo's virtues. Acceptance came in the summer of 1819.[19]

Not an exceptional student, Thomas had his share of infractions but remained a "respectable" cadet[20] and graduated in 1823, seventeenth in his class.[21] He spent his early career in Florida, and in 1833 he was assigned to the Adjutant General's Office in Washington, D.C. Thomas found his niche in staff work. Generating paper and maintaining the War Department's filing system gave his life form. By the outbreak of the Mexican War, he had achieved the rank of brevet major and was assistant adjutant general. Like many of his contemporaries, he wanted to go to Mexico, and in July 1846 he approached his superior, Brigadier General Roger Jones, about the possibility of serving on General Zachary Taylor's staff.[22] Thomas was certain to tell Jones that his purpose in requesting this assignment was not to cause problems with Taylor's adjutant, William Wallace Smith Bliss. He assured General Jones that his motives were noble and that the war in Mexico required his talents.[23] In his endorsement, Jones wrote that he was impressed with "the military spirit" of Thomas's request and wished to order him to report to Taylor.[24] Thomas did his work, obeyed orders, and was breveted as a lieutenant colonel in September 1848.[25] At the conclusion of the war, he was ordered back to Washington, where he resumed his rank as major in the 4th Infantry. He served as General Winfield Scott's chief of staff from 1853 to 1861.[26] Simon Cameron, Lincoln's first secretary of war, appointed him adjutant general in March 1861 with the rank of brevet brigadier general.[27] Cameron's tenure was brief, and in January 1862 Edwin McMasters Stanton ascended to the position of war secretary while Cameron became ambassador to Russia.[28]

Tall and garrulous, Thomas liked receiving and giving orders and enjoyed talking about his heroic role in carrying them out. His blunt manner and uninhibited arrogance irritated his fellow officers, particularly his penchant for never admitting wrongdoing. This trait manifested itself early in his career when in 1822, as a young cadet at the U.S. Military Academy, he was charged with having liquor in his room, court-martialed, found guilty, and dismissed from the army. Though reinstated in a few days,[29] he defended his behavior by reminding the court that it was close to Christmas, when everyone was expected to bend the rules.[30] In another incident, this time in the summer of 1864 outside Natchez, Mississippi, Thomas was returning to the city after an evening with a friend of his, a Mr. Kenny. A sentinel ordered the carriage stopped and demanded that Thomas and Kenny identify themselves. Thomas, remaining inside the carriage, refused, and the sentinel proceeded to arrest both men and escort them to the provost guard. Thomas was furious and later complained to Major General N. J. T. Dana, commander of the District of Vicksburg, that the sentinel was incompetent.[31] Clearly in the wrong, Thomas never admitted it.[32]

It was well known that Stanton did not like Thomas. In fact, some scholars argue that the secretary of war did not trust regular army officers in general and viewed them with suspicion.[33] But why Stanton had such an intense dislike of Thomas is not clear. Though some scholars have suggested that Thomas's alleged fondness for alcohol factored into his assignment to the Western Theater, it could also have stemmed from the fact that Thomas was a Cameron appointee and so did not have Stanton's trust. For certain, Stanton did not want him around. Colonel E. D. Townsend, Thomas's assistant and successor as adjutant general remembered how, during the days of the army's build-up in 1861, Cameron used Thomas to make speeches and represent him at functions. Under Stanton, however, the War Department "settled down to stern work, and glorifying ceased to be such a prominent element in military life," as Townsend put it.[34] With Stanton relying on Townsend more and more, a favorite method often used by the secretary of war to get Thomas out of town was to assign him mundane tasks in other cities. After Thomas returned from such a trip to muster out troops in Harrisburg, Pennsylvania, on March 23, 1863, Stanton abruptly ordered him to go on an inspection tour "of the armies, military posts, and military operations of the West." The "exigencies of the service" required it, he said, and issued the order on March 25.[35] Thomas did not question the wisdom of his out-of-town assignments, and this one was no different, or at least he did not record his feelings about being sent so far afield.[36] But it is clear that Stanton wanted him out of the office and away from Washington.

As ordered, Thomas stopped in Cairo, Illinois, on March 30, and it made a lasting impression on him. Along with the chaplain of the 14th Wisconsin Infantry, James B. Roberts, he visited the contraband camp where he found more than 1,500 men, women, and children in crowded barracks. Smallpox, pneumonia, and measles spread rapidly in these conditions, and many had died. Thomas ordered the Subsistence Department to provide food to the hospitals. For those healthy enough to work, Thomas proposed that they be sent to establish farms on Island No. 10. In this way, the chances for disease would be lessened, and the refugees would provide for themselves.[37] He was aware too that these unfortunate people could not be sent back to the homes they fled or to the border states where slavery still existed. Indeed, even in free states they would face prejudice, particularly among "those of Irish and German descent." The government needed to develop a policy of plantation leasing and arrange for their employment, he said.[38] He envisioned a system where these refugees, being employed on abandoned and confiscated plantations and farms, could cultivate and sell cotton to the benefit of everyone. He proposed a plan for such a system.[39]

Major General Lorenzo Thomas, adjutant general of the U.S. Army.
(National Archives, no. 111-BA-1434)

Thomas's major responsibility was to raise and organize black troops, however, and he began at a frantic pace. In getting his message to the troops, no command in the Valley was overlooked. Giving the same speech time and time again, he always made the presentations an event. He would have the troops parade, after which they would gather for his address. The commanding officers followed and echoed the adjutant general's remarks because "the view of many Generals and of the Officers . . . communicated directly to the Troops" was important to his success.[40] Grant, for one, was quickly won over. Writing to Halleck on April 19, Grant said that his corps commanders would "take hold of the new policy of arming negroes and using them against the rebels with a will."[41] In Memphis, Major General Stephen A. Hurlbut told Thomas that his corps would give its support too, and he wanted permission to enlist six hundred blacks as artillerists and train them to man the heavy guns around the city. Thomas gladly authorized him to raise six companies and to select the officers. Hurlbut knew "intelligent sergeants who will make good captains," Thomas said.[42] On April 9, 1863, Thomas was at Lake Providence, Louisiana, speaking to Major General James B. McPherson's corps and to General John Logan's division. Thomas proudly estimated that there were four thousand troops in attendance, all of whom were enthusiastic about the policy of arming blacks. Of the generals who spoke, Logan particularly impressed him because he proposed that each of McPherson's divisions raise two regiments of black troops. A confident Thomas arranged for the delivery of two thousand pairs of shoes and enough clothing and weapons to furnish the new regiments.[43]

Results came quickly. The next day, April 10, the 8th Regiment of Louisiana Volunteers of African Descent was organized under the command of Colonel Hiram Scofield.[44] On April 11, the 9th and 10th regiments were formed and mustered in.[45] On April 14, Thomas reported to Stanton that "the feeling of the troops in regard to the employment of blacks as soldiers is favorable in a high degree . . . and, so far, in my conversations with officers, I find no opponents to the policy."[46] To one observer, though, the picture was not so promising. Assistant Secretary of War Charles A. Dana, on a tour of the Mississippi Valley, wrote Stanton that "officers in this army, who three months ago, told me that they would never serve along with negro regiments, now say that Adjutant-General Thomas makes bad speeches to troops, but they shall obey orders, nevertheless."[47]

Many who heard Thomas speak did not agree with Dana because the adjutant general was an effective speaker. He spoke to large crowds with an orator's talent that emotionally appealed to and articulated the concerns of the assembled. One such occasion occurred on May 23, 1863, in Memphis, where any doubts of his oratorical ability were put to an end. Many freed people had gathered to hear the adjutant general, who began by expressing gratification at meeting "so many loyal black people." He was from a slave state, he said, and claimed to have owned slaves,[48] to have had a slave as a nurse in his infancy, and to have observed slaves on many plantations throughout the South.[49] His mission that day, though, was to tell them what he expected of them. Freedpeople were not to sit around; they were to work and—work for themselves, not a master. Thomas preached that they were now "free—free as I am, good as I am. We are all men; the only difference between us is I have had greater advantages than you. Now you are free, you can learn—learn to work. Learn to read."[50] Now they were to work for wages, and there were many loyal white men who had leased plantations and were eager to hire them. Furthermore, commanders wanted them to help crush the rebellion. In a brilliant oratorical stroke, Thomas said he believed that the rebellion had but one cause—slavery. He queried and lectured at the same time: "President Lincoln has set you free—will you fight? Suppose I would give you guns, and you should see a party of guerrillas in the woods, what would you do?" We'd kill them, the crowd roared. Thomas believed them, he said, and wanted them to enlist for this holy cause. Then he bellowed to the crowd: "I want to hear you sing." The air filled with voices, moving the reporter for the *New York Times* to remark: "To us it looked like a camp-meeting scene . . . my heart was surged with emotions."[51]

Five months later, on November 28, at Goodrich's Landing, Louisiana, Thomas spoke to another crowd. This speech was different, however, because planters, civilians, and members of the black regiments guarding the area had gathered. Dubbing it "one of the most interesting and important scenes of the War," the *New York Times* estimated that at least four thousand "unarmed free people" gathered that day.[52] They were "drinking into their thirsty ears words they had never heard before, spoken by an authority they had often heard of, but never realized, and hearing of duties and responsibilities which had never occurred to them, even in their dreams." With men in their Sunday best, women in their finest clothes, and the newly formed black regiments in uniform, the meeting opened with a prayer. Thomas then stepped forth and said: "I wish you all to listen to me . . . and mark what I say, for I shall not mince words." Black troops were told that prejudice against them was disappearing, particularly after their heroic accomplishments at Milliken's Bend and Fort Wagner. Officers were carrying out God's will and doing it brilliantly, Thomas told them. "Providence has decreed that the black men of the country should be soldiers." It was the "fixed desire of God. I know your hearts are in the work." Officers were to "elevate" these men and "improve their minds." He lectured the planters that profits were no longer to be their sole concern, for now they were there for the "good of the negroes" as well. They were to employ the women and children and the infirm. Marriages were to be protected, children were to be nurtured, and prejudice was to be erased. The *New York Times* observed that the "words sank deep into the hearts of all present, and the day will long be remembered with the sincerest pleasure by all who were so fortunate to be present." [53] Even the reporter for the more conservative *Harper's Weekly* was impressed: "it may safely be said that no singular and impressive scene has ever been enacted during the War as the Adjutant-General of the United States Army addressing negro soldiers, civilians, and women and children, on the duties and responsibilities of freedom." [54]

Though Thomas had much leverage and, in some sense, power, he still had to depend on the commanders of various departments and districts to provide recruits for the new regiments. Many blacks continued to go behind the lines and volunteer to become soldiers, but even so he wanted commanders to "gather the blacks" when on expeditions throughout the Mississippi Valley. Thomas recommended using black regiments to recruit other blacks, but he could not dictate to commanders. Some used whatever methods were at hand, including force. Also, there were times when circumstances required commanders to ignore the goals of the adjutant general. During the Vicksburg campaign, for example, when Grant pulled his forces from Louisiana, he left Thomas without a recruiting arm. In typical Thomas fashion he remained optimistic and predicted he would raise 20,000 men by the end of 1863. [55] Even Stanton could not ignore Thomas's "diligence and success." The secretary confessed that it had given him "great pleasure." [56] On May 20, Thomas telegrammed Stanton that the Third Mississippi Regiment of African Descent was organized. Clothing, "distinctive . . . of less cost . . . something a little more gay," would be provided. In addition, Thomas recommended Colonel Isaac Shepard, commander of the First Mississippi Regiment of African Descent, as a brigadier general. Shepard's "heart was in the work," Thomas said. Colonel Richard Ballinger was to take Shepard's place with the First Mississippi. [57] The pace was fast, and Thomas sent telegram after telegram, letter after letter, to the War Department. Between April 1, 1863, and the end of the year, the number of dispatches to the Adjutant General's Office in Washington numbered in the hundreds. In rapid-fire sentences he kept the Department apprised as to the organization of black troops, the responsibilities of officers of black troops, promotions of enlisted men to officer rank in black regiments, the assignment of officers from other regiments to black regiments, and reassignments and reorganizations. The pace was dizzying.[58]

As recruitment of blacks was being conducted on a national scale, the War Department realized that it had to control the work. To this end Congress created the Bureau for Colored Troops, and War Department General Orders No. 143, dated May 22, 1863, placed the new bureau in the Adjutant General's Office with the prime responsibility, of recording "all matters relating to the organization of Colored Troops." It established field offices and inspectors who supervised the organization of black troops and, among the bureau's other duties, administered the examinations of officers. Under the order, the names of regiments no longer reflected the place of origin. Now they would be regiments of the U.S. Colored Troops.[59] Because of his position as adjutant general of the army, Thomas continued to report directly to Stanton and to take his orders from the War Department rather than the bureau.

Thomas endorsed the new organization and frequently communicated with its commander, Colonel C. W. Foster, but his chief concern remained the recruitment and organization of black troops in the Mississippi Valley. Thomas became ill in June and was ordered back to Washington to convalesce. With his absence, recruitment slowed considerably between June and August, and the same old problems with refugees reoccurred.[60] He confessed to Colonel Townsend that the month had "closed with seemingly little done in the way of organizations of blacks." Those men he was able to get were now being used to fill the ranks of regiments already in the field. On July 11, 1863, Grant informed him that he had "broken up" a new colored regiment and transferred the men to those regiments already established. If regiments were to be maintained at regulation strength, there was no choice, Grant assured Thomas, and he was "anxious to get as many of these negro regiments as possible and to have them full and completely equipped."[61] Also, as a result of the military campaigns, so many blacks had been driven into the interior that Thomas had to attach recruiting officers to commands who were campaigning well beyond the banks of the Mississippi River.[62] He wrote to Major General John Schofield in St. Louis concerning a rumored expedition into Arkansas. If so, Thomas wanted Schofield to "collect as many blacks . . . as possible. The able bodied men you can organize into Regiments and I will commission such officers for them as you may designate. You will of course be careful to give me only such officers whose hearts are in the work."[63] After the battle at Milliken's Bend, Colonel Isaac Shepard complained that his Louisiana and Mississippi regiments were reduced by about half. He had 3,965 men and should have had 6,860.[64]

Isaac Shepard was the kind of soldier Thomas wanted to lead these regiments. Shepard was among the first officers to volunteer to raise a black regiment and had resigned as the commander of the Third Missouri Infantry to become the colonel of a black unit. In June 1863, while Shepard was temporarily in command of black troops in northeastern Louisiana, a soldier from a nearby white regiment "committed acts of wantonness against the negroes and their families." Shepard complained to the regimental commander and was ignored. Out of patience, he ordered the white soldier seized and tied up and then commanded black soldiers to whip him.[65] This was even too much for Thomas who, understanding the reasons behind Shepard's rage, regretted "exceedingly that you put him under the lash of the Negro soldiers. I trust this will not happen again."[66] Grant conducted an "informal investigation" and was "satisfied that the whole difficulty arose from the outrageous treatment of the Black Troops by some white ones, and the failure of their officers to punish the perpetrators."[67] Grant returned Shepard to duty on June 14.[68] Shepard's impetuosity notwithstanding, Thomas continued to have faith in him and strongly recommended him for a brigadiership on October 5, 1863. "His case is a special one," Thomas wrote, "he being the only Colonel who presented himself for a command of Colored Troops . . . at a time when I needed the support and co-operation of high officers."[69] Shepard received his brigadier's star on October 27.[70]

Officers of black troops, whether they shared Shepard's zeal or not, were to be white. In the early days of black recruitment, all noncommissioned officers and first sergeants were to be white as well.[71] This policy ended when Thomas concluded that the white noncommissioned officers lacked commitment to the cause. Accordingly, he "urged colonels to select intelligent blacks" to instruct and promote to these ranks.[72] When in September 1863 Daniel Ullman, brimming with enthusiasm and new to the Department of the Gulf, announced that he wanted to raise a regiment of Colored Troops and staff it with black officers, Thomas quickly revoked the plan. To Major General Nathaniel Banks, Thomas wrote that this had to be done "for obvious reasons," the least of which was that it was "highly injurious to the Organizations already authorized with entirely white officers."[73] Thomas had given the matter some thought, but he and the War Department in general did not want black officers commanding black regiments because they did not think them ready for the responsibility. These recruits had been brought up in slavery, Thomas told Senator Henry Wilson of Massachusetts, and were taught early on to be subservient to whites. Officers, being white, quickly won their respect and obedience. Thomas advised that black troops would not respond to black officers.[74]

Thomas was gratified that his efforts since the spring of 1863 appeared to be gaining acceptance. Indeed, he welcomed observers while continuing his tireless pace. One visitor was Brigadier General James S. Wadsworth, former aide-de-camp to General Irvin McDowell, veteran of the Battle of Gettysburg[75], and now on an inspection tour; he appeared at Thomas's headquarters in November 1863. The secretary of war sent Wadsworth to the Mississippi Valley to inquire if the organization of black troops was going as Thomas had said. Thomas welcomed him by placing everything at his disposal, even his "little steam-boat." Wadsworth used it to good effect, going to Baton Rouge, New Orleans, and Natchez to make inspections of the black units stationed there. Thomas could not have asked for a more positive report. Wadsworth made much of the fact that early officers of Colored Troops were frequently "second and third rate." But, Wadsworth said, incompetent officers had been weeded out, as had been the prejudice against blacks that had so clouded the initial organizational efforts in the spring of 1863. The troops were well disciplined but inadequately paid. Indeed, the pay for a private was equal to that of a noncommissioned officer. Because the troops lacked incentive to advance, an immediate pay increase was recommended.[76] Thomas agreed with all these points.

By the end of the year, Thomas reported that there were 20,830 men in various regiments throughout the Mississippi Valley, including 15,488 in infantry units. Five thousand had died of disease, he said, or had been captured or "lost to the service by other casualties." Thomas's report did not include the regiments in the Department of the Gulf.[77] General Wadsworth, on the other hand, included them, thus swelling the number of black troops in the Mississippi Valley to 27,000. Wadsworth reported that there were thirty-nine infantry regiments, four regiments of engineers, three cavalry, five heavy artillery, and three batteries of light artillery.[78]

Despite Wadsworth's favorable report, some of his fellow officers doubted the glowing reports coming from the adjutant general. Major General William T. Sherman, for example, cared little for the use of blacks as fighting soldiers and doubted Thomas's and Wadsworth's estimates regarding the number of blacks in units in the Mississippi Valley. Stanton wrote Thomas that "General Sherman seems to think that the colored troops reported to be raised by you on the Mississippi are chiefly on paper, and that the men are not to be found."[79] Thomas pointed out that Sherman failed to look at the logistics of the matter, for these troops were not concentrated but rather stretched along the length of the Mississippi and much of the Ohio Rivers and commanders depended on them.[80] Thomas wanted to clear the air of any ambiguity and wished to remind Sherman that his (Thomas's) "special duties" were "to organize Colored Troops, and I expect full co-operation on the part of all military commanders, to enable me to execute these Special Orders of the Secretary of War."[81] Not impressed, Sherman argued that blacks were best used as pioneers and laborers; if zealous recruiting agents continued to raid his laboring gangs, taking the able-bodied among them, he would be left with a "large class of Black Paupers."[82] Sherman was convinced that the "great mass of our soldering must be of the white race & the Black Troops should for some years be used with *caution*." It was a worthy endeavor, Sherman said, but "all I ask is that it be not forced beyond the laws of natural development."[83] Sherman complained to Thomas that his officers had actually recruited the men most fit to work on laboring gangs and as cattle drivers.[84] Sherman ordered recruiting in his command to cease and threatened to imprison recruitment officers. To him, Thomas and his recruiters were stealing a resource he badly needed. All of this was progressing too fast for Sherman. "For God's sake," he wrote Thomas, "let the negro question develop itself slowly & naturally & not be premature cultivation."[85] Thomas was furious. This would "stop enlistment from the colored men coming to his army," he complained to Stanton from Louisville, and the "threat to imprison the recruiting officers [is] especially harsh."[86] Not only was Sherman violating a rule Thomas held sacred, that is obeying orders, but he was trampling on a cause that Thomas had become to believe inviolable.

By the end of 1864, the organization and use of blacks as fighting soldiers could find no stronger advocate than the adjutant general. The successful exercise of his authority to raise black troops, give orders, and commission officers served to muffle the criticism of those opposed to his mission. His skills were tested, however, in the border states where slavery still existed and where, in certain instances, there was strong proslavery sentiment.

When Congress passed the Enrollment Act in March 1863, a rider was attached stating that loyal owners of slaves in the border states could receive compensation of up to $300 if a slave joined the military. The act also provided that all black males between the ages of twenty and forty-five were to be enrolled for the draft. If a slave was drafted into the service, his loyal owner was given a bounty of $100 and was required to file a claim for the remaining $200. A commission, appointed by the secretary of war, investigated the claim, and if the owner proved to be a Union man, the additional $200 was awarded. All troops drafted this way were to be mustered into the U.S. Colored Troops rather than into the various state militias.[87] Thomas soon discovered that, in the absence of political pressures and controls, recruiting blacks in states like Mississippi and Louisiana was straightforward. Doing the same in the border states, however, was not as clear-cut. In some states, Kentucky in particular, governors tenaciously held onto slavery as a system and reacted angrily when anyone tried to interfere with it. On the other hand, if a recruiting officer could prove that a slave belonged to a Confederate sympathizer, the slave could be recruited without regard for the law.

The question of loyalty remained a troubling one. Major General John Schofield, commander of the Department of the Missouri, observed in the autumn of 1863 that recruitment officers in the field decided questions of loyalty. Without criteria, the results were confusing and uneven, prompting Schofield to stop such recruiting.[88] In any case, there were not many potential recruits left in Missouri because, as Brigadier General William Pile, Thomas's recruiting agent in the state, reported, there were not more that one thousand "able bodied slaves" remaining and probably no more than three thousand altogether.[89] Even without Schofield's order, recruiting in Missouri remained lackluster, with only five infantry regiments organized and mustered in.[90]

Kentucky, however, was a different matter. While Governor Hamilton R. Gamble of Missouri cooperated with Thomas and the War Department, Kentucky governor Thomas Bramlette proved to be an obstructionist and a difficult chief executive.[91] Major General Ambrose Burnside, commander of the Department of the Ohio, warned Lincoln of the problems he would face in Kentucky when in June 1863 he advised the president that "it would be very unwise to enrol free negroes in that State. It would not add materially to our strength and I assure you it would cause much trouble."[92] Realizing this, Thomas approached Bramlette cautiously. Being headquartered in Louisville much of the time, Thomas could observe many able-bodied black men leaving the state and joining the army in Illinois or Indiana—or even Tennessee and as far away as Massachusetts. In a meeting with Bramlette, Thomas tried to convince him that if he were allowed to recruit openly in the state, Kentucky could easily meet the draft quotas required by the Provost Marshal General's Office in Washington. Bramlette counseled caution, however. Raising black troops in the state, he said, would endanger the Union cause. Besides, the governor said, Lincoln had promised him that recruitment of blacks would not take place in Kentucky.[93] The adjutant general reminded him that there already was a black regiment of heavy artillery in Paducah. Bramlette replied bitterly, saying that, yes, he knew this and that the citizens of the state were alarmed because they "have not schooled themselves to believe that the time has arrived for decisive action on their part for the entire abolition of slavery."[94] Even the commander of the District of Kentucky, Brigadier General Steven Gano Burbridge, recommended caution, advising Thomas that the people of the state continued to have "a deep-rooted prejudice against the abolition of slavery." To underscore the sensitive nature of the issue, Burbridge reminded the adjutant general that many of the state's leaders and influential citizens, including newspaper proprietors, owned slaves.[95] Sensitive or not, Burbridge was legally bound to enroll all males, black and white; consequently he issued General Orders No. 34 on April 18, 1864. According to the order, the provost marshal, not the adjutant general, was to be the sole agent of recruiting in the state. Furthermore, if a slave was drafted, the owner would be issued a certificate to be presented to the War Department for compensation.[96]

Thomas, however, in a move born from ignorance of Burbridge's order or out of a sense of prerogative, issued his own General Orders No. 20 on June 13, 1864. From his headquarters in Louisville, Thomas announced that the recruitment of blacks in Kentucky would proceed "as rapidly as possible, and [that] one or more officers will be placed in each county to receive the able-bodied men as they present themselves or are delivered by their owners." He was certain that Union men would "cheerfully" bring in their slaves, for they wanted the rebellion crushed; "if others do not, it makes no difference, as all who will present themselves for enlistment will be received and enlisted into the service of the United States."[97] At times Thomas did not seem to understand complex issues, since to assume, for example, that Union men would "cheerfully" bring in their slaves and be awarded a certificate valued at $300 was naive in the extreme. There had been nothing in his experience in Kentucky to encourage such an optimistic view. Nevertheless, to pacify the soon-to-be-enraged governor and General Burbridge, Thomas made it clear that Kentucky would receive full credit against its draft quota for all blacks recruited within its borders. To coordinate the recruiting effort, Thomas appointed Brigadier General Augustus L. Chetlain as supervisor of recruitment of black troops in the state. Chetlain was to receive his instructions from and report to Thomas, not Burbridge, and "colored troops will be used by General Chetlain for recruiting purposes, and will be distributed among the different camps of reception." Thomas purposely, but incorrectly, claimed that his actions were by order of the secretary of war.[98] It is not clear why Thomas did this, for it established two recruiting systems in a state whose commitment to the cause of the U.S. Colored Troops was tenuous at best. Thomas, having control of black recruitment in the states of the lower Mississippi Valley, did not seem to comprehend the tinderbox nature of the situation in Kentucky. To him, his orders of March 25, 1863, were clear-cut. The nuances generated by the politics of the state did not impress the adjutant general.

Thomas, however, was not one to disobey orders, and there is no indication that he requested guidance from the War Department for his policy regarding Kentucky. Even to a casual observer, it looked as though he had overstepped his authority. Reaction from Washington came quickly, and Thomas soon heard from both the War Department and a perturbed General Burbridge. Stanton directed Provost Marshal General James Fry to write Thomas to remind him that "on account of the peculiar condition of things in Kentucky," General Burbridge had been given control of the "recruitment service for both white and colored troops in their State." Burbridge and Major William Sidell, as superintendent of recruiting, had been "enlisting negroes in Kentucky" for several weeks, and the secretary did not want this disturbed. In fact, Stanton told Thomas to "give any aid in your power to carry out the plan General Burbridge is acting on, and to put under General Burbridge's control all officers whom you deem it best to connect with recruitment and organization in Kentucky."[99] In a terse letter to Thomas, Burbridge reminded him that he had been given the authority to raise colored troops by War Department Special Order No. 140 (1864) and that he (Burbridge), both as a Kentuckian and a "large slave holder," knew how sensitive the issue was. The General wanted it done with the "least possible feeling upon the subject by the people." Because of the hostile feelings of white Kentuckians, Burbridge planned to appoint natives of the state as officers of the black regiments and to send the white recruits to more active theaters of war, while using blacks to garrison forts. "The numerous cases of unpleasant perplexities arising out of this conflict of jurisdiction will readily suggest themselves to you," he wrote.[100]

Much of what Burbridge said must have angered Thomas, for he had labored long and hard to include black troops as active participants in the war. Having them assigned to garrison duty was a step backward. With his power over black recruitment in the state limited, he rescinded his General Orders No. 20, and Chetlain returned to his headquarters in Memphis.[101]

Always having to have the upper hand, though, Thomas told Burbridge that he was sending him a list of officers who were qualified for positions in black regiments. He was returning to several cities in the lower Mississippi, and "during my absence, I request that you will take the organization of colored troops into your hands and fill them up as rapidly as possible and will, of course, station them at such places as you may think best."[102] As Burbridge had the power anyway, this was a moot point. Nevertheless, Thomas correctly doubted that Burbridge would have time to oversee recruitment; indeed, Burbridge eventually gave the responsibility to Colonel J. S. Brisbin.[103]

The secretary of war must have breathed more easily after Judge Advocate General Joseph Holt, a Kentucky native, reported on his meeting with Governor Bramlette, General Burbridge, members of Burbridge's staff, and "knowledgeable" civilians. In his July 31, 1864, letter to Stanton, Holt painted a situation less troubled than heretofore reported. Holt estimated that around 10,000 blacks had enlisted in the state, and he predicted thousands more would join the army. In the beginning, Holt said, recruitment was characterized by outrages of various descriptions, "a shameful condition," but as the policy continued, all this disappeared. Opposition, such as it was, had been "fostered by unscrupulous politicians" who hoped to influence the presidential election in November 1864. Holt thought the experiment in Kentucky had been a success.[104]

Holt's rosy predictions appear ridiculous when seen through Governor Bramlette's eyes.[105] The governor was receiving letters daily from citizens describing outrages relating to the recruitment of blacks. In January 1864, the loyal citizens of Christian County sent the governor a petition telling them that the recruiting of blacks was draining the county of able-bodied slaves. "Some of our largest farmers & best Citizens . . . are losing all except the helpless ones."[106] S. P. Cope wrote Bramlette on July 8, 1864, informing him that a group of "four negro soldiers armed with muskets and bayonets entered his house while he and his family were at breakfast searching for my only remaining family Servant."[107] Cope claimed that his property had been destroyed, "my grounds laid waste, my produce and stock despoiled and killed."[108] He wanted to know what the governor could do. General Burbridge, as a commanding officer in the state, offered little solace. In June he wrote Bramlette that he was unable to determine the extent of the violations of laws of the state. As for the governor's concern regarding the abuse of the enrollment acts, Burbridge could only remind him that "my orders charge me with the execution of the laws . . . and I hope in doing so to have the cordial cooperation of your Excellency."[109] As late as September 1864, Bramlette was still on the offensive to stop black recruitment. In a letter to Lincoln, he wrote that, loyalty to the Union aside, "we are preserving the right and liberties of our own race, and . . . are not willing to sacrifice a single life, or imperil the smallest right of free white men for the sake of the negro."[110] Bramlette did not want the status of freedmen or slaves to be the basis for peace, and the governor wanted the U.S. Army to stay out of the affairs of the state of Kentucky.[111] Wisely, Lincoln and the War Department ignored Bramlette's ravings, and things soon settled down. By mid-September Bramlette was quiet, and Thomas could report that there were 14,000 blacks enlisted in Kentucky; he suspected that there would be 20,000 by the end of October.[112] Stanton was gratified.[113]

By December 1864 the situation in Kentucky was such that black recruitment continued—this time under Thomas's direction. After Lincoln's reelection in November, Governor Bramlette's histrionics receded, and General Burbridge was given another assignment.[114] Also the waning months of 1864 saw recruitment ebbing, particularly in the interior of the state where Confederate sentiment remained high and mounted troops were needed to protect recruiting officers. Nevertheless, Thomas informed Stanton in December that 9,623 men had been enlisted since his last report. Though he remarked that "recruitment continues dull" and that all the "able-bodied negroes in the cities and large towns, and the country adjacent . . . have been enlisted," his speculations of September, when he predicted a total of 20,000 black troops for the state, had been exceeded. In December 1864 the number of black troops enlisted in Kentucky was over 20,000.[115]

One potential source of recruits Thomas wanted to draw on were blacks who had escaped to the free states bordering Kentucky, particularly Illinois. He thought there were about one thousand men in the area around Mound City and Cairo.[116] Thomas requested that Brigadier General Solomon Meredith, commander of the District of West Kentucky, appoint an officer to go to Mound City and recruit those escaped Kentucky blacks. Major James McBride was appointed, and a more unfortunate choice could not have been made. When McBride arrived, he threw up pickets and forced any black man he could find to enroll. Few were Kentuckians. Most were Illinois natives and citizens of other states. McBride was ordered to stop and was arrested. To escape, he compelled the captain of a steamboat to take him and his "recruits" to Paducah.[117] The situation embarrassed Thomas, for it appeared to people on the scene that McBride had invaded Mound City and kidnapped these men, some of whom were navy employees. Apologizing to Illinois governor Richard Ogelsby, Thomas assured him that "there was no intention on my part to have any Negro removed from the state without his consent."[118] To Major General Joseph Hooker, Thomas wrote that McBride was to "*recruit* negroes not *seize* them" and that General Meredith had not relayed his orders to McBride clearly. Meredith promised a proper punishment for McBride. Everyone seemed satisfied.[119]

By February 1865, the system of recruitment in the Mississippi Valley had run its course. Many able-bodied former slaves and free black men had been recruited and were part of the U.S. Colored Troops. On April 9, 1865, Stanton ordered all recruitment for volunteer forces stopped.[120] Thomas returned to Washington, where Brigadier General E. D. Townsend had performed well in the Adjutant General's Office. Thomas strongly recommended that his staff, which included his two sons, Thomas and Evan, receive brevet promotions.[121] However, his relationship with the secretary of war had not improved. Stanton continued to send him on inspection tours, including one to Richmond in the summer of 1865.[122]

In his final report of October 3, 1865, Thomas reflected on his experiences in the Mississippi Valley. Stanton was reminded that the instructions to Thomas were given on short notice and that the issue of recruiting and arming blacks "was new to me;" "I entered upon the duty by no means certain at what I might be able to effect." Thomas, ever confident, concluded that "most of my military service was performed in the Slave States, and I was perfectly familiar with plantation life. I felt that I knew the peculiarities of the whole race."[123] Thomas was without a command when he went to the Mississippi Valley and had to depend on others much of the time. Furthermore, there was much chaos, and the previous raising of black regiments had been done without regard to regulations. Thomas ended this practice and ordered that all black regiments raised would conform to regulations of ten companies of one hundred men each.

The energy and capacity for work that Thomas brought to the effort impressed even his critics, and his efforts on behalf of freedpeople—a discussion of which is not within the scope of this essay—reflected an understanding and concern for their plight. Thomas's final report provides a glimpse of the complexities of the issues he confronted. In spite of the resistance, prejudice, and skepticism, Thomas estimated that 2,872 officers and 77,720 enlisted men entered into the service of the U.S. Colored Troops in the Mississippi Valley.[124] As a career officer, Thomas undertook assignments as ordered. With black recruitment, though, he brought energy and commitment to the cause.

Thomas continued in his role as adjutant general until 1868, when the events of that year proved his undoing following his embroilment in the impeachment crisis of President Andrew Johnson. Johnson told him that, after Stanton was fired, he was going to appoint him interim secretary of war. The president was clear that Thomas was to keep this to himself, but the talkative adjutant general did not heed the president's advice. He succeeded in embarrassing both himself and the president by announcing, while at a costume party, that he would be appointed the interim secretary of war. When he attempted to take over Stanton's office in the War Department, the secretary was already aware of the plot. The episode ended pathetically, and Thomas became a laughingstock to many.[125] He retired in 1868, living out his life in Washington, D.C., and dying of debility and congestion of the lungs on March 2, 1875, at the age of seventy-one.[126]

Notes

1. Benjamin P. Thomas and Harold M. Hyman, *Stanton: The Life and Times of Lincoln's Secretary of War* (New York: Alfred A. Knopf, 1962), 159; Dudley Taylor Cornish, *The Sable Arm: Black Troops in the Union Army, 1861–1865* (1956; Lawrence: University Press of Kansas, 1987), 113–15.

2. There is no collection of Thomas's private correspondence. Virtually all of his papers are official documents he wrote as a young officer and as adjutant general. After his retirement, he did not join the various veterans' associations; the Manuscript Division of the Library of Congress has only three items relating to him.

3. Cornish, *The Sable Arm*, 105–10. For a thoughtful overview of the recruitment of blacks into the Union army and how they were organized, see Ira Berlin, Joseph P. Reidy, and Leslie S. Rowland, eds., *The Black Military Experience* (Cambridge: Cambridge University Press, 1982), 1–45. See also Benjamin Quarles, *The Negro in the Civil War* (Boston: Little, Brown, 1953), 108–13.

4. War Department General Orders No. 143, May 22, 1863, "The Negro in the Military Service of the United States," 3 (1), Record Group (RG) 94, Records of the Adjutant General's Office, 1780s–1917, National Archives (NA), Washington, D.C. (hereafter cited as "The Negro").

5. Cornish, *The Sable Arm*, 235–37.

6. "Statement of Colored Troops in the Service of the United States, October 31, 1863, Compiled from the latest Official Reports," Annual Report of the Adjutant General Relating to the Colored Troops Division, RG 94, NA.

7. Cornish, *The Sable Arm*, 32–55.

8. The story is far more complex than this passage suggests. Ibid., 57–68.

9. Banks to Thomas, February 12, 1863, "The Negro," 3 (1).

10. Bussey to Curtis, January 13, 1863, "The Negro," 3 (2).

11. Curtis to Prentiss, March 9, 1863, ibid.

12. Cornish, *The Sable Arm*, 29; Quarles, *The Negro in the Civil War*, 162; "The Negro," 2:914–16.

13. Berlin et al., *The Black Military Experience*, 143–44.

14. Ibid.

15. Stanton to Thomas, March 25, 1863, in U.S. War Department, *The War of the Rebellion: A Compilation of the Official Records of the Union and Confederate Armies*, 128 vols. (Washington, D.C.: Government Printing Office, 1880–1901), 3rd ser., 3:100 (hereafter cited as *OR*).

16. The Census of 1820 shows no slaves owned by the family. Those of 1830 and 1840 show that Evan Thomas had two free black females residing in the household. See Population Schedules of the United States, 1820, microfilm roll 4, 137; 1830, microfilm roll 12, 121; 1840, microfilm roll 33, 186, RG 29, Records of the Bureau of the Census, NA.

17. Cadet Application Papers, file 22, 1819, RG 94, NA.

18. Ibid.

19. Ibid.

20. Major Alexander Macomb to Brevet Major William Jenkins Worth, January 31, 1823, Letters and Papers Received (irregular series) (F), Miscellaneous Military Academy Papers (F-77), 1813–25, RG 77, Records of the Office of the Chief of Engineers, NA.

21. George W. Cullum, *Biographical Register of Officers and Graduates of the U.S. Military Academy*, 7 vols. (New York: James Miller, Publishers, 1879), 1:247–48.

22. Thomas to Brigadier General Roger Jones, July 1, 1846, Letters Received, Main Series, RG 94, NA.

23. Ibid.

24. Ibid.

25. Thomas to Brigadier General Roger Jones, September 8, 1848, Letters Received, Main Series, RG 94, NA.

26. Cullum, *Biographical Register of Officers and Graduates of the U.S. Military Academy*, 1:247–48.

27. Ibid.

28. Ibid.

29. Major Alexander Macomb to Brevet Major William Jenkins Worth, January 31, 1823, Miscellaneous Military Academy Papers (F-77), 1813–25, RG 77, NA.

30. Court Martial file number Z29, Proceedings of Courts Martial, 1808–1940, RG 153, 34–59, Records of the Office of the Judge Advocate General, NA.

31. Thomas to General N. J. T. Dana, April 15, 1865, Letters Sent by Lorenzo Thomas, General's Papers and Books, RG 94, Records of the Adjutant General's office, 1780's–1917, NA (hereafter cited as Letters Sent).

32. The conflict between Dana and Thomas became acrimonious and bitter.

Thomas even tried to have Dana court-martialed for "malicious intent to in-jure and disgrace Brigadier General L. Thomas, Adjutant General U.S. Army," largely because Dana, angry with Thomas, questioned Thomas's handling of the case. By supporting the sentinel, Dana won the umbrage of the adjutant general. Fortunately, the case withered, and nothing more was heard of it. See Thomas to N. J. T. Dana, January 26, 1865, Letters Sent. See also Dana to Lieuten-ant Colonel C. T. Christensen, February 1, 1865, M-156-1865, Letters Received by the Division of West Mississippi, RG 393, Records of United States Conti-nental Commands, (1), Geographical Divisions and Departments and Military (Reconstruction) Districts, NA.

33. Thomas and Hyman, *Stanton*, 159.

34. E. D. Townsend, *Anecdotes of the Civil War in the United States* (New York: D. Appleton and Company, 1884), 78–79; Joseph T. Glatthaar, *Forged in Battle: The Civil War Alliance of Black Soldiers and White Officers* (New York: Free Press, 1990), 37.

35. Stanton to Thomas, March 25, 1863, *OR*, 3rd ser., 3:100–101.

36. Townsend, *Anecdotes of the Civil War*, 78–79.

37. Thomas to Stanton, April 1, 1863, and Final Report, October 3, 1865, Letters Sent.

38. Thomas to Stanton, April 1, 1863, Letters Sent.

39. Ibid.

40. Thomas to Stanton, October 3, 1865, Final Report, Letters Sent.

41. Grant to Halleck, April 19, 1863, "The Negro," 3 (1).

42. Thomas to Stanton, April 4, 1863, Letters Sent.

43. Thomas to Stanton, April 9, 1863, Letters Sent.

44. Special Order No. 5, April 10, 1863, Letters Sent.

45. Special Orders No. 9 and No. 10, April 14, 1863, Letters Sent.

46. Thomas to Stanton, April 14, 1863, Letters Sent.

47. Dana to Stanton, April 20, 1863, "The Negro," 3 (1). In his memoirs, Dana did not mention Thomas. He did, however, discuss the bravery of black troops at Milliken's Bend in 1863. See Charles A. Dana, *Recollections of the Civil War* (New York: Collier Books, 1963), 93–94.

48. This statement possibly was an oratorical flourish designed to speak to the emo-tions of Thomas's audience. If he indeed owned slaves, he did not do so in 1860; and it has not been discovered whether he did so before then. See the Eighth Census of the United States, Washington, D.C., 2nd Ward, Georgetown, 100, Eighth Census, Slave Schedules, 2nd Ward, (Georgetown) Washington, D.C., 99, 47–103, RG 29, NA.

49. *New York Times*, June 7, 1863.

50. Ibid.

51. Ibid.

52. *New York Times*, November 28, 1863.

53. Ibid.

54. "The Negro Troops in the Southwest," *Harper's Weekly* 7 (November 14, 1863): 721. There is an illustration on the front page accompanying the article depicting the event.

55. Thomas to Stanton, May 13, 1863, *OR*, 3rd ser., 3:212; Special Order No. 27, May 19, 1863, Letters Sent; Glatthaar, *Forged in Battle*, 64–65.

56. Stanton to Thomas, May 15, 1863, *OR*, 2nd ser., 3:212.

57. Thomas to Stanton, May 20, 1863, *OR*, 2nd ser., 3:214; Special Order No. 27, May 19, 1863, Letters Sent.

58. Registers of Letters Received, 1863, RG 94, NA. The Registers list the date received in the office, a synopsis of the letter or telegram, and whether it was referred to another office. Many of Thomas's communications were referred to Stanton, who then returned them to the Adjutant General's Office.

59. War Department General Orders No. 143, May 22, 1863, "The Negro," 3 (1). For a list of the unit designations that show regimental names before and after they became part of the USCT, see Brigadier General Richard C. Drum, comp., *List of Synonyms of Organizations in the Volunteer Service of the United States* (Washington, D.C.: Government Printing Office, 1885). For regimental histories of the USCT, see Frederick Dyer, *A Compendium of the War of the Rebellion* (1908; Dayton, Ohio: Morningside, 1978).

60. Special Order No. 45, August 18, 1863, Letters Sent; also in *OR*, 3rd ser., 3:686–87.

61. Grant to Thomas, July 11, 1863, in John Y. Simon, ed., *The Papers of Ulysses S. Grant*, 24 vols. to date (Carbondale: Southern Illinois University Press, 1967–), 9:23–24.

62. Thomas to Townsend, August 31, 1863, Letters Sent. Thomas referred specifically to General Frederick Steele's expedition into the interior from Goodrich's Landing on the Red River and to General John Schofield's move into Arkansas.

63. Thomas to Schofield, August 5, 1863, Letters Sent.

64. Shepard to Thomas, July 13, 1863, "The Negro," 3 (1).

65. Grant to Thomas, July 11, 1863, in Simon, *The Papers of Ulysses S. Grant*, 9:26; Thomas to Shepard, July 25, 1863, "The Negro," 3 (1).

66. Thomas to Shepard, July 25, 1863, Letters Sent.

67. Grant to Thomas, July 11, 1863, in Simon, *The Papers of Ulysses S. Grant*, 9:23–24.

68. Ibid., 26.

69. Thomas to Stanton, October 5, 1863, Letters Sent.

70. Francis B. Heitman, *Historical Register and Dictionary of the United States Army* (Washington, D.C.: Government Printing Office, 1903), 880.

71. Thomas to First Lieutenant R. Knox, Commissary of Musters, Seventeenth Army Corps, July 11, 1863, Letters Sent.

72. Thomas to Stanton, October 3, 1865, Final Report, Letters Sent.

73. Thomas to Banks, September 11, 1863, Letters Sent; also in *OR*, 3rd ser., 3:787.

74. Thomas to Henry Wilson, May 30, 1864, "The Negro," 4. See Cornish, *The Sable Arm*, 201–4, and Glatthaar, *Forged in Battle*, 176–79.

75. Heitman, *Historical Register and Dictionary*, 992.

76. Brigadier General James Wadsworth to Stanton, December 1863, "The Negro," 3 (1). In his May 30, 1863, letter to Senator Henry Wilson, Thomas argued for equal pay for blacks. For a thorough discussion, consult Cornish, *The Sable Arm*, chap. 10.

77. Thomas to Stanton, December 24, 1863, *OR*, 3rd ser., 4:733–34.

78. Wadsworth to Stanton, December ?, 1863, "The Negro," 4.

79. Stanton to Thomas, September 19, 1864, *OR*, 3rd ser., 4:733–34.

80. Thomas to Stanton, September 20, 1864, *OR*, 3rd ser., 4:734.

81. Thomas to Sherman, March 30, 1864, "The Negro," 4.

82. Sherman to Thomas, June 26, 1864, Letters Received by Brigadier General Lorenzo Thomas Relating to Colored Troops, RG 94, NA. See also John F. Marszalek, *Sherman: A Soldier's Passion for Order* (New York: Free Press, 1993), 271.

83. Sherman to Thomas, June 26, 1864, Letters Received by Brigadier General Lorenzo Thomas, RG 94, NA.

84. Sherman to Thomas, July 21, 1864, Letters Received by Brigadier General Lorenzo Thomas, RG 94, NA.

85. Ibid. Sherman's obsession with order is an important theme in his life. See Marszalek, *Sherman*, and Charles Royster, *The Destructive War: William Tecumseh Sherman, Stonewall Jackson, and the Americans* (New York: Alfred A. Knopf, 1991), 138–39. Both works stress Sherman's preoccupation with order and prove that his racial attitudes were not progressive.

86. Thomas to Stanton, June 15, 1864, *OR*, 3rd ser., 4:433–34.

87. *The Statutes at Large, Treaties, and Proclamations of the United States of America*, vols. 12–15 (Boston: Little, Brown, 1863–69), 13:6–9. For records relating to the Slave Commissions in the border states, see Records of Slave Commissions, RG 94, NA. The records give names of claimant, slave, and the amount, usually $300, paid as compensation. Sometimes, though not in every case, the regimental descriptive books of the regiments raised in the border states provide the same information. Regimental Books also are filed in RG 94, NA.

88. Schofield to Thomas, September 26, 1863, *OR*, 3rd ser., 3:849.

89. Thomas to Stanton, June 15, 1864, *OR*, 3rd ser., 4:433–34.

90. Thomas to Stanton, October 3, 1865, Final Report, Letters Sent.

91. There is a significant literature on black recruitment in Kentucky. See Victor B. Howard, *Black Liberation in Kentucky: Emancipation and Freedom, 1862–1884* (Lexington: University Press of Kentucky, 1983); John W. Blassingame, "The Recruitment of Colored Troops in Kentucky, Maryland, and Missouri, 1863–1865," *Historian* 29 (August 1967): 533–45; and John David Smith, "The Recruitment of Negro Soldiers in Kentucky, 1863–1865," *Register of the Kentucky Historical Society* 72 (October 1974): 364–90. Berlin et al., *The Black Military Experience*, chap. 4, documents the recruitment of blacks in Maryland, Missouri, and Kentucky.

92. Burnside to Lincoln, June 26, 1863, "The Negro," 3 (1).

93. This was true, though the recruitment began late in 1863. See Smith, "The Recruitment of Negro Soldiers in Kentucky," 374–75.

94. Thomas to Stanton, February 1, 1864, Letters Sent.

95. Burbridge to Thomas, April 5, 1865, "The Negro," 4.

96. General Orders No. 34, April 18, 1864, Headquarters, District of Kentucky, "The Negro," 4; Smith, "The Recruitment of Negro Soldiers in Kentucky," 385–86.

97. General Orders No. 20, Thomas to Stanton, June 13, 1864, *OR*, 3rd ser., 4:429.

98. Ibid.; the order was signed "By Order of the Secretary of War." On Chetlain's recruiting policies under General Orders No. 20, see Smith, "The Recruitment of Negro Soldiers in Kentucky," 385–86.

99. Fry to Thomas, July 3, 1864, *OR*, 3rd ser., 4:468.

100. Burbridge to Thomas, July 3, 1864, *OR*, 3rd ser., 4:468–69.

101. General Orders No. 24, Thomas to Stanton, July 6, 1864, Letters Sent. Thomas had a history of jurisdictional disputes. For example, in March 1864 he appointed Brigadier General William Pile to recruit in the Department of the Missouri, but General William S. Rosecrans, the department commander, had previously been authorized to do so. See General Orders No. 8, March 11, 1864, "The Negro," 4.

102. Thomas to Burbridge, July 24, 1864, *OR*, 3rd ser., 4:542–43. See also Letters Sent.

103. Thomas to Stanton, Final Report, October 3, 1865, Letters Sent.

104. Holt to Stanton, October 3, 1864, "The Negro," 4.

105. E. Merton Coulter, *The Civil War and Readjustment in Kentucky* (Chapel Hill: University of North Carolina Press, 1926), 211–13.

106. Citizens of Christian County to Bramlette, January 23, 1864, Governor Thomas Bramlette Papers, Military Correspondence, box 5, folder 98, Kentucky Department of Libraries and Archives, Frankfort, Ky. (hereafter cited as Bramlette Papers).

107. S. P. Cope to Bramlette, July 8, 1864, Bramlette Papers, box 5, folder 99.

108. Ibid.

109. Burbridge to Bramlette, June 16, 1864, Bramlette Papers, box 5, folder 100.

110. Bramlette to Lincoln, September 3, 1864, "The Negro," 4.

111. Ibid.; Coulter, *The Civil War and Readjustment in Kentucky*, 211–13.

112. Thomas to Stanton, September 19, 1864, *OR*, 3rd ser., 4:733.

113. Stanton to Thomas, September 19, 1864, *OR*, 3rd ser., 4:733.

114. Transferred to another command in February 1865, Burbridge was replaced by Major General John Palmer. See Coulter, *The Civil War and Readjustment in Kentucky*, 212–13.

115. I have used Thomas's figures to derive this number. Thomas to Stanton, December 27, 1864, *OR*, 3rd ser., 4:1017–18. The number of black recruits for Kentucky for the war was 23,703. Dyer, *A Compendium of the War of the Rebellion*, 11.

116. Ibid.

117. Thomas to Major General Joseph Hooker, January 20, 1865, Letters Sent.

118. Thomas to Gov. Richard Ogelsby, January 20, 1865, Letters Sent. A regiment raised in Indiana was staffed by Kentucky escapees, which was done peacefully. Thomas to Stanton, Final Report, October 3, 1865, Letters Sent.

119. Thomas to Hooker, January 20, 1865, Letters Sent.

120. James Fry to Thomas, April 9, 1865, Letters Received by General Lorenzo Thomas, RG 94, NA.

121. Thomas to Stanton, June 15, 1865, Letters Received by General Lorenzo Thomas, RG 94, NA.

122. Thomas to Stanton, June 5, 1865, Letters Sent.

123. Thomas to Stanton, Final Report, October 3, 1865, Letters Sent.

124. Ibid.

125. Leroy P. Graf et al., eds., *The Papers of Andrew Johnson*, 16 vols. (Knoxville: University of Tennessee Press, 1967–2000), 14:9–10; Thomas and Hyman, *Stanton*, 581–94; Townsend, *Anecdotes of the Civil War*, 124–37.

126. File T 631-CB-1864, Letters Received by the Commission Branch of the Adjutant General's Office, RG 94, NA; Jack D. Welsh, *Medical Histories of Union Generals* (Kent, Ohio: Kent State University Press, 1996), 337.

10

PROVEN THEMSELVES IN EVERY RESPECT TO BE MEN

Black Cavalry in the Civil War

Noah Andre Trudeau

In the course of one terrible night in 1865, Fannie Walker, a copying clerk in the Confederate Bureau of War, saw her whole world collapse. It began with her new nation. Most of the key personnel and agencies making up the Confederate States of America had fled when word arrived from besieged Petersburg that General Robert E. Lee was abandoning his lines. At once, a proudly defiant government became a woeful caravan of refugees on a road leading nowhere. If that were not enough, beautiful Richmond, a city Fannie had come to love, had been rocked throughout the night of April 2 by fires and explosions as if heaven itself had tried to wipe the Rebel capital from the map.

The crowning symbol of the changed order of things came at dawn on April 3, when Fannie looked out the window of the Valentine House, where she had sought safety while the city burned. What she saw, on the street below her, was something utterly unimagined in the culture of the white South. There, in blue uniform and on horseback was a Union cavalryman, a *black* Union cavalryman. Even as the terrified woman fought back the surge of racial horror bred of a lost world of genteel mores and the rigid caste system of slavery, she heard the Yankee trooper exclaim, "Richmond at last!"[1]

That lone African American mounted soldier represented a small and often overlooked group of black military outfits in the Civil War. While virtually all the glory and the lion's share of attention has been given to the "colored" infantry units organized during the conflict, it was the seven regiments of black cavalry that saw more constant and active field service than any comparable number of foot soldiers. Despite that record, the annals of those units remain obscure and are usually neglected in any general cavalry histories or amid the larger chronicles of the U.S. Colored Troops (USCT) infantry.

The door to enlisting African Americans into the U.S. military was kicked wide open by the Emancipation Proclamation. Before January 1, 1863, there were a handful of black regiments (all infantry) in the field. After it, the increase in the number of units authorized and organized was truly remarkable. By war's end there were some 120 infantry regiments, twelve heavy artillery units, ten batteries of light artillery, and seven cavalry regiments recorded by the Bureau for Colored Troops.[2]

The difficulties in raising black cavalry regiments stemmed from several causes. The first was systemic to all mounted troops, white or black. It cost more to equip a regiment on horse than it did one of infantry; it was also more expensive and difficult to maintain such a force in the field. Because of this, after the rush of volunteer regiments subsided in 1862 and greater governmental control was exercised, the general preference was to form infantry units rather than cavalry. As historian Stephen Z. Starr has pointed out, "cavalry . . . needed more gear than did the footsoldiers and the gunners." Thus this branch of the service, he says, "was beset by shortages to a greater extent than either the infantry or the artillery." Perhaps the most basic shortage facing prospective cavalry regiments was horseflesh. Despite the postwar claim of the army's quartermaster general that the Cavalry Bureau "promptly [met] all requisitions for the supply of public animals to our gallant armies in the field," combat losses and the generally poor level of animal care exercised by the men led to an enormous wastage of horses, which in turn made government officials reluctant to authorize new units, especially after 1863. There were training issues as well, since both man and beast needed more extensive drilling to learn their parts in the oftentimes complicated choreography of mounted maneuver.[3]

The other great difficulty faced in raising black cavalry regiments was a racist cultural blindness. It took a leap of faith for a white man to imagine that the primitive and childlike male African Americans could overcome the intellectual challenges of learning the art of the foot soldier. That leap widened considerably when the prospect of putting the black warrior on horseback was considered. Absent from this way of thinking was any knowledge of the skills practiced by the mounted slave herders (which would be later amply demonstrated by black cowboys). In a letter written in late 1864, Charles Francis Adams, Jr., then a major serving in the 5th Massachusetts Cavalry (Colored), articulated for the benefit of his ambassador father in London a "liberal" white opinion of that time:

> The negro makes a good soldier, particularly in those branches of the service where a high order of intelligence is less required. Negro infantry, properly officered [by whites], would I believe be as effective as any in the world. In regard to their efficiency as cavalry I somewhat share your doubt. After all a negro is not the equal of the white man. . . . He has not the mental vigor and energy, he cannot stand up against adversity. . . . He cannot fight for life like a white man. In this regiment if you degrade a negro who has once tried to do well, you had better shoot him at once, for he gives right up and never attempts to redeem himself. . . . He must and will sleep; no danger from the enemy and no fear of punishment will keep him awake. In infantry, which acts in large masses, these things are of less consequence than in cavalry; but in the service which our cavalry does, where individual intelligence is everything, and single men in every exposed position have only themselves and their own nerve, intelligence and quickness to rely on, it is a very different thing.[4]

Adams's attitude underscores the problems many whites had even conceiving of a black cavalry regiment. If one adds to that the problems facing cavalry units in general, then the seven regiments that were actually organized seem less a poor representation and more an amazing accomplishment.

The first mounted unit of African Americans to enter the War Department's ledger books appeared in New Orleans. It was the reluctant creation of the military commander of the Department of the Gulf, Major General Nathaniel P. Banks. Appointed to replace Major General Benjamin F. Butler, Banks was no friend of the black man. In fact, early in his tenure as department commander, he initiated a purge of the black officers in the three Louisiana Native Guard infantry regiments that Butler had mustered into Federal service in late 1862. This same Banks was a savvy political survivor who saw which way the political winds were blowing following the Emancipation Proclamation.[5]

On May 1, 1863, Banks announced the formation of what he styled "a corps d'armee of colored troops, to be designated as the 'Corps d'Afrique.'" True to his personal outlook and prejudice, these regiments were capped at five hundred men (normal regiments had one thousand—Banks did not believe that blacks could function in such large groupings) and an all-white officer corps. A significant aspect of Banks's scheme was that his "corps d'armee" was to embrace all arms—infantry, artillery, and cavalry. So, on September 12, 1863, the 1st Regiment of Cavalry Corps d'Afrique was formally organized at New Orleans. Seven months later, as part of a widespread War Department redesignation of most state-organized black units, the 1st Regiment became the 4th U.S. Colored Cavalry (USCC).[6]

The story of the second black cavalry regiment to be organized is inextricably bound up with the mission assigned in early 1863 to the army's adjutant general, Brigadier General Lorenzo Thomas. Ostensibly sent to the Mississippi Valley on an inspection tour, the sixty-year-old officer was given broad authority to raise African American units. Thomas was empowered to appoint officers (white, of course) and to channel War Department resources to the fledgling outfits. At a time when the preponderance of new regiments were being organized by the governors of various states, Thomas had been vested with an amazing amount of power. When he paused to catch his breath at the end of 1863, he could proudly lay claim to having had a hand in the formation of more than fifty "colored" regiments, with more to come.[7]

Thomas's inspection tour began at Cairo, Illinois, on April 1 and proceeded southward. September found him in Vicksburg, Mississippi, where his efforts received the full support of Major General Ulysses S. Grant. Grant already had cause to recognize the fighting abilities of African American troops. During his siege of Vicksburg, Confederates across the river attempted to disrupt his operations by attacking several important supply depots spotted along the Mississippi's west bank. At Milliken's Bend, on June 7, a force of Texas troops struck savagely at an encampment used to recruit black regiments. In bitter fighting that was at times hand-to-hand, the barely organized units held their positions. According to its regimental history, the 1st Mississippi Cavalry (African Descent) was authorized at Vicksburg by Thomas at the "suggestion of General Grant." The unit was formally mustered in on October 9, 1863, and was renamed the 3rd USCC on March 11, 1864.[8]

The first black cavalry regiments to be mustered directly into U.S. service were organized in Virginia. The moving force here was the same General Butler who had been replaced by Banks in Louisiana. Butler was a career politician-turned-general whose Massachusetts roots lent an abolitionist fervor to his pragmatic attitude toward blacks in the military. While essentially paternalistic in outlook, Butler consistently used his position to advance the organization of white-officered African American regiments. Prior to his taking over the military department that included lower Virginia, the pace of black recruitment there had been glacially slow, but once he was in control all that began to change.[9]

Butler obtained authorization for a cavalry regiment, and on December 22, 1863, the 1st USCC was formally organized at Camp Hamilton, Virginia. Eleven days earlier he proudly informed Washington that he had filled this regiment to the maximum number allowed, and so on December 26 Butler was given permission to organize a second, to be known as the 2nd USCC. By the time official sanction arrived in Virginia, formation of the 2nd was well under way at Fortress Monroe.[10]

Just as Banks was midwife to the 4th USCC, Lorenzo Thomas to the 3rd, and Butler to the 1st and 2nd regiments, it was the determined abolitionist governor of the Bay State, John A. Andrew, who played that part for the 5th Massachusetts Cavalry (Colored). According to a history of the regiment published in 1908, the unit "was recruited during the autumn and winter of 1863–64, and was mustered into the U.S. service by companies at dates ranging from January to May, 1864."[11]

Up to this point the black cavalry regiments had come into existence in either a strongly antislavery state (Massachusetts) or in occupied portions of Southern states (Louisiana, Mississippi, Virginia). The final pair of regiments entering the rolls posed a very different problem altogether. On July 24, 1864, Lorenzo Thomas reported to Washington that Brevet Major General Stephen G. Burbridge proposed to establish two such units in Kentucky, a pro-Union, proslavery border state whose congressional representatives had bitterly fought the Lincoln administration on every aspect of its black recruitment program. Anticipating the argument that the government could not supply the necessary horses, Thomas hastened to add that Burbridge intended to seize the necessary animals from Kentucky's citizenry. The plan called for loyal Unionist owners to be fully recompensed at war's end. Four days later Washington signaled its acceptance of these terms. On October 24 both the 5th and 6th USCC were entered on the army's ledgers.[12]

These thumbnail histories are only a small part of the story of the black Civil War cavalry regiments. Also worthy of consideration are questions of command leadership, the nature of the men who filled the ranks, life in the USCC, and the combat experiences of these units.

A common complaint about the new white cavalry regiments of 1863–65 was that most lacked a strong core of experienced officers. One critical professional was clearly thinking of the worst of them when he described this group as "insolent incapables who so foully disgraced their uniform." Ironically, here at least, the black cavalry regiments generally stood out for the right reasons. Their officers, in many cases, had significant cavalry experience before signing on. According to the white chaplain of the 1st USCC, "the officers . . . are, in soldiering knowledge and experience, a good deal above the average of officers in new regiments of white troops." In two notable cases, the men commanding black cavalry regiments brought with them from their previous unit a solid cadre of field-tested officers. Colonel Jeptha Garrard, who took over the 1st USCC on December 7, 1863, was accompanied by fellow members of the 3rd New York Cavalry, who together constituted what one of them boasted was "a thoroughly efficient and capable corps of officers." Even more impressive were the forty-three members of the 4th Illinois Cavalry who joined Embury D. Osband when he was put in charge of the 3rd USCC. Charles F. Adams, Jr., who succeeded Henry S. Russell in command of the 5th Massachusetts Cavalry (Colored), came from the ranks of the 1st Massachusetts Cavalry, while another alumni of the 3rd New York Cavalry, George W. Cole, took over the 2nd USCC. Historian Joseph T. Glatthaar has concluded that this recruitment of veteran cadres was a "positive development for both blacks who served under these officers and the American military establishment in general."[13]

For nearly every white joining a black cavalry regiment, the decision represented a carefully considered career move. Frederick W. Browne went from sergeant to lieutenant in the switch and was told by an admiring comrade that his transfer papers to the 1st USCC were worth $800.00. As noted by Lieutenant Robert Dollard (who became a captain in the 2nd USCC), there was, however, a price to be paid: "white men who accepted commissions as officers in regiments made up of such material were in a measure ostracized by their fellow officers of white regiments." Yet there could be rewards beyond money or advancement. A lieutenant in the 2nd USCC believed that helping black men fight for their freedom was something "glorious and ennobling." The man leading the 3rd USCC could boast that his troops were a "superb body of men, [and] I am very proud of them. I almost believe sometimes they could whip the whole Southern Confederacy."[14]

The few white cavalry officers who wrote about their wartime experiences left impressions of their men that reflect their cultural bias and their attitude toward their troopers. Captain Dollard termed his men "intelligent contrabands," suggesting that a certain elitism was associated with the mounted arm. Lieutenant Browne was sure that the 1st USCC, "being the first colored cavalry regiment, had in its ranks a rather better class of men than the infantry regiments had; some being from the North and some being the outlaw negroes who, in slavery times, had been able to maintain their liberty in the swamps of Eastern Virginia and North Carolina." Charles Francis Adams, Jr., whose opinion of blacks as cavalry has been mentioned, said this about the African Americans under his direct command: "They are docile and take readily to discipline and in large percentage of them, full as large as of the whites are decidedly soldierly in their bearing. As horsemen I think they are at least as good as the whites. . . . Of the courage in action of these men, at any rate when acting in mass, there can no doubt exist; of their physical and mental and moral energy and stamina I entertain grave doubts. . . . So far, as a whole, they more than fulfil every expectation which I entertained." Edward M. Main, an officer in the 3rd USCC, recalled that his regiment "was recruited from the camp-followers of the Union army — the colored servants, cooks, hostlers, teamsters and pioneers." Describing an episode in which two of his black sergeants risked their lives by carrying dispatches through enemy controlled territory in the guise of slaves, Main termed the men "young, brave and quick witted." It should be added that these descriptions are the exception rather than the rule for Main's history of the 3rd USCC, published in 1908. The book's text consists for the most part of biographies and anecdotes regarding the white officers, narrative descriptions of the regiment's various small-scale expeditions and excerpts from official reports. Just a handful of black troopers are mentioned by name, and the only roster covers the unit's officers, all of whom were white.[15]

With regard to the black men themselves, precious little is known of their thoughts and motivations. Because all seven regiments were drawn from largely slave populations, the number of letter writers or diary keepers is so small as not to have existed at all. We are left with a few suggestive snapshots of individuals, with little indication as to whether they are reliable samplings or unique expressions.

For example, George Washington Byrd was a North Carolina free black employed on a railroad when the war began. "I had never been a slave," he recollected in 1910, "and when I learned that the Confederate Government meant to force us free negroes into the service in some capacity I [decided] . . . to make myself scarce in that part of the country." Byrd wound up in Company A of the 1st USCC.[16]

The motive for Porter Brabston to join the 3rd USCC was pure clothes envy. In a statement he made to the government in 1893, he recalled that a friend who had enlisted visited Brabston's plantation near Vicksburg. The friend "had such nice clothes on with stripes on the arm of his coat & legs of his pants that I thought I would join his Company," he said. The reasons were substantially higher for J. O. Malone of the 5th Massachusetts Cavalry (Colored), who wrote in 1865: "As [the black soldiers] . . . have so great an interest in this land of their nativity, they appeal to all good men to keep nothing back that belongs to them as soldiers who have fought for the freedom of a country whose liberties were threatened by traitorous slaveholders and their infamous allies, the Copperheads of the North."[17]

A random sampling of five different regimental companies reveals a bit more about the enlisted men. Of the 113 credited to Company C of the 1st USCC, most (73) came from Virginia, with the next highest complement split between North Carolina (13) and Maryland (12). A great preponderance (82) were either farmers or laborers. For some reason, eight came to the regiment after having been waiters; four had been sailors, and one unabashedly listed his past experience as "huckster." The average age in this company was twenty-three. Company L of that same regiment must have recruited heavily in port areas such as Portsmouth and Norfolk because forty of its seventy-six troopers came from outside the United States, with seventeen from Canada and nineteen out of the Caribbean. Again, the most prevalent occupation was laborer (35), with service at sea as a sailor or steward second (15). The average age of this company was almost twenty-four.

North Carolina was the state most represented in Company A of the 2nd USCC with sixty Tar Heels out of 100 in the ranks. Virginia came second with twenty-five. Laborer was once more the most common occupation given (39), with a surprising number (56) of those asked not giving any previous occupation. The average age in this company was twenty-four.

Filling the ranks of Company A of the 3rd USCC, which operated in the Vicksburg area, were many Mississippi men (60 out of 126) who were farmers for the most part (104 of 126). Other states with some representation in the regiment were Virginia (13), Tennessee (10), South Carolina (8), Louisiana (8), North Carolina (7), Kentucky (7), and Alabama (5). The average age here was nearly twenty-seven.

While the designation of 5th Massachusetts Cavalry (Colored) would seem to suggest a unit whose ranks were filled by Northern blacks, analysis by historian Nick Salvatore indicates otherwise. Breaking down the composition of the 100 men of Company D he found that "[o]ne half (53 percent) of the privates were born in slave states or in the District of Columbia, and more than 30 percent listed a slave state as their last address. Seventy-nine percent of these men were thirty years of age or younger; as for their premilitary occupations, unskilled workers constituted almost 40 percent and farmers another 27 percent."[18]

Once recruited, the men underwent the Civil War equivalent of basic

"The War in Mississippi— The 1st Mississippi Negro Cavalry Bringing in to Vicksburg Rebel Prisoners Captured at Haines Bluff.—From a Sketch by Our Special Artist, Fred. B. Schell." (Frank Leslie's Illustrated Newspaper, *December 19, 1863, Special Collections Department, North Carolina State University Libraries)*

training. Colonel Jeptha Garrard's General Orders No. 11, issued January 18, 1864, established a seven-day schedule for the 1st USCC that included squadron and battalion drill, saber exercises and pistol firing. It is no wonder that Lieutenant Browne later would boast that the "constant drill soon made it [the unit] have the manner and bearing of soldiers." The white chaplain assigned to the 1st USCC agreed when he extolled its "exact drill and thorough discipline." A black trooper in the 5th Massachusetts Cavalry (Colored) informed the readers of the New York *Anglo-African* that the "men are fast learning the cavalry drill. They yet have to learn to train the horses to

the motion of different exercises." Captain Dollard of the 2nd USCC credited his men's readiness to their slave experiences. "They were submissive
and obedient and accommodated themselves to the exactions of the service
freely so that at the end of about sixty days we had them in fair shape to
take the field," he said.[19]

The condition of their equipment varied with location. In the West,
where shortages of horses and weapons plagued many of the cavalry regiments, the experience of the 3rd USCC was not unusual. According to
Lieutenant Frank W. Calais, "the regiment was inferiorly armed and poorly
mounted. By raiding the government corrals, a sufficient number of old
hacks, horses and mules were procured to mount the men on as fast as the
companies were organized. But these mounts were deemed fit only for drill
practice, and with no thought of taking the field with them." An inspection
report of this regiment that deemed it "about as good cavalry as we have,"
concluded it was a "pity they should not be immediately completely armed
and mounted and put to active service."[20]

In the East, thanks to General Butler's determined advocacy, the 1st and
2nd USCC began their campaigning as mounted units. However, by June
1864, in the wake of the great loss of animals during Grant's Overland
campaign and Butler's Bermuda Hundred campaign, the situation changed.
Lieutenant Browne of the 1st USCC observed that after Butler's forces were
bottled up on Bermuda Hundred, "the white cavalry became so short of
horses that we were dismounted." Captain Dollard reported that "[w]ith
the coming of the army of the Potomac all available troops were put into
the trenches and unnecessarily mounted troops were dismounted for this
purpose. Under this policy we had to give up the horses of our enlisted
men." The 5th Massachusetts Cavalry (Colored) entered its first action as
dismounted cavalry; it was not until the regiment was assigned to guard
POWs at Point Lookout, Maryland, and only after the energetic lobbying
of its second-in-command, that horses were procured.[21]

Problems of discipline and a poor officer cadre resulted in the dismounting of the 4th USCC per orders issued in New Orleans on October 17, 1864.
The regiment appears to have regained its horses by early 1865. The 5th and
6th USCC were organized relatively late in the war and, as already noted,
were allowed to form with the understanding that they would commandeer
their horses from the Kentucky population. Nevertheless, when some 600
untrained recruits from the two regiments were swept up in the unfortunate Saltville expedition in October 1864, there were significant problems.
According to the officer leading them in that action, "They were mounted

on horses that had been only partly recruited and that had been drawn with the intention of using them only for the purpose of drilling."[22]

There is ample evidence that the quality of supplies and munitions allotted to black cavalry regiments was often inferior to that provided white units. The report of one scout undertaken by the 3rd USCC notes that the "hard bread drawn [by the men] . . . was so wormy that they could not eat it." Another report says that at one plantation the officer "found eight pairs of boots, which were distributed among the soldiers that were without boots." An angry dispatch sent on April 9, 1864, by the commander of the 1st USCC complained that the "ammunition furnished to my command has been of the most worthless description."[23]

A closer examination of the matter, however, suggests that the real story may be less clear-cut. As historian Stephen Z. Starr has pointed out, black cavalry regiments did not have a monopoly on poor quality supplies and equipment. According to Starr, two Pennsylvania regiments were armed with Belgian infantry rifles, "about as worthless as a military weapon could be." The food was so bad for the 1st Iowa Cavalry that, as Starr tells it, "the men staged a full-scale riot." So while accounts of poor supplies sent to black units are certainly true, it is less certain that this represents any systematic or targeted racism. On the other hand, it would be naive to believe that black troopers received equal treatment from white quartermasters.[24]

A distinction that is more sharply drawn concerns the degree of punishment meted out to black soldiers in all branches of the service. Historian Joseph T. Glatthaar quotes one USCT officer as saying, "It is useless to talk about being lenient with them for if you give them an inch they will take a mile." After nine months in a top command position in the 5th Massachusetts Cavalry (Colored), an exasperated Charles Francis Adams, Jr., proclaimed, "I no longer wonder slave drivers were cruel. . . . I no longer have any bowels of mercy." In his account of service in the 1st USCC, Lieutenant Browne recounted the time an officer incited ten men to deliver some field justice to a conniving white sutler, who resisted and was killed by the troopers but not before wounding the officer. A few days later, one of the ten who had participated in the affair was "shot . . . dead in his tracks for disobedience of orders."[25]

Clearly the stereotype in the minds of most whites that savagery lurked just beneath the skin of black men prompted the extreme degrees of punishment suffered by those troopers. Yet a few of the black soldiers were not disposed to suffer in silence. When a private in the 5th Massachusetts Cavalry (Colored) was slapped with the flat of an officer's sword, he turned on the white man with his bayonet bared and declared, "God damn you! You would not strike *me* that way." A more public expression of frustration and anger was sent by a trooper of the 5th Massachusetts Cavalry (Colored) to the editor of New York's *Anglo-African* newspaper after witnessing a comrade strung up by his thumbs for ducking some fatigue duty.

> It is enough that we have been taken to Washington, half drilled in Cavalry tactics (organization for which we enlisted), dismounted, deprived of the arms we knew but little about, sent to the front with inexperienced officers to be made *pontoon bridges* of—sheep for the slaughter—to be treated as dogs by would-be *Christian men*, whose purpose it is to brutalize as much as possible those who, having [come forward to] . . . volunteer and sacrifice home, its tender endearments and luxuries, for the hardships and privations of camp life and the perils of the battle field, in defense of that country that has always considered them the *inferiors even of the inferior*![26]

The duties assigned to the black cavalry regiments brought into sharp focus the paradoxes of their status. Many black infantry units spent much of their time in uniform working as laborers. Cavalry was widely considered a specialized—even elite—branch of service, and the record for most of the black mounted regiments shows them more consistently engaged in military operations than the foot soldiers (though none escaped some period of heavy "fatigue" duty). Yet these seven African American cavalry units were almost never brigaded with white ones in a major field campaign. The likely posting for a black mounted regiment was outpost duty where its strength was dispersed across a wide area. Scouting, raiding, and reconnaissances made up most of its wartime activities.

An overview of the combat experiences of each of the African American mounted units will make this clearer. To avoid unnecessary narrative duplication, the stories of the 1st and 2nd USCC are treated together as are those of the 5th and 6th USCC.

At various points in its history, the 1st USCC was commanded by Colonel Jeptha Garrard, Major Harvey W. Brown, and Major William H. Seip. The 2nd USCC enjoyed a single commander throughout its term of service, Colonel George W. Cole. These two regiments served in southern Virginia (around Portsmouth and Norfolk) and on the Peninsula and took part in operations against Petersburg and Richmond. Prior to their participation in Butler's Bermuda Hundred campaign, the pair were engaged in a variety of reconnaissances, actions, and demonstrations. It was the 2nd USCC that took first battle honors when, on March 9, 1864, it skirmished with Rebel infantry (said to belong to Ransom's Brigade) near Bethel Church, outside Suffolk, Virginia. The black troopers were investigating a report (planted as it turned out) that some thirty unwilling Confederate conscripts were being held captive. As the men departed Suffolk, one company was sent to seal the likely escape route from the conscript pen while six others closed on it from the front.

Hardly had the larger column cleared the town when word came that the company sent to close the back door was under attack "by a superior force." Four companies were detached from the column. Coming up on the lone company they found themselves confronting enemy cavalry and artillery, backed with infantry. The black cavalrymen were pushed back to the out-skirts of Suffolk, where they made a stand. At one point Captain Dollard led a charge that momentarily halted the Rebel drive, only to see his counter-stroke fall apart because of his men's inexperience. The black troopers held their own for perhaps twenty minutes before they were, in Dollard's words, "driven from the field in considerable disorder."[27]

This skirmish cost the 2nd USCC eight killed, six wounded, and about a dozen missing. Captain Dollard's paternalism was showing when he said after this action, "I think some of us white folks lost our patience with colored soldiers for the time being, yet, considering their bringing up as slaves, and the short training they had as soldiers, they did well to do no worse under the conditions of attack by an overwhelmingly superior force." Dollard's opinion was perhaps overstated. An unidentified officer noted on the monthly returns for March that the men "deserve credit for their first battle." A correspondent for a Massachusetts daily who was present thought that the black troopers were "excellent horsemen, well acquainted with all the by-paths in this vicinity." In his official report Major General Benjamin F. Butler asserted that the troopers "behaved with the utmost courage, cool-ness, and daring." Always anxious to boost the case for black soldiers, Butler went on to declare, "I am perfectly satisfied with my negro cavalry."[28]

Lessons learned in the field were not always matters of life and death. The 2nd USCC next participated in a raid into North Carolina lasting from April 13 to 15, covering some 160 miles. While nothing occurred significant enough to warrant an official report, Captain Dollard privately thought the "way the men's caps were brushed off by the overhanging branches of the trees which lined the roadsides" taught them "the necessity of loosening the strap over the visor and placing it below the chin to keep the cap in place when collisions occurred."[29]

The 1st and 2nd USCC both took part in Butler's barren Bermuda Hundred campaign. Not surprisingly, they did so as unattached units appended to the cavalry division working with the Eighteenth Corps. As Butler's ship-borne invasion force ascended the James River from Fortress Monroe, the two black cavalry regiments carried out a diversion: by advancing along the river's north bank, they were to deceive the enemy into believing that Butler was following McClellan's 1862 route. When they were forced to swim their horses across the Chickahominy River at Bottom's Bridge, enough of the troopers lost their forage to cause the commander of the expedition to send most of the men back to Williamsburg to resupply. While crossing at Jones Bridge on the Chickahominy, Company E of the 1st USCC came under a heavy fire from a redoubt on the other side that cost it two men killed.[30]

This particular expedition was reported for the *New York Times* by its veteran military correspondent Henry J. Winser. His detailed narrative, one of the few extensive third party accounts of such actions, is worth some quotation:

> The [1st and 2nd USCC] . . . return from a raid on the Peninsula which has put the black regiments on their mettle for the first time, and demonstrated them to be made of sterling stuff. . . . The bushwhackers turned out in force to annoy them—these rascals attacking them from their coverts at every step of the way. . . . Wherever the raiding party appeared the inhabitants were stricken dumb with fear, which is not to be wondered at when it is considered what an infernal noise two thousand negro throats can add in the way of cheering to the clatter of four thousand hoofs, when throats and hoofs and all are hidden in an enveloping cloud of dust. . . . During the raid five of the colored soldiers were killed, and fifteen or twenty wounded; but it is thought that the bushwhackers paid dearly for this loss. . . . [The] entire body of cavalry reached the James River, at Harrison's Landing, and were brought up to [Bermuda Hundred] . . . on steamers. They seemed full of energy as they disembarked, notwithstanding their long ride. . . . I do not think I have ever seen prouder and more self-satisfied men than these black troopers appeared to be as they stepped from the boats tonight, in their dusty blouses and ragged blue pantaloons, each clanking his sabre and jingling his brazen spurs.[31]

Once General Butler consolidated his position on Bermuda Hundred and began to move inland, the two black cavalry regiments were given a more important assignment with the Army of the James. Instead of undertaking secondary operations, their new role, remembered Lieutenant Browne of the 1st USCC, was to take the "advance of Butler's army, being at the time the only cavalry he had." On May 9, a detachment of the 1st was ambushed while scouting northward along the Richmond Turnpike. The next day, with Butler's infantry battling near Chester Station, the 1st was held in reserve, while the 2nd effectively screened the vulnerable Union right flank.[32]

On May 11 Butler began a slow northward drive against the Confederate defenses at Drewry's Bluff, a movement that culminated with a large-scale battle fought on May 16. During the advance and in the course of the fighting, detachments of the 1st and 2nd USCC covered the Union right flank from the point where the infantry lines ended to the bank of the James River. Following Butler's defeat, the 2nd formed part of the rear guard that successfully kept back Rebel pursuit long enough to allow the Army of the James to entrench itself across the narrow neck of Bermuda Hundred. Even though Butler's campaign ended in failure, the two black cavalry regiments had proven themselves to be reliable and dependable combat units.[33]

Once Butler's campaign turned out to be fruitless, Grant ordered the Army of the Potomac to strangle Richmond by capturing Petersburg and its transportation hub south of the capital. To support this new operation, portions of Butler's army were appended to the Army of the Potomac. With the Potomac army came a sizeable cavalry force under Sheridan that quickly assumed most of the mounted duties south of the James, leaving Butler's comparatively tiny cavalry complement with little to do. The two black regiments were scattered across both fronts and had detachments posted along the James River. A glance through the company returns for June, July, and August 1864 shows such stations as Petersburg, Newport News, Fort Pocahontas, Cedar Level, Deep Bottom, Norfolk, and Fort Powhatan. Some of the duties noted include detached assignment "with ambulance corps," "guarding quartermaster stores," "escort" to telegraph construction teams, "guarding cattle on James River," and service as "teamsters."[34]

Butler's next major land action, part of a larger Union operation against Petersburg and Richmond in late September, involved the 2nd USCC with most of the black infantry in the Army of the James. The dismounted troopers served as skirmishers during the New Market Heights action on September 29 and then stood in reserve the next day. Later in the operation, these men held positions along the army's outpost line. (By this time the 1st USCC had been posted to garrison and patrol duty at Newport News and Portsmouth.) On February 18, 1865, the 2nd USCC was ordered to Norfolk, where it served until the war ended in the East.[35]

The surrender of Lee's army at Appomattox Court House and Joseph E. Johnston's force near Durham, North Carolina, marked the beginning of the rapid demobilization of the Union army in the East—save for the black units, most of which were retained in the service well into late 1865 and early 1866. When the U.S. government decided to reinforce heavily Union forces stationed in Texas, it drew on many African American units for the assignment. Both the 1st and 2nd USCC were included among the regiments dispatched to Texas, and it proved an unhappy coda to the generally positive service record of both units.

The orders transferring the 1st and 2nd USCC came as a bitter surprise to the men. It meant a painful separation from families and communities; it was even rumored that the men were to be sold to slave owners in South America and the Caribbean. The situation became a tinderbox waiting to explode, and the voyage down the James River proved the spark to set it off. There was an outright mutiny in the 1st USCC that was not put down until one of the revolt leaders was killed. It required a show of force by white soldiers and the arrest of several troopers to quash a similar reaction by members of the 2nd USCC. Once this unrest had been quelled, the two regiments completed their journey to Texas without incident; they served there until February 1866, when both were mustered out of U.S. service.[36]

The 3rd USCC, formerly the 1st Mississippi Cavalry (African Descent), was based in the West and operated largely out of Vicksburg. An ambitious and aggressive New Yorker, Embury D. Osband, commanded from the outset. In the regimental history (the only one for a black cavalry outfit), he is described as a man of "vigorous health, a perennial hopefulness, [and] an indomitable will." Osband was also, we are told, a "superb horseman" with "a genius for military operations." The officer was also a stickler for paperwork, so much so that of the fourteen extant after-action reports from black cavalry regiments in the *Official Records*, all but one came from the 3rd USCC.[37]

The 3rd USCC was a very busy regiment, though most of its engagements were on a small scale. The first combat action undertaken by the regiment involved only companies. On October 17, 1863, near Satartia, Mississippi, Company A, accompanying the 4th Illinois Cavalry, was engaged with "a large force of rebel cavalry" in a fight that was at times hand-to-hand. A second expedition, lasting from November 10 to November 13, included three of the regiment's companies. A small cavalry fight in late February 1864 resulted in nineteen of the USCC lost as prisoners. According to an account of this affair in the *New York Times*, "On the next morning . . . our troops found eight of the bodies of colored soldiers taken prisoners the day be-

"An Incident in the Battle of the Wilderness—The Rebel Generals Bradley Johnson and E. Stuart Taken to the Rear by Negro Cavalry, May 12." (Frank Leslie's Illustrated Newspaper, *June 4, 1864, Hargrett Rare Book and Manuscript Library, University of Georgia Libraries*)

fore. The clothing was stripped from their bodies and all were shot through the head."[38]

The first action of any consequence involving the 3rd USCC occurred on March 4, 1864. The regiment was part of a Federal force then occupying the small river port of Yazoo City, Mississippi, described by one of its officers as "pleasing to the eye and highly picturesque." The morning of March 4 found a detachment of the 3rd, numbering forty enlisted men and two officers, guarding the plank road that ran eastward from Yazoo City to Benton. The troopers, posted in a small redoubt at the foot of some rugged hills, suddenly were assailed by portions of Brigadier General Lawrence S. Ross's Texas Brigade. Estimates of the enemy force varied, with Ross reporting his total command (other portions of which were simultaneously attacking Yazoo City) at 1,300, while the 3rd USCC officer commanding in the redoubt was certain that he was holding out against an enemy "2,500" strong.[39]

This particular engagement underlines the stress faced by African American troopers in combat. As an officer in the 3rd put it, "capture meant death, and as the Texans were known to take no 'nigger' prisoners, the black soldiers had to face the alternative, victory or death." This statement is confirmed in the report of General Ross who said he was not prepared to "recognize negroes as soldiers or guaranty them nor their officers protection as such." One Texas account claims the justification of revenge, noting that the "negro troops a short time previous to this [fight], had caught and murdered two [men] of the Sixth Texas."[40]

As the Confederate main body swarmed into Yazoo City, one column drove in the USCC pickets on the Benton Road. The officer in command, Major Jeremiah B. Cook, pulled back into the redoubt. His forty troopers were joined by two companies of the 11th Illinois infantry, adding up to three hundred defenders altogether. Even as the rest of Ross's force struck with mixed success at Union positions in the town, Cook's command held off repeated efforts to overrun them. The Yazoo City fight bogged down into house-to-house actions that eliminated any chance for a quick victory as darkness came. Knowing that the next day would surely bring Federal gunboats to the scene, Ross withdrew, later reporting losses of six killed and fifty-one wounded. The history of the 3rd USCC tallies casualties of seventeen dead (two of them officers) and twenty-three wounded.[41]

An action on March 31, so small that it was not noted in the *Official Records* or even in the regimental history, also typifies the fate confronting many black soldiers in combat. A portion of Company G (thirty-eight men), led by Captain George Coykendall, met a larger enemy force while on a scout from Snyder's Bluff toward Yazoo City. According to the company's monthly return, the detachment charged the Rebels "and was repulsed and charged by the enemy in turn and followed ½ miles." The unnamed officer filling out the returns added the chilling note, "The enemy captured 16 men whom they put to death, not even excepting the wounded."[42]

The participation of the 3rd USCC in what was called the "Grierson Raid," from December 21, 1864, to January 13, 1865, marked one of the very few times a black cavalry regiment was brigaded with white ones in a field operation. Here the brigade commanded by Colonel Osband consisted of the 4th and 11th Illinois Cavalry, the 2nd Wisconsin Cavalry, and the 3rd USCC (which had moved from Vicksburg to Memphis in late November). Benjamin Grierson's force, numbering perhaps 3,500 men organized into three brigades, left Memphis on an easterly heading following the line of the Memphis and Charleston Railroad. After a short distance it turned south, raided the region around Brice's Crossroads, then moved east to strike the Mobile and Ohio Railroad. When scattered local Confederate defensive units attempted to consolidate, Grierson attacked them at Egypt Station on December 28, 1864. In this combat the 3rd USCC, fighting on foot, successfully overran an enemy stockade, then served as a rear guard when Grierson retired in the face of Rebel reinforcements. A few days later, several companies of the 3rd were detailed to slaughter some 1,000 hogs to prevent their use by the enemy.[43]

As he swung back toward the west, Grierson characteristically threw out a series of smaller columns to confuse the enemy as to his intentions. Colonel Osband and his brigade were engaged in just such a diversionary effort when they met an enemy force under Brigadier General Wirt Adams near Franklin, Mississippi, on January 2, 1865. The fight, which Adams termed "obstinately contested" and which Osband thought a draw, cost the regiment six killed and eight wounded.[44]

The 3rd USCC continued to operate out of Memphis until late April, when the regiment returned to Vicksburg, where it patrolled as far south as Natchez as part of a Federal dragnet aimed at preventing Confederate president Jefferson Davis from reaching the Trans-Mississippi. The unit remained on duty in the District of West Tennessee and the Department of Mississippi until it was mustered out of service on January 26, 1866.[45]

The history of the 4th USCC is largely a story of garrison and fatigue duties with only sporadic and very occasional employment in combat situations. For its first eleven months the regiment, commanded by Nathaniel C. Mitchell, then a major, was assigned to the defenses of New Orleans. (Subsequent commanders included Lieutenant Colonel Julius H. Alexander and Captain Otto Hefty.) A note in the 4th USCC's record of events for July 1864 says, "The entire Regiment worked on fortifications until July 10th when it is ordered to follow strictly the infantry drill of Casey." There is no evidence that the men were mounted before August, when the 4th was moved to Port Hudson. The entire regiment appears not to have received horses until August 18–24, 1864.[46]

Recruitment was an area where the 4th USCC did exceptionally well, largely through the efforts of one man, Major Joseph Warren Paine. The Boston-born Paine was a sometime insurance salesman and sometime writer, who edited a journal called the *Yankee Blade*. He had served in the 13th New York Cavalry before moving over to the 4th USCC, where he found his calling. "His plan of recruiting was peculiar," wrote a fellow officer.

> Taking a squad of colored cavalry, he would go outside of the lines, capture all the horses and mules he could lay hands on, and, mounting thereon all the recruits he could get, march back to camp. It was amusing to see him march his "ebony brigade" past the "starchy regiments" from Northern states. "Halloa! what have you got there?" would be the salutation. "Horace Greeley's body-guard," he would laughingly reply, and march on. And, what is more, he would not bring the husband and father, and leave the family to suffer.[47]

The 4th's major field action came even before all its men had been mounted. On August 23, four companies of the 4th USCC (so designated in an order of April 4) set out from Port Hudson as part of a 3,000-man column whose purpose was to threaten Clinton, Louisiana, to draw out the Rebel defenders. Once the Confederates had committed themselves, a fast-moving mounted force was to spring out of Port Hudson to catch the enemy in a pincer movement. The Clinton-bound column consisted mostly of infantry, with the 4th and the 2nd New York Cavalry the only mounted units.

While the expedition failed to tempt out a significant force of the enemy, it did initiate the 4th in combat. The regiment's record of events noted that the troopers of the 4th met "with the enemy on several occasions, in which each of the squadrons [did] themselves credit, capturing several of the enemy without loss to themselves, except one man wounded by accidental shot and one in the battle."[48]

The return of this expedition to Port Hudson marked the beginning of a decided downturn in the fortunes of the 4th USCC. According to the October 1864 entry in the record of events, "During the past month the Regiment has furnished heavy details for picket, escort, scouts and fatigue duty, which has prevented drill to a great extent. . . . Many of the horses are old remounts and diseased a great portion of the time. . . . [The men] have been without pay, have never had more than half a ration." Then, on

October 17, came orders dismounting the 4th USCC with the explanation that the "regiment has an unenviable reputation, both as to the incapacity of its officers and the laxity of discipline throughout."[49]

There is only one further record of the 4th in action; the regiment was included in an expedition from Port Hudson to Jackson on April 11–13, 1865. At the same time, a battalion of the 4th USCC set out from Port Hudson to provide security for a detachment of engineers and telegraph operators rebuilding the communications link between that point and Osyka, Mississippi. Knowing that the area was infested "with migratory bands of Confederates" and that the "Johnnies expected to take no prisoners alive," Lieutenant J. W. Evarts "selected 400 men, Sergeants, Corporals and privates, but no white officers" except himself.

Evarts's command set off on April 12. The repair party "moved forward rapidly, as most of the poles were standing," and they found "only occasional breaks in the wire." Reaching Osyka on April 17, Evarts encountered a large band of Confederate cavalry numbering, he estimated, "about 3,000." The Rebels had heard rumors of the cascading collapse of their nation, rumors Evarts confirmed for them from dispatches he carried. On April 18 the black troopers watched these veteran enemy soldiers disband their units and scatter back to their homes. Evarts "returned toward Port Hudson with 20,000 contrabands, the most motley crew conceivable, with every species of vehicle, cattle, mules, oxen, and horses stripped from neighboring plantations, that was ever beheld since the exodus of the Israelites from Egypt."[50]

Like many African American military units, the 4th USCC was retained in service throughout the general demobilization that began in June 1865. The troopers remained in the Port Hudson area until July of that year and then performed duty at various points in the Department of the Mississippi until the men mustered out of U.S. service on March 20, 1866.[51]

As previously noted, the 5th and 6th USCC were allowed to organize at Camp Nelson, Kentucky, only after assurances were given that the horses needed would be impressed from local citizens. Colonel L. Henry Carpenter took command of the 5th, while Colonel James F. Wade and Lieutenant Colonel James S. Brisbin assumed those responsibilities for the 6th regiment. Even before the units were formally mustered into U.S. service on October 24, 1864, portions of both took part in an expedition that resulted in one of the more infamous incidents of the war involving black cavalry.

It came at the end of a large-scale raid organized under the command of Brevet Major General Stephen G. Burbridge, which was targeted at Confederate salt production facilities in Southwest Virginia. Anxious to augment his strike force, Burbridge impressed six hundred African American recruits from the training facility at Camp Nelson, most of them intended for the 5th and 6th USCC. The grueling march from eastern Kentucky into southwestern Virginia was made especially difficult for the black troopers, who "were made the subject of much ridicule and many insulting remarks by the white troops, and in some instances petty outrages, such as the pulling off the caps of colored soldiers."[52]

Nothing went right on this raid. Burbridge moved too slowly; a critical supporting column was sent elsewhere; and Confederate defenders (a mix of home guard units and a miscellany of experienced troops) were able to take up a strong position outside Saltville, Virginia, which the Federals attacked on October 2, 1864. Burbridge withdrew after a day of stubborn fighting, even though the portion of his command that included the black troopers scored some success.[53]

The withdrawal was precipitate, leaving numbers of the wounded (black and white) behind. Afterward, reports circulated that many of the captured black soldiers had been wantonly murdered by their captors. The hatred felt in the Rebel ranks against the African American soldiers was real and intense, so much so that it prompted what historian William Marvel has termed "a boasting exaggeration of the slaughter." Although Confederates claimed as many as 155 of the black POWs were killed, Marvel's careful examination of personal service records has accounted for all but perhaps a dozen who might have been murdered. While still a telling indictment of racism, it does not suggest that Saltville should stand alongside Fort Pillow in the halls of infamy.[54]

When the Federals returned to Saltville in December, they were better organized and commanded. Both the 5th and 6th USCC participated in this expedition that successfully wrecked the salt-making facilities. In a January 2 communication to Washington from Lexington, Kentucky, Lorenzo Thomas boasted that in an engagement at Marion, Virginia, during this operation, "the negroes [in the 6th USCC] charged over open ground, and did not fire a gun until within thirty yards of the rebels." "I never yet saw anything in battle so terrible as an infuriated negro," said the officer commanding the 6th in this combat. After returning from this action, the two units were scattered across Kentucky guarding lines of communication and scouting. Both were transferred to the Department of Arkansas in December 1865 and were posted there when they were mustered out—the 5th USCC on March 20, 1866, and the 6th USCC on April 15.[55]

In his farewell address to the troopers of the 6th, Lieutenant Colonel

James S. Brisbin declared: "Go now black soldiers to your homes and become orderly, sober and industrious citizens. When the Government needs your service again it will call for you and you will come. The flag that now floats over us is as much yours as it is mine, and you must at all times be ready to defend it. Be as loyal to it in the future as you have been in the past. Teach your children to love it as you have loved it, to fight for it as you have fought for it, and if necessary to die for it, as your brothers did at Saltville and Marion."[56]

The 5th Massachusetts Cavalry (Colored), the only black cavalry unit to retain its state designation throughout its service, was organized at Camp Meigs, near Readville, Massachusetts, in the winter of 1863–64. Filling its roster of commanding officers were colonels Henry S. Russell, Samuel E. Chamberlain, and Charles F. Adams and Lieutenant Colonel Horace N. Weld. Private (soon to be sergeant) Amos Webber told the *Anglo-African* on April 24 that the men's health was "pretty good" and that the "officers are much respected." In early May 1864, the 5th Massachusetts Cavalry (Colored) was shifted by battalions of four companies each to Washington. There it was united and transferred to the Army of the James at Fortress Monroe, where "it was equipped as infantry."[57]

On June 9, 1864, dismounted troopers were part of a Union expedition sent against Petersburg. A soldier in the ranks calling himself "Africano" wrote a long description of this operation that appeared in the *Anglo-African*. Even though the whole endeavor failed to capture the Cockade City, "Africano" felt that the black troopers acquitted themselves well, several times driving the mostly home guard defenders "before the negro legions of Massachusetts."[58]

The regiment returned to Petersburg on June 15, still without horses and now brigaded with several black infantry units. As part of a far more substantial Union drive to capture Petersburg, the 5th Massachusetts Cavalry (Colored) joined in an attack on a Rebel outpost at Baylor's Farm. The Confederate position was backed by a battery of cannon that commanded the ground over which the advance had to move, and for a while, remembered Massachusetts private Charles Torrey Beman, "the shell, grape and canister came around us cruelly." "Africano" also made note of "a most terrific fire of shot, shell, grape, and canister, which poured like hail upon us."[59]

"Africano" stirred up a small hornet's nest by giving the 5th Massachusetts Cavalry (Colored) a decided pride of place in his account of the Baylor's Farm action. His letter to the *Anglo-African* was contradicted by one sent to the paper from a member of the 4th USCT who insisted that the mostly untried cavalrymen fired more into the backs of his regiment than into the faces of the enemy. Supporting the infantryman's case was a decision made later that same day by the officer commanding the black brigade in this operation not to commit the 5th Massachusetts Cavalry (Colored) to the assault on Petersburg. In his report he deemed the 5th Massachusetts Cavalry (Colored) so inefficient that again exposing it to enemy fire "would be a reckless and useless exposure of life to no purpose." This officer also termed the dismounted troopers "little other than an armed mob." By the end of June the regiment had been transferred to Point Lookout, Maryland, where it relieved the 36th USCT and took over the task of guarding the Rebel prisoners being held there.[60]

The only other Federal units posted to guard duty consisted of soldiers deemed too sick for active service but not ill enough for discharge. One Rebel prisoner caught the meaning of this assignment when he noted the arrival of the Bay State men, "ordered here, it is said, by Butler, for cowardice in presence of the enemy." Writing from Point Lookout on July 15, trooper G. Booth assured the *Anglo-African*'s readers that the Massachusetts men were doing "their duty cheerfully." He also passed along rumors that the regiment would soon be mounted. "Then we shall show ourselves one of the best cavalry regiments in the service," Booth boasted. Four months later, Sergeant Webber had to admit that the men still were not mounted, but they were drilling on a regular basis and learning "the art of managing a horse." On November 26 Webber reported that the Thanksgiving festivities included games, a dance, band music, and, of course, a turkey dinner with all the trimmings.[61]

The frustration began to show when "J. T." wrote to the *Anglo-African* on January 19, 1865, to complain that more than 330 men were being detailed every day for guard and camp duty. "I have never heard of a regiment being organized as ours is," he grumbled, "being cavalry and infantry at the same time." Discipline suffered. When a black sergeant struck a private for refusing an order to fall in, a scuffle broke out during which the black enlisted man cursed the noncommissioned officer as a "damned yellow nigger." In February Colonel Adams assumed command, and a month later the regiment was sent back to the Army of the James in time to make history.[62]

The new position of the 5th Massachusetts Cavalry (Colored) was along the Union line confronting Richmond's defenses. On the morning of April 3, 1865, the regiment was among the first U.S. troops to occupy the Rebel capital. "Our entry into the city I can not describe," wrote Lieutenant Edward J. Bartlett of the regiment. "We marched up Main Street at the head

of the column, a division of colored troops of the 25th Corps." Even iras-
cible Colonel Adams thought the moment one "which I should most have
desired as the culmination of my life in the Army." The view from Private
Beman's place in the ranks was more down to earth. "This is certainly a city
of hills," he told his father, "for it is going up and coming down all the time.
There are many fine buildings and nice-looking colored people here. They
shouted 'God bless you! we have been waiting for you and looking for you
a long time.'"[63]

Following two months of occupation duty in the Richmond-Petersburg
area, the 5th Massachusetts Cavalry (Colored) was included among the black
units sent to Texas. Old stereotypes were in full force, as details were made
from the regiment to provide "fatigue parties . . . [for] loading & unloading transports." Thanks to the influence exerted by its powerful state representatives, it was also one of the first black regiments to be demobilized,
mustering out of U.S. service on October 31, 1865. When the news of their
impending discharge reached the men at Clarksville, Texas, Quartermaster
Sergeant Thomas J. Laurel was greatly pleased that he and his comrades
would soon be back in Boston, "where our many near and dear friends will
be overjoyed to receive us, most particularly those who have young wives
and sweethearts."[64]

The 5th Massachusetts Cavalry (Colored) was the first mounted black
regiment to be discharged, and the 6th USCC was the last. In all they represented perhaps 7,500 men out of the more than 180,000 African Americans
who wore Union blue during the Civil War. If the service rendered by the
120 or so black infantry regiments barely registered on the postwar historical scales, that contributed by the seven cavalry units was imperceptible. Yet
it was not glory that called many of these men to arms; it was the desire to
prove to white society that that they were indeed human beings of the first
order. In the proud words of J. O. Malone of the 5th Massachusetts Cavalry (Colored), "The colored soldiers in this four years' struggle have proven
themselves in every respect to be men."[65]

Perhaps the greatest legacy of these African American troopers was the
act passed by Congress on July 28, 1866, authorizing two black cavalry regiments for the regular army. Thus were born the 9th and 10th United States
Cavalry—units that in time would gain renown as the Buffalo Soldiers. It
was the 10th Cavalry that in 1877 became home to the first black officer to
graduate from West Point, Henry Ossian Flipper, and ten years later the 9th
was the first assignment for the second African American West Pointer, John
Hanks Alexander.[66]

The record of the black cavalry regiments in the Civil War is one of credible (oftentimes exemplary) service, always in the face of a deeply seated racism that denied them the dignity of even having their accomplishments acknowledged. These young African Americans deserved better. Through their sacrifice and dedication, the black troopers contributed their voices to the larger and slowly growing chorus demanding equality of treatment and opportunity. The civil rights movement of the twentieth century had its roots, in part, in the groundbreaking steps first taken by the dedicated troopers of the Civil War's seven black cavalry regiments.

Notes

1. Burke Davis, *To Appomattox: Nine April Days, 1865* (New York: Rinehart, 1959), 132.

2. U.S. War Department, *The War of the Rebellion: A Compilation of the Official Records of the Union and Confederate Armies*, 128 vols. (Washington, D.C.: Government Printing Office, 1880–1901), 3rd ser., 5:138 (hereafter cited as *OR*).

3. Stephen Z. Starr, *The Union Cavalry in the Civil War*, 3 vols. (Baton Rouge: Louisiana State University Press, 1979–85), 3:7; *OR*, 3rd ser., 5:255. On the U.S. government's problems procuring horses after 1863, see *OR*, 3rd ser., 4:87, and Starr, *The Union Cavalry in the Civil War*, 2:14–16.

4. Worthington Chauncey Ford, ed., *A Cycle of Adams Letters: 1861–1865*, 2 vols. (New York: Houghton Mifflin, 1920), 2:216–17.

5. James G. Hollandsworth, Jr., *The Louisiana Native Guards: The Black Military Experience during the Civil War* (Baton Rouge: Louisiana State University Press, 1995), 43–45.

6. Dudley Taylor Cornish, *The Sable Arm: Black Troops in the Union Army, 1861–1865* (1956; Lawrence: University Press of Kansas, 1987), 126–27.

7. Ibid., 112–26.

8. Ibid., 144–45; Edward M. Main, *The Story of the Marches, Battles and Incidents of the Third United States Colored Cavalry: A Fighting Regiment in the War of the Rebellion, 1861–5* (Louisville: Globe Printing Company, 1908), 58.

9. Noah Andre Trudeau, *Like Men of War: Black Troops in the Civil War, 1861–1865* (Boston: Little, Brown, 1998), 115.

10. C. W. Foster to B. F. Butler, December 26, 1863, Records of the Adjutant General's Office, 1780s–1917, Colored Troops Division, 1863–89, Letters Sent, December 1863–March 1888, Record Group (RG) 94, National Archives (NA), Washington, D.C., vol. 2 of 21, entry 352.

11. *The Union Army: A History of Military Affairs in the Loyal States, 1861–65*, 8 vols. (1908; Wilmington, N.C.: Broadfoot Publishing Company, 1997), 1:215.

12. *OR*, 3rd ser., 4:549; John David Smith, "The Recruitment of Negro Soldiers in Kentucky, 1863–1865," *Register of the Kentucky Historical Society* 72 (October 1974): 364–90.

13. Starr, *The Union Cavalry in the Civil War*, 2:10; *Anglo-African* (New York), February 20, 1864; Frederick W. Browne, "My Service in the U.S. Colored Cavalry," in *Sketches of War History, 1861–1865: A Compilation of Miscellaneous Papers Compiled for the Ohio Commandery of the Loyal Legion, February 1885–February 1909* (1907; Wilmington, N.C.: Broadfoot Publishing Company, 1993), 213; Joseph T. Glatthaar, *Forged in Battle: The Civil War Alliance of Black Soldiers and White Officers* (New York: Free Press, 1990), 58–59; Main, *Story of the . . . Third United States Colored Cavalry*, 48.

14. Browne, "My Service in the U.S. Colored Cavalry," 213; Robert Dollard, *Recollections of the Civil War* (Scotland, S.Dak.: Published by the author, 1906), 99; Edward G. Longacre, *Army of Amateurs: General Benjamin F. Butler and the Army of the James, 1863–1865* (Mechanicsburg, Pa.: Stackpole Books, 1997), 57; Main, *Story of the . . . Third United States Colored Cavalry*, 48.

15. Dollard, *Recollections of the Civil War*, 99; Browne, "My Service in the U.S. Colored Cavalry," 213; Ford, *A Cycle of Adams Letters*, 2:218–19; Main, *Story of the . . . Third United States Colored Cavalry*, 21, 97.

16. *Washington National Tribune*, February 10, 1910.

17. Testimony of Porter Brabston in Pension File of Alexander Taylor, Company G, 3rd United States Colored Cavalry, NA; *Anglo-African*, June 17, 1865.

18. Records of the Adjutant General's Office, Regimental Books: 1st U.S. Colored Cavalry (Descriptive Book Cos. A to L); 2nd U.S. Colored Cavalry (Descriptive Book Cos. A to G and I to M); 3rd U.S. Colored Cavalry (Regimental Descriptive Book, vol. 1, no. 1), RG 94, NA; Nick Salvatore, *We All Got History: The Memory Books of Amos Webber* (New York: Times Books, 1996), 124.

19. Regimental Books 1st U.S. Colored Cavalry: Regimental Order Book Companies A–L, Company B Orders, RG 94, NA, 9; Browne, "My Service in the U.S. Colored Cavalry," 213; *Anglo-African*, February 20, 1864; May 7, 1864; Dollard, *Recollections of the Civil War*, 100.

20. Main, *Story of the . . . Third United States Colored Cavalry*, 270; Glatthaar, *Forged in Battle*, 187.

21. Browne, "My Service in the U.S. Colored Cavalry," 219–20; Dollard, *Recollections of the Civil War*, 128; Ford, *A Cycle of Adams Letters*, 2:186.

22. *OR*, 1st ser., 41 (4):27–28; Frederick H. Dyer, *A Compendium of the War of the Rebellion*, 2 vols. (1908; Dayton, Ohio: Morningside, 1994), 2:1721; *OR*, 1st ser., 39 (1):557.

23. *OR*, 1st ser., 39 (3):476; *OR*, 1st ser., 41 (1):295; J. Garrard to R. S. Davis, April 9, 1864, Regimental Books 1st U.S. Colored Cavalry: Regimental Letters Sent, vol. 1, no. 4, RG 94, NA, 21.

24. Starr, *The Union Cavalry in the Civil War*, 3:8; Ibid., 1:117.

25. Ford, *A Cycle of Adams Letters*, 2:269; Browne, "My Service in the U.S. Colored Cavalry," 220.

26. Salvatore, *We All Got History*, 138; *Anglo-African*, June 16, 1864.

27. Dyer, *A Compendium of the War of the Rebellion*, 2:1720; Dollard, *Recollections of the Civil War*, 102.

28. Dollard, *Recollections of the Civil War*, 101–7; Regimental Returns, 2nd U.S. Colored Cavalry, Company A, RG 94, NA; *Newburyport (Mass.) Daily Herald*, March 29, 1864; *OR*, 1st ser., 33:237–39, 665–66.

29. Dollard, *Recollections of the Civil War*, 109–10.

30. Herbert M. Schiller, *The Bermuda Hundred Campaign* (Dayton, Ohio: Morningside, 1988), 47–48, 68, 339; William Glenn Robertson, *Back Door to Richmond: The Bermuda Hundred Campaign, April–June 1864* (Newark, Del.: University of Delaware Press, 1987), 59, 259; Browne, "My Service in the U.S. Colored Cavalry," 213–14; Regimental Returns, 1st U.S. Colored Cavalry: Company E, RG 94, NA.

31. *New York Times*, May 11, 1864.

32. Browne, "My Service in the U.S. Colored Cavalry," 214; Schiller, *The Bermuda Hundred Campaign*, 155; Robertson, *Back Door to Richmond*, 127.

33. Browne, "My Service in the U.S. Colored Cavalry," 216; Schiller, *The Bermuda Hundred Campaign*, 181, 188, 215, 230, 238, 266; Robertson, *Back Door to Richmond*, 150, 173, 176, 234; *OR*, 1st ser., 36 (2):195–96.

34. Notations compiled from Regimental Returns 1st and 2nd U.S. Colored Cavalry, various companies, RG 94, NA.

35. Richard J. Sommers, *Richmond Redeemed: The Siege at Petersburg* (New York: Doubleday, 1981), 33, 174; Regimental Returns 2nd U.S. Colored Cavalry: Company G, RG 94, NA; Browne, "My Service in the U.S. Colored Cavalry," 220; Dyer, *A Compendium of the War of the Rebellion*, 2:1720.

36. Browne, "My Service in the U.S. Colored Cavalry," 221–22; Ira Berlin, Joseph P. Reidy, and Leslie S. Rowland, eds., *The Black Military Experience* (New York: Cambridge University Press, 1982), 723–24; Dollard, *Recollections of the Civil War*, 147–51; Dyer, *A Compendium of the War of the Rebellion*, 2:1720.

37. Dyer, *A Compendium of the War of the Rebellion*, 2:1343; Main, *Story of the . . . Third United States Colored Cavalry*, 46–47. Starr, *The Union Cavalry in the Civil War*, 3:200, suggests that the 1st Mississippi Cavalry (African Descent) and the 3rd USCC were different units, but the extant records clearly indicate they were the same.

38. Dyer, *A Compendium of the War of the Rebellion*, 2:1023; Main, *Story of the . . . Third United States Colored Cavalry*, 65–70, 74; *New York Times*, March 26, 1864.

39. Main, *Story of the . . . Third United States Colored Cavalry*, 74, 111, 120; *OR*, 1st ser., 32 (1):385.

40. Main, *Story of the . . . Third United States Colored Cavalry*, 115; *OR*, 1st ser., 32 (1):385; S. B. Barron, *The Lone Star Defenders* (New York: Neale Publishing Company, 1908), 181.

41. *OR*, 1st ser., 32 (1):387; Main, *Story of the . . . Third United States Colored Cavalry*, 118–23.

42. Regimental Returns 3rd U.S. Colored Cavalry: Company G, RG 94, NA; Record of Events 3rd U.S. Colored Cavalry, March 1864, RG 94, NA.

43. Main, *Story of the . . . Third United States Colored Cavalry*, 217–35; *OR*, 1st ser., 45 (1):844–47.

44. Main, *Story of the . . . Third United States Colored Cavalry*, 232; *OR*, 1st ser., 45 (1):858, 875.

45. Dyer, *A Compendium of the War of the Rebellion*, 2:1720–21.

46. Ibid., 2:1721; *OR*, 1st ser., 26 (1):895; *OR*, 1st ser., 34 (1):198; Record of Events 4th U.S. Colored Cavalry, July and August 1864, RG 94, NA.

47. William S. Studley, *Final Memorials of Major Joseph Warren Paine* (Boston: Press of John Wilson & Son, 1865), 17–18.

48. *OR*, 3rd ser., 4:214; *OR*, 1st ser., 41 (1):274–79; Record of Events 4th U.S. Colored Cavalry, July and August 1864, RG 94, NA.

49. Record of Events 4th U.S. Colored Cavalry, October 1864, RG 94, NA; *OR*, 1st ser., 41 (4):27–28.

50. *Washington National Tribune*, December 12, 1892.

51. Dyer, *A Compendium of the War of the Rebellion*, 2:1721.

52. Starr, *The Union Cavalry in the Civil War*, 3:557; *OR*, 1st ser., 39 (1):555–57.

53. William Marvel, *The Battles for Saltville: Southwest Virginia in the Civil War* (Lynchburg, Va.: H. E. Howard, Inc., 1992), 99–123; Trudeau, *Like Men of War*, 269–75.

54. Marvel, *The Battles for Saltville*, 121, 144–48; William Marvel, "What Makes A Massacre?" *Blue and Gray Magazine* 8 (August 1991): 52–53.

55. Marvel, *The Battles for Saltville*, 124–34; Starr, *The Union Cavalry in the Civil War*, 3:559–60; *OR*, 1st ser., 45 (2):495; Joseph T. Wilson, *The Black Phalanx: African American Soldiers in the War of Independence, The War of 1812, and the Civil War* (1890; New York: Da Capo Press, 1994), 311.

56. "The Negro in the Military Service of the United States," 4:3780, RG 94, NA.

57. *Anglo-African*, May 7, 1864; *The Union Army*, 1:215.

58. *Anglo-African*, June 25, 1864.

59. Edwin S. Redkey, ed., *A Grand Army of Black Men* (New York: Cambridge University Press, 1992), 99; *Anglo-African*, June 25, 1864.

60. *Anglo-African*, July 9, 1864, July 23, 1864; *OR*, 1st ser., 40 (2):490; Dyer, *A Compendium of the War of the Rebellion*, 2:1240; *The Union Army*, 1:215.

61. Salvatore, *We All Got History*, 133; *Anglo-African*, July 30, 1864, December 3, 1864; Redkey, ed., *A Grand Army of Black Men*, 119–20.

62. *Anglo-African*, February 18, 1865; Salvatore, *We All Got History*, 139; Dyer, *A Compendium of the War of the Rebellion*, 2:1240; *The Union Army*, 1:215.

63. Edward J. Bartlett to Brother, April 3, 1865, Bartlett Family Papers, Massachusetts Historical Society, Boston; Ford, *A Cycle of Adams Letters*, 2:261–62; *Anglo-African*, April 22, 1865.

64. Dyer, *A Compendium of the War of the Rebellion*, 2:1240; Record of Events 5th

Massachusetts Cavalry (Colored), Company L, May and June 1865, RG 94, NA; *Anglo-African*, October 21, 1865.

65. *Anglo-African*, June 17, 1865.

66. William H. Leckie, *The Buffalo Soldiers: A Narrative of the Negro Cavalry in the West* (Norman: University of Oklahoma Press, 1967), 6; John M. Carroll, ed., *The Black Military Experience in the American West* (New York: Liveright Publishing, 1973), 172–73.

11

IN THE SHADOW
OF JOHN BROWN

The Military Service of
Colonels Thomas Higginson,
James Montgomery, and
Robert Shaw in the
Department of the South

Keith Wilson

On June 28, 1863 Captain John Appleton wrote home to his wife: "One of Montgomery's men deserted, and was taken last night by the assistance of one of our sergeants of Co. B. At 7½ o'clock this morning the deserter was brought before Montgomery, who sat in an arm chair before his tent and said, 'Well what have you to say why sentence of death should not be passed upon you.' 'Nothing' says the man. 'Very well' says Montgomery, 'You die at half past nine' and went to his breakfast. The man was shot about three hundred yards from my tent."[1]

By itself, Colonel James Montgomery's summary execution of a black soldier appears as an individual miscarriage of military justice. However, when it is considered against the background of the rehearsal for reconstruction, the Port Royal Experiment that was developing in the Sea Islands of South Carolina, and the faltering attempts being made to make the enlistment of Southern blacks a national policy, the execution does point to critical tensions that were emerging in the movement to recruit blacks into the Union army.[2] This essay examines these tensions by analyzing the different strains of abolitionism represented by three unit commanders, Colonels Thomas Wentworth Higginson, James Montgomery, and Robert Gould Shaw. In particular it has as its objective an examination of the ways the officers' abolitionist beliefs shaped their attitude toward their troops and their perception of warfare.

Higginson, Montgomery, and Shaw all played critical roles in black recruitment and military service at a time—from November 1862 to July 1863—when a national policy in that regard was being formulated. They served together in the Department of the South, a department that officially consisted of the states of South Carolina, Georgia, and Florida but, in reality, was confined to several Federal enclaves dispersed along the Atlantic coast. All three commanders reflected on each other's military performance and personal character and sought to promote and publicize their military exploits and leadership. Even though all were committed to the abolitionist cause, each held very different views about the nature of the war and the performance of the black troops serving under them. These differences arose primarily from their contrasting racial beliefs, social backgrounds, and military experiences. These personal and social differences to some extent circumscribed the role they carved out for the black soldiers serving under them.

Shortly after the Emancipation Proclamation had been issued, the Sea Islands of South Carolina became an important center for the recruitment of black soldiers into the Union army. Located fifty miles southwest of Charleston, the South Carolina Sea Islands were occupied by Federal forces only seven months after the fall of Fort Sumter. Into these islands poured several hundred enthusiastic abolitionists intent on justifying emancipation by shaping the slave's experience of freedom. Here they toiled on the abandoned plantations to make the freedman a literate, self-reliant wage earner. Their faith in the Negro's productive capacity was closely linked to their belief in the fighting qualities of the former slaves. Therefore, from its beginning, the abolitionist experiment at Port Royal, in the Department of the South, was inextricably linked to the issue of black enlistment.[3]

In some ways what transpired in the Department of the South during the first crucial period of black enlistment, from November 1862 to July 1863, may be seen as a struggle between competing brands of abolitionism. The question that troubled the minds of those at the vanguard of the abolition movement, was not simply, would the Negro fight? But rather, how would he fight? Would he be influenced by the frontier abolitionism of James Montgomery, or would he allow himself to be led into civilized combat by Thomas Higginson and Robert Shaw, noble sons from Massachusetts?

Thomas Higginson (1823–1911) had impeccable credentials as a leading

Massachusetts abolitionist. Son of a wealthy merchant, Higginson graduated from Harvard's divinity school and then entered the Unitarian ministry. Higginson, an ardent social reformer and literary figure, wrote extensively on national issues in the *Atlantic Monthly*. During the decade immediately preceding the Civil War, he increasingly gained a national reputation as an antislavery advocate. He became a member of the Antislavery Vigilance Committee and was wounded in May 1854 trying to prevent the fugitive slave, Anthony Burns, from being returned to the South. In 1856 he went to Kansas on two occasions to support John Brown and the Free State settlers. During 1860 he became one of the "Secret Six" who financially supported John Brown's Harpers Ferry raid. After war was declared, Higginson received a captain's commission in the 21st Massachusetts Volunteers. It was while serving with this regiment that he accepted an invitation from Brigadier General Rufus Saxton, military governor of the Department of the South, to serve as colonel of the 1st South Carolina Volunteers (Colored).[4]

Unlike that of Thomas Higginson, the appointment of Robert Shaw (1837–63) to command a black regiment did not rest on his personal reputation as a militant abolitionist. Rather, Shaw's appointment to command the 54th Massachusetts Volunteers, the first black regiment raised in the North, was the result of his family's social standing and antislavery credentials. Shaw's family were members of the exclusive New England Brahmin caste, which was intent on providing intellectual and social leadership to the nation. His father, George Francis Shaw of New York, an heir of a wealthy Boston mercantile family, was well connected in Massachusetts abolitionist circles. Shaw entered Harvard in 1856 but withdrew in 1859 to work in his father's company. Although he was intellectually attracted to abolitionism, he had little personal involvement in the antislavery cause. When war broke out, Shaw enthusiastically joined the 2nd Massachusetts Volunteers and soon rose to the rank of captain. He fought bravely at Cedar Mountain and Antietam in August and September 1862. In February 1863, after some hesitation, he accepted Governor John A. Andrew's invitation to command the 54th Massachusetts Volunteers.[5]

The path taken by James Montgomery (1814–71) to the command of a black regiment contrasted sharply with that of the wealthy young aristocrat, Robert Shaw. A frontier schoolteacher and fighting clergyman, James Montgomery developed his antislavery convictions while fighting with John Brown in Kansas. From 1857 until the outbreak of war, Montgomery led his band of Jayhawkers on a bloody campaign to drive proslavery settlers from southern Kansas. When war was declared, he joined up with the forces of Senator James H. Lane who was fighting against the Rebels in Missouri. In search of a permanent command, Montgomery left Kansas for Washington in January 1863. There he managed to gain the patronage of Major General David Hunter, the commander of the Department of the South. At Hunter's request, Montgomery journeyed to the department in late January 1863 to begin the task of raising black regiments there.[6]

Although Montgomery, Shaw, and Higginson all opposed the institution of slavery and proudly commanded black troops, each was motivated by his own unique set of abolitionist beliefs. For example, Robert Shaw joined the Union army out of a sense of honor and duty. As a member of a distinguished family, Shaw believed he had a duty to save the Union by destroying the Southern slavocracy. On receiving Governor Andrew's offer to command the first black regiment raised in Massachusetts, Shaw initially rejected it, commenting, "If I had taken it, it would only have been from a sense of duty." When he finally accepted Andrew's offer, he did so with a strong sense of class pride, noblesse oblige, and a determination to please his mother, who was devoted to the abolitionist cause. Empathy with the suffering Negro slave did not figure prominently in his consideration.[7] Higginson, in contrast, was a zealous abolitionist. A romantic paternalist, Higginson welcomed the outbreak of war because he believed Union victory would save the childlike Negro from oppression by a morally corrupt feudal class. He urged blacks to aspire to citizenship, arguing that "enfranchisement of the black loyalists" was "the only way to prevent Congress from being replenished with plotting and disloyal men."[8]

James Montgomery's abolitionist beliefs had little in common with Shaw's concepts of honor and noblesse oblige or Higginson's militant activism and paternalism. Montgomery believed he was engaged in a holy war against slavery. For him the outbreak of the Civil War marked not the beginning of a new conflict but rather the consummation of a struggle for divine justice that began with John Brown in Kansas. His fervent opposition to slavery did not rest on notions of Negro rights, for he believed blacks to be a savage, inferior people who needed protection from further degradation at the hands of Southerners. Unlike Higginson, Montgomery was not interested in the citizenship rights of blacks. His vision of America was of a Christian nation in which white labor would be supreme and slavery destroyed. As a free settler in Kansas, Montgomery attacked slavery because he believed it undermined the moral fiber and Christian heritage of the nation.[9]

This sharp division between Montgomery's Western frontier abolitionism and Shaw and Higginson's "elite" Massachusetts abolitionism also influenced perceptions of what constituted legitimate warfare. Because Montgomery saw himself as a servant of God, an Old Testament avenger, he was
prepared to wage "hard war" on the civilian population of the South. "[A]
guerrilla company, to be effective, must be self-sustaining—must subsist
on the enemy. Therefore we feed ourselves at Pro-slavery larders and our
horses at Pro-slavery corn-cribs," boasted Montgomery when speaking of
his Kansas exploits. For Shaw and Higginson warfare meant something different. They believed that it was through warfare that a civilized people
demonstrated their high moral values. Both placed the blame for the war
primarily on the heads of the Southern slaveholders whom they accused of
duping the poor, ignorant people of the South.[10]

The strategies and tactics that Shaw and Higginson employed were also
influenced by the different values they attached to military service. Shaw
believed the army's performance depended on the values and standards of an
elite officer corps. Early in his military service he expressed his strong opposition to a "rotten military volunteer system" that appointed "3000 officers
without requiring them to pass any examination," everyone of whom could
be "unfit for his place as the most ignorant private in the ranks." Such an
unprofessional, disorganized system of officer selection caused serious disci-
plinary problems. He believed "the very reason that, in most volunteer regiments, the officers" had "so little control over their men" was "because they
owe their places to them." Convinced that combat success owed more to disciplined maneuvering than personal bravery, Shaw believed that the Yankee
volunteer had to be held under firm command. He strongly opposed "western" guerrilla warfare precisely because it was irregular, unprofessional, un-
scientific, and, above all, dishonorable. When accused of wantonly burning
the town of Darien, in the Department of the South, he defended himself by
claiming he had a "distaste for this barbarous sort of warfare." He had "gone
through the war so far without dishonor" and did not want "to degenerate
into a plunderer or robber."[11]

Shaw's commitment to civilized warfare influenced his reading habits.
While serving in Virginia with the 2nd Massachusetts Infantry, he spent
his leisure time reading Prince d'Orleans de Joinville's military accounts of
the Napoleonic wars and McCellan's Peninsula campaign. Shaw admired
de Joinville's military acumen and believed his views on the Union army's
"organization and discipline" were the "most sensible" he had "ever seen in
print." "Everything" he said about the "extravagance, inefficiency and al-

most total want of discipline inseparable from the volunteer system" was "true." Suspicious of the martial qualities of the volunteer, he found that de Joinville simply reinforced his view that the Yankee volunteer would only succeed in combat if he was subject to strict discipline and the codes of military warfare. Such a policy would prevent outrages from occurring.[12]

Higginson also had firm ideas about the role the officer corps should play in the Union army. Like Shaw, he believed military performance was dependent on good leadership. In "Regular and Volunteer Officers," an article appearing in the *Atlantic Monthly* in September 1864, Higginson praised the contribution of regular army officers by admitting that "on the whole, no regiment in the field made progress so rapid, or held their own so well, as those placed under regular officers." However, unlike Shaw, Higginson never wavered in his commitment to the Union volunteer. He rejoiced "to see how much the present war had done towards effacing the traditional jealousy between regular officers" and volunteer officers. The "two classes" of officers had "been so thoroughly intermingled, on staff-duties and in the field" that "it really cannot be said that there" was "much feeling of conscious separation left." This development did not surprise Higginson because he firmly believed that the Union's volunteer army was a noble representation of the society from which it sprung. Indeed, he advised the readers of the *Atlantic Monthly* that "[w]ar is not the highest of human pursuits, certainly; but an army comes very near to being the completest of human organizations, and he alone succeeds in it who readily accepts its inevitable laws, and applies them." War directed at Southern civilians was repugnant to Higginson because it undermined the moral integrity of the citizen soldier.[13]

Any study of the different perceptions of warfare held by Higginson, Shaw, and Montgomery must highlight the link between the enlistment of black troops and the changing character of the war. At the beginning of the Civil War, concepts of what constituted "civilized" or legitimate warfare were most clearly defined in Henry Wager Halleck's *International Law; or, Rules Regulating the Intercourse of States in Peace and War*, written in 1861 before Halleck became general in chief of the Union army. According to Halleck, civilized warfare was governed by two major principles. First, war should be fought on the battlefield and according to the rules of war. Captured enemy troops, for example, were to be treated as prisoners of war. Second, noncombatant immunity was to be rigorously enforced. Of course, these notions of civilized warfare were not universally adhered to by Union commanders. In some regions, principally the West, bloody guerrilla warfare was commonplace. As the Civil War dragged on, and Union victory eluded Union generals, Northern policy makers began to refine their definition of legitimate warfare. By 1863 it was becoming more permissible to wage "hard war" or "total war" on the economic resources of the Confederacy. In the West, Generals Ulysses S. Grant and William T. Sherman were developing a raiding strategy that aimed at crushing the Confederacy by waging war on a rebellious people and their property. Convinced that "all the South" was "in arms and deep in enmity," Sherman wrote to Grant from Memphis in October 1862 commenting, "they cannot be made to love us, but may be made to fear us, and dread the passage of troops through their country." Such hard war attitudes found strong support from veteran soldiers who wanted to punish the rebellious Southerners by inflicting on them the dreaded suffering of war. For these soldiers, aggressive foraging expeditions became effective vehicles for their revenge.[14]

The First and Second Confiscation Acts, the Militia Act, and, above all, the Emancipation Proclamation issued in January 1863 were important initiatives in the development of a total war policy because they allowed army commanders to use in the Union war effort slaves who had been the property of rebel slaveholders. This broader concept of war was eventually given official military endorsement in General Orders No. 100 issued by Major General Halleck in April 1863. General Orders No. 100 did not permit savagery or the wanton destruction of civilian property, but it did allow Union troops to destroy resources that would enable the enemy to wage war. Therefore, according to the principle behind this order it was both unjust and uncivilized to wage war on the Southern civilian population by wantonly destroying their homes and other assets that had no military value. Certainly Higginson and Shaw believed this mode of warfare was "uncivilized." The deployment of black troops, then, by Higginson, Shaw, and Montgomery, occurred at a time when notions of what constituted legitimate, civilized warfare were uncertain. This uncertainty helped to magnify the controversy surrounding the use of black troops in the Department of the South and gave it a national prominence that it might otherwise not have had.[15]

An analysis of black military service in the Department of the South during the critical period of November 1862 to July 1863 reveals three phases of development that were dominated in turn by Higginson, Montgomery, and Shaw. This threefold division of black military service in the Department of the South is somewhat arbitrary; each phase had no decisive beginning or end. Nevertheless, it is plausible to argue that black military service gained its original momentum with Higginson's arrival in November 1862 and that the formative phase closed with Shaw's death and Higginson's temporary retirement from the department in July 1863. It would be incorrect to see each developmental phase totally dominated by one officer, but there was a sense in which the focus of national attention did move successively from one officer to the other.

All three commanders forged relationships with each other. Although Higginson and Shaw never served together and met only once during the time they served in the Department of the South, they nonetheless did have a mutual respect for each other. After sharing a meal with Shaw, Higginson commented that he "should have known Shaw anywhere by his resemblance to his kindered." It did not take him "long to perceive that he [Shaw] shared their habitual truthfulness and courage." Shaw admired Higginson's commitment to his command. He had never seen anyone who "put his whole soul into his work as" Higginson had done. His "open-heartedness & purity of character" were admirable. In some ways James Montgomery provided the link between the two men because he served first with Higginson and then with Shaw, only a few weeks before Shaw was killed at Fort Wagner.[16]

Higginson arrived in the Department of the South in November 1862 and immediately embarked on the task of organizing his regiment, the 1st South Carolina Volunteers. In this formative period Higginson focused on drill and training because he knew that success depended heavily on battlefield performance. It was his firm belief that "forty rounds" would "marry us to the American Army, past divorcing, if we can only use them well." By late January 1863 his regiment was trained and ready to move.[17]

On January 23, 1863, Colonel Higginson left Beaufort, South Carolina, with a detachment of 462 officers and men in three ships bound for the St. Marys River, Florida. The aim of the expedition was to carry out a surprise attack on a Rebel cavalry company encamped at Township Landing, fifteen miles upriver. Although the Rebel cavalry company escaped largely unscathed, Higginson returned to Beaufort with his ships laden with lumber, iron railings, and bricks taken from Rebel properties. In his report to General Rufus Saxton, Higginson claimed the expedition was an outstanding success. Such was the fighting zeal of his men that they pleaded with him to allow them to pursue "the fleeing enemy and destroy his camp." In comments laced with paternalism, Higginson noted that the boyish enthusiasm of his soldiers had come to the fore when they journeyed by ship up the St. Marys River. Once his soldiers came under fire, they "actually fought each other for places at the few port-holes from which they could fire on the enemy." The "fiery energy" of his troops was so great that Higginson admitted that "it requires the strictest discipline to hold them in hand." Yet Higginson linked his condescending view of his soldiers with an admiration for their intense desire to escape from the horror of slavery. "They must fight or be slaves," Higginson informed Governor Andrew a few days before the expedition departed.[18]

News of Higginson's successful expedition received considerable publicity in the Northern press. The *New York Times* and *New York Tribune* endorsed Higginson's basic assertion that the Negro would fight. The *Christian Recorder*, the organ of the African Methodist Episcopal Church published in Philadelphia, proudly carried a report from one of Higginson's officers, Captain Charles T. Trowbridge, who asserted that the Rebels were "shot down like dogs by the negro volunteers, who fought like tigers." This favorable publicity occurred at a crucial time for the movement to enlist blacks. While the expedition was in progress, the House of Representatives was debating a bill introduced by Radical Republican congressman Thaddeus Stevens to enlist 50,000 blacks. At the same time, Governor John Andrew was seeking to raise black regiments in Massachusetts.[19]

In March 1863 Higginson embarked on another expedition, this time to Jacksonville, Florida. At first the expedition was very successful. Jacksonville fell without a shot being fired because Confederate general Joseph Finegan, commanding the District of Florida, was unaware of the invader's presence. However, much to Higginson's annoyance, before large-scale operations were begun General David Hunter recalled the entire expedition to Beaufort.[20]

During their withdrawal from Jacksonville, the Union troops set fire to large sections of the town. This action disturbed Higginson because it violated his notions of civilized warfare. "To think," he wrote in his journal, "that this was the end of our brilliant enterprise and the destruction of my beautiful city was a sadder thing than wounds or death." He attributed the fires to the "perfect insubordination" of the 8th Maine. In contrast, the military demeanor of the 1st South Carolina Volunteers was exemplary. "My men have behaved perfectly well," wrote Higginson; "though many were owned here . . . there has been no wanton outrage." Nevertheless, the Negro troops did enjoy the retribution being meted out to their former owners, and as the town burned they "sang and exhorted without ceasing."[21] Fortunately for Higginson, most of the Northern press exonerated the black troops from any involvement in the Jacksonville fire. This "piece of luck" so pleased Colonel Higginson that he ignored accusations that he had mistreated loyal white Southerners during the evacuation.[22]

After the Jacksonville expedition, Higginson's remaining period of military service proved relatively uneventful. His military duty included picket duty near Beaufort, South Carolina, and an abortive raid up the Coosaw River. In early July 1863 he was wounded while on an expedition up the South Edisto River. After a furlough in his hometown of Worcester, Massachusetts, he returned to South Carolina. Unable to fully recover from his wounds, he left military service in May 1864.[23]

Several weeks before going on furlough, Colonel Higginson commented on his military experience to the American Freedmen's Inquiry Commission. Established by the War Department in March 1863 to investigate the conditions and requirements of freedmen in Union-controlled territory, the commission took an interest in the performance of black troops. In his testimony Higginson described what he believed were the "strengths" and "weaknesses" of his black troops and presented arguments for employing them in combat.[24]

Higginson believed the blacks' courageous qualities were outward expressions of a childlike character. This paternal, essentially racist attitude reflected his class consciousness and his superior social standing. Invariably when Higginson explained the performance of his troops he called upon paternal imagery. His soldiers were "children," mere "boys." Commenting on the shelling of Jacksonville in *Army Life in a Black Regiment* (1869), Higginson wrote that his men shouted "with childish delight over every explosion." He also identified similar childlike excitement during the St. Marys expedition. On this occasion his men misunderstood orders and charged off into the darkness armed only with bayonets. When addressing the American Freedmen's Inquiry Commission, Higginson also employed paternal rhetoric to describe the performance of his troops. He commented that "once under fire they [were] excitable" and that there were dangers associated with controlling such "excitable" troops in battle.

Rather than try to excuse the weaknesses of the soldiers' combat performance, Higginson directed the commission's attention to the important role the army could play in raising the former slaves to "manhood." To this end, his troops had been "thoroughly tested in what may be called guerrilla warfare." He believed that an "education for men" best began "under fire in skirmishes." But the education could not stop there. His men had to be "empirically tested" in a "great battle," waged according to the rules of civilized warfare, before their manhood could be consummated.[25]

In order to support his demands for battlefield combat, Higginson emphasized the fine military qualities in the Negro's character. Foremost of these was a willingness to obey orders and an implicit faith in the officers.

Because discipline and training were key features of battlefield performance, Higginson believed the employment of black troops should not be limited to "a sort of guerrilla force." They should be "brigaded and thoroughly trained to fight in masses." When the commission probed this response and asked whether he was willing to trust colored men in the execution of "separate, distinct and isolated duty," Higginson boldly asserted that "it is not a question of color but of training. I should not have the slightest solicitude respecting my men if they had been properly trained for fighting in mass." Such remarks underscored Higginson's pride in his ability to train and discipline his men. In addition, they point to Higginson's belief in the educative powers of the officer corps. He firmly believed that the best officers were those who most closely resembled classroom teachers. "The officer makes command, as surely as, in educational matters, the teacher makes the school," wrote Higginson in the September 1864 issue of the *Atlantic Monthly*.[26]

Higginson wanted his troops to fight "in mass" partly because he believed they lacked self-reliance and "depended more upon their officers than white troops." In his opinion, the blacks' combat performance was modeled on that of their officers. "If their officers are intimidated they will be, and if their officers stand they will also." Higginson believed that battlefield command structures would ensure that the fighting spirit of the black soldiers could be fully controlled and exploited.[27]

Although Higginson was opposed to general campaigns of guerrilla warfare, he did not object to individual acts of justified retribution. In January 1863, during the St. Marys River expedition, he set the small town of St. Marys, located on the Georgia-Florida border, ablaze. Six months later, while on an expedition on Edisto Island, South Carolina, Higginson allowed liberated slaves to appropriate some of their masters' property. Even though these acts of retribution appeared to have some of the features of a guerrilla campaign, their motivation was very different. By imposing measured acts of retribution, Higginson believed that he was reinforcing the codes of civilized warfare. The Edisto slaves were able to take portable property from their masters because, he reasoned, it belonged to them. Higginson considered it their wages for having been slaves. However, Higginson did not permit the former slaves to engage in wanton plunder. In *Army Life in a Black Regiment*, Higginson commented that "no dwelling-houses were destroyed or plundered by our men,—Sherman's 'bummers' not having yet arrived." The burning of St. Marys also had a higher purpose, he explained. Union forces had been repeatedly fired on as they left this town. In his journal Higginson noted that "in such cases it is one's duty to burn the town."

Clearly, the Rebel civilians had to be taught a harsh lesson, a lesson to leave the fighting to the soldiers. After all, Higginson observed, "nothing benefits the manners like piracy."[28]

Higginson was acutely aware that he was engaged in a higher form of conflict, one that was far removed from the Kansas frontier. The conflict in Kansas had been essentially a war between border ruffians and bushwhackers, white frontiersmen living on the margins of society, far removed from the heartland of civilized society. Higginson believed that the Civil War differed from the Kansas conflict because it was a struggle for national survival. He interpreted the Civil War as a clash of cultures, a contest between Yankee civilization and Southern barbarism. "The ordeal by battle is a stern test of a nation," he reminded his *Atlantic Monthly* readers in 1861. Higginson confidently predicted a Union victory because the North was modern, progressive, educated, and "civilized." In contrast, the South had "made the mistake of confounding barbarism with strength." A militant abolitionist and an influential member of the Massachusetts intellectual elite, Higginson welcomed an opportunity to use the army as a vehicle to "elevate" black manhood and to demonstrate what he believed was the moral superiority of the North over the corrupt, proslavery South. The recruitment of Southern blacks into the Union Army was therefore of paramount importance to him not only because it dealt a telling blow to slavery, but also because it exposed the former slaves to an institution that encapsulated the North's moral and social values. In a letter to his friend George L. Stearns, Higginson noted that "military organization is certainly what these people need above all." Higginson firmly believed this, but then so too did Colonel James Montgomery, John Brown's lieutenant, who arrived in the Department of the South in January 1863.[29]

Montgomery arrived in the department in early January 1863 while Colonel Higginson was away on the St. Marys expedition. When he returned, Higginson warmly welcomed his old comrade, believing his presence in the department would give considerable impetus to black recruiting. Montgomery's reputation as a freedom fighter preceded him. "He understands my system of warfare exactly. He is a natural chieftain, and knows how to lead," John Brown explained to Richard J. Hinton, a British-born abolitionist, in 1858. Dr. Seth Rogers, Higginson's close friend, observed that he "had rarely heard" Higginson "express deeper confidence in any one." However, as Colonel Higginson became more familiar with Montgomery's strategy of plundering the Rebels and living off their land, he became increasingly disturbed. In July 1863 Higginson noted in his journal that he was pleased he was not brigaded with Montgomery, because Montgomery would "chafe so much" from serving under him. Then he added it would be "such hard work to coerce him into my notions of civilized warfare." Higginson considered Montgomery's "western" or "frontier" methods of fighting so "impulsive and changeable" that no sound military strategy could be developed from them. While not denying that Montgomery's guerrilla raids brought ample concrete rewards in the form of cotton and ex-slaves, Higginson nevertheless was disturbed about the impact these raids had on the black soldiers' morale and fighting spirit. Moreover, he believed only conventional warfare would enable the black soldier to gain military credibility and standing. Higginson was also disturbed by Montgomery's vigorous drafting campaign and harsh discipline. It was common knowledge that deserters from his regiment faced the threat of execution without even the formalities of a court-martial.[30]

A religious zealot, Montgomery lacked Higginson's indulgent, fatherly concern for his soldiers. When, on September 30, 1864, Montgomery addressed the 54th Massachusetts Volunteers, a regiment composed of free Northern blacks, and urged them to discard their campaign for wage justice, he declared: "You are a race of slaves. A few years ago your fathers worshipped snakes and crocodiles. Your features partake of a beastly character." Yet he claimed the situation was not hopeless. "You can be improved by education," Montgomery assured the men of the 54th. He believed that the army would play a vital role in this education because it would raise the slave to manhood by making him a Christian soldier. The "religious element is the only foundation on which we can build, in making soldiers of these freedmen," Montgomery informed Adjutant General Lorenzo Thomas. Montgomery wanted to make "the regiment a school in which the people may be prepared, not only for military duty, but for all the privileges and duties of social and civil life." Because he saw his men as degraded sinners in need of freedom and salvation, Montgomery encouraged his regiment's chaplain, the Reverend Homer H. Moore, to impose a strict Christian regime on his flock. In his chaplain's report of June 1, 1864, Moore wrote that "strict temper is the law of the camp." There was, allegedly, no drinking of alcoholic beverages, no tobacco chewing, no card playing, and no profane language in Colonel Montgomery's camp. Every night, the "voice of praise and prayer" was heard. Such behavior was not surprising, for Montgomery believed he was on a mission to inflict divine retribution on the slaveholding South; so each of his combat missions invoked God's blessing by beginning with a special church service.[31]

"Raid of Second South Carolina Volunteers among the Rice Plantations of the Combahee; from a Sketch by Surgeon Robinson." (Harper's Weekly, *July 4, 1863, N.C. Division of Historical Resources, Raleigh*)

On June 1, 1863, Colonel Montgomery led his newly organized regiment, the 2nd South Carolina Volunteers, on a daring raid up South Carolina's Combahee River. Assisting Montgomery in his venture was "General" Harriet Tubman, John Brown's chief spy.[32] Two days after its departure the expedition returned, an outstanding success. Confederate resistance had been so disorganized and intermittent that even Captain John F. Lay, the Confederate officer investigating the raid, reported that the expedition's "success was complete." The toast of Port Royal, Montgomery received much favorable comment in the Northern press, the *Boston Commonwealth* describing the raid as "a glorious consummation."[33]

Montgomery's raid marked a significant departure in the combat strategy heretofore employed in the Department of the South. Whereas Higginson's raids up the St. Marys and St. Johns Rivers had been primarily recruiting and foraging expeditions, Montgomery's Combahee River venture was a "western" guerrilla raid. The target of the raid was the wealthy rice planters' property that lined the river. Sluices were opened, fields were flooded, and mansions were burnt. Captain Lay called Montgomery's expedition an "Abolition raid" and concluded his official report by accusing Montgomery of having "disregarded all the rules of civilized warfare": his troops had "acted more as fiends than human beings." Even Higginson had reservations about Montgomery's methods of warfare. He admitted that Montgomery's "concepts of foraging were rather more Western and liberal than his." Although Higginson thought the Combahee raid was "a most brilliant success," he did not approve of "burning private houses."[34]

The commander of the Department of the South, Major General David Hunter, was particularly attracted to Montgomery's style of guerrilla warfare. His service in Montgomery's homeland as commander of the Department of Kansas (November 20, 1861–March 11, 1862), had left him well disposed to irregular warfare. An aggressive abolitionist, Hunter refused to wait for Washington's authorization to liberate and arm the slaves. In May 1862 he issued orders to free slaves in the Department of the South and to conscript blacks. These measures ran far ahead of Federal government policy and were disowned by Lincoln.[35]

On the day Montgomery returned from the Combahee expedition, Hunter informed Governor Andrew of Massachusetts that Colonel Montgomery had taken "but the initial step of a system of operations" that would "rapidly compel the Rebels, to withdraw all their slaves into the interior." This would leave "desolate the most fertile and productive of their counties along the Atlantic Seaboard." A few days earlier Hunter had sought permission from Lincoln to lead an army from the sea into the heartland of Georgia. This army would grow as thousands of liberated slaves joined its ranks. To arm these freedmen, Hunter requested that the War Department supply him with pikes. Yet Hunter was careful to reassure the government he was not seeking to provoke a chaotic, bloody servile insurrection. In a letter to Secretary of War Edwin M. Stanton, dated April 30, 1863, he asserted that the black troops who would spearhead this army of liberation had performed so nobly that "even our enemies . . . have not yet been able to allege against them a single violation of any of the rules of civilized warfare." Despite the lack of official interest in his proposed grand army of liberation, Hunter nonetheless continued to lobby for it even after he left the Department of the South.[36]

The question of "civilized warfare" and servile insurrection found expression in the department over the issuing of pikes rather than muskets to black soldiers. Perhaps this was so because many remembered that when

John Brown entered Harpers Ferry on October 16, 1859, he brought with him one thousand pikes to arm the rebellious slaves that he envisioned would form his army of liberation. On July 1 Captain John Appleton, 54th Massachusetts Volunteers, noted that "rumors were flying about" that the colored troops were going to be issued pikes. "We will resign," was the immediate cry that went up from the officers among the 54th Massachusetts Volunteers. However, gradually the mood changed. Appleton admitted that "he would not leave" his men behind and resign, "just when they needed me most." Most other officers adopted a similar stand. Appleton believed that "the Colonel had some trouble" convincing his superiors to abandon the policy. "Pikes against Minie balls is not fair play—especially in the hands of negroes whose great pride lies in being a soldier like white men," commented Colonel Shaw in a letter to his father. Shaw believed that soldiers who were armed only with pikes would be forced to fight like rebellious slaves and would be denied an opportunity to wage war in the way that trained, patriotic, white Union soldiers did. "I shall escape that," Shaw reassured his father, because his regiment was composed of free men. But the destiny of those commanding ex-slave regiments was less certain, Shaw believed; "Montgomery & Higginson . . . will have to come to it, unless the plan is given up." Fortunately for Montgomery and Higginson, the "plan was given up."[37]

Barely a week after the Combahee raid, Montgomery set out on an even larger expedition up Georgia's Altamaha River. During the course of this raid, Darien, Georgia's second largest port, was razed to the ground by Montgomery's troops. This event might have gone unreported by the Northern press, had it not been for the fact that black troops from Montgomery's 2nd South Carolina Volunteers and Shaw's 54th Massachusetts Volunteers were the "arsonists."[38]

Robert Shaw arrived in the Department of the South early in June 1863. Although he was enthusiastic in thinking that his regiment might strike a blow against slavery, Shaw nonetheless was uncertain about how his troops would perform on the battlefield. His perception of his soldiers' abilities was influenced by his racial prejudice. In letters written to friends early in the war, Shaw constantly referred to the blacks he encountered as "darkeys" and "niggers." These references became less common as Shaw became more familiar with the black troops serving under him. Nevertheless, his attitude toward his troops remained essentially condescending. Writing to his father in March 1863, Shaw described the enlistment and early training of his soldiers as if he were talking about a group of enthusiastic children. "We have

them examined, sworn in, washed & uniformed as soon as they arrive,—
and when they get into their buttons they feel about as good as a man can.
It is very laughable to hear the sergeants explain the drill to the men, as they
use words long enough for a Doctor of Divinity or anything else."[39]

Still, Shaw was motivated by a strong desire to "prove that a negro can be
made a good soldier," and he had great faith in the discipline and training
routines of the army. The alleged malleable nature of the Negro appealed to
him because he considered blacks more easily disciplined than white troops.
Shaw believed that African Americans would make a "fine army after a little
drill and could certainly be kept under better discipline" than "independent
Yankees."[40]

Because he was eager to engage in active combat duty, Shaw was pleased
that his regiment was placed in Colonel James Montgomery's brigade. On
June 5, 1863 he wrote to Governor Andrew, informing him that "Col. Montgomery is a good man to begin with, and though I don't admire his Indian
style of fighting, it is certainly better suited to this country and use of small
force than others." Clearly Shaw had reservations about Montgomery's
method of fighting. Nevertheless, when that "strange compound," "Bush-
whacker Montgomery," decided to lead a raid up the Altamaha River into
Georgia, Colonel Shaw and two of his companies participated enthusiastically.[41]

On arriving at Darien, situated on the Altamaha River, Montgomery's
expedition found the township largely deserted. After shelling the town for
some time, the Union forces landed unopposed. Shaw ordered his troops
to move only under the strict command of their officers. He allowed them
to break into the abandoned houses on the condition that they took only
property that would prove "useful in camp." In contrast, Colonel Montgomery allowed his soldiers to break ranks and plunder and burn the town.
Disturbed by this apparent collapse in army discipline, Shaw refused to join
in what he considered to be wanton destruction.[42]

In defense of his action, Montgomery argued "that the Southerners must
be made to feel that this was a real war, and that they were to be swept
away by the hand of God, like the Jews of old." Shaw believed that while
this justification "in theory" seemed "all right to some," he did not want to
be "made the instrument of the Lord's vengeance." Shaw considered Montgomery's excuse—that "we are outlawed, and therefore not bound by the
rules of regular warfare"—intolerable. In Shaw's opinion, it was "none the
less revolting to wreak our vengeance on the innocent and defenceless."[43]

Shaw always had opposed "pillage" and "barbarous warfare." Writing to his wife in January 1863, he condemned white Union soldiers for outrages committed in the Western Theater: "the pillage our soldiers are allowed to do in the West, shows that the discipline there is even worse than ours." He took comfort from the fact that as a member of Major General Henry Warner Slocum's Twelfth Corps, Army of the Potomac, he had witnessed less "pillage" in Virginia than he "could have believed possible in so large an army." Shaw attributed this situation more to the "intelligence and character of our men, than to the discipline." More important than intelligence, character, and discipline, however, was family commitment. Because "the majority" of the men had "families at home the thought of them" prevented his white troops "from robbing and maltreating defenceless old people and women and children."[44]

Shaw believed that the free black soldiers in his regiment also possessed these attributes. Moreover, because they were commanded by abolitionist officers from the best families of Massachusetts, he considered it unlikely they would commit any "outrages." Shaw even found some assurance in the events surrounding the burning of Darien. There, temptation to "barbarism" was strong, but his black soldiers resisted it. Shaw asserted that "the men themselves behaved well. They plundered and destroyed only by order of the commanding officer." Yet Shaw had serious doubts about the "energy and spirit of the ex-slave contraband regiments." Along with other officers in the 54th, including Captains John Appleton and Cabot Russel, Shaw believed that the former slaves were inferior to free blacks.[45]

In Shaw's view, the burning of Darien jeopardized the experiment of enlisting blacks in the Union army. Colonel Charles Russell Lowell, 2nd Massachusetts Cavalry, a close friend, also shared this concern. Writing to Shaw's sister, Josephine Shaw, he commented: "I don't wonder Rob feels badly about this burning and plundering—it is too bad. Instead of improving the negro character and educating him for civilized independence, we are redeveloping all his savage instincts." Some leading abolitionists also expressed shock at the news of the Darien outrage. George L. Stearns wrote to Governor Andrew claiming that the Darien conflagration was "dirty work" and "unwanton vandalism."[46]

Yet condemnation was not a universal response. Black abolitionist Frederick Douglass believed that the burning of Darien was justified because the Confederate government had violated the rules of civilized warfare by pledging to execute the officers of black troops and threatening to return black soldiers to slavery.[47]

General Hunter, a strong supporter of guerrilla warfare strategies, also supported Montgomery's tactics during the Altamaha River raid. On the eve of Montgomery's departure, Hunter had given him a copy of General Orders No. 100, Francis Lieber's *A Code for the Government of Armies* (1863), which outlined the army's rules for destroying civilian property used to aid the rebellion. Armed with Lieber's text, Montgomery may well have believed that he was being given a license to wage "hard war" on the South. Indeed, Montgomery admitted privately to Shaw that his actions at Darien were consistent with Hunter's orders. Although this admission made Hunter the true villain in the case, it did little to restore Shaw's faith in Montgomery as a commander of black troops. At first, Montgomery claimed he had some reservations about following Hunter's orders to "destroy all dwelling places he might find," but then, on reflection, he "finally changed his mind" and burnt the town.[48]

The Darien affair presented Shaw with two major concerns. First, he feared that his regiment would become a mere guerrilla force deployed to incite slave rebellions and wage a war against Southern property and defenseless civilians. The Darien affair had filled him with "disgust," he said, because it violated the so-called rules of civilized warfare that heretofore even the Rebel slaveholders had conformed to. To prove his point, Shaw referred to Confederate general J. E. B. Stuart's raid of October 9–12, 1862, which circled Union general George B. McCellan's forces and penetrated as far north as Chambersburg, Pennsylvania. In his report to Governor Andrew on the Darien affair, Shaw admitted that the conduct of Union troops "was in singular contrast to that of Stuart, when he entered Pennsylvania last autumn." Second, Shaw was afraid that the unique identity of his regiment would be lost. He feared that under the command of Montgomery, his brigade commander, the 54th Massachusetts would become just another contraband regiment. The regiment's mission of vindicating the ideals of New England abolitionism would be lost. Shaw endeavored to overcome his worries by adopting two strategies.[49]

The first was to lobby hard to have Montgomery removed as the brigade commander of black troops. Shaw suggested his friend Brigadier General Frank Barlow as Montgomery's replacement. Well known in Massachusetts abolitionist circles, Barlow had a reputation as a good battlefield commander. Shaw dismissed Montgomery's claims for leadership by arguing that while he was "a very brave and energetic man," he nonetheless had "never seen anything but a bushwhacking sort of war-fare." Shaw discounted Higginson's claims for leadership by simply arguing that he "had no experience at all."[50]

Shaw's efforts in this regard were largely unrewarded. Frank Barlow never came to the Department of the South, but, fortuitously for Shaw, Montgomery's influence in the department waned because Montgomery's poor health forced him to take lengthy periods of leave. When Hunter was replaced as commander of the department by Brigadier General Quincy A. Gillmore in June 1863, that also worked against Montgomery. Hunter was removed from his command so that Gillmore could accomplish what Hunter had failed to do, namely, capture Charleston.[51]

Shaw's second strategy was to expose his men to battlefield combat. He argued that in the past his men had participated only in "little miserable expeditions." Now they needed "a fair stand up fight, such as our Potomac Army is accustomed to." Shaw knew that the military reputation of his troops could only be made on the battlefield. Shortly after he had changed his mind and accepted Governor Andrew's offer to command a Massachusetts black regiment, he wrote to his sweetheart, Annie Haggerty, informing her that what "he had to do" was make the Negro a "good soldier." "All sensible men in the army, of all parties, after a little thought," believed that this was "the best thing" that could be done. He argued that those who opposed this initiative, "who are not brave or patriotic enough to enlist," should not ridicule the black patriots who were "going to fight for them." It was precisely because Shaw linked black enlistment to notions of American patriotism that he was so anxious to avoid having his regiment's reputation tarnished by Montgomery's "Indian" warfare. After all, the 54th Massachusetts Infantry had been raised in the Bay State to help save the Union, not to ignite servile insurrections.[52]

Even though Shaw believed blacks would "probably make a fine army after a little drill," doubts lingered in his mind about his soldiers' performance in battle. In the past he had even discussed with Higginson the possibility of placing his Massachusetts troops "between two fires . . . and so cutting off their retreat." In order to press his case for active combat, Shaw wrote to his brigade commander, Brigadier General George C. Strong, informing him that the 54th Massachusetts was "capable of better service than mere guerrilla warfare." Shaw wanted his black troops to fight alongside white troops "in order that they may have other witnesses besides their own officers to what they are capable of doing."[53]

Within two days Shaw had his reply. His regiment, one part of General Alfred Terry's division, would make a diversionary attack on James Island. In the course of the attack, the 54th Massachusetts Infantry distinguished itself by fighting a dogged rearguard action that saved the 10th Connecticut and probably General Terry's entire division. Colonel Shaw had every reason to feel satisfied. On July 15 he proudly wrote to his wife, informing her that "what we have done to-day wipes out the remembrance of the Darien affair."[54]

Although Colonel Shaw returned from the St. James Island expedition with a regiment of tired and hungry men, he gladly grasped at the opportunity to lead the renewed attack on Battery Wagner, a fort guarding the entrance to Charleston Harbor.[55]

In spite of a valiant charge by the 54th Massachusetts seven days later, Battery Wagner did not fall. A military failure, the unsuccessful attack by the 54th Massachusetts nevertheless had two positive results. First, the courage displayed by the black Massachusetts soldiers helped to convince skeptics in the North that the African American would fight for the Union and his freedom in a heroic manner and according to the conventions of war. Second, Shaw's death on the ramparts of the fort became a powerful symbol of the nobility of the abolitionist cause.[56]

There is little doubt that during the period from November 1862 to July 1863 the military exploits of Colonels Thomas Higginson, Robert Shaw, and James Montgomery in the Department of the South gave considerable impetus to the experiment to arm the black man. The combat performance of each unit commander contributed to the nation's war effort by proving that the black soldier would fight for his freedom and the Union. Yet the courage and patriotism of these commanders and their soldiers was not unique. Elsewhere in the South, black troops fought bravely at Port Hudson, Louisiana, in May 1863 and Milliken's Bend, Louisiana, in June 1863. What was distinctive about the Department of the South was the extensive and generally positive publicity that surrounded the military service of Colonels Higginson and Shaw. This appeared to vindicate not only the fighting qualities of black soldiers but also the powerful gospel of New England abolitionism. However, this vindication was never assured. On a number of occasions, Montgomery's guerrilla tactics and Hunter's grand military strategies threatened to undermine the experiment to arm the black Southerners.[57]

Higginson and Shaw represented particular strains of Massachusetts abolitionism that strongly opposed what they considered to be "uncivilized" warfare. While they were prepared to take their troops on foraging and recruiting raids, they condemned "uncivilized" guerrilla campaigns that deliberately targeted the homesteads and property of the Southern civilian population. Their opposition to this form of irregular warfare rested firmly on their social and racial beliefs. As a New England Brahmin, Robert Shaw wanted to fight a war that would honor his class and enhance its "aris-tocratic" leadership. Thomas Higginson, in contrast, was motivated by his militant abolitionism. He saw the war primarily as a clash of civilizations: the civilization and higher learning of the North versus the barbarism of the feudal South. Higginson expected the North would win simply because the Yankee citizen soldier represented the values of a more civilized society.

Essentially paternalist in outlook, Shaw and Higginson believed that black troops were emotionally unstable and lacking in self-reliance. They therefore feared how blacks would perform in guerrilla warfare. Given these racial parameters, Shaw and Higginson believed that black troops would make good soldiers only if they were subject to the discipline of the battlefield. Both Shaw and Higginson believed that black troops should be removed from campaigns of guerrilla warfare to combat positions on the battlefield. There, they believed, the troops would learn the art of civilized warfare from the elite officer corps that commanded them and from the example of the white citizen soldiers who fought alongside them.

Montgomery's abolitionism, bred in the West, differed significantly from that of Shaw and Higginson. A disciple of John Brown, Montgomery be-lieved he was waging a holy war against Southern slavery. Because he saw the Civil War essentially as the consummation of the Bleeding Kansas conflict, he waged "western" guerrilla warfare on the Rebels. Notions of "civilized warfare" meant little to him because they were not part of his military ex-perience. While he blamed slavery for brutalizing Southern blacks, Mont-gomery believed guerrilla warfare provided them with the best opportunity of seeking just revenge on their ex-masters.

This analysis of the different strains of abolitionism that shaped black military experience in the Department of the South suggests areas for future historical research. Historians James M. McPherson and Mark Grimsley both point to the issuing of the Emancipation Proclamation as a critical phase in the development of the Civil War. They argue that Lincoln's proc-lamation contributed to the blurring of the distinction between Southern civilians and Rebel soldiers. This evolution toward what McPherson calls "total war" and Grimsley calls "hard war" escalated with the movement and promotion of "fighting" generals such as Henry W. Halleck and Ulysses S. Grant from the West to commands in the East. The pursuit of "hard war" occurred first in the Department of the South, which Civil War historians should find a rich and challenging field for further study. War in this mili-tary department linked the employment of black troops with the evolving nature of legitimate warfare.

Notes

The author would like to thank the School of Humanities, Communications and Social Sciences, Monash University, for a research grant he received to help complete this essay.

1. J. W. M. Appleton Letterbook, June 28, 1863, 32–33, West Virginia University Library, Morgantown (hereafter cited as WVUL).

2. For a description of the Port Royal Experiment and the enlistment of black troops in the South Carolina Sea Islands, see Willie Lee Rose, *Rehearsal for Reconstruction: The Port Royal Experiment* (New York: Vintage Books, 1967), and James M. McPherson, *The Struggle for Equality: Abolitionists and the Negro in the Civil War and Reconstruction* (Princeton: Princeton University Press, 1972), 158–60, 162–69, 172–73, 175–77, 195–202.

3. Rose, *Rehearsal for Reconstruction*, xiii–xvi, 193–95; McPherson, *The Struggle for Equality*, 192–95, 197.

4. Reid Mitchell, *The Vacant Chair: The Northern Soldier Leaves Home* (New York: Oxford University Press, 1993), 55–56; McPherson, *The Struggle for Equality*, 197–98. For a discussion of Higginson's contribution to the abolitionist movement and black military service during the Civil War, see Tilden G. Edelstein, *Strange Enthusiasm: A Life of Thomas Wentworth Higginson* (New York: Atheneum, 1970); Howard N. Meyer, *Colonel of the Black Regiment: The Life of Thomas Wentworth Higginson* (New York: W. W. Norton, 1967); Mitchell, *The Vacant Chair*, chap. 4.

5. Ira Berlin, Joseph P. Reidy, and Leslie S. Rowland, eds., *The Black Military Experience* (Cambridge: Cambridge University Press, 1982), 86–87; Benjamin Quarles, *The Negro in the Civil War* (Boston: Little, Brown, 1969), 8–9; R. Shaw to Father, May 7, 1861, in Robert Gould Shaw, *Letters: RGS* (Cambridge, Mass.: Harvard University Press, 1864), 31; Peter Burchard, *One Gallant Rush: Robert Gould Shaw and His Brave Black Regiment* (New York: St. Martin's Press, 1965), 6, 14, 25; George M. Fredrickson, *The Inner Civil War: Northern Intellectuals and the Crisis of the Union* (New York: Harper Torchbooks, 1968), 151–56. For discussion of Robert Shaw's service with black troops see Burchard, *One Gallant Rush*; chaps. 10–18; Dudley Taylor Cornish, *The Sable Arm: Negro Troops in the Union Army, 1861–1865* (1956; New York: W. W. Norton, 1966), 148–56; Russell Duncan, ed., *Blue-Eyed Child of Fortune: The Civil War Letters of Colonel Robert Gould Shaw* (Athens: University of Georgia Press, 1992), 21–56, 282–388; Luis F. Emilio, *A Brave Black Regiment: The History of the Fifty-fourth Regiment of Massachusetts Volunteer Infantry, 1863–1865* (1891; New York: Arno Press, 1969); Fredrickson, *The Inner Civil War*, 151–56; Joseph T. Glatthaar, *Forged in Battle: The Civil War Alliance of Black Soldiers and White Officers* (1990; New York: Meridian, 1991), 136–41; James M. McPherson, *Drawn with the Sword: Reflections on the American Civil War* (New York: Oxford University Press, 1996), 99–109; Gary Scharnhorst, "From

Soldier to Saint: Robert Gould Shaw and the Rhetoric of Racial Justice," *Civil War History* 34 (December 1988): 308–22; Quarles, *The Negro in the Civil War*, 3–21. An important study of the role and legacy of Robert Gould Shaw and the men of the 54th Massachusetts Infantry has recently been published. See Martin H. Blatt, Thomas J. Brown, and Donald Yacovone, eds., *Hope and Glory: Essays on the Legacy of the Fifty-fourth Massachusetts Regiment* (Amherst: University of Massachusetts Press, 2001).

6. Cornish, *The Sable Arm*, 72–73, 78; Thomas Goodrich, *War to the Knife: Bleeding Kansas, 1854–1861* (Mechanicsburg, Pa.: Stackpole Books, 1998), 213–15, 218–19, 249, 252; John Van De Mark, "James Montgomery" (B.A. thesis, Washburn College, 1906), Kansas State Historical Society, Topeka (hereafter cited as KSHS); J. Montgomery to Robinson, August 3, 1862, J. Montgomery to G. L. Stearns, December 24, 1862, and J. Montgomery, "Sworn Statement Relating to Service in the War of Rebellion," June 12, 1871, James Montgomery Papers, KSHS; Geo. H. Hoyt to C. Robinson, August 13, 1862, Private Papers of Charles and Sara T. D. Robinson, KSHS; J. Montgomery to G. L. Stearns, December 26, 1862, George L. Stearns Papers, KSHS.

7. Fredrickson, *The Inner Civil War*, 152–55; Duncan, *Blue-Eyed Child of Fortune*, 245, 283; Blatt, Brown, and Yacovone, *Hope and Glory*, 54–55.

8. Thomas Wentworth Higginson, *Army Life in a Black Regiment* (1870; Williamstown, Mass.: Corner House Publishers, 1971), 41; Edelstein, *Strange Enthusiasm*, 143–44; Thomas Wentworth Higginson, "Fair Play the Best Policy," *Atlantic Monthly* 15 (May 1865): 630.

9. Montgomery, "Sworn Statement Relating to Service in the War of Rebellion," June 12, 1871, James Montgomery Papers, KSHS; Donald Yacovone, ed., *A Voice of Thunder: The Civil War Letters of George E. Stephens* (Urbana: University of Illinois Press, 1997), 39, 61, 273–74, 277–79.

10. Goodrich, *War to the Knife*, 219; Fredrickson, *The Inner Civil War*, 155–56; Thomas Wentworth Higginson, "The Ordeal by Battle," *Atlantic Monthly* 8 (July 1861): 88–95; Duncan, *Blue-Eyed Child of Fortune*, 195.

11. Duncan, *Blue-Eyed Child of Fortune*, 126, 132, 180, 191, 339, 343.

12. Ibid., 256–57, 261, 270, 351–52.

13. Thomas Wentworth Higginson, "Regular and Volunteer Officers," *Atlantic Monthly* 14 (September 1864): 348–49.

14. Both historians Mark Grimsley and James M. McPherson employ different terminology to describe war being waged to demoralize and defeat the South by destroying its economic resources. Grimsley uses the term "hard war" rather than "total war" because "hard war" refers to the limited mobilization of Northern society and was a term used by the participants in the Civil War. An additional attraction is that the term "hard war" refers distinctly to the Civil War. McPherson recognizes the Civil War was not a "total war" in the same way that World War II was. However, he believes this term best describes the scale of

the war and the kind of war waged by Sherman as he marched to the sea and by Sheridan as he raided the Shenandoah Valley. See Grimsley, *The Hard Hand of War: Union Military Policy towards Southern Civilians* (Cambridge: Cambridge University Press, 1995), 3–5; McPherson, *Drawn with the Sword: Reflections on the American Civil War* (New York: Oxford University Press, 1996), 67–69, 77–79, 83–85; Joseph T. Glatthaar, *Partners in Command: The Relationship between Leaders in the Civil War* (New York: Free Press, 1994), 144, 151, 153–54, 202–5; Major General W. T. Sherman to Major General U. S. Grant, October 4, 1862, in *The War of Rebellion: A Compilation of the Official Records of the Union and Confederate Armies*, 128 volumes (Washington, D.C.: Government Printing Office, 1880–1901), 1st ser., 17 (2):260–62 (hereafter cited as *OR*); Joseph T. Glatthaar, *The March to the Sea and Beyond: Sherman's Troops in the Savannah and Carolinas Campaigns* (1985; Baton Rouge: Louisiana State University Press, 1995), 133–35.

15. Issued in April 1861, the First Confiscation Act stated that a master who permitted his slaves to be used in Confederate service forfeited his claim to his slaves. In July 1862 the Second Confiscation Act freed all captured or fugitive slaves of Rebel masters and authorized the president to employ them in any way he thought necessary to crush the rebellion. The Militia Act, also issued in July 1862, enabled Lincoln to use "persons of African descent" as military laborers or in military or naval service "for which they may be found competent." The Emancipation Proclamation issued on January 1, 1863, freed slaves in Rebel-held territory and permitted their enlistment into military service to garrison forts and other military installations. See Berlin et al., *The Black Military Experience*, 4–5, 7–8; General Orders No. 100, April 24, 1863, *OR*, 3rd ser., 3 (3):148–64; Grimsley, *The Hard Hand of War*, 3–6, 13–17, 141, 144–50. Published in May 1861, Halleck's *International Law; or, Rules Regulating the Intercourse of States in Peace and War* drew heavily on Emmerich de Vattel's *The Law of Nations; or, Principles of the Law of Nature Applied to the Conduct and Affairs of Nations and Sovereigns* (London: G. G. and J. Robinson, 1797). See Grimsley, *The Hard Hand of War*, 1–16. General Orders No. 100 was commonly know as "Lieber's Code" because it drew heavily on two books written by Francis Lieber, *Manual of Political Ethics*, 2 vols. (1837; Philadelphia: J. B. Lippincott, 1890), and *On Civil Liberty and Self Government* (1853; Philadelphia: J. B. Lippincott, 1859). Lieber, a German-born jurist, admired John Brown's Harpers Ferry raid and actively campaigned against slavery. See Grimsley, *The Hard Hand of War*, 145–51; McPherson, *Drawn with the Sword*, 66–86; Mark E. Neely, Jr., "Was the Civil War a Total War?" *Civil War History* 37 (March 1991): 5–28; Eric T. Dean, Jr., "Rethinking the Civil War: Beyond 'Revolutions,' and the 'New Social History,' " *Southern Historian* 15 (1994): 28–50.

16. Higginson, *Army Life in a Black Regiment*, 225; Duncan, *Blue-Eyed Child of Fortune*, 339; Noah Andre Trudeau, *Like Men of War: Black Troops in the Civil War, 1862–1865* (Boston: Little, Brown, 1998), 63–64.

17. Although some soldiers from the 1st South Carolina Volunteers had already undertaken several forage expeditions along the coast of South Carolina and Georgia under the command of Lieutenant Colonel O. T. Beard, 48th New York Infantry, the regiment was not yet completely organized. Lieutenant Colonel O. T. Beard to Brigadier General R. Saxton, November 10, 1862, *OR*, 1st. ser., 14:191–92; T. W. Higginson, "Colored Troops under Fire," *Century Magazine* 54 (May 1897): 195; Higginson, *Army Life in a Black Regiment*, 61.

18. Edelstein, *Strange Enthusiasm*, 265–69; Glatthaar, *Forged in Battle*, 122; *OR*, 1st ser., 14:194–96, 198; Thomas Wentworth Higginson, Journal, February 4, 1863, Houghton Library, Harvard University (HUL). Higginson advocated the establishment of a chain of forts on the Eastern rivers deep in the heartland of the Eastern Seaboard slave states. These Union strongholds would be garrisoned by freedmen and would serve as recruiting bases. This plan received the enthusiastic endorsement of General Rufus Saxton. See *OR*, 1st ser., 14:194; T. Higginson to E. Atkinson, February 2, 1863, Edward Atkinson Papers, Massachusetts Historical Society, Boston (hereafter cited as MHS); T. Higginson to Governor Andrew, January 17, 1863, Executive Department Letters Received, 21b, 10, Massachusetts State Archives, Boston (hereafter cited as MSA).

19. *New York Times*, February 10, 1863; *New York Tribune*, February 11, 1863; *Christian Recorder*, February 14, 1863; Glatthaar, *Forged in Battle*, 123; Meyer, *Colonel of the Black Regiment*, 227.

20. *OR*, 1st ser., 14:232–36, 423; Higginson, *Army Life in a Black Regiment*, 99–100, 118, 125–29; T. W. Higginson, "The Reoccupation of Jacksonville in 1863," in *Civil War Papers Read before the Commandery of the State of Massachusetts, Military Order of the Loyal Legion of the United States*, 2 vols. (Boston: Published by the Commandery, 1900), 2:467–68, 473–74; Edelstein, *Strange Enthusiasm*, 273, 276–77; Seth Rogers, War-Time Letters of Seth Rogers, M.D., Surgeon of the First South Carolina. Afterwards the Thirty-Third USCT, 1862–1863, January 28, March 27–30, 1863, Military Order of the Loyal Legion of the United States, Massachusetts Commandery Collection, U.S. Army Military History Institute, Carlisle Barracks, Pa. (hereafter cited as USAMHI).

21. Mary T. Higginson, *Thomas Wentworth Higginson: The Story of His Life* (1914; Port Washington, N.Y.: Kennikat Press, 1971), 194–95; Higginson, *Army Life in a Black Regiment*, 125–28; Higginson, Journal, March 13, 30, 1863, HUL; Rogers, War-Time Letters, January 28, March 29, 30, 1863, USAMHI.

22. Higginson, *Army Life in a Black Regiment*, 127–29; Higginson, Journal, April 23, 1863, HUL; Cornish, *The Sable Arm*, 141; *National Antislavery Standard*, April 18, 1863; *Boston Commonwealth*, April 10, 1863; Higginson, *Thomas Wentworth Higginson*, 195–96; *OR*, 1st ser., 14:235–36.

23. Edelstein, *Strange Enthusiasm*, 281–95.

24. Testimony of Colonel T. W. Higginson, 1863, American Freedmen's Inquiry Commission Files, no. 3, 175, O-328 1863, Letters Received, 12th ser., Record

Group 94, National Archives, Washington, D.C. (hereafter cited as RG 94, NA); Preliminary Report of the American Freedmen's Inquiry Commission, *OR*, 3rd ser., 3:430–54; Final Report of the American Freedmen's Inquiry Commission, *OR*, 3rd ser., 4:289–382; McPherson, *The Struggle for Equality*, 182–88; John G. Sproat, "Blueprint for Radical Reconstruction," *Journal of Southern History* 23 (February 1957): 25–44.

25. Higginson, *Army Life in a Black Regiment*, 73, 125; Higginson, Journal, March 30, 1863; Testimony of Colonel T. W. Higginson, 1863, American Freedmen's Inquiry Commission Files, File no. 3, 175–76, 193–94, O-328 1863, Letters Received, 12th ser., RG 94, NA.

26. T. Higginson to E. Atkinson, February 2, 1863, Atkinson Papers; Testimony of Colonel T. W. Higginson, 1863, American Freedmen's Inquiry Commission Files, File no. 3, 175–76, 193–94, O-328 1863, Letters Received, 12th ser., RG 94, NA; Higginson, *Army Life in a Black Regiment*, 10, 15; Higginson "Regular and Volunteer Officers," 355.

27. Testimony of Colonel T. W. Higginson, 1863, American Freedmen's Inquiry Commission Files, File no. 3, 176, O-328 1863, Letters Received, 12th ser., RG 94, NA; Glatthaar, *Forged in Battle*, 166.

28. Higginson, *Army Life in a Black Regiment*, 176; "The term 'bummer' mostly applied to the regular or everyday forages. Members of the Twentieth Corps, particularly easterners, tended to use the term to refer to self-appointed or unauthorized foragers, but most troops in Sherman's army considered a bummer anyone who foraged on a regular basis, or without authority." See Glatthaar, *The March to the Sea and Beyond*, 122; Higginson, Journal, February 4, 1863.

29. Colonel T. Higginson to Major G. L. Stearns, July 6, 1863, Letters Received by Adjutant General L. Thomas 1863–1865, ser. 363, Colored Troops Division, RG 94, NA; Higginson, "The Ordeal by Battle," 88–95.

30. Higginson, Journal, February 23–25, March 14, 23, 24, May 25, July 7, 1863, HUL; W. E. Burghardt Du Bois, *John Brown* (1909; Armonk, N.Y.: M. E. Sharpe, 1997), 92; McPherson, *The Struggle for Equality*, 6; Rogers, War-Time Letters, February 24, 1863, USAMHI; Higginson, *Army Life in a Black Regiment*, 114–15; Edelstein, *Strange Enthusiasm*, 284; J. Montgomery to Mrs. G. L. Stearns, April 25, 1863, George L. Stearns Papers, KSHS; J. W. M. Appleton Letterbook, June 28, 1863, WVUL; E. L. Pierce to T. G. Adams, September 10, 1863, J. Montgomery Papers, KSHS.

31. Yacovone, *A Voice of Thunder*, 273–74, 278–80; Colonel J. Montgomery to General L. Thomas, May 2, 1863, Letter and Endorsement Book, 34th USCI, Regimental Books and Papers USCT, RG 94, NA; Chap. Homer H. Moore to Brigadier General L. Thomas, M-48, 1864, Letters Received, ser. 360, Colored Troops Division, RG 94, NA; R. Shaw to Father, June 22, 1863 in Shaw, *Letters: RGS*, 370; Duncan, *Blue-Eyed Child of Fortune*, 343.

32. Rose, *Rehearsal for Reconstruction*, 243–48; Benjamin Quarles, *The Negro in the Civil*

War (Boston: Little, Brown, 1969), 226–27; Major General D. Hunter to E. M. Stanton, June 3, 1863, *OR*, 1st. ser., 14:463.

33. *Boston Commonwealth*, July 10, 1863, quoted in Rose, *Rehearsal for Reconstruction*, 247; Report of Captain John F. Lay, C.S. Army, Inspector of Cavalry, June 24, 1863, *OR*, 1st ser., 14:306, and see also 299–308.

34. Report of Captain John F. Lay, C.S. Army, Inspector of Cavalry, June 24, 1863, *OR*, 1st ser., 14:298, 306, and see also 290–308; Higginson, *Army Life in a Black Regiment*, 114; Higginson, Journal, June 16, 1863, HUL; Christopher Looby, ed., *The Complete Civil War Journal and Selected Letters of Thomas Wentworth Higginson* (Chicago: University of Chicago Press, 2000), 282; Rose, *Rehearsal For Reconstruction*, 247, see also 244–47.

35. Berlin et al., *The Black Military Experience*, 6–7, 38–39; Edward A. Miller, Jr., *Lincoln's Abolitionist General: The Biography of David Hunter* (Columbia: University of South Carolina Press, 1997), 99–103, and, for discussion of Hunter's role as commander of the Department of Kansas, see 77–87. Hunter served briefly as commander of the Western Department. See Miller, *Lincoln's Abolitionist General*, 75–76; Mark M. Boatner III, *The Civil War Dictionary* (New York: David McKay, 1959), 418–19; *OR*, 1st ser., 6:263–64, 14:333, 341, 3rd ser., 2:29–31, 42–43, 50–60. Treasury officials in the Sea Islands of South Carolina opposed Hunter's conscription policy because they feared that it would drain male labor from the plantations, undermine the experiment in free labor, threaten the islands' food supply, and impact negatively on the morale of the freedmen. See Berlin et al., *The Black Military Experience*, 38.

36. Major General D. Hunter to Governor Andrew, June 3, 1863, Executive Department Letters, Letters Received, 21b, Andrew Papers, MSA; Major General D. Hunter to Hon. E. M. Stanton, April 30, 1863, *OR*, 3rd ser., 3:177–79; Major General D. Hunter to E. M. Stanton, August 31, 1863, *OR*, 3rd. ser., 3:740; Miller, *Lincoln's Abolitionist General*, 142–44.

37. Geoffrey C. Ward, Ric Burns, and Ken Burns, *The Civil War: An Illustrated History* (New York: Alfred A. Knopf, 1990), 2; J. W. M. Appleton Letterbook, July 1, 1863, 35, WVUL; Duncan, *Blue-Eyed Child of Fortune*, 365–67. For General Hunter's comments on his hero John Brown and his plan to issue pikes to liberated slaves, see Miller, *Lincoln's Abolitionist General*, 124, 144.

38. For discussion of the sacking of Darien, see: E. Merton Coulter, "Robert Gould Shaw and the Burning of Darien, Georgia," *Civil War History* 5 (Fall 1959): 363–73; Cornish, *The Sable Arm*, 149–50; Duncan, *Blue-Eyed Child of Fortune*, 43–45, 331, 342–46, 361, 369; Burchard, *One Gallant Rush*, 105–11.

39. Duncan, *Blue-Eyed Child of Fortune*, 18, 304.

40. Ibid., 18.

41. Ibid., 285–86. Originally, the 54th Massachusetts Volunteers was to be sent to serve in Brigadier General Edward A. Wild's brigade under Major General J. G. Foster. However, Colonel Shaw successfully lobbied Governor Andrew to have

his destination changed to the Department of the South. While Shaw feared that
Foster would use black troops only for fatigue duty, he believed that Major Gen-
eral David Hunter would readily commit them to combat. See Duncan, *Blue-
Eyed Child of Fortune*, 332–34, 338–40, 348–49; R. Shaw to Governor Andrew,
June 5, 1863, Executive Department Letters, Letters Received, 21b, 145, MSA;
J. W. M. Appleton Letterbook, June 7, 8, July 1, 10, November 27, 1863, 26, 33,
42, 113, WVUL.

42. Duncan, *Blue-Eyed Child of Fortune*, 43–45; Burchard, *One Gallant Rush*, 108–9.
43. Duncan, *Blue-Eyed Child of Fortune*, 343.
44. R. Shaw to Annie, January 5, 1863, in Shaw, *Letters: RGS*, 241.
45. R. Shaw to Governor Andrew, June 14, 1863 in "Robert Shaw Letters," *Magazine of History* 18 and 19 (January–December 1914): 25–27; J. W. M. Appleton Letter-book, June 9, 1863, 23–24, WVUL; C. Russel to Father, June 14, 1863, Cabot Jackson Russel Papers, New York Public Library; L. F. E. Letters, June 11, 1863, Fifty-fourth Massachusetts Infantry Regiment Papers, MHS. Disgust at James Montgomery's fighting tactics did not stop the Massachusetts officers from sa-voring the spoils of victory. For months following the Darien raid, furniture plundered from the town littered the Massachusetts camp.
46. R. Shaw to Governor Andrew, June 14, 1863, "Robert Shaw Letters," 25–27; Dun-can, *Blue-Eyed Child of Fortune*, 343; Higginson, *Thomas Wentworth Higginson*, 207–8; G. L. Stearns to Governor Andrew, June 23, 1863, Executive Department Letters, Letters Received, 21b, 150, MSA; C. Lowell to Miss Shaw, June 20, 1863, in Edward W. Emerson, *Life and Letters of Charles Russell Lowell, Captain Sixth United States Cavalry, Colonel 2nd Massachusetts Cavalry, Brigadier-General United States Volunteers* (Boston: Houghton Mifflin, 1907), 261.
47. Duncan, *Blue-Eyed Child of Fortune*, 44.
48. During his June 1864 Shenandoah Valley raid, Major General David Hunter de-stroyed a considerable amount of civilian property. He also torched the Virginia Military Institute. See Grimsley, *The Hard Hand of War*, 166–67, 178–81; Major General D. Hunter to Colonel J. Montgomery, June 9, 1863, *OR*, 1st ser., 14:466–67; Major General D. Hunter to Governor Andrew, June 3, 1863, Executive De-partment Letters, Letters Received, 21b, Andrew Papers, MSA; R. Shaw to Gov-ernor Andrew, July 2, 1863, Executive Department Letters, Letters Received, 59, 101, MSA; Duncan, *Blue-Eyed Child of Fortune*, 348–49, 356–57, 378–79.
49. R. G. Shaw to Governor Andrew, June 14, 1863, quoted from extract from *Boston [Journal]*, April 10, 1864, in Andrew Papers, 21b, 146, MSA; James M. McPher-son, *Ordeal By Fire: The Civil War and Reconstruction* (New York: Alfred A. Knopf, 1982), 300; James M. McPherson, *Battle Cry of Freedom: The Civil War Era* (New York: Oxford University Press, 1988), 536–37, 561.
50. R. G. Shaw to Governor Andrew, June 14, 1863, quoted from extract from *Bos-ton [Journal]* April 10 1864, in Andrew Papers, 21b, 146, MSA. Shaw considered former slave soldiers to be considerably inferior to free black Northern soldiers

because they had been subjected to the tyranny of slavery rather than the edifying benefits of Northern culture. Brigadier General Francis Channing Barlow commanded the 1st Division of the Eleventh Corps. In 1856 he tutored Robert Shaw for his Harvard entrance examinations. Barlow eventually married Shaw's sister Ellen. See Duncan, *Blue-Eyed Child of Fortune*, 11, 89, 193, 354, 381.

51. Governor Andrew wrote Secretary of War Stanton urging him to appoint General Barlow to command a black brigade. In his letter he repeated the substance of Shaw's criticism of the command capabilities of Higginson and Montgomery. Stanton took no action, perhaps because Barlow was wounded and captured at Gettysburg only a few days after Stanton received Andrew's letter. Barlow was not exchanged until March 1864. He never commanded a black brigade. See Duncan, *Blue-Eyed Child of Fortune*, 381–82; John A. Andrew to E. M. Stanton, June 29, 1863, *OR*, 3rd ser., 3:423–24; Miller, *Lincoln's Abolitionist General*, 145–46.

52. Duncan, *Blue-Eyed Child of Fortune*, 123, 285–86, 339, 351.

53. Ibid., 123, 354; Higginson, *Army Life in a Black Regiment*, 226; R. Shaw to General G. Strong, July 6, 1863, quoted in Emilio, *A Brave Black Regiment*, 49; Cornish, *The Sable Arm*, 150–51.

54. Duncan, *Blue-Eyed Child of Fortune*, 385; Burchard, *One Gallant Rush*, 121–26; Cornish, *The Sable Arm*, 151–52.

55. Cornish, *The Sable Arm*, 152–53.

56. Two brigades took part in the attack. The First Brigade under the command of General George C. Strong led the assault with the 54th Massachusetts being in the vanguard. Behind the First Brigade came the Second Brigade, commanded by Colonel Haldimand S. Putnam. See Cornish, *The Sable Arm*, 152–56; Emilio, *A Brave Black Regiment*, 64–104; Glatthaar, *Forged in Battle*, 123–35; McPherson, *The Struggle for Equality*, 211–12; Quarles, *The Negro in the Civil War*, 13–21; Blatt, Brown, and Yacovone, *Hope and Glory*, pts. 1, 2.

57. Glatthaar, *Forged in Battle*, 123–35.

12

HENRY MCNEAL TURNER
Black Chaplain in
the Union Army
Edwin S. Redkey

The Civil War marked a radical transformation in the lives of all African Americans. This was especially true for the young black men who fought in the war: they saw new places, met new people, thought new thoughts, and for the rest of their lives remembered the war as the Great Event. Few of those men, however, became well known to the public, either white or black. Their regiments, such as the 54th Massachusetts Volunteers, or their white officers, such as Thomas Wentworth Higginson, became heroes for a while. And in some of their battles, such as Fort Wagner, Olustee, Milliken's Bend, and Port Hudson, they won praise for showing that blacks could and would fight to defend the Union. But most of the men themselves remained anonymous. One exception was Henry McNeal Turner.

For Turner (1834–1915) the Civil War became an intense, invigorating crucible for his energetic talents. He served a black infantry regiment as chaplain. In that role he developed some of the ideas, attitudes, and skills that became manifest in his later career, in which he became a Reconstruction politician, a powerful churchman, and a national race leader. While serving in the army, Turner refined his thinking about the African race and its future. He worked with the freedmen and wrestled with the problems of their new status. Two specific activities propelled him to wide attention among both blacks and whites in both North and South. First, his newspaper letters from the battlefield attracted many readers and admirers in the North, and they launched him on a lifetime of journalism. His frequent letters and articles helped elevate him in church and public affairs. Second, in the first months after the war ended, he used his position as army chaplain to lead emancipated freedmen into his all-black church; this represented a significant culture shift for the ex-slaves and left a permanent mark on the South.

Born free in Newberry, South Carolina, Turner learned to read and write at the knee of his grandmother. When he was apprenticed to work in cotton fields beside slaves, he ran away and found a more interesting job sweeping a law office in Abbeville. There he impressed the lawyers and clerks with his intelligence; despite South Carolina's laws against educating African Americans, they gave the ambitious boy the rudiments of an education.[1]

When he was seventeen, Turner had a religious conversion under the guidance of white ministers of the Southern Methodist Church. Recognizing his ambition and education, the Methodists licensed him in 1853 to preach. With this authority, he traveled through several Southern states preaching in churches and revival meetings to both black and white audiences. He visited New Orleans in 1857. There he learned for the first time of the all-black African Methodist Episcopal (AME) Church, founded in Philadelphia in 1793 and based in the Northern and border states. In 1858 Turner decided to leave the Southern Methodists and join the AME Church.

Daniel Payne, the senior AME bishop, recognized Turner's potential and arranged for the young man to go to Baltimore. There he would study Hebrew, Greek, Latin, and theology under the watchful eyes of senior ministers of several churches, both black and white. In the African American community of Baltimore, it soon became clear that this bright, ambitious young man, a scholar and a powerful preacher, was destined for leadership.

When the Civil War broke out, Turner was still training in Baltimore. In April 1862, just as the government abolished slavery in the District of Columbia, he was assigned to the largest AME church in Washington, Israel Church on Capitol Hill, near both the heart of government and the war in Virginia. Congressmen and army officers frequently visited to hear Turner preach.[2]

Early in 1863, shortly after President Abraham Lincoln issued the Emancipation Proclamation, the War Department decided to use black soldiers to fight the Confederacy. The federal government had reluctantly accepted black soldiers for limited duty in Louisiana, South Carolina, and Kansas, but as the war dragged on and casualties rose, the Union needed more men and began organizing black troops. Many whites in the North considered this, at best, an experiment: Would black soldiers fight white opponents? Could they be relied on in battle? Many outspoken white soldiers resented fighting beside the colored troops and did not want to salute black officers, so Secretary of War Edwin M. Stanton ruled that only white men with military experience should be commissioned officers in the colored regiments. Some African Americans refused to enlist unless they had some black officers.[3]

In Massachusetts, where the state recruited three regiments of black soldiers, Governor John A. Andrew compromised with the War Department: He would appoint no black officers to command the colored troops, but African Americans could serve as chaplains. They would be commissioned officers, but, instead of having gold braid on their uniforms, they would wear simple suits of black. Eventually, fourteen black clergymen served as Union army chaplains. They included several men who would gain prominence after the war. Among them were Benjamin F. Randolph, William Waring, and William H. Hunter. Randolph, who became state chairman of the Republican Party in South Carolina, was assassinated for political reasons. Waring became an attorney and trustee of Howard University. Hunter became long-time editor of the *Christian Recorder*.[4] None, however, achieved the public attention of Turner.

In Washington, Turner recruited vigorously for the local unit, urging both free-born and "contrabands" to enlist in the 1st United States Colored Troops (USCT). While the men trained, he came regularly to preach for them, reminding them that the destiny of their race depended on their loyalty and courage. On occasion the regiment marched in a body to Israel AME Church to hear one of his patriotic sermons. In July 1863 the regiment, having filled its quota of a thousand men, prepared to leave for the war zone. By that time an African American clergyman had already been commissioned in the 55th Massachusetts Volunteer Infantry Regiment. Turner, having urged black men to risk their lives to free the slaves, began campaigning to get himself appointed chaplain of the Washington regiment. In November, at age thirty, he finally received his commission, becoming the only black officer in the 1st USCT.

Chaplain Turner discovered that the duties of a Union army chaplain in the Civil War were not well defined. Before the war, chaplains had only to teach school at army posts. When the war came those educational duties broadened to include holding worship services and prayer meetings, visiting the sick and wounded in hospitals, and burying the dead. Each chaplain had to work out his role in his regiment according to the expectations of his fellow officers, his men, and his own interests and talents.[5] For an energetic, ambitious man like Turner, the chaplaincy provided a tremendous opportunity to grow in influence. As soon as he had received his commission his portrait appeared in the widely read *Harper's Weekly*, an auspicious beginning.[6]

Turner served as army chaplain for two years. Shortly after reporting for duty with his regiment in Portsmouth, Virginia, he caught smallpox and spent months in a hospital. During a convalescent leave, he went to Philadelphia to attend the 1864 Quadrennial Conference of the AME Church. He returned to his regiment in May, just in time to participate in its first battle at Wilson's Wharf on the James River. From May through December, his unit shared in the heavy fighting around Petersburg and Richmond. At year's end, the 1st USCT and other black units participated in the massive amphibious attack against Fort Fisher, near Wilmington, North Carolina. Turner spent the spring of 1865 with his men as they joined Sherman's march through North Carolina. When the fighting ended, he was sent to Roanoke Island to help supervise a large settlement of ex-slaves. After his discharge in late September, he received another army commission as chaplain of a different African American regiment, which was assigned to the Freedmen's Bureau in Georgia. But shortly after arriving there he resigned and left the army. He turned his attention to politics, civil rights, black nationalism, and the development among the Southern freedmen of the AME Church.[7]

While in the army, Turner developed a life-long passion for journalism. He would later publish and edit several different newspapers, including the *Southern Recorder*, the *Voice of Missions*, and the *Voice of the People*. But throughout his life he frequently wrote his ideas and observations in the *Christian Recorder*, the weekly paper published in Philadelphia by the AME Church. During the time he lived in Baltimore, he began writing letters and occasional articles for the *Repository*, a church monthly. When he moved to Washington in 1862, he assumed the role of regular correspondent for the *Christian Recorder*, telling of events in the city, his church, and the black community. Washington, of course, was no ordinary community, and Turner's articles included more and more comment on national issues, especially race issues. When he joined the army as a chaplain, he continued to write frequently for the *Christian Recorder* and occasionally for the other national African American paper, the New York *Weekly Anglo-African*.

There is no precise measure of the circulation of these newspapers. The African American press was in its infancy; the *Christian Recorder* had barely survived the 1850s, and the *Weekly Anglo-African* had begun publishing in 1859. Although the *Anglo-African* would die in 1865, the *Recorder* was to survive as part of the rapid growth of black journals in the post–Civil War years. The *Recorder* had a wide influence because it was the journal of the AME Church. Preachers throughout the church drew on its articles and letters for their sermons and lectures. At a time when much of the general press dealt in stereotypes of blacks, the black press brought news of real people, especially of the soldiers. Turner became the most widely read and discussed African American reporter.[8]

In his army letters to the newspapers, Chaplain Turner wrote about a variety of subjects. Some dealt with battle accounts, some with race issues, some with church affairs, and some with his personal concerns. All were marked by his distinctive writing style, a vigorous, clear prose that contrasted with the murky, abstract articles of many other writers in the papers. Where others were circumspect, he had no fear of taking sides on an issue and calling his adversaries "timber heads." Turner was capable of polysyllabic words, Latin quotations, convoluted sentences, opaque paragraphs, purple prose, and outright bombast. After criticizing the Republicans in 1864 for being too slow to end slavery, he laced into the "Copperhead" platform of the Democrats and their presidential candidate, General George B. McClellan. "Who would have thought that an American heart could . . . publicly endorse such audacious resolutions as those incarnate devils at Chicago formed as the basis of a presidential campaign?" he wrote. "They are enough to revolt human modesty, and turn our most pridish [*sic*] promptings into confusion and burning shame. Never let the American people stand aghast at any thing again."[9]

But because he realized that journalism was a powerful tool for reaching black people, Turner's writing was normally like his speech: simple, direct, blunt, sometimes aggressive or sarcastic. Even when he wrote under such pseudonyms as "Uncle Sam," readers easily identified his style. He wrote from the front near Petersburg, Virginia, that his readers should not look for "anything like rhetorical flourishes . . . nor even excellence in composition," he wrote. "I am actually on the field of battle. . . . A man thinks very little about the niceties of literature when the bombs and balls are flying around his head."[10]

Turner's letters attracted readers for their content as well as their style. He told about the war, sometimes in thrilling detail, from the perspective of the black soldiers. He described their battles, praised their courage, and argued with rivals and politicians. His on-the-scene reports gratified the readers at home who were starved for information about their men and for positive news about African Americans. Furthermore, his letters inspired others to write, sometimes to add details or to call attention to different regiments or to argue with Turner over who did most to win a battle.

Turner's battle accounts demonstrated his talent as a vivid reporter of dramatic events. His regiment fought at least a dozen engagements with the Rebels, and he considered it one of his duties to inform the folks at home about the life-and-death doings of their men. Few professional newspaper reporters covered the black troops, and when they did they usually based their stories on official accounts told by the generals.[11] Turner, however, wrote as a participant, and his reports shared the strengths and weaknesses of first-hand observations.

Turner attracted many readers by his vivid descriptions of the action. Writing of his first exposure to Rebel fire at Wilson's Wharf, he wrote, "I was retiring from dinner, feeling very jolly over the idea of having eaten once more of a fat chicken. . . . Notwithstanding many were at dinner, down fell the plates, knives, forks, and cups, and few moments only were required to find every man, sick or well, drawn into the line of battle to dispute twice, if not thrice, their number of rebels." He continued, "The coolness and cheerfulness of the men, the precision with which they shot, and the vast number of rebels they unmercifully slaughtered, won for them the highest regard of both the General and his staff, and every white soldier that was on the field." If he exaggerated the victory and glorified the work of his men, his excitement is understandable; they had for the first time been under enemy fire and had been a credit to themselves and to their race. As the war went on, he became more objective, but he continued to write with vigorous detail and energy.[12]

In a lengthy description of the fighting for Fort Fisher, North Carolina, Turner wrote:

It was a noble sight to see our troops hanging on to the sides of the fort like so many leeches sticking to an afflicted man. Each embrasure was formed by high mounds of earth being thrown up on each side of the guns; and after our troops gained a foothold on the fort, each party would stick to those mounds and fight around them. You would constantly see them, by two's and three's, fall off and roll to the bottom and there lay weltering in their blood and gore, manifesting the greatest agony amid the death heaves which, too often, lasted but a few moments. . . . I was going up to where they were fighting to help a wounded man. Three balls in rapid succession came right by my left ear, which I thought was a warning to go back, and I turned immediately and ran to the rear, but not too soon to escape a load of grape[shot], which would have swept me, in a moment's time, into eternity.[13]

As a participant-reporter, Turner was limited in what he could see, and he was therefore biased toward his own regiment. After the Battle at Wilson's Wharf he reported that "the 1st Regiment of United States Colored Troops, with a very small exception, did all the fighting."[14] On June 15, 1864, African American troops, including the 1st USCT, distinguished themselves in the Union attack against Petersburg. Turner described the action in detail and with great emotion. He wrote that "my regiment then led the advance, and drove the rebels some five or six miles, keeping up a continual skirmish all the time." He added, "My regiment, in the advance, and the rest of the colored troops, lay under the galling fire of the rebel forts."[15] Such myopic comments dot his letters, and to read Turner's descriptions one might think his regiment won the war single-handedly: "The brave boys of the 1st Regiment, who have never given way in any skirmish, nor in nine battles, nor have ever failed to take any works they charged, and who have the confidence of every General in our corps, were there, and they stood firm, while the rebels poured the most galling fire into them that I ever saw poured into so few men in my life, and it is well known I have seen war wonders."[16]

Chaplain Turner was fond of reporting his own exposures to the dangers of battle, but his style of journalism exposed him to a different kind of hostile fire. His fellow AME pastor, Chaplain William H. Hunter of the 4th USCT, wrote a scathing critique of Turner's reporting blunders. Reminding him that his reports were read by the men who participated in the action, Hunter attacked Turner's eager account of a dying man's last words and his misuse of military terminology. He had rendered himself "ridiculous in the sight of all military men."[17] A sergeant in another black regiment did not "see how the 1st USCT could have done so much, for they were our support. . . . I cannot see where the 1st charged, for they were in the rear."[18] Turner replied, "It is very natural for every one to look upon his own regiment with a jealous eye, and it is his unquestionable prerogative to delineate its virtues and traits of excellence to any extent he chooses. . . . But for a man to speak disparagingly of other regiments to exult over his own is mean. . . . Copperheads and [James Gordon] Bennett's infamous [New York] *Herald* would want no better food than to have a rumpus take place amongst the 'nigger soldiers.'"[19]

Probably no amount of criticism would have stopped Turner, who wrote compulsively. He heard suggestions that his letters to the *Christian Re-*

corder were written for self-aggrandizement, but he replied to "these self-conceited timber-heads" that the task of journalism, especially African American religious journalism, called for the talents of all who could write to give leadership "in shaping public sentiment, developing the capacities of the contrabands, [and] moralizing our soldiers, whose unbridled lives . . . have almost hurled them headlong into the vortex of irrevocable profanity, vulgarity, and impoliteness."[20] He urged others, especially AME ministers, to take up the pen: "Nothing would be read more pleasantly and to more profit than a good, plain, yet practical gospel sermon."[21] In the meantime, however, Turner himself would continue to write.

Writing for the public, of course, had its rewards for Turner. He knew that people throughout the AME Church and the black communities in the North were reading his reports, for they spoke or wrote to him directly about them. James Lynch, the AME missionary at Hilton Head, South Carolina, wrote to the *Christian Recorder* that "from the battlefield, brother Turner keeps us well informed, and with great interest are his articles read."[22] Turner complained that he received more letters than he could answer personally. "But those three young ladies who have been writing to me, complimenting my letters to the *Recorder*, and desiring to correspond on the subject of matrimony, will allow me to inform them that I am a married man."[23]

The two national African American newspapers, the *Christian Recorder* and the *Weekly Anglo-African*, became important educational tools for Chaplain Turner. As a pastor he had campaigned to get his parishioners to read the *Christian Recorder* in order to raise their literacy and awareness of church affairs. As a chaplain he urged his men to read the papers. The weeklies, he reported, are "dearly prized by many of our gallant soldiers, who, I am happy to say, are trying to prepare for whatever position the future may offer them. Nothing," he added, "could have inspired a more eager ambition into the men of my regiment, for literary attainments, than the vast number of *Recorders* and *Anglos* which weekly find their way into our different companies."[24] When they saw their peers reading the newspapers, those who were illiterate were driven by envy and by their chaplain's constant urging that they learn to read. The education of blacks would be a life-long commitment of Turner's, and his own example of journalism would be one of his most powerful teaching tools.

Inevitably, Turner's newspaper articles dealt with race and race relations. He fully expected the end of slavery to open doors for blacks to merge fully into American life as soon as education and Christian morality improved the freedmen. Pride in the talents and potential of his race showed in all his

Bishop Henry McNeal Turner. (Moorland-Spingarn Research Center, Howard University)

writing. "I claim for [the freedmen] superior ability. . . . The ablest historian, the greatest orator, and the most skillful architect and mechanic I have
ever seen were all slaves in the South. . . . The fact that one negro is smart
argues the possibility of another, and another ad infinitum."[25] Of course,
he despised slavery and what it had done to both the nation and the slaves.
But he wanted more for them than just freedom—he strongly urged that
African Americans should have full rights and opportunities to fulfill the
American Dream.[26]

Later in his life, Turner grew bitter about American whites and would
exhort blacks to "emigrate or die."[27] He discussed the topic early in 1865:
"I would suggest the propriety to the colored politicians north of investigating that momentous subject, EMIGRATION." Turner did not at the time
advocate leaving the United States, but he predicted that "as soon as this
rebellion is over, it will be the chief topic of every legislative department,
from Congress on down to town councils." He urged his readers to study
the question and be ready to take one side or the other.[28] Throughout the
war, he remained generally optimistic about the future of the race.

Even though he was an army officer, Turner did not hesitate to criticize
the federal government. While his regiment was fighting in the trenches
before Richmond, the 1864 campaign for the presidency pitted Abraham
Lincoln against General George B. McClellan. Despite assailing McClellan's
Democrats for being proslavery, he blasted the Republican Lincoln for being
too slow to free the slaves and use black soldiers. If only Lincoln had adopted
the early emancipation policy of General John C. Frémont, and "had half
the encouragement been tendered to the negro which has been given to the
Copperheads, the Union might have rallied today over two hundred thousand colored soldiers, who would have struck terror to the heart of the rebellion." Turner idealized the black soldiers, but given the Southern whites'
fears of slave uprisings, earlier use of black troops would have had strong
effect. And the chaplain's work itself proved that able and talented African
Americans could become effective leaders.[29]

For eighteen months, the federal government refused to pay black soldiers the same as whites, and even colored chaplains received only half of
what a white private was paid. Many black soldiers, especially those in the
54th and 55th Massachusetts (Colored) Infantry, loudly protested and refused to accept any pay at all until Congress passed an equal-pay law. Turner
thought it unwise to complain too directly about the problem, but in his
newspaper letter he let the white soldiers make the case. He wrote after
the battle at Wilson's Wharf that because of the heroic fighting by Afri-

can Americans that day, "The universal expression among the white soldiers was, *That it was a burning shame for the Government to keep these men out of their full pay*." Turner added, "I do not care if Congress and the entire administration see the remark, *that unless the colored troops get their full pay very soon, I tremble and fear for the issue of things*. . . . God grant that the evil may be speedily remedied."[30]

Tension between the races frequently erupted on the regimental level, where white officers commanded black soldiers. If the officers had abolitionist sympathies, the friction was reduced, and that seemed to be the case in Turner's regiment. His letters mentioned his fellow officers in complimentary terms. For example, when his commanding officer, Colonel John Holman, returned to the regiment from sick leave, Turner wrote, "Such a shout never was heard, as the boys gave him; one unanimous ring reverberated through the adjacent woods and over the hills."[31] But many officers in other colored regiments had obtained their commissions in order to get the pay and privileges of rank, not to aid the African Americans. Occasionally, black soldiers would write to the newspapers complaining about their racist officers. Turner warned against too much complaining; he criticized a particular letter in which the soldier "compares every [white] officer in a colored regiment to everything that is low and mean, doing, I think, great injustice to thousands of as pure-hearted men as ever God let live." The chaplain observed, "There are officers to my knowledge in colored regiments, who are worth their thousands at home . . . men who came in for the purpose of helping to educate and develop the mental faculties of the black man."[32] Turner understood that if he, himself, were to be treated as a man, he must respond to his white officers as individuals. The ultimate goal would be an integrated society where talent and ambition would break down racial barriers. Meanwhile, he told his readers, the army was a good place to start.

Southern white Rebels brought out a different reaction from the chaplain. Early in 1865, after the conquest of Fort Fisher, his regiment was sent across the Cape Fear River to Smithville, North Carolina, to occupy the town and recruit black soldiers among the freedmen. "The white people, nearly without exception, showed a bitter and chagrined countenance," he wrote. The white women, especially, objected to the presence of victorious black soldiers. On his second day in town, Turner visited the home of an elderly black lady who had invited him to dinner. Not knowing he was there, several white women came into the yard and began arguing with his hostess about some firewood. "She told them it was Yankee wood, not theirs, and the tongue battle raged most furiously for some minutes, when one of the white women called her a liar, with another expression too vulgar to mention." Turner then "rose up, met them at the door, and cried out, 'Halt!' They said, 'Who are you?' 'A United States officer,' was my reply. 'Well, are you going to allow that negro to give us impudence? . . . We want you to know that we are white, and are your superiors. You are our inferior, much less she.' " "Well," said Turner, "all of you put together would not make the equal of my wife, and I have yet to hear her claim superiority over me." The chaplain thoroughly enjoyed the discomfiture of the "Southern aristocracy," and he told such stories with a chuckle and a light heart. Undoubtedly, the newspaper readers enjoyed reading about the change in race relations at Smithville.[33]

Turner's two years in the army as chaplain and journalist saw him develop his writing skills and sharpen his ideas for an audience eager to hear from a bold, articulate, educated black man. Throughout the rest of his long and active life, he built on that army experience, often reminding his readers of his wartime exploits. A powerful, outspoken preacher, Turner had strong opinions on many topics, religious and secular, especially civil rights. He was too energetic and ambitious to limit his ministry to one congregation; the regiment widened his vision, but through journalism he reached a nationwide following, especially in the AME Church.

"Reconstruction" in the South began in practical terms as soon as the Union army occupied Southern territory. The army itself became the agent of profound changes because it personified the victorious North, enforced emancipation, and upset traditional institutions, including the churches. In 1865 Chaplain Turner played a significant role in the first phase of religious reconstruction, "the process by which southern and northern, black and white Christians rebuilt the spiritual life of the South."[34]

If the duties of an army chaplain were ill defined during wartime, they were even more wide open when the army occupied Southern territory. When the fighting ended in any particular region, chaplains helped the victorious army deal with the local civilians, both black and white. Right up to the very end of the war in May 1865, the army still needed more men, so chaplains were ordered to recruit new soldiers among the freedmen. Chaplain Turner relished this assignment, for it gave him opportunities for working directly with the newly emancipated slaves. Because there were no official regulations to forbid it, he seized the chance to see that the freedmen had black-led churches of their own.

Turner worried most, of course, about the fate of Methodist freedmen. The Methodist Church had split in 1845 over the issue of slavery. The two divisions called themselves the Methodist Episcopal Church, or Northern Methodists, and the Methodist Episcopal Church, South, or Southern Methodist Church. The Southern Methodists, combining evangelical zeal with strong support for slavery, enrolled many African American members, both slave and free; many of these black Christians, like Chaplain Turner, had been converted and brought into the church by the Methodist plantation missionaries who devoted themselves to evangelizing blacks.[35] Black members usually worshiped in the same congregations as their white colleagues, but they sat or stood in strictly regulated places. In some larger towns the colored Methodists had their own church buildings; in most cases pious whites had provided the buildings for them, but others were built by the blacks themselves with their own labor and money. Most such black churches had white pastors, who, whatever else they may have preached, supported Southern racial traditions. Some churches had black ministers, many of whom, like the young Turner, became excellent preachers; but they were carefully supervised by whites who insisted on being present at every meeting.

As Union forces occupied more and more of the South, there developed among Methodists an intense competition for the loyalty of black members. Southern Methodists, of course, wanted to retain the 200,000 African Americans whom they had worked so hard to evangelize and nurture in the faith.[36] But Northern Methodist leaders held that Southern Methodists had sinned by supporting slavery. Assuming that the freed slaves would prefer to switch to an antislavery church, they sent eager missionaries into the South to win over the freedmen. But these biracial churches, which wanted to include Southern blacks in their white-dominated organizations, had to deal with the agents of the two Northern-based African Methodist churches, Turner's AME Church and the similar but smaller AME Zion Church. Each of these organizations believed that it could best give spiritual and practical guidance to Southern blacks. And they were both quite confident that the freedmen would prefer to be in a black-led church. There was little difference between the two denominations—both had broken from the Methodist Episcopal Church in the 1790s as a reaction to racial discrimination. Both believed the same doctrine, sang the same hymns, and organized themselves the same way. But because each had started in a different city and developed on its own course with its own leaders and traditions, the two had remained separate, sometimes bitter rivals, each sending its own missionaries to contest with the leaders of the two white-led Methodist churches.[37]

Chaplain Turner became alarmed at one early development in the struggle. Secretary of War Edwin M. Stanton late in 1863 authorized Northern churchmen to take over church buildings and congregations in the disloyal South. For the Methodists, this meant that the Northern Methodists could control Southern Methodists' churches, regardless of whether the parishioners were white or black. Turner wrote an open letter to the leaders of the AME and AME Zion Churches warning them of the danger. "Several of the ministers of the Methodist Episcopal Church are chaplains in the army, and being very zealous for their Church, they lay hold of these colored churches with an eager impetuosity." This meant that they would take over buildings and property that rightfully belonged to the black members. Worst of all, he wrote, "they have actually ordained [colored] elders and deacons . . . for the purpose of securing their allegiance . . . regardless of the qualifications of such preachers." He would be willing to concede to the Northern Methodists all the white congregations of the Southerners, "but not the colored; for colored soldiers, too, are fighting the battles of this country [and are] justly entitled to some of the spoils."[38] When he later had an opportunity, he energetically courted those black Southern Methodists for the AME Church. If the white Methodist chaplains could go after those spoils, so could Turner.

Ultimately, of course, it would be the Southern blacks themselves who would choose their churches. Some would opt to stay with the paternalistic Southern Methodists, comfortable with the status quo and concerned lest they antagonize the dominant whites. But most would choose to leave and follow the "gospel of freedom" as proclaimed by the Northern missionaries, especially the black churchmen.[39] Over 130,000 of the 200,000 colored members would leave the Southern Methodist Church in the late 1860s. They did so for several reasons: simply to get away from oppressive white people, to have their own churches, to have independent black preachers, and to get church-sponsored schooling for themselves and their children. They would accept Northern missionaries, white or black, so long as they supported the goals of the colored Southerners.[40] As the fighting drew to a close, Turner prepared to proclaim the AME Church to be the answer to all these needs.

Despite the head start of the white Northern Methodist missionaries, the black Methodists also rushed to bring Southern blacks into their organizations. The AME Church began its wartime expansion into the South by establishing a congregation in Alexandria, Virginia, across the river from Washington, D.C. In the spring of 1863 the church sent missionaries to the Sea Islands of South Carolina to establish congregations of freedmen. Later in 1863 AME churches were organized in Norfolk and Portsmouth, Virginia, and Bishop Daniel Payne claimed two black Methodist churches in Nashville, Tennessee, for the AME Church. Long before the fighting ended, the race was on to win the allegiance of the black Methodists of the South.[41]

Although he believed strongly in the merits of his all-black AME Church, Turner had a broader experience than most AME clergymen, and he also believed in cooperation with other denominations, even with the AME Zionists. He had been converted and had begun his preaching career in his native South Carolina under the Southern Methodist Church, and he always had warm feelings for some of his white colleagues there. While living in Baltimore (1858–62) he had been tutored by ministers and scholars of several denominations. In Washington he had led interdenominational efforts to aid the freedmen and to recruit black soldiers. And in the army he found himself the chaplain to a thousand men of various faiths. Consequently, despite (or because of) his energetic concern for the salvation and advancement of African Americans, he was not narrowly partisan for the AME Church.

As Chaplain Turner realized, the picture in the South was complicated by the presence of the AME Zion Church. Efforts to unite the two groups had failed. Instead, mutual suspicion, jealousy, and criticism marked their relations. As an energetic Methodist and devoted to his fellow blacks, but unlike many of his AME colleagues, Turner deplored this division. If he had his way, the two churches would merge and present a united front to both the white and black Methodists of the South. Through much of his life, he would try to unify the two denominations.

Turner made a major attempt to unite the two churches in 1864. He was then on convalescent leave from his army duties, and he attended the first week of the General Conference of the AME Church, held in Philadelphia. The General Conference, composed mostly of the senior ministers (elders) and bishops of the denomination, met every four years to transact business for the entire church. The conference held in 1864 was the first that Turner was eligible to attend, but he was certainly not a bashful newcomer. His proposal for merger with the AME Zion Church caused a stir among his colleagues. He had to return to army duty before the conference could act on his plan, but a negotiating committee met with an AME Zion committee late in May, and a joint Unification Committee met in June 1864, while Turner's regiment was attacking Petersburg.[42]

One of the AME Zion clergymen on the negotiating committee was an energetic young man from New England, James W. Hood, who like Turner, was enthusiastic about union between the two black churches. A congregation in New Haven had sent him as a missionary to establish AME Zion churches in and around New Bern, North Carolina. It seems that several members of the New Haven church and AME Zion pioneer Christopher Rush had come from New Bern. Hood had taken Andrew Chapel, a large African American congregation, into his denomination and had started several smaller groups, including one on Roanoke Island, where many freedmen had settled. Late in May 1864, Hood went to Philadelphia for meetings with the AME delegates. His experience in the South had persuaded him of the value of a united black Methodist Church, and he, like Turner, wanted the two denominations to combine. But Turner was in Virginia, not in Philadelphia where his AME colleagues stalled, demanding that the union be postponed for four years. It is interesting to speculate on what the results of that meeting might have been if Turner had been able to attend and exert his leadership in the debates. In the meantime, each church would do its best to win black Methodists in the South. The fortunes of war soon brought Hood and Turner into direct competition.[43]

At the end of January 1865, Turner moved from Fort Fisher across the Cape Fear River to Smithville (now Southport), North Carolina. He stayed there a month and although he was on official duty for the army, Turner saw a civilian field ripe for harvest. He did not ask or wait for permission from the army or from the bishops of his church but began proclaiming the "gospel of freedom."

> The second evening after my arrival, I told three young men to inform the colored people that I wanted to preach to them at night, and for that purpose I selected a large room in the house which I occupy. I expected to see eighteen or twenty, but, to my surprise, over a hundred came out. With these I had quite an interesting meeting. . . . I was in a very good talking humor, and . . . I tried to borrow eloquent terms from the lyric strains of the celestial hosts, and, poor as was my success, yet my descantation upon freedom, liberty, and justice to all men, irrespective of color, produced the wildest excitement I ever witnessed.[44]

At the conclusion of that meeting, a bold Turner announced that he would hold another service the following day. Instead of assembling in a private room, they would meet in the courthouse. "This made their eyes open much wider than usual, for colored people were never admitted into the Court House heretofore." He planned to preach in the morning and the evening, and to "organize an AME Church there, at 3 o'clock in the afternoon."[45]

The morning service in the courthouse on February 5 was well attended by blacks and by whites, "who came to the door and saw this colored brother occupying the judge's stand, and took with a polite leaving." In the smaller afternoon meeting, Turner "tried to speak at some length, holding the *Discipline* of the AME Church in one hand and the *Discipline* of the M.E. Church, South, in the other, reading and commenting from both." Turner then sat down to await the reaction of the people. The "leading men" of the congregation came forward, one by one, and enrolled in the AME Church, "each thanking God that the light had come."[46]

During the next week others came to the chaplain to add their names to his list. They told him about their religious experiences, but he believed that there were "not more than fifty pious persons in the town, and many of them had back-slidden in consequence of no care being taken of them. They had not met a [Bible] class for four years, nor heard of a prayer meeting, . . . and every sermon was a speech on slavery." Turner concluded that all the African American members of the Southern Methodist Church in Smithville would soon join the AME Church, but he despaired of finding a competent man whom he could license to take charge of the congregation. Nevertheless, he had taken his first prize in the emerging contest for black Methodists in North Carolina.[47]

Further success would not come so easily—other missionaries and chaplains were at work nearby. In Wilmington, recently taken by Union troops, there were two Methodist churches for African Americans: St. Stephen's and St. Luke's, better known as the Front Street Church. William H. Hunter, the AME chaplain of the 4th USCT had arrived with the conquering troops, and he claimed both congregations for the AME Church. On March 5, Turner rode on horseback the twenty miles to Wilmington to congratulate Hunter and visit the churches. But when he arrived for the evening service at St. Luke's, he found not only Hunter but also James W. Hood, of the AME Zion connection, who was preaching "a fine sermon." Turner also spoke, strongly advocating education for the freedmen. But he sensed a tension between Hunter and Hood.[48]

On the next day, the contest for Wilmington was joined in earnest. Turner learned that Hood was there to wrest St. Luke's away from Chaplain Hunter and the AME Church. Patiently, Turner listened to each man for two days. Both Hunter and Hood had participated in the "union convention" in Philadelphia the previous spring, so they already knew each other and the tensions between the denominations. "My heart sank within me immediately," wrote Turner, "for I could anticipate the troubles which would follow." He tried to mediate between his two friends. Hunter said that he had helped liberate and protect the people; therefore outsiders should not interfere with his work. Hood rejoined that, as an army chaplain, Hunter (and Turner) had no business interfering in civilian matters. Furthermore, he said, the AME Zion Church now had a "North Carolina Conference," and they had resolved to hold their next session in Wilmington, the largest city in the state.[49]

What bothered Turner was not so much the wrangling itself, but the impression it created among the Southern blacks. "The idea of these two connexions preaching the same gospel, believing the same doctrine, differing only on episcopacy, coming here among an innocent people to create a church schism is a burning shame." He did not blame Hood or Hunter so much as he criticized the very existence of the redundant organizations. When he had left the General Conference of the AME in Philadelphia, he thought there would be quick progress toward union. But Hood informed him that there had been no real change. "If it be a fact," Turner wrote, "in the name of all that is dear to our religion, let the better-thinking men rise in their great might and pity, and break down that wicked partition." He added, "I expect to quarrel with these two connexions until they unite. Rather than destroy the unity of the [black] Southern Methodists, I would prefer seeing the Bethel [AME] Church absorbed into [AME] Zion ten times. . . . I am for unity at all hazards. . . . Let us unite at once, and stop this connexional fizzling henceforth and forever."[50]

Chaplain Hunter proclaimed the AME Church to be the victor in Wilmington, for as he left town with his regiment, both St. Luke's and St. Stephen's Churches joined his denomination. But Hood, remaining in town after the army left, "worked ardently, and manipulated matters so that the St. Luke Church withdrew from the compact with [the AME Church] and came with Hood into Zion."[51]

Meanwhile, Chaplain Turner continued to do his best to bring the black Methodists of North Carolina into the AME Church. He and the other army chaplains had an advantage in that they could usually be the first to enter a newly conquered area. When Turner's regiment occupied Raleigh in early April 1865, he walked around town and asked about the churches. He found relatives of Chaplain Hunter and through them the colored Methodists. "I preached there . . . after which I received the leaders, 14; stewards, 7; members 450 or 500, and fine, sumptuous church and large lot, all paid for, into the AME Church. . . . This morning I licensed one preacher and one exhorter, which was the first thing of the kind in a generation of years."[52]

Confederate armies in North Carolina finally surrendered in April 1865, and in June Turner's regiment moved to occupy Roanoke Island. On his way there, he stopped at New Bern to visit Hood: "I went to his house, stayed all night, tried to preach in his splendid church, and had a pleasant time." Hood and Turner were much alike in their ideas and energy. "I find Brother Hood a strong advocate for union between our two connexions," wrote Turner. They discussed possible names for the to-be-merged denominations; Hood proposed "The United African Methodist Episcopal Church." Turner thought it should be simply "The United Methodist Episcopal Church." "I believe not only the African Church, but all other religious and moral institutions designated by local terms, are destined to die out. That little word, 'Unity' is going to eat up and annihilate, in God's own good time, every other phrase or sentence expressing man's upward march."[53]

At Roanoke Island, Turner labored to evangelize the freedpeople. On July 4, 1865, he delivered an oration, declaring that "the extremities of color, white and black" had transformed the recently reunited Union into "the world's theatre," and "that as soon as God would knock down the wall of prejudice between the whites and blacks, sectional division would crumble into dust throughout the entire Globe." But on Roanoke Island Turner found that Hood and his coworkers had already been there and enrolled the Methodist freedmen. The AME Zion work was just getting under way, and the people were still untutored in their religion. Turner inspected the various black churches, and his observations on the Methodists are noteworthy:

> The [Zion] Methodist Church, which I visited twice unobserved by the members, appeared to worship under a lower class of ideas, or to entertain a much cruder conception of God and the plan of salvation, than the Baptists—Hell fire, brimstone, damnation, black smoke, hot lead, &c., appeared to be presented by the speaker as man's highest incentive to serve God, while the milder yet more powerful message of Jesus was thoughtlessly passed by; that, of course, formed the key to their class of ideas. But, oh! what zeal and determination they manifest in their efforts to serve God! I have to admire it.[54]

The friendly competition with Hood and the AME Zion Church continued as long as Turner was stationed with his regiment in North Carolina. He heard about a black Methodist congregation in Edenton, about sixty-five miles away by steamboat, the only available transportation. "The colored people there have a splendid Methodist church, given to them several years ago by the whites," he wrote. The prospects of taking it into the AME Church, according to the chaplain, were excellent. Like the commanding general of an army, Turner planned to send one of his enlisted-man assistants to scout the situation and then go to Edenton himself for the conquest. But when the semimonthly steamer arrived, he learned that he had been outmaneuvered in the campaign. "There stood General Hood, armed to the teeth, with all his veteran force ready, and intent upon the capture of Edenton after a forced march from New Bern." Tasting sour grapes, Turner tried to persuade Hood that Edenton was not worth the effort. Hood, however, "went in, carried the place, left it well garrisoned, and returned yesterday, exultant in the glory of his conquest; and no one was more ready than I to lavish upon him my highest congratulations." "But," Turner confided, "had I even surmised Gen. Hood had any idea of the place, I would have been there before. Yet I shall never wrangle, by the grace of God, with a Zion brother." [55]

For Turner the end of the friendly internecine theological war meant that he had important decisions to make: Should he enter a busy but comfortable life as the pastor of a large church? Or should he return to the South as a missionary? After his discharge from the army in 1865 on Roanoke Island, he returned home to Washington and met with his superior, Bishop Daniel Payne, and the Missionary Board. Turner, it appears, was determined to return to the South as quickly as possible. He argued that the AME Church had a God-given mission to the freedpeople that must be tried. Most of his colleagues on the Mission Board gave him their blessing. The AME Church, however, had little money to finance his mission, so Turner, within a month of his having been mustered out, successfully petitioned to be reappointed chaplain, this time in a regular army black regiment attached to the Freedmen's Bureau in Georgia. He would try to build the church in Georgia while still in the army. [56]

Early in November he started a six-week journey southward, during which he was to visit friends and AME churches in Virginia, North Carolina, and South Carolina. He stayed overnight, again, with Hood, "whose high-toned Christian demeanor and exemplary hospitality ever make his house feel as welcome as my own." In New Bern, meanwhile, an AME Church had been established by George A. Rue, who had come from New England. Hood and Rue both welcomed Turner, who wrote, "I was proud to find such brotherly unity existing between the two divines. Yet each are [sic] strenuous advocates for their own branch of the Church." Moving on to Goldsboro, Raleigh, and Charlotte, North Carolina, Turner commented on the churches, the blacks, and the whites in each locale. At Charlotte he found that "the colored people have a fine church, and are very intelligent. They have all united with Zion Church, and several thought they had joined the regular AME Church, but they were proud to learn that we were going to unite. I told them we would if *timber heads* in both connexions did not raise the devil and prevent it."[57]

For Turner, at least, there was no bitterness or hostility toward the AME Zion Church, despite the fact that some of his colleagues may have seen it as "an enemy to be destroyed or discredited." The missionary impulse had made him an apostle of ecumenicity, just as it would do to others half a century later. In years to come he would continue to advocate unity among African American Methodists.[58]

When he reached Augusta, however, Chaplain Turner found that the main competition in Georgia was not the black AME Zion Church but the white Methodists. The black Methodists there were disturbed over a recent action of the Georgia Conference of the Methodist Church, South. In their wisdom, the Southern Methodists had assigned white pastors to all the colored Methodist churches in the state. Turner reported that several of the congregations had refused to accept the white preachers. "At Marietta, on last Sabbath, they voted the minister out, and he in the pulpit at the time." Bishop Payne and the AME Missionary Board had named Turner presiding elder, authorizing him to oversee the Georgia churches that had already come into the fold and to convert the multitudes. Despite the intransigence of the Southern Methodists, the new possibilities fairly dazzled Chaplain Turner. "Colored preachers from all quarters are calling upon me for authority to preach. I think we will soon be able to put a veto on the action of the [white] Georgia Conference."[59]

As a result of what he found on his tour through the seaboard states, Turner had begun to realize the tremendous opportunities and challenges that lay before him and his church. He wrote that he had preached to "about 30,000 freed people and many whites. Since my arrival in Georgia, I have addressed large crowds, and am still at work." Although army duties with the Freedmen's Bureau might have given him access to African Americans throughout Georgia, "by the time I had arrived in Augusta," he wrote, "I had made up my mind to resign the chaplaincy." In time he would enter Georgia politics, helping draft the new state constitution in 1867 and serving as a legislator (1868–70); he also was the postmaster in Macon and a customs inspector. But Turner's true work was building the AME Church in the South.[60]

As presiding elder for Georgia, Turner quickly brought thousands of black Methodists into his church. Being an army chaplain, however, had been the turning point of his career. He had attracted national attention and exerted leadership through his journalism. He had preached to the freed-people, creating AME Churches where none had existed before and persuading existing black congregations to join his all-black organization. He had matched wits and energy with both the Southern Methodists and the AME Zion missionaries, developing his belief in union for all black Methodists. And when the smoke of various battles had cleared, he had begun to challenge white domination of the lives and culture of the freedmen. Turner, who served as a bishop of the AME Church from 1880 to 1915, found his life's work in his two years as an army chaplain.

Notes

1. For Turner's life, see Stephen Ward Angell, *Bishop Henry McNeal Turner and African-American Religion in the South* (Knoxville: University of Tennessee Press, 1992); Edwin S. Redkey, *Black Exodus: Black Nationalist and Back-to-Africa Movements, 1890–1910* (New Haven: Yale University Press, 1969); Edwin S. Redkey, *Respect Black!: The Writings and Speeches of Henry McNeal Turner* (New York: Arno Press, 1971); Edwin S. Redkey, "Black Chaplains in the Union Army," *Civil War History* 33 (December 1987): 331–50.

2. Angell, *Bishop Henry McNeal Turner and African-American Religion*, 33–37.

3. Joseph T. Glatthaar, *Forged in Battle: The Civil War Alliance of Black Soldiers and White Officers* (New York: Free Press, 1990), 176–82.

4. Redkey, "Black Chaplains in the Union Army," 332; Thomas Holt, *Black over White: Negro Political Leadership in South Carolina during Reconstruction* (Urbana: University of Illinois Press, 1979) 105, 141; Carter G. Woodson, "The Waring Family," *Negro History Bulletin* 12 (February 1948): 99–107.

5. On the duties and problems of army chaplains, see Redkey, "Black Chaplains in the Union Army," and Warren B. Armstrong, *For Courageous Fighting and Confident Dying: Union Chaplains in the Civil War* (Lawrence: University Press of Kansas, 1998).

6. *Harper's Weekly*, December 12, 1863, reprinted in Angell, *Bishop Henry McNeal Turner and African-American Religion*, 55.

7. Angell, *Bishop Henry McNeal Turner and African-American Religion*, 60–67.

8. Ibid., 5.

9. Henry McNeal Turner (hereafter identified as HMT) to Editor, September 10, 1864, in *Christian Recorder*, September 17, 1864 (hereafter cited as *CR*).

10. HMT to Editor, June 30, 1864, in *CR*, July 9, 1864.

11. One exception was Thomas Morris Chester, a black journalist who reported

for the *Philadelphia Press* in the last months of the war. See R. J. M. Blackett, ed., *Thomas Morris Chester: Black Civil War Correspondent* (Baton Rouge: Louisiana State University Press, 1989). For excellent accounts of the battles fought by African American soldiers in the Civil War, see Noah Andre Trudeau, *Like Men of War: Black Troops in the Civil War, 1862–1865* (Boston: Little, Brown, 1998).

12. HMT to Editor, June 18, 1864, in *CR*, June 25, 1864.

13. HMT to Editor, January 18, 1865, in *CR*, February 4, 1865. See also Edwin S. Redkey, "Rocked in the Cradle of Consternation," *American Heritage* 31 (October/November 1979): 70–79.

14. HMT to Editor, June 13, 1864, in *CR*, June 25, 1864.

15. HMT to Editor, June 30, 1864, in *CR*, July 9, 1864.

16. HMT to Editor, April 5, 1865, in *CR*, May 6, 1865.

17. William H. Hunter to Editor, July 19, 1864, in *CR*, July 30, 1864.

18. "Wild Jack" to Editor, July 28, 1864, in *CR*, August 6, 1864.

19. HMT to Editor, July 20, 1864, in *Weekly Anglo-African* (New York), July 30, 1864.

20. HMT to Editor, May 15, 1865, in *CR*, June 3, 1865.

21. HMT to Editor, August 24, 1864, in *CR*, September 3, 1864.

22. James Lynch to Editor, n.d., in *CR*, September 3, 1864.

23. HMT to Editor, April 5, 1865, in *CR*, May 6, 1865.

24. HMT to Editor, November 28, 1864, in *CR*, December 17, 1864.

25. HMT to Editor, July 23, 1865, in *CR*, August 5, 1865.

26. Leon F. Litwack, *Been in the Storm So Long: The Aftermath of Slavery* (New York: Alfred A. Knopf, 1979), 450–52.

27. "Emigration or Extermination" was the front-page banner of the *Voice of the People*, a newspaper published by Turner from 1901 to 1907. See Redkey, *Black Exodus*, 252–87.

28. HMT to Editor, February 28, 1865, in *CR*, March 25, 1865.

29. HMT to Editor, September 10, 1864, in *CR*, September 17, 1864.

30. HMT to Editor, June 18, 1864, in *CR*, June 25, 1864. On the pay crisis, see Ira Berlin, Joseph P. Reidy, and Leslie S. Rowland, eds., *The Black Military Experience* (Cambridge: Cambridge University Press, 1982), 362–405; Howard C. Westwood, *Black Troops, White Commanders, and Freedmen during the Civil War* (Carbondale: Southern Illinois University Press, 1992), 125–66; Donald Yacovone, ed., *A Voice of Thunder: The Civil War Letters of George E. Stephens* (Urbana: University of Illinois Press, 1997), 58–79; Glatthaar, *Forged in Battle*, 169–76.

31. HMT to Editor, September 10, 1864, in *CR*, September 17, 1864; Glatthaar, *Forged in Battle*, 80–91, 176–82.

32. HMT to Editor, July 20, 1864, in *Weekly Anglo-African*, July 30, 1864.

33. HMT to Editor, February 4, 1865, in *CR*, February 25, 1865.

34. Daniel W. Stowell, *Rebuilding Zion: The Religious Reconstruction of the South, 1863–1877* (New York: Oxford University Press, 1998), 7. A number of recent

books have explored the transitions in Southern religion during and after the Civil War. Stowell examines the broad picture across the South and across denominational lines. Reginald F. Hildebrand, *The Times Were Strange and Stirring: Methodist Preachers and the Crisis of Emancipation* (Durham: Duke University Press, 1995), looks at all Methodists, North and South. Katharine L. Dvorak, *An African-American Exodus: The Segregation of the Southern Churches* (Brooklyn, N.Y.: Carlson Publishing Company, 1991), examines the racial separation in postwar churches. Clarence E. Walker, *A Rock in a Weary Land: The African Methodist Episcopal Church during the Civil War and Reconstruction* (Baton Rouge: Louisiana State University Press, 1982) focuses on one organization. Henry McNeal Turner is important in these accounts, and Angell's *Bishop Henry McNeal Turner and African-American Religion* sheds new light on the entire reconstruction of Southern religion. For an important collection of recent essays, see Randall M. Miller, Harry S. Stout, and Charles Reagan Wilson, eds., *Religion and the American Civil War* (New York: Oxford University Press, 1998).

35. William P. Harrison, ed., *The Gospel among the Slaves* (Nashville: Southern Methodist Publishing House, 1893), 232–40; Albert J. Raboteau, *Slave Religion: The Invisible Institution in the Antebellum South* (New York: Oxford University Press, 1978) 135–37; Ira Berlin, *Slaves without Masters: The Free Negro in the Antebellum South* (New York: Vintage, 1974), 291–94; William M. Wightman, *The Life of William Capers, D.D., One of the Bishops of the Methodist Episcopal Church, South, Including an Autobiography* (Nashville: Southern Methodist Publishing House, 1858).

36. Walker, *A Rock in a Weary Land*, 84.

37. For the origins of the African American Methodist churches, see Carol V. R. George, *Segregated Sabbaths: Richard Allen and the Emergence of Independent Black Churches, 1760–1840* (New York: Oxford University Press, 1973) and Harry V. Richardson, *Dark Salvation: The Story of Methodism As It Developed among Blacks in America* (Garden City, N.Y.: Doubleday, 1976).

38. HMT to Editor, September 21, 1864, in *CR*, September 24, 1864; Stowell, *Rebuilding Zion*, 30–31.

39. "The gospel of freedom" is Hildebrand's apt term. See Hildebrand, *The Times Were Strange*, xviii, 50–72.

40. Stowell, *Rebuilding Zion*, 25, 72–79.

41. Walker, *A Rock in a Weary Land*, 82–107.

42. *CR*, May 7, 1864; *Philadelphia Press*, May 6, 1864; David Henry Bradley, Sr., *A History of the AME Zion Church*, vol. 1, *1796–1872* (Nashville: Parthenon Press, 1956), 147–52; "General Conference Journal," reprinted in Charles S. Smith, *A History of the African Methodist Episcopal Church* (Philadelphia: AME Book Concern, 1922), 464–502; Angell, *Bishop Henry McNeal Turner and African-American Religion*, 60–67.

43. James W. Hood, *One Hundred Years of the African Methodist Episcopal Zion Church*

(New York: AMEZ Book Concern, 1895), 88–92, 290–91; Richardson, *Dark Salvation*, 204–6; David Henry Bradley, Sr., *A History of the AME Zion Church*, vol. 2, *1872–1968* (Nashville: Parthenon Press, 1970), 34–36.

44. HMT to Editor, February 4, 1865, in *CR*, February 25, 1865.

45. Ibid.

46. HMT to Editor, February 11, 1865, in *CR*, March 4, 1865.

47. Ibid.

48. HMT to Editor, n.d. [c. March 7, 1865], in *CR*, April 1, 1865.

49. Ibid.

50. Ibid.

51. William J. Walls, *The African Methodist Episcopal Zion Church: The Reality of the Black Church* (Charlotte, N.C.: AMEZ Publishing House, 1974), 188.

52. HMT to Editor, April 17, 1865, in *CR*, May 6, 1865.

53. HMT to Editor, June 14, 1865, in *CR*, June 24, 1865.

54. On Turner and the occupation of Roanoke Island, see Patricia C. Click, *Time Full of Trial: The Roanoke Island Freedmen's Colony, 1862–1867* (Chapel Hill: University of North Carolina Press, 2001), 147; HMT to Editor, June 23, 1865, in *CR*, July 1, 1865.

55. HMT to Editor, June 23, 1865, in *CR*, July 1, 1865.

56. Editorial, *CR*, October 14, 1865; James Lynch to Editor, October 26, 1865, in *CR*, November 4, 1865.

57. HMT to Editor, December 20, 1865, in *CR*, December 30, 1865.

58. Walker, *A Rock in a Weary Land*, 101; Walls, *The African Methodist Episcopal Zion Church*, 507; Angell, *Bishop Henry McNeal Turner and African-American Religion*, 101, 175.

59. HMT to Editor, December 20, 1865, in *CR*, December 30, 1865; Wesley J. Gaines, *African Methodism in the South, or Twenty-Five Years of Freedom* (Atlanta: Franklin Press, 1890), 8–10.

60. HMT to Editor, December 20, 1865, in *CR*, December 30, 1865; HMT to E. M. Stanton, December 15, 1865, Bureau of Refugees, Freedmen, and Abandoned Lands: Assistant Commissioner for Georgia: Letters Received: T63-1865 (Microcopy 798, Roll 13), Record Group 105, National Archives, Washington, D.C.

A DISTURBANCE
IN THE CITY
Black and White Soldiers
in Postwar Charleston
Robert J. Zalimas, Jr.

On February 18, 1865, fatigued Confederate troops reluctantly abandoned war-torn Charleston, South Carolina. Since the beginning of the war, Rebel soldiers had zealously defended the "cradle of secession" against a suffocating siege compounded by an intense barrage of Union artillery. Although Yankee shells nearly leveled the city, Southern troops held the port for most of the war, repelling several Union amphibious assaults. Recognized by its protectors as the "best-defended" city on the Atlantic coast, the port finally capitulated to Northern infantrymen.[1]

To be sure, the Yankee invaders expected some resistance, but they entered the port unopposed. Union soldiers from different regiments raced through Charleston Harbor in a desperate attempt to land on the shore first and hoist their own regimental flag on top of The Citadel. Off in the distance, naval escorts plodded through the mined harbor transporting occupation troops and provost guards to the coastal city. As the boats moved closer to the shore, those white Southerners who remained in Charleston soon recognized that the transports carried a fate that seemed worse than Union general William Tecumseh Sherman's depredations: the occupation of the city by black soldiers. Shocked white residents looked on in disgust as former slaves and sons of former slaves, armed with rifles and bayonets, marched through what long had been the symbol of Confederate resistance. For many white civilians, the sight was almost unbearable. "Night of horrors!" exclaimed botanist Henry Ravenel from his plantation outside

Charleston. Likewise, Emma Holmes, a Charleston refugee, moaned in desperation. "I should feel thankful to know that all my aged relatives there were resting quietly in their graves rather than be exposed to such torture of soul."[2]

That afternoon, the 21st U.S. Colored Troops (USCT), a unit composed of former slaves from South Carolina, Florida, and Georgia, cautiously entered the port city.[3] An onrushing cloud of smoke from fires set by the retreating Confederates greeted the black liberators. Along with members of other white and black Union regiments, the men of the 21st moved quickly into the city and worked their way through Charleston's rubble to extinguish the raging inferno. To slow the Union advance, retreating Confederate soldiers engulfed Charleston with flames by setting afire cotton warehouses, buildings, bridges, the railroad depot, and several naval vessels. By nightfall on Sunday, February 19, the *Charleston Daily Courier* reported that four square miles of the city had burned down.[4]

After the black and white troops extinguished the flames, Union officers posted black detachments throughout Charleston and ordered them to clean up the debris, find shelter for incoming black refugees, and seek out new recruits. As soon as Union forces took control of the city, Lieutenant General Ulysses S. Grant ordered all white soldiers to leave Charleston and pursue fleeing Rebels up the Cape Fear River. Grant then directed the commander of the Department of the South (South Carolina, Georgia, and Florida), Major General Quincy A. Gillmore, to hold the men of the 21st USCT in Charleston, "where they have been raised and where their families are." Due to the large African American population in the city, Grant wanted these soldiers to keep potential black refugees from fleeing the port while the massive and swift Union offensive rolled through the Carolinas. Thus, in one of the war's rich ironies, Grant's order briefly gave the former slaves control over the home of secession and what would become one of the centers of Southern resistance toward the federal government's reconstruction policies.[5]

During the final year of the war, this scene was repeated throughout the South. As more and more Rebel territory fell under Federal control, Union commanders increasingly used black regiments to occupy several Confederate cities. These assignments released more white regiments to serve on the front lines and allowed Union field commanders to relegate African American men to the more tedious rear-echelon labor details. The presence of these armed black men offended white Southerners, however, and created an obstacle in swinging their loyalty back to the Union. Consequently,

Union commanders followed a strategy designed to minimize racial clashes by typically replacing black occupation troops with white soldiers while moving the African Americans beyond the pale of Southern towns.[6]

By positioning black soldiers in outlying areas, Union commanders achieved two goals. After helping the Northern invaders defeat Confederate troops, black regiments usually stayed behind advancing forces and constructed refugee camps for homeless and vulnerable former slaves. It was the intent of U.S. military officials that these camps would keep large refugee bands isolated and prevent them from impeding Union army food and supply trains. Because the black refugees and black soldiers resided outside Southern cities, the location of the camps in remote areas also assuaged bitter white Southerners and their fears of black insurrections.[7]

Although Union field commanders relied on black regiments to secure Confederate cities and territories, some Northern generals tended to share the racial prejudices of many white Southerners and felt uncomfortable placing black men in dominant positions over whites. Major General Sherman, for example, practiced racial segregation during his occupation of Savannah (December 21, 1864–February 1, 1865) and connived to move his black soldiers from the city to coastal fortifications. In late December 1864, while preparing to invade South Carolina, Sherman telegraphed Lieutenant General Grant and suggested transferring a white regiment from Maryland to replace the black regiment occupying Savannah. He expressed his concern about using black troops and noted that white Southerners "are dreadfully alarmed lest we garrison the place with Negroes." Sherman recognized the importance of racial separation to white Southerners, and in fact he sympathized with them. "Now no matter what the Negro soldiers are," Sherman concluded, "you know that people have prejudices which must be regarded."[8]

The presence of Charleston's large black population in late February 1865, however, convinced Union leaders to station both black and white provost guards in the city. (By 1870 the city's black population would grow to 26,173 representing 53 percent of the city's total population.) Once Union soldiers gained control of Charleston, military officials suspended civil government and declared martial law over the city. Black and white troops then occupied civic buildings, including police headquarters, and served in Charleston as military policemen from February to November 1865.[9] The men of the 21st USCT received orders to patrol Charleston's black community, while the white soldiers of the 127th New York Volunteers were assigned to the city's white neighborhoods. In this capacity, African American soldiers could act as a buffer between the white and black populace, assisting former slaves in the transition from slavery to freedom while protecting them from retaliation by whites. A conflict in the summer of 1865 between black and white Union troops disrupted this plan as white soldiers openly challenged the authority of black military policemen. Five months after black troops gained control of Charleston, these tensions eventually culminated in a violent race riot that tore the city apart, leaving several soldiers and citizens wounded and one freedman dead. In a city known for its secessionist sympathies, the conflict between the two regiments brought to light the frustrations of many African American soldiers in their struggle to gain respect within the Union ranks.[10] Moreover, the white soldiers' aggressive reaction foreshadowed the use of racial violence by white Southerners during the Reconstruction era, prefiguring their future efforts to keep blacks subordinate.[11]

Initially, the occupation of Charleston resembled previous garrison duty in which the African American soldiers worked as laborers to clean up the destruction left by war. The relentless wartime bombardment had demolished large parts of the city, compelling rich whites to evacuate while leaving blacks and poor whites to endure Union occupation alone. In addition to putting them on labor details, Brigadier General Alexander Schimmelfennig, the Union commander for Charleston, also granted the black soldiers firm authority over the city, ordering them to arrest any soldier, white or black, who tried to enter Charleston without a pass. Although the order was consistent with their role as provost guards, the black soldiers recognized this authority as a step toward racial equality with white soldiers.[12] Like most African American soldiers, the black men of the 21st USCT viewed equality within the Union army as a step toward full citizenship. As was true of white soldiers, military service constituted a test of manhood for black males. Subsequently, they felt the war would give them a chance to eradicate the myth of black inferiority. "We are now recognized as soldiers," proclaimed a black sergeant then stationed at nearby Mount Pleasant, South Carolina, "and as men who are fighting for liberty, union, and equal rights."[13]

Originally named the 3rd South Carolina Infantry, the 21st USCT was mustered into service on June 19, 1863, at Hilton Head, South Carolina. Until it received the honor of being the first Union regiment to enter Charleston on February 18, 1865, the unit spent the war occupying the South Carolina Sea Islands as well as positions in northeastern Florida. In December 1864, the 3rd, 4th, and 5th South Carolina Infantry were consolidated into one

regiment and redesignated the 21st USCT.[14] Prior to their postwar assignment, the men of the 21st gained a reputation for challenging their subordinate position in the Northern army. In November 1863 a portion of the regiment stacked arms to protest the difference between their pay and that of
their white counterparts. The frustrated troops demanded a change in policy
and refused to return to duty until the Union army resolved the inequity.
The soldiers quickly abandoned their protest after their white commanding
officer, Lieutenant Colonel Augustus Bennett, charged them with mutiny
and executed a black sergeant for instigating the revolt. Fifteen months after
this incident, these former slaves found themselves patrolling the streets of
Charleston and welcomed the opportunity once again to prove their manhood and gain respect from Southern civilians as well as their Northern
white comrades.[15]

By the end of the regiment's first week on occupation duty (February 25, 1865), however, Schimmelfennig compromised their authority over
the port. The Union commander ordered a contingent from the 21st USCT
to move thirty miles north of Charleston and support white regiments in
pursuit of Confederate soldiers. The decision to move some of these black
troops away from Charleston may have cost Schimmelfennig his postwar
command. The next day he was suddenly relieved and reassigned as commander for the "Defenses of Charleston." At various times during the war,
Schimmelfennig suffered from smallpox and malaria, so the move may have
resulted from his poor health. (Seven months later, he in fact died from a
virulent type of tuberculosis.) But Gillmore may have demoted Schimmelfennig as a punishment for disobeying Grant's directive to keep the black
regiment in Charleston. For whatever reason, Brigadier General John P.
Hatch, commanding the coast division, replaced Schimmelfennig as commander for the port district.[16]

Soon after the black companies marched northward, Hatch took command of Union forces in Charleston. A native New Yorker, Hatch graduated
from West Point in 1845. During the Civil War, he served as a division commander in the Army of Potomac and was severely wounded in September
1862 at South Mountain in the Maryland campaign. Hatch recuperated for
a year and returned to the Union army in October 1863, serving in administrative positions and garrison posts for the rest of the war.[17]

With a depleted occupation force in Charleston, Hatch designated the
127th New York Volunteers as the permanent garrison force for the port
on February 26, 1865. He transferred the white soldiers from the coast and
immediately moved them into the city. Organized in Staten Island, New

York, the regiment spent most of the war occupying the South Carolina Sea Islands and then participated in the siege operations against Charleston. The regiment also fought in a number of small operations along the South Carolina coastline, including the Battle of Honey Hill. Originally, the organizers of the unit sought to make the regiment a beacon for men of "good moral character" in order to minimize the "demoralizing influences of camp and army life." To find these men, Union officers recruited white males in a number of New York's Presbyterian churches, using the Thirteenth Street Presbyterian Church in New York City as headquarters. The regiment's officers came from these congregations, where many had taught Sunday school. They called themselves the "Monitors" because each soldier was expected "to exert a 'monitorial' restraining influence over the others." Although the men of this new regiment maintained a pious facade in New York City, a recruit from Maine reported that, once these "praying men" left New York, he witnessed "no *sign* of temperance" among them. Like many white Union troops, these vigilant soldiers failed to recognize black equality, and most held conservative racial attitudes when they arrived in Charleston at full strength on February 27, 1865.[18]

In the same order granting control of Charleston to the New Yorkers, Hatch also ordered the 21st USCT to form a biracial garrison force with the 127th New York Volunteers. One day after the white regiment arrived in Charleston, Hatch actively pushed for the return of the black detachments. The general then designated the 21st USCT as "part" of the garrison force for Charleston. Those black soldiers not assigned to provost duty would soon return to work as laborers on defensive fortifications and the reconstruction of a bridge twenty miles north of Charleston.[19]

Although it is not quite clear why Hatch recalled members of the African American regiment, he may have wanted some black military presence in the port to defuse the growing animosity between white soldiers and black Charlestonians. After the Union army swept through South Carolina in February 1865, black refugees flocked into Charleston. While the black population grew, racial confrontations proliferated as the men of the 127th New York reportedly tormented the freedmen, especially black merchants. "The 127th N.Y.V.I. insulted the colored people everywhere," one observer noted, "stoned them, knocked them down, and cut them."[20] In response to these disturbances, Hatch divided the city into sectors in which the 127th New York occupied the southern streets of Charleston while the 21st USCT garrisoned Charleston's black neighborhood located in the northern section of the port.[21]

While the behavior of the white troops disrupted racial relations, their actions as an occupying force reflected the attitudes of many Northern soldiers toward Southerners in general. Late in the war, some Union commanders allowed their soldiers to take whatever they wanted from Southern merchants, farmers, and slaves. In Charleston, many observers reported that the Union soldiers and freed people looted indiscriminately during the early days of occupation. This practice continued in the postwar era as white provost guards took advantage of unprotected blacks and whites. Subsequently, when the men of the 21st USCT returned to Charleston in full force, they attempted to stop this mistreatment and immediately resumed their role as protectors of the former slaves by aggressively patrolling the marketplace where the freedpeople exchanged their goods.[22]

The strained relations between the black and white soldiers may have convinced Hatch to remove the 21st USCT and replace it with another regiment composed of former slaves. Several months later, after the free black community celebrated the end of the war and the return of the U.S. flag to Fort Sumter on April 14, 1865, Hatch again divided the black regiment and sent detachments to coastal fortifications on the Sea Islands off the coast of Charleston.[23] There he used the African American troops to reinforce breastworks.[24] He then assigned the 35th USCT, stationed at nearby Mount Pleasant in Charleston Harbor to replace the 21st USCT in the northern section of Charleston. Originally known as the 1st North Carolina Volunteers, the unit was mustered into service in June 1863 at New Bern, North Carolina. Under the command of Colonel James C. Beecher, an abolitionist and evangelical preacher (and the youngest child of Lyman Beecher and brother to Harriet Beecher Stowe), the unit fought at the Battle of Olustee, Florida, on February 20, 1864, and with the 127th New York at the Battle of Honey Hill, South Carolina, on November 30, 1864. Afterward, the regiment followed the 21st USCT to Charleston and performed fatigue duty on Charleston's Sea Islands.[25]

While the black soldiers from North Carolina moved into the city, many of the port's black males joined the Union army and reported to camps outside the city limits. At this time, Major Martin Delany—a renowned abolitionist, army recruiter, and public supporter of black nationalism as well as the first African American to receive a field-grade commission in the Union army—moved to Charleston with orders to raise new USCT regiments. As he publicly admonished Charleston's freedpeople vigorously to resist white aggression, he gained a presence in the city that inspired the black community. "*Do anything; die first! But don't submit again to them—never again be slaves,*"

Delany bellowed to an enthusiastic crowd of former slaves, black soldiers, and white abolitionists during the flag-raising ceremony at Fort Sumter on April 14, 1865. Throughout the spring of 1865, many of Charleston's black men reacted positively to Delany and joined the Union ranks. By mid-April 1865, Hatch reported that since February of that year a thousand men from Charleston's black population had enlisted in the Union army and had been transferred to training camps.[26]

Unfortunately for the black residents of Charleston, the transfer of their men to army camps outside the city came at an inopportune time. By Hatch's own account, the removal of the new black recruits left more than five thousand black women and children without the protection of males. Moreover, the army medical inspector for Charleston also reported that accumulated debris created an environment susceptible to a contagious epidemic. The inspector feared that the matter would decompose under the hot summer sun, harboring a "most fruitful source of danger and disease." He unfairly blamed the freed black population for the unsanitary conditions and recommended either moving them to the Sea Islands or forcing the unemployed among them to clean up the city. The next day, Generals Gillmore and Hatch endorsed the report and called for the impressment of all unemployed black men as laborers.[27]

In addition to the threat of disease during the spring of 1865, the port city was also running out of food. Without federal support to alleviate the misery found in this unforgiving environment, Colonel William Gurney, the commander for the 127th New York Volunteers, sent an urgent request for assistance to the president of the New York Produce Exchange. He reported that the sudden influx of soldiers and refugees had drained the city of supplies and emptied food stores. Gurney sent the letter in vain, however, for by mid-June 1865 private charitable food lines, run and operated by the city's black elite, closed for lack of support. Heightening the famine's impact, a smallpox epidemic soon wreaked havoc on the African American community. On a visit to the city in May 1865, Major General Sherman found himself stunned by the widespread despair ravaging Charleston's white and black communities and immediately left the port in disgust. "Anyone who is not satisfied with war should go and see Charleston," he reported chillingly, "and he will pray louder and deeper than ever that the country may in the long future be spared any more war."[28]

While black Charlestonians suffered under these intense psychological and physical pressures, the white New Yorkers soon added to their woes by resuming their mistreatment of the freedmen. The white provost guards forced unsuspecting blacks to work as laborers and smashed stalls in the blacks' marketplace located in the northern sector of the city. In addition to pillaging homes and businesses owned by black Charlestonians, the white Yankees also reportedly beat and raped the former slaves. "Peaceable colored citizens have been kicked out of their homes, knocked down in the streets, bled with brickbats and bayonets, cut with knives, pounded and mauled in the places of business, by United States soldiers," observed a reporter for the *Boston Commonwealth*. Witnesses also reported that the white New Yorkers embraced former white Rebels while rejecting "the true loyalist [that is, the Southern black]." According to these reports, white soldiers expected former slaves to maintain antebellum racial etiquette by deferring to white Northerners on the sidewalks of Charleston. If African Americans failed to move aside when white soldiers approached, white soldiers were known to remove forcibly the offending parties with a "boot or perhaps the point of a bayonet." This constant harassment of African Americans by white soldiers finally forced white Union leaders to intercede and to issue broad proclamations condemning the conduct of the 127th New York Volunteers. Gurney admitted that some members of his regiment beat and insulted Charleston's freedpeople and issued general orders promising "severe punishment" if any white soldier continued to mistreat blacks. Under pressure from Charleston's black elite, Hatch also condemned the misconduct of the 127th and promised to remove the New Yorkers if they persisted in their behavior. The efforts of the white commanders provided little relief, however, and black Charlestonians often retaliated against the white troops, challenging the soldiers' rifles and bayonets with knives and bottles.[29]

In addition to charging them with physical abuse, blacks also accused the white New Yorkers of attempting to deny black citizens their political and civil rights. During the spring and summer of 1865, African Americans in Charleston held meetings and local conventions to promote political activism. Besides holding their own meetings in black churches, the leaders of the local freed community demanded their place at public meetings and took exception to military officials who blocked their efforts to participate in civic affairs. In April 1865 freedmen reported that white loyalists used "bayonets" to keep black Charlestonians from attending a meeting called to propose a resolution condemning the assassination of President Abraham Lincoln. Later that summer, in June and July 1865, black leaders again were aroused when Major General Gillmore closed two African American meetings called to raise grievances against white occupation troops in the city. Buttressing the protests from black leaders, white abolitionists joined in assailing members of the 127th New York Volunteers for hindering black political participation. In one highly visible incident on May 11, 1865, a white officer, Lieutenant A. S. Bodine of the 127th New York, expelled black businessmen from a public meeting at Hibernian Hall called to consider the reorganization of the South Carolina state government. When the Union officer directed the black merchants to take seats behind their white counterparts, the African Americans refused, and in turn the white officer ordered their removal. The freedmen immediately returned, led by the fiery white abolitionist James Redpath (1833–91), who demanded the integration of the hall and the right of blacks to attend public meetings. Angry whites quickly adjourned the assembly and left abruptly. Afterward, the remaining white and black citizens managed to pass a series of resolutions pledging allegiance to the United States.[30]

A longtime abolitionist and former supporter of John Brown, Redpath then resided in Charleston and served as superintendent of schools. Born in Scotland, Redpath emigrated to America in 1849 and quickly landed a job as a correspondent for Horace Greeley's *New York Tribune*. Prior to the war, Redpath traveled throughout the South reporting on the conditions of the Southern slave and eventually published his newspaper articles in book form. Working as a war correspondent for the *Boston Journal*, Redpath was once again hired by the *New York Tribune* as their front-line reporter in January 1865. As an abolitionist, he submitted biased reports and called for harsher treatment of white Charlestonians and for the opening up of public schools for the freedpeople. In March 1865 federal authorities turned to Redpath and asked him to serve as superintendent of public schools. He immediately made his presence known and infuriated white Charlestonians by integrating nine public schools and organizing a memorial service for dead Union soldiers. Three Union regiments attended the services, including the 35th and 104th USCT, as well as over three thousand black schoolchildren who led the congregation in singing "John Brown's Body." Afterward, Redpath turned his full attention to the forced removal of Charleston's freedmen from the political meeting held on May 11. Recognizing an opportunity to bring the abuses of the white regiment to national attention, the angry Scotsman openly called for charges against Lieutenant Bodine.[31]

Pressured by the impassioned Redpath and members of the African American community, Major General Gillmore court-martialed Bodine for his actions, charging him with "unwarrantable exercise of arbitrary power" and "conduct prejudicial to good order and military discipline." The court-martial met on June 14, 1865, and made the front pages of both national and local newspapers three weeks later. The trial quickly turned into an open-and-shut case with a number of credible witnesses, including Redpath and Superintendent of Freedmen Gilbert Pilsbury, testifying that Lieutenant Bodine had wrongfully turned away black men from a public meeting. Not surprisingly, Bodine defended his order as proper and within his authority. Because the meeting was open only to citizens of South Carolina, he questioned whether black Charlestonians possessed the same legal rights as white citizens of the state. For Redpath and other defenders of the African Americans in Charleston, Bodine's rejection of black citizenship typified the attitudes and actions of white soldiers toward Charleston's freed community. If white Union officers and enlisted men refused to recognize blacks as citizens, then mistreatment of the former slaves would continue with impunity.[32]

Following Bodine's trial, Redpath continued to complain to Union authorities about the conduct of several Union commanders whom he deemed "unfriendly" toward the freedpeople. He threatened to seek the court-martial of Colonel Gurney, whom he blamed for the disorderly conduct of the white New Yorkers. In addition, Redpath sent letters of complaint against General Hatch for refusing to allow Charleston's blacks to participate in upcoming Fourth of July celebrations. After several of the letters reached the head of the Freedmen's Bureau, Major General Oliver Otis Howard, Gillmore finally addressed the embarrassing racial conflicts and removed the rowdy New York unit from Charleston.[33]

Gillmore discharged the New Yorkers several months before their scheduled release, siding with Redpath and the former slaves. "The regiment was carefully chosen for its good discipline," he wrote to Howard, "but street quarrels have taken place . . . arising from insolence and brutality of soldiers toward the negroes." Although Gillmore recognized that the local black merchants sometimes instigated the rows, he blamed the white regiment for its lack of discipline. These statements nevertheless appear to have been written to placate Redpath and other critics. From the beginning of the war, Gillmore opposed black enlistment and blamed black occupation forces for the postwar disturbances in his department, and he later pushed to remove the African American regiments from the state. Hence Gillmore confided to Howard that the racial disputes between the 127th New York Volunteers and black soldiers from various units were isolated incidents sparked by individual disagreements. Because he spent most of his time in Savannah, Gillmore clearly did not recognize the contest between black and white troops in Charleston over the future role of African Americans in postwar

Southern society. Conversely, he downplayed the racial tensions dividing the city and replaced the white New Yorkers with another white New York regiment then stationed in Georgia, the 165th New York Volunteers (also known as the 2nd Duryee's Zouaves).[34]

The 165th New York Volunteers had been mustered into the Union army on November 28, 1862, at Staten Island, New York. The regiment served at the siege of Port Hudson and skirmished with Mosby's Rangers during Sheridan's Shenandoah Valley campaign, but spent most of the war on garrison duty. The unit wore flamboyant uniforms patterned after the French colonial light infantry, consisting of red baggy pants, a short, open blue jacket, and a turban. While on occupation duty in Louisiana, the men of the 165th New York quickly displayed a lack of respect toward their fellow Union soldiers. Private George A. Hussey of the 165th New York, a new recruit who joined the regiment in the summer of 1864, instantly disliked the Zouaves. He felt the men of the 165th regiment projected an overt brazenness that Hussey partly attributed to the unconventional attire worn by its members. Sent to the unit in June 1864 with four new companies, Hussey reported that the unit lacked organization and that a "majority" engaged in criminal activity, including petty larceny. They stole from soldiers in other units, as well as from each other, forcing Hussey to sleep with "my things under my head." For Hussey, this behavior was not surprising after he learned that one hundred members of the unit allegedly had served some time in jail before the war. Recognizing their lack of character, he predicted that many of these former convicts would desert once they received back pay. Although Hussey reported that the regiment had a good reputation within the Union army, he sent home monthly reports documenting misconduct among the Zouaves and anxiously hoped for a transfer "away from this miserable organization."[35]

The 165th New York Volunteers entered Charleston with a checkered past on race relations as well. Before its transfer to Charleston in late June 1865, the unit anticipated an early release from the Union army. After spending the last months of the war guarding Confederate prisoners in Delaware, the regiment moved to Washington, D.C., on June 1, 1865, a short week after other white regiments from the Army of Potomac participated in the Grand Review (a two-day parade down Pennsylvania Avenue before thousands of cheering spectators in Washington on May 23–24). Because members of those white regiments left for home immediately after the ceremony, soldiers from the 165th also expected to receive their discharge as soon as they arrived in the nation's capital. Instead, the anxious Zouaves received orders to go to Georgia, moving Hussey to remark that he and the "boys are disappointed." In addition to their frustration, the unexpected transfer to Georgia may have created animosity among the New Yorkers toward the coastal freedpeople. On their arrival in Savannah in June 1865, the Zouaves were ordered to patrol the streets of Savannah because the city's freedmen allegedly were causing "much trouble of late ending frequently in murder." While performing guard duty in that city, some of the men refused to accept postings with soldiers from a black Union regiment. "It was the intention of the whole regiment to refuse to be so closely connected with negro troops," Hussey asserted, noting that only "the force of bayonets" prevented a mutiny among the Zouaves. The commander of the 165th New York Volunteers, Lieutenant Colonel Gouvenor Carr, immediately arrested the rebellious white soldiers and posted the interracial assignments without further incident. Shortly afterward, the regiment moved to Charleston.[36]

Although members of the 165th New York Volunteers may have griped at the prospect of once again patrolling a Southern area alongside black men, their racial prejudices would soon provoke a violent reaction in Charleston from the most respected black unit in the country. In June 1865 the renowned 54th Massachusetts Volunteers replaced the 35th USCT (except for Company C) as the protectors of Charleston's African American community. The first African American regiment raised in the North, the 54th Massachusetts gained an enduring reputation for its heroic assault against Battery Wagner (a Confederate fort guarding Charleston) on July 18, 1863. Although it lost the battle and suffered over 40 percent casualties, the regiment's exploits gained national attention and helped eradicate the myth of black inferiority, inspiring many African Americans to enlist in the Union army. Like the men of the 21st and 35th USCT regiments, the Northern black soldiers of the 54th Massachusetts (whose companies were filled with sons and grandsons of Northern abolitionists including Frederick Douglass, William Lloyd Garrison, and Sojourner Truth) understood the symbolic importance of black men garrisoning the "cradle of secession" and were determined to quash any semblance of white oppression, especially if it came from white Union soldiers. "Thank God, Massachusetts has at last come to the assistance of South Carolina, and through her sable sons, shown us the true path to honor and usefulness," recorded a joyous black Charlestonian on the arrival of the 54th Massachusetts Volunteers. "Let the credit of our lifting up be to him who comes from the Old Bay State, and standing here in this accursed city, boldly announce that all men are free, and that never again shall we call any man master."[37]

The arrival of the 54th Massachusetts Volunteers, the presence of detachments of the 21st and 35th USCT, and the transfer of the white New Yorkers to Charleston served to exacerbate already tense race relations in the city. While in transit to their new assignment, the Zouaves received warnings about "disturbances" between white and black soldiers and uncovered rumors that the streets of Charleston were not safe for white soldiers after dark. On arriving in Charleston on July 1, 1865, the New York enlisted men received passes and instantly engaged in street fights with members of the 21st and 35th USCT as well as of the 54th Massachusetts Volunteers. "The first night proved the rumors to be true," Hussey noted, "for some of the boys returned somewhat the worse from brick bats etc used on them by negros [*sic*]." Lieutenant Colonel Carr pointed to the easy access to liquor and the lack of a unified military police force as factors contributing to the brawls. A correspondent for the *New York Times* reported, however, that taunting among the opposing units caused the fights. He observed that from the "very first day they occupied the post it became evident that they [the 165th New York Volunteers] and the colored troops could not live together." "The latter," he continued, "appeared to be envious of the showy uniforms of the Zouaves, and the Zouaves were impressed with the idea that the colored soldiers took special pains to insult them." A reporter for the *Charleston Daily Courier* confirmed this animosity between the regiments and acknowledged that nightly "feuds" occurred in Charleston between the white and black soldiers.[38]

In spite of these confrontations, General Hatch designated the 165th New York Volunteers for police duty. For their first assignment, Hatch ordered the New Yorkers "held in readiness" to suppress a rumored black insurrection on the Fourth of July. Ironically, the 165th New York Volunteers had received the same orders in Savannah and were warned there that the "negros are to raise on that day to sack the town." Like most rumors concerning black uprisings on Christmas and the Fourth of July, the supposed revolts never materialized in either city, and the holiday passed without incident.[39]

But tensions continued to rise between the white and black troops. In a letter to President Andrew Johnson, Lieutenant Colonel Carr surmised that black troops resented the designation of his unit as policemen. His subordinates charged that the African American soldiers believed that the white provost guards infringed on their own responsibilities as occupation troops and that the blacks retaliated by attacking individual white soldiers who walked their "beats" alone. Carr insisted that only a few of his men participated in racial fighting and blamed Hatch for not taking the prompt action to stop these alleged assaults. The correspondent for the *New York Times* confirmed Carr's assertions, reporting that the white troops assumed certain privileges, which they believed had not been extended to the black soldiers, while the African American troops identified themselves as the "sole guardians of the city." Once again, white and black soldiers demonstrated their conflicting interpretations of the meaning of Union victory over Southern slaveholders. While white troops rejected black equality within army ranks, black soldiers considered their role as military policemen a significant opportunity to claim openly their rights as citizens. In defense of his black soldiers, Hatch denied Carr's allegations and condemned the Zouaves' misconduct, claiming that they immediately "showed ill feeling towards the colored people" resulting in "frequent disturbances." As tensions escalated, Hatch curiously took no immediate action to resolve the situation. More than likely, he recognized the rows as minor street fights, not uncommon occurrences in postwar Charleston.[40]

On July 8, 1865, these almost daily street fights erupted into a major race riot between the white soldiers, black soldiers, and Charleston's freedpeople. Various newspaper accounts state either that white soldiers attacked the freedmen or that the freedmen attacked the Zouaves. Regardless of who started it, the riot lasted for several days, with an observer commenting that the number of dead "never will be known." The *Charleston Daily Courier* reported first and confirmed Carr's allegations that black soldiers attacked individual white military policemen. According to the reporter's sources, a mixed group of freedmen and black soldiers, mostly from the 21st USCT and the 54th Massachusetts Volunteers, assaulted a Zouave in the downtown marketplace. The soldier called for help, and a squad from the 165th New York Volunteers rushed forward in defense of their comrade. The black soldiers quickly took positions and fired at the oncoming white unit, but they missed their intended targets and hit James Bing, an innocent black merchant, killing him instantly. Stray bullets also hit two other merchants, who luckily received only minor wounds. Eventually, a full company of Zouaves arrived from the city barracks and dispersed the black soldiers.[41]

The correspondent for the *New York Times* provided a slightly different account of the event, based on discussions with members of the Zouaves. According to his report, a single freedman approached one of the Zouaves with a knife. Then, a squad of fifteen white military policemen, "with loaded muskets and fixed bayonets," chased the culprit through the market. As the Zouaves moved through the stalls, a group of black soldiers suddenly appeared and fired on the white infantrymen. The New Yorkers returned fire, and the Union soldiers clashed for twenty minutes. Following the skirmish, fights between blacks and whites continued until dawn and rioting persisted for several more days. "All that night confusion reigned in Charleston," the journalist continued, adding that "[t]he disturbances were not confined to any particular locality, but they prevailed throughout the city." After the arrival of a white infantry regiment on July 10, 1865, the installment of an 8:00 P.M. curfew on July 12, 1865, by the new post commander, General William T. Bennett, and the subsequent arrest of various instigators, the fighting receded. Finally, peace was restored.[42]

Initially, Hatch play downed the riots and, because only one black man was killed, called the racial fighting "very much exaggerated." He blamed both white and black soldiers for the three-day disturbance as well as "lower class" whites who "encouraged the white soldiers and in some cases got them drunk for the purpose of bringing on trouble." Because black and white soldiers in Charleston fought during the entire occupation period, Hatch attached little importance to the July riot. After months of racial disturbances in the city, he continued to miss the significance of efforts by black Charlestonians to define their place in the postwar South by defying white oppression.[43]

Not surprisingly, Charleston's black community interpreted the three-day riot differently. Many considered the racial fighting a call to arms. Again asserting their newfound political activism, black Charlestonians held a community meeting on July 10, 1865, and issued a strong resolution condemning the abuse of their civil rights. Threatening to bring their grievances to Washington, the freed community demanded an investigation by military leaders into their continued mistreatment at the hands of the white New York soldiers. Furthermore, they demanded protection and announced their determination to stop "any intrusions upon our rights as loyal citizens."[44]

Although it is not entirely clear who started the Charleston riot, Major General Gillmore immediately accused the New Yorkers of instigating the affair and transferred the regiment to Morris Island the next day. Fuming after another embarrassing racial confrontation, Gillmore decided to eliminate the fighting between the black and white troops once and for all. He directed the officers and enlisted men of the 165th New York Volunteers to remain on the island and prohibited them from visiting Charleston for any reason. The banishment alone did not satisfy Gillmore, who also wanted to humiliate the New Yorkers. To do so, he struck at the very heart of a Civil War regiment by sending an officer from the 21st USCT to disarm the white troops and to seize their regimental colors. On the battlefield, the regimental flag was "the most visible badge of pride" for Civil War soldiers and many infantrymen bravely risked their lives to carry it during treacherous charges across open fields of fire. If a unit lost its colors to the enemy during the heat of battle, shame and cowardice swept through the ranks. Thus, because soldiers had killed and died to prevent their colors from falling into enemy hands, Gillmore clearly meant to embarrass the white New Yorkers.[45]

Due to the conflicting reports of the Charleston riot, Gillmore also transferred the 21st USCT to Hilton Head, South Carolina, believing that men in the unit were among the first to fire shots at the Zouaves. He then ordered Hatch, now a brevet major general and commander of the northern district for the Department of the South, to transfer black soldiers from other USCT regiments to the 21st to reduce the number of black soldiers in the city. Gillmore suggested that Hatch put an additional fifty to one hundred black soldiers on fatigue duty at Hilton Head "to get them away from doing harm." After months of racial tensions between white and black soldiers in Charleston, Gillmore reverted to the Union wartime policy of using only white troops to occupy Southern towns. Although the 54th and 55th Massachusetts Volunteers (in addition to a detached company from the 35th USCT stationed at The Citadel) remained in Charleston awaiting their discharges, Gillmore appointed the white 47th Pennsylvania Volunteers as the sole military policemen for Charleston. The unit had rushed into the port on the morning of July 10, 1865, and quickly ended the racial fighting by acting as a wedge between the white New Yorkers and the black soldiers.[46]

These events in Charleston had a major impact on national policy. After the July 1865 riot, Grant directed Gillmore to reduce his occupation force by discharging all white regiments in the state. This order was consistent with official military policy because white troops were being discharged more rapidly than black soldiers. Grant gave them priority because many white soldiers enlisted before black soldiers could join the Union army. Denied enlistment for the first two years of the war, black men did not officially join the Union army until President Abraham Lincoln issued his final Emancipation Proclamation on January 1, 1863. In addition to taking into account their earlier enlistment dates, Grant recognized that white soldiers had the right to vote, while Southern and most Northern black men did not.[47]

On receiving the dispatch, Gillmore suggested a modification to Grant's order, hoping to retain most of his white regiments. At the time, 14,000 Union soldiers occupied South Carolina (11,200 blacks and 2,800 whites).

" 'Marching on!' — The Fifty-fifth Massachusetts Colored Regiment Singing John Brown's March in the Streets of Charleston, February 21, 1865." (Harper's Weekly, *March 18, 1865, N.C. Division of Historical Resources, Raleigh)*

Gillmore asked to release only one white unit, the 165th New York Volunteers, leaving him with 2,500 white soldiers to occupy the major cities in the state. Gillmore did so because he did not favor having Northern black soldiers in his command. Gillmore blamed these African American troops for disrupting labor relations between plantation owners and black laborers. Following emancipation, white planters and former slaves struggled to establish a viable free labor system regulated by legal contracts. Black field hands sought fair compensation in wages or crops, while white planters hoped to bind workers to yearly labor agreements. Both grappled with the new system, and both frequently broke the pacts they made. In Gillmore's estimation, many black laborers on large plantations failed to honor their labor contracts because of what he called the "pernicious influence of a few bad colored soldiers." Thus Gillmore suggested removing black regiments organized and raised in the North, including the 54th and 55th Massachusetts Volunteers, and two African American units organized and raised in the former Confederate states, the "not well disciplined" 35th

USCT and the "not well officered and badly disciplined" 21st USCT. Not surprisingly, Gillmore considered it "unwise" to release any more black soldiers from regiments raised in the South, identifying these black veterans as an undesirable addition to Charleston's already troublesome African American community.[48]

After receiving these suggestions, Grant ordered Gillmore to discharge only the Northern-raised black units while retaining African American soldiers from Southern states as "surplus subject to orders." By keeping blacks in uniform, Grant wished to discharge more white soldiers while impeding the postwar exodus of black refugees into Southern white communities. Following a request for garrison units numbering twenty-five or more men for coastal posts, Grant offered two of the Southern black regiments in South Carolina to the Union commander in North Carolina in order to "dispense with white troops by having colored troops sent to him." Again, Grant's action continued Union wartime policy of using black regiments to replace white soldiers engaged in what was considered to be undesirable duty. On his return to Washington in September 1865, Grant incorporated the initiatives employed in South Carolina as official policy and urged the War Department to release all Northern-raised black troops from military service.[49]

While New York and Massachusetts regiments received early discharges and a heroes' welcome in the North, the 21st USCT continued to serve the federal army in the South. Gillmore split the regiment into detachments and placed the African Americans in garrison posts throughout rural South Carolina and Georgia until October 1866. Although the transfer ended tensions between black and white soldiers in Charleston, the shift in postwar policy hurt the future role of the black soldier in the U.S. Army, as Northern leaders once again segregated African American men to areas beyond white contact. This was meant in part to protect black troops from attacks by whites in urban centers. But the decision to post them primarily in isolated rural areas also left large communities of freedpeople unprotected. As federal officials feared, the abuse by white soldiers of Southern blacks did not subside after the black troops left Charleston. In August 1865 Gilbert Pilsbury, the Freedmen's Bureau agent for the city, reported that white soldiers continued to abuse former slaves, especially black refugees. "Not an hour of the day passes," he wrote to Brevet Major General Rufus Saxton, the assistant commissioner of the Freedmen's Bureau for South Carolina, "but witnesses groups of wretched disconsolate negroes, dragged under guard to the Prov. Marshall, or the Chief of Police, to jail, or to the court of justice." "If anything is missing in the city," he added, "it affords a sufficient opportunity to exhibit negro hatred."[50]

This boded ill, of course, for the success of the entire Reconstruction experiment. Because some of the most powerful figures in the Union army excused racial violence among and against their own soldiers, these commanders allowed the 1865 Charleston riot and other bloody attacks to influence military policy throughout the South. By condoning racial divisions, Generals Gillmore and Grant approved a segregation of U.S. occupation troops and opened the door to future retaliation against blacks by former Confederates. White Southerners thus used attacks on African Americans to force the complete removal of black soldiers from the South, an appeasement that eventually led to the return of white hegemony over black Southerners.[51]

Notes

1. John Johnson, *The Defense of Charleston Harbor, Including Fort Sumter and the Adjacent Islands, 1863–1865* (Charleston: Walker, Evans & Cogswell Company, 1890), 259; E. Milby Burton, *The Siege of Charleston, 1861–1865* (Columbia: University of South Carolina Press, 1970), 313. For other works on Charleston's defensive fortifications, see also Warren Ripley, ed., *Siege Train: The Journal of a Confederate Artilleryman in the Defense of Charleston* (Columbia: University of South Carolina Press, 1986); C. A. Bennett, "Roswell Sabin Ripley: 'Charleston's Gallant Defender,' " *South Carolina Historical Magazine* 95 (July 1994): 225–42; and Edward G. Longacre, ed., " 'It Will Be Many a Day before Charleston Falls': Letters of a Union Sergeant on Folly Island, August 1863–April 1864," *South Carolina Historical Magazine* 85 (April 1984): 108–34.

2. Captain Samuel Cuskaden to Lieutenant H. A. Mott, March 6, 1865, in *The War of the Rebellion: A Compilation of the Official Records of the Union and Confederate Armies*, 128 vols. (Washington, D.C.: Government Printing Office, 1880–1901), 1st ser., 53:60–61 (hereafter cited as *OR*); Joel Williamson, *After Slavery: The Negro in South Carolina during Reconstruction, 1861–1877* (Chapel Hill: University of North Carolina Press, 1965), 22; Wilbert L. Jenkins, *Seizing the New Day: African Americans in Post–Civil War Charleston* (Bloomington: Indiana University Press, 1998), 31; Arney Robinson Childs, ed., *The Private Journal of Henry William Ravenel, 1859–1887* (Columbia: University of South Carolina Press, 1947), 212; John F. Marszalek, ed., *The Diary of Miss Emma Holmes, 1861–1866* (Baton Rouge: Louisiana State University Press, 1979), 408. For other works on Sherman's march through South Carolina, see Marion Brunson Lucas, *Sherman and the Burning of Columbia* (College Station: Texas A&M University Press, 1976); Joseph T. Glatthaar, *The March to the Sea and Beyond: Sherman's Troops in the Savannah and Carolinas Campaigns* (New York: New York University Press, 1985);

and George C. Rable, *Civil Wars: Women and the Crisis of Southern Nationalism* (Urbana: University of Illinois Press, 1989), 171–80.

3. This unit was formerly known as the 3rd South Carolina Volunteers.

4. Cuskaden to Mott, March 6, 1865, *OR*, 1st ser., 53:60–61; Major General Quincy A. Gillmore to Major General Henry W. Halleck, February 18, 1865, *OR*, 47 (2):483–84; *Charleston Daily Courier*, February 20, 1865; Gerald Schwartz, ed., *A Woman Doctor's Civil War: Esther Hill Hawks' Diary* (Columbia: University of South Carolina Press, 1984), 117; Luis F. Emilio, *A Brave Black Regiment: History of the Fifty-fourth Regiment of Massachusetts Volunteer Infantry, 1863–1865* (1894; New York: Arno Press, 1969), 281–84; Donald Yacovone, ed., *A Voice of Thunder: The Civil War Letters of George E. Stephens* (Urbana: University of Illinois Press, 1997), 80–81; Robert N. Rosen, *Confederate Charleston: An Illustrated History of the City and the People during the Civil War* (Columbia: University of South Carolina Press, 1994), 138–41; and Noah Andre Trudeau, *Like Men of War: Black Troops in the Civil War, 1862–1865* (Boston: Little, Brown, 1998), 353–64.

5. Walter J. Fraser, Jr., *Charleston! Charleston!: The History of a Southern City* (Columbia: University of South Carolina Press, 1989), 269–70; Lieutenant General Ulysses S. Grant to Edwin M. Stanton, February 26, 1865, in John Y. Simon, ed., *The Papers of Ulysses S. Grant*, 24 vols. to date (Carbondale: Southern Illinois University Press, 1967–), 14:55. The 21st USCT "is almost wholly composed of Charleston blacks," observed a Northern reporter. See *New York Tribune*, March 11, 1865.

6. For a discussion on Union policy toward black troops, see Brooks D. Simpson, *Let Us Have Peace: Ulysses S. Grant and the Politics of War and Reconstruction, 1861–1868* (Chapel Hill: University of North Carolina Press, 1991), 38–46; George Washington Williams, *A History of the Negro Troops in the War of the Rebellion, 1861–1865* (New York: Harper & Brothers, 1888), 106–9, 122, 161–66; Mary Frances Berry, *Military Necessity and Civil Rights Policy: Black Citizenship and the Constitution, 1861–1868* (Port Washington, N.Y.: Kennikat Press, 1977), 77; and Robert J. Zalimas, Jr., "Black Union Soldiers in the Postwar South, 1865–1866" (M.A. thesis, Arizona State University, 1993). For a similar discussion highlighting the initial use of black soldiers as "auxiliary forces," see Dudley Taylor Cornish, *The Sable Arm: Black Troops in the Union Army, 1861–1865* (1956; Lawrence: University Press of Kansas, 1987), 185–86, and Joseph T. Glatthaar, *Forged in Battle: The Civil War Alliance of Black Soldiers and White Officers* (New York: Free Press, 1990), 182–85.

7. Simpson, *Let Us Have Peace*, 38–46; Williams, *A History of Negro Troops in the War of the Rebellion*, 106–9; and Berry, *Military Necessity and Civil Rights Policy*, 77. For recent studies on Union military policy toward white Southerners, see Mark Grimsley, *The Hard Hand of War: Union Military Policy toward Southern Civilians, 1861–1865* (Cambridge: Cambridge University Press, 1995), and Stephen V. Ash, *When the Yankees Came: Conflict and Chaos in the Occupied South, 1861–1865*

(Chapel Hill: University of North Carolina Press, 1995). For descriptions of black refugee camps, see Cam Walker, "Corinth: The Story of a Contraband Camp," *Civil War History* 20 (March 1974): 5–22, and Marion B. Lucas, "Camp Nelson, Kentucky, during the Civil War: Cradle of Liberty or Refugee Death Camp?" *Filson Club Historical Quarterly* 63 (October 1989): 439–52.

8. Sherman to Grant, December 31, 1864, in Simon, *The Papers of U. S. Grant*, 13:171n; Stanley P. Hirshson, *The White Tecumseh: A Biography of General William T. Sherman* (New York: John Wiley, 1997), 265–77; *New York Tribune*, March 1, 1865. In Savannah (unlike Atlanta), Sherman implemented a "hands-off" policy in order to sway the civilian population back to the Union. For a discussion of Sherman's racial attitudes, see John F. Marszalek, *Sherman: A Soldier's Passion for Order* (New York: Free Press, 1993), 309–13, and Michael Fellman, *Citizen Sherman: A Life of William Tecumseh Sherman* (New York: Random House, 1995). For a modern-day debate on the racial attitudes of General Grant, see William S. McFeely, *Grant: A Biography* (New York: W. W. Norton, 1981), and Brooks D. Simpson, "Butcher? Racist?: An Examination of William S. McFeely's *Grant: A Biography*," *Civil War History* 33 (March 1987): 63–83.

9. Fraser, *Charleston! Charleston!*, 269–76. Following the November 1865 elections, the commander for South Carolina, Major General Daniel E. Sickles, allowed Charleston's civil government to resume control of the city. See ibid., 275–76. Black Charlestonians, however, did not join the city's regular police force until November 1868. See W. Marvin Dulaney, " 'Breaking the Spirit of Our People': Black Police Officers in Charleston during Reconstruction," *Avery Review* 1 (Spring 1998): 69–86.

10. For a discussion of the lack of respect for black officers among white Union soldiers, see James G. Hollandsworth, Jr., *The Louisiana Native Guards: The Black Military Experience during the Civil War* (Baton Rouge: Louisiana State University Press, 1995).

11. For a discussion of the use of violence by white Southerners during Reconstruction, see George C. Rable, *But There Was No Peace: The Role of Violence in the Politics of Reconstruction* (Athens: University of Georgia Press, 1984).

12. Special Order No. 30, Headquarters, Northern District, Department of the South, February 20, 1865, *OR*, 1st ser., 47 (2):508; Gillmore to Halleck, February 18, 1865, *OR*, 1st ser., 47 (2):483–84; Circular, Headquarters, Northern District, Department of the South, February 20, 1865, *OR*, 1st ser., 47 (2):508; Yacovone, *A Voice of Thunder*, 81; Williams, *A History of Negro Troops in the War of the Rebellion*, 164–65; Eric Foner, *Reconstruction: America's Unfinished Revolution, 1863–1877* (New York: Harper and Row, 1988), 80–81; Leon F. Litwack, *Been in the Storm So Long: The Aftermath of Slavery* (New York: Alfred A. Knopf, 1979), 292–301. Although Brigadier General Alexander Schimmelfennig designated the 21st USCT as the main occupation force for Charleston, other black regiments were stationed in Charleston at various times, including the 33rd, 35th,

and 102nd USCT as well as the 54th and 55th Massachusetts Volunteers. See Bernard Powers, "Community Evolution and Race Relations in Reconstruction Charleston, South Carolina," *South Carolina Historical Magazine* 95 (January 1994): 28, and Yacovone, *A Voice of Thunder*, 81. For biographical sketches of Schimmelfennig, see Stewart Sifakis, *Who Was Who in the Civil War* (New York: Facts on File, 1988), 572; Ezra J. Warner, *Generals in Blue: Lives of the Union Commanders* (Baton Rouge: Louisiana State University Press, 1964), 424; and Harry W. Pfanz, *Gettysburg—Culp's Hill and Cemetery Hill* (Chapel Hill: University of North Carolina Press, 1993), 371. For a discussion of black support for the Union armies, see Clarence L. Mohr, *On the Threshold of Freedom: Masters and Slaves in Civil War Georgia* (Athens: University of Georgia Press, 1986). For a discussion of Charleston's free black community, see Michael P. Johnson and James L. Roark, eds., *No Chariot Let Down: Charleston's Free People of Color on the Eve of the Civil War* (Chapel Hill: University of North Carolina Press, 1984).

13. First Sergeant H. D. Dudley, Company K, 35th USCT to Editor, *Christian Recorder*, May 20, 1865 (hereafter cited as *CR*).

14. Janet B. Hewett, ed., *Supplement to the Official Records of the Union and Confederate Armies*, vol. 77, ser. 89, pt. 2: *Record of Events* (Wilmington, N.C.: Broadfoot Publishing Company, 1998), 547–56 (hereafter cited as *SOR*); Mohr, *On the Threshold of Freedom*, 86, 89.

15. Ira Berlin, Joseph P. Reidy, and Leslie S. Rowland, eds., *The Black Military Experience* (Cambridge: Cambridge University Press, 1982), 391–95. For a discussion of manhood in the African American regiments, see Jim Cullen, " 'I's a Man Now': Gender and African American Men," in Catherine Clinton and Nina Silber, eds., *Divided Houses: Gender and the Civil War* (New York: Oxford University Press, 1992), 72–91; Hollandsworth, *The Louisiana Native Guards*, 104–16; Cornish, *The Sable Arm*, 289–91; Eugene D. Genovese, *Roll, Jordan, Roll: The World the Slaves Made* (New York: Vintage Books, 1974), 155–58. For a discussion of the pay issue, see Berlin et al., *The Black Military Experience*, 20–21, and Cornish, *The Sable Arm*, 186–95.

16. Brigadier General Alexander Schimmelfennig to Brigadier General E. E. Potter, February 25, 1865, *OR*, 1st ser., 47 (2):577–78; Captain J. W. Dickinson to Commanding Officer 21st USCT, February 25, 1865, *OR*, 1st ser., 47 (2):578; Berlin et al., *The Black Military Experience*, 40–41. Potter abandoned the offensive after the retreating Confederates burned the Santee River Bridge. The black detachments, however, stayed on provisional duty with Potter until ordered to return to Charleston. See Emilio, *A Brave Black Regiment*, 284.

17. Warner, *Generals in Blue*, 423–24, 216–17; Sifakis, *Who Was Who in the Civil War*, 292–93.

18. General Orders No. 6, Headquarters Northern District, Department of the South, February 26, 1865, *OR*, 1st ser., 47 (2):593; Frederick H. Dyer, *A Compendium of the War of the Rebellion*, vol. 3, *Regimental Histories* (New York: Thomas

Yoseloff, 1958), 1454; Franklin McGrath, *The History of the 127th New York Volunteers* (n.p., n.d.), 6–7, 117–51; Solomon Bates Starbird to Marianne Starbird (sister), August 12, 26, September 13, 1862, Starbird Letters, Clements Library, University of Michigan, Ann Arbor.

19. General Orders No. 6, Headquarters Northern District, Department of the South, February 26, 1865, *OR*, 1st ser., 47 (2):593; Brigadier General John P. Hatch to Brigadier General Edward E. Potter, February 28, 1865, *OR*, 1st ser., 47 (2):616–17; Hatch to C. H. Van Wyck, February 28, 1865, *OR*, 1st ser., 47 (2):618.

20. Loyal Citizen to *Standard* Editor, *National Anti-Slavery Standard*, September 30, 1865.

21. In 1860 the black population of Charleston numbered 16,600 (41 percent of the total population) and by 1870 would grow to 26,173 (53 percent). After the war, the black population of the South's ten largest cities doubled between 1865 and 1870, while the white population in these cities rose only 10 percent. See Foner, *Reconstruction*, 81–82, and Ash, *When the Yankees Came*, 155. For reports that black and white regiments controlled separate sections of Charleston, see Frank A. Rollin, *Life and Public Services of Martin R. Delany* (1883; New York: Arno Press, 1969), 220–21, and Frances Perkins Beecher, "Two Years with a Colored Regiment: A Woman's Experience," *New England Magazine* 17 (January 1898): 539.

22. Powers, "Community Evolution and Race Relations," 27–28; *Charleston Daily Courier*, May 25, 1865; Yacovone, *A Voice of Thunder*, 84–85, 87. See also Berry, *Military Necessity and Civil Rights Policy*, 89; Genovese, *Roll, Jordan, Roll*, 152–54. For a discussion of racial violence between Charleston's freedmen and white military police force, see Bernard Powers, *Black Charlestonians: A Social History, 1822–1888* (Fayetteville: University of Arkansas Press, 1994), 76–77. For first hand accounts of abuse by white Union troops against slaves and their property, see George P. Rawick, ed., *The American Slave: A Composite Autobiography*, vol. 2, *South Carolina Narratives Parts 1 and 2* (Westport, Conn.: Greenwood Publishing Company, 1972), 12, 40, 43, 53, 69, 72–73, 77, 105, 128, 145. On the same day that he demanded the return of the 21st USCT, February 28, 1865, Hatch also helped to inflame the already tense occupation environment. Unsubstantiated reports had reached his desk accusing former slaves of committing murders at Thirteen-Mile Hill, a black community located near Goose Creek north of Charleston. Reacting quickly, Hatch immediately sent four companies under the command of Colonel Edward N. Hallowell of the 54th Massachusetts with orders to uproot the entire African American community and relocate it to Charleston under gunpoint. The soldiers complied, and the reluctant migrants moved into the port, increasing the size and racial tensions of the black community. See First Lieutenant Leonard B. Perry (Acting Assistant Adjutant General) to Colonel E. N. Hallowell, February 28, 1865, *OR*, 1st ser., 47 (2):618.

23. The 21st USCT as well as African American sailors joined Charleston's freedmen in March to celebrate the end of slavery in South Carolina. In April, African

American soldiers in Charleston helped Northern politicians, preachers, and abolitionists to raise the Union flag at Fort Sumter. See McGrath, *A History of the 127th New York*, 152; Lieutenant H. A. Batterson (Acting Assistant Adjutant General) to Rear Admiral John A. Dahlgren, and Batterson to Lieutenant Colonel A. G. Bennett, March 20, 1865, *OR*, 1st ser., 47 (2):929; Thomas Holt, *Black over White: Negro Political Leadership in South Carolina during Reconstruction* (Urbana: University of Illinois Press, 1977), 11; James Brewer Stewart, *William Lloyd Garrison and the Challenge of Emancipation* (Arlington Heights, Ill.: Harlan Davidson, 1992), 190–93; Edward A. Miller, Jr., *Gullah Statesman: Robert Smalls from Slavery to Congress, 1839–1915* (Columbia: University of South Carolina Press, 1995), 24–25.

24. Hewett, *SOR*, 549; Special Order No. 68, Headquarters, Northern District, Department of the South, April 2, 1865, *OR*, 1st ser., 47 (3):89.

25. Special Order No. 68, Headquarters, Northern District, Department of the South, April 2, 1865, *OR*, 1st ser., 47 (3):89; Hewett, *SOR*, 762–79; Dyer, *A Compendium of the War of the Rebellion*, 1729; Return of the United States Forces Charleston S.C. for April 1865, Returns from U.S. Military Posts 1800–1916, Record Group (RG) 393, M617, roll 198, National Archives (NA), Washington, D.C. For a biographical sketch of James C. Beecher and an account of the famous Beecher family, see Lyman Beecher Stowe, *Saints, Sinners and Beechers* (Indianapolis: Bobbs-Merrill, 1934). For a discussion of Beecher's mental illness and subsequent postwar suicide, see Glatthaar, *Forged in Battle*, 240–41.

26. Special Order No. 68, Headquarters, Northern District, Department of the South, April 2, 1865, *OR*, 1st ser., 47 (3):89; Rollin, *Life and Public Services of Martin Delany*, 195–96, 200–202, 209–13. Other observers confirmed that 1,000 black Charlestonians had joined the Union army since February 1865. See *CR*, March 18, 1865, and *National Anti-Slavery Standard*, March 25, 1865.

27. Peter Pineo, U.S. Army Medical Inspector to Major Burger, April 7, 1865, *OR*, 1st ser., 47 (3):126–27; Endorsement of Major General Quincy A. Gillmore, April 10, 1865, *OR*, 1st ser., 47 (3):127; Endorsement of Brigadier General John P. Hatch, April 11, 1865, *OR*, 1st ser., 47 (3):127; Yacovone, *A Voice of Thunder*, 86–87; Schwartz, *A Woman Doctor's Civil War*, 137, 149–50. The medical inspector's remarks are significant because he raised concerns about the spread of disease before most physicians accepted germ theory.

28. Colonel William Gurney to George D. Cragin, Esq., President Produce Exchange, New York City, April 3, 1865, in *OR*, 1st ser., 47 (3):94–95; Fraser, *Charleston! Charleston!*, 274–75; Sherman quoted in ibid., 273. Massive starvation also rampaged through the adjacent sea islands. See Schwartz, *A Woman Doctor's Civil War*, 141–42.

29. Yacovone, *A Voice of Thunder*, 86–87; *Boston Commonwealth*, June 17, 1865, quoted in Yacovone, *A Voice of Thunder*, 87; *CR*, June 10, 1865; General Orders No. 44, May 21, 1865, Headquarters, City of Charleston, in *CR*, June 10, 1865; James

Redpath to Editor, *National Anti-Slavery Standard*, July 22, 1865; *Charleston Daily Courier*, May 25, 1865.

30. Holt, *Black over White*, 11–13; *New York Tribune*, May 8, 1865; *Charleston Daily Courier*, July 8, 1865; John R. McKivigan, "James Redpath in South Carolina: An Abolitionist's Odyssey in the Reconstruction Era South," in Randall M. Miller and John R. McKivigan, eds., *The Moment of Decision: Biographical Essays on American Character and Regional Identity* (Westport, Conn.: Greenwood Press, 1994), 196; Yacovone, *A Voice of Thunder*, 87; *New York Times*, May 22, 1865.

31. McKivigan, "James Redpath in South Carolina," 191–93, 196; *New York Tribune*, May 13, 1865; Jenkins, *Seizing the New Day*, 37.

32. McKivigan, "James Redpath in South Carolina," 196–98; *New York Tribune*, May 13, 1865; *Charleston Daily Courier*, July 8, 1865. For a discussion of racism among U.S. soldiers, see Reid Mitchell, *Civil War Soldiers* (New York: Penguin Books, 1988), 121–23, and Edwin S. Redkey, ed., *A Grand Army of Black Men: Letters from African-American Soldiers in the Union Army, 1861–1865* (Cambridge: Cambridge University Press, 1992), 249–68.

33. McKivigan, "James Redpath in South Carolina," 196–98; *Charleston Daily Courier*, July 8, 1865. Other Northern observers echoed Redpath and reported that Hatch "hated" African American soldiers and "encouraged arbitrary arrests of all blacks." See Yacovone, *A Voice of Thunder*, 88. After the trial, Redpath and his wife returned north in mid-June, so he was not in Charleston for the July riot. In September 1865 he contacted Major General O. O. Howard and requested a reappointment to his old post. Howard, eager to avoid the national attention Redpath brought to the Freedmen's Bureau, encouraged the superintendent for South Carolina, Brevet Major General Rufus Saxton, to appoint the "less controversial" Pennsylvania Quaker Rufus Tomlinson. See McKivigan, "James Redpath in South Carolina," 198.

34. Gillmore to Howard, July 2, 1865, Letters Sent, Department of the South, RG 393, NA; Warner, *Generals in Blue*, 176–77; and Whitelaw Reid, *Ohio in the War: Her Statesmen, Her Generals, and Soldiers*, vol. 1, *History of the State During the War, and the Lives of Her Generals* (New York: Moore, Wilstach & Baldwin, 1868), 617–55.

35. *History of the Second Battalion Duryee Zouaves, One Hundred and Sixty-fifth Regiment New York Volunteer Infantry* (New York: n.p., 1904), 9–35; Dyer, *A Compendium of the War of the Rebellion*, 1466; Ron Spicer and Roger D. Stureke, "The 165th New York Volunteer Infantry Regiment, 1863," *Military Collector and Historian* 20 (Summer 1968): 49–51; Private George A. Hussey to Mary Jane Alexander Hussey (mother), August 21, 1864, Hussey to Mary Hussey (sister), November 4, 1864, Hussey-Wadsworth Families Collection, Clements Library, University of Michigan, Ann Arbor (hereafter cited as HW). See also "Zouave" in Mark Mayo Boatner III, *The Civil War Dictionary* (New York: David McKay, 1988), 954. The unit patterned itself after Major General Abraham Duryee's 5th New York Volunteers, known as Duryee's Zouaves.

36. Hussey to Mother and Sister, June 3, 7, 28, July 17, 1865, HW; Lieutenant Colonel Gouvenor Carr to President Andrew Johnson, July 14, 1865, File No. C2112 (V. 5) 1865, Volunteer Service Branch, Office of the Adjutant General, RG 94, NA. The soldiers placed under arrest were quickly released to enable them to join the transfer of the 165th to Charleston. For other reports that discuss problems between white Zouave units from New York and black regiments, see Virginia M. Adams, ed., *On the Altar of Freedom: A Black Soldier's Civil War Letters from the Front: Corporal James Henry Gooding* (Amherst: University of Massachusetts Press, 1991), 110. For a report on the Grand Review, see James M. McPherson, *Ordeal by Fire: The Civil War and Reconstruction* (New York: McGraw-Hill, 1992), 485.

37. Hewett, *SOR*, 766; Return of the United States Forces Charleston S.C. for June 1865, Returns from the U.S. Military Posts 1800–1916, RG 393, M617, roll 198, NA; James M. Sanders to Editor, *CR*, June 10, 1865. The reputation of the 54th Massachusetts was well known to Gillmore, who ordered the assault on Battery Wagner. Afterward, while under his command in the Department of the South, the 54th also received high praise for its performance of excessive fatigue duty on South Carolina's Sea Islands. See Cornish, *The Sable Arm*, 147–56, 246. The history of the 54th Massachusetts is well documented. See Emilio, *A Brave Black Regiment*; Peter Burchard, *One Gallant Rush: Robert Gould Shaw and His Brave Black Regiment* (New York: St. Martin's Press, 1965); Russell Duncan, ed., *Blue-eyed Child of Fortune: The Civil War Letters of Colonel Robert Gould Shaw* (Athens: University of Georgia Press, 1992); Adams, *On the Altar of Freedom*; Yacovone, *A Voice of Thunder*.

38. Hussey to Mother and Sister, July 17, 1865, HW; Carr to Johnson, July 14, 1865, RG 94, NA; *New York Times*, July 24, 1865; *Charleston Daily Courier*, July 11, 1865. During a short trip to South Carolina's Sea Islands, Hussey observed that the freedmen treated the Zouaves well but "seemed shy of us most likely on account of our dress." See Hussey to Mother and Sister, June 28, 1865, HW.

39. *New York Times*, July 24, 1865; *Charleston Daily Courier*, July 11, 1865; General Orders No. 59, July 6, 1865, Headquarters, City of Charleston, Bound Records, 165th New York Infantry, RG 94, NA; Hussey to Mother and Sister, June 28, 1865, HW. For a discussion of how white Southerners used the black insurrection scare as an instrument of white unity and a justification to rearm themselves, see Dan T. Carter, "The Anatomy of Fear: The Christmas Day Insurrection Scare of 1865," *Journal of Southern History* 42 (August 1976): 346–64.

40. Carr to Johnson, July 14, 1865, and Hatch to Lieutenant Colonel William Burger, August 22, 1865, File No. C2112 (V.5) 1865, Volunteer Service Branch, Office of the Adjutant General, RG 94, NA. Hussey also noted that the "disturbances" between black and white soldiers were "frequent." See Hussey to Mother and Sister, July 17, 1865, HW.

41. *Charleston Daily Courier*, July 10, 1865; *Edgefield (S.C.) Advertiser*, July 19, 1865. At the time of the riot, Gillmore was at his headquarters in Savannah, Georgia. See *New York Times*, July 24, 1865. In one account, a prominent freedman recounted

rumors that the Zouaves disrupted Bing's egg stand and then stabbed him with bayonets after he protested. See *Boston Journal*, July 23, 1865, reprinted in *New York Tribune*, July 24, 1865. In *Black Charlestonians*, 78, Powers places the 127th New York Volunteers at the riot instead of the 165th New York Volunteers.

42. *New York Times*, July 24, 1865; General Orders No. 61, July 12, 1865, Headquarters, City of Charleston, in *Charleston Daily Courier*, July 13, 15, 1865. Although the 165th New York Volunteers constituted the main white force during the racial rioting, members of the 157th New York Volunteers, a white unit awaiting transport home, also took part in the rows. See Captain T. D. Hodges (Acting Assistant Adjutant General) to Lieutenant Colonel J. C. Carmichael, Commanding 157th New York Volunteers, July 13, 1865, Letters Sent, Department of the South, RG 393, NA. Several historians have mentioned the Charleston riot in their works. See Yacovone, *A Voice of Thunder*, 87; Williamson, *After Slavery*, 258; Melinda Meek Hennessey, "Racial Violence during Reconstruction: The 1876 Riots in Charleston and Cainhoy," *South Carolina Historical Magazine* 86 (April 1985): 102; Brooks D. Simpson, LeRoy P. Graf, and John Muldowny, eds., *Advice after Appomattox: Letters to Andrew Johnson, 1865–1866* (Knoxville: University of Tennessee Press, 1987), 117 n. 28; and Powers, *Black Charlestonians*, 77–78.

43. *National Anti-Slavery Standard*, August 19, 1865.

44. Ibid., July 29, 1865.

45. Gillmore to Brevet Major General Hatch, July 13, 1865, Letters Sent, Department of the South, RG 393, NA. For the importance of regimental colors, see James I. Robertson, Jr., *Soldiers Blue and Gray* (Columbia: University of South Carolina Press, 1988), 223–24. Lieutenant Colonel Carr refused to hand over the colors, forcing Gillmore to raise charges against him. Gillmore then disarmed the 165th New York Volunteers and placed the regiment under arrest at Battery Wagner. A court-martial found Carr guilty of insubordination, and he received a dishonorable discharge. See General Orders No. 25, Headquarters, Department of South Carolina, August 30, 1865, Court Martial File OO1347, General Courts Martial 1812–1938, Office of the Judge Advocate General, RG 153, NA. Hussey reported that the unit played a "Yankee trick" on Gillmore and handed him two empty poles with covers. See Hussey to Mother and Sister, July 17, 1865, HW.

46. William M. Burger (Assistant Adjutant General) to Hatch, July 15, 1865, Letters Sent, Department of the South, RG 393, NA. Although peace was restored, tensions remained high in Charleston, and the local paper reported several back-alley brawls between individual members of the 54th Massachusetts Volunteers and the 47th Pennsylvania Volunteers. See *Charleston Daily Courier*, August 5, 7, 8, 1865, and Yacovone, *A Voice of Thunder*, 88–89. Four days after the riot, a white assistant inspector from Ohio visited Charleston and reported the "disgraceful" and "slovenly" demeanor of the 47th Pennsylvania Volunteers while praising Company C of the 35th USCT, who "carry themselves as soldiers." See Major E. C. Culp to Brevet Major George E. Gourand, July 14, 1865, Let-

ters Sent by the Acting Assistant Inspector at Charleston, Department of the South, RG 393, NA. Although Esther Hill Hawks, a white teacher and doctor attached to the 21st USCT lamented returning to "that forsaken island," she reported that some enlisted men embraced the transfer because their families resided at Mitchelville, an African American community located near Hilton Head. See Schwartz, *A Woman Doctor's Civil War*, 166. When various black regiments were stationed on South Carolina's Sea Islands, wives of white officers and black enlisted men joined their husbands and served as nurses and teachers to assist former slaves in their transition from slavery to freedom. See Beecher, "Two Years with a Colored Regiment," 533–43; and Susie King Taylor, *A Black Woman's Civil War Memoirs: Reminiscences of My Life in Camp with the 33rd U.S. Colored Troops, Late 1st South Carolina Volunteers*, ed. Patricia W. Romero (New York: Markus Weiner, 1988).

47. Gillmore to Brigadier General Lorenzo Thomas, July 20, 1865, Letters Sent, Department of South Carolina, RG 393, NA; Berlin et al., *The Black Military Experience*, 373; editorial, *Chicago Tribune*, n.d., reprinted in *National Anti-Slavery Standard*, September 16, 1865. For a discussion of black enlistment, see Benjamin Quarles, *The Negro in the Civil War* (Boston: Little, Brown, 1953), 182; James M. Guthrie, *Camp-Fires of the Afro-American; or, The Colored Man as a Patriot* (Philadelphia: Afro-American Publishing Company, 1899), 360, and Cornish, *The Sable Arm*. Although black suffrage remained a controversial issue in both Northern and Southern states, Thomas Morris Chester, an African American reporter for the *Philadelphia Press*, reported that some black soldiers in the Army of the James did vote in the election of 1864. See R. J. M. Blackett, ed., *Thomas Morris Chester, Black Civil War Correspondent: His Dispatches from the Virginia Front* (Baton Rouge: Louisiana State University Press, 1989), 189.

48. Gillmore to Brigadier General Lorenzo Thomas, July 20, 1865, Letters Sent, Department of South Carolina, RG 393, NA; Berlin et al., *The Black Military Experience*, 373; Brevet Colonel Theodore S. Bowers to Grant, July 29, 1865, in Simon, *The Papers of U. S. Grant*, 15:290n. For a discussion highlighting this period of adjustment and experimentation in South Carolina labor arrangements, see Julie Saville, *The Work of Reconstruction: From Slave to Wage Laborer in South Carolina, 1860–1870* (Cambridge: Cambridge University Press, 1994), 72–101, and Roger L. Ransom and Richard Sutch, *One Kind of Freedom: The Economic Consequences of Emancipation* (Cambridge: Cambridge University Press, 1977), 57–61. After an inspection tour of South Carolina, Major General George G. Meade called the charges against the black soldiers "groundless" and ascertained that white plantation owners generated the rumors concerning the disruption of labor contracts. See Major General Meade to Edwin M. Stanton, September 20, 1865, in Simpson et al., *Advice after Appomattox*, 231. Grant later used these "groundless" reports to argue against using black soldiers as occupation troops in the South. See Grant to President Andrew Johnson, December 18, 1865, in

Simon, *The Papers of U. S. Grant*, 15:435. For Southern white reaction to black laborers in the postwar South, see Michael Les Benedict, *The Fruits of Victory: Alternatives in Restoring the Union, 1865–1877* (Lanham, Md.: University Press of America, 1986), 83–85.

49. Grant to Bowers, July 31, 1865, in Simon, *The Papers of U. S. Grant*, 15:290; Circular No. 44, War Department, Adjutant General's Office, September 9, 1865, *OR*, 3rd ser., 5:108. In his September report, Meade also noted that Gillmore planned to reduce the size of his remaining black regiments. Gillmore already had discharged physically unqualified black soldiers and intended to consolidate the five Southern-raised units into two or three regiments. See Meade to Stanton, September 20, 1865, *OR*, 3rd ser., 5:108.

50. Gilbert Pilsbury to Brevet Major General Rufus Saxton, August 27, 1865, Reports of Conditions and Operations, July 1865–December 1866, Records of the Assistant Commissioner for the State of South Carolina, Bureau of Refugees, Freedmen, and Abandoned Lands, 1865–70, RG 105, M869, roll 34, NA. In November 1865 Saxton reported from Charleston that the "condition of the freedmen is now strongly worse than when he was in slavery." Saxton to Dr. J. Milton Hawks, November 7, 1865, Esther Hill Hawks Papers, Manuscript Division, Library of Congress, Washington, D.C. For similar reports, see Redkey, *A Grand Army of Black Men*, 183–85, and Schwartz, *A Woman Doctor's Civil War*, 200. On Saxton, see Paul A. Cimbala, *Under the Guardianship of the Nation: The Freedmen's Bureau and the Reconstruction of Georgia, 1865–1870* (Athens: University of Georgia Press, 1997).

51. For a discussion of how white South Carolinians used racial violence to regain control of the state, see Richard Zuczek, *State of Rebellion: Reconstruction in South Carolina* (Columbia: University of South Carolina Press, 1996).

14

USCT VETERANS
IN POST–CIVIL WAR
NORTH CAROLINA
Richard Reid

On the morning of February 22, 1865, Union troops under the command of General Alfred H. Terry marched into the smoke-shrouded city of Wilmington, North Carolina, hard on the heels of General Braxton Bragg's retreating Confederates. Among the many soldiers filing through the city that day were the men of General Charles Paine's all-black division, including the 37th U.S. Colored Troops (USCT), a regiment raised in North Carolina. One of the men, recognized and embraced by his mother, was described in a fellow soldier's letter in a way that would have resonated with many black enlisted men. "He had left his home a slave," the letter's author, who was in the 4th USCT, wrote, "but he returned in the garb of a union soldier, free, a man."[1] Both mother and son would have been aware of the new aspirations and expectations of equal treatment that were formed as part of the black military experience. The black veterans had been changed in diverse ways. Many had achieved a degree of literacy, while black noncommissioned officers had developed leadership abilities and learned to handle a range of new responsibilities. All the soldiers had their personal worlds broadened as they tramped through parts of the nation that they had never seen. Most would have agreed with Frederick Douglass that when a black man could "get an eagle on his button, and a musket on his shoulder, and bullets in his pocket," then no one could deny that he had earned the rights of citizenship.[2]

Yet if black veterans looked forward eagerly to new changes as a result of their military service, it was equally clear that much of Southern white society clung to the values and attitudes of the past. One of the black soldiers occupying Kinston, North Carolina, in the summer of 1865 described the anger and frustrations of the townspeople there. He wrote of them "calling in all manner of names that were never applied to the Deity, to deliver them from the hands of the *smoked Yankees*."[3] When God did not respond promptly enough, some ex-Confederates took matters into their own hands and murdered at least one black soldier in Kinston.[4] The killing was not an isolated event. A few months later, Private Henry Cotanch of the 37th USCT was shot at Morehead City by a white Southerner for whom the war was not yet over. About the same time, Bill Jones, who had served in the 14th U.S. Colored Heavy Artillery (USCHA), was lynched in Greene County.[5] These events involved attitudes and conflicts that framed the veterans' experiences in the decades after the war. Few of them had left the service without undergoing fundamental changes, some positive and some not. The world that they carved out for themselves was in the midst of a larger society clinging to older values.

An increasing amount of scholarship has been produced in recent years outlining the Reconstruction experiences of Southern African Americans, but less has been done on the postwar readjustments of the region's black Union veterans.[6] Indeed, the most recent study of Civil War soldiers in war and peace gives only a few pages to the experiences of Southern black veterans.[7] Interesting new studies have been completed on individual black regiments, but they have not followed the soldiers' careers after discharge.[8] When broader studies have made passing references as to what impact Union military service had on Southern blacks, these works have tended to portray such service as a positive force in the veterans' later lives. For some historians, the years in the military served, at least for a select group, as a means of achieving successful postwar careers. Other writers, when discussing the veterans' postwar lives, have seen little evidence of what a later generation would call postcombat (or posttraumatic) stress disorder. Thus historian Eric Foner has argued that "[f]or black soldiers, military service meant more than an opportunity to help save the Union, even more than their own freedom and the destruction of slavery as an institution. For men of talent and ambition, the army flung open a door to advancement and respectability. From the army would come many of the political leaders of Reconstruction."[9] Historian Joseph T. Glatthaar also believes that military service acted for black veterans, as it had for so many others, as a springboard into politics or other careers.[10] In addition, he has argued that while the black veterans' postwar experiences were diverse and while some, like a large number of their white officers, suffered personal and emotional problems in the postwar years, "for most black soldiers, psychological adaptation to a peace-time environment seems to have gone quite smoothly."[11] Glatthaar cites as proof a very low divorce rate and few cases of opium addiction or mental problems. He does make it clear, however, that there is limited reliable information by which to judge properly the veterans' peacetime readjustments. One implication of his argument is that the ease of the transition back to civilian life was helped by the support of the local black community. Historian Larry Logue's recent study of postwar readjustment among both white and black soldiers deals with only a few specific problems facing the Southern black veterans. Regional studies, however, suggest that, in addition to suffering from the endemic white violence that in parts of the South affected all African Americans, newly mustered-out veterans had difficulty competing for jobs with black civilians who had not been in the war.[12] The problem of job competition was aggravated for the men of most Southern black regiments by their late dates of discharge. Whereas most Northern black regiments were demobilized during 1865, Southern black regiments remained in service as late as 1867.

It is therefore worth examining the postwar experiences of black veterans from one state or region in order to test some of the conclusions reached by historians such as Foner, Glatthaar, and Logue about the positive benefits of military service. The experience of different groups of black veterans may vary considerably depending on the region in which they lived. One might also expect that the postwar experience of the black veterans would differ considerably depending on where they had been recruited, what their pre-war situation had been, and what kind of military experience they had had in the war. Black veterans returning to a victorious and prosperous Northern state could expect a response very different from the one encountered by African American ex-soldiers being discharged in a Southern state crippled economically and in the throes of social readjustment. Wartime experiences altered the veterans in different ways. Some black units had traveled extensively across the nation and had developed an esprit de corps as the result of successful military service. Other units had served only locally, functioning more as a uniformed labor force.

The black veterans from North Carolina offer a useful case study of how one group of ex-servicemen created new lives following the war. These soldiers could persuasively claim that they, more than others in their state, had been an important part of the struggle to end slavery and, also, that during their Reconstruction service they had frequently been the only force preventing or limiting white abuse directed at the freedpeople. Did these credentials translate into personal success for the veterans after they were discharged? Did their lives differ significantly from those of other men who had not volunteered? The first part of the essay will look at what the patterns of mobility and residency reveal about the social readjustments of the veterans. The next part will assess whether or not the veterans were able to translate military service into political leadership in the years after 1865. Did these credentials predict success at the polls in North Carolina? Or were other factors more important among the electorate? The last section will look at the personal lives of the men and how they may have been changed by their time in the service.

The group of men used for this study of postwar adjustment and change were African Americans recruited in 1863 and 1864 from eastern North Carolina.[13] Initially, the impetus for recruitment came from abolitionist-minded politicians and military figures from Massachusetts. The governor of that state, John A. Andrew, and General Edward A. Wild wanted to use this group of men as part of a brigade of black infantry, Wild's "African Brigade," in order to demonstrate to the nation the effectiveness of black troops. The brigade, as envisioned by its planners, would consist of the 55th Massachusetts Volunteers and four regiments to be raised in North Carolina. The brigade was never fully formed, and it was soon broken up. Only three infantry regiments were organized from North Carolina, and they were used in several different departments. The regiments were established as the 1st, 2nd, and 3rd North Carolina Colored Volunteers, but on February 8, 1864, they were redesignated the 35th, 36th, and 37th USCT. Toward the end of the war, an artillery regiment, the 1st North Carolina Colored Heavy Artillery, was also formed in eastern North Carolina to serve local defense needs and to act as a handy source of labor. In March 1864 this regiment was also renamed, becoming the 14th USCHA. In all, from June 1863 until the end of the war, Union recruiters were able to enlist more than 5,000 black soldiers from the occupied parts of the state.[14]

Most of these soldiers served in the four regiments discussed above, and they constitute the sample for the present study.[15] Each of the four regiments that had been created, three of infantry and one of heavy artillery, enrolled in excess of a thousand men into their ranks during the war, for a total of 4,653 soldiers. Of these, almost 4,100 would survive the war.[16] Recruited over a two-year period, they were initially all drawn from the same region of North Carolina, the northeastern counties that had been occupied by Union forces in 1862. Only late in the war were significant numbers

"Colored Troops under General Wild, Liberating Slaves in North Carolina."
(Harper's Weekly, *January 23, 1864, N.C. Division of Historical Resources, Raleigh*)

of volunteers drawn from outside this pool, from the eastern edges of the North Carolina Piedmont as well as from some parts of Virginia.

The men who made up the regiments under study shared a number of qualities with black troops recruited throughout other parts of the South. The vast majority of the North Carolina soldiers had been illiterate slaves, had worked as agricultural laborers, and were between eighteen and twenty-eight years of age when they joined the service. Many had enlisted in the army after fleeing the control of their slave owners. Once in the army, they shared other common experiences as well. Virtually all of their commissioned officers were white, with most coming from Massachusetts.[17] These enlisted men, like all other black soldiers, initially received a lower rate of pay than the white enlisted men in the army and were more likely to be equipped with substandard material. In addition, as black troops, they were more commonly employed in fatigue or garrison duties than in combat and were more likely to suffer a higher mortality rate because of disease.[18] Like all Civil War soldiers, these men experienced periods of boredom, privation, elation, and terror. On the other hand, military service allowed some of these African Americans to develop and hone a range of skills in their roles as noncommissioned officers, and it enabled even more to take the first steps toward literacy. Moreover, the men of the infantry regiments served, in varying degrees, outside their home state, and this may have changed their worldviews.

While they shared some common wartime experiences, the men in the four regiments differed in significant ways according to where, when, and how their units were used, and these factors had an influence on their postwar lives. Though some of these soldiers never left North Carolina, others traveled extensively as part of their war service and became very familiar with other parts of the South. When the war ended, two regiments, the 37th USCT and the 14th USCHA, were serving in North Carolina, and that is where they finished their military service, close to friends and families. The 36th USCT had served in Virginia, but in May 1865 the regiment was sent to Texas as part of the all-black Twenty-fifth Corps. It served on the Rio Grande border until late 1866. The 35th USCT had left the state almost as soon as it had been organized and fought in South Carolina and Florida; it then did all of its postwar service in the area around Charleston. During the war, some of these infantry regiments had developed a proud fighting tradition, while the men of the artillery regiment spent more of their time as stevedores than as soldiers. In the end, the regiments were released from service over a fourteen-month period. The artillerymen were mustered out in December 1865, but the 37th USCT remained in service until early 1867. The two regiments in Texas and South Carolina were mustered out in those states, and the soldiers were offered transportation back to North Carolina.[19] As a result, the opportunities and timing for both political leadership and employment varied considerably among the veterans.

With the end of the war and the beginnings of demobilization, the black veterans had to make complex decisions as to where they wished to live as a precondition to what they wanted to do. Where they chose to live revealed much about the veterans' expectations and values and what types of lives they hoped to have in the future. Many of the men had spent years outside their home state and had served alongside African Americans born in other Southern states as well as white officers from Northern states. It would seem reasonable that the wider the men's wartime experience, the wider the range of possibilities that they would see for their futures. Demobilization meant immediate decisions for many. Government regulations stipulated that regiments that were to be mustered out would go "generally to that point in the State where mustered in" and be paid off and disbanded.[20] Policy for the USCT differed. Often the regiments were mustered out in the locale where they were serving, although transportation was provided, for those who wished, back to where they had been mustered in. Thus the men mustered out in Texas and South Carolina had to decide whether they would accept government assistance to return to North Carolina or would prefer to remain where they were. This may have been a relatively easy decision for the men in Texas, for service along the border had been very hard. The chaplain of one black regiment had claimed that no "set of men in any country ever suffered more severely than we did in Texas. Death has made fearful gaps in every regiment."[21] Deciding whether or not to return to their home state was clearly a more difficult choice for the men who had served in South Carolina. Some had married South Carolina women, and many had made friends in that state. When the commander of the 35th USCT, Colonel James Beecher, polled his men to see if they wished to be discharged at New Bern or Charleston, they were evenly split. As time passed, more favored being mustered out in New Bern, but the colonel noted that "there seems to be considerable vacillation as the time approaches and the results may be different every day it was taken."[22] A different decision faced the veterans demobilized in North Carolina. They had to decide if they wished to stay with familiar surroundings and be close to families and friends or to explore new possibilities and engage in new opportunities outside of the state.

It is possible to get some sense of what decisions these men made regarding their futures by locating the veterans at later points in time. In the case of ex-soldiers who had left the state, locating them can be an extremely difficult task. As for those who remained in North Carolina, later censuses allow significant numbers of veterans to be located. There are a series of methodological problems, however, that make it impossible for even the most diligent researcher to find all of the veterans. One of the standard sources available to historians, the 1870 national census, turns out to be one of the least accurate censuses for the South. It probably underenumerated all blacks living in North Carolina by as much as 20 percent.[23] Moreover, anyone trying to link individuals using both their military service records and later census information faces additional problems. Many of the veterans used aliases after they had been discharged from the army. Of course, researchers familiar with nineteenth-century records who are tracking someone named Pierce will, as a matter of course, also check for Pearse, Peirce, or Peerse. Further complicating the matter, most African Americans had chosen surnames as one of their first acts of freedom. How they picked their names and their willingness to replace their first choices varied enormously. Many selected their surnames on the same grounds as did Daniel Hill, who wrote,

"I took the name after my owner."[24] Others may have simply been recorded that way by Union recruiters, thus ensuring that at least some would later wish for new surnames. Some of the ex-soldiers who changed their names did so for the same reasons that prompted former private Jeremiah Gray of the 36th USCT to become Jeremiah Walker: "I enlisted under [the] name Jeremiah Gray, my master's name," he wrote. "Since I came out of the war I changed my name to that of my father and now I vote and pay taxes under [the] name of Jeremiah Walker."[25]

Sometimes the veterans continued to be known under both names. Thus the son of one veteran who had served in the 35th USCT wrote that his father had "enlisted under the name of America Etheridge or America Baum, his real name being Etheridge, but was owned by Mr. Baum, either name being correct." The same son later wrote of "my father America Ethe-ridge (real name America Baum)."[26] In other cases, names that seemed appropriate when selected in 1863 were altered over time (thus Allen Newborn later was called Allen Newton). Moreover, because these names were recorded by regimental clerks and census enumerators whose level of literacy was sometimes only slightly higher than that of the enlistees, wide variations in spelling were inevitable. Other soldiers may have had an experience similar to that of Lucas Creech, who explained that his name at the start of the war was Lucas Barrow, after his owner Renben Barrow. When asked why he had enlisted in the 14th USCHA under the name Lucas Bond, the veteran explained, "I gave my name as I recollect as Lucas Barrow, and they put it down as Lucas Bond, and I served under that name."[27]

Despite the methodological problems involved in tracking down the veterans, an insight into the postwar mobility of these soldiers can be gained by selecting a representative sample of the soldiers from each regiment and locating as many as possible who still resided in North Carolina in 1870 and 1890.[28] By contrasting the postwar experiences of the different groups of veterans, it is possible to measure what influence out-of-state service may have had on the soldiers' later lives. Of the soldiers selected in the sample, some had died; some were living outside the state; and some could just not be found. Nevertheless, about 40 to 50 percent of the veterans from the various regiments could be located in 1870 and between 15 to 25 percent in 1890. Assuming an equal mortality rate for all ex-soldiers after 1865 and similar difficulties in locating veterans from any unit, the differing numbers should reflect the percentage of veterans from each regiment who were living outside North Carolina after the war.[29]

When a comparison is made of the postwar residences of different groups of veterans, several patterns become clear. The more extensive their service outside the state, the less likely it is that one can locate the veterans within North Carolina in their later years.[30] The regiment with the fewest veterans living in postwar North Carolina, the 35st USCT, had operated entirely outside the state during the war and had been mustered out in Charleston. The largest percentage of veterans that could be located in North Carolina had served in the artillery regiment that had never left the eastern part of the state.[31] Almost 25 percent fewer members of the 35th USCT could be found in North Carolina than could be found in the case of the artillery veterans. Nevertheless, the ties to the home state were strong because even with regard to the 35th USCT a large majority of the men returned to their home state and remained there. Twenty years later, after death had thinned the ranks of the veterans, the pattern remained uncharged. Indeed, the men of the 35th USCT made up an even smaller percentage of the state's black veterans in 1890 than they had in 1870.[32] Clearly, some of the soldiers who had served outside the state during the war chose to remain where they were demobilized or to return to locales outside North Carolina where they had served and where they had developed close personal ties. Service outside their state may have made these men more receptive to new opportunities beyond North Carolina. Certainly, in the decades after the war, the veterans who had traveled extensively outside their state seemed more open to relocation and may have been more inclined to join the various migration schemes and economic incentives offered to North Carolina blacks to leave their state.[33] Taken as a group, the soldiers who had never left North Carolina appear to have been more cautious about starting anew in regions unknown to them.[34]

Although many of the veterans who chose to live outside the state left little in the way of records to trace them, a few can be tracked, and case studies of them reveal a wide spectrum of options available to North Carolina's black veterans.[35] Some of the men mustered out in Texas and South Carolina never returned to their state of enlistment, and most of these men simply disappeared from government records. Only a small number of these men can be traced. Some veterans like Private Louis Belk (Belt, then Williams), who had served in the 14th USCHA, chose to reenlist in the new black regiments that were established in the regular army. Belk was not typical, however, for by the time he had been discharged from the 10th U.S. Cavalry and applied for a pension, he was living in Alabama and had lost contact with all his old comrades, who, he wrote, had "scatered [sic] like the chaff before the wind."[36]

More commonly, the soldiers who did not return to North Carolina maintained contact with other comrades, and these ties help explain why they had not gone back to their home state. Pension records, compiled decades after the war ended, show a cluster of men from the 35th USCT living around Summerville, South Carolina, a region where the regiment had served during the first year of Reconstruction. Several of these men, while still in the army, had married women from the local community. In a similar pattern, a number of veterans from the 36th USCT settled in and around Norfolk, Virginia, a locale where the regiment had been stationed during the war and from where it had recruited some of its soldiers. Returning to Norfolk allowed Henry Clarke, a former musician in the 36th USCT who had grown up in Plymouth, North Carolina, to stay in contact with some of his Virginian-based comrades while maintaining ties with North Carolina. It also allowed him to sign on and serve with the U.S. Navy for several years.[37]

The records suggest that men who left North Carolina did so because of the influence of friends or kin, to pursue employment of a limited term, or just to satisfy a sense of adventure. Some left almost as soon as they were mustered out of the service, only to return after a few years. Still others stayed in the state through part of Reconstruction before they left. For Simon McIver (Bostic), formerly of the 14th USCHA, who had enlisted at New Bern but who had been born in Marlboro County, South Carolina, leaving North Carolina meant going home. For John Jack, who had served in the 37th USCT, out-of-state migration was a short-term employment strategy.[38] Private Abram Bissel left North Carolina looking for seasonal labor outside the state and never returned, living the remainder of his life first in Georgia and then in Florida.[39] Other veterans traveled outside North Carolina only for brief periods of time after they left the army. George Gaylord, a private in the 35th USCT, was seriously injured at the Battle of Olustee and was discharged in the fall of 1864 after losing the sight in one eye. On being paid off, he took a steamer to New York, stayed there for two weeks, and then returned to Hyde County and never left.[40]

A few of the veterans, perhaps influenced by their officers, moved north immediately following demobilization, while others left only as the political climate in North Carolina changed. Nicholas Clairborne of the 37th USCT, for instance, departed for Boston as soon as he had been mustered out. Nathaniel Spellman, a former artilleryman, waited until 1874 before he followed one of his friends from the 14th USCHA, Henry E. Dewell (Duert), to take up residence in Brooklyn, New York, and Dewell was in-

Unidentified private, U.S. Colored Troops, with woman, ca. 1865. (Ada Tharp Photograph Album, PH 038, Special Collections Department, University of Texas at El Paso Library)

fluenced by his sister, Annie, who left Roanoke Island for New York late in the war. She met him while visiting Elizabeth City in 1867 or 1868 and told him about the opportunities in the North.[41] It is likely that other veterans moved north to try to rejoin loved ones. During the war, Union officials repeatedly tried to persuade black women on Roanoke Island to relocate to domestic service jobs in the Northern states. Because Roanoke had been a designated settlement for the families and dependents of Wild's soldiers, some of the women who had moved north from the island, like Annie, very likely were the wives or relatives of the soldiers.[42]

In the years after the war, as some African Americans became pessimistic about life in the reconstructed South, migration to another country became an increasingly attractive option, and a few Southern blacks dreamed of a life free of oppression and sorrow in Africa.[43] By the late 1860s, interest in the American Colonization Society (ACS) and its activities in Liberia generated a response in northeastern North Carolina in ways that involved at least some of the veterans. Unfortunately, the limited surviving records offer only tantalizing clues as to how many veterans were involved in the migration movement. A group of 200 freedmen from Martin County headed by A. W. Powers, likely a former private in the 35th USCT, told the ACS that they would be ready to emigrate to Africa by May 1870.[44] Another veteran of the 35th USCT, Private Peter Mountain, headed a group of 163 African Americans who left Windsor, North Carolina, in November 1871, for Liberia. John F. Shepherd, who had served in Company B, 35th USCT, had led an even larger group that departed from Windsor in the previous year.[45] Because only the leaders of these groups were identified in their correspondence with the ACS, it is not possible to estimate how many other veterans may have been involved. It is also not clear from the ACS records whether the people who asked for passage actually left North Carolina or, if they left, remained in Africa.

In early 1877, for instance, Samuel Wiggins, formerly of the 14th USCHA, applied to move his family from Plymouth to Liberia. His application was one of sixteen letters received by the ACS from North Carolina that year. The records do not show whether Wiggins went to Africa and then returned or whether he ever in fact left the state. But Wiggins nonetheless resided in Plymouth in 1890.[46] As interest in migrating to Liberia waned in North Carolina, it was replaced by plans to resettle blacks hoping to escape oppression in other states such as Kansas and Indiana. In 1879, approximately 1,000 left North Carolina for the West, with an unknown number following in later years. Although no veterans were among the organizers who can be identified, the migrants were recruited from an area of the state where numerous veterans resided, and the migrants may have included some of the ex-soldiers.[47]

Given how widely dispersed the veterans who left the state became, the residence pattern of the veterans who remained in North Carolina is very striking. The majority of the veterans who can be located in the 1870 census had returned either to their county of recorded birth or to an adjoining county. Twenty-five years after the war was over, virtually all of the almost 700 ex-soldiers found in the Civil War Veterans Census of 1890 lived in the easternmost areas of the state, close to where they had been born and where they had enlisted. Just over half the veterans, some 360 men, lived in six counties near or by the coast: Beaufort, Bertie, Craven, Halifax, Pasquotank, and Washington.[48] Indeed, the 1890 residencies were more closely clustered in the eastern counties than the pre-1860 residencies had been. No more than two or three of the veterans lived west of the eastern fringe of the Piedmont.[49] Few veterans had even returned to the counties along the Piedmont's eastern edge that had yielded significant numbers of recruits during the war.[50] Instead, large numbers of these old soldiers lived in the Tidewater region, especially in or close to coastal towns and cities such as New Bern, Elizabeth City, and Wilmington.[51] In the countryside where many of the veterans still resided, they were frequently found in close proximity to other members of their old units.

For example, in 1890 more than three dozen black veterans, including twenty-five from the 14th USCHA, gave their postal address as the small town of Windsor.[52] This clustering of veterans was frequent throughout the northeastern counties. As numerous pension records confirm, clustering allowed many black veterans to remain in close contact with old comrades whom they could see on a weekly basis and from whom they could draw various forms of assistance. Besides the potential support network it offered to these old soldiers, the residence pattern testified to the importance of kinship, friendships, and local attachments to these men. Moreover, the presence of a large number of veterans, especially if in close proximity to each other, created a sense of security lacked by African Americans elsewhere in the state.

Gun ownership, especially the possession of pistols and shotguns, was common among the veterans, and the white militia or police forces seem to have had less success in disarming these men than they did in the case of blacks elsewhere in the state. When local white militiamen confiscated pistols and shotguns from black veterans returning to Hertford County in

December 1865, the ex-soldiers appealed to the Freedmen's Bureau assistant commissioner for assistance. The weapons that the veterans had purchased when they were being discharged were returned.[53] Owning weapons and demonstrating a willingness to use them offered these freedmen a security not available to others. In some areas of the state, Confederate veterans had taken over the newly formed county police forces in order to intimidate blacks and Unionists. These groups used violence and assault to overawe the freedmen; if arrested by U.S. soldiers, the perpetrators found county courts sympathetic and country jails porous.[54] The black veterans were able to counter such intimidation in some of the northeastern counties by public displays of their military preparedness. For example, on July 4, 1866, Horace James, a white reformer, invited three hundred to four hundred blacks to his plantation in Pitt County for fireworks, food, and a public demonstration of the martial readiness of the local veterans. James described the events that followed dinner: "Target practice with Springfield rifles and ball cartridges elicited spirited competition, in which exercise the two best shots were made by colored men. An extempore organization of infantry and of cavalry (mule-mounted) drilled, fired, charged, and marched, to their own intense delight."[55] Although white-on-black violence was widespread in the state, it was more frequent and more visible in the central and western counties than it was in the northeast.[56] While local demographics, conflicts within the white communities, and political struggles explain some of the variation, the presence of large numbers of black veterans in close proximity no doubt discouraged some white violence.[57]

The location of so many veterans in northeastern North Carolina offered them the potential of strong postwar political influence and leadership. Blacks in North Carolina began to organize politically within months of the official ending of hostilities, and some of the emerging leaders had been involved in the war effort as members of USCT regiments. Moreover, the areas with the most political activity—the coastal regions and the eastern cities of the state—were precisely those counties where black recruitment had been the greatest. In May 1865 a group of ex-soldiers held a meeting to demand political changes that included the right to vote. As soldiers who "had the privilege of fighting for our country," they had become anxious, the veterans argued, "to show our countrymen that we can and will fit ourselves for the creditable discharge of the duties of citizenship. We want the privilege of voting."[58] By the summer of 1865, Equal Rights Leagues or Union Leagues had emerged in Wilmington, Beaufort, New Bern, and Kinston.[59]

Indeed, the strongest supporters of the first freedmen's convention in the state, convened in Raleigh on September 29, 1865, were the black residents of New Bern, the city that had supplied so many black recruits.[60] And yet, when that convention met, as was true of the one that followed it a year later, the delegates included almost none of the North Carolina veterans.

Of course, in the summer and fall of 1865, only a minority of North Carolina's black soldiers were in a position to become involved in political activities of the state's black community. When the freedmen's convention was called in the fall of 1865, none of the regiments had been mustered out, although two units, the 14th USCHA and the 37th USCT, were serving within the state. When the next convention was called one year later, only the veterans of the artillery regiment had reentered civilian life. The 37th USCT continued to serve in North Carolina, while the soldiers of the 35th and 36th USCT had just been mustered out. Many of the men in the latter regiments had not yet returned to North Carolina.[61] At the first convention, out of over one hundred delegates, many of whom remain anonymous, only Sergeant Hezekiah Foster of the 14th USCHA can be identified from among the black troops at the meeting. Because the limited description left of him was that of a man "of few words and careful deeds," it is reasonable to assume that his role at the convention was limited.[62] Present, however, were more prominent men who had military credentials and who would provide greater leadership.

One of the most radical men behind the convention movement was Abraham H. Galloway, a mulatto who had escaped the state in 1857 and moved first to Philadelphia, then to Ohio, and then to Canada. He returned to North Carolina as soon as Union troops occupied the eastern part of the state and became a major force in encouraging recruits for Wild's brigade. Although he did not enlist, Galloway may have been involved in intelligence work for the Union army. He later became the most influential black politician before his sudden death in 1870.[63] A more moderate member of the convention was the Reverend George A. Rue, who had ministered for six years in Massachusetts before becoming chaplain of the 32nd USCT, a unit formed in Pennsylvania. Rue was appointed chaplain of the convention. The actual leader of the convention, according to reporter Sidney Andrews, was James H. Harris, a free mulatto from Granville County who had moved first to Ohio and then to Canada at the start of the war. In 1863 Harris had helped to raise men in Indiana for the 28th USCT, although he had not joined that regiment. Two other eastern delegates who played important roles in the convention and who had encouraged black recruitment were the Reverend James W. Hood and John P. Sampson. Hood had moved from Pennsylvania to New Bern in 1863 to take over the city's African Methodist Episcopal Zion church. While the minister had assisted black recruitment, he had also protected his congregation from unscrupulous white officers.[64] Hood was elected president of the convention. Sampson, a free mulatto from Wilmington, had moved north, was educated in Ohio, and published the *Cincinnati Colored Citizen*. He was almost as radical and influential as Galloway.

Both the first and second conventions are interesting because they operated at two seemingly conflicting levels. During the debates the delegates discussed radical issues. But afterward they issued guarded, cautious public statements. Thus the first convention's public address to the Constitutional Convention of North Carolina, coming after several days of radical debate, was moderate to the point of being almost apologetic. Then the convention resolved itself, upon adjournment, into a state Equal Rights League. Public notice of the next convention in 1866, however, referred to the meeting as a "Colored Educational Convention."[65] Certainly the second convention, which had a more militant tone in many of its debates, showed no significant increase of veterans among its delegates, even though three of the North Carolina regiments had been discharged and the fourth was then serving in the state.

The lack of direct political involvement by the veterans became clearer in the years following the state election of 1868. Although the veterans provided little political leadership, other blacks in North Carolina filled a number of important roles. At least sixty African Americans were elected to state and local offices during the years of Reconstruction. Another fifty-five state and national representatives won seats in the years from 1877 to 1900. Yet among the 115 blacks elected to office, only one man, John S. W. Eagles, a former private in the 37th USCT, was a veteran of the North Carolina regiments, and he only served out a partial term after a member elected in 1868 resigned.[66] A few more veterans from these regiments can be found in appointed positions such as magistrates, justices of the peace, and election registrars. But that is all. In contrast, twice as many black elected officials had spent part of the war as servants in North Carolina military units.[67]

In addition to Eagles, however, at least ten more black North Carolina elected officials had fought for the Union, two in the navy and eight in the army. But they were recruited outside North Carolina. Among the ex-soldiers, George M. Arnold worked as a reporter for the African Methodist Episcopal Church's *Christian Recorder* before joining the 4th USCT, a regiment raised in Baltimore. George L. Mabson, the slave son of a prominent white Wilmington citizen, was sent to Boston in 1854 for an education, and it was there that he joined the 5th Massachusetts Cavalry. Benjamin Morris, born in New Bern, was also educated in the North before enlisting. Henry E. Scott was born in Ohio and educated in Wisconsin before he joined the Union army, and John A. White, a native of Virginia, served in the war in a Pennsylvania regiment. Parker Robbins and his brother Augustus, free property-owning mulattoes in Bertie County before the war, joined the 2nd U.S. Colored Cavalry. After the war, both men represented Bertie in the state assembly.[68]

The military service records of these politicians may have won them some votes. More likely, what the electoral successes of these men reveal is the political advantage of having some Northern credentials. Success at the polls, of course, depends foremost on the character of a candidate (and or perhaps the weakness of the opponent), but it was not coincidental that among the most influential of the early black politicians were men who carried with them a Northern cachet. Such a group would include Galloway, both George L. and William P. Mabson, and North Carolina's leading black politician, James H. Harris, who was elected to the North Carolina Senate in 1872. Significantly, the man who in many ways replaced Harris in influence, James E. O'Hara, was raised and educated in New York City. He was elected to the U.S. Congress in 1882.[69]

Why were the black veterans who served in the four regiments raised in North Carolina underrepresented among the elected and appointed political black leadership? It may have had as much to do with the personal characteristics of the North Carolina veterans as with voter preference. Certainly the profile of the "average" soldier differed from that of the successful black Reconstruction politician. Both the current historical literature and the data from postwar North Carolina indicate that the early black leadership was lighter-skinned, wealthier, more literate, and more inclined to have been free and to reside in urban centers than the bulk of the black population.[70] Although there were significant numbers of mulattoes among the first soldiers recruited, only a tiny percentage of North Carolina's veterans had the credentials that the voters desired.[71] Most of North Carolina's USCT veterans were rural, black, and poor.

In addition, military service did not automatically transfer into white Republican support for the black veterans. When white political appointments were made in Reconstruction North Carolina, or when white Republicans voted, the chief concern generally was the "loyalty" of the candidate. When the same appointments were made among blacks, loyalty was assumed, and the greatest concern often was literacy. One example of this can be seen in the appointment of white and black election registrars in 1867. The search for white registrars focused on "northern men" or men from North Carolina's white Union regiments. The "loyalty" of the black population never was seen as an issue. Instead, the primary concern was to find men who could "read or write sufficiently to be of any use to the Board of Registration." Even though the black registrars who were appointed included some USCT veterans, the search by white officials frequently seemed restricted to ministers and teachers.[72]

The fact that veterans did not hold numerous offices, however, did not mean that they were politically unimportant. The bulk of the veterans lived in the state's famous "Black Second" Congressional District, which would continue to elect Republican candidates until the end of the century.[73] Conservatives had gerrymandered this district in an attempt to minimize black voting power. The veterans in the "Black Second" helped elect three important black politicians, O'Hara, Henry Plummer Cheatham, and George H. White.[74] Even in the "Black Second," however, success depended on attracting white as well as black voters. Local black veterans were not the best candidates to attract votes from the white electorate.

The limited political success of the veterans was paralleled in other aspects of their postwar careers. Just as the army had not provided a springboard for them into politics, neither did it open financial doors for most of the ex-soldiers. The limited amounts of money that veterans received during the war in bounties and wages did not allow them, as a class, to achieve financial independence. Of course, few enlisted men, white or black, came out of the war financially enriched. Indeed, North Carolina's veterans seem quite similar to their black counterparts from Ohio, who "returned to virtually the same conditions from which they had left."[75]

Many of the veterans emerged from the war the worse for wear—physically, if not psychologically, disabled. A significant number were unable to take care of themselves, let alone launch successful business or political careers. Although their pension records are full of accounts of the black veterans' disabilities, white contemporaries often viewed the cries for assistance with considerable skepticism. Nevertheless, regimental records make clear that even before the war ended, many of the soldiers had become sufficiently disabled for various reasons to be discharged and that many would remain permanently impaired and limited in doing whatever work they could obtain.[76] Some had been disabled from wounds, while others had contracted diseases that left them with permanent physical disabilities. Even soldiers who had never seen the enemy could suffer problems. For example, Isaac Bryant of the 14th USCHA spent more of his service as a stevedore than he did firing ordnance, but he did not escape injury. In December 1864, while unloading ammunition boxes, his comrades slipped, and the full weight of the box that they were handling fell on him. He suffered a "rupture of both sides laying him up two or three weeks at a time. . . . His guts came down so that he is not able to do anything like work having to wear truses [*sic*] to keep up."[77] Bryant's case was not unique.

Many USCT enlisted men suffered serious but less identifiable personal damage. Glatthaar has argued that the psychological adjustment of the black veterans seems to have been relatively easier than for the white officers, at least as measured by such things as psychological problems and divorce. In part this speaks to the fact that few whites cared enough or were in a position to record black psychological problems or to see them as similar in nature to those that afflicted white veterans. The best documented case of a mental disorder among men who had served in the USCT regiments was, not surprisingly, that of a prominent white officer, Colonel James C. Beecher, who both before and after his service in the 35th USCT suffered breakdowns. After years of anguish and periods in asylums, he committed suicide. The U.S. Pension Office agreed that his being "exposed to all of the vicissitudes of army life" had exacerbated Beecher's condition.[78]

Pension officials, however, tended to be less sympathetic to black veterans who claimed that an ailment, especially diminished mental competence, had resulted from their military service. When the daughter of Charles Oats, formerly of the 37th USCT, applied for a pension, she described her father's illness. The daughter had "learned from comrades of the Regt. that her father contracted a disease of [the] head by exposure and cold at Chaplin [Chaffin's] Farm causing him to be very lightheaded and to act as if he were not very bright—would at times wander away from camp."[79] James H. Moore claimed in his application that he had received such severe sunstroke while serving in the 14th USCHA that it left him a wreck. After the war, Moore claimed that he "would be giddy and weak headed and at times crazy and have fits." Sometimes, "he would be out of his mind" for over a month.[80] Neither of the men, however, received a disability pension for these ailments.

In some of the extreme cases, black veterans who, like Colonel Beecher, were driven by their own private demons later committed suicide. Washington Newby left far fewer records to make his actions understandable than did the New England colonel, but he also took his own life. After a long period of hospitalization, Newby had been discharged from the 36th USCT in June 1865 and had returned to North Carolina. Years later his mental health declined, and the veteran began to suffer from a series of physical ailments. His widow explained that "we had to watch him constantly and one night we fell asleep and he got out and we could not find him." By the time that they located Newby, he had drowned himself. "It was said," his widow wrote, "that he went crazy from the roaring of the guns in the war."[81]

According to their correspondence with government officials, the war had as deleterious an impact on the domestic lives of North Carolina's USCT veterans as it had on so many Northern white veterans. Assessing those postwar problems, however, is complicated by the contemporary social perceptions of black marriages by whites and by the legal problems involved with understanding relationships that the soldiers had begun before the war. Although not recognized as legal marriages, stable slave marriages clearly existed, usually with the consent of owners and the recognition of the community. There were also common-law relationships enforced by slave owners and perceived as transitory by African Americans. Several examples illustrate the variety of marriages between black men and women.

Chester Amieny had married Francis Reddick with the consent of their owners before the war. When Chester enlisted in the 14th USCHA in February 1864, he arranged for Francis to live with a friend, Daniel Weeks, and his family. When he could, Chester sent back part of his pay to help his wife. After the war, Weeks testified that "we all belonged to the same church and a rule came in the church for us to be remarried under special act of Legislature and my wife and I and Chester Amieny and his wife Francis Amieny and about 60 other couples got married by Rev. Hull Grimes."[82] This long and stable marriage thus was unaffected by the wartime transitions of black life.

A more complex and troubled relationship was that of John Banks and his wife, Julia. They had married while the 35th USCT was stationed in South Carolina in 1866. Despite conflicting accusations, it appears that some years later, after Julia "took up with" her deceased daughter's husband, John left his wife. Although a friend of the veteran testified that Banks had left "because Gaddes was too intimate with his wife," Julia claimed that she had tried unsuccessfully to get him back. His reply, she testified, had been "that he was too old to work for me, that he wanted to live off his pension."[83] Another case involved Peter Downing, who had been discharged from the 36th USCT after losing his right arm in fighting around Deep Bottom, Virginia, and had returned to Plymouth, North Carolina. By 1870, he had married twice and was collecting a disability pension. His third marriage, to Eliza Garrick, was a disaster. Eventually Downing moved out because, he wrote, she treated him "so mean." The old soldier testified that "she has not a good character and used to go away and remain away for days and when I would ask her where she had been, she would say that it was none of my business." Downing was clearly intimidated by Garrick, for he failed to contest her demand that she receive half his pension. Years later, the old veteran bitterly complained that his wife "is untrue to me and She gets one half of my Bounty and I am obliged to go very short in my Dealings and after She gets ½ of my Money She puts it on other men. . . . She is a very bad woman."[84] The special agent investigating the claim had trouble deciding whom to believe. His uncertainty was understandable. Unlike Eliza, large numbers of women had great difficulties in obtaining widows' pensions because of their clouded legal status, which attests to the inherent problems in assessing the stability of the marriages of North Carolina's USCT veterans.

In addition to the range of physical and emotional problems that the veterans may have experienced, other factors constricted the financial fortunes of these men. The fact that the veterans had to reenter the work force months and sometimes years after the Confederate surrender put them at a disadvantage compared to men of both races whose businesses were already established. A year before the war ended, at least eighteen black businessmen, turpentine farmers, and grocers working in the areas under Union control were reporting annual incomes of $1,000 or more.[85] Thus they began the postwar years with a significant advantage over the men just coming out of the service. Moreover, black veterans in Southern states generally were poorly positioned to succeed in business enterprises that depended on the good will and patronage of the surrounding white community.[86]

Blacks were able to leave the Union army with some financial benefits if they had been frugal and fortunate. Not many enlisted men could save much from their wages, however, especially if they had dependents at home to whom they were sending money. The men who had enlisted first were the least fortunate, for they had received little in the way of bounties. Only the men who had enlisted late in the war qualified for bounties of up to $300. For some soldiers, a bounty could be the start of modest property ownership. Unfortunately, many veterans who were owed money by the government for bounties or back wages were at the mercy of the agents and lawyers who handled their postwar applications. At the very best, veterans could expect to pay $10 to $25 plus expenses to these agents in order to obtain relatively small amounts of money. At worst, a veteran might lose most or all of what he was entitled to. One black veteran who used an unscrupulous attorney found that after various fees, expenses, and stationery were deducted from his $100 check, he received only $19.20.[87] Even when the legal fees charged were reasonable, few veterans achieved a secure financial future from the money they received for their military service.

This does not mean that the veterans emerged from the war without any benefits. What it does suggest is that the benefits were limited or intangible. By the end of the war, black soldiers received not only the same pay as whites but also, in some instances, bounties of almost equal value.[88] The money allowed some veterans who managed to avoid fraudulent practices to emerge from the war as modest property owners or small-scale tradesmen. Even the limited veteran pensions, which varied from only a few dollars to, by 1912, perhaps $12 a month, proved important enough to elderly ex-soldiers. The pensions may have let some of them enter into tacit understandings with young women, exchanging support for them in their old age for the benefits of a widow's pension. The fact that the amount of money was quite small did not mean that it was not desperately important to many impoverished veterans.

In a few cases, veterans—such as Sergeant Richard Etheridge—were able to translate their military careers into long-term government appointments. Etheridge was a free black from Roanoke Island who during the war had served as regimental commissary sergeant in the 36th USCT. After the war, he worked first as a fisherman and then as a surfman at the lifesaving station at Bodie Island. In 1879 the former sergeant was appointed the first black commander of a station in the history of the U.S. Lifesaving Service.[89] At his death in 1900, Etheridge was earning $900 a year, but after a long and distinguished career he was able to leave only a modest estate of $1,055.[90] Another case, that of John S. W. Eagles, perhaps suggests that the success of the veterans should not just be measured in the short term. As significant as his role was in helping to establish the Republican Party in New Hanover County and in serving as a policeman and registrar there, perhaps Eagles's career should be measured by the success of his offspring. His son, Dr. John Eagles, a graduate of the Leonard School of Pharmacy at Raleigh's Shaw University, established one of the major black drugstores in the state and became a member of the black elite.[91]

Etheridge and Eagles were, however, exceptional cases. Financial or political success among North Carolina's USCT veterans was uncommon.[92] While the veterans may have been insulated and supported by their local community, few became wealthy. They could draw great comfort from knowing that they had played a major role in freeing the slaves and launching the freedom generation. Like the soldier at the fall of Wilmington, they emerged from the war not only with their freedom but also with their manhood. Having served their race and their country, most returned to friends and kin, perhaps moving to coastal towns as their health declined and living out quiet lives of destitution.

Notes

1. Edwin S. Redkey, ed., *A Grand Army of Black Men: Letters from African-American Soldiers in the Union Army, 1861–1865* (Cambridge: Cambridge University Press, 1992), 167.

2. Frederick Douglass, "Address for the Promotion of Colored Enlistments" (July 6, 1863), *Douglass' Monthly*, August 1863, in Philip S. Foner, ed., *The Life and Writings of Frederick Douglass*, 5 vols. (New York: International Publishers, 1952–75), 3:365.

3. Redkey, *A Grand Army of Black Men*, 173.

4. Ibid.

5. A. H. Stein, *History of the Thirty-Seventh Regiment, U.S.C. Infantry* (Philadelphia: King & Baird Printers, 1886), 129; "Lucas Creech, (Bond)," Civil War Pension Files, Record Group (RG) 15, National Archives, Washington, D.C. (hereafter cited as CWPF, NA).

6. Some examples include Howard N. Rabinowitz, ed., *Southern Black Leaders of the Reconstruction Era* (Urbana: University of Illinois Press, 1982); Leon Litwack and August Meier, eds., *Black Leaders in the Nineteenth Century* (Urbana: University of Illinois Press, 1988); Peter Kolchin, *First Freedom: The Response of Alabama's Blacks to Emancipation and Reconstruction* (Westport, Conn.: Greenwood Press, 1975); Roberta Sue Alexander, *North Carolina Faces the Freedmen: Race Relations during Presidential Reconstruction* (Durham: Duke University Press, 1985); and Joseph P. Reidy, *From Slavery to Agrarian Capitalism in the Cotton Plantation South: Central Georgia, 1800–1880* (Chapel Hill: University of North Carolina Press, 1992). For a detailed study of black veterans in the decades after the Civil War, see Donald R. Shaffer "Marching On: African American Civil War Veterans in Postbellum America, 1865–1951" (Ph.D. diss., University of Maryland, College Park, 1996). Shaffer examines the lives of 1,044 randomly sampled veterans plus those of another 200 ex-soldiers who had notable postwar careers.

7. Larry M. Logue, *To Appomattox and Beyond: The Civil War Soldier in Peace and War* (Chicago: Ivan R. Dee, 1996), 84–85.

8. Examples of recent scholarship on black regiments include Jonathan William Horstman, "The African-American's Civil War: A History of the 1st North Carolina Colored Volunteers" (M.A. thesis, Western Carolina University, 1994);

Versalle Freddrick Washington, "Eagles on Their Buttons: The Fifth Regiment of Infantry, United States Colored Troops in the American Civil War" (Ph.D. diss., Ohio State University, 1995), published as *Eagles on Their Buttons: A Black Infantry Regiment in the Civil War* (Columbia: University of Missouri Press, 1999); James Kenneth Bryant II, " 'A Model Regiment': The 36th Colored Infantry in the Civil War" (M.A. thesis, University of Vermont, 1996); John Dwight Warner, "Crossed Sabres: A History of the Fifth Massachusetts Volunteer Cavalry: An African American Regiment in the Civil War" (Ph.D. diss., Boston College, 1997); Pia Seija Seagrave, ed., *A Boy Lieutenant: Memoirs of Freeman S. Bowley, 30th United States Colored Troops Officer* (1906; Fredericksburg, Va.: Sergeant Kirkland's Museum and Historical Society, 1997); James M. Paradis, *Strike the Blow for Freedom: The 6th United States Colored Infantry in the Civil War* (Shippensburg, Pa.: White Mane Books, 1998); Edward A. Miller, Jr., *The Black Civil War Soldiers of Illinois* (Columbia: University of South Carolina Press, 1998); and Shana Renee Hutchins, " 'Just Learning to Be Men': A History of the 35th United States Colored Troops, 1863–1866" (M.A. thesis, North Carolina State University, 1999).

9. Eric Foner, *Reconstruction: America's Unfinished Revolution, 1863–1877* (New York: Harper and Row, 1988), 9.

10. Joseph T. Glatthaar, *Forged in Battle: The Civil War Alliance of Black Soldiers and White Officers* (New York: Free Press, 1990), 248.

11. Ibid., 237.

12. In Rhode Island, for example, the unemployment rate of black veterans was five times as high as that of black civilians. See Logue, *To Appomattox and Beyond*, 87.

13. As a first step, a database of all the soldiers in the four regiments was created from the various military records, roster lists, military description books, and morning reports held at the National Archives. In addition, an ongoing sample of pension records generated by these veterans was incorporated into the database. The pension information comes from two different repositories. Data have been selected from 195 of the Civil War Pension Files held at the National Archives as well as from 110 pension applications handled by the black lawyer Frederick C. Douglas. The pension applications from black veterans in the New Bern area are now held in three collections at the J. Y. Joyner Library, East Carolina University. The combination of information allowed for the linking and verification of these veterans with the national Census of 1870 and the special Civil War Veterans Census of 1890 as well as with any records appearing in printed accounts and manuscript records. It was possible then to identify veterans who had achieved success during Reconstruction. Of course, many of the veterans either changed their names or had their names recorded in different ways. This, plus the paucity of extant records concerning these men, makes certain linkages very difficult.

14. Some 5,035 recruits were officially credited to North Carolina, but recruiters

from Northern states such as Massachusetts, Rhode Island, New York, and Connecticut all enlisted African Americans in North Carolina who were credited to the Northern states. See Ira Berlin, Joseph P. Reidy, and Leslie S. Rowland, eds., *The Black Military Experience* (Cambridge: Cambridge University Press, 1982), 12.

15. Although the men from these regiments accounted for the vast majority of recruits from North Carolina, a sizable number of black North Carolinians were scattered through regiments raised in states such as Tennessee, Arkansas, Indiana, and Louisiana. A few others served in the navy or in the 2nd U.S. Colored Cavalry, a unit raised around Portsmouth and Norfolk, Virginia, which sent recruiters to Plymouth, North Carolina.

16. Although the number of survivors amounted to about 6 or 7 percent of the state's adult black male population as a whole, in the eastern counties where they were to be found, veterans constituted perhaps as much as 20 percent of the adult black male population.

17. The exceptions were the officers in the artillery regiment, who came from a wide range of Northern states.

18. The disease mortality rate for all African American soldiers in the Civil War was about one in seven, while the rate for white Union soldiers was one in seventeen. See Washington, "Eagles on Their Buttons," 186.

19. According to army regulations, the units should have been discharged where they had been mustered in. In the case of the 35th USCT, its commander took a straw poll among the enlisted men and chose to discharge them in Charleston. The case of the 36th USCT is less clear: some of the soldiers had finished their three-year service before the regiment as a whole was mustered out; these men left Texas as early as the summer of 1866.

20. U.S. War Department, *The War of the Rebellion: A Compilation of the Official Records of the Union and Confederate Armies*, 128 vols. (Washington: Government Printing Office, 1880–1901), 3rd ser., 5:2.

21. Redkey, *A Grand Army of Black Men*, 202.

22. Colonel J. Beecher to Brigadier General O. H. Hart, May 21, 1866, Descriptive and Letter Book, 35th USCT, RG 94, Adjutant General's Office (AGO), NA.

23. The best of the nineteenth-century censuses probably missed about 10 percent of the population. Moreover, the parts of society marginalized by class or ethnicity, as well as transients and young adults, constituted a disproportional segment of those missed. In 1870 the census operated under very difficult circumstances in the Southern states, and the results reflected those problems. See Richard Reid, "The 1870 United States Census and Black Underenumeration: A Test Case from North Carolina," *Histoire Sociale/Social History* 28 (November 1995): 487–99.

24. "Daniel Hill," CWPF, NA.

25. "Jeremiah Gray," CWPF, NA.

26. "America Baum," CWPF, NA.

27. "Lucas Creech (Bond)," CWPF, NA.

28. The year 1890 was selected because the Civil War Veterans Census of 1890 picked up most, if not all, of the remaining veterans. See Richard Reid, "Residency and Black Veterans in North Carolina, 1865–1890" (paper presented at the annual meeting of Southern Historical Association, New Orleans, November 1995).

29. It was initially postulated that active military campaigning, such as that experienced by the 35th USCT, might have contributed to greater physical disability after the war. Pension records suggest, however, that the men of the 14th USCHA had as many health problems, or at least they reported as many, as the soldiers of the other regiments.

30. It is very difficult to assess accurately the number of the veterans of the four regiments who were living in North Carolina at any given time. The 1870 census underenumerated blacks by probably as much as 20 percent, while another significant number of the veterans, perhaps also 20 percent, used at least two different names through this period. The problems of locating the North Carolina veterans in other Southern states are even greater. See Reid, "The 1870 United States Census and Black Underenumeration," 488–99.

31. The author made a random selection of from 250 to 300 soldiers mustered out from each regiment and then attempted to locate the men in the general manuscript census of 1870.

Regiment	No. of Cases	Located/1870 Census
35th USCT	278	105 (37.8%)
36th USCT	243	98 (40.3%)
37th USCT	301	139 (46.2%)
14th USCHA	251	124 (49.4%)

32. The Civil War Veterans Census of 1890 attempted to locate all Union veterans by state, giving their postal location and their former units.

Regiment	Men Mustered Out	Veterans Located in 1890
35th USCT	881	134 (15.2%)
36th USCT	578	118 (20.4%)
37th USCT	796	211 (26.5%)
14th USCHA	883	220 (25.0%)

33. William Cohen, *At Freedom's Edge: Black Mobility and the Southern White Quest for Racial Control, 1861–1915* (Baton Rouge: Louisiana State University Press, 1991), 69, 85, 187–97. In addition to the well-known plans to resettle Southern blacks in Liberia, Kansas, and Indiana, labor agents recruited men in North Carolina for railroad work in other Southern states. Unfortunately, in most cases only the leaders' names have been recorded, making it impossible to assess accurately the number of veterans involved in each group.

34. It is important to note, of course, that even the men of the 14th USCHA may have been more willing to emigrate than other North Carolina blacks. In other words, the act of enlisting itself may have indicated a greater willingness to take risks.

35. Most of the men found outside the state were located because they, or people connected to them, submitted various claims to the government for pensions, bounties, or back pay.

36. "Louis Belk (alias Williams)," CWPF, NA.

37. "Henry Clarke," CWPF, NA.

38. "Simon McIver (alias Bostic)," "Noah Willis," CWPF, NA. John Jack had testified in the pension application of Noah Willis.

39. "Abram Bissel, alias Harwell, Howell," CWPF, NA.

40. "George Gaylord Pension Application," Frederick C. Douglas Papers, J. Y. Joyner Library, East Carolina University, Greenville, N.C. East Carolina University has three manuscript collections holding veterans' pension applications handled by the lawyer Frederick C. Douglas.

41. "Nicholas Clairborne," "Nathaniel Spellman (alias Thompson)," CWPF, NA.

42. On women at Roanoke Island, see Patricia L. Click, *Time Full of Trial: The Roanoke Island Freedmen's Colony, 1862–1867* (Chapel Hill: University of North Carolina Press, 2001).

43. For a discussion of the postwar interest in "the African Dream," see Cohen, *At Freedom's Edge*, 138–67.

44. The regimental books of the 35th USCT indicate that Andrew Powers, age twenty, of Martin County, had enlisted in 1863. Muster Rolls and Returns, Regimental Descriptive and Letter Book, 35th USCT, RG 94, AGO, NA.

45. The 1870 census for North Carolina lists a Peter Mountain of Windsor Township, Bertie County, as having the same age and complexion as that of Private Peter Mountain, Company I, 35th USCT. See "Applications for Passage," American Colonization Society Papers (ACS), Manuscript Division, Library of Congress (LC).

46. "Applications for Passage," ACS, LC; Sandra L. Almasy, ed., *North Carolina 1890 Civil War Veterans Census* (Joliet, Ill.: Kensington Glen Publishers, 1990), 219.

47. The center of recruitment was Lenoir County, home to a large number of veterans of the 14th USCHA and some from the 35th USCT. See Cohen, *At Freedom's Edge*, 176, 187–95.

48. The total is compiled from Almasy, *North Carolina 1890 Civil War Veterans Census*.

49. The Civil War Veterans Census of 1890, a supplementary census, began with lists from the Grand Army of the Republic and responses from newspaper inquiries; it augmented that information with thousands of letters to locate men missed by the enumerators. The census presupposed that veterans would identify themselves as such. It is possible that some black veterans living in central or western parts of the state did not wish to be identified as veterans. If so, it would support an argument of a less hostile climate in the northeastern counties.

50. For example, Sampson, Wayne, Nash, and Halifax Counties had provided 154 recruits to the four regiments, chiefly after April 1864. Of these counties, only Halifax, with almost forty, had a significant number of veterans in 1890.

51. This is consistent with Shaffer's findings that veterans were more urbanized than other African Americans. It also explains the presence of some eighty veterans who were living in Wilmington in 1890, although few recruits had come from New Hanover County.

52. Almasy, *North Carolina 1890 Civil War Veterans Census*, 20–26.

53. The owning and wearing of pistols, in the face of hostile white civilians, forced Union commanders to try, unsuccessfully, to stop the practice. See General Order No. 10, 9 May 1864, Letters, Endorsement and Order Books, 36th USCT, RG 95, AGO, NA. The black veterans returning to Hertford County believed that they were being targeted because they had served in the Union army. See Berlin et al., *The Black Military Experience*, 801–2.

54. William McKee Evans, *Ballots and Fence Rails: Reconstruction in the Lower Cape Fear* (Chapel Hill: University of North Carolina Press, 1966), 68–73, 77, 81, 99.

55. Stephen E. Reilly, "Reconstruction through Regeneration: Horace James' Work with the Blacks for Social Reform in North Carolina, 1862–1867" (Ph.D. diss., Duke University, 1983), 170.

56. Counties with the greatest recorded violence included Rutherford, Alamance, Caswell, Lincoln, Cleveland, Gaston, Mecklenburg, Guilford, Orange, Randolph, Montgomery, and Moore. For a discussion, see Jeffrey J. Crow, Paul D. Escott, and Flora J. Hatley, *A History of African Americans in North Carolina* (Raleigh: North Carolina Division of Archives and History, 1992), 89–91.

57. Evans credits local black militia led by Union veterans for resisting in Wilmington in 1868 white terrorists who were trying to intimidate black voters. See Evans, *Ballots and Fence Rails*, 98–102.

58. *New York Daily Tribune*, May 19, 1865.

59. Alexander, *North Carolina Faces the Freedmen*, 16.

60. John Richard Dennett, *The South As It Is, 1865–1866* (New York: Viking Press, 1965), 148. New Bern had been the center of black recruitment, and many of the soldiers' families remained there or in James City during the war. Veterans of the 14th USCHA had begun returning to the area by December 1865.

61. Political involvement for the veterans, while difficult, would not have been impossible, especially if they had had the assistance of Republican leaders and Reconstruction officials. After all, by December 1865 there were hundreds of veterans from the 14th USCHA living in the state who could have become politically active.

62. Sidney Andrews, *The South since the War* (Boston: Ticknor & Fields, 1866), 125. When Foster was recommended as an election registrar in 1867, he was described as "intelligent." Records of the Bureau of Refugees, Freedmen, and Abandoned Lands, North Carolina, RG 105, reel 32, NA.

63. On Galloway's career, see David S. Cecelski, "Abraham H. Galloway: Wilmington's Lost Prophet and the Rise of Black Radicalism in the American South," in Cecelski and Timothy B. Tyson, eds., *Democracy Betrayed: The Wilmington Race Riot of 1898 and Its Legacy* (Chapel Hill: University of North Carolina Press, 1998), 43–72, and Cecelski, *The Waterman's Song: Slavery and Freedom in Maritime North Carolina* (Chapel Hill: University of North Carolina Press, 2001), chap. 7.

64. Bishop J. W. Hood, *One Hundred Years of the African Methodist Episcopal Zion Church; or, The Centennial of African Methodism* (New York: Book Concern of the A.M.E. Zion Church, 1895), 292–96.

65. *Weekly North Carolina Standard* (Raleigh), October 17, 1866.

66. It is possible, given the limited information known of some of the representatives, that a few more veterans might have been elected because names and approximate ages were similar to those of several of the legislators. Significantly, if these men were veterans, they chose to achieve electoral success without invoking their military past.

67. The men were Hawkins W. Carter, who served in the North Carolina House of Representatives (1874–80) and the North Carolina Senate (1881–83), and Isham Sweat, who was elected to the House of Representatives from Cumberland County in 1868 for one term. In addition, James H. Jones, formerly the personal servant of President Jefferson Davis, served as a Raleigh alderman from 1873 to 1889.

68. Robert C. Kenzer, *Enterprising Southerners: Black Economic Success in North Carolina, 1865–1915* (Charlottesville: University Press of Virginia, 1997), 87.

69. Although Eric Foner lists O'Hara as born in New York and removed to the West Indies as a child, George W. Reid locates his birth in the West Indies with his family moving to New York in 1850. Both agree that he was educated in New York City. See Foner, *Freedom's Lawmakers: A Directory of Black Officeholders during Reconstruction* (New York: Oxford University Press, 1993), 96–97, and Reid, "Four in Black: North Carolina's Black Congressmen, 1874–1914," *Journal of Negro History* 64 (Summer 1979): 231–33.

70. Alexander, *North Carolina Faces the Freedmen*, 23–24, 84–85; Foner, *Reconstruction*, 116; Foner, *Freedom's Lawmakers*, xv–xxvi; Richard Lowe, "Local Black Leaders during Reconstruction in Virginia," *Virginia Magazine of History and Biography* 103 (April 1995): 181–206; Edmund L. Drago, "Georgia's First Black Voter Registrars During Reconstruction," *Georgia Historical Quarterly* 78 (Winter 1994): 760–93.

71. In the four regiments, from 7.5 percent to 14 percent of the men enlisted were recorded as other than "black" or "dark," and about 90 percent of all the soldiers had their occupation listed as laborer or farmer. A description of the characteristics of the earliest recruits can be found in Richard Reid, "Raising the African Brigade: Early Black Recruitment in Civil War North Carolina," *North Carolina Historical Review* 70 (July 1993): 283–85.

72. Among the limited number of veterans selected were Sergeants Hezekiah Fos-

ter of the 14th USCHA, John Monroe of the 35th USCT, Richard Etheridge and Frank James of the 36th USCT, and Charles Sheppherd of the 37th USCT. Because first sergeants were responsible for some paperwork, two possible reasons explain their selections. In the case of Frank Pieson, a "printer" and "late pvt. 37th USCT," who was one of the twenty-one black registrars in Ware County, or Reuben Mezell (Mazell), a teacher and late private in the 35th USCT, occupation may have been more important than service. See Registers and Reports of Registrars Recommended for the Election of Delegates, RG 105, NA.

73. The congressional district was the creation, in 1872, of the Conservative-controlled legislature. By gerrymandering the district in such a way as to maximize the black vote here, the Conservatives hoped to emasculate black electoral strength in other districts. See Eric Anderson, *Race and Politics in North Carolina, 1872–1901: The Black Second* (Baton Rouge: Louisiana State University Press, 1981).

74. Crow, Escott, and Hatley, *A History of African Americans in North Carolina*, 109.

75. Washington, "Eagles on their Buttons," 190.

76. In the 35th USCT, by the summer of 1864, between thirty and forty of the men were physically incapacitated, although Colonel Beecher was having great trouble obtaining their discharges. By the end of the year, forty-four men had been discharged for various reasons, and the examples in the other regiments reflect the same problem. Colonel J. C. Beecher to Lieutenant A. Coates, 13 July 1864; Colonel J. C. Beecher to Captain M. Bailey, June 29, 1864; Annual Returns . . . December 31, 1864, Descriptive and Letter Book, 35th USCT, RG 95, AGO, NA.

77. "Isaac Bryant," CWPF, NA.

78. "James C. Beecher," CWPF, NA.

79. "Charles Oats," CWPF, NA. Apparently Oats either wandered away from camp or deserted shortly before the regiment was discharged.

80. "James H. Moore," CWPF, NA.

81. "Washington Newby," CWPF, NA.

82. "Chester Amieny," CWPF, NA.

83. "John Banks," CWPF, NA.

84. "Peter Downing," CWPF, NA.

85. Horace James, *Annual Report of the Superintendent of Negro Affairs in North Carolina, 1864, with an Appendix Containing the History and Management of the Freedmen in this Department up to June 1st, 1865* (Boston: W. F. Brown & Company, 1865), 11–12. James received information from 305 blacks involved in trades and professions in the region around New Bern after he had posted a request for the data. The average reported incomes were highest for barbers ($675), grocers ($678), and carpenters ($510), but average incomes also were significant for blacksmiths ($468), coopers ($418), and masons ($402).

86. On attracting white customers and the disadvantage of starting businesses after the war, see Kenzer, *Enterprising Southerners*, 38–49.

87. "William Latham," CWPF, NA.

88. By late 1864, Northern recruiting agents were offering black recruits state bounties of several hundred dollars. In 1873 a law retroactively equalized bounties
for black soldiers with those of white recruits.

89. Joe A. Mobley, *Ship Ashore!: The U.S. Lifesavers of Coastal North Carolina* (Raleigh:
North Carolina Division of Archives and History, 1994), 94–98.

90. "Richard Etheridge," CWPF, NA.

91. Foner, *Freedom's Lawmakers*, 68; Kenzer, *Enterprising Southerners*, 115.

92. None of the veterans, for instance, show up among the most prosperous North
Carolina blacks. See Loren Schweninger, *Black Property Owners in the South,
1790–1915* (Urbana: University of Illinois Press, 1990), 295–300.

CONTRIBUTORS

John David Smith is Graduate Alumni Distinguished Professor of History at North Carolina State University. He is the author or editor of fifteen books, including *An Old Creed for the New South* (1985), *Black Voices from Reconstruction* (1996), and *Black Judas: William Hannibal Thomas and "The American Negro"* (2000), which received the Mayflower Society Award for Nonfiction.

Anne J. Bailey is professor of history at Georgia College and State University. She is the author or editor of six books on the Civil War. Her most recent works include *Civil War Arkansas: Beyond Battles and Leaders* (2000) and *The Chessboard of War: Sherman and Hood in the Autumn Campaigns of 1864* (2000), winner of the Richard Barksdale Harwell Award.

Arthur W. Bergeron, Jr., is the Historian at Pamplin Historical Park and the National Museum of the Civil War Soldier near Petersburg, Virginia. He is the author, coauthor, or editor of nine books, including *The Civil War Reminiscences of Major Silas T. Grisamore, CSA* (1993), *Confederate Mobile, 1861–1865* (1991), and *Guide to Louisiana Confederate Military Units, 1861–1865* (1989).

John Cimprich is professor of history at Thomas More College in Crestview Hills, Kentucky. He is the author of *Slavery's End in Tennessee, 1861–1865* (1985) and has a work in progress on Fort Pillow.

Lawrence Lee Hewitt is professor of history (retired) at Southeastern Louisiana University. He is the author or editor of nine books, including *Port Hudson, Confederate Bastion on the Mississippi* (1987), *The Confederate High Command and Related Topics* (1990), *Leadership during the Civil War* (1992), and *Louisianians in the Civil War* (2001).

Richard Lowe is Regents Professor of History at the University of North Texas. He is the author or editor of several books and articles on the American Civil War and Reconstruction, including *Republicans and Reconstruction in Virginia, 1856–70* (1991), *The Texas Overland Expedition of 1863* (1996), and *A Texas Cavalry Officer's Civil War* (1999).

Thomas D. Mays is assistant professor of history at Quincy University in Quincy, Illinois. He is the author of *The Saltville Massacre* (1995) and the editor of *Let Us Meet in Heaven: The Civil War Letters of James Michael Barr, 5th South Carolina Cavalry* (2001).

Michael T. Meier is a program officer with the National Historical Publications and Records Commission. He received his Ph.D. in 1982, writing his dissertation on "Caleb Goldsmith Forshey: Engineer of the Old Southwest, 1813–1881." He is the author of several book reviews and articles.

Edwin S. Redkey is professor emeritus of history at Purchase College, State University of New York. He is the author of *Black Exodus: Black Nationalist and Back-to-Africa Movements, 1890–1910* (1969) and the editor of *Respect Black!: The Writings and Speeches of Henry McNeal Turner* (1971) and *A Grand Army of Black Men: Letters from African-American Soldiers in the Union Army, 1861–1865* (1992).

Richard Reid is associate professor of history at the University of Guelph, Ontario, Canada. He has published extensively in both Canadian and American history.

William Glenn Robertson is the Command Historian of the United States Army Combined Arms Center and Fort Leavenworth, Kansas. A Civil War specialist, he is the author of *Back Door to Richmond: The Bermuda Hundred Campaign* (1987) and *The Petersburg Campaign: The Battle of Old Men and Young Boys* (1989), as well as numerous articles on Civil War military subjects.

Noah Andre Trudeau lives in Washington, D.C. He has written or edited six books about the Civil War, including *Bloody Roads South: The Wilderness to Cold Harbor, May–June 1864* (1989), which received the Fletcher Pratt Award, and *Like Men of War: Black Troops in the Civil War, 1862–1865* (1998), winner of the Jerry Coffey Memorial Book Prize.

Keith Wilson is lecturer in history at Monash University Gippsland Campus, Australia. He is the author of *"Campfires of Freedom": The Camp Life of Black Soldiers during the Civil War* (2002).

Robert J. Zalimas, Jr., is assistant professor of history at Morris College in Sumter, South Carolina. He is completing his doctoral dissertation at The Ohio State University on black Union soldiers and their role in the postwar South.

INDEX

Note: Italic page numbers refer to illustrations.

Freeman, Thomas D., 41
Frémont, John C., 12, 19, 22, 345
Fribley, Charles W., 138, 139, 140–41
Fry, James, 265
Fugitive Slave Laws, 3, 13
Fugitive slaves: and Emancipation
    Proclamation, 4; as military laborers,
    11, 14–15, 17, 21; and arming of slaves,
    19; recruitment of, 20

Galloway, Abraham H., 405, 406, 407
Gamble, Hamilton R., 263
Gardner, William H., 215, 217
Garland, J. P., 82
Garrard, Jeptha, 281, 284, 287
Garrick, Eliza, 411
Garrison, William Lloyd, 3, 22, 97, 373
Gaylord, George, 400
Geary, John White, 2
General Orders No. 11 (1864), 284
General Orders No. 20 (1864), 264, 265
General Orders No. 21 (1864), 41
General Orders No. 24 (1864), 202
General Orders No. 34 (1864), 264
General Orders No. 100 (1863), 46, 312,
    324, 330 (n. 15)
General Orders No. 143 (1863), 259
General Orders No. 163 (1863), 49
General Orders No. 252 (1863), 47
Georgia, 11, 21, 44, 230, 242 (n. 8),
    372–73
Germanna Ford, 177
Gillem, Alvan C., 206, 208
Gillmore, Quincy A.: and Florida, 136–
    37; and Hincks, 173, 196 (n. 7); and
    Montgomery, 325; and 21st USCT,
    362, 377; and Schimmelfennig, 365;
    and disease risk in Charleston, 368;
    and black political activism, 369; and
    Bodine, 370; and tensions between
    black and white troops, 371–72,
    376–77, 388 (n. 45); and Charleston

racial violence, 376; and reduction
    of occupation forces, 377–79, 390
    (n. 49); and segregation of occupa-
    tion troops, 377–79, 380
Giltner, Henry L., 206, 207, 208
Gladstone, William A., 43
Glasgow (colonel), 122
Glatthaar, Joseph T., xiii, xiv, 42, 55,
    281, 286, 392–93, 409
Glory (film), xiii
Gooch, Daniel, 153
Gooding, James Henry, 40, 50
Gooding, Oliver P., 84, 93
Goodrich's Landing, Louisiana, 257
Grant, Susan-Mary, 42
Grant, Ulysses S.: and black enlistment,
    24, 251–52, 256, 259; and Dana, 55;
    and Petersburg, 56, 187–88, 189, 201,
    290; and Battle of the Crater, 58,
    61, 62; losses of, 95; and Vicksburg,
    100; and Vicksburg campaign, 111–
    12, 114, 116, 126, 258; and Milliken's
    Bend executions, 126; and prisoners
    of war, 145, 241 (n. 4); and Burnside,
    170; and Virginia campaign, 171, 173,
    177, 178, 182, 201; and black troops'
    assignments, 228, 379; as general in
    chief, 228; and Lincoln, 240 (n. 3);
    and Thomas, 279; Overland cam-
    paign of, 285; raiding strategy of,
    312; and total war policy, 327; and
    Charleston, 362, 365, 377, 379; and
    segregation of occupation troops,
    377, 379, 380
Gray, Jeremiah, 398
Greeley, Horace, 16, 370
Greenleaf, Halbert S., 98
Grierson, Benjamin H., xix, 55, 97,
    294
Grierson Raid, 294
Grimes, Hull, 410
Grimsley, Mark, 327, 329–30 (n. 14)